Payroll Accounting 2021

Seventh Edition

Jeanette M. Landin, Ed.D., M.B.A.
Landmark College

Paulette Schirmer, D.B.A., M.B.A.
University of Alaska Southeast

PAYROLL ACCOUNTING 2021, SEVENTH EDITION

Published by McGraw Hill LLC, 1325 Avenue of the Americas, New York, NY 10121. Copyright © 2021 by McGraw Hill LLC. All rights reserved. Printed in the United States of America. Previous editions © 2020, 2019, and 2018. No part of this publication may be reproduced or distributed in any form or by any means, or stored in a database or retrieval system, without the prior written consent of McGraw Hill LLC, including, but not limited to, in any network or other electronic storage or transmission, or broadcast for distance learning.

Some ancillaries, including electronic and print components, may not be available to customers outside the United States.

This book is printed on acid-free paper.

1 2 3 4 5 6 7 8 9 LWI 24 23 22 21 20

ISBN 978-1-260-24797-8 (bound edition)
MHID 1-260-24797-X (bound edition)
ISBN 978-1-260-48122-8 (loose-leaf edition)
MHID 1-260-48122-0 (loose-leaf edition)

Portfolio Manager: *Steve Schuetz*
Product Developers: *Sarah Sacco*
Marketing Manager: *Claire McLemore*
Content Project Managers: *Fran Simon; Brian Nacik*
Buyer: *Laura Fuller*
Designer: *Beth Blech*
Content Licensing Specialists: *Beth Cray*
Cover Image: *Venomous Vector/Shutterstock*
Compositor: *SPi Global*

All credits appearing on page or at the end of the book are considered to be an extension of the copyright page.

Library of Congress Control Number: 2020908794

About the Authors

©Tom Raffelt

Jeanette Landin

Landmark College
Jeanette Landin is an associate professor of business and accounting at Landmark College in Putney, Vermont, where she teaches undergraduate accounting and business courses to an at-risk student population. She is a baccalaureate student advisor and works with students to prepare them for employment. Dr. Landin earned her BA degree from the University of California at Irvine before receiving her MBA and EdD from the University of Phoenix, where she conducted research into college success strategies for at-risk students. She has earned master's certificates in accounting and in autism spectrum disorders.

Dr. Landin is an active member of the Institute for Management Accountants (IMA), the American Accounting Association, Teachers of Accounting Curriculum at Two-Year Colleges (TACTYC), the Association of Certified Fraud Examiners (ACFE), and Vermont Women in Higher Education (VWHE), and she previously served as an active member of the California Business Educators Association and the Western Business Educators Association. Dr. Landin has served as the chair of the IMA's Committee for Academic Relations and as a peer reviewer for the American Accounting Association. She is a peer reviewer for the *Transnational Journal of Business* and the Associate Editor for Accounting with the Multimedia Educational Resource for Learning and Online Teaching (MERLOT).

©Ryan Kauzlarich

Paulette Schirmer

University of Alaska Southeast
Paulette Schirmer is an assistant professor of accounting with the University of Alaska Southeast for its accounting courses. She received her BS in accounting from Metropolitan State College of Denver (now Metropolitan State University of Denver), her MBA from Regis University, and her DBA from the University of Phoenix, where she conducted research on globalization strategies for small businesses.

Dr. Schirmer was also recently an accountant with the Division of Finance for the State of Alaska, where she worked as the statewide training coordinator and assisted with the development and troubleshooting of the reporting system for the accounting program. Dr. Schirmer was active in the preparation of Alaska's Comprehensive Annual Financial Report and assisted with the budgetary implementation, departmental accounting, and structure training.

Dedications

The authors dedicate this book to the following individuals:

For Chris, Kierstan, and Meaghan, who are the center of my universe, and for Dad, who believed in me until the very end.

—Jeanette Landin

For Royce and Elizabeth, who kept me grounded and reminded me to have fun. For Christina, who remind me to stop and breathe.

—Paulette Schirmer

A Note from the Authors

We are excited to share the new edition of *Payroll Accounting 2021* with you. Payroll accounting is detailed, deadline-driven, and of utmost importance for the successful functioning of a business. The changing, detailed nature of payroll accounting involves legal challenges, economic changes, technological advances, and—above all—governmental obligations. Our text takes a modern approach to payroll accounting, incorporating coverage of real-world issues that many students will face in their careers, such as cyber security, payroll fraud, labor planning, and labor costs. We believe that information contained in this textbook and its ancillary materials contribute to a comprehensive understanding of payroll accounting in the 21st century and that it will make accounting students more valuable to the organizations they work for in their careers.

But as educators, we understand that providing the content is not enough, so we provide multiple opportunities for students to practice in Connect. Whether you are teaching face-to-face, hybrid, or online, *Payroll Accounting 2021* is flexible enough to be used in courses as short as 3 weeks and as long as 15 weeks. We are proud of what we have accomplished with this text, and we thank the faculty and students who have provided feedback to refine the content in this edition. We strongly believe that we have taken payroll accounting education to a higher level of rigor.

Our approach to payroll accounting is different from other existing texts because of our perspective about payroll's role in business. To us, payroll is more than pressing buttons, writing checks, and submitting forms—payroll is the story of **people.** These people include the ones within the business who make decisions about the company's directions and the people who work for the business and depend on their paychecks to support their livelihoods. We wrote this text because we wanted students to develop a sense of how business directly affects employees' lives and vice versa.

To foster the connection between business and people, each chapter's introductory story contains recent events involving payroll accounting that highlight the connections among payroll, legislation, business decisions, and people affected by all the decisions made. In Chapter 1 and Chapter 2, we highlighted specific challenges stemming from the Tax Cuts and Jobs Act and effects of the SECURE Act on employers. In Chapter 3, we explored the debate of the minimum wage versus a "living wage" and how it affected governmental workers in Missouri. In Chapter 4, we explore the latest trends in employee fringe benefits, one of which being financial literacy and wellness. We have also explored the effects of the Families First Coronavirus Response Act on fringe benefits to Chapter 4. Chapter 5 now has the information about federal income tax with the changes to the employee Form W-4 that was implemented as of January 1, 2020. We have introduced a new tool available from the IRS to assist with manual computations of federal income tax and have retained the information regarding pre-2020 Forms W-4 because of the likelihood that students will see both types of forms in the workplace for the foreseeable future. In Chapter 6, we highlighted the effect of employee labor costs on the business's overall expenses, especially as it relates to the employer reporting dates in response to the COVID pandemic. Finally, our Chapter 7 introduction highlights a payroll fraud case that was discovered in early 2020 in a tiny town in Vermont, which is still evolving as of the publication of this text.

What makes this text a modern approach is that we believe that payroll is the connection between financial and managerial accounting and that it has everyday connections to businesses, people, and the greater economy in a myriad of ways. Our approach is to encourage students to know the **how** of computing payroll as well as the **why** because we believe strongly that the future of the accounting profession involves knowledge of both the process and the purpose within the broader scheme of business. We have included materials to demonstrate the integration of payroll in other aspects of both managerial and financial accounting as well as business operations. Within Appendixes D and E, we have provided information that allows readers to connect their learning about payroll within the context of their own state's legal framework and links to each state's revenue department to facilitate specific learning. We are passionate about college education because we are both accounting faculty, and we bring a wealth of experience in accounting, education, industry, and governmental settings that informs our writing.

Our text features many interesting real-world connections. We've drawn examples from many different disciplines to help make payroll accounting come alive for teachers and students alike. We want to call specific attention to two discussions that are unique to our text: (1) the content in Chapter 6 that explores labor planning (Learning Objectives 6-5 and 6-6) and (2) the discussion in Chapter 7 about the function of labor costs in business and employee benefit reports as strategic tools (Learning Objectives 7-5 and 7-6). We believe that this information contributes to a comprehensive understanding of payroll accounting in the 21st century and that it will make accounting students more valuable as emerging accountants embarking upon their careers. We have added notes regarding COVID-19 and payroll throughout the text to bring attention to the effects of the pandemic on this essential business function.

We strongly believe that payroll accounting needs to be applied, so we provide both a continuing problem, located at the end of each chapter and a comprehensive problem, located in Appendix A, that may be presented in either three-month or one-month versions. Technological integration of the continuing problem and Appendix A within Connect provides an excellent tool for student learning and faculty assessment of course learning objectives. SmartBook 2.0, LearnSmart, and guided example videos of tax-form completion lead to reinforcement of both concepts and key terminology. We are excited to produce this work through McGraw-Hill because of its top-quality teaching and learning resources available through Connect. Teaching traditional payroll accounting and Internet-based financial accounting via McGraw-Hill's Connect platform for several years has been a wonderful experience for both our students and ourselves.

The AACSB guidelines encourage the achievement of the highest possible standards in business education. We believe that students should understand both how payroll should be completed as well as how it can be manipulated for personal gain. Payroll fraud continues to be a major source of loss for companies, and it is surprising to find how common it is. We've included examples of the frauds that employees have perpetrated in recent years. According to the Government Accounting Office, payroll fraud of all types, including misclassification of workers, costs the federal government $16 billion annually. We hope that these stories enliven and enrich your class discussions. We've also updated the payroll processing options in Chapter 1 to reflect an accurate representation of the current state of the available technology used by businesses of any size (Learning Objective 1-5). In Chapter 2, we explored situations in which an individual may have multiple employers and changes implemented by the USCIS and the U.S. Department of Health and Human Services for Multistate employers (Learning Objective 2-2). We believe that this information about multiple employers and multistate employees is a growing issue that will challenge employers.

Another new piece in this edition is the updated Employee Earnings Register to capture data provided by employees on Form W-4 and apply it to federal income tax computations (Learning Objective 5-1). We have updated our section about cryptocurrency as a means of transmitting payroll amounts due. It is important to understand that cryptocurrency as a means of paying employees, while being considered, is a complicated issue because of its connection to the stock market, as opposed to a central bank, as a basis for its value. This topic is evolving and we are certain that we will witness the evolution of payment methods that will involve some sort of cryptocurrency in the future as far as regulating its use and protecting employee pay and employer tax remittance.

We continue to rely on the guidance of our colleagues, instructor feedback, and student suggestions to keep us grounded and to push us to deliver the best possible content. We hope you enjoy reading this book as much as we enjoy writing it!

Jeanette Landin
Paulette Schirmer

Changes to the Seventh Edition

Based on feedback from our reviewers and users, we have included additional content in this seventh edition of *Payroll Accounting*. During the process of updating the content for the seventh edition, we explored the changes to payroll taxes stemming from the Tax Cuts and Jobs Act of 2017, most of which are in Chapter 5. We explored the Final Rule, enacted in January 2020, in Chapter 1 and its effect on the minimum wage for salaried workers in Chapter 3. We added a discussion of SUTA taxes and tips for employers to reduce their SUTA tax rate in Chapter 6. We included a new tool produced by the IRS in 2020 to assist in the computation of federal income tax for Forms W-4 completed in 2020 and for the Forms W-4 completed in prior years and showed how it compared to the use of the wage-bracket and the percentage methods based on Publication 15-T in Chapter 5.

We have maintained our content about the available payroll certification exams. A correlation guide is included in Appendix F that aligns the learning objectives in the text with the topics included on payroll certification examinations offered by the National Association of Certified Professional Bookkeepers (NACPB), the American Institute of Professional Bookkeepers (AIPB), and the American Payroll Association (APA).

We appreciate all feedback and user recommendations we have received because they have helped us create a stronger, more complete text. The changes we have made have added clarity, updated information, and given additional opportunities for students to demonstrate their understanding of the concepts presented.

The following are specific changes to each chapter.

Chapter 1

In Chapter 1, we updated payroll-related legislation to reflect as many changes as possible prior to publication. We discussed the Final Rule, the SECURE Act, and the changes to the e-Verify system. We added information about *qui tam* rewards and clarified the provisions of the various sections of the SOX Act. We updated our discussion of Work Opportunity Tax Credit provisions as they relate to the PATH act. We expanded the discussion of ACA reporting requirements and added information about the employer's role in child support enforcement through payroll garnishments.

Chapter 2

Chapter 2 now has an expanded explanation of H-1B visas and the full multistate employer form. We updated the graph depicting the trend of average hours worked per week. We updated the discussion of the effects of the gig economy on employer documentation by exploring the joint employer rule. We included a link to the Massachusetts Institute of Technology's living wage calculator to help explain the difference between minimum wage and living wage. We discussed Regulation Z as it pertains to paycard regulation and employee access to earned funds.

Chapter 3

Chapter 3 opens with updated minimum wage and tipped minimum wage information. We added a discussion of overtime computations for piece-rate workers to clarify the differences between piece-rate and other types of overtime pay. We introduced an updated payroll register format to match the new requirements from the 2020 Form W-4. We expanded our discussion of compensation for on-call time.

Chapter 4

We have expanded the discussion of fringe benefits in Chapter 4. We discussed that certain states consider paid time, such as sick and vacation time, as fringe benefits and include that time in taxable income computations, regardless of the employee's use of the time. We added a reference table for garnishments to foster deeper understanding of the percentages allowed for each type with an emphasis on the percent of total compensation that may be garnished, We expanded a discussion of labor unions with an example that highlighted the current use of labor unions in the tech industry and added information regarding fringe benefits enacted in response to the COVID-19 pandemic.

Chapter 5

Chapter 5 contains an explanation of the differences between federal income tax computations based on the changes to the W-4. We devoted a section of the chapter to explain the new withholding guidelines, which are more closely aligned with the tax return guidelines for marital status and dependents as well as including the computations for employees whose Forms W-4 are pre-2020. We included an Excel-based income tax assistant that is available from the IRS for manual payroll computation.

Chapter 6

In Chapter 6, we updated employer payroll tax information and all tax forms with the current year's editions. We included a new section detailing ways for employers to reduce SUTA tax rates, thus reducing the overall cost of labor. We expanded our presentation of state and local tax remittances and included examples of completed state and local tax return forms to prepare students for real-world situations. We have explored temporary changes to reporting requirements due to the COVID pandemic. We discussed the penalty for willfully not depositing employee-share payroll taxes, as mandated by IRS code. We concluded the chapter with a discussion of the purpose of completing benefit analysis reports within the context of industry partners and company strategy.

Chapter 7

Chapter 7 explores the increased need for critical thought as a function of the payroll accountants' responsibilities because artificial intelligence (AI) is increasing its role in the accounting process. We highlighted the shift in the payroll accountant's duties to involve less data entry and more data and trend analysis. We concluded the chapter with a discussion of how the Internet of Things (IoT) affects payroll, especially as it relates to report generation and accurate financial reports. We have streamlined the overall view of the payroll process from beginning to end to provide students with a concise guide to completing payroll.

COVID-19 specific payroll information contained in this edition:

As the federal response to the COVID-19 pandemic was continuously evolving as we wrote this edition, we were unable to include application of the Paycheck Protection Program (PPP) to examples and problem materials in this edition. However, it is important to note the following information about the (PPP) Final Rule:

- Payroll costs are eligible for PPP. Specific payroll costs are:
  - Salaries, wages, commissions, tips, or other compensation are covered. Employers may use tip records or a reasonable estimate of tips, provided the tips were in cash.
  - Other covered payroll costs include paid time off for vacation, FMLA-related leave, sick leave, separation, or dismissal pay.
  - Health care coverage, insurance premiums, retirement costs, and remittance of state and local taxes pertaining to employee payroll are covered. "Retirement costs" are not yet defined as of May 22, 2020.
  - Bonuses and hazard pay are considered payroll costs.
  - Owner-employees may receive 8/52 of their 2019 compensation.
- Loans will be forgiven for tips during the covered period. The covered period is either eight weeks from loan disbursement or an Alternative Payroll Covered Period if employees are paid biweekly or more frequently. Employers will not have forgiveness for payroll costs that are incurred between disbursement of the PPP loan and the Alternative Payroll Covered Period. The Alternative Payroll Covered Period expires as of June 30, 2020.
- Loan forgiveness does not include employer reduction in full-time employees (or equivalent if the employee works 40 or more hours per week). However, if an employee does not return due to illness, death, or rejection of an offer to return to work, the employer will not be penalized.
- Employers who reduce employee hours or pay rate by more than 25% will not receive loan forgiveness for those employees.
- Employers must retain records of the PPP documentation for six years after the date of forgiveness or repayment in full.
- The AICPA has a loan forgiveness spreadsheet and instructions available at https://www.aicpa.org/content/dam/aicpa/interestareas/privatecompaniespracticesection/qualityservicesdelivery/ussba/downloadabledocuments/coronavirus-ppp-loan-forgiveness-calculation-steps.pdf

Appendix A: Comprehensive Payroll Project

In Appendix A, we continued the emphasis on completion of the payroll register and the transfer of data to both employees' earnings records and accounting entries. We moved the comprehensive project to remove the state withholding tax because of the changes resulting from the implementation of the Tax Cuts and Job Act since many states had not finalized income tax procedures at the time of publication.

Appendix C: Federal Income Tax Tables

We updated both the percentage and the wage-bracket methods of determining federal income tax withholding to reflect the most current tax rates available. We have included both Publication 15 and Publication 15-T in this appendix.

Appendix D: State Income Tax Information

We updated the tax rates for each state in Appendix D.

Appendix F: Payroll Certification Information

We continued correlating the learning objectives in this text with the topics included on payroll certification examinations offered by the National Association of Certified Professional Bookkeepers (NACPB), the American Institute of Professional Bookkeepers (AIPB), and the American Payroll Association (APA). We included the certification exam requirements and contact information for each certification organization.

Text Features

Chapter Opener

Each chapter opens by focusing on a payroll accounting topic related to a real-world company to set the stage for the topic of the chapter.

Chapter One

Payroll Practices and System Fundamentals

Payroll systems are an integral part of job planning and strategic human resource management, cost management for products and services, and benefits analysis for a company. A company's payroll system has historically connected human resources and accounting departments. In contemporary businesses, payroll has taken on a strategic role in terms of company direction and future plans. The continual evolution of technological tools to manage company resources, including monetary and human, provides both opportunities and challenges to employers in terms of employee access and protection of private information. A well-designed payroll system is a critical element in company management; for this reason, an understanding of payroll foundations is imperative. In this chapter, we will explore the need for a payroll system, legal requirements, ethical guidelines, best practices, and variations in payroll practices among different-sized companies.

LEARNING OBJECTIVES

After studying Chapter 1, you should be able to:

LO 1-1   Identify Legislation That Pertains to Payroll and Business

LO 1-2   Discuss the Legal Framework Specific to Payroll Accounting

Stop & Check

The Stop & Check feature allows students to review their understanding of the content just read. It also enables instructors to conduct formative assessments at multiple points throughout each chapter, testing the students' understanding informally as well as offering opportunities to expand on the material.

Which Law?

Stop & Check

1. Requires employers to verify the employee's legal right to work in the United States?
2. Protects the rights of disabled workers?
3. Governs the management of retirement plans?
4. Protects discrimination of workers older than age 40?
5. Creates safe work environments for employees?
6. Mandates equal pay for equal work?
7. Extends medical benefits for terminated employees?
8. Ensures that child support obligations will be paid?
9. Protects workers and families with preexisting medical conditions?
10. Enforces payment of monetary damages because of discrimination?
11. Requires internal controls on payroll practices of public companies?
12. Gives small employers incentives to establish retirement plans?

a. COBRA
b. ERISA
c. Civil Rights Act of 1991
d. PRWOR
e. SOX
f. ADEA
g. HIPAA
h. ADA
i. OSHA
j. Equal Pay Act of 1963
k. IRCA
l. SECURE

Trends to Watch

Each chapter contains a feature box that connects payroll-related recent events with industry trends that shape the future of the profession. These trends offer instructors more opportunities to expand upon chapter topics, fostering discussion and application.

Trends to Watch

LEGAL ENVIRONMENT

To say that the legal environment of payroll is continually evolving is an understatement. Since 2017, we have witnessed the following legal challenges:

- Increasing numbers of private employers and localities raising the minimum wage significantly to close the gap between the minimum wage and the living wage.
- Challenges to the Affordable Care Act related to the overturn of the individual mandate for health care coverage.
- Supplemental wage rate changes for payments of bonuses.
- State enforcement of predictive scheduling, fair/flexible scheduling laws on changing employee's schedules.
- Re-framing the federal income tax structure, treatment for nonresident aliens, supplemental wage withholding rates, and inflation adjustments.

Some trends to watch include the following:

- An increase in the demand for flexible work schedules as younger employees enter the workforce.
- The expansion of artificial intelligence (AI) into the payroll process that connects it more closely to HR and other company functions.
- An increase in the use of Human Resource information systems that connects company functions into an integrated platform.
- A reduction of paper in the payroll function through the use of Internet-based systems that connect departments within a company and employees via web portals and portable apps.
- Acceleration in businesses moving to a completely cloud-based operations management and payroll process.

End-of-Chapter Assessments

Students can demonstrate their understanding through assessments designed to complement the chapter's learning objectives. Each chapter has review questions, exercises, and problems, with the exercises and problems having two sets each chapter (Set A and Set B). Each type of assessment is designed to measure student learning as follows:

- Questions for review are designed to check for students' remembrance of concepts.
- Exercises check for understanding and application of chapter concepts.
- Problems allow students to apply and analyze payroll accounting principles.

Exercises Set A

E1-1A.
LO 1-1, 1-2
Lupore Fabrics obtained a contract in Watts Mills, South Carolina that involves the production of materials for military uniforms, a project contracted with the federal government for $2,800,000. What laws govern the wages Lupore Fabrics pays to its workers for this project? (Select all that may apply.)
1. Davis–Bacon Act
2. Sarbanes–Oxley Act
3. Walsh–Healey Act
4. FLSA

E1-2A.
LO 1-1, 1-2
Martine Piccirillo works as the payroll clerk for Centinix, a security company that hires many part-time and temporary workers who are paid on an hourly basis. What law governs the hiring or documenting of these workers?
1. ADEA
2. FLSA
3. IRCA
4. USERRA

Critical Thinking Exercises

Want to challenge your students further? The Critical Thinking Exercises require students to consider complex real-world situations that build confidence and turn learning into mastery. These exercises offer possibilities for team presentations or class debate.

Critical Thinking

CT1-1. You have been hired as a consultant for Dynozz Medical Software, which an IRS audit of its accounting records. During your review, you notice and the payroll system involving overpayments of labor and payments to te employees. What should you do?

CT1-2. Liliya Milic is the accountant for Syiva, a local nonprofit organization. She tasked with managing the costs of the payroll so that staffing levels ma the same even if funding levels change. She considers outsourcing the a payroll processing company. What are some factors that Liliya should in her decision? Why are these factors important?

In the Real World: Scenarios for Discussion

Each chapter contains a discussion scenario that is drawn from real-world events. These scenarios encourage the expansion of chapter content and allow students to apply their learning to real situations.

In the Real World: Scenario for Discussion

Domino's Pizza franchises in New York were sued by the state of New York in 20 wage theft at 10 stores. Under New York law, a corporation and a franchiser ar employers if they meet certain criteria regarding employee control. The state four Domino's met the criteria for being a joint employer because it mandates a sign number of policies with which franchisers must comply. The problem arose when Do mandated the use of PULSE payroll software, which the pizza company knew to be and did not attempt to remedy. The flawed software led to employees being paid a below the legal minimum wage, failed to pay overtime, did not reimburse employe vehicle use, and abused tip credit guidelines.

Internet Activities

The Internet Activities at the end of each chapter offer students the chance to use their web navigation skills to expand on their learning. These exercises attract tech-savvy learners, allowing them to form their own understanding of payroll concepts on their own terms.

Internet Activities

1-1. Using the website www.jstor.org, search for articles about payroll-related laws or relevant employment legislation. Once you find an article, summarize the article and explain how the legislation influenced contemporary payroll practices.

1-2. Visit the website of the American Payroll Association at www.americanpayroll.org. On the right side of the Home page, you will find articles about recent developments in payroll practices and legislation. Choose an article and create a presentation to your class about how its content affects payroll practice.

1-3. Want to know more about the specifics of some of the concepts in this chapter? Check out these websites:

Continuing Payroll Project: Prevosti Farms and Sugarhouse

Toni Prevosti is opening a new business, Prevosti Farms a Sugarhouse, which is a small company that will harvest, refine, and s maple syrup products. In subsequent chapters, students will have t opportunity to establish payroll records and complete payroll inform tion for Prevosti Farms and Sugarhouse.

Toni has decided that she needs to hire employees for the bu ness to grow. Complete the application for Prevosti Farms and Sugarhouse's Employ Identification Number (Form SS-4) with the following information:

Prevosti Farms and Sugarhouse is located at 820 Westminster Road, Bridgewat Vermont, 05520 (which is also Ms. Prevosti's home address), phone number 802-55 3456. Bridgewater is in Windsor County. Toni, the responsible party for a Limited Liabil Corporation created in the United States with one member (disregarded entity), h decided that Prevosti Farms and Sugarhouse, will pay its employees on a biweekly bas Toni's Social Security numb 5-22-0443. The beginning the busine

Sianc/Shutterstock

Continuing Payroll Project: Prevosti Farms and Sugarhouse

Starting with Chapter 1, each chapter has an integrated, continuing payroll project—about a fictional company Prevosti Farms and Sugarhouse—that matches the chapter content and affords students a macro-level understanding of how each piece of payroll fits together.

Comprehensive Payroll Project: Wayland Custom Woodworking

The Comprehensive Payroll Project (Appendix A) allows students to track a quarter's worth of payroll transactions for a company. This Comprehensive Payroll Project offers instructors increased flexibility in teaching and assessment by offering a simulation equivalent to a full quarter of a fictitious company's payroll activities, including payroll transactions, pay processing, and tax form completion. The Comprehensive Payroll Project may be presented in different lengths—as short as one month or in its three-month entirety—to meet curricular needs. Instructors may assign this in connection with many chapters of the book or use it as a final project for their courses.

Appendix A

Comprehensive Payroll Project: Wayland Custom Woodworking

Wayland Custom Woodworking is a firm that manufactures custom cabinets and woodwork for business and residential customers. Students will have the opportunity to establish payroll records and to complete a month of payroll information for Wayland.

Wayland Custom Woodworking is located at 12850 Old Highway 50, Glenbrook, Nevada, 89413, phone number 775-555-9877. The owner is Mark Wayland. Wayland's EIN is 91-7444533I and the Nevada Employer Account Number is E6462582020-6. Wayland has determined it will pay its employees on a semimonthly basis. Federal income tax should be computed using the percentage method.

Students will complete the payroll for the final quarter of 2020 and will file the fourth quarter and annual tax reports on the appropriate dates. At the instructor's discretion, students may complete a short version, which contains the payroll transactions beginning December 4. Directions for completion of the short version follow the November 30 transactions.

Rounding can create a challenge these exercises, the rate for the individual round So take their salary and 2,080 (52 weeks at 40 hours per week hour

Connect for *Payroll Accounting 2021*

- **SmartBook 2.0®** A personalized and adaptive learning tool used to maximize the learning experience by helping students study more efficiently and effectively. SmartBook 2.0 highlights where in the chapter to focus, asks review questions on the materials covered and tracks the most challenging content for later review recharge. SmartBook 2.0 is available both online and offline.

- **End-of-Chapter** Content is a robust offering of review and question material designed to aid and assess the student's retention of chapter content. The end-of-chapter content is composed of both static and algorithmic exercises, problems, critical thinking exercises, and continuing payroll projects, which are designed to challenge students using McGraw Hill's state-of-the-art online homework technology. Guided example videos are also provided with select end-of chapter problems, which help walk students through complex payroll processes. Instructors can also assign test bank questions to students in both static and algorithmic versions.

- **Auto-Graded Payroll and Tax Forms** are integrated into Connect and are assignable. Students can complete the forms in these problems to gain a better understanding of how payroll forms are prepared in today's digital world.

- **Guided example videos** are also provided with select end-of-chapter problems, which help walk students through complex payroll processes. Instructors can also assign test bank questions to students in both static and algorithmic versions.

- The **Comprehensive Payroll Project** from Appendix A is available on Connect in an auto-graded format. Students will apply skills, such as preparing tax forms and payroll registers, to complete the payroll process for a company from start to finish. Instructors can choose from the full three-month version or the shorter one-month version for their Connect assignment.

- **The Test Bank** for each chapter has been updated for the seventh edition to stay current with new and revised chapter material, with all questions available for assignment through Connect. Newly available within Connect, Test Builder is a cloud-based tool that enables instructors to format tests that can be printed or administered within a LMS. Test Builder offers a modern, streamlined interface for easy content configuration that matches course needs, without requiring a download. Test Builder provides a secure interface for better protection of content and allows for just-in-time updates to flow directly into assessments.

Auto-Graded Forms

Comprehensive Payroll Project

Instructors: Student Success Starts with You

Tools to enhance your unique voice

Want to build your own course? No problem. Prefer to use our turnkey, prebuilt course? Easy. Want to make changes throughout the semester? Sure. And you'll save time with Connect's auto-grading too.

65%
Less Time
Grading

Laptop: McGraw Hill; Woman/dog: George Doyle/Getty Images

Study made personal

Incorporate adaptive study resources like SmartBook® 2.0 into your course and help your students be better prepared in less time. Learn more about the powerful personalized learning experience available in SmartBook 2.0 at **www.mheducation.com/highered/connect/smartbook**

Affordable solutions, added value

Make technology work for you with LMS integration for single sign-on access, mobile access to the digital textbook, and reports to quickly show you how each of your students is doing. And with our Inclusive Access program you can provide all these tools at a discount to your students. Ask your McGraw Hill representative for more information.

Solutions for your challenges

A product isn't a solution. Real solutions are affordable, reliable, and come with training and ongoing support when you need it and how you want it. Visit **www.supportateverystep.com** for videos and resources both you and your students can use throughout the semester.

Padlock: Jobalou/Getty Images

Checkmark: Jobalou/Getty Images

Students: Get Learning that Fits You

Effective tools for efficient studying

Connect is designed to make you more productive with simple, flexible, intuitive tools that maximize your study time and meet your individual learning needs. Get learning that works for you with Connect.

Study anytime, anywhere

Download the free ReadAnywhere app and access your online eBook or SmartBook 2.0 assignments when it's convenient, even if you're offline. And since the app automatically syncs with your eBook and SmartBook 2.0 assignments in Connect, all of your work is available every time you open it. Find out more at **www.mheducation.com/readanywhere**

> *"I really liked this app—it made it easy to study when you don't have your textbook in front of you."*
>
> - Jordan Cunningham,
>   Eastern Washington University

Calendar: owattaphotos/Getty Images

Everything you need in one place

Your Connect course has everything you need—whether reading on your digital eBook or completing assignments for class, Connect makes it easy to get your work done.

Learning for everyone

McGraw Hill works directly with Accessibility Services Departments and faculty to meet the learning needs of all students. Please contact your Accessibility Services Office and ask them to email accessibility@mheducation.com, or visit **www.mheducation.com/about/accessibility** for more information.

Acknowledgments

This seventh edition of *Payroll Accounting* would not have been possible without the patience, guidance, and encouragement of Steve Schuetz, executive portfolio manager; the diligence and commitment of Sarah Sacco, product developer; the support and leadership of Fran Simon and Brian Nacik, content project managers; the incredible form templates designed by Kitty O'Donnell; and the amazing artwork of Beth Blech, designer. We further want to thank Claire McLemore, marketing manager; Beth Cray, content licensing specialist; Kevin Moran, director of digital content; Xin Lin, lead product manager; and the composition team at SPi Global. Thanks go to our project development team who handled every formatting request with professionalism. Special thanks to Carmela Gordon, Trident Technical College, for her contributions to verify the accuracy of our content.

Countless other colleagues have offered their feedback, insights, and inspiration during various stages of this project. We want to extend sincere thanks to the reviewers who helped us shape the seventh edition:

Angel Luper
Tri-County Technical College

April Mohr
Jefferson Community and Technical College

Beth Vaughn
Zane State College

Carmela Gordon
Trident Technical College

Debbie Trumbo
Gwinnett Technical College

Denice Pardee
Arapahoe Community College

Edwina Phillips
Rhodes State College

Erol Tucker
Victoria College

Gerald Childs
Waukesha County Technical College

Jeanine Metzler
North Hampton Community College

Jennifer Alderman
Highland Community College

Jeremy Germann
Centralia College

Joseph Nicassio
Westmoreland County Community College

Lori Parry
Eastern Gateway Community College

M. Jeff Quinlan
Madison College

Marina Grau
Houston Community College

Martha Cranford
Rowan-Cabarrus Community College

Matthew Njoku
Central Piedmont Community College

Rhonda O'Quinn
Helena College University of Montana

Ronald Carter
Patrick Henry College

Saturnino Gonzalez
El Paso Community College

Tanya Haddad
Southwestern College of California

Victoria Badura
Metropolitan Community College

William Lyle
Georgia Piedmont Technical College

Our heartfelt thanks to all who have helped us continue to improve this text.

Jeanette Landin

Paulette Schirmer

Brief Contents

Contents

Payroll Accounting 2021

Chapter One

Payroll Practices and System Fundamentals

Payroll systems are an integral part of job planning and strategic human resource management, cost management for products and services, and benefits analysis for a company. A company's payroll system has historically connected human resources and accounting departments. In contemporary businesses, payroll has taken on a strategic role in terms of company direction and future plans. The continual evolution of technological tools to manage company resources, including monetary and human, provides both opportunities and challenges to employers in terms of employee access and protection of private information. A well-designed payroll system is a critical element in company management; for this reason, an understanding of payroll foundations is imperative. In this chapter, we will explore the need for a payroll system, legal requirements, ethical guidelines, best practices, and variations in payroll practices among different-sized companies.

LEARNING OBJECTIVES

After studying Chapter 1, you should be able to:

LO 1-1   Identify Legislation That Pertains to Payroll and Business

LO 1-2   Discuss the Legal Framework Specific to Payroll Accounting

LO 1-3   Discuss the Ethical Guidelines for Payroll Accounting

LO 1-4   Identify Contemporary Payroll Practices

LO 1-5   Compare Payroll Processing Options for Different Businesses

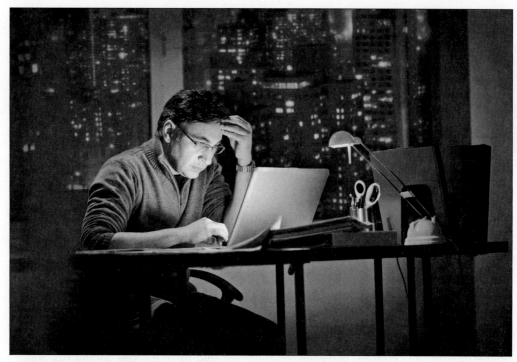

JGI/Tom Grill/Blend Images LLC

The Final Rule: FLSA Updated

The U.S. Department of Labor issued a Final Rule that was enforced in early 2020 and addressed which employee payments may be excluded from overtime rates. This was an important clarification because the last update to FLSA about overtime pay was 50 years earlier. Some of the employee benefits that do not need to be included in their regular pay rate include:

- Unused paid leave, either sick time or paid time off.
- Certain types of referral and sign-on bonuses.
- Discretionary bonuses stemming from exceptional events.
- Sporadic or infrequent payments.
- "Right to rest" pay and "Clopening" (i.e., closing and opening) pay.

These Final Rule guidelines address new employment situations that were not problems 50 years ago but have become frequent enough that legislative guidance was deemed necessary. Corporate human resources and payroll personnel undertake a critical function in their companies. They must ensure that payroll is not only disbursed in a timely and accurate manner, and they must also abide by an ever-changing legal landscape.

(Source: Morgan Lewis)

Employment legislation is highly complex and dynamic. Large or small, employers must abide by the law and be aware when it changes. In Chapter 1, we will explore the basics of payroll systems, including legal and ethical issues involved with employee pay.

LO 1-1   Identify Legislation That Pertains to Payroll and Business

Alexander Kirch/Shutterstock

Unlike many other types of accounting, payroll affects most (if not all) members of an organization. Payroll errors can lead to serious internal and external problems. Internal errors may cause a company to pay excessive wages for unneeded overtime, underpay employees, forgo profits, or employ the wrong number or type of workers during seasonal or other workflow changes. Managers use internal reports about labor usage, staffing levels, and employee compensation trends to ensure operational effectiveness. Organizational decision-makers use these reports to control labor costs, hire additional employees to meet surge demands, and manage the cost of goods sold. Payroll errors can result in governmental fines, taxes, or legal charges related to the violation of labor laws. Employers provide external reports to the Internal Revenue Service (IRS), state government tax departments, and many more agencies, depending upon the nature of the company.

> The Louisiana Department of Revenue took action in 2018 against three companies for underreporting employee tax liabilities. The Government Against Misclassified Employees Operational Network (GAME ON) Task Force found that these three companies had deliberately misclassified workers as independent contractors instead of employees to avoid employee income tax liability. During the three years investigated, the total of tax liabilities, penalties, and interest due for the three companies was approximately $250,000. (Source: Louisiana Department of Revenue)

According to the United States Bureau of Labor Statistics as of 2018, employment in accounting jobs is expected to increase 6 percent through 2028, which is the average growth for business professions. Salaries average $44,761 for payroll clerks, $78,829 for payroll supervisors, and $99,623 for payroll managers, according to the 2020 salary guides available via www.salary.com.

The legislative framework governing employers' payroll systems is complex. Although several fundamental laws still exist, payroll and human resource laws tend to reflect societal evolution over time. Note how some of these laws have been challenged or changed since their inception.

The *Equal Pay Act of 1963* mandated that males and females be paid equally for equal work. As of 2020, 48 states have enacted legislation that clarifies and/or extends the original 1963 act. Any employees who feel they have been paid unequally based upon gender have legal options to rectify the situation:

- First, they should gather documentation regarding the differential and determine if other employees in question are willing to substantiate the difference.
- Second, they should speak with their supervisor to question the pay differential.
- Should the supervisor be unwilling to discuss or adjust the pay discrepancy, an attorney may become a necessary third step.

This act was modified by the *Lilly Ledbetter Fair Pay Act of 2009*, which removed the 180-day statute of limitations on claims of unequal treatment.

> In 1979, Lilly Ledbetter, an employee of Goodyear Tire and Rubber Company, started at the same rate of pay as males in the same position. Over time, management declined her raises based on negative reviews that Ms. Ledbetter later claimed were discriminatory. Under the provisions of the 1963 Equal Pay Act, the claimant had 180 days to file a complaint. Although the U.S. Supreme Court agreed with her discrimination claims, it ruled in favor of Goodyear because of the lack of timeliness of Ms. Ledbetter's filing. This ruling ultimately led to the Lilly Ledbetter Fair Pay Act of 2009. (Source: U.S. EEOC)

CREATISTA/Getty Images

The *Civil Rights Act of 1964* prohibited discrimination based on race, creed, color, gender, and national origin. Since 1964, this act has been extended by Executive Order 11478 to protect people with AIDS, pregnant workers, people with different sexual orientations, and people with disabilities. In June 2015, the U.S. Supreme Court ruled in *Obergefell v. Hodges* (U.S. Supreme Court No. 14-556) that same-sex marriage was legal and could not be banned in any state. This extension of the 1964 Civil Rights Act represented another step toward the legal protection of worker dignity.

The *Age Discrimination in Employment Act of 1967 (ADEA)* prevents mandatory retirement of older employees (older than age 40) and prohibits age-based discrimination in hiring.

> An AARP survey conducted in Oregon found that 62% of workers over the age of 40 who have applied for employment have been discriminated against due to their age. Approximately 35% of job applicants over the age of 40 have been asked age-related questions during job interviews, which is a violation of ADEA. However, older workers are the most rapidly growing group of workers in Oregon. The Oregon legislature is seeking legal remedies for this issue as of 2020. (Source: AARP)

NicolasMcComber/Getty Images

The *Occupational Safety and Health Act of 1970 (OSHA)* defined and enforced healthy and safe working environments for employees. Employee safety programs and personal protective equipment represent an additional cost to the employer, but fines for noncompliance and payments made following workplace injuries are often far more costly: fines range from $13,494 per serious violation to $134,937 (2020 figures) for willful or repeated violations.

The *Employee Retirement Income Security Act of 1974 (ERISA)* regulates the management of retirement and pension plans. ERISA has been extended by the *Consolidated Omnibus Budget Reformation Act of 1985 (COBRA)*. During the recession of 2007–2009, the value of some employee retirement funds decreased, causing employees to postpone retirement. The Internal Revenue Service imposes limitations on retirement plan contributions, and those limits have shifted to reflect the need for employees to recoup losses sustained during the recession. Since that time, employee retirement benefits have shifted from being a financial burden to becoming an employee hiring and retention strategy, and retirement researchers are contemplating proposing a mandatory retirement savings law.

COBRA extended medical benefits for terminated employees at the employee's expense. The repeal of the Defense of Marriage Act (DOMA) in 2013 forced employers to offer COBRA coverage to same-sex spouses. As of 2020, terminated employees who opt not to enroll in COBRA plans may enroll in *Marketplace* plans for up to 60 days post-termination.

COBRA benefits currently extend to beneficiaries including employees, dependent spouses, and children. Benefits are paid to beneficiaries in the event of reduced hours or separation of employment for any reason excluding gross misconduct and upon the death of the employee. In the event that the company offers retiree benefits, COBRA coverage also extends to beneficiaries in the event of Chapter 11 bankruptcy.

In 2020, the *Setting Every Community Up for Retirement Enhancement (SECURE) Act* granted small employers tax incentives if they implemented an automatic retirement plan enrollment for their employees. Alternatively, the act allows small employers to form a group that would allow the employees of each business to have better access to retirement plans than the employer could offer by itself.

A development in 2019 involved the IRS approval of an employer connecting employee 401(k) contributions toward payment of their student loans. In one instance, the guidelines for an employer's contribution to the employee's student loan were that the employees were paying at least 2 percent of their salary toward their student loans during a given period. Other companies, such as Abbott, offer an expanded 401(k) employer match for employees who meet similar guidelines as far as their student loan repayment. (Source: Employee Benefit News)

The *Immigration Reform and Control Act of 1986 (IRCA)* requires employers to verify that employees are legally able to work in the United States. Form I-9 is the most common payroll-related application of this law. Immigration and citizenship laws require the collection of information within an I-9, and retention is three years from the date of hire or one year from date of termination (whichever is longer).

Information collected on Form I-9 is monitored closely to ensure that the employee is legally authorized to work in the United States. Employers may also use the *E-verify* system to confirm legal employment eligibility. Note that the E-verify system does not replace the completion of the I-9 but does offer employers the opportunity to check legal employment eligibility rapidly via the Internet.

Westend61/Getty Images

The *Americans with Disabilities Act of 1990 (ADA)* extended the provisions of the Civil Rights Act of 1964 by ensuring that people with disabilities have the same opportunities as those without mental or physical impairment. This law applies to employers with 15 or more employees on the payroll, including full-time and part-time workers. The enactment of the *Americans with Disabilities Act Amendments Act (ADAAA)* in 2008 extended the definition of disability to include a greater number of disabilities. Final Regulations on the ADAAA in 2011 clarified the definitions of disability and the required accommodations to include the following:

- The expansion of the definition of disability includes a lower standard of the definition of impairment.
- The determination of impairments requires the employee to be assessed individually.
- With the exception of corrective lenses, the determination of disability does not include devices that provide relief or mitigation of the condition, such as hearing aids.
- Impairments that occur periodically or episodically or that are in remission are still considered impairments.
- Any disability determination must not require analysis that is extensive,

The *Civil Rights Act of 1991* granted employees who have been discriminated against the chance to be paid monetary damages through legal proceedings. This act applies to American employers and American-controlled employers with internationally based operations.

Workplace diversity and inclusion has become an increasing priority at workplaces during the last decade. As of 2020, *Forbes* posted its listing of the best workplaces for diversity and inclusion, sourced from polls of 60,000 Americans who worked for companies with a minimum of 1,000 employees. The top three employers included the following:

1. SAP Software
2. Henry Ford Health System
3. Procter & Gamble

(**Source:** *Forbes*)

Pixtal/AGE Fotostock

The *Family and Medical Leave Act of 1993 (FMLA)* granted employees the right to take medical leave under reasonable circumstances without fear of job loss. The employee may have to take unpaid leave, but medical benefits must continue under FMLA provisions. Upon return from family leave, the employer must provide an equivalent position with equivalent pay, benefits, and terms of employment. The employer has many responsibilities under the FMLA that involve employee notification of benefits and processes while on leave.

As of 2020, several states have enacted higher levels of paid family leave legislation: California, Connecticut, New Jersey, New York, Oregon, Rhode Island, Washington D.C. (July 2020), and Massachusetts (January 2021). More states are considering paid family leave, which will lead to further clarification about paid family leaves, limits, and specific provisions.

At the end of 2017, the *Tax Cuts and Jobs Act* (Public Law 115-97) was passed by legislators in Washington. This provided a tax credit to employers who offer their employees paid leave under the FMLA. Employers may receive from 12.5 percent to 25 percent, whereas the rate of payment to the employee is 50 percent or more of what the employee would normally be paid during the normal course of work for the company. Eligibility limits of the type of employer and employee exist under the regulations (see Sec. §13403).

The Tax Cuts and Jobs Act (TCJA) has led to specific areas of focus for employers. These areas of focus include

- Compliance: Tax computations have changed, which may force employers to file amended tax returns for 2018 and ensure that 2019 returns follow the tax code changes.

- Controversy: When the TCJA provisions expire, companies may need to re-file tax returns, which makes record-keeping and changes made due to the TCJA enactment a critical function in payroll.

- International tax: For companies with an international presence, including employees, the TCJA may result in new tax liabilities.

- Compensation for executives: TCJA affected the tax treatment of highly compensated employees and fringe benefits offered to workers. This has led to scrutiny of compensation plans and their legal compliance.

- State taxes: Because of TCJA provisions, some states have witnessed tax increases for employees. Since each state has different tax laws and not all states have chosen to comply with TCJA provisions, state taxation has become increasingly complex.

(Source: AICPA)

The *Uniformed Services Employment and Reemployment Rights Act of 1994 (USERRA)* governs the rights of military service members in terms of length of military service, return to work, and accommodations for injured veterans. USERRA was amended as to service members' rights in 2005. In 2011, USERRA was further amended by the Veterans Opportunity to Work Act, which allowed USERRA to recognize claims of a hostile work environment resulting from an individual's military status.

The U.S. Department of Labor investigates many cases involving service members' rights. Army veteran Lisa Slater returned to her job as a security officer, in which she had 13 years with her company, after deployment on active duty. However, upon her return to her employment, she found that she was classified as a new employee, which was found to be a violation of USERRA. She received approximately $20,000 in back wages, and her seniority was restored following arbitration. (Source: U.S. DOL)

The *Personal Responsibility and Work Opportunity Reconciliation Act of 1996 (PRWOR)* mandated that employers file a new hire reporting form within 20 days after an employee initially commences work. This act protects children and needy families by enforcing child support obligations. The child support provisions of PRWOR were strengthened by the passage of the *Personal Responsibility, Work and Family Promotion Act of 2002*, which reauthorized PRWOR when it expired.

> According to the Office of Child Support Enforcement, distributed collections of child support for the fiscal year 2018 totaled in excess of $28 billion. This number represented a decrease of 0.10 percent from the fiscal year 2017. (Source: Office of Child Support Enforcement)

Jeanette Landin

The *Health Insurance Portability and Accountability Act of 1996 (HIPAA)* protects workers and their families who have preexisting medical conditions from discrimination based on those conditions. The Ebola outbreak in 2014 led to additional guidance about HIPAA rights and notifications to interested parties, including employers, during emergency situations.

> HIPAA protections continue even after a business ceases operations. Filefax Inc. of Illinois was ordered to pay approximately $100,000 in fines because of HIPAA violations, although the company is no longer in business. The issue leading to the fines involved a lack of secure storage of employee health records following an investigation by the Office of Civil Rights. (Source: U.S. HHS)

The *Defense of Marriage Act of 1996 (DOMA)* restricted payroll-related taxes and benefits to include only traditionally married couples, denying married status to people in same-sex unions. The U.S. Supreme Court overturned DOMA in its ruling in *U.S. v. Windsor* on September 6, 2013; the Internal Revenue Service subsequently mandated that all married same-sex couples must be treated as married for all tax purposes. The repeal of DOMA had a ripple effect throughout all phases of payroll because of the need to amend business and personal tax return filings back to 2011, owing to the three-year amendment rule. The effects of DOMA's repeal also have had a ripple effect on employee rights, highlighting the need for an additional legislative clarification.

The repeal of DOMA provoked the need to clarify the term "family member." Following the U.S. Supreme Court decision in *Obergefell v. Hodges (2015),* the U.S. Department of Labor updated the definition of spouse to include same-sex marriages, regardless of where they live.

Maskot/Getty Images

In *U.S. v. Windsor,* Ms. Windsor and her wife were recognized as a married couple by the state of New York, and her compensation was taxed accordingly. However, the IRS sued Windsor for unpaid taxes because her same-sex marriage violated DOMA. The U.S. Supreme Court found that DOMA violated Windsor's Fifth Amendment right to liberty and overturned DOMA. The IRS subsequently dropped its lawsuit. (Source: U.S. Supreme Court)

The *Sarbanes–Oxley Act of 2002 (SOX)* provided criminal penalties for violations of ERISA. SOX provides protections for whistle-blowers (Sec. § 806) and mandates the rotation of auditors among publicly owned companies (Sec. § 203). SOX Section 302 mandates that corporate officers must attest to the accuracy and completeness of the contents of the financial statements. An additional consideration for public companies of SOX regarding payroll is that the internal controls of a payroll system must be reported under the law's guidelines (Sec. § 404). Costs of SOX compliance have sparked discussion about the act's effectiveness,

> In 2020, SOX and the Dodd–Frank Act, which involved consumer protection and oversight of trading via the New York Stock Exchange, intersected to strengthen consumer protections (known as *qui tam* rewards). The intersection led to a bill introduced in Congress to create an independent board to oversee auditor conduct in publicly held companies, thus limiting conflicts of interest and thus protecting individuals who invest in companies traded on the stock market. (Source: National Law Review)

The *American Recovery and Reinvestment Act of 2009 (ARRA)* provided tax credits for employers and employees through the Making Work Pay provisions. Although ARRA's provisions have expired, parts of it were reinstated through the *American Taxpayer Relief Act of 2012 (ATRA)*. Many of the ATRA provisions were extended through 2015 by the extension of the Work Opportunity Tax Credit and extended through 2021. The *Protecting Americans from Tax Hikes (PATH) Act* of 2015, which also prevented certain types of tax fraud, extended the ATRA provisions by offering employers tax credits for hiring qualified veterans and individuals who have endured long-term unemployment.

As times change, new legislation will be enacted, and existing laws are sometimes repealed and amended. An example of evolving legislation includes new local laws regarding fairness in scheduling employees' shift work schedules. Right-to-work laws are another example of employment-related legislation. As of 2020, 27 U.S. states and Guam have enacted right-to-work legislation that promotes an employee's right to opt-out of union membership. West Virginia's law has been deemed unconstitutional, and the case will likely go to the state's Supreme Court of Appeals. At the time of this writing, the notion of the right to work without forcing union participation is being considered by the U.S. Congress.

The payroll accountant's job is one of consistent and continual learning and research to ensure that the company is complying with all current regulations and reporting requirements. Many states, but not all, have additional payroll tax laws. Federally mandated payroll laws will be addressed in the next section.

See https://www.thebalancecareers.com/right-to-work-2071691 for more information about state-specific legislation.

Which Law?

Stop & Check

1. Requires employers to verify the employee's legal right to work in the United States?
2. Protects the rights of disabled workers?
3. Governs the management of retirement plans?
4. Protects discrimination of workers older than age 40?
5. Creates safe work environments for employees?
6. Mandates equal pay for equal work?
7. Extends medical benefits for terminated employees?
8. Ensures that child support obligations will be paid?
9. Protects workers and families with preexisting medical conditions?
10. Enforces payment of monetary damages because of discrimination?
11. Requires internal controls on payroll practices of public companies?
12. Gives small employers incentives to establish retirement plans?

a. COBRA
b. ERISA
c. Civil Rights Act of 1991
d. PRWOR
e. SOX
f. ADEA
g. HIPAA
h. ADA
i. OSHA
j. Equal Pay Act of 1963
k. IRCA
l. SECURE

Stoatphoto/Shutterstock

LO 1-2   Discuss the Legal Framework Specific to Payroll Accounting

Why did businesses start withholding taxes from employees' paychecks? Federal income tax withholding was temporarily instituted in 1861 as a way to recover from the high costs of the Civil War; however, this tax was repealed in 1872. Throughout the 19th century, cities were growing in the wake of the Industrial Revolution, as factories and companies increased automation and institutionalized mass production. People were moving from rural to urban areas in unprecedented numbers, and the need for infrastructure and civil services grew. Roads needed to be built, law enforcement personnel needed to be increased, and outbreaks of disease prompted a need for sanitation systems. Therefore, the U.S. Congress formalized the permanent continuation of the federal income tax instituted during the Civil War as a means to fund the infrastructure improvements of the booming cities. After many failed attempts to reinstate a federal income tax, Congress passed the *Sixteenth Amendment to the U.S. Constitution*, in 1909, which was ratified by states in 1913. This version incorporated a tiered income tax, including exemptions and deductions to limit the tax imposed on wages earned; it was the harbinger of many employment-related laws (see Figure 1-1).

During the Great Depression of the 1930s, the stock market collapsed, financial institutions went bankrupt, and companies released workers or ceased business operations. The government needed money to fund programs that would stimulate economic recovery. Additionally, the need for a social welfare system emerged as the number of displaced workers increased. The 1930s became a decade of landmark employment legislation that defined the legal environment for employers and employees, most of which remains enforced in 2020.

In 1931, Congress passed the *Davis–Bacon Act*, creating a standard of wages for governmental contracts totaling more than $2,000. The increased standard wages created under the Davis–Bacon Act brought additional revenue to small businesses and the communities where the contract workers lived, bought groceries, and purchased other services or goods. The Davis–Bacon Act comprised more than 60 different federal statutes, providing a prevailing wage and wage classification strategy to guide employers and contractors. As of 2020, the minimum wage for all employees affected by the Davis–Bacon Act is $10.80 per hour, unless the local prevailing minimum wage rate is higher.

FIGURE 1-1
Timeline of Payroll Legislation

> The determination of wages to be paid to workers affected by the Davis–Bacon Act varies by geographic area, contract, and type of work performed. To facilitate wage determination, the U.S. Department of Labor maintains a website (https://www.wdol.gov/dba.aspx) in which employers may access their specific contract in question and research the provisions of the contract to ensure that employees are paid appropriately. (Source: U.S. Department of Labor)

The *Walsh–Healey Public Contracts Act* of 1936 affected governmental contractors providing goods or services exceeding $10,000. The act required companies to pay workers a minimum wage for all hours worked under 40 per week and time and a half (regular pay times 1.5) per hour for any hours over 40 per week. The Walsh–Healey Public Contracts Act also prohibited the employment of individuals younger than 16 years of age. Compliance with this act is enforced through the Employment Standards Administration Wage and Hour Division of the Department of Labor. These standards also apply to workers within the District of Columbia.

In 1935, the *Social Security Act (SSA)*, also known as the *Federal Insurance Contributions Act (FICA)*, established a contribution-driven fund to help the average U.S. worker in response to the social and financial distress caused by the Great Depression. Originally, the Social Security tax was designed such that younger workers supported retired, disabled workers and surviving families of deceased workers. It is important to note that the worker does not need to die or become disabled to receive Social Security benefits; the truth is that age and disability are components in the decision but are not the only factors considered when awarding Social Security benefits. A contribution-driven fund's employees and employers pay a percentage of gross earnings into the Social Security fund. Originally, the fund was designed to be earmarked for a specific individual upon retirement, but the fund currently provides assistance for families who experience diminished wages and working situations because of the infirmity of the worker or a family member, as well as monetary benefits to dependents of retired or deceased workers. Social Security is synonymous with *Old-Age, Survivors, and Disability Insurance (OASDI)*. *Medicare*, a government-mandated health insurance program for individuals was also included in the SSA legislation. As of 2020, the age at which individuals may receive full retirement benefits is 66 years and eight months for people born after 1958. The full retirement age will increase two months each year until it reaches the full retirement age of 67. However, individuals may begin receiving permanently reduced benefits as early as age 62, but their Social Security payments will be reduced by 25 percent because of the additional months of social security benefits that the person will receive between age 62 and the full retirement age. Similarly, people who retire at age 65 will receive 93.3 percent of the full retirement benefit. (Source: Social Security Administration)

> As of 2020, Social Security paid 8.4 million disabled workers a monthly benefit. This figure represented a milestone for the Social Security Administration because that number was the highest that had ever been paid. Furthermore, the Social Security agency estimated that approximately 62 percent of American retirees depended on their Social Security checks for basic needs such as food and shelter and the funds received from Social Security reduces the poverty rate among senior citizens. The amount of Social Security payouts varies based on age, years of work, and the highest wages earned. (Source: Motley Fool)

As another part of its social welfare legislation, the U.S. Congress passed the *Federal Unemployment Tax Act (FUTA)* as a way to help displaced workers, individuals from the workforce who find themselves unemployed and meet certain state or federal qualifications. FUTA and its state counterpart, the *State Unemployment Tax Act (SUTA)*, are based upon the wages earned by the employees. Unlike Social Security taxes, only employers pay FUTA. Some states require both employers and employees to contribute to SUTA. For example, Alaskan

Parinya Maneenate/Shutterstock

employees contribute up to an annual amount of $207.50 (2020 figure) to SUTA, which is collected at a rate of 0.50 percent of wages; employers contribute up to 1.59 percent of employee wages until they reach $41,500 in annual gross earnings (2020 figure). Should an employee have more than one employer, the employee is allowed to request a return for the amounts over the annual earnings maximum in the following year. The COVID-19 pandemic strained states' unemployment funds in 2020, and changes to the SUTA rates and policies may be significant in future years.

The enactment of the *Fair Labor Standards Act (FLSA)* of 1938 required more detailed record-keeping and worker protection. This act regulates the minimum wage, a topic with which most workers are familiar, stated as the lowest an individual under certain classifications can be paid. Less commonly known, the minimum wage applies only to workers at businesses that meet certain conditions. For example, small businesses that conduct no interstate commerce, such as a restaurant that serves only locally obtained food from one state, are not subject to the minimum wage provisions of FLSA. Additionally, tipped employees, such as restaurant servers, are exempt from minimum wage standards under FLSA. In the contemporary business world, a business that does not conduct interstate commerce is rare, but the provision in FLSA remains in effect.

An important fact about FLSA wage guidelines is that no maximum wage cap exists. Securities and Exchanges Commission (SEC) regulations stipulate that the compensation packages of high-ranking employees of public companies must be published with the company's mandatory annual report.

The minimum wage may differ from a "living wage," which is an amount needed to meet basic subsistence needs. As of 2020, 70 cities and 39 states have enacted living wage legislation to rise in relation to the Consumer Price Index. The following cities are examples of places with living wage ordinances:

- San Leandro, California
- Pine Bluff, Arkansas
- Asheville, North Carolina
- Pittsburgh, Pennsylvania
- Albuquerque, New Mexico
- Portland, Maine
- Prince George's County, Maryland

(**Source:** Economic Policies Institute)

FLSA guidelines define maximum hours, minimum age, pay rates, and mandatory break times. This part of the FLSA is an outgrowth of the industrial environment of the early 20th century when no such guidelines existed. Horror stories about working conditions and children working 12- to 14-hour days abounded during the 1930s. The FLSA created the classifications of exempt and nonexempt workers. Exempt workers are salaried workers who are not subject to certain wage and overtime provisions of FLSA. Nonexempt workers are protected by the provisions of the FLSA and are therefore subject to wage and overtime provisions.

Additionally, FLSA regulation does not apply to pay periods or to the amount of paid time off given to employees. Those two items are at the discretion of the employer. Paid time off has become a topic of discussion since 2010, and companies such as McDonald's began offering it to nonexempt employees in 2015 as a regular part of employee benefit packages in response to pressure from labor leaders. Eleven states, including Massachusetts, Oregon, Connecticut, California, Washington, Arizona, and Vermont, and more than 30 municipalities have instituted paid sick leave for employees as of 2020.

The third class of workers, independent contractors, is not subject to the payment provisions of the FLSA. *Independent contractors* are typically treated as vendors of a business. Independent contractors are not employees of the business and are not reflected in payroll records. The IRS uses *Form SS-8* to help determine employee or independent contractor status. The Department of Labor ruled that improper classification of workers diminished workers' legal protections under the FLSA and declared that the following items must be considered when classifying a worker as an employee or an independent contractor:

1. The extent to which a worker is an integral element of the employer's business.
2. Whether the worker's managerial skills affect his or her opportunity for profit or loss.
3. Relative investments in facilities and equipment by *both* the employee and the employer.
4. The extent to which the worker exercises independent business judgment.
5. The permanent nature of the working relationship between the employer and employee.
6. The type and extent of the control that the employer has over the employee.

(Source: U.S. Department of Labor)

> Penalties for misclassification of employees as independent contractors can be high. If the misclassification is found to be intentional on the part of the employer, the monetary amount of the penalty is higher. In the case of *Fair v. Communications Unlimited Inc.,* the U.S. District in Missouri found that the employer had deliberately miscategorized workers in 10 states as independent contractors to avoid paying overtime wages required under the FLSA. The employer was ordered to provide the names and other contact information to the court in order to determine appropriate overtime compensation awards. (Source: Google Scholar)

To obtain the remittance of employers' withholding taxes, the federal government needed a way to standardize the collection of taxes from employers. Before the *Current Tax Payment Act (CTPA) of 1943*, no formalized guidelines for remittance of taxes existed. During the time before the CTPA, the remittance of taxes from employers was inconsistent and unreliable as a funding source for governmental projects. The CTPA was passed during World War II as a means of guaranteeing a source of funds to support the country's involvement in the war. The CTPA created the requirement for the submission of estimated taxes on wages earned during the year of earning instead of after the end of the year as previously required.

Another employer obligation is *workers' compensation*, commonly known as *workers' comp.* Unlike other payroll-specific laws, state laws govern workers' compensation laws. Employer requirements for providing workers' comp coverage vary from state to state and are not required in certain states if the employer has fewer than a certain minimum number of employees. Because workers' compensation is an insurance program, it is not considered a tax, but it is a state-mandated employer payroll expense.

Workers' compensation is an insurance policy carried by employers to provide wage continuation and to pay for medical services for workers injured in the course of doing business. The amounts assigned to the policy vary by type of work being performed and associated risks for various professions. For example, heavy equipment operators would have a higher workers' comp rate than office workers because their exposure to injury is deemed higher by the insurance industry. The impact of the COVID-19 pandemic on certain businesses such as meat-packing plants, may lead to changes in workers' compensation insurance procedures in future years.

Halfpoint/Shutterstock

Workers' compensation plans are subject to annual audits and are based upon payroll wages less any employees exempted from the coverage, typically working owners. Employers must report all wages earned by the employee; however, only one-third of overtime hours are reported to the workers' compensation auditor. Each state has different requirements for coverage and eligibility. The number of employees over which workers' compensation insurance is required varies per state, as shown in Table 1-1.

The *Affordable Care Act (ACA)* of 2010 was one of the most significant changes in payroll accounting in recent years. Although the primary focus of the act was to ensure health care coverage for all Americans, employers have several reporting responsibilities related to the act. One of the responsibilities included in Section 1003 is the disclosure and justification for

TABLE 1-1
Workers' Compensation Laws by State

STATE	MINIMUM NUMBER OF EMPLOYEES
Alaska	1 (may be self-insured)
Alabama	5
Arizona	1
Arkansas	3
California	1
Colorado	1
Connecticut	1 (including uninsured subcontractors)
Delaware	1
D.C.	1
Florida	4 (except noted industries), 1 (construction), 6 (agricultural), 12 (seasonal)
Georgia	3
Hawaii	1
Idaho	1 (including part-time workers)
Illinois	1 (including part-time workers)
Indiana	1
Iowa	1 (excluding very low salary employers)
Kansas	1 (exempt if annual gross payroll is less than $20,000 or agricultural employer. Sole proprietors and LLC members are exempt from coverage)
Kentucky	1
Louisiana	1 (including part-time, either employees or subcontractors, exceptions for agriculture only employers)
Maine	1 (subcontractors must also be covered)
Maryland	1 (agricultural employers must have at least 3 employees or a payroll of less than $15,000 annually)
Massachusetts	1 (domestic workers must be covered if they work more than 16 hours per week)
Michigan	1 (certain family members who are employees may be exempt, certain very small employers are exempt), 3 (private employers)
Minnesota	1
Mississippi	5 (certain subcontractors' employees are covered, excludes domestic, farm, non-profit fraternal, charitable, religious or cultural organizations)
Missouri	5 (includes full and part-time, seasonal, temporary), 1 (construction), except farm laborers, domestic servants, certain real estate agents, direct sales, commercial motor-carrier owner-operators
Montana	1
Nebraska	1
Nevada	1
New Hampshire	1 (including part-time workers)
New Jersey	1
New Mexico	3 (construction employers must cover any employees)
New York	1
North Carolina	3 (only 1 employee for businesses that involve radiation exposure)
North Dakota	1 (including part-time, seasonal, temporary workers)
Ohio	1
Oklahoma	1 (when a business has 5 or fewer family members as employees, the family members are exempt from coverage)
Oregon	1
Pennsylvania	1
Rhode Island	4
South Carolina	4 (some occupations exempt if <$3,000 in annual payroll), (including part-time workers)
South Dakota	1
Tennessee	6 (construction, subcontractors, and coal businesses must always have it)
Texas	No mandatory coverage except government contractors
Utah	1
Vermont	1 (agricultural/farming employers with annual payroll <$10,000 are exempt) (including part-time workers)
Virginia	3 (including part-time workers)
Washington	1
West Virginia	1 (independent contractors, agricultural employers with <3 employees, and casual employers are exempt)
Wisconsin	3 (including part-time workers, compliance time requirement varies by industry)
Wyoming	1

Source: NFIB and WCC.

rates of plans and any increases in premiums. Another reporting requirement is the number of full-time equivalent (FTE) employees, the cost of insurance coverage provided to employees, and the elimination of a waiting period for health insurance coverage. The legislation of the Affordable Care Act covers 974 pages and contains many provisions and contingencies, including a requirement for continuing premium review. In 2017, a mandate of the Affordable Care Act that levied a financial penalty on individuals who elected not to have medical insurance was overturned by Executive Order 13765. In 2018, a judge in Texas ruled that Executive Order 13765 caused the ACA to be unconstitutional. As of the release of this edition, the future of the ACA in light of the Texas judge's ruling has been appealed, which led to a group of 20 states working to have the entire law repealed. However, the provisions and requirements of the ACA are still in force and employers must comply with the existing requirements.

According to the Internal Revenue Service, employers must report whether they provide Minimum Essential Coverage that is part of their company-sponsored benefits including any group health plans, COBRA plans, or preexisting insurance coverage. Health insurance coverage is reported on IRS Form 1095 A, B, or C as follows:

- Form 1095-A is for individuals who have purchased insurance from the Healthcare Marketplace, not through an employer. This form is issued by the Marketplace.

- Form 1095-B is to report information to the IRS for individuals who have minimum essential coverage through group insurance plans provided by governmental employers and qualified private-sector employers. Additionally, employers who are not applicable large employers but who sponsor self-insured group health plans must report information about employees (and their spouse and dependents) who enroll in the coverage to their employees, even though the employers are not subject to the employer shared-responsibility provisions or the information reporting requirements for applicable large employers.

- Form 1095-C is for applicable large employers who provide health insurance where the employer is responsible for the shared responsibility provision of the act. This form is issued by employers who offer coverage but are not self-insured, and who have 50 or more full-time and/or full-time equivalent employees.

The employer must file IRS form 1095-B or 1095-C and furnish a copy to the insured if the insured received medical insurance benefits for as few as one day of one month during a calendar year.* The transmittal form, which contains a summary of all Form 1095 issued, required the IRS is Form 1094-A, B, or C, depending on the type of 1095 issued. (Source: IRS)

*It should be noted that the parts of the Affordable Care Act have been changed and others are being debated as of the time of publication.

Legislative provisions and reporting requirements remain in effect until the formal repeal of the legislation. The United States Supreme Court has refused to expedite the appeal that would overturn the Affordable Care Act as of January 2020. Changes in 2020 include the following:

- Reduced affordability standard: The percentage of an employee's monthly household income that would be used to obtain affordable coverage is 9.86 percent.
- Certain preventive care items are included, such as aspirin for adults over 50 who are at risk for cardiovascular issues, blood pressure screening, depression screening, and many other items.

(Source: Healthcare.gov)

The 2017 ***Tax Cuts and Jobs Act*** and represented sweeping changes to the tax code. This law had a profound effect on payroll taxes, especially employee federal income tax liability, and required a comprehensive reframing of employee income tax computation. Specific changes to payroll included a change to the Social Security wage base, adjustments to non-resident alien withholding, adjustments for inflation, and decreases in supplemental wage withholding rates. The Internal Revenue Service issued new mid-year tax withholding tables and forms in response to the changes mandated in this act and introduced a new Employee's Withholding Certificate (Form W-4) and tax guide in 2020.

The *Consolidated Appropriations Act of 2018* increased the funding for the E-Verify program, which is an Internet-based system that offers employers instant verification of an employee's eligibility to work in the United States. It is important to note that the E-Verify program does not replace the need for the completion of Form I-9 upon employee hire because it is a voluntary service. The following table from the USCIS compares the E-Verify program against the I-9 requirement.

Form I-9	E-Verify
Mandatory	Voluntary for most businesses
Requires a Social Security number	Requires a Social Security number
No photo required on identity documents	Photo is required on identity documents
MUST be used to re-verify expired employment authorization	MAY NOT be used to re-verify expired employment authorization

(Source: USCIS)

Another important part of the Consolidated Appropriations Act included monetary penalties of $1,000 per instance (plus damages) for employers who withhold employee tip earnings inappropriately. This section of the act repealed a 2017 Department of Labor regulation that prevented employers from requiring that all tips be placed into a pool for tipped and nontipped employees. Although the act did not remove the use of tip pools, it prevented managers and supervisors from participating in the tip pools.

Which Payroll Law?

Stop & Check

1. Established requirements for employer record keeping?
2. Provided government assistance for workers who are too old or infirm to work?
3. Established protection for displaced workers?
4. Required employers to file taxes collected in a timely manner?
5. Set aside funds for health insurance?
6. Regulated wages for employees whose employer engaged in governmental contracts?
7. Is governed on a state-to-state basis and protects employees injured during the course of work activities?
8. Is responsible for reporting requirements of essential health coverage for full-time equivalent employees?
9. Restructured payroll tax calculations, supplemental withholding allowances, and the Social Security wage base?
10. Funded E-Verify programs for employee eligibility to work?

a. Social Security Act
b. Workers' compensation
c. Current Tax Payment Act
d. Fair Labor Standards Act
e. Tax Act (PL 115-97)
f. Federal Unemployment Tax Act
g. Medicare
h. Consolidated Appropriations Act
i. Affordable Care Act
j. Davis–Bacon Act

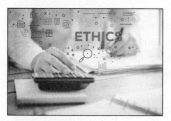

Garagestock/Shutterstock

LO 1-3   Discuss the Ethical Guidelines for Payroll Accounting

Professional *ethics* is critical in any accounting context, and especially so in payroll accounting. After the Enron accounting scandal and the passage of the Sarbanes–Oxley Act of 2002 (SOX), ethics became a focus of the accounting profession as a whole. Even with the SOX framework, the payroll industry is rife with ethical violations including fraud and theft.

The payroll accountant is entrusted to handle money belonging to the firm and rightfully owed to the government and company employees. Payment of these monies becomes a moral contract between the company and the recipients; therefore, ethics are a vital element in payroll accounting. Several accounting organizations, including the American Institute of Certified Public Accountants (AICPA), Institute of Management Accountants (IMA) and International Federation of Accountants (IFAC) has delineated codes of ethics that are applied in the accounting profession. The basic guidelines of an ethics code include the following tenets, shown in Figure 1-2.

FIGURE 1-2

Basic Guidelines of a Code of Ethics

Ethisphere maintains an annual list of the most ethical companies in the world. In 2020, the list included many companies based in the United States, such as 3M, Allstate, LinkedIn, T-Mobile, and several others. Although the companies on the list are in a variety of industries, certain ethical principles are common to all: integrity, social responsibility, care for all stakeholders, and honesty and transparency in all business dealings. (Source: Ethisphere)

Confidentiality

An accountant is responsible for maintaining confidences and exercising moral judgment in all actions. A payroll accountant deals with sensitive personnel information that must remain confidential. Social Security numbers, employee legal obligations, and an employer's tax liabilities are a few examples of information that a payroll accountant must protect.

The state of New Jersey enacted the Diane B. Allen Equal Pay Act, which strengthened existing antidiscrimination laws by preventing pay differences based on traits protected under other civil rights laws. It also protected employees who discussed pay with other employees. However, it should be noted that the payroll accountant is still responsible for maintaining the confidentiality of employee records in order for this law to function in the way it was intended. (Source: State of New Jersey 2018 Legislature)

GaudiLab/Shutterstock

Professionalism

Accountants must uphold *professionalism* by maintaining confidentiality, maintaining the public's trust, and upholding professionalism in their practice. In terms of payroll accounting, professionalism includes honoring the needs of the firm, its employees, and associated governmental entities. A payroll accountant must complete all tasks and adhere to deadlines, despite any personal issues. Personal honesty and transparency of transactions are the core of acting professionally.

Brinker International, the parent entity for restaurants such as Maggiano's Little Italy and Chili's, outlines its ethical policy and expectations for employee compliance, especially as they pertain to the Brinker International Payroll Company, L.P., in its Ethical Business Policy. An emphasis on transparency, integrity, and action in the public interest are key components of the policy. (Source: Brinker International)

Integrity

In the workplace, integrity is the most important asset a professional can possess. *Integrity* involves doing the right thing despite any external pressure, personal temptations, or conflicts of interest. The main question when weighing the integrity of a decision is: Am I doing what is right and just for everyone concerned? Any course of action that lacks integrity potentially restricts the rights of interested parties and compromises the best interests of the company. The AICPA code of ethics includes express direction about not covering up mistakes as part of an accountant's integrity.

Payroll fraud can happen anywhere that pressures, opportunities, and rationalizations exist. A payroll specialist for a District of Columbia consulting firm was indicted on embezzlement charges involving fictitious employees. The payroll specialist stole over $250,000, including amounts deposited for payroll taxes, by changing the pay disbursement details of terminated employees. Instead of leaving the employees' files in a "terminated" status, the altered detail allowed automatic salary payments to continue—but to be deposited to the payroll specialist's personal account. The payroll specialist, who plead guilty to wire fraud, was ordered to repay the employer $250,000 and was sentenced to 21 months in prison. (Source: U.S. Department of Justice)

Objectivity and Independence

Accountants must take care to be independent of any pressures that would compromise the integrity of their work. These pressures can come from business or personal relationships that may affect a payroll accountant's judgment concerning the best interests of all concerned in a given situation. *Objectivity* in accounting means that the accountant considers only facts relevant to the task at hand, independent of all other pressures. The Public Company Accounting Oversight Board (PCAOB) specifies that *independence* may be compromised if any of the following situations occur:

- Commitment to a future purchase of a financial interest in a client's business.
- Personal or family ownership in excess of 5 percent of a client's business.
- Professional engagement with a client's firm in which the payroll professional had a personal interest such as partial ownership.

Social obligations may compromise a payroll accountant's objectivity. The AICPA Code of Ethics Section 17 specifically addresses social club membership as a factor in the loss of an accountant's independence or objectivity. Such club membership could create a social debt that may cause an accountant to commit payroll fraud. (Source: AICPA)

FatCamera/Getty Images

Professional Competence and Due Care

Professional competence and *due care* revolve around an accountant's competence and assume that the accounting professional is equally competent as other people in a similar role. In payroll accounting, due care is an ongoing process that involves education, training, and experience. According to the AICPA, an accountant must remain current with accounting practices and legal developments to comply with due care requirements. Payroll laws and tax guidelines change regularly. As a payroll accountant, it is extremely important to remain aware of annual changes that the IRS and other accounting bodies publish through participation in professional accounting organizations, subscriptions to accounting industry publications, and participation in discussions at accounting conferences.

Staying current with payroll changes is an ongoing task. Some of the sources for this information include

- IRS (www.irs.gov).
- AICPA (www.aicpa.org).
- Financial Accounting Standards Board (FASB) (www.fasb.org).
- American Payroll Association (www.americanpayroll.org).
- U.S. Department of Labor (www.dol.gov).
- Compliance Tools for HR Professionals (www.hr.blr.com).

What's Ethical?

1. Giles Montragon is the payroll accountant for his company. His boss informs him that the company is considering switching payroll systems and asks for his input. What are some ethical concerns involved in changing accounting software?

2. Liza Beals, the payroll manager, is in a sorority. At a social event, she discovers that one of her sorority sisters works for the same company. Her sorority sister asks Liza for confidential information about one of the employees in her department, claiming that the sorority oath requires Liza's compliance. What should Liza do?

Rawpixel.com/Shutterstock

LO 1-4 Identify Contemporary Payroll Practices

Contemporary accounting practices reflect the effects of technology and electronic communications on business. Payroll practices have adapted to include modern tools that facilitate data transmission, and new challenges have emerged. Examples include the following:

- Direct deposit regulations for employee pay and tax remittances.
- Electronic filing requirements.
- New timekeeping methods.
- The availability of paycards as a method of wage and salary disbursement.
- Government contract influences on the payroll.
- International employees.
- Simultaneous in-house and outsourced payroll personnel.
- Integration of payroll into other company functions.
- Security of confidential, electronic personnel information.
- Cloud-based software designed for security, accessibility, and portability of data.

Payroll is no longer a stand-alone department. Integrated software packages offered by mainstream accounting software providers, such as QuickBooks and Sage 100cloud, allow business owners to view data across departments and synthesize the information to make large-scale decisions. Contemporary payroll systems serve as a tool for strategic planning, performance measurement, and customer/vendor relations using mobile, cloud-based platforms that may be accessed through Internet-connected devices. Payroll accountants are a key element in the decision-making process and must remain educated about legal and compliance issues as well as remain current in their understanding of software applications and relevant technological concerns.

The payroll accountant plays a vital role in a company's structure, no matter how large or small. Payroll and other employee benefits often represent the largest category of a company's expenses. Chipotle Mexican Grill Inc. (CMG), originally started as a subsidiary of McDonald's but currently a separate entity, reported nearly $1.5 billion in payroll expenses in its stores during the fiscal year 2019, which represented an 11 percent increase over 2018. As an innovative company in the fast-food market, CMG has integrated technology and sustainability measures to engage customers and promote the use of locally sourced ingredients to support local farmers. Notice in the following table how, despite technology integration, CMG's labor expenses are nearly as large as its product-related expenses.

CHIPOTLE MEXICAN GRILL INC.			
OPERATING COSTS AND EXPENSES (in millions, selected data)			
Company-operated restaurant expenses	**2019**	2018	2017
Food, beverage, and packaging	**1,847.9**	1,600.8	1,535.4
Labor	**1,472.1**	1,326.1	1,206.0
Occupancy	**363.1**	347.1	327.1
Other operating costs	**760.8**	680.0	651.6
General, & administrative expenses	**451.6**	375.5	296.4
Total operating expenses	**5,142.4**	4,606.6	4,205.6
Operating income	**444.0**	258.4	270.8

Source: SEC

Payroll Preparation Options

Several options exist for payroll preparation. The most frequently used methods for contemporary payroll preparation are electronic accounting programs. Other options available are the manual calculation of payroll using spreadsheets and charts prepared by the Internal Revenue Service and payroll preparation by outsourcing the process to a third party such as ADP, Paychex®, and myPay Solutions. A hybrid solution that allows the company to outsource certain payroll functions to an external provider exists with online accounting software provided by companies such as Intuit and Sage, creators of QuickBooks and Sage 100cloud, respectively.

Online banks are starting to enter the payroll industry as a means to facilitate payroll access via smartphones. Chime Bank advertises access to directly deposited funds up to two days prior to the employer's pay date, based on the employer's funds availability. Another option targeted for small employers includes Amboy Bank, which offers payroll processing, reporting, and banking services that simplify the payroll process for both employers and their employees.

Regardless of the payroll preparation method, it is important for the payroll accountant to understand how the process should work. In the event of hardware failure, legislative actions, or tax changes, the accountant must ensure accurate payroll preparation. Companies can lose credibility as the result of flawed payroll, as well as be subject to substantial fines, IRS audits, and civil litigation. Cases in which companies have paid fines for improper payroll practices abound.

Chuy's Mesquite Broiler in Arizona was fined in excess of $20,000 in late-payment penalties and had to pay employees nearly $115,000 in unpaid overtime pay. The employer chose to pay its employees the first 40 hours of work via check and overtime in a separate check or cash. The problem was that the separate check for the overtime was paid at regular pay rates that did not include the overtime premium required by FLSA. (Source: *KOLD)*

Some companies have seriously shortchanged employees' paychecks, paying fines in addition to the standard payroll expenditures. Other tales of employee overpayment highlight problems in payroll systems, such as computer glitches that have delayed payment of the company's wages. Because the computer glitches are ultimately the responsibility of a company's president or CEO and represent a potential for ethical breaches, the volume of legislation and stories of problems involving payroll administration point to the need for a well-established payroll system. Despite the numerous federal and state legislative actions concerning payroll practices, none delineate the format and design of a payroll system.

The information contained in the personnel records is highly sensitive and must be protected against intrusion from unnecessary parties. The *Privacy Act of 1974* guarantees the safeguarding of information contained in private personnel records and mandates information safekeeping as well as due process rights to individuals. Consider the implications of the legal requirements of information safekeeping:

- Personnel records contain information about an individual's marital status, children, other dependents, and legal residence—sensitive information that must be protected under the Privacy Act of 1974.

- Payroll records generally have information about the hourly rate and salary information for each employee. Access to these records is protected by provisions of the *Equal Employment Opportunity Commission (EEOC)* and could provoke or inhibit discrimination lawsuits.

- The information contained in payroll records influences the accuracy and integrity of a company's accounting records. The recording of payroll expenses and liabilities affect the profitability of a company, which influences investor and customer relations.

- Companies engaging in business with the federal government must comply with the Davis–Bacon Act (for federal contracts) and potentially the *Copeland Anti-Kickback Act* of 1934 (or construction projects, protecting taxpayers from unethical pay practices).

- The number of hours worked by an employee must comply with the provisions of the Fair Labor Standards Act.

- Deductions for payroll, especially for retirement plans, must be documented and verified in accordance with the Sarbanes–Oxley Act of 2002.

Employers are required to file tax deposits for employee withholding, Social Security, Medicare, FUTA, and SUTA taxes according to an identified timeline depending upon the size of the company's payroll. Taxes may be remitted via telephone, Internet, mail, or the company's payroll software program. Additional reports are required from the employer on either a quarterly or an annual basis. A company has many responsibilities within its payroll system:

- Tax withholding must be done consistently, reflecting the requirements of federal, state, and local authorities.

- Employers must match amounts withheld from employee paychecks for certain payroll taxes.

- Withholding of deductions that the employee voluntarily elects, such as health care, insurance, and investments, must be correctly recorded and reported.
- Timely and accurate payment must be made to the employee, government agencies, and companies for which the employee has designated the voluntary deductions.
- Tax and other liabilities must be reported to governmental agencies in accordance with established deadlines.

An accurate payroll system allows managers to focus on the firm's business, not payroll administration. As such, a well-designed system benefits the employees and governmental agencies, and thus the firm. The timely forwarding of any monies withheld from employees, either by governmental regulation or voluntary election, is critical to a firm's success.

Besides administrating employee pay, a well-designed and accurately maintained payroll system is necessary during inevitable governmental audits or potential business operation interruptions, as seen during the COVID-19 pandemic during 2020. An audit is a process by which a third-party organization, either a public accounting firm or a government agency, inspects the accounting records of a firm for accuracy, integrity, and compliance with federal rules and regulations. During a payroll audit, the auditor inspects the company's records of employee pay, tax remittance, and voluntary deduction maintenance. The thought of audits instills fear into the hearts of even the most seasoned accounting professionals. Their salvation, however, is to establish and maintain an accurate payroll system.

Consider the growth of selected companies:

- Tom's of Maine started in 1968 as a local organic personal care product company and is now a nationally recognized leader in environmental stewardship and sustainability. (Source: www. tomsofmaine.com)
- Ben and Jerry's, which started with a $5 correspondence course in ice-cream making and a $12,000 investment in 1978, has become an icon of premium ice cream and environmental causes. Ben and Jerry's has since been purchased by the Unilever Corporation and maintains an independent board of directors. (Source: www.benjerry.com)

Rh2010/123RF

- McDonald's Corporation was started in 1955 by the McDonald brothers when they sold their hamburger business to Ray Kroc. The brand is now an international icon for fast food, serving approximately 68 million customers in 120 countries each day.

These companies share similar beginnings: one location, a few employees, and a relatively simple payroll. As each company has grown, so has the payroll complexity, including multiple departments and facilities in many states and countries. At the heart of each company is a well-run business model and a sound payroll system that has evolved with it.

Tracking and monitoring employee hours, locations, and applicable governmental requirements within various nations require knowledgeable payroll staff, willing to remain current with accounting trends and international regulations. Sophisticated payroll systems enable companies to create, populate, and file a multitude of documents using current software and Internet technology.

Alexander Supertramp/Shutterstock

Privacy Protection

A company must make every reasonable effort to protect personnel information contained in payroll records. This is a critical part of any payroll accountant's job. Several federal privacy acts exist to protect the information contained in payroll and personnel records. Additionally, 13 states have enacted specific data privacy legislation. Each state's privacy law refers to "reasonable" steps that companies must take to protect customer's information.

The privacy acts include (but are certainly not limited to):

- U.S. Department of Health and Human Services Privacy Act 09-40-0006, which pertains to eligibility of public employees for pay, entitlements, raises, and benefits.

- Common-Law Privacy Act, which pertains to freedom from misuse or abuse of one's private affairs.
- Privacy Act of 1974, pertaining to the use of information about private citizens.
- Computer Fraud and Abuse Act (CFAA) of 1986, which addresses cybercrime, an issue that has grown in importance in recent years.

The General Accounting Office of the federal government has been working to revise guidelines about the privacy of records and the release of information as the Internet and e-business evolve. The United States Congress has sought ways to address contemporary computer-based cyber threats, but as yet has not passed legislation at the federal level. States have enacted privacy laws, especially as they pertain to social media, to protect employees against cyber hacks.

Online privacy is a growing concern, and it affects the security of payroll data. Employees at New-York-based Barney's went unpaid in early 2020 when a hacker group gained control of the payroll system on one of its servers. Employees were unpaid for over a week and some employees terminated their employment in protest. (Source: *Page Six*)

Benoit Daoust/Shutterstock

The common element among these laws is the protection of sensitive employee information such as addresses, dependents, compensation amounts, and payroll deductions. The payroll accountant is also responsible for discretion in discussing pay rates, bonuses, or other compensation-related topics with employees and management. Sensitive topics should never be discussed with anyone other than the employee or appropriate managers. All employment-related items may be viewed during an audit of payroll records, and auditors must treat the information with absolute confidentiality.

One way that the federal government keeps track of employers is with Employer Identification Numbers (EINs). The EIN allows the IRS to know which companies may have employees, therefore generating employment tax revenue for the government and creating tax liabilities for employers. Form SS-4 (see Figure 1-3) is used to apply for an EIN by providing the personal Social Security number, type of business, and the existence of any prior EINs for a business owner. The EIN is required for all tax deposits, tax returns, and informational returns. It will appear on the company's Form W-2s, 940s, 941s, any state tax forms, and the annual tax return for the company. Form SS-4 may be completed either on paper or through an online request portal processed by the IRS that contains the same information as the paper form.

Confidential Records

Stop & Check

You are the payroll clerk of a company. A group of students approaches you to work on a class project and asks to see confidential personnel and payroll records. What would you do? What are the laws regarding the situation?

FIGURE 1-3
Example of Form SS-4

Form **SS-4**	**Application for Employer Identification Number**	OMB No. 1545-0003
(Rev. December 2019)	(For use by employers, corporations, partnerships, trusts, estates, churches, government agencies, Indian tribal entities, certain individuals, and others.)	EIN
Department of the Treasury Internal Revenue Service	▶ Go to *www.irs.gov/FormSS4* for instructions and the latest information. ▶ See separate instructions for each line. ▶ Keep a copy for your records.	

Type or print clearly.

1 Legal name of entity (or individual) for whom the EIN is being requested

Thomas Braden

2 Trade name of business (if different from name on line 1)	**3** Executor, administrator, trustee, "care of" name
Braden Fisheries	

4a Mailing address (room, apt., suite no. and street, or P.O. box)	**5a** Street address (if different) (Don't enter a P.O. box.)
1234 Coastal Highway	
4b City, state, and ZIP code (if foreign, see instructions)	**5b** City, state, and ZIP code (if foreign, see instructions)
Anchorage, AK 99509	

6 County and state where principal business is located

Anchorage, Alaska

7a Name of responsible party	**7b** SSN, ITIN, or EIN
Thomas Braden	445-54-4554

8a Is this application for a limited liability company (LLC) (or a foreign equivalent)? . . . . ☑ Yes ☐ No

8b If 8a is "Yes," enter the number of LLC members . . . . . . ▶   3

8c If 8a is "Yes," was the LLC organized in the United States? . . . . ☑ Yes ☐ No

9a **Type of entity** (check only one box). **Caution:** If 8a is "Yes," see the instructions for the correct box to check.

☐ Sole proprietor (SSN) _____
☐ Partnership
☐ Corporation (enter form number to be filed) ▶ _____
☐ Personal service corporation
☐ Church or church-controlled organization
☐ Other nonprofit organization (specify) ▶ _____
☑ Other (specify) ▶ **Disregarded Entity**

☐ Estate (SSN of decedent)
☐ Plan administrator (TIN)
☐ Trust (TIN of grantor)
☐ Military/National Guard   ☐ State/local government
☐ Farmers' cooperative   ☐ Federal government
☐ REMIC   ☐ Indian tribal governments/enterprises

Group Exemption Number (GEN) if any ▶

9b If a corporation, name the state or foreign country (if applicable) where incorporated

State	Foreign country

10 **Reason for applying** (check only one box)

☑ Started new business (specify type) ▶ Commercial Fishing
☐ Hired employees (Check the box and see line 13.)
☐ Compliance with IRS withholding regulations
☐ Other (specify) ▶

☐ Banking purpose (specify purpose) ▶ _____
☐ Changed type of organization (specify new type) ▶ _____
☐ Purchased going business
☐ Created a trust (specify type) ▶ _____
☐ Created a pension plan (specify type) ▶ _____

11 Date business started or acquired (month, day, year). See instructions.

05/01/2020

12 Closing month of accounting year   December

14 If you expect your employment tax liability to be $1,000 or less in a full calendar year **and** want to file Form 944 annually instead of Forms 941 quarterly, check here. (Your employment tax liability generally will be $1,000 or less if you expect to pay $5,000 or less in total wages.) If you don't check this box, you must file Form 941 for every quarter. ☐

13 Highest number of employees expected in the next 12 months (enter -0- if none). If no employees expected, skip line 14.

Agricultural	Household	Other
		15

15 First date wages or annuities were paid (month, day, year). **Note:** If applicant is a withholding agent, enter date income will first be paid to nonresident alien (month, day, year) . . . . ▶   05/15/2020

16 Check **one** box that best describes the principal activity of your business.
☐ Construction   ☐ Rental & leasing   ☐ Transportation & warehousing
☐ Real estate   ☐ Manufacturing   ☐ Finance & insurance
☐ Health care & social assistance   ☐ Wholesale-agent/broker
☐ Accommodation & food service   ☐ Wholesale-other   ☐ Retail
☑ Other (specify) ▶ **Commercial Fishing**

17 Indicate principal line of merchandise sold, specific construction work done, products produced, or services provided.

Fish and Seafood

18 Has the applicant entity shown on line 1 ever applied for and received an EIN?   ☐ Yes   ☑ No

If "Yes," write previous EIN here ▶

Third Party Designee	Complete this section **only** if you want to authorize the named individual to receive the entity's EIN and answer questions about the completion of this form.	
	Designee's name	Designee's telephone number (include area code)
	Address and ZIP code	Designee's fax number (include area code)

Under penalties of perjury, I declare that I have examined this application, and to the best of my knowledge and belief, it is true, correct, and complete.

Name and title (type or print clearly) ▶ Thomas Braden, President	Applicant's telephone number (include area code) 907-555-1346
Signature ▶ *Thomas Braden* Date ▶ 05/01/2020	Applicant's fax number (include area code) 907-555-9876

For Privacy Act and Paperwork Reduction Act Notice, see separate instructions.   Cat. No. 16055N   Form **SS-4** (Rev. 12-2019)

Source: Internal Revenue Service.

LO 1-5 Compare Payroll Processing Options for Different Businesses

Companies have several options for payroll processing. The option a company chooses depends on the size of the business, the complexity of the business in terms of geographic placement and business model, the capital available for payroll processing, and the availability of trained personnel.

Jeanette Landin

During the middle of the 20th century, employers measured workers' time by using punch clocks and handwritten timesheets. Contemporary time collection devices serve as more than simple time clocks. Although the old-fashioned punch clocks still exist, companies have integrated different time-collection systems as part of their office security and computer access procedures. Time clocks are used as part of a security system to log in people as they enter a building for work, which can yield analysis of simple on-site versus working-hour time.

Many companies now use biometric devices such as fingerprint readers to collect time for their hourly employees. Systems such as Kronos offer biometric badges and time-collection devices that connect with office telephones. Using computer access as another type of collection device serves a similar function and can offer the additional functionality of specific task tracking and precise timekeeping. With the growth of mobile connectivity, companies now have a large number of smartphone apps, such as WhenIWork and ExacTime, to track employee attendance and productivity. Practices relating to time collection are a vital element in payroll accuracy.

The basic elements of a payroll system are similar for all companies, but this is a case when size does matter. However, it is not only the size of the company but also the complexity of the laws that affect payroll procedures. Let's look at the differences between large and small company payrolls and then explore certified payroll issues.

Large Businesses

Large companies present intricate problems for payroll accountants. Companies such as Apple, Alphabet (Google), and Microsoft have multiple divisions, many of which exist in different geographical locations. General Electric (GE) has different companies that operate as separate entities within GE's framework. Payroll procedures reflect the intricacy of the company's structure and may take many forms.

Metamorworks/Shutterstock

One of the major challenges in larger organizations is the existence of multiple departments in which an individual employee may work on any given day. Some companies can have shared employees, who will have allocable time to more than one department; for example, one employee may work for both the marketing and the production departments. When this occurs, the payroll accountant will have to record the time worked for each department, and pay rates may differ based on the tasks that the employee performs for each department.

A common payroll procedure with large companies involves employee portals on company websites. On the company's payroll website, employees may enter vacation time, overtime, and other issues that pertain to the employee's payroll data. Through the same website, employees may change withholding allowances and voluntary deductions and maintain certain other aspects of their employees' files. Such web-based portals contain highly sensitive information, and the security of the information is an obvious concern for the companies who use them. Multiple identity checks and security measures are in place to ensure the privacy of employee data, such as SSL (secure sockets layer) encryption, *VPN* (virtual private network), and CAPTCHA programs that are designed to differentiate between humans and other computer programs.

To overcome some of the issues with payroll processing, large companies may rely heavily on payroll service vendors to assist with payroll preparation and human resources integration. Providers such as myPay Solutions and ADP work with the security needs of the company

Providing employees with Internet-based access to their personnel files is a challenging issue. Federal laws do not grant employees the right to access their personnel files, and companies must be aware of state laws before providing access. Questions of assigning access to other parties (such as union representatives), access to file artifacts, and the right of the employee to challenge items contained in their file are issues that a firm should address when creating a web portal through which employees may access payroll records. In addition, issues of cybersecurity and online privacy must be addressed. (Source: SHRM)

to offer websites that are secure and integrate multiple personnel functions seamlessly. Some larger firms will work with software engineers to develop independent systems specifically meeting unique company needs.

Large companies face other issues related to accurate timekeeping, such as the volume of employee records. Companies with computerized time-measurement systems may link employees' computer logins, telephone logins, or building access with the payroll system. Companies working with radio frequency time cards and electronic payroll monitoring can properly allocate employee time to specific machines or production lines. With the computer software and services currently available, large companies have many options to maintain the accuracy and integrity of their payroll systems.

Small Businesses

One apparent difference between large and small businesses is the volume and handling of payroll records. A small number of employees generally leads to fewer payroll-related transactions. Manual payroll systems may be maintained in very small businesses, including the use

valentinrussanov/Getty Images

of handwritten time cards. Outsourcing of payroll activities may not be as prominent. With a small company, the amount of time to complete payroll-related tasks may be less than in a large company. For a small company, the task can be performed without disrupting the revenue-producing tasks of the business.

Small companies have the option of processing payroll in-house with a minimum of difficulty. However, small companies may lack specifically trained payroll personnel, which may place the responsibility for employee pay and benefits on other personnel and may increase the risk of pay or tax inaccuracies. The human resource director, office manager, and payroll professional may be roles performed by the same person. Using payroll software and a properly designed payroll system, the task of payroll for a small company is generally manageable by minimal company staff. Small companies may choose to explore outsourcing as the company grows. Outsourcing payroll may be a viable option if the task becomes unwieldy or legal obligations become unmanageable.

Small companies have an option to use hosting services as a way to access cloud-storage, subscription-based services that possess security comparable to on-site accounting software. Hosted payroll accounting software can change in scale without the need for additional software licensing, update issues, or specific hardware.

For more information about hosted payroll, check out these top-rated services:

- Paychex
- Intuit Payroll
- Gusto
- OnPay
- SurePayroll

Source: Business News Daily

Depending on the size of the company, number of employees, and complexity of the payroll process, the company may choose to purchase a computer-based accounting system, it may continue to prepare worksheets and manual payroll checks, or it can decide to *outsource* the payroll preparation and associated tasks to an external vendor. Contemporary best practices often include the use of cloud-based software due to the frequency and necessity of software updates and the file size. Whichever decisions the company makes as it grows, the importance of understanding the mechanics of the payroll process is paramount. Whether a company performs the payroll process in-house or outsources it, the company is liable for payroll-filing compliance. The next section provides an overview of the various computer-based systems available.

Common payroll mistakes made by small firms include

- Misclassifying employees as independent contractors.
- Paying payroll late.
- Omitting the value of gift cards awarded to employees as part of their taxable income.
- Failure to make timely and/or accurate payroll tax deposits.
- Improper treatment of expense reimbursements made to employees.
- Incorrect treatment of taxable fringe benefits.

(Source: *Accounting Today*)

Large vs. Small

1. What are three payroll processing issues faced by large companies?
2. How does payroll processing differ between large and small companies?

Computer-Based Systems

Various accounting software packages exist to facilitate payroll-related accounting tasks, including QuickBooks, Sage 100cloud, and Microsoft Dynamics GP. The use of computerized payroll systems eliminates approximately 80 percent of payroll processing time and errors. Computerized accounting systems foster the integration of payroll data with other company financial functions through Enterprise Resource Planning (ERP), which allows decision-makers to develop a comprehensive understanding of the operational needs of the company. Although payroll professionals must verify employee data and update the software at regular intervals, computerized systems reduce the burdens of manual pay calculations, pay disbursement, and report compilation from the payroll accountant.

When used properly, small companies may benefit from a computerized payroll system. Although concerns about the confidentiality of personnel records exist, electronic access to records may streamline certain tasks, such as employee information updates and overtime reporting. Additionally, as the year-end approaches, companies can deliver the employees' W-2 (see Figure 1-4) tax forms electronically, ensuring employees' rapid access to their tax documents.

A trend in payroll processing involves the issuance of electronic paycards, much like preloaded credit cards, as opposed to paper checks. Paycards offer the employees the flexibility of not having to wait for their paycheck to be deposited at a bank. Companies that offer direct deposit as a payment option must offer paycards as an option to employees who do not have bank accounts. However, a paycard can be lost or stolen, and with it, the employee's paycheck. Additionally, employers may be charged fees for loading a paycard. When companies

FIGURE 1-4
Form W-2 Wage and Tax Statement

	a Employee's social security number				
22222	444-44-4444	OMB No. 1545-0008			

b Employer identification number (EIN) 12-1234567		1 Wages, tips, other compensation 21689.20	2 Federal income tax withheld 1858.00
c Employer's name, address, and ZIP code Some Company 123 Main Street Anywhere, Anystate 00000		3 Social security wages 22396.20	4 Social security tax withheld 1386.89
		5 Medicare wages and tips 22369.20	6 Medicare tax withheld 324.74
		7 Social security tips	8 Allocated tips
d Control number		9	10 Dependent care benefits
e Employee's first name and initial Last name Suff. Connie Barnes P.O. Box 11211 Sioux City, IA 73217		11 Nonqualified plans	12a DD 707.00
		13 Statutory employee ☐ Retirement plan ☒ Third-party sick pay ☐	12b
		14 Other	12c
			12d
f Employee's address and ZIP code			

15 State Employer's state ID number IA 1866748	16 State wages, tips, etc. 21689.20	17 State income tax 976.01	18 Local wages, tips, etc.	19 Local income tax	20 Locality name

Form **W-2** Wage and Tax Statement   **2020**   Department of the Treasury—Internal Revenue Service

Copy 1—For State, City, or Local Tax Department

Source: Internal Revenue Service.

consider paycards as an option, it is important to communicate to employees an understanding that there may be costs assessed by the card issuer.

Internet-Based Systems

Internet-based accounting software is an option for a company that does not have the need for or the resources to purchase a computer-based accounting system. Computer-based accounting systems such as QuickBooks, Microsoft Dynamics GP, and Sage 100 Standard offer both desktop and Internet-based services for businesses. In addition, companies such as Xero and Wave have developed Internet-only accounting packages that are accessible for a monthly fee. The advantages of using Internet-based services include the ease of access for accounting personnel and managers and automatic software updates. A potential disadvantage of relying on Internet-based software for a company's accounting is information security issues.

Accounting Today conducted case studies with firms that had used Internet-based accounting software and highlighted the following:

Positive Aspects	Challenges
Timely identification of financial issues because of the ease of access to company records	Users cannot usually customize certain information layouts to suit specific company needs
Low price for software access and "real-time" knowledge of business information	Not suitable for highly complex businesses such as large manufacturing operations
Increased opportunity for collaboration in the business planning and monitoring process	Employee resistance to learning about new software and company accounting process
Continual software updates for changes in tax rates or other related practices	More options available than company personnel knew how to use

It is estimated that advances in predictive software and Artificial Intelligence-based systems will make accounting software more useful for small businesses, enabling companies to engage in real-time business analysis that had been previously out of their reach. Additionally, software advances will enable business owners to be more flexible in the way they conduct business as far as the work location, information demands, and data transmittal. (Source: *Accounting Today*)

Manual Systems

With manual payroll systems, the payroll employee relies on deduction percentages that come presented in publications from the Internal Revenue Service. *Publication 15* (also known as *Circular E*) is the manual payroll accountant's best friend, along with periodic updates and supplemental publications.

RapidEye/Getty Images

The largest challenges the manual payroll preparer faces are time constraints and updated tax tables. Companies can determine the length of time between the end of the payroll period and the employee payments with some degree of latitude. However, employers must make every reasonable effort to pay their employees in a timely and accurate manner to avoid ethical breaches and potentially costly litigation.

Manual payroll accountants may use spreadsheet programs, such as Microsoft Excel, in which the accountant can create lookup formulas or other connecting formulas to facilitate the accurate completion of the payroll process. Spreadsheets with formulas or macros should be used only if the accountant understands the formulas and can verify the linkage prior to finalizing payroll to ensure that calculations are correct.

> According to the IRS, approximately 40% of all small businesses make payroll errors, averaging $845 in fines per year. The most common errors include missed or late payments. (Source: *Journal of Accountancy*)

Outsourced Payroll Systems

Outsourced payroll processing has become rather popular as a way to ensure compliance with the changing legal structure and withholding requirements. When a company chooses to use an outsourcing firm for the completion of the payroll processes, there are several considerations: records retention, confidentiality, compliance, timeliness, and thoroughness. Managers should review the cost/benefits of outsourcing a firm's payroll processes prior to making the commitment.

External payroll providers offer flexibility and advanced data analysis that might be challenging for smaller internal departments. During a survey of more than 2,000 accounting professionals, an overwhelming margin stated they would prefer to outsource payroll functions because of the time involved in the process. External payroll management providers such as ADP and Paychex® assist company owners and managers with strategic planning and related human resources issues. However, outsourcing is not a wise decision for all companies. For a small company, outsourcing may not be cost-effective. For large or international companies, outsourcing may be the only option to manage payroll complexity.

A recent trend in payroll accounting involves cloud-based computing, meaning that the data is housed on a server external to the firm and accessible via an Internet connection. Companies such as ADP offer cloud-based payroll and human resource functions for businesses. These services reduce costs by allowing a company to avoid hardware and software costs associated with payroll. However, issues have arisen with payroll vendor stability and information security.

> In late 2019, payroll provider MyPayrollHR terminated business operations abruptly, which left hundreds of thousands of employees without the pay they were due from the thousands of employers that relied on the service. FBI investigators have warned companies to complete thorough background and reliability checks on outsourced payroll vendors before entrusting employee payroll to them. Source: American Payroll Association

FIGURE 1-5
Form WH-347 Certified Payroll

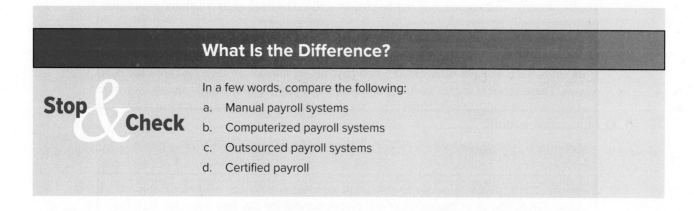

Source: U.S. Department of Labor.

Certified Payroll

Companies who do business with the federal government under the Davis–Bacon Act are required to file a report (see Figure 1-5 for Form WH-347) delineating the payroll paid as part of the government contract with each payroll. *Certified payroll* is a way that the federal government keeps track of the money spent as part of government contracts. Davis–Bacon Act–related wages and the state versions of those regulations require special handling and knowledge. Certified payroll facilitates governmental internal accountability and verifies that Davis–Bacon Act requirements are met.

Information needed to complete a Certified Payroll report includes the following:

✓ Company-specific identifying information.
✓ The job being worked on and its duration.
✓ Employee information that includes social security number and address.
✓ Hours worked on each job and the pay rate associated with it.
✓ Gross pay earned for the week.
✓ Taxes, withholdings, and fringe benefits.
✓ Net pay earned per employee.

What Is the Difference?

Stop & Check

In a few words, compare the following:

a.   Manual payroll systems

b.   Computerized payroll systems

c.   Outsourced payroll systems

d.   Certified payroll

Trends to Watch

LEGAL ENVIRONMENT

To say that the legal environment of payroll is continually evolving is an understatement. Since 2017, we have witnessed the following legal challenges:

- Increasing numbers of private employers and localities raising the minimum wage significantly to close the gap between the minimum wage and the living wage.
- Challenges to the Affordable Care Act related to the overturn of the individual mandate for health care coverage.
- Supplemental wage rate changes for payments of bonuses.
- State enforcement of predictive scheduling, fair/flexible scheduling laws on changing employee's schedules.
- Re-framing the federal income tax structure, treatment for nonresident aliens, supplemental wage withholding rates, and inflation adjustments.

Some trends to watch include the following:

- An increase in the demand for flexible work schedules as younger employees enter the workforce.
- The expansion of artificial intelligence (AI) into the payroll process that connects it more closely to HR and other company functions.
- An increase in the use of Human Resource information systems that connects company functions into an integrated platform.
- A reduction of paper in the payroll function through the use of Internet-based systems that connect departments within a company and employees via web portals and portable apps.
- Acceleration in businesses moving to a completely cloud-based operations management and payroll process.

Summary of Payroll Practices and System Fundamentals

Accounting practices have existed for centuries, and a need continually exists for employers to compensate employees for the work they have performed. Once the United States began taxing personal income, payroll processing became increasingly complex. During the 20th century, payroll practices evolved to include provisions for withholding taxes from employees, remitting payroll taxes to government agencies, maintaining accurate and confidential records, and incorporating civil rights-related legislation. Payroll accounting is a field that, due to its changing nature, requires precision and attention to minute details. Additionally, because of the nature of their work, payroll accountants must adhere to ethical guidelines including due care, objectivity, and independence, professional competence, integrity, and confidentiality.

The establishment of a 21st-century payroll system involves careful, deliberate planning. The framework used for the payroll system must have ample room for company growth, structure to ensure system stability, and trained payroll personnel to ensure that company and government deadlines are met. Using the best practices outlined in this chapter may help a company implement a robust payroll system, whether the system is maintained by company personnel, outsourced, completed manually, or accomplished through the use of specifically designed software. Robust payroll system design may reduce or prevent problems with employees and governmental entities.

Key Points

- Legislation that has affected employees' working conditions has mandated many aspects of the workplace, including civil rights, retirement and health benefits, and reinvestment in American workers.
- Payroll-specific legislation has influenced working hours and employee wages and was updated in 2020 to address contemporary employer concerns.
- Employer and employee tax laws have been enacted, and the remittance of tax obligations has been mandated.
- Payroll accountants must adhere to ethical guidelines because of the nature of the work performed.
- The ethical principles of confidentiality, integrity, objectivity, independence, and professional competence and due care guide the payroll accounting profession.
- Payroll practices include the electronic transmission of employee pay and tax obligations.
- The security of employee information is an ongoing concern for companies, especially with electronic transmission of sensitive data.
- Payroll may be processed at a central corporate site or through an outsourced payroll processing company.
- Many companies use payroll accounting software such as QuickBooks and Sage 100cloud.
- Cloud-based payroll processing has offered many resources for companies, including partial or total payroll preparation services.
- Payroll security and privacy are critical to ensure employer legal compliance and to protect employees.

Vocabulary

ACA	Equal Pay Act of 1963	Protecting Americans from Tax Hikes (PATH) Act
ADA	ERISA	
ADAAA	Ethics	
ADEA	FICA	Professional competence
ARRA	FLSA	Professionalism
ATRA	FMLA	PRWOR
Certified payroll	FUTA	Publication 15
Circular E	HIPAA	SECURE
Civil Rights Act of 1964	Independence	Sixteenth Amendment to the U.S. Constitution
Civil Rights Act of 1991	Independent contractor	
COBRA	Integrity	Social Security Act (SSA)
Consolidated Appropriations Act of 2018	IRCA	SOX
	Lilly Ledbetter Fair Pay Act of 2009	SUTA
		Tax Cuts and Jobs Act
Copeland Anti-Kickback Act	Medicare	USERRA
	OASDI	VPN
Current Tax Payment Act of 1943	Objectivity	Walsh–Healey Public Contracts Act
	OSHA	
Davis–Bacon Act of 1931	Personal Responsibility, Work and Family Promotion Act of 2002	Workers' compensation
DOMA		
Due care		
EEOC	Privacy Act of 1974	

Review Questions

1. What is the purpose of a payroll system?
2. What are two of the differences between large- and small-company payroll practices?
3. What is certified payroll? Which companies must use it?
4. Why might it be a good idea to let employees manage their payroll records? What are some of the pitfalls?
5. What are two ways that a payroll system may protect a company in the event of a visit from a government auditor?
6. What is payroll outsourcing? When might a company consider outsourcing its payroll?
7. What are three examples of federal laws that are essential to ensure legal, fair hiring practices?
8. What are the major types of payroll processing methods?
9. What are two laws governing the taxes that employers must withhold from employees?
10. What are the guidelines for FLSA in terms of overtime and pay rate?
11. Why was the Social Security Act of 1935 created? What were its provisions?
12. What are two of the advantages of a computerized payroll system over a manual system?
13. Which act created the term "Full-Time Equivalents"?
14. How has cloud-based payroll processing affected contemporary payroll practices?
15. What are two of the differences between the completion of the I-9 and the use of E-Verify systems?
16. What was the purpose of the SECURE Act?
17. What are two of the challenges that arise from the use of outsourced payroll systems?

Exercises Set A

E1-1A.
LO 1-1, 1-2

Lupore Fabrics obtained a contract in Watts Mills, South Carolina that involves the production of materials for military uniforms, a project contracted with the federal government for $2,800,000. What laws govern the wages Lupore Fabrics pays to its workers for this project? (Select all that may apply.)
1. Davis–Bacon Act
2. Sarbanes–Oxley Act
3. Walsh–Healey Act
4. FLSA

E1-2A.
LO 1-1, 1-2

Martine Piccirillo works as the payroll clerk for Centinix, a security company that hires many part-time and temporary workers who are paid on an hourly basis. What law governs the hiring or documenting of these workers?
1. ADEA
2. FLSA
3. IRCA
4. USERRA

E1-3A.
LO 1-1, 1-2

Benson Rake is a member of the hiring board for Quambo Dynamics, a software firm. As the board reviews candidates for a position, one of the other board members wants to exclude Nicholas Mathers, a man in his 50s, because his age might mean that he would be retiring within the next 10 years. What law protects Nicholas against this practice?
1. FLSA
2. ADEA
3. ADA
4. Civil Rights Act of 1991

E1-4A.
LO 1-1, 1-2

Ovenet Inc. is a qualified private-sector company that provides health insurance to its employees. The company is self-insured. Which of the following forms should the company provide its employees to comply with the Affordable Care Act?
1. 1095-A
2. 1095-B
3. 1095-C

E1-5A.
LO 1-3

Julia Chaudhari is the new payroll accountant for Insulose Chemicals. She is a member of a local young professionals networking organization. At a social gathering of the organization, her brother-in-law, Osher Nicastro, approached her about reviewing the company's payroll records to help her make sure they were correct. What ethical guidelines should Julia consider before agreeing to meet? (Select all that apply.)
1. Confidentiality
2. Objectivity and independence
3. Professional competence and due care
4. Integrity

E1-6A.
LO 1-4, LO 1-5

Merlin Anson owns Uninix Computers, a company with five employees. As a small business owner, he has several options for payroll processing. What factors should he consider when deciding on which payroll processing option is best for Uninix Computers? (Select all that apply.)
1. The number of independent contractors.
2. The physical size of the office facility.
3. The amount of money he has to spend on payroll processing.
4. The computer technology used by the business.

Match the following terms with their definitions:

E1-7A.	Manual payroll	a.	A preloaded credit card used to pay employees.
E1-8A.	Timecard	b.	The process of gathering information about hours worked for one or more employees.
E1-9A.	Paycard	c.	A web-based application wherein employees can modify certain payroll-related information.
E1-10A.	Employee Internet portal	d.	Governs accounting for firms with federal government contracts in excess of $2,000.
E1-11A.	Certified payroll	e.	A record of the time worked during a period for an individual employee.
E1-12A.	Outsourced payroll	f.	Examples of companies used for outsourcing payroll processing.
E1-13A.	Auditor	g.	Provided funding for the E-Verify program.
E1-14A.	ADP and Paychex®	h.	Payroll administration using a paper payroll register.
E1-15A.	Time collection	i.	The use of an external company to track time and benefits and pay employees.
E1-16A.	Davis–Bacon Act	j.	A person or group who examines a company's accounting records for accuracy.
E1-17A.	Consolidated Appropriations Act	k.	A way for governmental agencies to track the payroll associated with a government contract.

Problems Set A

P1-1A.
LO 1-2

Hayim Accardi is the accounting manager for a small, local firm that has full- and part-time staff. How do FLSA guidelines regarding working hours apply to Hayim's employees?

P1-2A.
LO 1-4, 1-5

Jessalyn Poulsen is an accountant for her firm, a medium-sized company with 125 employees. The firm has traditionally maintained the administration of its payroll. Her co-worker, the only other accountant in the firm, retires. Because of budget concerns, the firm chooses not to refill the position. What options does Jessalyn have regarding the administration of the payroll?

P1-3A.
LO 1-1, 1-2

Elias Motta is the office manager and payroll clerk for his company, which is composed of 12 employees. An employee, Sylvia Gladwin, stops by Elias's office and wants to view her payroll record. What privacy regulations must Elias consider before granting his co-worker access?

P1-4A.
LO 1-2

A group of employees, who read on a website that income tax collection is illegal, approach Hawa Furst, the controller for a large company. They request that he stop withholding income taxes from their pay unless he can explain what laws govern income tax collection. What should Hawa tell them?

P1-5A.
LO 1-1, 1-2

Kalea Germain is a warehouse worker for a small grocery market. As she was moving some merchandise, the loading dock door unexpectedly fell and injured her. How does OSHA apply to Kalea for this type of injury?

P1-6A.
LO 1-4

Ennis Locatelli is a new payroll accountant at Avata Electronics. In his review of previous manual payroll records, he noted several errors that required the issuance of additional checks to employees for unpaid payroll amounts. What are Ennis's options to avoid similar problems in the future?

P1-7A.
LO 1-3

Libbi Alberighi and Flavia van Peij are friends who work for the same company. Libbi manages a manufacturing department and Flavia supervises the payroll clerks. Which ethical guidelines or rules would these friends need to remember when discussing work?

P1-8A.
LO 1-1, 1-2

At Denniston Industries, employees have the option of choosing employer-sponsored health insurance. What responsibilities does the employer have according to COBRA upon the termination of an employee?

P1-9A.
LO 1-5

Katelijn Preston is a new manager at Resterra Inc. She is looking at using the E-Verify process for new hires. What recommendations can you give her about the differences between having an employee complete the I-9 and the E-Verify process?

P1-10A.
LO 1-4

Cahya Russell is a new employee in the payroll department for Winhook Industries. She has had several employees approach her with questions but is unsure how privacy regulations could affect her response. What advice would you give her about privacy laws and payroll?

Exercises Set B

E1-1B.
LO 1-1, 1-2

Emmett Colquhoun is a military veteran who requires many absences for medical reasons. His boss at Betri Farms has demanded that he reduce the number of sick days unless he provides his medical history. Which law(s) protect Emmett? (Select all that apply.)
1. ADA
2. FLSA
3. USERRA
4. HIPAA

E1-2B.
LO 1-1, 1-2

Gale Rana is a production worker at Gexo Manufacturing, which produces air conditioning systems. After working there for 10 years, she discovers through conversations with a colleague with the same title and similar seniority that her wage is 20 percent lower than his wage. She feels that she has been a victim of discrimination. Which law(s) govern her situation?
1. FLSA
2. Civil Rights Act of 1964
3. ADEA
4. Equal Pay Act

E1-3B.
LO 1-4, 1-5

Mathias Acker is the new bookkeeper for Meganyx Enterprises, a small business consulting firm, and was hired to replace a long-time employee who retired. Upon starting the position, Mathias notices that the prior bookkeeper used a purely manual system. The company owner has said that Mathias may update the payroll system. What options are available?

E1-4B.
LO 1-2

Paula Aggio is the accounting manager for Sugent Communications. The company has a staff that includes five full-time employees and eight on-call workers who independently determine the number of hours and their work location. The on-call consultants claim that they should be classified as employees. What criteria should Paula use to determine the workers' employment status? (Select all that apply.)
1. The extent to which the on-call workers control their hours and working locations.
2. The number of hours worked by the on-call workers.
3. The number and types of job-specific tools that the employer provides.
4. How the workers are compensated for their work, by the job or by hours.

E1-5B.
LO 1-3

Erkan Dioli is the payroll accountant for Prosario Imports. His most recent experience with accounting was when he was in college, which was eight years ago. Which ethical guideline addresses his need to remain current with accounting practice?
1. Integrity
2. Professionalism
3. Professional competence and due care
4. Confidentiality

E1-6B.
LO 1-5

Khaled Watson is the payroll accountant for Antizio Electronics, a company that engages in work on federal contracts. He wants to ensure that the company is compliant with the provisions of the Davis–Bacon Act. What is the name of the process used to monitor payroll compliance in this situation?
1. Contracted payroll
2. Davis–Bacon verification
3. Certified payroll
4. Outsourced payroll

Match the following items with their definitions:

E1-7B.	USERRA	a.	A provision of the Sarbanes–Oxley Act.
E1-8B.	*U.S. v. Windsor*	b.	Instituted a tiered income tax on workers.
E1-9B.	Internal controls documentation	c.	Prohibited employment of individuals younger than 16 years of age.
E1-10B.	HIPAA	d.	Strengthened the child support provisions of PRWOR.
E1-11B.	Lilly Ledbetter Fair Pay Act	e.	Legislation that governs the treatment of military service personnel.
E1-12B.	Sixteenth Amendment	f.	A worker who is not subject to a company's direction or its payroll laws.
E1-13B.	Walsh–Healey Public Contracts Act	g.	Repealed the 180-day statute of limitations on equal pay complaints.
E1-14B.	Independent contractor	h.	Reframing federal employee income tax computations.
E1-15B.	Personal Responsibility, Work and Family Promotion Act of 2002	i.	The case responsible for the U.S. Supreme Court's repeal of DOMA
E1-16B.	IRCA	j.	Protects the confidentiality of employee medical records.
E1-17B.	Tax Cuts and Jobs Act	k.	Mandates completion of Form I-9.

Problems Set B

P1-1B.
LO 1-4, 1-5

Albina Kravitz is the payroll administrator for Exity Enterprises. Because of economic conditions, her boss has assigned her the additional duties of office management, and Albina is considering outsourcing her payroll duties. What are the pros and cons of outsourcing the company's payroll?

P1-2B.
LO 1-1, 1-2

Jolana Thomas is the payroll clerk for Telemba Communications. One of the company's employees, Darijo Boon, informs Jolana that he feels that he was the victim of unequal pay three years prior. What law(s) provide guidance about Darijo's complaint?

P1-3B.
LO 1-3

Clara Hudnall is Conosis Incorporated's payroll accountant. During a casual conversation with co-workers, she learns that Thorben Vinkovic, a co-worker, is deliberately overstating the number of hours worked during each pay period because of a personal economic situation. Which ethical guidelines pertain to this situation? What should Clara do with this knowledge?

P1-4B.
LO 1-4

Perpetua Holguin is a payroll accountant for Marore Industries. She is asked to explain the differences between manual and computerized accounting practices. What differences should she highlight in her explanation?

P1-5B.
LO 1-1, 1-2, 1-3

During a review of payroll records, Osvaldo Morena notices that a female employee in Department A is receiving a significantly lower salary than similarly skilled male employees in the same department. What actions should Osvaldo take in this situation?

P1-6B.
LO 1-3

Samuel Alescio is an accountant for Diado, a large, multinational firm. During payroll processing, he notices that the new state payroll tax updates have not been installed in the firm's software. What ethical guidelines govern his behavior in this situation?

P1-7B.
LO 1-2

Nitza Croce is an employee of Autonder, a contractor that provides governmental construction services in Washington, DC. The current contract is for $250,000. Nitza is 22 and is paid $9.50 per hour. How does the Walsh–Healey Public Contracts Act affect her?

P1-8B.
LO 1-4

Eugene Robertson works as a payroll clerk at Hyperend Inc. He shares an office with three other co-workers and must examine documents containing personal information as a regular part of his duties. Based on the provisions of the Privacy Act of 1974, what responsibilities does Eugene have regarding the payroll records he handles?

P1-9B.
LO 1-5

Larissa Abiodun is a senior payroll administrator for Falcive Landscape Design. The company has 15 employees and annual revenues of $10 million. She has been using and maintaining manual payroll records for the last 20 years of her career, and the president of Falcive Landscape Design wants to explore options for computerized payroll processing. Which payroll option is the most suitable for both Larissa and Falcive Landscape Design? Why?

P1-10B.
LO 1-2

Alfredo Bellini is the payroll accountant for Pyrondo Fireworks and he has been asked for information about employees and independent contractors. What are three of the key differences between employees and independent contractors?

Critical Thinking

CT1-1. You have been hired as a consultant for Dynozz Medical Software, which is facing an IRS audit of its accounting records. During your review, you notice anomalies in the payroll system involving overpayments of labor and payments to terminated employees. What should you do?

CT1-2. Liliya Milic is the accountant for Syiva, a local nonprofit organization. She has been tasked with managing the costs of the payroll so that staffing levels may remain the same even if funding levels change. She considers outsourcing the payroll to a payroll processing company. What are some factors that Liliya should consider in her decision? Why are these factors important?

In the Real World: Scenario for Discussion

Domino's Pizza franchises in New York were sued by the state of New York in 2016 for wage theft at 10 stores. Under New York law, a corporation and a franchiser are joint employers if they meet certain criteria regarding employee control. The state found that Domino's met the criteria for being a joint employer because it mandates a significant number of policies with which franchisers must comply. The problem arose when Domino's mandated the use of PULSE payroll software, which the pizza company knew to be flawed and did not attempt to remedy. The flawed software led to employees being paid at rates below the legal minimum wage, failed to pay overtime, did not reimburse employees for vehicle use, and abused tip credit guidelines.

Food for thought:

1. Should the franchisers be held liable as joint employers with Domino's? Why or why not?

2. Which laws pertain to employee wages? How would they apply in this situation?

3. What could be done to ensure future legal compliance?

Internet Activities

1-1. Using the website www.jstor.org, search for articles about payroll-related laws or relevant employment legislation. Once you find an article, summarize the article and explain how the legislation influenced contemporary payroll practices.

1-2. Visit the website of the American Payroll Association at www.americanpayroll.org. On the right side of the Home page, you will find articles about recent developments in payroll practices and legislation. Choose an article and create a presentation to your class about how its content affects payroll practice.

1-3. Want to know more about the specifics of some of the concepts in this chapter? Check out these websites:

www.dol.gov/whd/

www.taxhistory.com/1943.html

www.workerscompensationinsurance.com

www.Kronos.com

www.adp.com

www.paychex.com

1-4. Would it help to see a video explanation of FLSA coverage? Go to the link below and select Topic 1: Coverage. https://www.dol.gov/whd/flsa/videos.htm

1-5. Check out www.employer.gov to see the Department of Labor's Office of Compliance site. This site contains guidelines for employers about their specific responsibilities to employees, compliance deadlines, posters, and other resources. Its employee-focused website, www.worker.gov, contains worker-focused resources geared to foster understanding of employee rights under the law.

1-6. Using the website www.ncsea.org search for research about child support statistics, collections per year, and payroll professionals' role in the process.

Sianc/Shutterstock

Continuing Payroll Project: Prevosti Farms and Sugarhouse

Toni Prevosti is opening a new business, Prevosti Farms and Sugarhouse, which is a small company that will harvest, refine, and sell maple syrup products. In subsequent chapters, students will have the opportunity to establish payroll records and complete payroll information for Prevosti Farms and Sugarhouse.

Toni has decided that she needs to hire employees for the business to grow. Complete the application for Prevosti Farms and Sugarhouse's Employer Identification Number (Form SS-4) with the following information:

Prevosti Farms and Sugarhouse is located at 820 Westminster Road, Bridgewater, Vermont, 05520 (which is also Ms. Prevosti's home address), phone number 802-555-3456. Bridgewater is in Windsor County. Toni, the responsible party for a Limited Liability Corporation created in the United States with one member (disregarded entity), has decided that Prevosti Farms and Sugarhouse, will pay its employees on a biweekly basis. Toni's Social Security number is 055-22-0443. The beginning date of the business is February 1, 20XX. Prevosti Farms and Sugarhouse will use a calendar year as its accounting year. Toni anticipates that she will need to hire six employees initially for the business, three of whom will be agricultural and three who will be office workers. The first date of wage disbursement will be February 14, 20XX. Toni has not had a prior EIN.

Form **SS-4**	**Application for Employer Identification Number**	OMB No. 1545-0003
(Rev. December 2019) Department of the Treasury Internal Revenue Service	(For use by employers, corporations, partnerships, trusts, estates, churches, government agencies, Indian tribal entities, certain individuals, and others.) ▶ Go to *www.irs.gov/FormSS4* for instructions and the latest information. ▶ See separate instructions for each line. ▶ Keep a copy for your records.	EIN

Type or print clearly.

1	Legal name of entity (or individual) for whom the EIN is being requested

2	Trade name of business (if different from name on line 1)	3	Executor, administrator, trustee, "care of" name

4a	Mailing address (room, apt., suite no. and street, or P.O. box)	5a	Street address (if different) (Don't enter a P.O. box.)
4b	City, state, and ZIP code (if foreign, see instructions)	5b	City, state, and ZIP code (if foreign, see instructions)

6	County and state where principal business is located

7a	Name of responsible party	7b	SSN, ITIN, or EIN

8a	Is this application for a limited liability company (LLC) (or a foreign equivalent)? . . . . ☐ Yes ☐ No	8b	If 8a is "Yes," enter the number of LLC members . . . . . . ▶

8c	If 8a is "Yes," was the LLC organized in the United States? . . . . ☐ Yes ☐ No

9a Type of entity (check only one box). **Caution:** If 8a is "Yes," see the instructions for the correct box to check.

☐ Sole proprietor (SSN) _____

☐ Partnership

☐ Corporation (enter form number to be filed) ▶ _____

☐ Personal service corporation

☐ Church or church-controlled organization

☐ Other nonprofit organization (specify) ▶ _____

☐ Other (specify) ▶

☐ Estate (SSN of decedent) _____

☐ Plan administrator (TIN) _____

☐ Trust (TIN of grantor) _____

☐ Military/National Guard   ☐ State/local government

☐ Farmers' cooperative   ☐ Federal government

☐ REMIC   ☐ Indian tribal governments/enterprises

Group Exemption Number (GEN) if any ▶

9b	If a corporation, name the state or foreign country (if applicable) where incorporated	State	Foreign country

10 **Reason for applying** (check only one box)

☐ Started new business (specify type) ▶ _____

_____

☐ Hired employees (Check the box and see line 13.)

☐ Compliance with IRS withholding regulations

☐ Other (specify) ▶

☐ Banking purpose (specify purpose) ▶ _____

☐ Changed type of organization (specify new type) ▶ _____

☐ Purchased going business

☐ Created a trust (specify type) ▶ _____

☐ Created a pension plan (specify type) ▶ _____

11	Date business started or acquired (month, day, year). See instructions.	12	Closing month of accounting year
13	Highest number of employees expected in the next 12 months (enter -0- if none). If no employees expected, skip line 14.	14	If you expect your employment tax liability to be $1,000 or less in a full calendar year **and** want to file Form 944 annually instead of Forms 941 quarterly, check here. (Your employment tax liability generally will be $1,000 or less if you expect to pay $5,000 or less in total wages.) If you don't check this box, you must file Form 941 for every quarter. ☐

Agricultural	Household	Other

15	First date wages or annuities were paid (month, day, year). **Note:** If applicant is a withholding agent, enter date income will first be paid to nonresident alien (month, day, year) . . . . ▶

16 Check **one** box that best describes the principal activity of your business.

☐ Construction   ☐ Rental & leasing   ☐ Transportation & warehousing

☐ Real estate   ☐ Manufacturing   ☐ Finance & insurance

☐ Health care & social assistance

☐ Accommodation & food service

☐ Other (specify) ▶

☐ Wholesale-agent/broker

☐ Wholesale-other   ☐ Retail

17	Indicate principal line of merchandise sold, specific construction work done, products produced, or services provided.

18	Has the applicant entity shown on line 1 ever applied for and received an EIN? ☐ Yes ☐ No If "Yes," write previous EIN here ▶

Third Party Designee	Complete this section **only** if you want to authorize the named individual to receive the entity's EIN and answer questions about the completion of this form.	
	Designee's name	Designee's telephone number (include area code)
	Address and ZIP code	Designee's fax number (include area code)

Under penalties of perjury, I declare that I have examined this application, and to the best of my knowledge and belief, it is true, correct, and complete.

Name and title (type or print clearly) ▶

	Applicant's telephone number (include area code)
Signature ▶ Date ▶	Applicant's fax number (include area code)

For Privacy Act and Paperwork Reduction Act Notice, see separate instructions.   Cat. No. 16055N   Form **SS-4** (Rev. 12-2019)

Source: Internal Revenue Service.

Answers to Stop & Check Exercises

Which Law?
1. k
2. h
3. b
4. f
5. i
6. j
7. a
8. d
9. g
10. c
11. e
12. l

Which Payroll Law?
1. d
2. a
3. f
4. c
5. g
6. j
7. b
8. i
9. e
10. h

What's Ethical?
1. Answers will vary. Some concerns include data privacy and integrity in the software switchover, tax and employee pay integrity on the new software, and employee pay methods.
2. Answers will vary. Liza could choose to ignore her sorority sister's request, claiming confidentiality. She could also discontinue active participation in the sorority. In any case, Liza must not consent to her sorority sister's request for confidential information.

Confidential Records
As a payroll clerk, your task is to protect the privacy and confidentiality of the information you maintain for the company. If a student group—or any personnel aside from the company's payroll employees and officers—wishes to review confidential records, you should deny their request. If needed, you should refer the group to your department's manager to discuss the matter in more depth. The laws that apply to this situation are the Privacy Act of 1974, U.S. Department of Labor OCFO-1, and potentially HIPAA.

Large vs. Small
1. Large companies face issues with multiple departments, employee access to online personnel portals, employee data security, and timekeeping accuracy.
2. For small companies, the cost of outsourcing the payroll function needs to be considered. On one hand, a small company may not have personnel who are proficient with payroll regulations and tax reporting requirements, which leaves a company vulnerable to legal actions and stringent fines. However, engaging a payroll service company may be cost prohibitive. The decision to outsource the payroll for a small company should take into account the number of personnel, locations, and types of operations in which the company engages.

What Is the Difference?
a. Manual payroll systems involve the use of paper-and-pencil record keeping or a spreadsheet program, such as Microsoft Excel. This is most appropriate for very small firms.
b. Computerized payroll systems can be used by any company, regardless of size. Examples of computerized systems include QuickBooks, Sage 100cloud, and Microsoft Dynamics GP. These computer packages range in price, depending on the company size and operational scope.
c. Outsourced payroll involves the engagement of a third party to manage a company's payroll data, issue employee compensation, and prepare tax forms.
d. Certified payroll pertains to companies with employees who work on federal government contracts. Certified payroll ensures that a company reports payroll expenditures of contractually allocated money.

Chapter Two

2

Payroll System Procedures

Payroll procedures have a dual focus: (1) governmental rules and (2) the company's needs. The company must abide by the applicable governmental and industrial regulations or face potential fines, sanctions, or closure. To comply with regulations, a company must make several decisions: pay frequency, pay types (e.g., direct deposit, paycards, or paper checks), employee benefits, and handling of pay advances. The payroll accountant must prepare for the integration of new hires, transfer of employees among departments, and terminations that occur during the normal course of business. Employee benefits and government-required payroll deductions complicate the employee payment process.

Accountants handle documents that have varying levels of confidentiality. Some items include receipts for expenses, invoices from vendors, and other business-related documents that are not confidential. Employee-related documents that payroll accountants handle are usually private and often contain highly sensitive personal information. Various regulations regarding the length of retention and storage procedures apply to payroll documents. An important note about financial or personnel documentation is this: Any documents connected with fraudulent activity have no time limit for retention purposes. In the event of suspected fraud, investigators may request relevant fraud-related documents at any time.

LEARNING OBJECTIVES

After studying Chapter 2, you should be able to:

LO 2-1   Identify Important Payroll Procedures and Pay Cycles

LO 2-2   Prepare Required Employee Documentation

LO 2-3   Differentiate between Exempt and Nonexempt Workers

LO 2-4   Explain Pay Records and Employee File Maintenance

LO 2-5   Describe Internal Controls and Record Retention for a Payroll System

LO 2-6   Discuss Employee Termination and Document Destruction Procedures

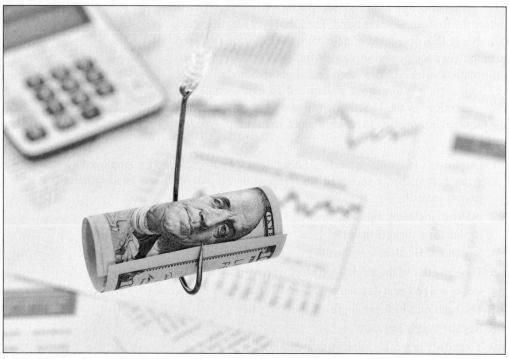

William Potter/Shutterstock

Fraud Revealed by Payroll Record Audit

In Greenwood, Indiana, a payroll clerk for Center Grove Community Schools managed to steal nearly $300,000 between 2016 and 2019. The clerk committed the theft by continuing to pay terminated employees and depositing that pay into her own bank account. Additionally, she diverted the worker's compensation pay for another employee to her bank account. The payroll clerk's misdeeds were found through an audit of the payroll records conducted by state investigators after another employee came forward as a whistleblower.

Center Grove Community Schools responded to the theft by reviewing their payroll record-keeping processes and implementing stronger internal controls. As a public school system, Center Grove corporate officers were aware of their fiduciary responsibility with taxpayer funds. Corporate officers reviewed IRS filings to resolve inconsistencies arising from the multi-year theft and continued to work with state officials to resolve any other financial crimes that would be discovered in the continuing investigation.

(Source: Daily Journal)

Personnel and payroll files are closely related. In Chapter 2, we will explore payroll system procedures, including information about file security, legally required documents, and internal controls.

LO 2-1 Identify Important Payroll Procedures and Pay Cycles

The documentation required for paying employees starts before the first employee is hired. The Employer Identification Number (EIN), obtained online from the IRS, is the first step in employer documentation, closely followed by the employee information files. Under the Fair Labor Standards Act (FLSA), certain information is required in every employee file. According to the U.S. Department of Labor, the list of the required information to be maintained in the employee file includes

PhuShutter/Shutterstock

1. Employee's full name as used for Social Security purposes, and the employee's identifying symbol or number, if such is used in place of the employee's name on any time, work, or payroll records.
2. Address, including zip code.
3. Birthdate, if younger than 19.
4. Sex and occupation.
5. Time and day of the week when employee's workweek begins.
6. Hours worked each day and total hours worked each workweek.
7. The basis on which employee's wages are paid.
8. Regular hourly pay rate.
9. Total daily or weekly straight-time earnings.
10. Total overtime earnings for the workweek.
11. All additions to or deductions from the employee's wages.
12. Total wages paid each *pay period*.
13. Date of payment and the pay period covered by the payment.

Payroll documentation regulations protect employees by ensuring that they receive accurate paychecks. These regulations also keep employers in compliance with tax regulations and provide an audit trail for government bodies. *New hire reporting* requirements ensure that employees pay legal obligations such as child support and garnishments. Figure 2-1 shows a sample Employee Information Form, which contains elements of the information from the employee file. Note that the employee file is maintained by the firm's human resources department, and the employee information form shown in Figure 2-1 is maintained by the payroll department, so some FLSA elements may not appear on the form.

FIGURE 2-1

Sample Employee Information Form

NAME	Jonathan A. Doe	Hire Date	1/1/2020		Dependent child <17	2
ADDRESS	100 Main Street	Date of Birth	4/16/1983		Dependent other	2
CITY/STATE/ZIP	Anytown, MD 21220	Position	Sales	PT /(FT)	Step 4a W-4 Info	none
TELEPHONE	202-555-4009	Filing Status	Married/Joint		Step 4b W-4 Info	none-standard
SOCIAL SECURITY NUMBER	987-65-4321	Pay Rate	$15.00	Hr / Wk / Mo	Step 4c W-4 Info	none

Period Ended	Hrs Worked	Reg Pay	OT Pay	Gross Pay	Social Sec Tax	Medicare	Fed Inc Tax	State Inc Tax	401(k)	Total Deduc	Net Pay	YTD
1/16/2020	80	1,200.00	-	1,200.00	74.40	17.40	-	25.25	25.00	142.05	1,057.95	1,057.95

The Equal Employment Opportunity Commission's protection of employee rights, especially when it leads to a lawsuit, involves the firm's personnel documentation. Accurate and correctly maintained payroll records are especially important because they reflect the firm's treatment of its employees. In certain states, such as Illinois, employees have the right to inspect their personnel files and to issue rebuttals for incorrect items.

When a company develops or reviews its payroll system, the payroll accountant faces a multifaceted task. The employer must answer several questions:

- How will the company handle new hires?
- What information will be maintained in employee personnel files?
- Where will files be stored and who is responsible for file security?
- What will the procedure be when an employee transfers from one department to another?
- What is the procedure to follow upon employee termination?
- What processes should the company establish to ensure government compliance?
- How will employee time and attendance be tracked?
- How long do employee files need to be retained after an employee leaves the company?
- Do employees have the legal right to inspect their files, and what procedures should be in place when employees request to see their files?
- Where will the mandatory FLSA Minimum Wage Poster (Figure 2-2) be displayed?

Pay Cycles

Let's start with a basic question: How often should the company pay its employees? Regardless of which accounting system the company is using, the determination of pay cycle, or pay periods, is the first thing a new company needs to establish. Options for payroll cycles include the following:

Daily payroll is typically paid at the end of the day or by the end of the next business day. This method of payroll processing is typical in day labor situations; however, it should be noted that day labor could be treated as independent contractor work and thus not be subject to payroll, payroll taxes, or a W-2. Daily payroll could potentially have 365 or 366 pay periods.

Weekly payroll is typically used in a five-day workweek. The employees receive their paychecks the following Friday. Several types of companies use a weekly payroll system, including grocery stores, construction, and professional offices. This pay frequency may lead to 52 pay periods per year.

Biweekly payroll is typically processed based on a two-week period, and employees receive their paychecks approximately a week after the end of the pay period. Pay dates may be any weekday. This pay frequency generally has 26 pay periods per year. On rare occasions there may be 27 pay periods in a biweekly payroll; however, this is rare, and typical calculations will use 26.

Semimonthly payroll is paid twice a month. Examples of semimonthly payroll pay dates include (1) the 1st and 15th of the month and (2) the 15th and last day of the month. This is not the same as biweekly payroll, and taxation and hours paid are different. Employees receive 24 pay disbursements per year when using a semimonthly payroll system.

Monthly payroll is less frequently used than other methods. Some companies process payroll once per month and may allow a semimonthly draw to the employees. When employees are allowed to draw their wages at mid-month, the employer may or may not take payroll taxes out of the draw. If the mid-month draw does not have payroll taxes withheld, the month-end payroll will need to recover all taxes and withholdings for the month from the employee.

Figure 2-3 shows the different types of pay cycles a company can offer its employees.

FIGURE 2-2
FLSA Minimum Wage Poster

EMPLOYEE RIGHTS
UNDER THE FAIR LABOR STANDARDS ACT

FEDERAL MINIMUM WAGE
$7.25 PER HOUR
BEGINNING JULY 24, 2009

The law requires employers to display this poster where employees can readily see it.

OVERTIME PAY

At least 1½ times the regular rate of pay for all hours worked over 40 in a workweek.

CHILD LABOR

An employee must be at least 16 years old to work in most non-farm jobs and at least 18 to work in non-farm jobs declared hazardous by the Secretary of Labor. Youths 14 and 15 years old may work outside school hours in various non-manufacturing, non-mining, non-hazardous jobs with certain work hours restrictions. Different rules apply in agricultural employment.

TIP CREDIT

Employers of "tipped employees" who meet certain conditions may claim a partial wage credit based on tips received by their employees. Employers must pay tipped employees a cash wage of at least $2.13 per hour if they claim a tip credit against their minimum wage obligation. If an employee's tips combined with the employer's cash wage of at least $2.13 per hour do not equal the minimum hourly wage, the employer must make up the difference.

NURSING MOTHERS

The FLSA requires employers to provide reasonable break time for a nursing mother employee who is subject to the FLSA's overtime requirements in order for the employee to express breast milk for her nursing child for one year after the child's birth each time such employee has a need to express breast milk. Employers are also required to provide a place, other than a bathroom, that is shielded from view and free from intrusion from coworkers and the public, which may be used by the employee to express breast milk.

ENFORCEMENT

The Department has authority to recover back wages and an equal amount in liquidated damages in instances of minimum wage, overtime, and other violations. The Department may litigate and/or recommend criminal prosecution. Employers may be assessed civil money penalties for each willful or repeated violation of the minimum wage or overtime pay provisions of the law. Civil money penalties may also be assessed for violations of the FLSA's child labor provisions. Heightened civil money penalties may be assessed for each child labor violation that results in the death or serious injury of any minor employee, and such assessments may be doubled when the violations are determined to be willful or repeated. The law also prohibits retaliating against or discharging workers who file a complaint or participate in any proceeding under the FLSA.

ADDITIONAL INFORMATION

- Certain occupations and establishments are exempt from the minimum wage, and/or overtime pay provisions.
- Special provisions apply to workers in American Samoa, the Commonwealth of the Northern Mariana Islands, and the Commonwealth of Puerto Rico.
- Some state laws provide greater employee protections; employers must comply with both.
- Some employers incorrectly classify workers as "independent contractors" when they are actually employees under the FLSA. It is important to know the difference between the two because employees (unless exempt) are entitled to the FLSA's minimum wage and overtime pay protections and correctly classified independent contractors are not.
- Certain full-time students, student learners, apprentices, and workers with disabilities may be paid less than the minimum wage under special certificates issued by the Department of Labor.

 ≡WHD **WAGE AND HOUR DIVISION**
UNITED STATES DEPARTMENT OF LABOR

1-866-487-9243
TTY: 1-877-889-5627
www.dol.gov/whd

WH1088   REV 07/16

Source: U.S. Department of Labor.

FIGURE 2-3
Pay Periods

Daily	• 365 or 366 periods
Weekly	• 52 periods
Biweekly	• 26 periods
Semimonthly	• 24 periods
Monthly	• 12 periods

What's in the File?

Stop & Check

1. Which of the following artifacts must be included in the employee file?
   a. Full name and address.
   b. Occupation.
   c. Mother's maiden name.
   d. Pay rate.
   e. Date of payment.
   f. Spouse's name.

Match the pay frequencies: The number of pay periods:

2. Monthly   a. 26 or 27
3. Semimonthly   b. 12
4. Biweekly   c. 52
5. Weekly   d. 24

LO 2-2   Prepare Required Employee Documentation

Employees versus Independent Contractors

People who work for a company may be classified as either employees or independent contractors depending on the nature of the work and the withholding of payroll-related taxes from the worker's compensation. According to the Internal Revenue Service (IRS), millions of workers have been misclassified, which has led to employers not depositing the full amount of taxes due and employees missing out on benefits. IRS Form SS-8, the Determination of Worker Status for Purposes of Employment Taxes and Income Tax Withholding, is a way that employers may receive official guidance about worker classification. This form is available from the IRS and elicits information about the behavioral control, financial control, and the relationship of the worker to the firm as ways to determine the correct status of the worker as an employee or an independent contractor. When the employer submits this form, the IRS makes the final determination of employee status.

Rawpixel.com/Shutterstock

Employees

The determination of a worker as an employee has two primary criteria according to labor laws. The first is the *work direction,* which means that the employer substantially directs the worker's performance. The employer provides the primary tools that an employee uses; for example, the employee may be given the use of a desk, computer, company car, or other items needed to complete the assigned work. The other criterion is the *material contribution,* which means that the work that the employee completes must involve substantial effort. An employer withholds payroll taxes from an employee's compensation, provides company-specific benefits, and includes the worker on governmental reports.

10'000 Hours/DigitalVision/
Getty Images

Independent Contractors

Classification of a worker as an independent contractor (IC) means that the employer does not direct the worker's specific actions and does not provide the tools needed to complete the work. For example, if a worker performed accounting services for a company but used a privately owned computer and printer, as well as determined the number and timing of the hours worked for the company, the worker could be classified as an independent contractor. An independent contractor may or may not perform work that constitutes a material contribution to the employer.

Another identifier of an independent contractor is the duration of the relationship with the employer. Independent contractors tend to have shorter-term relationships with the business than employees do. Furthermore, an independent contractor will not share in profits or losses of the company in the same manner as employees. Finally, independent contractors are not subject to FLSA provisions for minimum wage and overtime pay.

Payment records for independent contractors, although maintained separately from payroll records, are an instance in which payroll accountants must be aware of employee classification and record-keeping requirements to avoid fraudulent activity. The independent contractor generally works for specified fees that they bill to the company, which typically pay them through their accounts payable department, not payroll. Independent contractors are also responsible for their own payroll taxes. The topic of worker classification as an employee or independent contractor has become increasingly important in the past decade as many employers have sought to reduce governmental fines and other liabilities stemming from the incorrect classification of workers.

The IRS uses three common-law tests to clarify whether a worker is an employee or an independent contractor:

1. **Behavioral Control:** To what extent does the employer have the right to control and direct the worker's actions?
2. **Financial Control:** This guideline pertains to the worker's unreimbursed expenses, investment in job-related tools, availability of worker's services to other entities outside the company, and how the worker is paid.
3. **Relationship of the Parties:** This includes details related to any work-related contracts between the employer and the worker, benefits offered, permanency of the relationship, and the relationship between the worker's services and the firm's normal business operations.

A contemporary issue in worker classification is the gig economy, in which people choose to work multiple short-term contracts or freelance jobs. In November 2019, the state of New Jersey required Uber to pay $649 million for multiple years of unpaid employment taxes. This decision was pursuant to a suit filed in 2018 claiming that Uber drivers should be treated as employees because the company controlled the

(continued)

(concluded)

hours of work and directed their work activities, thus meeting the criteria for drivers being classified as employees instead of independent contractors. As of 2019, approximately 57 million workers in the United States participated in the gig economy as secondary or tertiary work, although the Bureau of Labor Statics does not have a method to capture precise data about the actual number of gig-economy workers. (Source: MarketWatch)

Further clarification about determining employment status may be located in IRS Publication 1779. Upon request, the firm may request official guidance from the IRS by submitting Form SS-8. Penalties are levied on employers who deliberately misclassify employees in an effort to cut payroll costs; in addition to penalties, the employers may have to provide unpaid wages to misclassified employees. As of 2018, the Wage and Hour Division of the Department of Labor had recovered in excess of $1.3 billion in back wages due to misclassified workers over the past five years and reported an additional $322 million recovered during 2019.

Reporting New Employees

Reporting newly hired employees is considered important by governmental bodies. Why is this so?

- First, reporting employees creates a registry to monitor people who owe child support or other court-ordered garnishments.
- Second, it helps immigration agencies track immigrants to ensure that they are still legally able to work in the United States.
- Third, for certain professions such as teaching, the new-hire reporting system can be used to communicate issues such as ethical violations for which the professional has been censured by governmental or accrediting bodies.
- Finally, the new hire reporting system assists with the administration of COBRA medical benefits.

All newly hired employees must provide specific documentation. For legal purposes, the minimum amount of documentation allowed is Form *W-4* (see Figure 2-4) and the *I-9* (see Figure 2-5). Form W-4 is a publication of the Internal Revenue Service. The main purpose behind the W-4 is to help the employer determine the correct amount of federal income taxes to withhold from the employee's payroll. Employees may make changes to the information on Form W-4 at any time during the year. A best practice with regard to Form W-4 is to request that employees file a new form each January. States may have similar withholding forms, which should similarly be completed. Since Form W-4 was significantly changed in 2020, it is worth noting that employees hired prior to 2020 do not need to complete a new Form W-4, but those hired after January 1, 2020, must complete the form.

Notice that the 2020 Form W-4 is significantly different from prior years.

- Step 1: Personal information, including full name, address, social security number, and marital status
- Steps 2-4: These are used only for employees with additional income through a spouse's job, deductions for dependents, and additional income tax adjustments based on worksheets contained in the full form.
- Step 5: Employee and employer's signature and date.

FIGURE 2-4

Form W-4 Employee Withholding Certificate (Completed Example)

Form **W-4** Department of the Treasury Internal Revenue Service	**Employee's Withholding Certificate** ▶ Complete Form W-4 so that your employer can withhold the correct federal income tax from your pay. ▶ Give Form W-4 to your employer. ▶ Your withholding is subject to review by the IRS.

OMB No. 1545-0074

20**20**

Step 1:

Enter Personal Information

(a) First name and middle initial	Last name	(b) Social security number
Jonathan W	Doe	987-65-4321

Address

123 Main Street

City or town, state, and ZIP code

Anytown, KS 54932

▶ **Does your name match the name on your social security card?** If not, to ensure you get credit for your earnings, contact SSA at 800-772-1213 or go to *www.ssa.gov.*

(c) ☑ Single or Married filing separately

☐ **Married filing jointly** (or Qualifying widow(er))

☐ **Head of household** (Check only if you're unmarried and pay more than half the costs of keeping up a home for yourself and a qualifying individual.)

Complete Steps 2–4 ONLY if they apply to you; otherwise, skip to Step 5. See page 2 for more information on each step, who can claim exemption from withholding, when to use the online estimator, and privacy.

Step 2:

Multiple Jobs or Spouse Works

Complete this step if you (1) hold more than one job at a time, or (2) are married filing jointly and your spouse also works. The correct amount of withholding depends on income earned from all of these jobs.

Do **only one** of the following.

(a) Use the estimator at *www.irs.gov/W4App* for most accurate withholding for this step (and Steps 3–4); **or**

(b) Use the Multiple Jobs Worksheet on page 3 and enter the result in Step 4(c) below for roughly accurate withholding; **or**

(c) If there are only two jobs total, you may check this box. Do the same on Form W-4 for the other job. This option is accurate for jobs with similar pay; otherwise, more tax than necessary may be withheld . . . . . ▶ ☐

TIP: To be accurate, submit a 2020 Form W-4 for all other jobs. If you (or your spouse) have self-employment income, including as an independent contractor, use the estimator.

Complete Steps 3–4(b) on Form W-4 for only ONE of these jobs. Leave those steps blank for the other jobs. (Your withholding will be most accurate if you complete Steps 3–4(b) on the Form W-4 for the highest paying job.)

Step 3:

Claim Dependents

If your income will be $200,000 or less ($400,000 or less if married filing jointly):

Multiply the number of qualifying children under age 17 by $2,000 ▶ $ _____ 0

Multiply the number of other dependents by $500 . . . . ▶ $ _____ 0

Add the amounts above and enter the total here . . . . | **3** | $ _____ 0

Step 4 (optional):

Other Adjustments

(a) Other income (not from jobs). If you want tax withheld for other income you expect this year that won't have withholding, enter the amount of other income here. This may include interest, dividends, and retirement income . . . . | **4(a)** | $ _____ 0

(b) Deductions. If you expect to claim deductions other than the standard deduction and want to reduce your withholding, use the Deductions Worksheet on page 3 and enter the result here . . . . | **4(b)** | $ _____ 0

(c) Extra withholding. Enter any additional tax you want withheld each **pay period** . | **4(c)** | $ _____ 0

Step 5:

Sign Here

Under penalties of perjury, I declare that this certificate, to the best of my knowledge and belief, is true, correct, and complete.

▶ *Jonathan W. Doe*
Employee's signature (This form is not valid unless you sign it.)

▶ 05/01/2020
Date

Employers Only

Employer's name and address	First date of employment	Employer identification number (EIN)

For Privacy Act and Paperwork Reduction Act Notice, see page 3.   Cat. No. 10220Q   Form **W-4** (2020)

(Source: Internal Revenue Service.)

FIGURE 2-5
I-9 Employment Eligibility Verification Form

Employment Eligibility Verification **Department of Homeland Security** U.S. Citizenship and Immigration Services	**USCIS** **Form I-9** OMB No. 1615-0047 Expires 10/31/2022	

▶ **START HERE: Read instructions carefully before completing this form. The instructions must be available, either in paper or electronically, during completion of this form. Employers are liable for errors in the completion of this form.**

ANTI-DISCRIMINATION NOTICE: It is illegal to discriminate against work-authorized individuals. Employers **CANNOT** specify which document(s) an employee may present to establish employment authorization and identity. The refusal to hire or continue to employ an individual because the documentation presented has a future expiration date may also constitute illegal discrimination.

Section 1. Employee Information and Attestation *(Employees must complete and sign Section 1 of Form I-9 no later than the **first day of employment**, but not before accepting a job offer.)*

Last Name *(Family Name)*	First Name *(Given Name)*	Middle Initial	Other Last Names Used *(if any)*		
Doe	Jonathan	W			

Address *(Street Number and Name)*	Apt. Number	City or Town	State	ZIP Code
123 Main Street		Anytown	KS	54932

Date of Birth *(mm/dd/yyyy)*	U.S. Social Security Number	Employee's E-mail Address	Employee's Telephone Number
05/17/1991	9 8 7 - 6 5 - 4 3 2 1	jonathandoe@anymail.com	(620) 555-2299

I am aware that federal law provides for imprisonment and/or fines for false statements or use of false documents in connection with the completion of this form.

I attest, under penalty of perjury, that I am (check one of the following boxes):

☒ 1. A citizen of the United States

☐ 2. A noncitizen national of the United States *(See instructions)*

☐ 3. A lawful permanent resident   (Alien Registration Number/USCIS Number): N/A

☐ 4. An alien authorized to work   until (expiration date, if applicable, mm/dd/yyyy): N/A
     Some aliens may write "N/A" in the expiration date field. *(See instructions)*

Aliens authorized to work must provide only one of the following document numbers to complete Form I-9:
An Alien Registration Number/USCIS Number OR Form I-94 Admission Number OR Foreign Passport Number.

1. Alien Registration Number/USCIS Number: N/A
              OR
2. Form I-94 Admission Number: N/A
              OR
3. Foreign Passport Number: N/A
   Country of Issuance: N/A

QR Code - Section 1
Do Not Write In This Space

Signature of Employee *Jonathan W. Doe*	Today's Date *(mm/dd/yyyy)* 05/01/2020

Preparer and/or Translator Certification (check one):
☒ I did not use a preparer or translator.   ☐ A preparer(s) and/or translator(s) assisted the employee in completing Section 1.
(Fields below must be completed and signed when preparers and/or translators assist an employee in completing Section 1.)

I attest, under penalty of perjury, that I have assisted in the completion of Section 1 of this form and that to the best of my knowledge the information is true and correct.

Signature of Preparer or Translator	Today's Date *(mm/dd/yyyy)*	

Last Name *(Family Name)*	First Name *(Given Name)*		

Address *(Street Number and Name)*	City or Town	State	ZIP Code

 Employer Completes Next Page

Employment Eligibility Verification

Department of Homeland Security

U.S. Citizenship and Immigration Services

USCIS
Form I-9

OMB No. 1615-0047
Expires 10/31/2022

Section 2. Employer or Authorized Representative Review and Verification

(Employers or their authorized representative must complete and sign Section 2 within 3 business days of the employee's first day of employment. You must physically examine one document from List A OR a combination of one document from List B and one document from List C as listed on the "Lists of Acceptable Documents.")

Employee Info from Section 1	Last Name (Family Name) Doe	First Name (Given Name) Jonathan	M.I. W	Citizenship/Immigration Status 1

List A Identity and Employment Authorization	OR	List B Identity	AND	List C Employment Authorization

List A	List B	List C
Document Title N/A	Document Title Driver's license issued by state/territory	Document Title Social Security card (unrestricted)
Issuing Authority N/A	Issuing Authority Kansas	Issuing Authority Social Security Administration
Document Number N/A	Document Number G93847562	Document Number 987654321
Expiration Date (if any) (mm/dd/yyyy) N/A	Expiration Date (if any) (mm/dd/yyyy) 05/17/2022	Expiration Date (if any) (mm/dd/yyyy) N/A
Document Title N/A		
Issuing Authority N/A	Additional Information	QR Code - Section 2 Do Not Write In This Space
Document Number N/A		
Expiration Date (if any) (mm/dd/yyyy) N/A		
Document Title N/A		
Issuing Authority N/A		
Document Number N/A		
Expiration Date (if any) (mm/dd/yyyy) N/A		

Certification: I attest, under penalty of perjury, that (1) I have examined the document(s) presented by the above-named employee, (2) the above-listed document(s) appear to be genuine and to relate to the employee named, and (3) to the best of my knowledge the employee is authorized to work in the United States.

The employee's first day of employment (mm/dd/yyyy): 05/01/2020   *(See instructions for exemptions)*

Signature of Employer or Authorized Representative *Jessica Stolpp*	Today's Date (mm/dd/yyyy) 05/01/2020	Title of Employer or Authorized Representative Human Resources
Last Name of Employer or Authorized Representative Stolpp	First Name of Employer or Authorized Representative Jessica	Employer's Business or Organization Name Homestead Retreat

Employer's Business or Organization Address (Street Number and Name) 9010 Old Manhattan Highway	City or Town Olathe	State KS	ZIP Code 59384

Section 3. Reverification and Rehires *(To be completed and signed by employer or authorized representative.)*

A. New Name (if applicable)			B. Date of Rehire (if applicable)
Last Name (Family Name)	First Name (Given Name)	Middle Initial	Date (mm/dd/yyyy)

C. If the employee's previous grant of employment authorization has expired, provide the information for the document or receipt that establishes continuing employment authorization in the space provided below.

Document Title	Document Number	Expiration Date (if any) (mm/dd/yyyy)

I attest, under penalty of perjury, that to the best of my knowledge, this employee is authorized to work in the United States, and if the employee presented document(s), the document(s) I have examined appear to be genuine and to relate to the individual.

Signature of Employer or Authorized Representative	Today's Date (mm/dd/yyyy)	Name of Employer or Authorized Representative

LISTS OF ACCEPTABLE DOCUMENTS
All documents must be UNEXPIRED

Employees may present one selection from List A
or a combination of one selection from List B and one selection from List C.

LIST A **Documents that Establish Both Identity and Employment Authorization**	OR	LIST B **Documents that Establish Identity**	AND	LIST C **Documents that Establish Employment Authorization**
1. U.S. Passport or U.S. Passport Card		1. Driver's license or ID card issued by a State or outlying possession of the United States provided it contains a photograph or information such as name, date of birth, gender, height, eye color, and address		1. A Social Security Account Number card, unless the card includes one of the following restrictions: (1) NOT VALID FOR EMPLOYMENT (2) VALID FOR WORK ONLY WITH INS AUTHORIZATION (3) VALID FOR WORK ONLY WITH DHS AUTHORIZATION
2. Permanent Resident Card or Alien Registration Receipt Card (Form I-551)				
3. Foreign passport that contains a temporary I-551 stamp or temporary I-551 printed notation on a machine-readable immigrant visa		2. ID card issued by federal, state or local government agencies or entities, provided it contains a photograph or information such as name, date of birth, gender, height, eye color, and address		2. Certification of report of birth issued by the Department of State (Forms DS-1350, FS-545, FS-240)
4. Employment Authorization Document that contains a photograph (Form I-766)		3. School ID card with a photograph		3. Original or certified copy of birth certificate issued by a State, county, municipal authority, or territory of the United States bearing an official seal
5. For a nonimmigrant alien authorized to work for a specific employer because of his or her status: a. Foreign passport; and b. Form I-94 or Form I-94A that has the following: (1) The same name as the passport; and (2) An endorsement of the alien's nonimmigrant status as long as that period of endorsement has not yet expired and the proposed employment is not in conflict with any restrictions or limitations identified on the form.		4. Voter's registration card		
		5. U.S. Military card or draft record		4. Native American tribal document
		6. Military dependent's ID card		5. U.S. Citizen ID Card (Form I-197)
		7. U.S. Coast Guard Merchant Mariner Card		6. Identification Card for Use of Resident Citizen in the United States (Form I-179)
		8. Native American tribal document		
		9. Driver's license issued by a Canadian government authority		7. Employment authorization document issued by the Department of Homeland Security
6. Passport from the Federated States of Micronesia (FSM) or the Republic of the Marshall Islands (RMI) with Form I-94 or Form I-94A indicating nonimmigrant admission under the Compact of Free Association Between the United States and the FSM or RMI		**For persons under age 18 who are unable to present a document listed above:** 10. School record or report card 11. Clinic, doctor, or hospital record 12. Day-care or nursery school record		

Examples of many of these documents appear in the Handbook for Employers (M-274).

Refer to the instructions for more information about acceptable receipts.

(Source: USCIS.)

In the following example, Jonathan W. Doe was born on 5/17/1981 and lives at 123 Main Street, Anytown, Kansas 54932. He is single and claims one withholding allowance. His Social Security number is 987-65-4321. His employer is Homestead Retreat at 9010 Old Manhattan Highway, Olathe, Kansas 59384, with an Employer Identification Number of 92-1117654. His email address is jonathandoe@anymail.com, and his phone number is (620) 555-2299. When he filled out his new hire paperwork on May 1, 2020, Jessica Stolpp in Human Resources for Homestead Retreat verified his identity with both his Social Security card and his driver's license (G93847562), which expires on his birthday in 2022.

Additional Withholding

If an employee has more than one job or a spouse who works, an option to avoid having to owe taxes at the end of the year is to withhold additional federal income taxes out of each check. Additional withholdings are requested within the employee's Form W-4. This can be either a straight dollar value or an additional percentage. These amounts are withheld from the employee and submitted with the normal federal payroll tax deposits by the employer. Employees may elect to include backup withholding amounts in Step 4 of Form W-4, which directs the employer to withhold additional tax amounts. Backup withholding may occur in situations where the employee received additional, nontaxable income (such as dividends, royalties, or interest payments) or in situations when the IRS notified the employee of underreported income issues.

The I-9 form is published by the Department of Homeland Security, which stipulates that all new hires be reported within 20 days of their start date. Registration of employees by using the I-9 form minimizes negative implications associated with monitoring legally authorized workers in the United States and tracking people with legal obligations such as child support and other garnishments.

The final page of the I-9 form contains the documents the employee provides to verify identity and eligibility to work in the United States. Employees must provide either one item from List A *or* one item from both List B *and* List C.

The U.S. Citizen and Immigration Service (USCIS) implemented new changes in 2020:

- A fillable PDF version of the form with drop-downs for dates and prefilled lists.
- A new citizenship/immigration status section.
- Form availability in Spanish.

The E-Verify system was implemented in 2017 to provide employers with a fast, free way to verify an employee's legal eligibility to work in the United States. It should be noted that participation in E-Verify is *voluntary* and that completion of the I-9 is *mandatory.* (Source: USCIS)

The payroll accountant should retain a copy of the Employment Eligibility Verification Form (I-9) and a current Employee Withholding Allowance Certificate (W-4) in every employee's permanent file, although no legislation mandates that practice. The employer should request a new Form W-4 from employees annually in January to ensure that all addresses, life situations, and other information remain current. Because of the timing constraints on the release of annual tax documents such as Forms W-2 and W-3, employers should verify employees' Form W-4 information as close as possible to January 1 each year.

Hiring Packet Contents

The **hiring packet** maintained by many companies may be as basic as a simple Form W-4 and I-9 or may be incredibly complex if foreign workers and multiple types of voluntary or mandated deductions are involved. Common items in a hiring packet are the federal forms mentioned earlier,

Elnur/Shutterstock

state and local withholding allowance forms, elections for voluntary deductions, insurance paperwork, and the offer letter that specifies the pay rate and start date. Not all companies have the same items in the hiring packet, and no federal legislative guidelines exist. The firm's management, after reviewing the needs of the company and the legal requirements for the position, determines the hiring packet contents. Many companies also are including diversity self-declaration paperwork to ensure compliance with equal opportunity legislation, requirements under federal contracts, and other special requirements in the event of a payroll audit.

Notification of New Hires to State Offices

The Immigration Reform and Control Act mandates that employers notify state offices within 20 days of an employee's start date. State forms for fulfilling this requirement vary and states offer online registration for new hires. One purpose of registering new hires with states is to maintain databases for child support enforcement. Fines for nonreporting of new hires vary, both on the number of unreported new hires and for incomplete information. The penalty for noncompliance is strictly enforced and ranges from $25 per unreported employee to $500 for intentional nonreporting.

> According to the Office of Child Support Enforcement (OSCE), employers assisted in the collection of over $24 billion during 2018 through their timely reporting of new hires. Additionally, the Temporary Assistance for Needy Families (TANF) for child support in arrears decreased by 11% between 2008 and 2018. (Source: OCSE)

Reporting of new hires is a complex task with high potential for errors for companies with employees in multiple states. The Office of Management and Budget (OMB) has designed a form (see excerpt in Figure 2-6) for multistate employers to register and designate one state as the primary place to which they will send new hire reports. They can designate on the form the other states in which they have employees. The use of the multistate registry helps employers ensure they remain in compliance with the law.

Another issue to consider is the multiple employer rule. For individuals with multiple, and sometimes joint, employers, the issue of withholding appropriate taxes arises. According to the U.S. Department of Labor, the joint employer test involves four factors:

1. Who hires/fires the employee.
2. Which employer substantially controls the employee's work.
3. Which employer determines the employee's pay rate and method.
4. Who maintains the employee's employment records.

Foreign Workers

Employers who hire foreign citizens face additional challenges. The employer must verify that the employee is legally allowed to work in the United States. Generally, the I-9 form serves this purpose, but there may be occasions when the prospective employee does not have an appropriate government-issued visa for working in the United States. If no visa exists, the employer may file a petition with the U.S. Citizenship and Immigration Services office to gain permission for the foreign employee to work in the United States through an *H-1B visa*. The H-1B visa is authorized for employers to hire foreign workers who have specialized university-level expertise that would benefit the company. As of 2019, the maximum number of regular H-1B visas permitted by USCIS was 65,000 employees. An additional 20,000 H-1B visas were available for foreign workers with advanced degrees. The fees for permanent workers not in the protected classes can range from $500 to $5,000, depending on the classification of the worker's preference, the size of the employer, and the employee's non-immigrant status. In the case of foreign workers, the employer must file Form 1042 for any

FIGURE 2-6
Multistate Employer Registration Form

OMB Control No: 0970-0166
Expiration Date: 07-31-2022

MULTISTATE EMPLOYER REGISTRATION FORM FOR NEW HIRE REPORTING

Employers who have employees working in two or more states may use this form to register to submit their new hire reports to one state or make changes to a previous registration. Multistate employers may also visit https://ocsp.acf.hhs.gov/OCSE/ to register or make changes electronically.

Federal law (42 USC 653A(b)(1)(A)) requires employers to supply the following information about newly hired employees to the State Directory of New Hires in the state where the employee works:

- Employee's name, address, Social Security number, and the date of hire (the date services for remuneration were first performed by the employee)
- Employer's name, address, and Federal Employer Identification Number (FEIN)

If you are an employer with employees working in two or more states, AND you will transmit the required information or reports magnetically or electronically, you may use this form to designate one state where any employee works to transmit ALL new hire reports to the State Directory of New Hires.

If you are no longer a multistate employer OR you are a multistate employer but no longer report to a single state, check "No Longer a Multistate Employer" in the box below.

☐ **No Longer a Multistate Employer (If checked, complete items 1-4 and 6-7 and return the form via email (preferred), fax, or mail (see last page for return information).**

If you need help completing this form, call the Multistate Employer Help Desk at 1-800-258-2736, Option #1 (8:00 a.m.- 5:00 p.m. ET).

Please note that all fields are required unless otherwise noted as optional.

1. **Enter your company's Federal Employer Identification Number (FEIN) without hyphen. This is the nine-digit number used by the IRS to identify your company.**

   FEIN: [   ]

2. **Enter today's date in MM/DD/YYYY format.**

   Date: [   ]

3. **Enter your company's name. This is the name associated with the FEIN in item 1.**

   Employer Name: [   ]

   Enter your company's address, including city, state, and ZIP code. This is the address associated with the FEIN in item 1. If your company's FEIN address is a foreign address, print the country's name and Postal code.

   Employer Address: [   ]

   City: [   ]   State: [   ]

   ZIP code: [   ]

   (For foreign addresses only) Country Name: _____   Country Postal Code: _____

<u>Subsidiary Information:</u> **Please go to www.acf.hhs.gov/css/resource/multiple-fein-spreadsheet to access the Multiple FEIN Spreadsheet, enter information about all your company's subsidiaries, and submit it with this form. Subsidiaries are companies wholly controlled by your company.**

We need the below information about your company's subsidiaries.

FEIN	Organization Name	Address Line1	Address Line2	Address Line3	City	State	Province	Country	ZIP/ Postal Code	Address Delivery Type (Optional)
										■ **Payroll/Income Withholding Order** ■ **National Medical Support Notice** ■ **Verification of Employment** ■ **Workers Compensation**

4. **Enter the name of the state or U.S. territory your company designated to report new hire information to.**

   NOTE: The state you choose must be a state in which you have one or more employees. Refer to the state listing shown in item 5.

5. **Check the box next to the additional states or U.S. territories where your company has employees working. Do not put a check next to the state or territory you selected in item 4. You must select at least one state or territory in this list to register as a multistate employer.**

☐ Alabama   ☐ Alaska   ☐ Arizona   ☐ Arkansas   ☐ California   ☐ Colorado

☐ Connecticut ☐ Delaware   ☐ Dist. of Col ☐ Florida   ☐ Georgia   ☐ Guam

☐ Hawaii   ☐ Idaho   ☐ Illinois   ☐ Indiana   ☐ Iowa   ☐ Kansas

☐ Kentucky   ☐ Louisiana   ☐ Maine   ☐ Maryland   ☐ Massachusetts ☐ Michigan

☐ Minnesota   ☐ Mississippi   ☐ Missouri   ☐ Montana   ☐ Nebraska   ☐ Nevada

☐ New Hampshire ☐ New Jersey   ☐ New Mexico   ☐ New York   ☐ North Carolina ☐ North Dakota

☐ Ohio   ☐ Oklahoma   ☐ Oregon   ☐ Pennsylvania ☐ Puerto Rico   ☐ Rhode Island

☐ South Carolina ☐ South Dakota ☐ Tennessee   ☐ Texas   ☐ Utah   ☐ Vermont

☐ Virgin Islands ☐ Virginia   ☐ Washington   ☐ West Virginia ☐ Wisconsin   ☐ Wyoming

☐ All States and Territories

6. **Enter your name, title, work phone number, work email address (do not use Gmail, Yahoo, MSN, or Hotmail email addresses), and work fax number.**

   Company's Business Contact Name:

   Phone: Fax (optional):

   Email:

7. **BE SURE TO SIGN THIS FORM. By completing this form, I certify that the information provided is accurate and that I am authorized to complete this form on my company's behalf.**

   Signature of the person completing this form:

Source: United States Department of Health and Human Services.

payments made. For information about the Permanent Worker Visa Preference Categories, please visit the U.S. Citizenship and Immigration Services website (www.uscis.gov).

The purpose of H-1B visas is to facilitate the employment of foreign workers who possess specialized skills, as defined by U.S. statute 20 CFR § 655.700. "Specialty occupation" is defined as possessing specialized knowledge, with the minimum educational requirement being a bachelor's degree or commensurate experience, or a distinguished fashion model. (Source: Cornell Law School)

Image Source

Statutory Employees

Some personnel who would normally be classified as independent contractors must be treated as employees for tax purposes. The IRS classifies *statutory employees* as personnel who meet any of the following guidelines:

- A driver who distributes beverages (other than milk) or meat, vegetable, fruit, or bakery products or who picks up and delivers laundry or dry cleaning, if the driver is a single company's agent or is paid on commission.

- A full-time life insurance sales agent whose principal business activity is selling life insurance or annuity contracts, or both, primarily for one life insurance company.

- An individual who works at home on materials or goods that a company supplies and that must be returned to that company or a designated agent in accordance with furnished specifications for the work to be done.

- A full-time traveling or city salesperson who works on a single company's behalf and turns in orders from wholesalers, retailers, contractors, or operators of hotels, restaurants, or other similar establishments. The goods sold must be merchandise for resale or supplies for use in the buyer's business operation. The work performed for that single company must be the salesperson's principal business activity.

Recall that the primary differences between an employee and an independent contractor are that the independent contractor sets his or her own hours and provides the tools necessary to complete the task. Statutory employees are a hybrid of an employee and an independent contractor. To ensure proper and timely remittance of employment taxes, the IRS has mandated that the employer withhold FICA taxes from statutory employees in the same manner as other company personnel; however, federal income taxes are not withheld from statutory employees' pay.

The term *statutory employee* may be applied to other types of workers on occasions. In 2019, Slawomir Fiedziuszko, an aerospace engineer who was semi-retired at the time, performed consulting work for a contractor of Space Systems Loral (now called Maxam). He contested the withholding of employment taxes, claiming that he was a consultant, not an employee. The judge in the case upheld the decision to classify Mr. Fiedziuszko as an employee because he worked from home doing work designed specifically to meet Maxam's specifications. Under the definition of a statutory employee, Mr. Fiedziuszko met the third criteria to be considered a statutory employee because his work was completed using Maxam's proprietary software in accordance with established specifications. (Source: *Forbes*)

U.S. Workers in Foreign Subsidiaries

Many companies have foreign subsidiaries and divisions that employ U.S. expatriate workers. The *Foreign Account Tax Compliance Act (FATCA)* of 2010 requires employers to report to the IRS the wages of employees who are permanent U.S. citizens working in foreign

FIGURE 2-7
Employee Database Information Sample

Personal Information

Salary

Vacation

Tax Details

Benefits & Deductions

Employee Files

Direct Deposit

Employee History

$14.59/hour

Salary History

Amount	Effective on
$14.59/hour	04/04/2016
$13.75/hour	01/01/2015

locations in order to facilitate the appropriate taxation of such workers. Under the IRS Foreign Earned Income Exclusion, expatriate workers must file Form 673 with their employer to exclude the first $107,600 of annual wages (2020 figure) from U.S. taxation but must pay income tax on income in excess of that amount and declare foreign assets.

Entering New Employees into the Database

The method of entering a new employee into the payroll system depends upon the system that the employer chooses to utilize. A manual system would require tasks such as adding the employee to the federal, state, and local lists for taxes withheld as well as adding the new hire to the list of employees to pay. Manual systems should have a checklist of all employees to ensure that no one is missed in the process.

Setting up a new employee in an automated system involves many more steps. The payroll employee enters in the pertinent data (see Figure 2-7). Employee number, name, address, Social Security number, wage, pay frequency, withholding information from W-4, department, and contact information are typically included. The payroll employee must designate a worker's compensation classification, state of employment, and local jurisdiction (when local taxes are applicable). Depending on state requirements and employer preferences, additional location codes, job classification codes, and other identifying characteristics may also be required.

Who Are You?

1. Go to the website for the U.S. Citizenship and Immigration Services, located at www.uscis.gov, and type I-9 into the search box on the website. Click on the link for the PDF version of the I-9 form to obtain a digital copy. What are two different ways that you would be able to prove your eligibility for work in the United States?

2. Go to the IRS website, located at www.irs.gov, and type W-4 into the search box on the website. Click on the link for the PDF version of the W-4 to obtain a digital copy. Assume you have more than one job and estimate the amount to include as income from other jobs. Complete the multiple job worksheet. Was your estimate close? Explain.

3. What are three examples of statutory employees?

LO 2-3 Differentiate between Exempt and Nonexempt Workers

Gajus/Shutterstock

Company employees may be classified as either exempt or nonexempt workers. The distinction between the two terms is how the wage and hour provisions of FLSA apply to the worker. *Exempt* workers are not subject to (i.e., are exempt from) the FLSA wage and hour provisions; wage and hour laws usually apply to *nonexempt* workers. The details of the worker's classification as exempt or nonexempt are always maintained in payroll records, but the inclusion of this information in other personnel records is at the employer's discretion.

Many different types of employees are classified as exempt from FLSA provisions, including certain computer professionals and outside salespersons. Companies will typically classify highly skilled workers such as accountants, general managers, human resource managers, and upper management as exempt, salaried employees. Because job titles alone are not a basis for classification of employees as exempt from FLSA provisions, the U.S. Department of Labor has issued guidelines for the most common types of employees. Note that for workers to be classified as exempt, they must meet *all* elements in the following tests to achieve exempt status.

- Executive Exemption
  - Salary compensation must be no less than $684 per week.
  - Managing the firm must be a primary duty of the employee.
  - The employee must supervise and otherwise direct the work of at least two other full-time employees (or an equivalent).
  - The employee must have the authority to hire and fire other employees.
- Administrative Exemption
  - Salary compensation must be no less than $684 per week.
  - The primary duty must include the performance of office or other non-manual labor that relates directly to the management of the firm's operations.
  - The employee must exercise independent judgment in the performance of normal duties.
- Professional Exemption
  - Learned Professional
    - Salary compensation must be no less than $684 per week.
    - This employee must perform work that is characterized by advanced learning or that is primarily academic in nature and requires consistent discretion and judgment.
    - The employee's advanced knowledge must be in a field that involves science or learning.
    - The employee must have acquired that knowledge through specialized intellectual education.
  - Creative Professional
    - Salary compensation must be no less than $684 per week.
    - This employee's primary work duty must involve invention, imagination, or originality that requires judgment and discretion.

(Source: DOL)

When workers are employed on a salary basis, they are paid to perform a specific job regardless of the number of hours worked to accomplish that job. A Morning Consult online poll (see Figure 2-8) reflected that a significant portion of American workers surveyed worked in excess of 40 hours per week; however, it should be noted the law currently provides that if salaried employees show up or are called by their employer for even an hour, the company may be required to pay them for the full eight-hour day.

FIGURE 2-8
Total Number of Hours Worked per Week

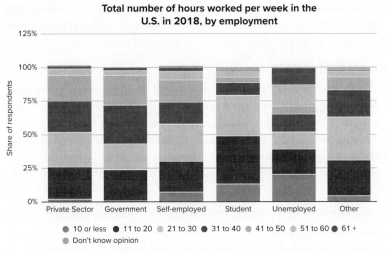

Source: Statista 2019

A primary difference is that nonexempt salaried individuals receive overtime pay for any hours exceeding 40 per week. The difference between salaried and hourly workers in reference to overtime calculation is that salaried workers will receive their normal shift hours of pay, even when not working the full shift, and do not receive overtime when they work more than 40 hours per week.

Hourly nonexempt employees receive a predetermined amount per hour of work performed (or fraction thereof). Some employers may make an election that permits four 10-hour shifts; should the election be made, the employee would be subject to overtime rates only after the 40 hours have been performed. It should be noted that some employers have a company policy stating that they pay overtime for employees who work in excess of 8 hours per day (or 10 hours, if that is the normal work shift); however, paid overtime is only mandated by the FLSA on a weekly basis. According to the Bureau of Labor Statistics (see Figure 2-9), the average number of hours worked per week in the United States is less than 40 hours.

Classifying employee wages as to salary versus hourly is a basic determination, linked to the type of work performed and the position within the company. Salaried *exempt* employees are not

FIGURE 2-9
Average Working Hours of All Employees

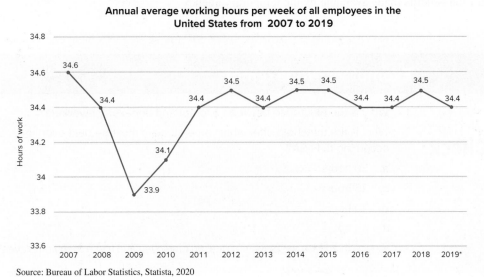

Source: Bureau of Labor Statistics, Statista, 2020

subject to overtime, are paid to do a specific job, and fulfill the FLSA requirement of self-direction; however, not all salaried employees are classified as exempt. Certain jobs such as nurses, police officers, and upper-level administrators may earn a fixed salary but are classified as *nonexempt* because of the nature of management direction in their function. Nonexempt workers do not generally supervise other employees and generally work under the direction of a supervisor.

Leased and Temporary Employees

Employers occasionally experience a need to have an additional employee but do not have the time to use a traditional hiring process. In this event, employers may opt either to lease an employee or to contact a temporary employment agency. Although these terms may sound similar, the difference between the leased and temporary employees involves the determination of employer intent and liability for worker injuries and errors.

Under IRS code section 414(n), an employee is classified as a *leased employee* if all the following conditions exist:

1. A formal agreement exists between the employer and the employee leasing organization.
2. The employee works on a full-time basis.
3. Employee actions are directed by the recipient company (i.e., the lessee).

Leased employees are considered common-law employees and are eligible for the same benefits as regular employees, including compensation practices, employer contributions, and so forth. The IRS stipulates that no more than 20 percent of a company's employees may be leased employees.

The Tax Cuts and Jobs Act of 2017 included a provision in which employers who leased employees from Professional Employer Organizations (PEOs) could qualify for a 20 percent profit deduction under section 199A of the Act. PEOs serve companies by acting as the hiring body and human resource managers for workers. in January 2019, the IRS clarified under §1.199A-2(b)(2)(ii) that employers who use third-party employees through a PEO could consider those leased employees as common-law employees and would qualify for the profit deduction and subsequent decrease in tax liability. (Source: JDSupra)

A temporary employee differs from a leased employee in the direction of the employee's actions. The *temporary employee* is an employee of the employment agency, which directs them to fill specific short-term needs of a variety of employers. Temporary employees may work either full-time or part-time, depending on the needs of the employer, and are only eligible for the benefits made available by the temporary agency.

Exempt vs. Nonexempt

1. What is the difference between exempt and nonexempt workers?
2. What is the threshold after which an employee must be paid overtime, according to FLSA?
   a. 30 hours
   b. 35 hours
   c. 40 hours
   d. 45 hours
3. What is the difference between a leased employee and a temporary employee?

LO 2-4 Explain Pay Records and Employee File Maintenance

Robert Nicholas/OJO Images/
Getty Images

One of the most important parts of any payroll system is the maintenance of employee pay records, especially considering the classification of exempt versus nonexempt employees and the legislation that pertains to overtime pay. The maintenance of accurate and detailed records that reflect the pay period, pay date, pay rate, and deductions are critical not only because it is a legal requirement in terms of delivering accurate pay, but also for positive employee relations. Employers retain physical copies of employees' time records, pay advice, and any other documentation processed with the paycheck. Other types of documentation include

- Request for a day off.
- Reports of tardiness or absenteeism.
- Detailed records of work completed during that day's shift.
- Records of overtime worked.

Technological advances allow employers to scan and save this information digitally, such as using an Adobe Acrobat file within the payroll accounting system.

> The best payroll apps allow for multiple payment methods and payment of independent contractors and part-time workers by scanning images directly into the software. Some of the best apps available include
>
> - Payable
> - Square Payroll
> - eFileCabinet
> - Trinet

The availability of digital copies facilitates managerial, auditor, or authorized executives' review, approval, or commentary on the documentation attached to payroll documents. Digital copies also permit transparency of records between the employer and employee, reducing miscommunication and payroll discrepancies, and facilitating the use of Internet employee record portals.

Pay Records

Employee wages involve far more than simple hourly rates or periodic salary payments. The first payroll decision a company should make is the company's pay frequency (daily, weekly, biweekly, semimonthly, monthly). The choice of payment frequency affects the applicable amounts for employee income tax withholding. Separate schedules for federal income taxes are provided in IRS Publication 15-T (available at www.irs.gov), which is released in November for the following year (i.e., 2021 tax information would normally be released during November 2020). Once the employer determines the pay frequency, the payroll accountant can establish the payroll record submission and pay disbursement schedule for company employees.

Pay Rate

The pay rate is the amount per hour per pay period the company determines the employee should be compensated. The determination of pay rate depends upon many employee variables: experience, education, certifications, governmental regulations (minimum wage, Davis–Bacon wages, etc.), hours worked, or a combination of all of the above. Employers may also pay specific rates for jobs performed. For example, employees working in a

Department of the Treasury
Internal Revenue Service

Publication 15-T
Cat. No. 32112B

Federal Income Tax Withholding Methods

For use in **2020**

Contents

Source: Department of the Treasury Internal Revenue Services

manufacturing environment may be subject to a different pay scale when cross-trained and working in a sales capacity. Minimum wage rates vary per state, and different parts of the same state may have different wages and may increase minimum wage amounts at various times during the year.

The idea of paying a living wage continues to be a prominent issue. A living wage is defined as the amount of money needed to sustain the desired lifestyle. In Virginia, the Richmond Living Wage Program is a certificate program co-sponsored by state and local leaders to encourage businesses to focus more on the needs of employees than on the business's profitability. This program encourages consumers to patronize businesses that have demonstrated their dedication to delivering a living wage to their employees.

The Massachusetts Institute of Technology (MIT) created a living wage calculator to facilitate awareness of the cost of living in different communities in the United States. This calculator is located at http://livingwage.mit.edu/ (Source: Virginia Business)

EXAMPLE: PAY PERIOD COMPUTATION, BIWEEKLY EMPLOYEE

Juan de la Cruz is a manager for a textiles firm. He earns $52,000 per year, is classified as an exempt employee and is paid biweekly. He normally works 40 hours per week.

During June, the following occurred:
Pay period ending June 15: Juan worked 85 hours.
Pay period ending June 29: Juan worked 78 hours.
Salary for the June 15 pay period = $52,000/26 periods per year = $2,000
Salary for the June 29 pay period = $52,000/26 periods per year = $2,000

Juan's salary for each pay period would be the fixed amount no matter how many hours he worked because he is classified as an exempt employee.

Hourly employees are protected by the FLSA and eligible for overtime pay. When overtime pay is applied, hourly employees may earn more than their salaried counterparts. Overtime rules and rates are determined by FLSA; however, some states may have additional requirements for overtime pay. Overtime is calculated at one-and-a-half times the employee's hourly rate. For FLSA, overtime applies only to hours worked exceeding 40 in a week (with some exceptions). Some states, such as California, may also require that employees receive overtime pay for any hours worked exceeding 8 per day in addition to the 40 hours per week, making it possible for an hourly employee to earn overtime pay without reaching the 40 hours in the week. In this textbook, nonexempt employees receive overtime pay for hours worked in excess of 40 hours per week, unless otherwise noted.

> The concept of a fluctuating workweek for salaried nonexempt employees has been a source of confusion for employers. Some salaried nonexempt employees work in industries that require them to be available at different times based on company needs. Employees who are nonexempt and salaried but have hours that are changeable due to the nature of the job may receive overtime during periods when they work more than 40 hours in a given week.

Commissions and piece-rate compensation offer employees incentives for specific jobs. A *commission* is a percentage of sales or services performed by an individual. An example of a commission would be a sales representative receiving 1 percent of all sales he or she initiates. *Piece rate* connects employee compensation with the production of a good or service. Piece rate compensation was widely used in the United States prior to industrialization and automated manufacturing. For example, when a shoe was being made, the person preparing the sole would receive a set rate per item.

> The California state legislature passed Assembly Bill (AB) 1513, which established guidelines about productive time and rest time for piece-rate employees. This bill also established a specified time period for employers to pay employees back pay because of the legal change. AB 1513 affected employees in a variety of industries, including spas and salons in which workers' compensation was connected to the number of treatments completed. (Source: California DIR)

Compensation structures can become complex if the employee is compensated using multiple payment types. A sales representative may receive a salary and commissions while working on the sales floor but receive hourly and piece rate if filling in on the manufacturing floor. Proper classification of the various aspects of the employee's workday becomes exceptionally important for the correct processing of the payroll.

Entering Hours

When it is time to prepare the payroll, an automated system will provide the payroll employee with a simple form to complete, typically including wage type and number of hours worked. In complex organizations, an additional classification of job location may be required if the employee works in multiple departments or locations. The automated systems will complete the mathematics to obtain gross pay, and most automated systems will calculate overtime and shift differentials (i.e., higher pay for working during times not considered "normal business hours").

ImYanis/Shutterstock

Many web-based applications exist to track employee attendance and calculate pay. TimeStation, ClockShark, and TimeDock use Quick-Read (QR) codes, employee PINs, and GPS location tagging to verify employee work. These apps may be useful tools for companies with employees at remote locations. Apps such as CalculateHours allow employees to calculate their hours worked and to email the timesheet to a supervisor. Other apps, such as the iTookOff paid leave tracker, allow employees to manage their paid time off through a synchronized app.

Calculations of Weekly Regular Time and Overtime

Even with the use of automated systems, the payroll accountant must determine the break-down of each employee's regular and overtime hours. Recall the discussion regarding the FLSA standard of 40 hours in a week. This is where the calculation of overtime becomes important. The employee's hours are added up, the total for the pay period is computed to determine if the employee worked more than 40 hours total for any given week, and overtime is separated from regular hours worked for wage calculations. If the employee did not work more than 40 hours, the total regular hours are noted on the time card. If the employee did work more than 40 hours, hours worked will be divided between the 40 regular hours and the overtime pay computation.

Depending upon company policy, the existence of paid holidays or sick days may alter payroll calculations. However, holiday hours, sick time taken, and vacation days are not usually included in the worked hours to determine overtime. Figure 2-10 shows a few examples of states and locations that offer mandatory paid sick leave.

According to the FLSA, employers are not required to pay for employee sick time; however, many states have either passed legislation or have pending bills that would mandate employer-paid sick time. Since 2008, more than 30 separate locations, including cities and entire states, have passed paid sick time legislation. This is a partial list of areas that have legislated paid sick leave.

FIGURE 2-10
Locations with Mandatory Paid Sick Leave

States/Districts	Counties	Cities
Washington, DC	Orange County, FL	Pittsburgh, PA
Arizona	Montgomery County, MD	Milwaukee, WI
California	Cook County, IL	Seattle, WA
Connecticut	Westchester County, NY	Plainfield, NJ
Massachusetts		Elizabeth, NJ
Maryland		New Brunswick, NJ
Michigan		Jersey City, NJ
New Jersey		Tacoma, WA
Oregon		Newark, NJ
Rhode Island		New York City, NY
Vermont		Passaic, NJ
Washington		East Orange, NJ
		Paterson, NJ
		Irvington, NJ
		Montclair, NJ
		Trenton, NJ
		Minneapolis, MN
		Philadelphia, PA
		Bloomfield, NJ
		Chicago, IL

(Source: ABetterBalance.org)

Note: States that have passed mandatory sick-time laws may have cities whose sick-time laws differ.

Worker Facts

1. Which classification of workers is subject to the wage and hour provisions for overtime in the Fair Labor Standards Act?

2. What is the difference between exempt and nonexempt employees in overtime pay requirements?

3. What is the difference between commission and piece-rate pay as far as the basis for the compensation?

4. What is the difference between the minimum wage and a "living wage"?

LO 2-5 Describe Internal Controls and Record Retention for a Payroll System

destinacigdem/123RF

Internal controls are critical to ensure the integrity of a payroll system. The confidentiality of payroll information is one of the most important controls in establishing a payroll system. Pay records such as time records are considered confidential documents, and personnel who handle or maintain such records must ensure the privacy of the information they contain. Small firms may be able to maintain the confidentiality of hand-written time sheets; however, multi-facility companies may need to use more secure time-collection methods to ensure information privacy.

Strategic planning of the payroll system prior to its inception can prevent data errors and losses related to inadequate *internal controls*. Most importantly, the payroll system design should be reviewed at regular intervals to determine its effectiveness and appropriateness for the company size and to correct errors before they become magnified.

Internal controls are a necessity, especially for small companies. The median loss to companies where fraud has occurred is $108,000. Examples of easily implemented internal controls include

- Transparency in the flow of money in and out of the organization.

- Involvement in cost management and expense disbursal.

- Engagement of multiple employees in the record-keeping process.

- Attentiveness to employee behavior.

- Recognition that any organization may become a fraud victim.

The need for internal controls increases as a company engages more fully with internet portals such as time-tracking and payroll processing sites. Technological changes introduce a new level of vulnerability into a company's data, so robust internal control practices are vital. (Source: *Strategic Finance*)

A company with many departments and many employees will generally have a more complex *review process* than a small company will. In an organization that has one office and a dozen or fewer employees, certain steps of the verification process may be omitted and fewer people are required to conduct it. Conversely, a large organization with several departments and many employees could have several levels of verification in the *payroll review* process.

FIGURE 2-11
Payroll Review Process: Steps to Ensure Accurate Payroll

Employee completes time card.	Manager verifies the employee's time card.	Payroll clerk computes the period wages for the employee.	Payroll supervisor verifies the payroll clerk's math.	Employee's check is presented with payroll register for verification and signatures.

Even outsourced payroll requires levels of the review process. The payroll executed by an external company is only as accurate as the data provided. For instance, a company could have a payroll review process such as the one shown in Figure 2-11.

An extremely important issue within internal controls is the determination of authorized signers. A common (and good!) practice in a company is to have more than one designated signatory for payroll checks. Often, these signers are different people than those involved in the review process. In many companies, more than one person signs the payroll checks as another level of review of the accuracy. Remember that the most important part of payroll is *accuracy*. The extra time it takes to review and obtain the necessary signatures is time well spent, as long as it prevents costly errors.

Documentation of the payroll process is vital. As should be clear by now, the execution of payroll is not merely writing checks to employees. Proper documentation of payroll entails a well-delineated procedure and properly trained personnel. Table 2-1 contains examples of different documentation controls, the activities involved in each, and the personnel who may be required.

TABLE 2-1
Documentation Controls

Procedure	Example of Internal Control Activities	Could Be Performed by
Review and approval of time data from time cards or other time collection devices	Completion of the time collection procedure Review of time collection for accuracy and approval	Employee's supervisor
Overtime approval	Approve the amount and type of overtime to be paid	Employee's supervisor
Approval for leave of absence or other unpaid time off	Obtain all prior approvals for unpaid time away due to FMLA or other reasons	Employee's supervisor
Timely entering of payroll data	Enter the payroll data into the payroll system in a timely manner, and check for data integrity and accuracy	Payroll clerk
Payroll system security	Make sure that only designated employees or payroll vendors have access to payroll data	Payroll supervisor
Approval of the payroll prior to issuance	Obtain the approval from signatory prior to issuing checks	Authorized signer(s)
Maintenance of paid time off (e.g., vacation, sick, etc.)	Ensure that employees receive the exact amount agreed upon	Payroll clerk; employee; supervisor; other designee
Access to payroll data	Ensure that payroll data is confidential and secure	Payroll supervisor
Separation of duties	Make sure that different people verify data, enter data, verify checks	Payroll supervisor
Training of payroll staff	Ensure that payroll department employees and other department supervisors are aware of and follow company payroll policies	Payroll supervisor

Review of Time Collected

All workers hours reported manually on time cards or electronically through other methods must be verified for accuracy prior to the completion of any payroll. Simple issues in employee underpayment (which can cause federal penalties) or overpayment (which can erode the company's available cash) can occur even with sophisticated systems. Time collection and employee payment errors can lead to reduced employee morale, lawsuits, and fines.

> One of the largest payroll fraud schemes involved $70 million in payroll deposits made to MyPayrollHR, a New York-based company that engaged in cloud-based payroll processing. Although the clients had done everything correctly, the owner of MyPayrollHR abruptly stopped operating after collecting employer funds and not disbursing payroll amounts due to employees for two consecutive pay periods. (Source: KrebsonSecurity)

Overtime Approval

Hourly employees are subject to federal overtime provisions, commonly known as time-and-a-half, but may include other pay bases such as double-time and so forth. FLSA guarantees nonexempt employees' rights to appropriate pay for the hours worked; however, employees can misreport the overtime they work, costing the company money in the process. Therefore, a good practice is to obtain supervisor approval on all employee-reported overtime. Computerized systems can also affect the reported overtime. The data is only as accurate as the person who entered it. One of the authors worked at a company that once paid her for 75 hours of overtime in one pay period—when she should have had only 7.5! This kind of error can cause chaos for both the employee, who must return the money, and the employer, who should not have paid it in the first place. Once again, improper pay can erode the morale of the employees. Overpayment on hours can create many other overpayments, including (but not limited to) federal withholding taxes, Medicare, Social Security taxes, and pension or 401(k) contributions that are driven by gross wages.

> A significant percentage of corporate fraud involves payroll tampering or embezzlement. A payroll and accounting manager in Atlanta, Georgia, pled guilty to wire fraud after investigators discovered that she had embezzled $1.5 million over a six-year period through improper payroll deposits. The employee had created a fake employee and instructed the outsourced payroll company to direct deposit that employee's pay into her own personal bank account. The employee had a file for the fictitious worker. A multiperson payroll verification process could have shortened the duration and reduced the amount of the embezzlement. (Source: *Accounting Today*)

Approval for Leave of Absence or Other Unpaid Time Off

The employee's supervisor is one level of oversight to ensure that the payroll data reaches the payroll department accurately and in a timely fashion. Supervisors work closely with their employees and should approve overtime and paid time off. Supervisors review individual timesheets for accuracy prior to delivery to the payroll department. Control of time away from work is the responsibility of the employee's supervisor, at the very minimum. The department supervisor should approve the time off. This approval needs to be tracked and maintained by the payroll department to ensure integrity in the payroll records. A suggested best practice is to keep requests for time away attached to the payroll stub for the affected pay period. The use of leave forms provides companies with a paper trail used to clarify perceived discrepancies in pay.

Web-based services facilitate requests, approvals, and tracking for paid time off. Apps such as Zenefits allow managers to adjust paid time off, approve and track employee requests, synchronize calendars, and download reports detailing employee time away from work. (Source: Zenefits)

File Security

Based on the amount of legislation regarding the privacy and security of personnel information, it is important to understand that all files pertaining to payroll, whether paper or electronic, must be kept secure from tampering. Another reason for *file security*, or restriction of personnel file access, is the firm's governmental payroll obligations. The tax information contained in the payroll records is required to prepare timely and accurate payment of payroll taxes, a factor that is nearly as important as paying the employees. Examples of methods to secure payroll records include multiple passwords for system access, locking of file cabinets with controlled key disbursement, and encryption programs.

Because payroll data contains highly personal and private information, security of the information is important. To maintain file security, access to payroll records is restricted to a relatively small number of people. Paper-based payroll data is stored in a secure location; similarly, electronic payroll data is securely backed up and encrypted.

Data privacy and fund protection are a high priority for companies and legislators. Preventing breaches of payroll record security is a high priority and an evolving issue. The Electronic Fund Transfer Act of 1978, created to prevent problems with newly created ATM cards, has been expanded to address fraud and theft issues with *paycards*, a preloaded credit card that allows an employee to access funds without needing a bank account. Paycard use for payroll disbursement was estimated to be nearly $57 billion in 2015 and continues to be the fastest-growing payroll method in the United States, with 5.9 million active paycards being used as of 2017 and is expected to grow annually as paycard regulation and protections expand. With the growth of the gig economy and the number of unbanked employees, paycards are a relatively secure method of disbursing immediately accessible pay.

In *Jessie Chavez v. PVH Corporation* (2013), the defendant had to pay $1.85 million to Chavez because of fees deducted from the plaintiff's payroll card, which meant that the full amount of the wages was reduced; additionally, the plaintiff had not agreed to paycard use in advance. The Consumer Financial Protection Bureau (CFPB) proposed legislation in 2014 that would include specific language on paycards, informing employees of their right to request another form of pay disbursement. As of October 2016, the CFPB issued a rule that regulated the posting of accounting, disclosures, and overdraft credit that became effective as of October 2017.

The Electronic Funds Transfer Act, of which Regulation E is the most pertinent to payroll cards, implemented specific protections for employees who use paycards to receive their pay. This ruling that was effective in 2019 added Regulation Z that mandated disclosure of all paycard-related fees and other paycard-related information to employees. (Source: American Payroll Association; Law360)

Alternating Duties and Cross-Training

The cross-training of payroll professionals can act as a safeguard of payroll information. One of the goals of the Sarbanes–Oxley Act of 2002 was to protect the integrity of accounting data by legislating document retention requirements, corporate officer responsibility for financial accuracy, and the rotation of duties by auditors. The same principle applies to payroll system

Who Does Which Job?

Imagine that you have been approached to assist a business owner who is concerned about the security of his or her company's payroll. In a team of three or four people, decide how you would distribute payroll responsibilities to implement excellent internal control procedures. How did you divide the responsibilities? Explain.

workers. Cross-training and alternating the duties of the people in the payroll process may avoid or minimize errors and potential issues stemming from corruption. Furthermore, cross-training and rotation of duties foster professional development and proficiency with multiple tasks. This rotation of payroll duties refers only to personnel within the payroll department, not opening the payroll processing to non-accounting departments.

> Cross-training employees has more benefits than fraud deterrence. Offering employees the chance to learn other duties empowers them in their professional development, which fosters a sense of fulfillment among employees. Cross-training also grants employees the opportunity to consider different perspectives and to gain a broader understanding of the company's operations. Finally, cross-training is linked to better problem-solving ability because employees understand diverse tasks. (Source: *Forbes*)

Best Practices Involved in Employee File Maintenance

Maintenance of employee files is as important as the protection of employee information. IRS Regulation 26 CFR 1.6001 clearly states that the method of *file maintenance* is the responsibility of the employer. The Internal Revenue Code recommends record labeling, creation of backup copies, and secure record storage. An important note is that despite the choice of record maintenance, the employer retains all liability for auditor access to the information upon demand. Items such as time and work records, including time cards and electronic work records, must be maintained to be available for auditors because these items are vital components of a payroll system audit.

> **26 CFR 1.6001–1 Records.**
>
> (a) *In general.* Except as provided in paragraph (b) of this section, any person subject to tax under subtitle A of the Code (including a qualified State individual income tax which is treated pursuant to section 6361(a) as if it was imposed by chapter 1 of subtitle A), or any person required to file a return of information with respect to income, shall keep such permanent books of account or records, including inventories, as are sufficient to establish the amount of gross income, deductions, credits, or other matters required to be shown by such person in any return of such tax or information. (Source: GPO)

Ninun/123RF

Payroll record maintenance is important for employees at all levels of the organization. IRS Revenue Procedure 98-25, 1998-1 CB 689, was enacted in 1998 to govern the maintenance procedures and duration of record-keeping for companies with employees. Provisions of the law include payroll transaction details such as time worked, pay dates, employee status, record reconciliation, and correlation of IRS reports and employee records. With regard to executive-level pay, the company must keep records of how the executive's pay was derived, including benchmarks from similar companies, payout period, and scheduled increases. All pay disbursed must be justified according to the amount and type of work performed, regardless of employee level or classification. A company's payroll and legal department should work closely to determine and implement a maintenance and record destruction program that complies with IRS requirements but avoids the inaccessibility of data that occurs with information overload.

According to FLSA, the following records must be maintained for a minimum of **three** years:

- Payroll and other related records
- Union Contracts
- Contacts involving exclusions from the regular pay rate
- Any agreements pertaining to overtime rates
- Any certificates pertaining to workers who would receive sub-minimum wages
- Records referring to sales that would form the basis for employee commissions

Similarly, the following records must be retained for a minimum of **two** years under FLSA:

- Employment and earnings records
- Any tables used to compute company wage rates
- Worker schedules to support time worked
- Any other records that contain information about wage additions or deductions.

Note that no guidelines exist for any particular order of these documents, but any copies of these records must be clear if copied or otherwise transmitted.

Electronic Records

Many companies have moved to electronic scanned copies of payroll records that allow immediate access to employee files from a password-protected format. In remote locations, payroll accountants can send the managers and employees Adobe Acrobat files requiring a password to access pay records. Several data encryption programs are currently on the market, allowing payroll managers to select the best fit for their individual company. All hard copies (i.e., paper versions) of payroll information must be in a locked file cabinet with limited access.

Andrey_Popov/Shutterstock

Computers have become a necessary part of a business and offer significant benefits to the accounting department. Most accounting software for the preparation of payroll includes password requirements that the company can control, limiting access to electronic information about employees, pay, and personal information. Many regulatory agencies have addressed the issue of record security and safeguarding procedures; for example, the Food and Drug Administration enacted 21 CFR Part 11 that delineates electronic record security and safeguarding procedures.

Payroll accounting, according to the definition by the Internal Revenue Code, is a closed system because only certain employees are granted access to the information contained in the electronic records. All aspects of information security are the employer's responsibility, including access to, creation of, and maintenance of electronic personnel and pay records. Record identifiers would log who had accessed an electronic file, when, and from what location. Record logging provides an additional measure of security and protection against unauthorized access (also called "hacking") as well as tracking whether unauthorized changes occur on records.

According to the FBI, more than $1 billion per year has been lost to hackers using ransomware. Ransomware is malicious code placed into a computer system by hackers, aimed at obtaining a monetary fee to release access to a company's computerized information. The city of Atlanta, Georgia, encountered ransomware that was

(continued)

(concluded)

downloaded onto the city's computer system during a city-related Internet search. As a result of the attack, the city's daily operations were halted because workers could not access their computers. (Source: ArsTechnica, TrendMicro)

Like other payroll records, electronic records, especially those accessible over the Internet, must be safeguarded to prevent fraudulent activity and data corruption. Employers can provide access to information via a company's intranet (inside the organization) or via the Internet using encryption programs, passwords, and secured website locations. It is important to note that once a company has allowed Internet access to its payroll files, the company is opening itself up to additional risks from hacking or wrongful use of the payroll information. It is the payroll accountant's responsibility to report any suspicious activity to company managers or the information security department of the company.

Payroll as a Non-Solo Effort

One best practice is to have more than one person involved in the generation and maintenance of payroll records. Many errors can occur when the total payroll responsibility rests with one person. Errors that occur may be the result of a complex hacking effort or a simple failure to remove the system access from a former employee.

- Nonexistent or "ghost" employees could be created and paid via the payroll system. The person committing the fraud could circumvent the payroll system and divert the funds to himself or an accomplice.

- Terminated employees could continue to be paid via the payroll system, or the funds could be subverted to someone else perpetrating the fraud.

- Sales commission plans, employee bonus plans, incentive programs, and other arrangements intended to induce particular behaviors are subject to the employee's and management's manipulation.

- The payroll checks distributed to employees could be stolen individually or en masse prior to their distribution. In addition, check fraud could be perpetrated using actual checks or just the account information.

- The company's payroll system or payroll service provider could suffer a breach of the security protocols protecting the computer systems, which could allow any combination of fraud or theft to be perpetrated.

Other instances of payroll fraud could have been avoided with a *separation of duties*, which involves the division of related tasks to prevent fraud. Internal controls promote improved accuracy when more than one person is involved in payroll preparation and disbursement. A division of record maintenance, employee verification, and the spread of pay disbursement responsibilities among different employees, depending upon the size of the company, would prevent many of the preceding problems. This not only protects the employer from complaints and potential legal issues stemming from payroll anomalies, but also provides a level of protection and verification to employees. Auditors look for well-defined internal controls within organizations to ensure legal compliance and file integrity.

- A payroll worker, disgruntled with his job, stole almost $300,000 from different companies by transferring the organizations' money into different bank accounts that he owned.

- A former bookkeeper forged $80,000 in payroll checks before the company owner discovered the discrepancy.

- In the Los Angeles Unified School District, internal inspectors found that the pay system was issuing paychecks to deceased employees.

(continued)

(concluded)

- In an audit of Department of Transportation records in Florida, the auditors found that the paper files supporting the payroll system had been discarded to make room in the office. The audit revealed overpayments to employees caused by an incorrect calculation and a lack of payroll verification. Of the employees who were overpaid, only one returned the money.

In the event of a data breach, the company must act quickly to contain the damage and prevent additional issues. The American Payroll Association offered the following action steps that companies should take when they experience a breach in their accounting data software:

Step 1   Prevent the spread of the data breach by taking payroll systems to an offline state and restrict access to records.

Step 2   Determine the scale of the threat or breach. Gather all related data and facts involving the breach and assess any vulnerabilities in the system.

Step 3   Contact the appropriate law enforcement officials to notify them of the crime and to open an investigation. Notify the Federation of Tax Administrators at www.taxadmin.org to engage their service in the investigation.

Step 4   Review the company's data storage, retention, and authorization policies to identify ways to prevent future occurrences.

Document Retention Requirements

According to IRS Regulation 26 CFR 1.6001, records pertaining to any financial transaction must remain available for *payroll audit*, the inspection by regulating bodies, at all times. The purpose of the tax code is to maintain records for legal purposes in the event of the suspicion of fraudulent activity. IRS Regulation 26 CFR 1.6001 pertains to both manual and computerized records, including payroll records prepared by third-party sources. Both manual and electronic documents must be maintained in such a way that they maintain accessibility for the duration similar to tax record retention.

When a company institutes a retention schedule, the requirements of legislation and the IRS must be considered. The retention period does not begin until the disbursement of pay occurs or the employee terminates employment, whichever occurs last. Remember: In the event of fraudulent activity, retention requirements no longer apply, and all company records can be requested by the courts.

Companies must abide by both state and federal law regarding document retention. Employee payroll records, consisting of all forms and payroll compensation statements, must be retained following *termination* or separation. Although no regulations exist for the retention and archiving of internal payroll documents (e.g., a *payroll register*), a general guideline is that the internal documents should be stored with the other payroll accounting records and destroyed in accordance with accounting record guidelines.

When an employee is terminated, records for the employee and reason for termination must be retained for a period of one year. If an employee qualifies under ADEA, all payroll records must be retained for a period of three years. The Lilly Ledbetter Fair Pay Act created a record retention requirement of an additional three years for primary records (pay records or bargaining agreements) and two years for supplementary data (time cards, wage rate tables, piece rate records). As a good practice to meet the various requirements, many businesses will set document retention at three years for all files.

In 2018, the state of Massachusetts discovered that the state comptroller's website had not listed the Massachusetts State Police salaries in its reports since 2010. Because most of the State Police earn more than $150,000 annually, the omitted amount was

(continued)

(concluded)

substantial. The governor requested an overtime audit to detect potential abuses that could leave the state vulnerable to legal proceedings. (Source: WBUR News)

Agencies that have the right to audit payroll records include

- The Internal Revenue Service (IRS).
- Federal and state Departments of Labor.
- Department of Homeland Security.
- Other state and local agencies.
- Labor unions.

The following is a chart that explains federal record retention requirements, including relevant laws and types of documents.

Payroll Records (time sheets, electronic records, etc.)	• 3-year retention period • An additional 5-year post-termination retention is recommended due to Lilly Ledbetter Act • Includes employee data, any pay records, and all compensation, financial and nonfinancial
Employee Federal, State, and Local Tax Records	• 4 years from date the tax is due or paid • Includes all W-4s, state and local tax withholding forms, requests for additional tax withholding, and tax remittances
Form I-9 and Accompanying Employment Eligibility Documents	• 3 years after hire OR • 1 year after termination, whichever is longer
Employee Benefits and Contributions	• 6 years • All retirement plan contributions, plan changes, records pertaining to any other employee voluntary deductions
Health Plan Documentation	• No written guidelines, but a minimum of 6 years is recommended • All written notices about changes in health coverage, especially for health coverage after termination of employment

Even if your company outsources payroll activities, it is still accountable for all records and the information transmitted to the payroll service companies. The third-party payroll service provider attends only to the processing of company payroll but is not responsible for payroll tax payments. Tax remittance remains the liability of the company. Instances in which companies have diverted payroll tax liabilities for personal purposes have resulted in sizable fines and sanctions for companies.

In 2017, the IRS levied a $1 million lien against the property of CCH Oncology of Buffalo, New York. The company failed to remit or file returns for income, Social Security, and Medicare taxes for both the employees' and the employer's shares starting approximately July 2016. The lien amount included failure to pay and failure to file penalties as well as interest. (Source: *The Buffalo News*)

Internal Controls and Audits

Stop & Check

1. Which of these is *not* a payroll internal control procedure?
   a. Overtime approval.
   b. Removal of payroll oversight.
   c. Cross-training.
   d. File security.

2. Which of these records should be retained in the event of a payroll audit?
   a. Employee medical records.
   b. Employee reviews.
   c. Employee time and work records.
   d. Employee nonpayroll correspondence.

LO 2-6   Discuss Employee Termination and Document Destruction Procedures

When employees are terminated, either voluntarily (i.e., resignation) or involuntarily (i.e., termination), the employer has payroll issues unique to the situation. The common element to each termination is the paperwork needed. When an employer terminates a worker's employment involuntarily, the burden of proof for the termination is on the employer, should the case ever require legal scrutiny.

In *Graziadio v. Culinary Institute of America* (2016), the plaintiff was terminated involuntarily after taking two consecutive three-week leaves to care for her children because the Culinary Institute of America claimed that Graziadio had not filed the required paperwork for leave under the FMLA. At first, the court ruled in favor of the Culinary Institute of America because the proper paperwork was not on file. However, further investigation found that the human resources director of the Culinary Institute of America, who refused to allow Graziadio to return to work, had not responded to Graziadio's numerous email requests for FMLA paperwork to justify her absence and to return to work. (Source: FindLaw)

Steve Debenport/Getty Images

Employee Termination

There are two different methods of separation of an employee from the company: *termination* and *resignation*. When an employee leaves a company, the payroll accountant must complete several steps with regard to the employee's and the firm's records. The employee's final paycheck will reflect a culmination of hours worked, and possibly, depending on the company policies, vacation earned and not taken and sick time earned and not taken. Depending on the company's policies, if the employee's compensation is commission-based, there should be an agreement between management and the employee regarding their sales and the timing of the final paycheck to ensure the payment of all earned commissions.

Final hours are calculated the same as for any normal pay period. The employee's daily hours are calculated to determine regular and overtime, and the worked hours are added together to determine weekly hours and weekly overtime. If the employee earned any vacation or sick time, then those hours may also need to be paid out on the final paycheck. Vacation and sick time are not included in the worked hours for the determination of overtime.

A limited amount of legislation exists about the payment of a severance package upon termination. In general, two situations exist in which severance packages may be required by legislation: The closure of a company facility and a large number of employee layoffs. In the event that a large number of employees are laid off, a severance package may be required if any promise, written or oral, of a severance package exists or if the company has a history of paying severance packages to laid-off employees. For specific guidelines, the state's employment department would be the primary resource for official guidance (see Appendix E for state contact information).

In terms of payroll accounting, a major difference between the termination and the resignation of an employee, besides the circumstances surrounding the employee's separation from the company (layoff, termination for cause, resignation, etc.), is the timing of the delivery of the final pay disbursement. When an employee quits, any compensation due will be processed and disbursed on the company's next scheduled pay date. However, when the employee is terminated, the company may be mandated to issue the final paycheck immediately or within a short time frame to comply with state labor laws. There is no federal regulation for the timing of the issuance of the employee's final pay, although the Department of Labor explicitly mandates back pay owed to former employees. Table 2-2 contains information about states' employee termination pay guidelines.

Document Destruction

Ingram Publishing/SuperStock

Although many state and federal laws delineate the time requirement for document retention, there are also several methods for regulated ***document destruction*** of sensitive payroll data. How must confidential payroll-related documents be destroyed? It is not as simple as throwing old payroll documents in the trash. Preferred destruction methods of confidential payroll documents include incineration, confidential shredding services, or pulping of the paper records. Electronic records must be purged from the server. Although specific destruction procedures and regulations vary among states and localities, the basic guidelines of confidential destruction after the required retention period are common to most areas. From small-scale record destruction using in-office paper shredders to large-scale operations such as ProShred, Iron Mountain, and many other companies, destruction of confidential business documents is a serious concern because of the federal privacy laws governing payroll documents.

A best practice in terms of document destruction is to create a policy regarding document retention and destruction schedules. An employee in charge of these schedules would be tasked with ensuring that all paper records are stored appropriately and retained for the proper legal time. Another best practice is to separate payroll-related documentation into the following categories:

- Private personnel information such as Forms W-4 and I-9, court-ordered garnishments, wage information, and direct deposit instructions.
- Employee benefits paperwork including benefit elections, FMLA documentation, workers' compensation evidence, and flexible spending account information.
- Any investigative information maintained separately because of the absence of a statute of limitations on employee fraud.

By separating the employee paper files into these categories, document retention and destruction guidelines may be observed more efficiently.

Electronic Records

Rawpixel.com/Shutterstock

As the use of electronic payroll records has grown, the need to define appropriate destruction procedures has become increasingly apparent. Simply deleting a website or a portion of the data does not guarantee the security of confidential information. Details of the website's design and

TABLE 2-2
States' Termination and Resignation Pay Guidelines

State	Guideline	State	Guideline
AL	No termination pay guidelines	MO	Immediately upon termination; no law for resignation
AK	Within three working days upon termination; at the next regular pay date that is at least more than three days upon resignation	MT	Immediately upon termination unless the employer's written policy extends the time to the next regular payday; next regular pay date or 15 days, whichever is earlier, for resignation
AZ	Within seven working days or the end of the next pay period, whichever is sooner	NE	Next regular payday or within two weeks, whichever is sooner for both termination and resignation
AR	Within seven days of discharge (railroad employees only); no law exists for resignation	NV	Immediately upon termination; next scheduled pay date or seven days, whichever is sooner upon resignation
CA	Immediately upon discharge for termination; within 72 hours upon resignation	NH	Within 72 hours upon termination; next pay date in the event of a layoff
CO	Immediately upon discharge (i.e., within 6 hours of the next business day or 24 hours if payroll is processed off-site) for termination; next scheduled pay date upon resignation	NJ	Next regularly scheduled payday for both termination and resignation
CT	No later than the next business day upon termination; next scheduled pay date upon resignation	NM	Within five days upon termination; next scheduled pay date upon resignation
DE	Next regularly scheduled payday for termination and resignation	NY	Next regularly scheduled payday for both termination and resignation
DC	No later than the next business day following termination; next scheduled pay date or within seven days upon resignation	NC	Next regularly scheduled payday for both termination and resignation
FL	No termination or resignation pay guidelines	ND	Next regularly scheduled payday or within 15 days whichever occurs first; next regularly scheduled payday
GA	No termination or resignation pay guidelines	OH	No termination pay legislation; within 15 days upon resignation
HI	At time of termination unless conditions render pay impossible, next business day in that case; next business day if resignation with notice	OK	Next regularly scheduled payday for both termination and resignation
ID	Next regular payday or within 10 days, excluding weekends and holidays, whichever occurs first; within 48 hours upon employee written request for both termination and resignation	OR	By the end of the next business day upon termination; within 48 hours days upon resignation with notice or next scheduled payday without notice
IL	Next regularly scheduled payday for both termination and resignation	PA	Next regularly scheduled payday for both termination and resignation
IN	Next regularly scheduled payday for both termination and resignation	RI	Next regularly scheduled payday for both termination and resignation
IA	Next regularly scheduled payday for both termination and resignation	SC	Within 48 hours or next scheduled payday, not to exceed 30 days upon termination; no law exists for resignation
KS	Next regularly scheduled payday for both termination and resignation	SD	Next regularly scheduled payday or whenever the terminated employee returns all the employer's property for both termination and resignation
KY	Next regular payday or 14 days, whichever is later for both termination and resignation	TN	Next regularly scheduled payday or 21 days, whichever comes later for both termination and resignation
LA	Next regular payday or 15 days, whichever is sooner for both termination and resignation	TX	No later than six days after termination; by the next scheduled pay date upon resignation
ME	Next scheduled payday or within two weeks after a demand from the employee, whichever is sooner for both termination and resignation	UT	Within 24 hours upon termination; next scheduled pay date upon resignation
MD	Next regularly scheduled payday for both termination and resignation	VT	Within 72 hours upon termination; next scheduled pay date or the following Friday (if not pay date) upon resignation
MA	Immediately upon termination; next scheduled pay date or the following Saturday upon resignation	VA	Next regularly scheduled payday for both termination and resignation
MI	Next regularly scheduled payday for both termination and resignation	WA	Next regularly scheduled payday
MN	Immediately upon termination; next regular pay date upon resignation unless there is less than five days until payday, then 20 days after last day of work under resignation	WV	On or before the next scheduled payday upon termination; next scheduled pay date upon resignation
MS	No termination or resignation pay guidelines	WI	Next regularly scheduled payday or within one month, whichever is sooner upon termination; within 24 hours if layoff; next scheduled pay date upon resignation
		WY	Within five business days for both termination and resignation

Source: FindLaw

system change documentation must be maintained to facilitate record disposal. Guidelines for electronic records disposition include

- Data disposition instructions including dates and authorized administrators.
- Record destruction schedules involving security encryption.
- Technical documentation for each record system.
- Identifying information for file indexes and unique records.
- If a website is involved, technical documentation of the site architecture should be maintained.

> The proliferation of electronic accounting records, especially payroll-related data, has led to the adoption of the Department of Defense Data Wipe Method, commonly referred to as DoD 5220.22-M, which sanitizes electronic records. Various data wiping tools have this software tool, including DBAN, CBL Data Shredder, and ErAse. (Source: Lifewire)

Destroy and Terminate

1. How should paper payroll records be destroyed? How about electronic records?
2. Charlie, a resident of Hawaii, is terminated without cause from his job on October 11. He is terminated at the end of the day after the payroll manager has left. When must he receive his final pay? Is the employer required to pay him a severance package? Explain.

Trends to Watch

PAYROLL PROCEDURES

As we move further into the digital age, payroll procedures are changing to meet employer needs, technological availability, and employee accessibility. Some procedures that have changed since 2014 include the following:

- Affordable Care Act employer reporting requirement clarification.
- An increase in the use of Internet-based employee files, which requires increasingly sophisticated security software and company protocols.
- Changes to limitations on the number of and fees related to visas for foreign workers.
- Increased "job swapping" that requires employees to be cross-trained and employers to consider the compensation needs of different positions.
- An increase in the "virtual marketplace," in which employers and employees will telecommute or otherwise perform work from geographically dispersed locations.

Some trends to watch include the following:

- Tighter security protocols regarding electronic data and restricting access to electronic records to prevent cyber hacking and fraud.
- An increase in cloud-based computing and record storage for payroll and personnel records.
- More mobile-friendly workplaces and payroll management.
- Increased use of big data and artificial intelligence in payroll management and corporate integration.
- Enterprise resource planning integrating the ability for searching and retrieving information throughout a company.

Summary of Payroll System Procedures

The establishment of a payroll system involves careful planning and deliberation. The framework used for the payroll system needs to have enough room for company growth and enough structure to make sure that company and governmental deadlines are met. Using the best practices outlined in this chapter can help a company implement a robust payroll system, whether the system is maintained by company personnel or outsourced, completed manually or electronically with the use of specifically designed software. Adequate payroll system design can save a company from problems with employees and governmental entities and may prevent data breaches and fraud.

Although pay processes and methods vary among companies, the framework of internal review and the necessity for accuracy remain the fundamental aspects of any payroll system. Documentation of an employee's eligibility to work in the United States as well as the compensation method, rates, tax liabilities, and voluntary withholdings are critical elements of employee files that the payroll accountant needs to produce accurate payroll disbursements. The process of entering items into a payroll system varies depending on the type of work done and the compensation rates, for which the payroll accountant must have documentation. Depending on the company's preferences, anything from manual records to computerized records to external payroll vendors may be used to track the payroll. At employee termination, final payment must be issued, but the timing of that final pay depends on state legislation.

Payroll record-keeping and maintenance are complex issues and subject to several federal and state regulations. Employee personal information must be safeguarded at all times, and information privacy is paramount. Now that many companies are resorting to electronic pay records, information safeguarding is especially important, and encryption efforts are multidimensional, involving the accounting, legal, and information systems departments of an organization. Destruction of payroll-related documents after the required retention period is a serious concern, and an entire industry focuses on document retention and destruction.

Key Points

- Communication protocol varies among companies and departments within companies.
- Upon employment, company personnel must ensure completion of Form W-4 and the I-9 to determine accurate taxes and legal eligibility to work in the United States.
- Ethical payroll practices require the protection of information and dissemination only to the employee or specifically relevant supervisory staff.
- Employees are classified as either exempt or nonexempt from FLSA provisions.
- To be classified as an exempt employee requires an examination of job duties.
- Control of the payroll system involves regular system design review and delineation of specific tasks.
- Payroll, whether completed internally or by an outsourced vendor is only as accurate as the information provided.
- Pay periods are at the discretion of the company. The IRS has developed *tax tables* (i.e., tax withholding amounts) for each pay interval that are contained in Publication 15-T, an annual IRS guide to payroll that was updated in 2020.
- File security is of utmost importance, especially when files are stored electronically and accessed via an Internet portal.
- Documentation for payroll exceptions such as time away from work should be maintained separately from regular work time documentation.
- Calculations of pay can involve many variables and require a review of each employee's information prior to pay issuance.
- Final pay needs to reflect all earned compensation, paid time off, and deductions up to the date of termination.

- The timing of final pay disbursement when an employee is terminated depends on state law.
- Document retention and destruction procedures are important for data security and audit purposes.

Vocabulary

Biweekly payroll	Internal control	Piece rate
Commission	Leased employee	Resignation
Daily payroll	Monthly payroll	Review process
Document destruction	New hire reporting	Semimonthly payroll
Exempt	Nonexempt	Separation of duties
File maintenance	Outsourced vendor	Statutory employee
File security	Pay period	Tax table
Foreign Account Tax Compliance Act (FATCA)	Paycard	Temporary employee
	Payroll audit	Termination
Hiring packet	Payroll register	W-4
I-9	Payroll review	Weekly payroll

Review Questions

1. What are the necessary elements of internal control for a payroll department?

2. Why should more than one person prepare/verify payroll processing?

3. What documents should be included in all new-hire packets?

4. Why are new hires required to be reported to the state's employment department?

5. For the state in which you live, when must a terminated employee be paid his or her final paycheck?

6. What are the five main payroll frequencies?

7. What are two of the best practices in establishing a payroll system?

8. What are the important considerations in setting up a payroll system?

9. What are two different tasks involved in payroll accounting?

10. What agencies or organizations can audit a company's payroll records?

11. How long should employee records be retained?

12. Why are independent contractors not paid through a company's payroll system?

13. What is the difference between termination and resignation?

14. What are the differences among daily, weekly, biweekly, semimonthly, and monthly pay periods?

15. What differentiates exempt and nonexempt employees?

16. What challenges does a company face when using cloud-based payroll and personnel records?

17. What two regulations pertain to employee paycard use?

Exercises Set A

E2-1A.
LO 2-1, 2-4

Krystal Valdez, a nonexempt employee at Misor Investments, works a standard 8:00–5:00 schedule with an hour for lunch each day. Krystal received overtime pay for hours in excess of 40 per week. During the week, she worked the following schedule:

- Monday: 7.5 hours
- Tuesday: 8.25 hours
- Wednesday: 8 hours
- Thursday: 8.5 hours
- Friday: 10 hours

How many hours of overtime did Krystal work this week?
1. 0 hours
2. 1.5 hours
3. 2 hours
4. 2.25 hours

E2-2A.
LO 2-1

Roger Ortega receives his pay twice per month working for Megaveo Enterprises. Which of the following choices describes his pay frequency?
1. Biweekly
2. Semimonthly
3. Weekly
4. Monthly

E2-3A.
LO 2-2

Lila Rivera is a new employee for Divera Glass. Which federal forms must she complete as part of the hiring process? (Select all that apply.)
1. W-4
2. W-2
3. SS-8
4. I-9

E2-4A.
LO 2-5, 2-6

Wilbur Matthews, a resident of Wisconsin, ended his employment with Bovill Farms on December 4, 2020. The next pay date for the company is December 18. By what date should he receive his final pay?
1. December 7
2. December 11
3. December 18
4. December 31

E2-5A.
LO 2-5

Charlene Kelley is a new nonexempt sales clerk for Oyondo Retail Stores. She completes her time card for the pay period. To ensure proper internal control, what is the next step in the payroll review process?
1. Submit the time card to the payroll clerk.
2. Have a friend check her math for accuracy.
3. Submit the time card to her manager for review.
4. Enter the time card data directly into the payroll system.

E2-6A.
LO 2-6

Alfonso Silva needs additional filing space at the end of the year in the company's off-site, secured storage. He sees several boxes of payroll records marked for the current year's destruction. What methods can Alfonso use to dispose of the payroll records? (Select all that apply.)
1. Contact an off-site record destruction service.
2. Place the boxes containing the records in the company trash disposal.
3. Shred the records, and then dispose of the shredded paper.
4. Incinerate the payroll records marked for destruction.

E2-7A.
LO 2-1

Ed Myers is verifying the accuracy and amount of information contained in the employee records for his employer, Genible Industries. Which of the following items should be present in the employee information? (Select all that apply.)
1. Job title
2. Social Security number
3. Birth date, if greater than 19
4. Employee address

E2-8A.
LO 2-2

Ginger Klein is the payroll clerk for Neolane Transportation. A colleague who is classified as an independent contractor requests to be classified as an employee. What factors should Ginger consider? (Select all that apply.)
1. Relationship of the parties
2. Behavioral control
3. Method of compensation
4. Financial control

E2-9A.
LO 2-2

What are the forms of identification that establish *identity* for the I-9? (Select all that apply.)
1. Driver's license
2. Native American tribal document
3. Voter registration card
4. Social Security account card

E2-10A.
LO 2-2

What are the forms of identification that establish *employment authorization* for the I-9? (Select all that apply.)
1. U.S. Citizen I.D. Card
2. U.S. Passport
3. School record
4. Certified copy of the birth certificate

E2-11A.
LO 2-3

Jamie Patil is a candidate for the position of a sales manager with Retrozz Furniture. She is going to be required to supervise several employees and can determine the direction in which she will complete the assignments given to her. What guidelines should she follow when classifying workers as exempt or nonexempt? (Select all that apply.)
1. OSHA
2. FLSA
3. Department of Labor
4. IRS

E2-12A.
LO 2-3

Susana Robledo is the office manager for Wardley and Sons Auto Detailing. Because it is a small office, she is required to keep track of all employee records and pay both employees and contractors. Which of the following are legal factors that will differentiate exempt from nonexempt employees? (Select all that apply.)
1. Number of hours worked
2. Type of work performed
3. Employee age and education
4. Amount of supervisor-given direction

Problems Set A

P2-1A.
LO 2-1

Henrietta Morales is a salaried employee earning $75,000 per year. What is Henrietta's period pay for each of the following pay frequencies?
1. Biweekly
2. Semimonthly
3. Weekly
4. Monthly

P2-2A.
LO 2-2, 2-3

Beth Caldwell is in the payroll accounting department of Acerill Films. An independent contractor of the company requests that Social Security and Medicare taxes be withheld from future compensation. What advice should Beth offer?

P2-3A.
LO 2-5

You are the new payroll supervisor for your company. Which payroll documentation control procedures are now your responsibility?

P2-4A.
LO 2-2

Leona Figueroa is a new employee in the payroll department of Octolium Computers. After working at the company for one week, she asks you why it is so important to submit new hire documentation. What guidance will you offer her?

P2-5A.
LO 2-4

You are the payroll accounting clerk for your company, Conose Advertising, which has 50 employees. The controller has recently switched the firm from an in-house payroll system to an outsourced payroll provider. What are your responsibilities within the company for payroll records and employee file issues?

P2-6A.
LO 2-2

Aaron Tallchief is a citizen of the Northern Pomo Indian Nation. In completing his I-9, he provides an official Northern Pomo Indian Nation birth certificate to establish identification and employment eligibility. Is this sufficient documentation? Why or why not?

P2-7A.
LO 2-3

Ian Burns is the new payroll accountant for ECG Marketing. Certain employees have been requesting changes in classification from nonexempt to exempt. How do the U.S. Department of Labor guidelines help him answer the employees' questions?

P2-8A.
LO 2-6

Twinte Cars, a California corporation, has internal corporate requirements that stipulate a three-year payroll document retention period. It enters into a contract with an international company that mandates a six-year payroll document retention requirement. How should Twinte Cars balance these requirements?

P2-9A.
LO 2-2

Ted McCormick is a full-time life insurance agent with Centixo Insurance, a small insurance company. The company has classified him as an employee, and he feels that he should be classified as an independent contractor because he receives no company benefits and sets his own office hours. Should he be reclassified as an independent contractor? Why or why not?

P2-10A.
LO 2-2

Evelyn Hardy is an employee of Polyent Plastics, a company with headquarters in Rock Island, Illinois. She lives and works in Doha, Qatar, and earns an annual salary of $97,300. The company has been withholding U.S. federal income taxes from her pay, but Evelyn believes that she should be exempt because she is an expatriate. What course of action should Evelyn take?

P2-11A.
LO 2-2, 2-4

Complete the W-4 for employment at Superore Wheels starting 3/16/2020, the employer's address is 6150 Speedtrack Road, Montrose, CO 81401 and EIN is 91-1701225.
Erma Jane Grant
441 West Hill Road
Montrose, Colorado 81401
SSN: 432-55-6792
Marital status: Single
Does not require any additional amount to be withheld

P2-12A.
LO 2-2, 2-4

Complete the I-9 for employment at Superore Wheels at 6150 Speedtrack Road, Montrose, Colorado 81401. Erma is starting 3/16/2020. Be sure to complete Section 2 of Form I-9.
Erma Jane Grant
441 West Hill Road
Montrose, Colorado 81401
SSN: 432-55-6792
Maiden name: Grant
Marital status: Single
Date of Birth: June 12, 1986
U.S. Citizen
Erma presented her passport for her employer to review.
Passport number 389049392, issued by the United States Department of State, expires April 1, 2026
Administrative assistant Samantha Cook verified the information for the company.

Form W-4

Form W-4

Department of the Treasury
Internal Revenue Service

Employee's Withholding Certificate

▶ Complete Form W-4 so that your employer can withhold the correct federal income tax from your pay.
▶ Give Form W-4 to your employer.
▶ Your withholding is subject to review by the IRS.

OMB No. 1545-0074

2020

Step 1: Enter Personal Information	(a) First name and middle initial	Last name	(b) Social security number
	Address		▶ **Does your name match the name on your social security card?** If not, to ensure you get credit for your earnings, contact SSA at 800-772-1213 or go to *www.ssa.gov*.
	City or town, state, and ZIP code		

(c) ☐ Single or Married filing separately
☐ Married filing jointly (or Qualifying widow(er))
☐ Head of household (Check only if you're unmarried and pay more than half the costs of keeping up a home for yourself and a qualifying individual.)

Complete Steps 2–4 ONLY if they apply to you; otherwise, skip to Step 5. See page 2 for more information on each step, who can claim exemption from withholding, when to use the online estimator, and privacy.

Step 2:

Multiple Jobs or Spouse Works

Complete this step if you (1) hold more than one job at a time, or (2) are married filing jointly and your spouse also works. The correct amount of withholding depends on income earned from all of these jobs.

Do **only one** of the following.

(a) Use the estimator at *www.irs.gov/W4App* for most accurate withholding for this step (and Steps 3–4); **or**

(b) Use the Multiple Jobs Worksheet on page 3 and enter the result in Step 4(c) below for roughly accurate withholding; **or**

(c) If there are only two jobs total, you may check this box. Do the same on Form W-4 for the other job. This option is accurate for jobs with similar pay; otherwise, more tax than necessary may be withheld . . . . . ▶ ☐

TIP: To be accurate, submit a 2020 Form W-4 for all other jobs. If you (or your spouse) have self-employment income, including as an independent contractor, use the estimator.

Complete Steps 3–4(b) on Form W-4 for only ONE of these jobs. Leave those steps blank for the other jobs. (Your withholding will be most accurate if you complete Steps 3–4(b) on the Form W-4 for the highest paying job.)

Step 3:

Claim Dependents

If your income will be $200,000 or less ($400,000 or less if married filing jointly):

Multiply the number of qualifying children under age 17 by $2,000 ▶ $ _____

Multiply the number of other dependents by $500 . . . . ▶ $ _____

Add the amounts above and enter the total here . . . . | **3** | $ |

Step 4 (optional):

Other Adjustments

(a) **Other income (not from jobs).** If you want tax withheld for other income you expect this year that won't have withholding, enter the amount of other income here. This may include interest, dividends, and retirement income . . . . | **4(a)** | $ |

(b) **Deductions.** If you expect to claim deductions other than the standard deduction and want to reduce your withholding, use the Deductions Worksheet on page 3 and enter the result here . . . . | **4(b)** | $ |

(c) **Extra withholding.** Enter any additional tax you want withheld each **pay period** . | **4(c)** | $ |

Step 5:

Sign Here

Under penalties of perjury, I declare that this certificate, to the best of my knowledge and belief, is true, correct, and complete.

▶ _____   ▶ _____
Employee's signature (This form is not valid unless you sign it.)   Date

Employers Only	Employer's name and address	First date of employment	Employer identification number (EIN)

For Privacy Act and Paperwork Reduction Act Notice, see page 3.   Cat. No. 10220Q   Form **W-4** (2020)

Source: Internal Revenue Service.

Employment Eligibility Verification
Department of Homeland Security
U.S. Citizenship and Immigration Services

USCIS
Form I-9
OMB No. 1615-0047
Expires 10/31/2022

▶ **START HERE:** Read instructions carefully before completing this form. The instructions must be available, either in paper or electronically, during completion of this form. Employers are liable for errors in the completion of this form.

ANTI-DISCRIMINATION NOTICE: It is illegal to discriminate against work-authorized individuals. Employers **CANNOT** specify which document(s) an employee may present to establish employment authorization and identity. The refusal to hire or continue to employ an individual because the documentation presented has a future expiration date may also constitute illegal discrimination.

Section 1. Employee Information and Attestation *(Employees must complete and sign Section 1 of Form I-9 no later than the **first day of employment**, but not before accepting a job offer.)*

Last Name *(Family Name)*	First Name *(Given Name)*	Middle Initial	Other Last Names Used *(if any)*
Address *(Street Number and Name)*	Apt. Number	City or Town	State	ZIP Code

Date of Birth *(mm/dd/yyyy)*	U.S. Social Security Number	Employee's E-mail Address	Employee's Telephone Number

I am aware that federal law provides for imprisonment and/or fines for false statements or use of false documents in connection with the completion of this form.

I attest, under penalty of perjury, that I am (check one of the following boxes):

☐ 1. A citizen of the United States

☐ 2. A noncitizen national of the United States *(See instructions)*

☐ 3. A lawful permanent resident   (Alien Registration Number/USCIS Number): _____

☐ 4. An alien authorized to work   until (expiration date, if applicable, mm/dd/yyyy): _____
       Some aliens may write "N/A" in the expiration date field. *(See instructions)*

Aliens authorized to work must provide only one of the following document numbers to complete Form I-9:
An Alien Registration Number/USCIS Number OR Form I-94 Admission Number OR Foreign Passport Number.

QR Code - Section 1
Do Not Write In This Space

1. Alien Registration Number/USCIS Number: _____
                 OR
2. Form I-94 Admission Number: _____
                 OR
3. Foreign Passport Number: _____
     Country of Issuance: _____

Signature of Employee	Today's Date *(mm/dd/yyyy)*

Preparer and/or Translator Certification (check one):
☐ I did not use a preparer or translator.   ☐ A preparer(s) and/or translator(s) assisted the employee in completing Section 1.
(Fields below must be completed and signed when preparers and/or translators assist an employee in completing Section 1.)

I attest, under penalty of perjury, that I have assisted in the completion of Section 1 of this form and that to the best of my knowledge the information is true and correct.

Signature of Preparer or Translator	Today's Date *(mm/dd/yyyy)*
Last Name *(Family Name)*	First Name *(Given Name)*

Address *(Street Number and Name)*	City or Town	State	ZIP Code

🛑 *Employer Completes Next Page* 🛑

Form I-9 10/21/2019

Page 1 of 3

Employment Eligibility Verification
Department of Homeland Security
U.S. Citizenship and Immigration Services

USCIS
Form I-9
OMB No. 1615-0047
Expires 10/31/2022

Section 2. Employer or Authorized Representative Review and Verification

(Employers or their authorized representative must complete and sign Section 2 within 3 business days of the employee's first day of employment. You must physically examine one document from List A OR a combination of one document from List B and one document from List C as listed on the "Lists of Acceptable Documents.")

Employee Info from Section 1	Last Name *(Family Name)*	First Name *(Given Name)*	M.I.	Citizenship/Immigration Status

List A Identity and Employment Authorization	OR	List B Identity	AND	List C Employment Authorization

Document Title

Issuing Authority

Document Number

Expiration Date *(if any) (mm/dd/yyyy)*

Document Title

Issuing Authority

Document Number

Expiration Date *(if any) (mm/dd/yyyy)*

Document Title

Issuing Authority

Document Number

Expiration Date *(if any) (mm/dd/yyyy)*

Document Title

Issuing Authority

Document Number

Expiration Date *(if any) (mm/dd/yyyy)*

Document Title

Issuing Authority

Document Number

Expiration Date *(if any) (mm/dd/yyyy)*

Additional Information

QR Code - Sections 2 & 3
Do Not Write In This Space

Certification: I attest, under penalty of perjury, that (1) I have examined the document(s) presented by the above-named employee, (2) the above-listed document(s) appear to be genuine and to relate to the employee named, and (3) to the best of my knowledge the employee is authorized to work in the United States.

The employee's first day of employment *(mm/dd/yyyy)*: _____ *(See instructions for exemptions)*

Signature of Employer or Authorized Representative	Today's Date *(mm/dd/yyyy)*	Title of Employer or Authorized Representative
Last Name of Employer or Authorized Representative	First Name of Employer or Authorized Representative	Employer's Business or Organization Name

Employer's Business or Organization Address *(Street Number and Name)*	City or Town	State	ZIP Code

Section 3. Reverification and Rehires *(To be completed and signed by employer or authorized representative.)*

A. New Name *(if applicable)*			**B.** Date of Rehire *(if applicable)*
Last Name *(Family Name)*	First Name *(Given Name)*	Middle Initial	Date *(mm/dd/yyyy)*

C. If the employee's previous grant of employment authorization has expired, provide the information for the document or receipt that establishes continuing employment authorization in the space provided below.

Document Title	Document Number	Expiration Date *(if any) (mm/dd/yyyy)*

I attest, under penalty of perjury, that to the best of my knowledge, this employee is authorized to work in the United States, and if the employee presented document(s), the document(s) I have examined appear to be genuine and to relate to the individual.

Signature of Employer or Authorized Representative	Today's Date *(mm/dd/yyyy)*	Name of Employer or Authorized Representative

Form I-9 10/21/2019

Page 2 of 3

LISTS OF ACCEPTABLE DOCUMENTS
All documents must be UNEXPIRED

Employees may present one selection from List A
or a combination of one selection from List B and one selection from List C.

LIST A	LIST B	LIST C
Documents that Establish Both Identity and Employment Authorization OR	**Documents that Establish Identity** AND	**Documents that Establish Employment Authorization**
1. U.S. Passport or U.S. Passport Card	1. Driver's license or ID card issued by a State or outlying possession of the United States provided it contains a photograph or information such as name, date of birth, gender, height, eye color, and address	1. A Social Security Account Number card, unless the card includes one of the following restrictions: (1) NOT VALID FOR EMPLOYMENT (2) VALID FOR WORK ONLY WITH INS AUTHORIZATION (3) VALID FOR WORK ONLY WITH DHS AUTHORIZATION
2. Permanent Resident Card or Alien Registration Receipt Card (Form I-551)		
3. Foreign passport that contains a temporary I-551 stamp or temporary I-551 printed notation on a machine-readable immigrant visa	2. ID card issued by federal, state or local government agencies or entities, provided it contains a photograph or information such as name, date of birth, gender, height, eye color, and address	2. Certification of report of birth issued by the Department of State (Forms DS-1350, FS-545, FS-240)
4. Employment Authorization Document that contains a photograph (Form I-766)	3. School ID card with a photograph	3. Original or certified copy of birth certificate issued by a State, county, municipal authority, or territory of the United States bearing an official seal
	4. Voter's registration card	
5. For a nonimmigrant alien authorized to work for a specific employer because of his or her status:	5. U.S. Military card or draft record	
a. Foreign passport; and	6. Military dependent's ID card	4. Native American tribal document
b. Form I-94 or Form I-94A that has the following:	7. U.S. Coast Guard Merchant Mariner Card	5. U.S. Citizen ID Card (Form I-197)
(1) The same name as the passport; and	8. Native American tribal document	6. Identification Card for Use of Resident Citizen in the United States (Form I-179)
(2) An endorsement of the alien's nonimmigrant status as long as that period of endorsement has not yet expired and the proposed employment is not in conflict with any restrictions or limitations identified on the form.	9. Driver's license issued by a Canadian government authority	7. Employment authorization document issued by the Department of Homeland Security
	For persons under age 18 who are unable to present a document listed above:	
6. Passport from the Federated States of Micronesia (FSM) or the Republic of the Marshall Islands (RMI) with Form I-94 or Form I-94A indicating nonimmigrant admission under the Compact of Free Association Between the United States and the FSM or RMI	10. School record or report card	
	11. Clinic, doctor, or hospital record	
	12. Day-care or nursery school record	

Examples of many of these documents appear in the Handbook for Employers (M-274).

Refer to the instructions for more information about acceptable receipts.

Form I-9 10/21/2019

Source: United States Citizenship and Immigration Services.

Exercises Set B

E2-1B.
LO 2-1, 2-4

Stacy Romero, a nonexempt employee of Prosaria Publishers, works a standard 6:00 a.m. to 3:00 p.m. schedule with an hour for lunch. Stacy works in California, a state that requires overtime pay for hours exceeding 8 per day and for those exceeding 40 in a week. During the week, she worked the following schedule:

- Monday: 8.25 hours
- Tuesday: 8 hours
- Wednesday: 8.75 hours
- Thursday: 7 hours
- Friday: 9 hours

Based on the requirements above, how much overtime has Stacy worked during the period?

1. 2 hours
2. 0.5 hour
3. 1 hour
4. 3 hours

E2-2B.
LO 2-1

Grant Saunders is a salaried employee earning $84,000 per year. He receives his payroll every other week. Which of the following best describes the pay frequency?

1. Biweekly
2. Semimonthly
3. Weekly
4. Monthly

E2-3B.
LO 2-4, 2-6

On October 30, 2020, Dolores Goodman quit her job after 10 years with Omnivue Optics in Utah. Omnivue Optics pays employees weekly on Fridays. Upon quitting, Dolores had 38.5 hours of vacation accrued that she had not used, and she had worked 45 hours, 5 hours of which was subject to overtime. When must she receive her final paycheck?

1. On the next pay date
2. Within seven days
3. Immediately upon discharge
4. Within 24 hours

E2-4B.
LO 2-4, 2-6

Adrienne Norman ended her employment with Univee Inc. on December 16, 2020. When is the earliest that Univee Inc. may destroy her payroll records?

1. December 16, 2021
2. December 16, 2022
3. December 16, 2023
4. December 16, 2024

E2-5B.
LO 2-5

Elijah Brown is a new payroll clerk at Zata Imports, a company with 250 employees. He has completed entering all timecard data for the pay period. What should Elijah's next step in the payroll review process be?

1. Ask employees to verify that the time Elijah entered is accurate.
2. Generate paychecks and prepare them for signature.
3. Ask his supervisor to verify the accuracy of the payroll data.
4. Have another payroll clerk verify the data accuracy.

E2-6B.
LO 2-6

Elaine Wheeler needs additional filing space at the end of the year in the company's office and chooses to use off-site, secured storage. Upon arriving at the storage facility, she discovers that the unit is nearly full and sees several boxes marked for destruction at the end of the calendar year. What are Elaine's options regarding the destruction of the payroll records marked for destruction? (Select all that apply.)

1. She should take the oldest year's boxes to the closest recycling facility.
2. She should make arrangements to pulp or burn the paper payroll records marked for destruction.
3. She should arrange to have a document destruction service pick up the boxes marked for destruction.
4. She should bring a shredding machine to the storage facility and prepare to shred the records marked for destruction.

E2-7B.
LO 2-1

Gerardo Rogers is conducting a review of the payroll files for each employee at Meejo Games. Which of the following items must be present in the file? (Select all that apply.)
1. Basis upon which compensation is paid.
2. Overtime pay earned during each pay period.
3. Hours worked during each pay period.
4. Break times taken each day.

E2-8B.
LO 2-2

Jane McCarthy is preparing to compute employee pay and needs to determine the amount of employee federal income taxes to be withheld. Which of the following should she consult?
1. USCIS I-9
2. IRS Publication 15-T
3. DHS Schedule F
4. SSA Schedule 8

E2-9B.
LO 2-2

John Franklin is a new employee of Camidel Clothiers. Which of the following will provide proof of *identity* for the completion of the I-9? (Select all that apply.)
1. U.S. Passport
2. U.S. Military Identification Card
3. U.S. Citizen Identification Card
4. New York driver's license

E2-10B.
LO 2-2

Sheri Jennings is completing the I-9 for her new employment at Insulend Tours. Which of the following provides proof of her *employment authorization*? (Select all that apply.)
1. Social Security card
2. Certificate of birth abroad, issued by the U.S. Department of State
3. Louisiana driver's license
4. U.S. Passport

E2-11B.
LO 2-3

Laverne Watkins is a candidate for the position of marketing clerk with the promotions department of Paramba Productions, earning $10.25 per hour. She will work occasional overtime in her new position and will not have managerial or supervisory duties as a regular part of her job description. Why should Laverne be classified as a nonexempt employee? (Select all that apply.)
1. Her annual wages are lower than the minimum exempt salary.
2. She has no supervisory or managerial duties.
3. She has the term *clerk* in her job title.
4. She will work occasional overtime.

E2-12B.
LO 2-3

Rex Marshall manages a ski resort with year-round and seasonal employees. Assuming that the ski resort engages in interstate commerce, which are the FLSA requirement(s) that Rex should consider? (Select all that apply.)
1. Hourly wages paid to employees.
2. Safety of the working conditions.
3. Number of hours worked per week.
4. Employee age and weekly work schedule.

Problems Set B

P2-1B.
LO 2-2

Tasha Webb is an independent contractor for Antimbu Exports, where you are the payroll accountant. She feels that she should receive employee benefits because of the number of hours that she dedicates to the company. What guidance could you offer Tasha?

P2-2B.
LO 2-6

Joseph Lyons was terminated for cause from Telecy Industries in Hawaii on August 21, 2020. As of the date of his termination, he had worked 22 hours of regular time. Employees at Telecy Industries are paid semimonthly on the 15th and last day of the month. Joseph would like to know when he will be paid for the accrued hours. What will you tell him?

P2-3B.
LO 2-2

Sara Northman is a member of the Algonquin Indian Nation and is a new employee at Predeo Game Designs. During the process of completing her I-9, she claims that the only way to prove her identity is the Algonquin Indian Nation official birth certificate. Is this document sufficient to prove employment authorization for the purposes of the I-9? Why or why not?

P2-4B.
LO 2-2

Abraham Manning is a new employee of Symity Batteries. He is curious about the purpose of the requirements for new hire documentation to be forwarded to government agencies. What should you tell him?

P2-5B.
LO 2-1

Frances Perez wants to start her own company. As a seasoned payroll professional, she approaches you for guidance about the differences among weekly, biweekly, and semimonthly pay periods. What would you tell her?

P2-6B.
LO 2-5

Katrina Wilkins is a new payroll clerk for Remm Plumbing. She is curious about the purpose of the different steps in the payroll review process and asks you, her supervisor, for guidance. What would you tell her?

P2-7B.
LO 2-4

George Andrews started as a payroll accountant at Portose Herbals, a company with 70 employees. He soon notices that the former payroll accountant had been processing payroll manually and suggests that the company immediately switch to cloud-based payroll. Although the company is switching to an electronic payroll processing system, what types of paper documentation must be maintained in employee records?

P2-8B.
LO 2-5

Tara Morris, a payroll clerk, has received a promotion and is now the payroll supervisor for Fligen Enterprises. What document control items could now become her responsibility?

P2-9B.
LO 2-2

Herman Watkins is in the payroll department of Neombee Plastics, a multistate company. The company has historically been filing employee information with each state. What alternative exists for multistate employers?

P2-10B.
LO 2-1

Derek Allen is the payroll supervisor for Caposis Freight. His company is preparing to merge with another distribution company that has a different pay cycle. The president of the company wants to know the difference between biweekly and semimonthly pay cycles as far as to pay dates and payment amounts are concerned. What should Derek tell him?

P2-11B.
LO 2-2, 2-4

Complete the W-4 for employment at Equtri Farms located at 8541 Brook Road, Taylorville, IL 62556 with an EIN of 92-6643122, effective 6/17/2020:
Linda Ellen Marshall
8924 County Line Road
Taylorville, Illinois 62555
SSN: 129-53-2309
Married filing jointly
They do not wish to withhold additional amounts.
Linda earns $32,000 at her primary job. She has a second job as a delivery driver for Tazio Labs, where she earns $12,000/year.

P2-12B.
LO 2-2, 2-4

Complete the I-9 for employment effective 7/23/2020 at Ecovee Energy located at 244 Winston Drive, Gretna, Virginia 24557. Be sure to complete Section 2 of Form I-9.
Lloyd Gregory Flowers
SSN: 382-10-0392
Date of Birth: 11-20-1993
1298 Chatham Road
Gretna, Virginia 24557
U.S. Citizen
Lloyd presented his driver's license and Social Security card to the Human Resources Manager, Amanda Weeble, to review.
Virginia Driver's License #293034293, Expires 11/20/2023

Form **W-4**	**Employee's Withholding Certificate**	OMB No. 1545-0074
Department of the Treasury Internal Revenue Service	▶ Complete Form W-4 so that your employer can withhold the correct federal income tax from your pay. ▶ Give Form W-4 to your employer. ▶ Your withholding is subject to review by the IRS.	**2020**

Step 1:

Enter Personal Information

(a) First name and middle initial   Last name

(b) Social security number

Address

▶ **Does your name match the name on your social security card?** If not, to ensure you get credit for your earnings, contact SSA at 800-772-1213 or go to *www.ssa.gov*.

City or town, state, and ZIP code

(c) ☐ Single or Married filing separately
☐ **Married filing jointly** (or Qualifying widow(er))
☐ **Head of household** (Check only if you're unmarried and pay more than half the costs of keeping up a home for yourself and a qualifying individual.)

Complete Steps 2–4 ONLY if they apply to you; otherwise, skip to Step 5. See page 2 for more information on each step, who can claim exemption from withholding, when to use the online estimator, and privacy.

Step 2:

Multiple Jobs or Spouse Works

Complete this step if you (1) hold more than one job at a time, or (2) are married filing jointly and your spouse also works. The correct amount of withholding depends on income earned from all of these jobs.

Do **only one** of the following.

(a) Use the estimator at *www.irs.gov/W4App* for most accurate withholding for this step (and Steps 3–4); **or**

(b) Use the Multiple Jobs Worksheet on page 3 and enter the result in Step 4(c) below for roughly accurate withholding; **or**

(c) If there are only two jobs total, you may check this box. Do the same on Form W-4 for the other job. This option is accurate for jobs with similar pay; otherwise, more tax than necessary may be withheld . . . . . . ▶ ☐

TIP: To be accurate, submit a 2020 Form W-4 for all other jobs. If you (or your spouse) have self-employment income, including as an independent contractor, use the estimator.

Complete Steps 3–4(b) on Form W-4 for only ONE of these jobs. Leave those steps blank for the other jobs. (Your withholding will be most accurate if you complete Steps 3–4(b) on the Form W-4 for the highest paying job.)

Step 3:

Claim Dependents

If your income will be $200,000 or less ($400,000 or less if married filing jointly):

Multiply the number of qualifying children under age 17 by $2,000 ▶ $ _____

Multiply the number of other dependents by $500 . . . . . ▶ $ _____

Add the amounts above and enter the total here . . . . | **3** | $

Step 4 (optional):

Other Adjustments

(a) Other income (not from jobs). If you want tax withheld for other income you expect this year that won't have withholding, enter the amount of other income here. This may include interest, dividends, and retirement income . . . . | **4(a)** | $

(b) Deductions. If you expect to claim deductions other than the standard deduction and want to reduce your withholding, use the Deductions Worksheet on page 3 and enter the result here . . . . | **4(b)** | $

(c) Extra withholding. Enter any additional tax you want withheld each **pay period** . | **4(c)** | $

Step 5:

Sign Here

Under penalties of perjury, I declare that this certificate, to the best of my knowledge and belief, is true, correct, and complete.

▶ _____   ▶ _____

Employee's signature (This form is not valid unless you sign it.)   **Date**

Employers Only

Employer's name and address

First date of employment

Employer identification number (EIN)

For Privacy Act and Paperwork Reduction Act Notice, see page 3.   Cat. No. 10220Q   Form **W-4** (2020)

Form W-4 (2020)

Step 2(b)—Multiple Jobs Worksheet *(Keep for your records.)*

If you choose the option in Step 2(b) on Form W-4, complete this worksheet (which calculates the total extra tax for all jobs) on **only ONE** Form W-4. Withholding will be most accurate if you complete the worksheet and enter the result on the Form W-4 for the highest paying job.

Note: If more than one job has annual wages of more than $120,000 or there are more than three jobs, see Pub. 505 for additional tables; or, you can use the online withholding estimator at *www.irs.gov/W4App*.

1 **Two jobs.** If you have two jobs or you're married filing jointly and you and your spouse each have one job, find the amount from the appropriate table on page 4. Using the "Higher Paying Job" row and the "Lower Paying Job" column, find the value at the intersection of the two household salaries and enter that value on line 1. Then, **skip** to line 3 . . . . **1** $ _____

2 **Three jobs.** If you and/or your spouse have three jobs at the same time, complete lines 2a, 2b, and 2c below. Otherwise, skip to line 3.

    a Find the amount from the appropriate table on page 4 using the annual wages from the highest paying job in the "Higher Paying Job" row and the annual wages for your next highest paying job in the "Lower Paying Job" column. Find the value at the intersection of the two household salaries and enter that value on line 2a . . . . **2a** $ _____

    b Add the annual wages of the two highest paying jobs from line 2a together and use the total as the wages in the "Higher Paying Job" row and use the annual wages for your third job in the "Lower Paying Job" column to find the amount from the appropriate table on page 4 and enter this amount on line 2b . . . . **2b** $ _____

    c Add the amounts from lines 2a and 2b and enter the result on line 2c . . . . **2c** $ _____

3 Enter the number of pay periods per year for the highest paying job. For example, if that job pays weekly, enter 52; if it pays every other week, enter 26; if it pays monthly, enter 12, etc. . . . . **3** _____

4 **Divide** the annual amount on line 1 or line 2c by the number of pay periods on line 3. Enter this amount here and in **Step 4(c)** of Form W-4 for the highest paying job (along with any other additional amount you want withheld) . . . . **4** $ _____

Step 4(b)—Deductions Worksheet *(Keep for your records.)*

1 Enter an estimate of your 2020 itemized deductions (from Schedule A (Form 1040 or 1040-SR)). Such deductions may include qualifying home mortgage interest, charitable contributions, state and local taxes (up to $10,000), and medical expenses in excess of 7.5% of your income . . . . . . **1** $ _____

2 Enter:
    { • $24,800 if you're married filing jointly or qualifying widow(er)
      • $18,650 if you're head of household
      • $12,400 if you're single or married filing separately } . . . . **2** $ _____

3 If line 1 is greater than line 2, subtract line 2 from line 1. If line 2 is greater than line 1, enter "-0-" . . **3** $ _____

4 Enter an estimate of your student loan interest, deductible IRA contributions, and certain other adjustments (from Part II of Schedule 1 (Form 1040 or 1040-SR)). See Pub. 505 for more information **4** $ _____

5 **Add** lines 3 and 4. Enter the result here and in **Step 4(b)** of Form W-4 . . . . **5** $ _____

Married Filing Jointly or Qualifying Widow(er)

Higher Paying Job Annual Taxable Wage & Salary	Lower Paying Job Annual Taxable Wage & Salary											
	$0 - 9,999	$10,000 - 19,999	$20,000 - 29,999	$30,000 - 39,999	$40,000 - 49,999	$50,000 - 59,999	$60,000 - 69,999	$70,000 - 79,999	$80,000 - 89,999	$90,000 - 99,999	$100,000 - 109,999	$110,000 - 120,000
$0 - 9,999	$0	$220	$850	$900	$1,020	$1,020	$1,020	$1,020	$1,020	$1,210	$1,870	$1,870
$10,000 - 19,999	220	1,220	1,900	2,100	2,220	2,220	2,220	2,220	2,410	3,410	4,070	4,070
$20,000 - 29,999	850	1,900	2,730	2,930	3,050	3,050	3,050	3,240	4,240	5,240	5,900	5,900
$30,000 - 39,999	900	2,100	2,930	3,130	3,250	3,250	3,440	4,440	5,440	6,440	7,100	7,100
$40,000 - 49,999	1,020	2,220	3,050	3,250	3,370	3,570	4,570	5,570	6,570	7,570	8,220	8,220
$50,000 - 59,999	1,020	2,220	3,050	3,250	3,570	4,570	5,570	6,570	7,570	8,570	9,220	9,220
$60,000 - 69,999	1,020	2,220	3,050	3,440	4,570	5,570	6,570	7,570	8,570	9,570	10,220	10,220
$70,000 - 79,999	1,020	2,220	3,240	4,440	5,570	6,570	7,570	8,570	9,570	10,570	11,220	11,240
$80,000 - 99,999	1,060	3,260	5,090	6,290	7,420	8,420	9,420	10,420	11,420	12,420	13,260	13,460
$100,000 - 149,999	1,870	4,070	5,900	7,100	8,220	9,320	10,520	11,720	12,920	14,120	14,980	15,180
$150,000 - 239,999	2,040	4,440	6,470	7,870	9,190	10,390	11,590	12,790	13,990	15,190	16,050	16,250
$240,000 - 259,999	2,040	4,440	6,470	7,870	9,190	10,390	11,590	12,790	13,990	15,520	17,170	18,170
$260,000 - 279,999	2,040	4,440	6,470	7,870	9,190	10,390	11,590	13,120	15,120	17,120	18,770	19,770
$280,000 - 299,999	2,040	4,440	6,470	7,870	9,190	10,720	12,720	14,720	16,720	18,720	20,370	21,370
$300,000 - 319,999	2,040	4,440	6,470	8,200	10,320	12,320	14,320	16,320	18,320	20,320	21,970	22,970
$320,000 - 364,999	2,720	5,920	8,750	10,950	13,070	15,070	17,070	19,070	21,290	23,590	25,540	26,840
$365,000 - 524,999	2,970	6,470	9,600	12,100	14,530	16,830	19,130	21,430	23,730	26,030	27,980	29,280
$525,000 and over	3,140	6,840	10,170	12,870	15,500	18,000	20,500	23,000	25,500	28,000	30,150	31,650

Single or Married Filing Separately

Higher Paying Job Annual Taxable Wage & Salary	Lower Paying Job Annual Taxable Wage & Salary											
	$0 - 9,999	$10,000 - 19,999	$20,000 - 29,999	$30,000 - 39,999	$40,000 - 49,999	$50,000 - 59,999	$60,000 - 69,999	$70,000 - 79,999	$80,000 - 89,999	$90,000 - 99,999	$100,000 - 109,999	$110,000 - 120,000
$0 - 9,999	$460	$940	$1,020	$1,020	$1,470	$1,870	$1,870	$1,870	$1,870	$2,040	$2,040	$2,040
$10,000 - 19,999	940	1,530	1,610	2,060	3,060	3,460	3,460	3,460	3,640	3,830	3,830	3,830
$20,000 - 29,999	1,020	1,610	2,130	3,130	4,130	4,540	4,540	4,720	4,920	5,110	5,110	5,110
$30,000 - 39,999	1,020	2,060	3,130	4,130	5,130	5,540	5,720	5,920	6,120	6,310	6,310	6,310
$40,000 - 59,999	1,870	3,460	4,540	5,540	6,690	7,290	7,490	7,690	7,890	8,080	8,080	8,080
$60,000 - 79,999	1,870	3,460	4,690	5,890	7,090	7,690	7,890	8,090	8,290	8,480	9,260	10,060
$80,000 - 99,999	2,020	3,810	5,090	6,290	7,490	8,090	8,290	8,490	9,470	10,460	11,260	12,060
$100,000 - 124,999	2,040	3,830	5,110	6,310	7,510	8,430	9,430	10,430	11,430	12,420	13,520	14,620
$125,000 - 149,999	2,040	3,830	5,110	7,030	9,030	10,430	11,430	12,580	13,880	15,170	16,270	17,370
$150,000 - 174,999	2,360	4,950	7,030	9,030	11,030	12,730	14,030	15,330	16,630	17,920	19,020	20,120
$175,000 - 199,999	2,720	5,310	7,540	9,840	12,140	13,840	15,140	16,440	17,740	19,030	20,130	21,230
$200,000 - 249,999	2,970	5,860	8,240	10,540	12,840	14,540	15,840	17,140	18,440	19,730	20,830	21,930
$250,000 - 399,999	2,970	5,860	8,240	10,540	12,840	14,540	15,840	17,140	18,440	19,730	20,830	21,930
$400,000 - 449,999	2,970	5,860	8,240	10,540	12,840	14,540	15,840	17,140	18,450	19,940	21,240	22,540
$450,000 and over	3,140	6,230	8,810	11,310	13,810	15,710	17,210	18,710	20,210	21,700	23,000	24,300

Head of Household

Higher Paying Job Annual Taxable Wage & Salary	Lower Paying Job Annual Taxable Wage & Salary											
	$0 - 9,999	$10,000 - 19,999	$20,000 - 29,999	$30,000 - 39,999	$40,000 - 49,999	$50,000 - 59,999	$60,000 - 69,999	$70,000 - 79,999	$80,000 - 89,999	$90,000 - 99,999	$100,000 - 109,999	$110,000 - 120,000
$0 - 9,999	$0	$830	$930	$1,020	$1,020	$1,020	$1,480	$1,870	$1,870	$1,930	$2,040	$2,040
$10,000 - 19,999	830	1,920	2,130	2,220	2,220	2,680	3,680	4,070	4,130	4,330	4,440	4,440
$20,000 - 29,999	930	2,130	2,350	2,430	2,900	3,900	4,900	5,340	5,540	5,740	5,850	5,850
$30,000 - 39,999	1,020	2,220	2,430	2,980	3,980	4,980	6,040	6,630	6,830	7,030	7,140	7,140
$40,000 - 59,999	1,020	2,530	3,750	4,830	5,860	7,060	8,260	8,850	9,050	9,250	9,360	9,360
$60,000 - 79,999	1,870	4,070	5,310	6,600	7,800	9,000	10,200	10,780	10,980	11,180	11,580	12,380
$80,000 - 99,999	1,900	4,300	5,710	7,000	8,200	9,400	10,600	11,180	11,670	12,670	13,580	14,380
$100,000 - 124,999	2,040	4,440	5,850	7,140	8,340	9,540	11,360	12,750	13,750	14,750	15,770	16,870
$125,000 - 149,999	2,040	4,440	5,850	7,360	9,360	11,360	13,360	14,750	16,010	17,310	18,520	19,620
$150,000 - 174,999	2,040	5,060	7,280	9,360	11,360	13,480	15,780	17,460	18,760	20,060	21,270	22,370
$175,000 - 199,999	2,720	5,920	8,130	10,480	12,780	15,080	17,380	19,070	20,370	21,670	22,880	23,980
$200,000 - 249,999	2,970	6,470	8,990	11,370	13,670	15,970	18,270	19,960	21,260	22,560	23,770	24,870
$250,000 - 349,999	2,970	6,470	8,990	11,370	13,670	15,970	18,270	19,960	21,260	22,560	23,770	24,870
$350,000 - 449,999	2,970	6,470	8,990	11,370	13,670	15,970	18,270	19,960	21,260	22,560	23,900	25,200
$450,000 and over	3,140	6,840	9,560	12,140	14,640	17,140	19,640	21,530	23,030	24,530	25,940	27,240

Source: Internal Revenue Service.

Employment Eligibility Verification
Department of Homeland Security
U.S. Citizenship and Immigration Services

USCIS
Form I-9

OMB No. 1615-0047
Expires 10/31/2022

▶**START HERE:** Read instructions carefully before completing this form. The instructions must be available, either in paper or electronically, during completion of this form. Employers are liable for errors in the completion of this form.

ANTI-DISCRIMINATION NOTICE: It is illegal to discriminate against work-authorized individuals. Employers **CANNOT** specify which document(s) an employee may present to establish employment authorization and identity. The refusal to hire or continue to employ an individual because the documentation presented has a future expiration date may also constitute illegal discrimination.

Section 1. Employee Information and Attestation *(Employees must complete and sign Section 1 of Form I-9 no later than the **first day of employment**, but not before accepting a job offer.)*

Last Name *(Family Name)*	First Name *(Given Name)*	Middle Initial	Other Last Names Used *(if any)*

Address *(Street Number and Name)*	Apt. Number	City or Town	State	ZIP Code

Date of Birth *(mm/dd/yyyy)*	U.S. Social Security Number	Employee's E-mail Address	Employee's Telephone Number
	☐☐☐-☐☐-☐☐☐☐		

I am aware that federal law provides for imprisonment and/or fines for false statements or use of false documents in connection with the completion of this form.

I attest, under penalty of perjury, that I am (check one of the following boxes):

☐ 1. A citizen of the United States

☐ 2. A noncitizen national of the United States *(See instructions)*

☐ 3. A lawful permanent resident   (Alien Registration Number/USCIS Number): _____

☐ 4. An alien authorized to work   until (expiration date, if applicable, mm/dd/yyyy): _____
       Some aliens may write "N/A" in the expiration date field. *(See instructions)*

Aliens authorized to work must provide only one of the following document numbers to complete Form I-9:
An Alien Registration Number/USCIS Number OR Form I-94 Admission Number OR Foreign Passport Number.

QR Code - Section 1
Do Not Write In This Space

1. Alien Registration Number/USCIS Number: _____
           OR
2. Form I-94 Admission Number: _____
           OR
3. Foreign Passport Number: _____
     Country of Issuance: _____

Signature of Employee	Today's Date *(mm/dd/yyyy)*

Preparer and/or Translator Certification (check one):

☐ I did not use a preparer or translator.   ☐ A preparer(s) and/or translator(s) assisted the employee in completing Section 1.
(Fields below must be completed and signed when preparers and/or translators assist an employee in completing Section 1.)

I attest, under penalty of perjury, that I have assisted in the completion of Section 1 of this form and that to the best of my knowledge the information is true and correct.

Signature of Preparer or Translator	Today's Date *(mm/dd/yyyy)*

Last Name *(Family Name)*	First Name *(Given Name)*

Address *(Street Number and Name)*	City or Town	State	ZIP Code

🛑 *Employer Completes Next Page* 🛑

Form I-9 10/21/2019

Page 1 of 3

Employment Eligibility Verification
Department of Homeland Security
U.S. Citizenship and Immigration Services

USCIS
Form I-9
OMB No. 1615-0047
Expires 10/31/2022

Section 2. Employer or Authorized Representative Review and Verification

(Employers or their authorized representative must complete and sign Section 2 within 3 business days of the employee's first day of employment. You must physically examine one document from List A OR a combination of one document from List B and one document from List C as listed on the "Lists of Acceptable Documents.")

Employee Info from Section 1	Last Name *(Family Name)*	First Name *(Given Name)*	M.I.	Citizenship/Immigration Status

List A Identity and Employment Authorization	OR	List B Identity	AND	List C Employment Authorization

List A	List B	List C
Document Title	Document Title	Document Title
Issuing Authority	Issuing Authority	Issuing Authority
Document Number	Document Number	Document Number
Expiration Date *(if any) (mm/dd/yyyy)*	Expiration Date *(if any) (mm/dd/yyyy)*	Expiration Date *(if any) (mm/dd/yyyy)*
Document Title		
Issuing Authority	Additional Information	QR Code - Sections 2 & 3 Do Not Write In This Space
Document Number		
Expiration Date *(if any) (mm/dd/yyyy)*		
Document Title		
Issuing Authority		
Document Number		
Expiration Date *(if any) (mm/dd/yyyy)*		

Certification: I attest, under penalty of perjury, that (1) I have examined the document(s) presented by the above-named employee, (2) the above-listed document(s) appear to be genuine and to relate to the employee named, and (3) to the best of my knowledge the employee is authorized to work in the United States.

The employee's first day of employment *(mm/dd/yyyy)*: _____ *(See instructions for exemptions)*

Signature of Employer or Authorized Representative	Today's Date *(mm/dd/yyyy)*	Title of Employer or Authorized Representative
Last Name of Employer or Authorized Representative	First Name of Employer or Authorized Representative	Employer's Business or Organization Name

Employer's Business or Organization Address *(Street Number and Name)*	City or Town	State	ZIP Code

Section 3. Reverification and Rehires *(To be completed and signed by employer or authorized representative.)*

A. New Name *(if applicable)*			**B.** Date of Rehire *(if applicable)*
Last Name *(Family Name)*	First Name *(Given Name)*	Middle Initial	Date *(mm/dd/yyyy)*

C. If the employee's previous grant of employment authorization has expired, provide the information for the document or receipt that establishes continuing employment authorization in the space provided below.

Document Title	Document Number	Expiration Date *(if any) (mm/dd/yyyy)*

I attest, under penalty of perjury, that to the best of my knowledge, this employee is authorized to work in the United States, and if the employee presented document(s), the document(s) I have examined appear to be genuine and to relate to the individual.

Signature of Employer or Authorized Representative	Today's Date *(mm/dd/yyyy)*	Name of Employer or Authorized Representative

Form I-9 10/21/2019

Page 2 of 3

LISTS OF ACCEPTABLE DOCUMENTS
All documents must be UNEXPIRED

Employees may present one selection from List A
or a combination of one selection from List B and one selection from List C.

LIST A **Documents that Establish Both Identity and Employment Authorization**	**OR**	LIST B **Documents that Establish Identity**	**AND**	LIST C **Documents that Establish Employment Authorization**
1. U.S. Passport or U.S. Passport Card		1. Driver's license or ID card issued by a State or outlying possession of the United States provided it contains a photograph or information such as name, date of birth, gender, height, eye color, and address		1. A Social Security Account Number card, unless the card includes one of the following restrictions: (1) NOT VALID FOR EMPLOYMENT (2) VALID FOR WORK ONLY WITH INS AUTHORIZATION (3) VALID FOR WORK ONLY WITH DHS AUTHORIZATION
2. Permanent Resident Card or Alien Registration Receipt Card (Form I-551)				
3. Foreign passport that contains a temporary I-551 stamp or temporary I-551 printed notation on a machine-readable immigrant visa		2. ID card issued by federal, state or local government agencies or entities, provided it contains a photograph or information such as name, date of birth, gender, height, eye color, and address		2. Certification of report of birth issued by the Department of State (Forms DS-1350, FS-545, FS-240)
4. Employment Authorization Document that contains a photograph (Form I-766)		3. School ID card with a photograph		3. Original or certified copy of birth certificate issued by a State, county, municipal authority, or territory of the United States bearing an official seal
5. For a nonimmigrant alien authorized to work for a specific employer because of his or her status: a. Foreign passport; and b. Form I-94 or Form I-94A that has the following: (1) The same name as the passport; and (2) An endorsement of the alien's nonimmigrant status as long as that period of endorsement has not yet expired and the proposed employment is not in conflict with any restrictions or limitations identified on the form.		4. Voter's registration card		
		5. U.S. Military card or draft record		4. Native American tribal document
		6. Military dependent's ID card		5. U.S. Citizen ID Card (Form I-197)
		7. U.S. Coast Guard Merchant Mariner Card		6. Identification Card for Use of Resident Citizen in the United States (Form I-179)
		8. Native American tribal document		
		9. Driver's license issued by a Canadian government authority		
6. Passport from the Federated States of Micronesia (FSM) or the Republic of the Marshall Islands (RMI) with Form I-94 or Form I-94A indicating nonimmigrant admission under the Compact of Free Association Between the United States and the FSM or RMI		**For persons under age 18 who are unable to present a document listed above:** 10. School record or report card 11. Clinic, doctor, or hospital record 12. Day-care or nursery school record		7. Employment authorization document issued by the Department of Homeland Security

Examples of many of these documents appear in the Handbook for Employers (M-274).

Refer to the instructions for more information about acceptable receipts.

Critical Thinking

2-1. When Omnimia Graphics was looking to implement a payroll accounting system, the manufacturing firm had several options. With only 40 employees, the manual preparation of payroll through spreadsheets and handwritten time cards was a comfortable option for the firm. Another option was to convince the senior management of Omnimia Graphics to implement a software program for payroll processing. How should the company handle the maintenance of the current payroll records? What internal control issues should be addressed?

2-2. You have been hired as a consultant for Semiva Productions, a company facing an IRS audit of its accounting records. During your review, you notice anomalies in the payroll system involving overpayments of labor and payments to terminated employees. What would you do?

In the Real World: Scenario for Discussion

The Lilly Ledbetter Fair Pay Act of 2009 centered on a case in which Ms. Ledbetter discovered documents that revealed discrimination against her that resulted in unequal pay practices. The company argued that the documents were confidential and scheduled for destruction and that Ms. Ledbetter should not have had access to the information. What are the issues in this case in terms of document privacy and retention? How could the situation have been prevented in the first place?

Internet Activities

2-1. Using a search engine such as Google, Yahoo, or Bing, search the Internet for the term "new hire packet contents." Compile a list of the different new hire packet items that you find in at least three companies. What are some unique items that you found on the companies' lists? Check out the IRS's video about determining the correct amount of withholding allowances for your Form W-4, https://www.youtube.com/watch?v=BBuAzW43K1A&feature=youtu.be.

2-2. Go to www.irs.gov and search for IRS e-file security. List the facts that the IRS cites about why e-filing is secure. What about these practices makes the customer's information secure? How could the IRS improve e-filing security?

2-3. Want to know more about some of the concepts discussed in this chapter? Check out

www.uscis.gov

www.irs.gov/businesses

www.archives.gov/federal-register/cfr/subject-title-26.html

www.proshred.com

www.ironmountain.com

2-4. The Massachusetts Institute of Technology (MIT) has created a website with a living wage calculator. This tool is designed to help people compute the wages they need to earn in order to achieve their desired lifestyle. Check it out at Living Wage Calculator, http://livingwage.mit.edu.

Continuing Payroll Project: Prevosti Farms and Sugarhouse

Prevosti Farms and Sugarhouse pays its employees according to their job classification. The following employees make up Sugarhouse's staff:

Employee Number	Name and Address	Payroll information
A-Mille	Thomas Millen 1022 Forest School Rd Woodstock, VT 05001 802-478-5055 SSN: 031-11-3456 401(k) deduction: 3% Section 125 deduction: $155	Hire Date: 2-3-2020 DOB: 12-16-1982 Position: Production Manager PT/FT: FT, exempt M/S: Married/Joint Pay Rate: $35,000/year Dependents under 17: 3 Dependents over 17: 1 Step 4 information: none

Employee Number	Name and Address	Payroll information
A-Towle	Avery Towle 4011 Route 100 Plymouth, VT 05102 802-967-5873 SSN: 089-74-0974 401(k) deduction: 5% Section 125 deduction: $100	Hire Date: 2-3-2020 DOB: 7-14-1991 Position: Production Worker PT/FT: FT, nonexempt M/S: Single Pay Rate: $12.00/hour Dependents under 17: 0 Dependents over 17: 0 Step 4 information: none
A-Long	Charlie Long 242 Benedict Road S. Woodstock, VT 05002 802-429-3846 SSN: 056-23-4593 401(k) deduction: 2% Section 125 deduction: $155	Hire Date: 2-3-2020 DOB: 3-16-1987 Position: Production Worker PT/FT: FT, nonexempt M/S: Married/Joint Pay Rate: $12.50/hour Dependents under 17: 2 Dependents over 17: 0 Step 4 information: none
B-Shang	Mary Shangraw 1901 Main Street #2 Bridgewater, VT 05520 802-575-5423 SSN: 075-28-8945 401(k) deduction: 3% Section 125 deduction: $100	Hire Date: 2-3-2020 DOB: 8-20-1994 Position: Administrative Assistant PT/FT: PT, nonexempt M/S: Single Pay Rate: $11.00/hour Dependents under 17: 0 Dependents over 17: 1 Step 4 information: none
B-Lewis	Kristen Lewis 840 Daily Hollow Road Bridgewater, VT 05523 802-390-5572 SSN: 076-39-5673 401(k) deduction: 4% Section 125 deduction: $155	Hire Date: 2-3-2020 DOB: 4-6-1960 Position: Office Manager PT/FT: FT, exempt M/S: M Pay Rate: $32,000/year Dependents under 17: 2 Dependents over 17: 1 Step 4 information: none
B-Schwa	Joel Schwartz 55 Maple Farm Way Woodstock, VT 05534 802-463-9985 SSN: 021-34-9876 401(k) deduction: 5% Section 125 deduction: $100	Hire Date: 2-3-2020 DOB: 5-23-1985 Position: Sales PT/FT: FT, exempt M/S: Married/Joint Pay Rate: $24,000/year base plus 3% commission per case sold Dependents under 17: 2 Dependents over 17: 0 Step 4 information: none
B-Prevo	Toni Prevosti 820 Westminster Road Bridgewater, VT 05520 802-555-3456 SSN: 055-22-0443 401(k) deduction: 6% Section 125 deduction: $155	Hire Date: 2-3-2020 DOB: 9-18-1967 Position: Owner/President PT/FT: FT, exempt M/S: Married/Joint Pay Rate: $45,000/year Dependents under 17: 3 Dependents over 17: 2 Step 4 information: none

The departments are as follows:

Department A: Agricultural Workers

Department B: Office Workers

1. You have been hired to start on February 3, 2020, as the new accounting clerk. Your employee number is B-XXXXX, where "B" denotes that you are an office worker and "XXXXX" is the first five letters of your last name. If your last name is fewer than five letters,

<table>
<tr><td colspan="3">

Form **W-4**

Department of the Treasury
Internal Revenue Service
</td><td colspan="3">

Employee's Withholding Certificate

▶ Complete Form W-4 so that your employer can withhold the correct federal income tax from your pay.
▶ Give Form W-4 to your employer.
▶ Your withholding is subject to review by the IRS.
</td><td>

OMB No. 1545-0074

20**20**
</td></tr>
</table>

Step 1:

Enter Personal Information

(a) First name and middle initial	Last name	(b) Social security number

Address

City or town, state, and ZIP code

▶ **Does your name match the name on your social security card?** If not, to ensure you get credit for your earnings, contact SSA at 800-772-1213 or go to *www.ssa.gov*.

(c) ☐ **Single or Married filing separately**
☐ **Married filing jointly** (or Qualifying widow(er))
☐ **Head of household** (Check only if you're unmarried and pay more than half the costs of keeping up a home for yourself and a qualifying individual.)

Complete Steps 2–4 ONLY if they apply to you; otherwise, skip to Step 5. See page 2 for more information on each step, who can claim exemption from withholding, when to use the online estimator, and privacy.

Step 2:

Multiple Jobs or Spouse Works

Complete this step if you (1) hold more than one job at a time, or (2) are married filing jointly and your spouse also works. The correct amount of withholding depends on income earned from all of these jobs.

Do **only one** of the following.

(a) Use the estimator at *www.irs.gov/W4App* for most accurate withholding for this step (and Steps 3–4); **or**

(b) Use the Multiple Jobs Worksheet on page 3 and enter the result in Step 4(c) below for roughly accurate withholding; **or**

(c) If there are only two jobs total, you may check this box. Do the same on Form W-4 for the other job. This option is accurate for jobs with similar pay; otherwise, more tax than necessary may be withheld . . . . . ▶ ☐

TIP: To be accurate, submit a 2020 Form W-4 for all other jobs. If you (or your spouse) have self-employment income, including as an independent contractor, use the estimator.

Complete Steps 3–4(b) on Form W-4 for only ONE of these jobs. Leave those steps blank for the other jobs. (Your withholding will be most accurate if you complete Steps 3–4(b) on the Form W-4 for the highest paying job.)

Step 3:

Claim Dependents

If your income will be $200,000 or less ($400,000 or less if married filing jointly):

Multiply the number of qualifying children under age 17 by $2,000 ▶ $ _____

Multiply the number of other dependents by $500 . . . . ▶ $ _____

Add the amounts above and enter the total here . . . . | 3 | $

Step 4 (optional):

Other Adjustments

(a) **Other income (not from jobs).** If you want tax withheld for other income you expect this year that won't have withholding, enter the amount of other income here. This may include interest, dividends, and retirement income . . . . | 4(a) | $

(b) **Deductions.** If you expect to claim deductions other than the standard deduction and want to reduce your withholding, use the Deductions Worksheet on page 3 and enter the result here . . . . | 4(b) | $

(c) **Extra withholding.** Enter any additional tax you want withheld each **pay period** . | 4(c) | $

Step 5:

Sign Here

Under penalties of perjury, I declare that this certificate, to the best of my knowledge and belief, is true, correct, and complete.

▶ _____
Employee's signature (This form is not valid unless you sign it.)

▶ _____
Date

Employers Only

Employer's name and address	First date of employment	Employer identification number (EIN)

For Privacy Act and Paperwork Reduction Act Notice, see page 3.   Cat. No. 10220Q   Form **W-4** (2020)

Employment Eligibility Verification

Department of Homeland Security

U.S. Citizenship and Immigration Services

USCIS
Form I-9

OMB No. 1615-0047
Expires 10/31/2022

▶**START HERE:** Read instructions carefully before completing this form. The instructions must be available, either in paper or electronically, **during completion of this form. Employers are liable for errors in the completion of this form.**

ANTI-DISCRIMINATION NOTICE: It is illegal to discriminate against work-authorized individuals. Employers **CANNOT** specify which document(s) an employee may present to establish employment authorization and identity. The refusal to hire or continue to employ an individual because the documentation presented has a future expiration date may also constitute illegal discrimination.

Section 1. Employee Information and Attestation *(Employees must complete and sign Section 1 of Form I-9 no later than the **first day of employment**, but not before accepting a job offer.)*

Last Name *(Family Name)*	First Name *(Given Name)*	Middle Initial	Other Last Names Used *(if any)*

Address *(Street Number and Name)*	Apt. Number	City or Town	State	ZIP Code

Date of Birth *(mm/dd/yyyy)*	U.S. Social Security Number	Employee's E-mail Address	Employee's Telephone Number
	☐☐☐ - ☐☐ - ☐☐☐☐		

I am aware that federal law provides for imprisonment and/or fines for false statements or use of false documents in connection with the completion of this form.

I attest, under penalty of perjury, that I am (check one of the following boxes):

☐ 1. A citizen of the United States

☐ 2. A noncitizen national of the United States *(See instructions)*

☐ 3. A lawful permanent resident   (Alien Registration Number/USCIS Number): _____

☐ 4. An alien authorized to work   until (expiration date, if applicable, mm/dd/yyyy): _____
     Some aliens may write "N/A" in the expiration date field. *(See instructions)*

Aliens authorized to work must provide only one of the following document numbers to complete Form I-9:
An Alien Registration Number/USCIS Number OR Form I-94 Admission Number OR Foreign Passport Number.

> QR Code - Section 1
> Do Not Write In This Space

1. Alien Registration Number/USCIS Number: _____

   OR

2. Form I-94 Admission Number: _____

   OR

3. Foreign Passport Number: _____

   Country of Issuance: _____

Signature of Employee	Today's Date *(mm/dd/yyyy)*

Preparer and/or Translator Certification (check one):

☐ I did not use a preparer or translator.   ☐ A preparer(s) and/or translator(s) assisted the employee in completing Section 1.
(Fields below must be completed and signed when preparers and/or translators assist an employee in completing Section 1.)

I attest, under penalty of perjury, that I have assisted in the completion of Section 1 of this form and that to the best of my knowledge the information is true and correct.

Signature of Preparer or Translator	Today's Date *(mm/dd/yyyy)*

Last Name *(Family Name)*	First Name *(Given Name)*

Address *(Street Number and Name)*	City or Town	State	ZIP Code

STOP   *Employer Completes Next Page*   STOP

Employment Eligibility Verification

Department of Homeland Security

U.S. Citizenship and Immigration Services

USCIS

Form I-9

OMB No. 1615-0047
Expires 10/31/2022

Section 2. Employer or Authorized Representative Review and Verification

(Employers or their authorized representative must complete and sign Section 2 within 3 business days of the employee's first day of employment. You must physically examine one document from List A OR a combination of one document from List B and one document from List C as listed on the "Lists of Acceptable Documents.")

Employee Info from Section 1	Last Name *(Family Name)*	First Name *(Given Name)*	M.I.	Citizenship/Immigration Status

List A	OR	List B	AND	List C
Identity and Employment Authorization		**Identity**		**Employment Authorization**

List A	List B	List C
Document Title	Document Title	Document Title
Issuing Authority	Issuing Authority	Issuing Authority
Document Number	Document Number	Document Number
Expiration Date *(if any) (mm/dd/yyyy)*	Expiration Date *(if any) (mm/dd/yyyy)*	Expiration Date *(if any) (mm/dd/yyyy)*
Document Title		
Issuing Authority	Additional Information	QR Code - Sections 2 & 3 Do Not Write In This Space
Document Number		
Expiration Date *(if any) (mm/dd/yyyy)*		
Document Title		
Issuing Authority		
Document Number		
Expiration Date *(if any) (mm/dd/yyyy)*		

Certification: I attest, under penalty of perjury, that (1) I have examined the document(s) presented by the above-named employee, (2) the above-listed document(s) appear to be genuine and to relate to the employee named, and (3) to the best of my knowledge the employee is authorized to work in the United States.

The employee's first day of employment *(mm/dd/yyyy)*: _____   *(See instructions for exemptions)*

Signature of Employer or Authorized Representative	Today's Date *(mm/dd/yyyy)*	Title of Employer or Authorized Representative
Last Name of Employer or Authorized Representative	First Name of Employer or Authorized Representative	Employer's Business or Organization Name

Employer's Business or Organization Address *(Street Number and Name)*	City or Town	State	ZIP Code

Section 3. Reverification and Rehires *(To be completed and signed by employer or authorized representative.)*

A. New Name *(if applicable)*			B. Date of Rehire *(if applicable)*
Last Name *(Family Name)*	First Name *(Given Name)*	Middle Initial	Date *(mm/dd/yyyy)*

C. If the employee's previous grant of employment authorization has expired, provide the information for the document or receipt that establishes continuing employment authorization in the space provided below.

Document Title	Document Number	Expiration Date *(if any) (mm/dd/yyyy)*

I attest, under penalty of perjury, that to the best of my knowledge, this employee is authorized to work in the United States, and if the employee presented document(s), the document(s) I have examined appear to be genuine and to relate to the individual.

Signature of Employer or Authorized Representative	Today's Date *(mm/dd/yyyy)*	Name of Employer or Authorized Representative

Form I-9   10/21/2019

Page 2 of 3

LISTS OF ACCEPTABLE DOCUMENTS
All documents must be UNEXPIRED

Employees may present one selection from List A
or a combination of one selection from List B and one selection from List C.

LIST A		LIST B		LIST C
Documents that Establish Both Identity and Employment Authorization	OR	**Documents that Establish Identity**	AND	**Documents that Establish Employment Authorization**
1. U.S. Passport or U.S. Passport Card		1. Driver's license or ID card issued by a State or outlying possession of the United States provided it contains a photograph or information such as name, date of birth, gender, height, eye color, and address		1. A Social Security Account Number card, unless the card includes one of the following restrictions: (1) NOT VALID FOR EMPLOYMENT (2) VALID FOR WORK ONLY WITH INS AUTHORIZATION (3) VALID FOR WORK ONLY WITH DHS AUTHORIZATION
2. Permanent Resident Card or Alien Registration Receipt Card (Form I-551)				
3. Foreign passport that contains a temporary I-551 stamp or temporary I-551 printed notation on a machine-readable immigrant visa		2. ID card issued by federal, state or local government agencies or entities, provided it contains a photograph or information such as name, date of birth, gender, height, eye color, and address		
4. Employment Authorization Document that contains a photograph (Form I-766)				2. Certification of report of birth issued by the Department of State (Forms DS-1350, FS-545, FS-240)
		3. School ID card with a photograph		

5. For a nonimmigrant alien authorized to work for a specific employer because of his or her status:
 a. Foreign passport; and
 b. Form I-94 or Form I-94A that has the following:
   (1) The same name as the passport; and
   (2) An endorsement of the alien's nonimmigrant status as long as that period of endorsement has not yet expired and the proposed employment is not in conflict with any restrictions or limitations identified on the form.
		4. Voter's registration card		3. Original or certified copy of birth certificate issued by a State, county, municipal authority, or territory of the United States bearing an official seal

		5. U.S. Military card or draft record		
		6. Military dependent's ID card		
		7. U.S. Coast Guard Merchant Mariner Card		4. Native American tribal document
				5. U.S. Citizen ID Card (Form I-197)
		8. Native American tribal document		6. Identification Card for Use of Resident Citizen in the United States (Form I-179)
		9. Driver's license issued by a Canadian government authority		
		For persons under age 18 who are unable to present a document listed above:		7. Employment authorization document issued by the Department of Homeland Security
6. Passport from the Federated States of Micronesia (FSM) or the Republic of the Marshall Islands (RMI) with Form I-94 or Form I-94A indicating nonimmigrant admission under the Compact of Free Association Between the United States and the FSM or RMI		10. School record or report card		
		11. Clinic, doctor, or hospital record		
		12. Day-care or nursery school record		

Examples of many of these documents appear in the Handbook for Employers (M-274).

Refer to the instructions for more information about acceptable receipts.

Source: United States Citizenship and Immigration Services.

use the first few letters of your first name to complete the employee number. Your Social Security number is 555-55-5555, and you are full-time, nonexempt, and paid at a rate of $34,000 per year. You have elected to contribute 2 percent of your gross pay to your 401(k) and will have $100 per pay period for Section 125. Complete the W-4 and the I-9 to start your own employee file. You are single with only one job. You live at 1644 Smitten Road, Woodstock, VT 05001. You will not be claiming anything for section 4 of the W-4. Your phone number is (555) 555-5555. Your date of birth is 01/01/1991. You are a citizen of the United States and provide a Vermont driver's license #88110009 expiring 01/01/23 in addition to your Social Security card for verification of your identity. Mary Shangraw verified the information for the company. Prevosti Farms and Sugarhouse is located at 820 Westminster Road, Bridgewater, VT, 05520. Prevosti has an EIN of 22-6654454.

2. Complete the employee information form for each employee. Enter the pay rate earnings for each employee.

Employee Earnings Register

NAME					Hire Date				Dependent child <17			
ADDRESS					Date of Birth				Dependent other			
CITY/STATE/ZIP					Position		PT / FT		Step 4a W-4 Info			
TELEPHONE					Filing Status				Step 4b W-4 Info			
SOCIAL SECURITY NUMBER					Exempt/Nonexempt				Step 4c W-4 Info			
					Pay Rate			Hr / Wk / Mo / Yr				

Period Ended	Hrs Worked	Reg Pay	OT Pay	Comm	Gross Pay	Social Sec Tax	Medicare	Fed Inc Tax	State W/H Tax	Sect 125	401(k)	Total Deduc	Net Pay	YTD

Source: United States Citizenship and Immigration Services.

EMPLOYEE EARNING RECORD

NAME	_____	Hire Date	_____
ADDRESS	_____	Date of Birth	_____
CITY/STATE/ZIP	_____	Exempt/Nonexempt	_____
TELEPHONE	_____	Married/Single	_____
SOCIAL SECURITY NUMBER	_____	Pay Rate	_____
POSITION	_____		_____

Period Ended	Hrs Worked	Reg Pay	OT Pay	Holiday	Comm	Gross Pay	Ins	401(k)	Taxable Pay for Federal	Taxable Pay for FICA

Taxable Wages for Federal	Taxable Wages for FICA	Federal W/H	Social Sec. Tax	Medicare Tax	State Inc. Tax	Total Deduc	Net Pay	YTD Net Pay	YTD Gross Pay

EMPLOYEE EARNING RECORD

NAME _____ Hire Date _____

ADDRESS _____ Date of Birth _____

CITY/STATE/ZIP _____ Exempt/Nonexempt _____

TELEPHONE _____ Married/Single _____

SOCIAL SECURITY NUMBER _____ Pay Rate _____

POSITION _____

Period Ended	Hrs Worked	Reg Pay	OT Pay	Holiday	Comm	Gross Pay	Ins	401(k)	Taxable Pay for Federal	Taxable Pay for FICA

Taxable Wages for Federal	Taxable Wages for FICA	Federal W/H	Social Sec. Tax	Medicare Tax	State Inc. Tax	Total Deduc	Net Pay	YTD Net Pay	YTD Gross Pay

EMPLOYEE EARNING RECORD

NAME _____ Hire Date _____

ADDRESS _____ Date of Birth _____

CITY/STATE/ZIP _____ Exempt/Nonexempt _____

TELEPHONE _____ Married/Single _____

SOCIAL SECURITY NUMBER _____ Pay Rate _____

POSITION _____

Period Ended	Hrs Worked	Reg Pay	OT Pay	Holiday	Comm	Gross Pay	Ins	401(k)	Taxable Wages for Federal	Taxable Wages for FICA

Taxable Wages for Federal	Taxable Wages for FICA	Federal W/H	Social Sec. Tax	Medicare Tax	State Inc. Tax	Total Deduc	Net Pay	YTD Net Pay	YTD Gross Pay

EMPLOYEE EARNING RECORD

NAME _____   Hire Date _____

ADDRESS _____   Date of Birth _____

CITY/STATE/ZIP _____   Exempt/Nonexempt _____

TELEPHONE _____   Married/Single _____

SOCIAL SECURITY NUMBER _____   Pay Rate _____

POSITION _____

Period Ended	Hrs Worked	Reg Pay	OT Pay	Holiday	Comm	Gross Pay	Ins	401(k)	Taxable Pay for Federal	Taxable Pay for FICA

Taxable Wages for Federal	Taxable Wages for FICA	Federal W/H	Social Sec. Tax	Medicare Tax	State Inc. Tax	Total Deduc	Net Pay	YTD Net Pay	YTD Gross Pay

EMPLOYEE EARNING RECORD

NAME _____   Hire Date _____

ADDRESS _____   Date of Birth _____

CITY/STATE/ZIP _____   Exempt/Nonexempt _____

TELEPHONE _____   Married/Single _____

SOCIAL SECURITY NUMBER _____   Pay Rate _____

POSITION _____

Period Ended	Hrs Worked	Reg Pay	OT Pay	Holiday	Comm	Gross Pay	Ins	401(k)	Taxable Pay for Federal	Taxable Pay for FICA

Taxable Wages for Federal	Taxable Wages for FICA	Federal W/H	Social Sec. Tax	Medicare Tax	State Inc. Tax	Total Deduc	Net Pay	YTD Net Pay	YTD Gross Pay

EMPLOYEE EARNING RECORD

NAME _____   Hire Date _____

ADDRESS _____   Date of Birth _____

CITY/STATE/ZIP _____   Exempt/Nonexempt _____

TELEPHONE _____   Married/Single _____

SOCIAL SECURITY NUMBER _____   Pay Rate _____

POSITION _____   _____

Period Ended	Hrs Worked	Reg Pay	OT Pay	Holiday	Comm	Gross Pay	Ins	401(k)	Taxable Pay for Federal	Taxable Pay for FICA

Taxable Wages for Federal	Taxable Wages for FICA	Federal W/H	Social Sec. Tax	Medicare Tax	State Inc. Tax	Total Deduc	Net Pay	YTD Net Pay	YTD Gross Pay

EMPLOYEE EARNING RECORD

NAME _____   Hire Date _____

ADDRESS _____   Date of Birth _____

CITY/STATE/ZIP _____   Exempt/Nonexempt _____

TELEPHONE _____   Married/Single _____

SOCIAL SECURITY NUMBER _____   Pay Rate _____

POSITION _____   _____

Period Ended	Hrs Worked	Reg Pay	OT Pay	Holiday	Comm	Gross Pay	Ins	401(k)	Taxable Pay for Federal	Taxable Pay for FICA

Taxable Wages for Federal	Taxable Wages for FICA	Federal W/H	Social Sec. Tax	Medicare Tax	State Inc. Tax	Total Deduc	Net Pay	YTD Net Pay	YTD Gross Pay

EMPLOYEE EARNING RECORD

NAME _____   Hire Date _____

ADDRESS _____   Date of Birth _____

CITY/STATE/ZIP _____   Exempt/Nonexempt _____

TELEPHONE _____   Married/Single _____

SOCIAL SECURITY NUMBER _____   Pay Rate _____

POSITION _____

Period Ended	Hrs Worked	Reg Pay	OT Pay	Holiday	Comm	Gross Pay	Ins	401(k)	Taxable Pay for Federal	Taxable Pay for FICA

Taxable Wages for Federal	Taxable Wages for FICA	Federal W/H	Social Sec. Tax	Medicare Tax	State Inc. Tax	Total Deduc	Net Pay	YTD Net Pay	YTD Gross Pay

Answers to Stop & Check Exercises

What's in the File?
1. a, b, d, e
2. b
3. d
4. a
5. c

Who Are You?
1. Student answers will vary. One possible way to prove both identity and employment is a current U.S. passport. Alternatively, a current state-issued driver's license and a Social Security card will work for the purposes of the I-9.
2. Student answers will vary. When evaluating the earnings of more than one job, the breakdown of includable amount by pay period is often overlooked.
3. Student answers will vary. Examples of statutory employees include the following: A driver who distributes beverages (other than milk) or meat, vegetable, fruit, or bakery products or who picks up and delivers laundry or dry cleaning if the driver is a single company's agent or is paid on commission. A full-time life insurance sales agent whose principal business activity is selling life insurance or annuity contracts, or both, primarily for one life insurance company. An individual who works at home on materials or goods that a company supplies and that must be returned to that company or a designated agent in accordance with furnished specifications for the work to be done. A full-time traveling or city salesperson who works on a single company's behalf and turns in orders from wholesalers, retailers, contractors, or operators of hotels, restaurants, or other similar establishments. The goods sold must be merchandise for resale or supplies for use in the buyer's business operation. The work performed for that single company must be the salesperson's principal business activity.

Exempt vs. Nonexempt

1. Exempt workers are exempt from the overtime provisions of FLSA. Exempt workers tend to be employees in a company's managerial or other leadership functions, in which they may need to work more than 40 hours per week to complete their tasks. Exempt workers usually receive a fixed salary per period that is not based on the number of hours worked. Nonexempt workers tend to be compensated on an hourly basis and often do not have managerial or leadership responsibilities. It should be noted that some nonexempt workers do have managerial or leadership responsibilities and may receive a fixed salary; however, these particular employees are covered by the overtime provisions of FLSA.
2. c (40 hours)
3. The leased employee is a common-law employee of the firm, whereas the temporary employee is an employee of the temporary agency.

Worker Facts

1. Hourly workers and nonexempt workers are protected by FLSA
2. Exempt workers receive a fixed amount of money and generally direct the actions of other employees; nonexempt workers are eligible for overtime and generally have their work directed by a manager.
3. Commission workers are typically tied to sales completed by the individual; piece-rate pay is determined by the number of pieces the employee completes during a shift or period.
4. Student answers may vary but should include: minimum hourly rate is set by the U.S. Federal government. Minimum wage rates can and do vary per state, and different parts of the same state may have different minimum wages. The minimum wage may differ from a "living wage", which is an amount needed to meet basic subsistence needs. A calculating tool was provided in the chapter for discussion on various location living wages.

Who Does Which Job?

Student answers will vary. The answer should reflect a clear separation of duties, cross-training, rotation of tasks, and security protocols.

Internal Controls and Audits

1. b
2. c

Destroy and Terminate

1. Paper payroll records should be shredded or burned. Computer records should be purged from the server and all other storage devices.
2. Charlie should receive his final pay on October 11, and no later than October 12. His employer is not required to provide him with a severance package, although he may be eligible for his accrued vacation pay.

Chapter Three

Gross Pay Computation

Two important terms in payroll accounting are gross pay and net pay. *Gross pay* is the total amount of wages earned before deducting amounts for taxes or other deductions. *Net pay* is the amount of money the employee actually receives in a paycheck after all taxes and other deductions have been subtracted. In this chapter, we will focus on computing gross pay.

The calculation of an employee's gross pay is the first step for payroll processing. Employee pay may be calculated in different ways. *Hourly* employees are paid for each hour, or fraction thereof, that they work on a given day. Salaried employees are broken into two classifications based on FLSA legislation: *exempt* and *nonexempt*. Salaried exempt employees receive pay based on the job they perform, regardless of the number of hours it takes to perform the job. Salaried nonexempt employees may receive both *salary* and *overtime*. Another class of employees works on a *commission* basis, which means that some or all of their wages are based on sales revenue. The final classification is *piece-rate* employees. Typically found in manufacturing environments, employees are paid based upon the number of pieces completed during a work shift.

LEARNING OBJECTIVES

After studying Chapter 3, you should be able to:

LO 3-1 Analyze Minimum Wage Pay for Nonexempt Workers

LO 3-2 Compute Gross Pay for Different Pay Bases

LO 3-3 Calculate Pay Based on Hours and Fractions of Hours

LO 3-4 Calculate Overtime in Various Situations

LO 3-5 Create a Payroll Register

LO 3-6 Apply Combination Pay Methods

LO 3-7 Explain Special Pay Situations

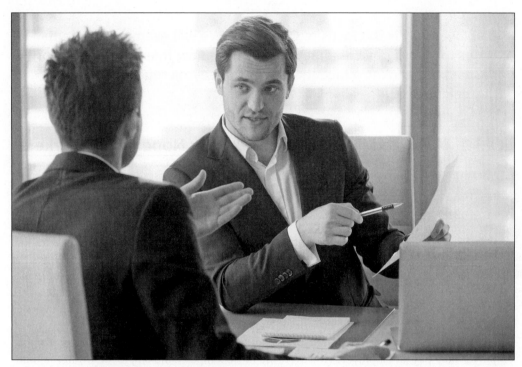

Aleksandr Davydov/fizkes/123RF

The Minimum Wage vs. a Living Wage

The Fair Labor Standards Act (FLSA) established a minimum wage and standard weekly working hours to protect workers. The federal standard for regular weekly working hours is 40, and the act states that employees who work in excess of 40 hours per week must receive overtime wages of at least one and a half times their regular hourly wage. The Federal minimum wage has been $7.25 per hour since 2009.

In early 2020, the managers of Jackson County, Missouri, faced the issue of the difference between the wages it paid to its employees and earnings of non-governmental employees in the county, based on a study conducted in 2017. County managers realized that employees were leaving government positions because of a relatively low wage that did not provide enough income for their employees to meet their financial needs. The current minimum wage in the state of Missouri is $9.45 per hour. However, many residents of Jackson County live in Kansas City, where the minimum wage does not provide enough to meet financial needs. The solution, as decided by the county manager, was to raise County employee wages to $12.50 per hour immediately, which is approximately a 17 percent pay increase for the employees alone. For the county, the cost will be nearly $9 million for compensation costs alone.

The quandary about federal, state, and living wages is one that employers face in many parts of the country. Many cities, counties, and states have a minimum wage that exceeds the federal minimum wage, sometimes by a large margin. The conundrum occurs when the employer must choose between profits and employees. In the case of Jackson County, the additional money required to increase employee compensation would not be as simple as other employers because it is a government entity. The government budget must be examined and choices made to pay for the wage increase without raising taxes, which would cause other problems for county residents.

(Sources: KSHB)

Employee pay is the focus of Chapter 3. We will examine different bases for gross pay computations, discuss how these compensation bases differ and introduce the use of the payroll register as a tool in pay calculation.

LO 3-1 Analyze Minimum Wage Pay for Nonexempt Workers

Wavebreakmedia/iStock/Getty Images

Two primary classifications of employees exist: exempt and nonexempt. These classifications refer to the provisions of the Fair Labor Standards Act (FLSA). The FLSA provisions protect nonexempt employees, including clerical, factory, and other nonmanagerial employees. Nonexempt employees are operative workers whose workdays may vary in duration, whose tasks do not meet the U.S. Department of Labor guidelines for exempt employees, and who do not generally have supervisory or managerial duties. Exempt employees include employees who meet the U.S. Department of Labor guidelines for exempt classification, which includes job titles such as Department Supervisor or Warehouse Manager.

For hourly workers, FLSA contains wage provisions that stipulate the *minimum wage* an employer may pay an employee. However, the law exempts some employers from the minimum wage requirements. According to the U.S. Department of Labor, the following conditions exempt an employer from paying the federal minimum wage:

- Firms that do not engage in interstate commerce as part of their business production.
- Firms with less than $500,000 of annual business volume.

Note that certain firms are always covered by the FLSA provisions, regardless of their participation in interstate commerce or annual business volume. These businesses include hospitals, schools for mentally or physically disabled or gifted children, preschools, schools of any level, and governmental agencies. Under FLSA section 3(y), law enforcement and fire protection employees may have specified work periods ranging from 7 to 28 days, during which employees would be paid for overtime only after a predefined number of working hours.

FLSA was modified in 1974 to include explicit provisions about domestic workers. Since 1974, minimum wage provisions cover domestic service workers, such as nannies and chauffeurs. Note that the 1974 modification specifically excluded occasional babysitters and employees who provide domestic companion services for the elderly. In 2015, the U.S. Congress further amended FLSA to include caregivers and other direct care employees who provide in-home companionship services as being subject to the federal or state minimum wage, whichever is higher. It should be noted that domestic workers who reside on the employer's premises permanently or for an extended time period are exempt from FLSA provisions.

> For live-in domestic service workers who are essentially on duty 24 hours per day, the U.S. Department of Labor has issued a sleep-time requirement of 8 hours per day, of which 5 hours must be consecutive, and adequate sleeping facilities must be provided. According to Fact Sheet 79D, if the employee's sleep time is interrupted for any reason, the employee must be compensated for that time. (Source: DOL)

Minimum Wage

An important consideration with the minimum wage provision of the FLSA is the existence of separate tiers of the minimum wage. Wages for *tipped employees* are lower than those of nontipped employees. Federal wage and hour laws as of 2020 stipulate a federal minimum wage of $7.25 and a minimum hourly wage of $2.13 for tipped employees. States may enact additional minimum wage laws to address the specific economic needs of their population. This minimizes federal legislative needs to revisit the minimum wage annually.

Most American nonexempt employees receive a wage higher than the federal minimum wage, and the majority of minimum wage employees work in the restaurant industry. Certain states such as California and Washington permit municipalities to enact ordinances mandating a higher minimum wage. However, other states such as Iowa and Florida have state constitutions that prohibit cities from instituting higher minimum wages. The challenge for employers, especially for those who operate in multiple areas, is to understand the minimum wage provisions for each location and how they affect the business and the employees. As of 2019, two-thirds of Americans favor an increase in the minimum wage to $15 per hour. (Source: Pew Research Center)

As of 2020, 29 states and the District of Columbia have minimum wage rates that are higher than the federal minimum wage. Note that five states have a minimum wage that is less than the FLSA minimum wage or is not specified. When the minimum wage is not specified, the federal minimum wage applies. These lower minimum wages may be paid by employers who are not subject to FLSA provisions because they do not conduct interstate commerce. A map depicting minimum wages for 2020 is shown in Figure 3-1, and the details of specific minimum wage rates are shown in Table 3-1. Examples involving employee pay with different minimum wages follow.

EXAMPLE 1: STATE MINIMUM WAGE LOWER THAN FEDERAL MINIMUM WAGE

Don Mayer works for a Georgia employer that conducts no interstate commerce and whose annual business volume is less than $300,000. He is a janitor in a manufacturing plant and earns the minimum wage for Georgia. How much would he earn for a 40-hour pay period?

Georgia minimum wage: $5.15 per hour

40 hours × $5.15/hour = $206

Because the employer does not meet the requirements that would force it to pay Don the federal minimum wage, it may pay the state's minimum wage.

FIGURE 3-1
Minimum Wage Hourly Rates for 2020

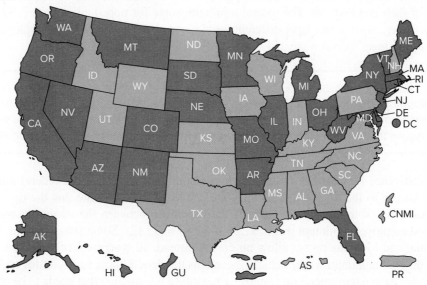

(Source: U.S. Department of Labor, 2020)

Legend: The states highlighted in dark blue have minimum wage amounts that are higher than the federal minimum wage of $7.25 per hour.

TABLE 3-1

Minimum Wage Hourly Rates by State

AK	$10.19	IA	$7.25	MS	None†	PA	$7.25
AL	None†	ID	7.25	MT	$8.65*	RI	10.50
AR	10.00	IL	9.25	NC	7.25	SC	None†
AZ	12.00	IN	7.25	ND	7.25	SD	9.30
CA	12.00*	KS	7.25	NE	9.00	TN	None†
CO	12.00	KY	7.25	NH	7.25	TX	7.25
CT	11.00	LA	None†	NJ	11.00	UT	7.25
D.C.	14.00	MA	12.75	NM	9.00	VA	7.25
DE	9.25	MD	11.00	NV	8.25*	VT	10.96
FL	8.56	ME	12.00	NY	11.80*	WA	13.50*
GA	5.15†	MI	9.65	OH	8.70*	WI	7.25
HI	10.10	MN	10.00*	OK	7.25*	WV	8.75
		MO	9.45	OR	11.25	WY	5.15†

Source: U.S. Department of Labor, 2020.

*These states have stipulations that change the minimum wage based on different variables. Consult the state's revenue office for specific details.

†In states with no minimum wage or one lower than the federal minimum wage, the federal minimum wage prevails as long as they meet FLSA revenue and interstate commerce thresholds.

> **EXAMPLE 2: STATE MINIMUM WAGE HIGHER THAN THE FEDERAL MINIMUM WAGE**
>
> Wendy Roberts is a minimum wage worker in the state of Washington. She works for a national restaurant chain and has a standard 37.5-hour workweek. How much would she earn during a 75-hour, two-week pay period?
>
> Washington minimum wage: $13.50 per hour
>
> 75 hours × $13.50/hour = $1,012.50
>
> Because Wendy works for a national chain restaurant, it is safe to assume that the company conducts interstate commerce and earns more than $500,000 in revenues per year. She would be compensated at the state minimum wage in any case.

Tipped Employees

Workers in professions such as waiters, waitresses, bartenders, food service workers, and some hotel service personnel may receive an hourly wage less than the minimum wage rates listed in Table 3-1. The rationale for the decreased minimum wage is that these employees have the opportunity to earn tips (***tipped wages***) from patrons of the establishments as a regular part of their employment. The federal minimum wage for tipped employees is $2.13 per hour; however, many states have different regulations about how much the employee must earn in tips to meet federal wage and hour laws.

> In 2018, voters in Washington, DC, approved Initiative 77, which will gradually increase the tipped wage through 2026 until it meets the minimum wage for the area. Initiative 77 was a controversial measure because of the growing restaurant economy and wage gap issues that the measure was intended to remedy. (Source: *Vox, Washington Post*)

The difference between the tipped employee minimum wage and the federal minimum wage is known as the ***tip credit***. Federal wage and hour laws mandate that the tip credit is $5.12 per hour. Note that the tip credit is the difference between the minimum wage and the tipped employee minimum wage ($7.25 − $2.13 = $5.12). Some states such as Alaska, California, and Montana do not allow tip credit; instead, all workers receive the prevailing federal or local minimum wage. Table 3-2 contains the details about tip credit for each state. Some states have requirements on employers regarding information that needs to be obtained prior to applying a tip credit. For example, North Carolina requires a monthly or per pay period affidavit from employees of the total amount of tips received.

TABLE 3-2
Table of 2020 Minimum Hourly Wages for Tipped Employees by State

Jurisdiction	Basic Combined Cash and Tip Minimum Wage Rate	Maximum Tip Credit Against Minimum Wage	Minimum Cash Wage	Definition of Tipped Employee by Minimum Tips Received (monthly unless otherwise specified)
Federal: Fair Labor Standards Act (FLSA)	$7.25	$5.12	$2.13	More than $30
State Law Does Not Allow Tip Credit				
Note: The minimum rate is the same for tipped and non-tipped employees				
Alaska			10.19	
California 25 or fewer employees			12.00	
26 or more employees			13.00	
Minnesota:				
Large employer Annual receipts > $500,000 per year			10.00	
Small employer Annual receipts < $500,000 per year			8.15	
Montana:				
Business with gross annual sales exceeding $110,000			8.65	
Business with gross annual sales of $110,000 or less			4.00	
Nevada			8.25	With no health insurance benefits provided by the employer and received by the employee
			7.25	With health insurance benefits provided by the employer and received by the employee
Oregon			11.25	
Washington			13.50	
State Law Allows Tip Credit				
Arizona	12.00	3.00	9.00	Not specified
Arkansas	10.00	7.37	2.63	More than $20
Colorado	12.00	3.02	8.98	More than $30
Connecticut:	11.00			At least $10 weekly for full-time employees or $2.00 daily for part-time in hotels and restaurants. Not specified for other industries.
Hotel, restaurant		4.62	6.38	
Bartenders who customarily receive tips		2.77	8.23	
Delaware	9.25	7.02	2.23	More than $30
District of Columbia (D.C.)[2]	14.00	9.55	4.35	Not specified
Florida	8.56	3.02	5.54	
Hawaii	10.10	0.75	9.35	More than $20
Idaho	7.25	3.90	3.35	More than $30
Illinois	9.25	40% of applicable minimum wage (3.70)	5.55	$20
Indiana	7.25	5.12	2.13	Not specified
Iowa	7.25	2.90	4.35	More than $30
Kansas	7.25	5.12	2.13	More than $20
Kentucky	7.25	5.12	2.13	More than $30

(continued)

Jurisdiction	Basic Combined Cash and Tip Minimum Wage Rate	Maximum Tip Credit Against Minimum Wage	Minimum Cash Wage	Definition of Tipped Employee by Minimum Tips Received (monthly unless otherwise specified)
Maine	12.00	6.00	6.00	More than $30
Maryland	11.00	7.37	3.63	More than $30
Massachusetts	12.75	7.80	4.95	More than $20
Michigan	9.65	5.98	3.67	Not specified
Missouri	9.45	50% (4.72)	4.73	Not specified
Nebraska	9.00	6.87	2.13	Not specified
New Hampshire	7.25	55% of applicable minimum wage (3.99)	45% of applicable minimum wage (3.26)	More than $30
New Jersey	11.00	7.87	3.13	Not specified
New Mexico	9.00	6.65	2.35	More than $30
New York	See website[3]			Not specified
North Carolina	7.25	5.12	2.13	More than $20
North Dakota	7.25	33% of applicable minimum wage (2.39)	4.86	More than $30
Ohio: *Applies to employees of businesses with annual gross receipts of greater than $305,000 per year.*	8.70	4.35	4.35	More than $30
Oklahoma	7.25	5.12	2.13	Not specified
Pennsylvania	7.25	4.42	2.83	More than $30
Rhode Island	10.50	6.61	3.89	Not specified
South Carolina			2.13	Not specified
South Dakota	9.30	50% (4.65)	4.65	More than $35
Tennessee			2.13	
Texas	7.25	5.12	2.13	More than $20
Utah	7.25	5.12	2.13	More than $30
Vermont: *Employees in hotels, motels, tourist places, and restaurants who customarily and regularly receive >$120/ month in tips for direct and personal customer service*	10.96	5.46	5.46	More than $120
Virginia	7.25	5.12	2.13	Not specified
West Virginia	8.75	70% (6.13)	2.62	Not specified
Wisconsin	7.25	4.92	2.33	Not specified
Wyoming	7.25	5.12	2.13	More than $30

Source: U.S. Department of Labor, 2020.

[2] As of July 1, 2017, in Washington, DC, the minimum cash tip will increase in increments.

[3] See https://labor.ny.gov/formsdocs/factsheets/pdfs/p717.pdf. Note: States not listed fall under FLSA minimum cash paid rate at $2.13/hour.

EXAMPLE: TIPPED EMPLOYEE IN OKLAHOMA, MINIMUM WAGE MET

Abigail Hansford is a tipped employee in Stillwater, Oklahoma. During a 40-hour work-week and pay period, she earned $220 in tips.

Hourly tipped minimum wage: $2.13 per hour

$2.13 per hour × 40 hours = $85.20 in wages

Tips earned: $220

Total wages and tips earned during the pay period:

$220 + $85.20 = $305.20

The federal and state minimum wage is $7.25 per hour. The minimum wage for a 40-hour workweek:

$7.25 per hours × 40 hours = $290

Therefore, Abigail has earned more than the federal and state minimum wage. The employer does not need to contribute to Abigail's pay during the pay period.

As of mid-2019, the debate of minimum wage for gig economy workers changed when the federal government ruled that certain service workers, such as domestic cleaners and drivers for companies like Uber and Lyft, were actually independent contractors because they provided their own work equipment in the form of cleaning supplies and vehicles. The federal Department of Labor further stipulated that the employers did not specify the procedures for job completion, such as cleaning methods or driving routes. (Source: *The New York Times*)

EXAMPLE: TIPPED EMPLOYEE IN RHODE ISLAND, MINIMUM WAGE *NOT* MET

Grayson Jeffries is a tipped waiter in Warwick, Rhode Island. During a 40-hour work and pay period, he earned $75 in tips.

Hourly tipped minimum wage: $3.89 per hour

$3.89 per hour × 40 hours = $155.60 in wages

Tips earned: $75

Total wages and tips earned during the pay period:
$155.60 + 75 = $230.60

The state minimum wage for Rhode Island is $10.50 per hour. During a 40-hour workweek and pay period, the minimum pay for an employee is

$10.50 per hour × 40 hours = $420.00

Because Grayson has not earned the minimum wage, the employer must pay the difference between the earned wages and tips and the minimum wage:

$420.00 − $230.60 = $189.40 to be added to Grayson's pay by the employer to bring his pay to the minimum wage.

Pay Your Employees Correctly

Stop & Check

1. Heather Pai works as a clerk receiving minimum wage for a pharmaceutical company in North Carolina that pays its employees on a biweekly basis. She is classified as nonexempt, and her standard workweek is 40 hours. During a two-week period, she worked 88 hours and received $638.00. Was Heather's pay correct? Explain.

2. Tony Dupuis works as a publisher's representative receiving minimum wage in Maryland. He works 39.5 hours during a one-week period. How much should he receive?

3. Mary Lindquist is a temporary worker for a popular radio station, which is a large employer in Minnesota. She receives the minimum wage and works 32 hours per week. How much should she receive for two weeks of work?

4. Tony Hardwick is a tipped minimum wage worker for a Minnesota company with $615,000 in annual revenues. He worked 75 hours during a biweekly pay period, in which he earned $1,000 in tips. What is his gross pay (excluding tips)?

Kzenon/Shutterstock

LO 3-2   Compute Gross Pay for Different Pay Bases

Salaried Workers

Employees in highly technical, qualification-driven positions within a company are generally classified as exempt from FLSA regulations. Accountants, engineers, lawyers, managers, and supervisors are included in this classification. Section 13(a)(1) of the FLSA defines the eligible exempt employees in the following job descriptions: executives, administrative personnel, professionals, and outside sales representatives. Section 13(a)(17) of the FLSA also allows specific computer-related employees to be included in the classification of salaried workers. The FLSA provides a minimum wage for salaried workers of not less than $684 per week, per the Final Rule that went into effect as of January 2020. In addition, the Final Rule, according to 29 CFR 778.114, stipulates an employer may use the fluctuating workweek method if the employee works hours that vary from week to week and receives a fixed salary as straight time compensation. The hourly rate is then computed by dividing the salary amount by the number of hours actually worked. (Source: U.S. DOL)

> Companies often use a technique called "job leveling" to determine salaries for exempt employees. This technique uses job analysis to define common types of responsibilities in an effort to generate pay grades. Although the intent of this technique is to determine objective pay criteria, this practice has led to staffing imbalances, multiple titles for similar jobs, and issues with employee morale. Solutions to the job-leveling issue include a comparison of each employee's duties and a holistic view of the actual size of the job. Once these variables are measured, the job is compared to similar roles in the industry to determine appropriate compensation. (Source: SHRM)

The division of salaried workers into exempt and nonexempt statuses has historically correlated with company policy more than legal requirements. However, in 2015 the U.S. Department of Labor began to investigate employee classifications to ensure compliance with FLSA stipulations. IRS Form SS-8 is designed to help employers determine the proper classification (employee or independent contractor) under the law.

For nonexempt salaried workers, the employment contract entered into between the employee and the employer determines at what level of hourly work they would receive overtime pay. Many salaried nonexempt worker contracts, when specified, are for 45 hours per week. If the contract stipulates that 45 hours per week is the standard workweek for a salaried, nonexempt employee, then the employee is still subject to FLSA overtime rules for hours worked past 40. For the purpose of this textbook, the standard workweek is five days out of a seven-day week.

> ### EXAMPLE: SALARIED, NONEXEMPT EMPLOYEE
> Brad Hammond, a salaried, nonexempt employee, earns $1,000 per week and has a standard 45-hour workweek.
>
> Hourly compensation: $1,000/45 hours = $22.22 per hour
> Overtime rate = $22.22 × 1.5 = $33.33 per hour
>
> Because this employee is classified as nonexempt according to FLSA guidelines, the employee is subject to overtime compensation, and the hourly rate is needed to compute overtime pay.
>
> For the same salaried, nonexempt employee, if the contract between employee and employer stated that all hours *exceeding* 45 were considered for overtime, then the individual would need to work 45.25 hours or more in the week to qualify for overtime.
>
> However, *if* the contract stated that only 40 hours were required before the overtime rates are applied, then the 5 hours would be paid at overtime rates.
>
> **Note:** A salaried *exempt* worker would be paid $1,000 per week regardless of the number of hours worked.

Employers may not prorate a salaried worker's pay when the number of hours worked is fewer than the contractual hour requirement. An exception to this would be time away from work in accordance with the employer's sick or vacation policy. The company would allow employees to take paid time off under either of these programs to supplement their missed wages. Companies may also offer salaried employees the option of leave without pay for missed days; however, contractual hours covered under leave without pay must be documented and signed by both a manager and the employee.

Salary Translation to Hourly Rates

The calculation of gross pay for salaried employees depends on the firm's choice of pay periods. An employee's gross pay is determined by dividing the annual pay by the number of pay periods in a year. For instance, if a firm paid employees on a monthly basis, then the salary calculation would be $\frac{1}{12}$ of the yearly amount. It is occasionally necessary to determine the hourly rate for salaried employees. To get the hourly rate, you would use the following equation:

$$\text{Hourly rate} = \frac{\text{Annual amount}}{\text{Total hours worked per year}}$$

To arrive at the total number of hours worked per year, multiply the number of weeks in a year (52) by the number of hours worked in a standard workweek without overtime.

$$\text{Hourly rate} = \frac{\text{Annual salary}}{\text{Number of hours in a standard worksheet} \times 52 \text{ weeks/year}}$$

Because the calculation of overtime, holiday, or vacation time for salaried workers could be based upon the hourly rate of the individual, knowing how to calculate that amount will enable accurate pay.

EXAMPLE

Jackie Ainsley earns a salary of $60,000 per year for ABD Industries. ABD Industries pays its employees on a monthly basis.

Gross pay = $60,000 per year/12 months = <u>$5,000 per month</u>

If she were a nonexempt employee, it would become necessary to calculate her hourly rate. When calculating the hourly rate, using the correct number of hours in a regular workweek is critical in determining the overtime pay rate. Note the following examples computing the hourly rate using different regular workweeks.

Number of Hours in the Regular Workweek	$\dfrac{\text{Annual salary}}{\text{Number of hours} \times 52 \text{ weeks}}$	Hourly Rate
40	$\dfrac{60{,}000}{(40 \times 52)}$	$28.85
37.5	$\dfrac{60{,}000}{(37.5 \times 52)}$	$30.77
35	$\dfrac{60{,}000}{(35 \times 52)}$	$32.97

What happens if the salaried employee decides to take unpaid leave during a pay period? That amount must be deducted from the gross pay amount. In the case of unpaid leave, the amount of time taken and the number of regular hours in the pay period are the major factors.

EXAMPLE: UNPAID LEAVE

Michelle Barre wants to take two extra days off around a holiday but has no paid time off remaining for the year. ABD Industries pays Michelle on a biweekly basis, and there are 80 hours in a pay period. At 8 hours per day, she will be taking 16 hours of unpaid leave (8 hours × 2 days).

Using the example for Michelle's work with ABD Industries with her regular working hours as 40 hours per week, her normal salary is

80 hours × $28.85/hour = $2,308 per pay period

To calculate her pay, including the unpaid leave, we need the proportion of her paycheck that will be unpaid. We calculate the proportion of the total paycheck she will be taking as unpaid leave.

Unpaid portion: 16 hours

Normal hours per pay period: 80

Unpaid portion = 16/80 = 0.20

That means she will receive 100 − 0.20 = 0.80 (or 80 percent) of her normal gross pay.

Gross pay per period with 16 hours unpaid time:

$2,308 × 0.80 = <u>$1,846.40</u>

Note: Using a rounded hourly rate (as shown in this example) to compute period pay will differ from results using nonrounded hourly rates. We have also not separated out the holiday pay intentionally for this example.

In many instances, nonexempt employees are paid on a salary basis to avoid paperwork such as *time cards* or pay sheets if they consistently work a fixed number of hours per week. According to 29 CFR 778.113(a), the employer and employee must agree on the standard number of hours to be worked each week for which the employee shall receive fixed pay. If the employee is classified as a nonexempt worker, however, the FLSA requires that these salaried workers are eligible for overtime. For a nonexempt salaried worker, the hourly rate is necessary to compute pay beyond the agreed-upon weekly hours per 29 CFR 778.113(a).

If the employee works less than the agreed-upon number of hours during the week, some states have provisions by which the employee's salary may be reduced. In this case, the hourly rate is again necessary to make sure the gross pay is correctly calculated.

Salaried Workers and Minimum Wage Comparisons

In the case of a salaried nonexempt worker for whom FLSA provisions apply, the fixed weekly salary must adhere to minimum wage guidelines. The minimum wage applies to salaried non-exempt employees whose wages do not exceed $684 per week. The U.S. Department of Labor has established this salary level as one of the tests for exemption from FLSA provisions.

EXAMPLE: SALARIED NONEXEMPT EMPLOYEE PAY

Sally Albritton is a receptionist for KTC Incorporated, located in California. She is salaried and works 40 hours per week, but she is nonexempt because her job classification is nonmanagerial.

If she were paid $275 per week

Hourly wage = $275/40 hours per week = <u>$6.88/hour</u>

This amount is below the federal minimum wage test for exempt employees. Sally would need to be paid a minimum of $290 per week for her work to meet FLSA minimum wage requirements because of her weekly 40-hour work agreement with her employer. Considering that California has a much higher minimum wage than federal minimum wage, it would be necessary to determine the appropriate minimum wage for her location and company size. To meet the minimum wage requirement, the employer must contribute additional money to meet the minimum wage requirement.

Hourly Workers

Hourly workers are paid for any hours or fraction of the hours they work. These employees may be either skilled or unskilled. Hourly employees must receive overtime for hours worked in excess of 40 per week, according to FLSA. Overtime is the same for hourly workers as it is for salaried nonexempt workers. Hourly workers may be paid for each minute worked, and the computation of those minutes depends upon company policy. Companies may offer different work shifts and workday lengths, such as four 10-hour shifts or five 8-hour shifts, to reach the 40 hours needed. State regulations may require the company with the 10-hour shifts to file an election to pay no overtime for the two additional hours per day. The reason stated should not be overtime avoidance, but a deemed economic benefit for the longer schedules. For example, setup time in a manufacturing environment can eliminate anywhere from half an hour to an hour of productive time. By working the longer schedules, manufacturing efficiency can be improved.

> In Asheville, North Carolina, the city changed the working hours for employees in the public works department to be 10-hour shifts. The change in working hours has led to increased employee satisfaction. Additionally, the department consumed less electricity and natural gas by closing the office one day per week. Although a four-day workweek is not appropriate for all departments and job functions, it is an option that employers may consider. (Source: WLOS)

Hourly Workers in More Than One Job Classification

An employee working for an hourly wage may work in more than one job classification. When this occurs, the employee's pay per classification may vary. For example, a manufacturing employee may work on the sales counter where the pay differential provides an additional $1.50 per hour. When situations like this occur, the payroll accountant must be informed of hours performed for each of the job classifications to provide accurate pay, classification, and reporting. Methods used to communicate this include notes on the time card, schedules provided to the payroll clerk, or job duty notification forms.

> ### EXAMPLE: HOURLY PAY WITH DIFFERENT RATES
> Merrill Cabral is an hourly worker for a fast-food establishment in Louisiana and earns $7.25 per hour. He occasionally is the crew chief, during which he receives a $2.00 per hour differential. During a 40-hour workweek, he worked 16 hours as a crew chief and 24 hours as a regular employee. His pay would be calculated as follows:
>
> Regular pay: 24 hours × $7.25/hour = $174
>
> Crew chief pay: $7.25/hour + $2.00/hour differential = $9.25/hour
>
> 16 hours × $9.25/hour = $148
>
> Gross pay = $174 + $148 = $322

Commission Work

Commissions are compensation based on a set percentage of the sales revenue for a product or service that the company provides. Commission-based compensation is appropriate in the following types of situations:

- Retail sales personnel.
- Automotive sales personnel.
- Media databases or monitoring that pertains to media relations.
- Marketing sales agents.

EXAMPLE: COMMISSION WORKER PAY

An ice machine company may have sales representatives earning 5 percent commission on all sales made. If sales representative A sells $100,000 worth of ice machines during July, the commission due is computed as follows:

Sales price × Commission rate = $100,000 × 5% = $5,000

Note: Commissions may be contingent upon the company's commissions return/warranty policy.

If sales representative A had returns of $7,500 during August, the commission for that month could be reduced:

Returns × Commission rate = deduction from commissions $7,500 returns × 5% commission rate = $375 deducted from commissions during August.

Note that the commission deduction policy varies among employers and is not mandated by any legislation.

An important classification of a sales representative's job is the difference between inside and outside sales. An inside sales representative is one who conducts business via telephone, email, or other electronic means and may not travel to customer sites. An outside sales representative meets with customers either at the customer's facility or another agreed-upon location. Some inside sales representatives are covered under the FLSA and must receive at least minimum wage for their labors. Outside sales representatives are excluded from minimum wage requirements under FLSA. In a 2010 circuit court decision, the judge ruled that inside sales representatives are nonexempt from FLSA wage and hour provisions, whereas outside sales and retail sales representatives are exempt.

EXAMPLE: INSIDE SALES REPRESENTATIVE, LESS THAN MINIMUM WAGE

Helen Steinel works as an inside sales representative in the company store and receives a 5 percent commission for all sales she makes during her shift. During the week, she made 15 sales via telephone with a total dollar value of $1,500.

Commissions = Dollar value of sales × Commission rate

Commissions = $1,500 × 5% = $75

Based upon a 40-hour workweek, she would have effectively earned **$1.88** per hour; thus, the employer would be responsible for meeting the minimum wage requirements under FLSA. The employer would have to adjust Helen's compensation to meet the minimum wage requirements for the specific location and local laws.

EXAMPLE: OUTSIDE SALES REPRESENTATIVE, LESS THAN MINIMUM WAGE

Samantha Durant works as an outside sales representative for the same company. She made sales this week of $2,000 and has an agreed-upon commission percentage of 10 percent of her total sales revenue. Commission = 2,000 × 10% = $200; $200 per week/40 hours = $5.00 hour. Because she is an outside sales representative, she is exempt from minimum wage regulations under FLSA.

Gross Pay for Commission-Based Employees

In situations where the employee is principally engaged in the sale of a product or service but in no way engaged in the manufacturing of the item, a commission pay basis is appropriate. In some states, the commission-based employee may receive commissions for work, even after termination, if the sale was completed prior to termination. In many ways, commission-based pay is a contract between the employer and the employee to sell a product. The payment for such a contract may not be reneged upon, even after termination of employment. It should be noted that many states prohibit deductions pertaining to the cost of doing business from an employee's commission. In other words, if a customer received a product that was damaged, lost, or otherwise destroyed, the employee's commission would not be affected.

EXAMPLE

Sonja Hinton works as an outside salesperson with Bayfront Watercraft in California. Her whole function with Bayfront is to sell the company's products to customers at the customer's facility or other agreed-upon locations, for which she receives a commission of 5 percent based on the retail price of all sales she makes. During May, she sold $20,000 of products during one week.

Commission = $20,000 × 0.05 = $\underline{\underline{\$1,000}}$

Digital Vision/SuperStock

Commission pay can vary by employer, by client, by sales volume, and by employee based on his or her seniority or experience with the company. For instance, sales made by an employee to Client A may have a different commission rate than sales made to Client B, as well as be different for all other clients. Different products may also have varying commission rates, and changes in sales volume can alter commission rates. A sample of a commission-tracking sheet follows.

EXAMPLE: COMMISSION TRACKING SHEET

Salesperson	Client	Product or Service	Total Sales Price	Rate	Commission
Anthony Bauer	Thompson Milbourne	RR-223	$1,245	2%	$24.90
Anthony Bauer	Kockran Heights	RS-447	$2,016	5%	$100.80
Anthony Bauer	Hoptop Ranges	RT-11	$892	3.5%	$31.22

It is important that commissions earned be tracked closely for a variety of reasons:

- Employees' pay accuracy.
- Sales employee performance.
- Sales tracking.
- Job order tracking.
- Returns/reductions of commissions paid accuracy.

Commission pay must still meet FLSA minimum wage standards unless the employee is classified as an exempt worker. Similar to salaried nonexempt employees, commission-based employees are subject to the 40-hour workweek as a basis for FLSA minimum wage computations.

EXAMPLE: EFFECTIVE PAY RATE, EXCEED MINIMUM WAGE

In the example concerning Sonja Hinton at Bayfront, Sonja's pay was $1,000 for 40 hours of work.

Sonja's effective wage = $1,000/40 hours = $\underline{\underline{\$25/\text{hour}}}$

EXAMPLE: EFFECTIVE PAY RATE, LOWER THAN THE MINIMUM WAGE

Anita Edward, another inside sales commission-based employee at Bayfront Watercraft, made only $250 in commission for the week during which she worked 40 hours.

Effective hourly rate = $250/40 hours = $\underline{\underline{\$6.25/\text{hour}}}$

This amount is below the minimum wage in California. It is the employer's responsibility to compensate the employee at the appropriate minimum wage, so Bayfront would have to adjust Anita's compensation to meet FLSA requirements.

Piece-Rate Work

Piece-rate work involves paying employees for each unit they manufacture or each action they perform. This type of pay, based on task completion, is one of the oldest forms of performance-based pay. Dating back to the 16th century, piece-rate pay is thought to have evolved from journeyman artisans whose masters paid them per unit they completed. Prior to computations of hourly wages, piece-rate was an accurate measure of how productive an employee was. Frederick Taylor wrote about a piece-rate system in 1896, citing that it placed an emphasis on efficiency and production. A criticism of Taylor's analysis, however, is that the piece-rate system overemphasizes production and may create an adversarial relationship between workers and managers.

> California's AB 1513, passed in 2016, amended California Labor Code 226.2 and mandated that piece-rate workers be paid for nonproductive time during the workday. Pay during the nonproductive time would be at a different rate than the normal piece-rate work. This nonproductive time includes the time that the employee is under the employer's control, but not on a rest or recovery break. The argument for paid nonproductive time for piece-rate workers is that the employee remains under the control of the employer despite the lack of productivity. (Source: California Department of Industrial Relations)

FLSA requirements subjected the piece-rate system to minimum wage requirements. Piece-rate workers must be paid no less than the minimum wage for their location, forcing employers to track their work hours accurately. In many ways, piece-rate pay is more difficult to track and to administer than other types of pay. Not only must the employees be compensated for the work they complete, but they are also subject to FLSA minimum and daily break provisions, including lunch and other breaks. Piece-rate work has also fallen under some suspicion regarding the quality of work being performed, this can add an additional review to the completed work.

EXAMPLE: PIECE-RATE PAY, EXCEED THE MINIMUM WAGE

John Samuelson is a piece-rate worker in Tennessee who receives $15 per completed piece of work. During a week, he completes 30 pieces and works 40 hours.

John's pay = $15/per piece completed × 30 pieces completed = $450

Hourly rate equivalent = $450/40 hours = $11.25/hour

John's pay exceeds the FLSA minimum wage for his location, so the employer does not have to adjust John's compensation.

EXAMPLE: PIECE-RATE WORKER, BELOW MINIMUM WAGE

Sarah McDowell works for the same employer as John and receives the same rate of pay. She completes 15 pieces during the week.

Sarah's pay = $15/piece × 15 = $225

Hourly rate equivalent = $225/40 = $5.63/hour

Sarah's pay does not meet the minimum wage requirement, so the employer would have to examine Sarah's work and pay rates to ensure that she meets the FLSA minimum wage requirements.

A wide variety of occupations benefit from piece-rate pay systems. Some of these occupations are

Vineyard workers	Inspectors
Carpenters	Property Assessors
Machinists/fabricators	Production workers
Sheep shearers	Forest workers

Ariel Skelley/DigitalVision/Getty Images

The common thread is that each position has an output that is quantifiable and linked to some aspect of a manufacturing or service industry. The important part of piece-rate work is that a quantifiable base must be linked with a specified standard rate per amount of work.

Vineyard workers: Tons of grapes harvested
Inspectors: Number of items inspected
Installers: Number of items installed
Customer service agents: Number of customers assisted
Machinists/fabricators: Number of items produced
Sheep shearers: Pounds of wool gathered
Forest workers: Amount of wood chopped and/or processed

At Bayfront Watercraft, the manufacturing department has different types of fabricators, installers, and other production workers in addition to Pat (the hull maker). Let us assume that Joanna works in the upholstery department where she constructs vinyl covers for seats. Rick is in the assembly department and assembles steering mechanisms for the boats.

EXAMPLE: PIECE-RATE COMPUTATION, DIFFERENT EMPLOYEES

Worker	Number of Items	Rate per Item	Gross Pay
Pat Wu	30 hulls	$100	$3,000
Joanna Yoder	100 seat covers	25	2,500
Rick Karmaran	25 steering mechanisms	40	1,000

Each worker is compensated based on the work he or she completes. In some companies, workers may work on multiple items for which different rates exist. In cases where one worker completes multiple pieces at different rates, the rates for each different piece must be computed.

EXAMPLE: TOTAL PAY, ONE PIECE-RATE EMPLOYEE

Worker	Item	Number of Items	Pay per Item	Total Pay
John Brichacek	Motor installation	10 motors	$50 per motor	$500
	Rudder installation	15 rudders	20 per rudder	300
			Total pay for John:	$800

A separate record for each employee is important in the case of piece-rate pay, especially when the employee works with multiple production items at different rates. Overtime rates for piece-rate workers are computed differently than for hourly workers. Once the standard number of pieces per hour is determined, the amount per hour per piece can be computed. Since the hourly rate now includes the overtime hours worked, the specific overtime hours would only be multiplied by 1/2 instead of the 1-1/2 of other workers.

EXAMPLE: PIECE RATE WITH OVERTIME PAY

Bayfront determines that 50 ignition assemblies can reasonably be completed in a 40-hour workweek by one worker. Ignition assemblies are paid at a rate of $25 per assembly.

Standard amount paid per 40-hour workweek: $1,250

50 assemblies × $25/assembly = $1,250

Hourly amount = $1,250/40 hours = $31.25/hour

If the employee worked overtime, the rate would be computed as follows:

Overtime wages = Hourly rate + (0.5 × Hourly rate × Overtime hours)

(continued)

(concluded)

If an employee worked a 45-hour workweek, the pay would be computed as

Standard amount per week + Overtime pay

= $1,250 + ($31.25/hour × 5 hours overtime) + ($15.625 × 5 hours overtime)

= $1,484.375, which would be <u>$1,484.38</u> (rounded)

According to FLSA provisions, piece-rate workers must have a standard number of items that can be reasonably completed each day that allows for breaks and rest periods. To increase compensation, it could be very easy for an employee to engage in overwork so that he or she could complete more items. According to 29 CFR 525.12(h)(2)(ii), piece-rate employees must have a standard number of items per period, and most are subject to minimum wage provisions. However, if an employee is paid a different rate for nonproductive time, the regular rate is the average of the regular rate and the nonproductive rate.

Computations for Different Bases

1. Natasha Uttrecht is a marketing representative who earns a 3 percent commission based on the revenue earned from the marketing campaigns she completes. During the current pay period, she completed a marketing campaign with $224,800 revenue. How much commission will she receive from this campaign?

2. Jeremy Wikander is a specialty artisan for a luxury car maker based in South Carolina. He makes handcrafted dashboards and receives $550 per completed assembly. During a semimonthly pay period, he completes two dashboard assemblies and works 90 hours. How much does he receive for the completion of the assemblies? Does this amount comply with minimum wage requirements? Explain.

3. Lanea Kiehn is a salaried worker making $57,000 per year for a company using biweekly payroll. Her standard schedule is 40 hours over five days per week. She has used all of her vacation time prior to this pay period and fell ill for three days. What effect does this have on the current pay period? Will her gross pay be the same as if she had vacation time available? (Note: Only round final calculations.)

LO 3-3   Calculate Pay Based on Hours and Fractions of Hours

Employees, both salaried nonexempt and hourly, are paid based upon the number of hours, or fractions thereof, worked. The payroll accountant must learn how to convert a fraction of a 60-minute clock into a fraction of 100. While accounting software packages are able to convert minutes into payable units, typically the payroll accountant does this math. Fortunately, the math for this calculation is fairly straightforward.

EXAMPLE: CONVERSION OF MINUTES TO DECIMALS AND FRACTIONS

If an employee works 30 minutes, then the computation for pay purposes is

30 minutes ÷ 60 minutes/hour = 0.5 hour or 50/100

If an employee works 33 minutes, the payroll computation is

33 minutes ÷ 60 minutes/hour = <u>0.55</u> hour, or <u>55/100</u>

Note: This calculation is necessary when the employer pays using the hundredth-hour method instead of the quarter-hour method. If this had been a quarter-hour computation, the number of minutes would have been rounded to the closest 15-minute increment, which is 0.50 hours.

Calculations of employee wages are broken down by the hour or fraction thereof. Regardless of the classification of the employee, a determination of pay per pay period causes the payroll accountant to break down all wages. Salaries are determined based upon a yearly salary and therefore need to be broken down per pay period (monthly, semimonthly, weekly, or biweekly). Companies may pay employees by fractions of an hour (hundredth-hour basis) or by the quarter-hour (rounded to the nearest 15-minute interval), depending upon company policy. The next section will walk you through the calculations of both the hundredth and quarterly processes.

Hourly Calculations

Depending on the company's policy, time payments can be paid either by the individual minute or rounded to the nearest designated interval. Hourly calculations are a combination of minutes and hours. Hours are broken into two categories: regular and overtime. When determining the hourly wage for a salaried individual, the number of average hours required under the salary must be known.

EXAMPLE: HOURLY WAGE COMPUTATION, SALARIED EMPLOYEE

If a manager is expected to work 45 hours per week at $75,000 per year, the effective hourly wage would be

$75,000/(45 × 52 weeks) = $75,000/2,340 = $32.05 per hour

EXAMPLE: WEEKLY PAY INCLUDING PAID SICK TIME

Jason Taylor worked four days during the payroll week. He worked 7.5 hours the first day, 8.75 hours the second day, 7 hours the third day, and 9.5 hours the fourth day. He used 8 hours of his paid sick time on one day during the week. He is paid overtime for any hours worked in excess of 40 per week.

Regular hours: 7.5 + 8.75 + 7 + 9.5 = 32.75 hours

He will also receive 8 hours of sick time.

Jason's gross pay = 32.75 regular hours + 8 sick = 40.75 hours

Even though Jason has more than 40 hours on his payroll, 8 are not considered "worked" and would therefore not be included in the calculation for the determination of overtime.

EXAMPLE: WEEKLY PAY INCLUDING PAID HOLIDAY TIME

Karen Golliff worked four days during the week with a holiday on Monday. Her hours worked were 8.25 hours the first day, 9 hours the second day, 7.75 hours the third day, and 8.5 hours the fourth day. The company pays 8 hours for the holiday. She is paid for any hours worked in excess of 40 hours per week.

Regular hours: 8.25 + 9 + 7.75 + 8.5 = 33.5 hours

She will also be paid 8 hours regular pay for the holiday.

Karen's gross pay will contain 41.5 hours of regular pay, which includes 8 hours of holiday pay. Karen has not worked in excess of 40 hours because the holiday is not included in *worked* hours, so she will not receive overtime.

Quarter-Hour System

Some employers compensate employees based upon rounding working hours to the nearest 15 minutes, a system widely known as the *quarter-hour system*. The payroll accountant becomes responsible for rounding the time either up or down consistently across all individuals and pay periods. If an individual worked 8 hours and 6 minutes, he would be paid for 8 hours. However, if that same individual were to work for 8 hours and 8 minutes, he would be paid for 8 hours plus 15 minutes of overtime, if the company pays for overtime on any hours worked over 8 in a day.

EXAMPLE: ROUNDING MINUTES FOR THE QUARTER-HOUR SYSTEM

0–7 minutes past the previous 15-minute interval rounds *down* to the previous 15-minute interval.

Example: 10:06 a.m. would count as 10:00 a.m. in the quarter-hour system.

8–15 minutes past the previous 15-minute interval rounds *up* to the next 15-minute interval.

Example: 10:09 a.m. would count as 10:15 a.m. in the quarter-hour system.

EXAMPLE: QUARTER-HOUR SYSTEM COMPUTATION, ROUNDING TO THE PREVIOUS QUARTER-HOUR

Amanda Leong worked from 8 a.m. until noon. She took one hour for lunch and returned to work at 1 p.m. At the end of the day, Amanda ended up leaving work at 4:20 p.m. Using the quarter-hour system

   From 8 a.m. to noon: 4 hours

   From 1 p.m. to 4:20 p.m.: 3.25 hours

   because 4:20 p.m. rounds down to 4:15 p.m. under the quarter-hour system.

   Total time: 4 + 3.25 = <u>7.25 hours</u>

EXAMPLE: QUARTER-HOUR SYSTEM COMPUTATION, ROUNDING TO THE NEXT QUARTER-HOUR

Justin Fretwell worked from 8 a.m. until 12:30 p.m. before taking a half-hour lunch. He returned at 1 p.m. and worked until 4:10 p.m. His employer pays on the quarter-hour system, so Justin would be paid as follows:

   From 8 a.m. to 12:30 p.m.: 4 hours, 30 minutes = 4.5 hours

   From 1 p.m. to 4:10 p.m.: 3.25 hours

   because 4:10 p.m. rounds up to 4:15 p.m. under the quarter-hour system.

   Total time for the day: <u>7.75 hours</u>

Hundredth-Hour System

The *hundredth-hour system* is similar to the quarter-hour system in that it calculates partial hours of work performed. Instead of rounding the employee's time to 15-minute intervals, the hundredth-hour system divides the hour into increments. The calculation of partial minutes is simple:

$$\text{Conversion of minutes to hundredth hour} = \frac{\text{Number of minutes in partial hour}}{60 \text{ minutes per hour}}$$

EXAMPLE: CONVERSION FROM MINUTES TO HUNDREDTH-HOUR

If an employee worked 4 hours and 16 minutes,

4 hours + 16 minutes/60 minutes per hour = <u>4.27 hours</u>

EXAMPLE: HUNDREDTH-HOUR TIME COMPUTATION

Leslie Mellor works an 8-hour shift that had 15 minutes of additional overtime. Her normal hourly rate is $10/hour. Her pay would be computed as follows:

8 hours × $10 per hour = $80 regular pay

15 minutes overtime = 15/60 = 0.25 hour

Overtime = 0.25 hours × $10/hour × 1.5 = $3.75

Total pay for the day = $80 + $3.75 = <u>$83.75</u>

Following is an example of how the time may appear on an individual's time card. Note that an employer should choose only one method of computing partial hours—quarter-hours or hundredth-hours—and apply it to all situations and all employees.

EXAMPLE: QUARTER-HOUR COMPUTATION, WEEKLY PAY DETAILS

Amanda Parker: Employee Number 1776M

Clock In	Clock Out	Clock In	Clock Out	Hours Worked
08:00	11:00	12:00	16:54	7 hours 54 minutes = 8.00 hours
08:00	11:30	12:30	17:05	8 hours 5 minutes = 8.00 hours
07:00	12:09	13:15	17:30	9 hours 24 minutes = 9.5 hours
07:30	12:21 rounds down	13:24	17:30	8 hours 57 minutes = 8.75 hours
			Total	34.25 hours

In the next example, notice how the same employee with the same amount of time worked would have different hourly computations based on hundredth-hour computations. The difference in the hourly computations leads to a difference in compensation for the period.

EXAMPLE: HUNDREDTH-HOUR COMPUTATION, WEEKLY PAY DETAILS

Amanda Parker: Employee Number 1776M

Clock In	Clock Out	Clock In	Clock Out	Hours Worked
08:00	11:00	12:00	16:54	7 hours 54 minutes = 7.9 hours
08:00	11:30	12:30	17:05	8 hours 5 minutes = 8.08 hours
07:00	12:09	13:15	17:30	9 hours 24 minutes = 9.4 hours
07:30	12:21	13:24	17:30	8 hours 57 minutes = 8.95 hours
			Total	34.33 hours

Quarter-Hour vs. Hundredth-Hour

Stop & Check

1. Blue Sky Manufacturing has historically paid its employees according to the quarter-hour system. Software changes have caused them to change to the hundredth-hour system. What is the number of hours worked under the quarter-hour system? What is the time worked under the hundredth-hour system?

Employee	Time In	Time Out	Time In	Time Out	Total
Ann Gottlieb	8:06 a.m.	12:25 p.m.	1:20 p.m.	4:57 p.m.	Quarter-hour: Hundredth:
Nevada Lofkin	7:58 a.m.	12:02 p.m.	1:02 p.m.	5:05 p.m.	Quarter-hour: Hundredth:
Pat Blackburn	8:32 a.m.	11:54 a.m.	1:05 p.m.	5:32 p.m.	Quarter-hour: Hundredth:

2. Why do discrepancies exist between the quarter-hour time and the hundredth-hour time totals?

3. Why would it be worthwhile for Blue Sky Manufacturing to switch to the hundredth-hour system?

LWA/Dann Tardif/Blend Images LLC

LO 3-4   Calculate Overtime in Various Situations

Nonexempt employee overtime may occur in a variety of situations. When an employee works past the FLSA maximum hours per week, the employee must be compensated at a rate of 1.5 times the regular hourly rate. However, situations exist when employees must be compensated at more than the standard overtime premium, and others exist when exempt employees may receive overtime pay. We will explore examples of overtime compensation in a variety of situations.

Standard Overtime Pay

In general, FLSA-stipulated overtime includes any hours worked in excess of 40 during a 7-day, 168-hour week. No limit on the number of hours that an employee may work per week exists for employees over the age of 16. No legislation stipulates that employees must be paid at overtime rates on Saturdays and Sundays as long as the total number of hours worked is less than 40 during a period of seven consecutive days. An important fact to note is that the regular pay rate may not be below the FLSA or state-based minimum wage, especially in the case when overtime pay has been earned.

According to the Bureau of Labor Statistics, the average number of weekly overtime hours as of 2020 was 3.15 per employee. Although this may seem to be a relatively low number, employee overtime can become a significant amount for a large employer. As an example, the city of Las Cruces, New Mexico, failed to pay overtime for employees who worked at local events, citing a flex-time agreement. The city was forced to pay over $8,500 in overtime pay for a single event in early 2020. (Sources: Bureau of Labor Statistics, *Las Cruces Sun News*)

The first example explains basic overtime pay computation for a nonexempt employee with a 40-hour workweek. The second part of the example reflects the payment of a bonus as a normal part of the employee's pay.

Overtime on retail or service salaries with commission have two rules that must be met in order for the commissions to be included in the wage base for the overtime calculations: (1) the employee's regular pay must be in excess of 1-½ times the statutory minimum wage and (2) more than one-half of the employee's compensation must be from the commissions.

EXAMPLE: NONEXEMPT PAY CALCULATION

Monique Martin works as a maintenance worker at a busy office building. She earns $52,000 annually, is paid weekly, and is classified as nonexempt. Her standard workweek is 40 hours. Since Monique is classified as a nonexempt worker, she is eligible to receive overtime for any hours worked in excess of 40 per week per her employment contract.

During the pay period ending April 22, Monique worked 50 hours. As a result, Monique would receive her weekly pay *plus* overtime calculated to include the non-discretionary bonus. To determine her hourly wage, divide her annual pay by the total hours worked during the year. Her gross earnings for the April 22 pay period would be as follows:

Name	M/S	#Dep	Hourly Rate	No. of Regular Hours	No. of Overtime Hours	Regular Earnings	Overtime Earnings	Gross Earnings	401(k)	Insurance	Taxable Wages for Federal W/H	Taxable Wages for FICA
Monique Martin	S	1	25.00	40	10	1,000.00	375.00	1,375.00				

Note that Monique's regular pay and her overtime pay are calculated separately and then added together to determine the gross pay.

Hourly rate plus bonus

If Monique was eligible for a bonus as part of her employment agreement, her bonus would be added to her regular pay to determine the hourly rate on which the overtime is based. In this example, if Monique received a $120 bonus for her work, the overtime computation would be as follows:

Name	M/S	#Dep	Hourly Rate	No. of Regular Hours	No. of Overtime Hours	Bonus	Regular Earning	Overtime Earning	Gross Earning	401(k)	Insurance	Taxable Wages for Federal W/H	Taxable Wages for FICA
Monique Martin	S	1	25.00	40	10	120.00	1,000.00	420.00*	1,540.00				

*Calculation: $40 * 25 = $1,000 + 120 = $1,120 / 40 = $28 * 1.5 = $42 * 10 = $420

Overtime for Employees of Hospitals and Residential Care Facilities

One instance when the overtime computation differs from the standard rate involves employees who work at hospitals and residential care facilities. FLSA section 7(j) applies a rule to these workers known as the *Eight and Eighty (8 and 80)* rule. According to the 8 and 80 rule, the number of consecutive days is 14 instead of 7; similarly, the threshold for overtime is 80 hours during the work period instead of 40. An example reflecting the 8 and 80 rule follows.

EXAMPLE: 8 AND 80 OVERTIME CALCULATION

Victor Garner is a Licensed Professional Nurse (LPN) at Fountainside Hospital. During the period starting June 5 and ending June 18, he worked 95 hours. Victor is classified

(continued)

(concluded)

as nonexempt and earns an hourly wage of $31.50. Victor's pay for the two-week period would be as follows:

Name	M/S	#W/H	Hourly Rate	No. of Regular Hours	No. of Overtime Hours	Regular Earning	Overtime Earning	Gross Earning	401(k)	Insurance	Taxable Wages for Federal W/H	Taxable Wages for FICA
Victor Garner	S	1	31.50	80	15	2,520.00	708.75	3,228.75				

Note that the first 80 hours are paid at the regular hourly rate. The 15 additional hours are paid at the overtime premium rate.

A study conducted by New York University found that new nurses work 12-hours shifts on average and most average 39.4 hours per week. Of these new nurses, about half reported working mandatory overtime. (Source: *Medical Express*)

Tipped Employee Overtime

Another overtime situation involves tipped employees. According to the FLSA, employers may consider tips earned by the employee when computing overtime pay. A best practice when the employer chooses to use the tips earned as part of the overtime computation is to notify the employee in advance that their tips will be included in the overtime pay calculation. An example of both situations, with and without tips included, will show how the wage computations differ.

EXAMPLE: TIPPED EMPLOYEE OVERTIME

Elsie Morales is a nonexempt tipped employee at the Love House Bar and Grill in Arvada, Colorado. The minimum cash wage in Colorado is $8.98 per hour, and the tip credit is $3.02 per hour (i.e., the minimum wage for Colorado is $12.00 per hour). During the pay period beginning January 31, 2020, and ending February 7, 2020, Elsie worked 48 hours and earned $300 in tips.

Without the consideration of tips, and based on the state minimum wage, Elsie must be paid $624.00 for the 48 hours worked, as follows:

Name	M/S	#W/H	Hourly Rate	No. of Regular Hours	No. of Over-time Hours	Tips	Regular Earning	Overtime Earning	Gross Earning	401(k)	Insurance	Taxable Wages for Federal W/H	Taxable Wages for FICA
Elsie Morales	S	1	12.00	40	8		480.00	144.00	624.00				

Overtime pay with tips included as part of the hourly wage

If the employer counted the $300 in tips earned toward the minimum cash over-time wage, Elsie would not be eligible for any further compensation for the overtime because the gross earnings exceed the minimum due.

Name	M/S	#W/H	Hourly Rate	No. of Regular Hours	No. of Over-time Hours	Tips	Regular Earning	Overtime Earning	Gross Earning	401(k)	Insurance	Taxable Wages for Federal W/H	Taxable Wages for FICA
Elsie Morales	S	1	8.98	40	8	300.00	659.20	197.76	856.96				

Earnings calculation

Regular earnings: $300 + (8.98 × 40) = $300 + 359.20 = 659.20
Overtime earnings: $659.20/40 = $16.48/hour × 1.5 = $24.72 × 8 = $197.76

Overtime pay excluding tips as part of the hourly wage

If the employer did not count Elsie's tips toward the hourly wage, her pay would be computed as follows:

Name	M/S	#W/H	Hourly Rate	No. of Regular Hours	No. of Over-time Hours	Tips	Regular Earning	Overtime Earning	Gross Earning	401(k)	Insurance	Taxable Wages for Federal W/H	Taxable Wages for FICA
Elsie Morales	S	1	8.98	40	8		359.20	107.76	466.96				

In this case, the employer would need to pay Elsie the difference between the minimum wage and the minimum tipped wage:

$466.96 / 40 = 11.674 / hour

40 hours × $12.00 per hour = $480.00

$480.00 − $466.96 = $13.04

Note that state laws vary as to the inclusion of tips in tipped employee overtime calculations.

Piece-Rate Employee Overtime

Piece-rate workers are eligible for overtime on a similar basis to hourly nonexempt employees. However, because they are paid on a piece-rate basis, the overtime computation is based on the number of pieces completed and the total number of productive hours worked during the consecutive seven-day period.

EXAMPLE: PIECE-RATE EMPLOYEE OVERTIME

Edmund Dennis is a piece-rate employee at Snowy Day Sculptures in Terrace Lake, New Mexico. He earns $75 per finished sculpture. During the week of February 27, he worked 48.5 hours and completed 12 sculptures. He is paid minimum wage (i.e., $7.50 per hour) for nonproductive time; during the week of February 27, he had four hours of nonproductive time. His overtime would be calculated based on the productive time of 44.5 hours as follows:

Name	M/S	#W/H	Piece Rate	# of Pieces Completed	No. of Regular Hours	No. of Over-time Hours	Piece Rate Earnings	Regular Earning	Over-time Earning	Gross Earning	401(k)	Insurance	Taxable Wages for Federal W/H	Taxable Wages for FICA
Edmund Dennis	S	1	75	12	40	4.5	900.00	30.00	45.51	975.51				

Earnings calculation

Piece-rate earnings: 12 × $75 = $900

Regular earnings = 4 × $7.50 = $30

Overtime = $900/44.5 × .5 = $10.11 × 4.5 = $45.51

Note that the overtime earnings are computed based on the piece-rate earnings divided by the total number of productive hours, which yields an effective hourly rate. That hourly rate is multiplied by 1.5 and the number of overtime productive hours to determine the overtime pay.

Salaried Nonexempt Overtime

In cases when the employee is a salaried nonexempt worker, the standard number of working hours per week depends on the hiring agreement. If the number of hours agreed upon is 40 per week, then the standard overtime examples should be followed. However, if the number of agreed-upon hours is 45 per week, then the overtime is calculated using 45 hours to determine the hourly rate and time worked in excess of 45 hours is subject to overtime premiums. The same principle applies to employees who work four 10-hour shifts, shifts that have differential rates, or other similar arrangements.

EXAMPLE: SALARIED NONEXEMPT POSITION WITH A NORMAL 45-HOUR WORK SCHEDULE

Clay Curtis is an administrator for Strickland Farms and earns $52,000 annually, paid biweekly. He is a salaried nonexempt employee with a standard 45-hour workweek. During the two-week pay period ending September 25th, Clay worked 99 hours. His overtime would be computed as follows:

Name	M/S	#W/H	Salary	No. of Regular Hours	No. of Overtime Hours	Regular Earning	Overtime Earning	Gross Earning	401(k)	Insurance	Taxable Wages for Federal W/H	Taxable Wages for FICA
Clay Curtis	S	1	2,000.00	90	9	2,000.00	300.00	2,300.00				

Earnings calculation

Overtime rate = $52,000/(45 × 52) = $22.22 × 1.5 = $33.33 × 9 = $300

Edwin de Luz Trucking and Gravel LLC was ordered to pay nearly $60,000 in back pay and wages due to a failure to record all time worked. The discrepancy resulted from the company's policy of automatically deducting the mandatory 30-minute lunch break from every worker, regardless of the actual time taken. Accurate record-keeping is critical for compliance with FLSA regulations. (Source: *KHON*)

Overtime for Employees Who Work in Two or More Separate Functions

Suppose an employee works in two separate functions in the company and earns a different rate for each function. For example, the employee may work in accounts payable and as a front desk receptionist, each with different pay rates. In this case, the overtime rate is often calculated using the average of the two pay rates.

EXAMPLE: EMPLOYEE WITH TWO DIFFERENT PAY RATES FOR DIFFERENT FUNCTIONS

Kiana Mancuso works equally for Sidwell Industries as both an accounts payable clerk and a front desk receptionist. She earns $18.50 per hour for accounts payable and $15 per hour for reception work. During the week ending October 27, Kiana worked 50 hours; 26 hours were in accounts payable, and the rest were at the front desk. Her pay would be computed as follows:

Name	M/S	#W/H	Hourly Rate	No. of Regular Hours	No. of Overtime Hours	Regular Earning	Overtime Earning	Gross Earning	401(k)	Insurance	Taxable Wages for Federal W/H	Taxable Wages for FICA
Kiana Mancuso—accounts payable	S	1	18.50	20	6	370.00	166.50	536.50				
Kiana Mancuso—front desk	S	1	15.00	20	4	300.00	90.00	390.00				
Total Earnings								926.50				

Note that company policies on overtime pay may vary from the situations described. When in doubt, the payroll accountant should refer to the FLSA overtime calculator advisor published by the U.S. Department of Labor.

How Does Overtime Affect Gross Pay?

Stop & Check

1. Tommy Grubb is a hospital worker with the city of Keene, New Hampshire. Which rule governs his overtime pay?

2. Michaele Gerald is a salaried nonexempt employee who earns $39,000 per year, paid biweekly, and commission is based on sales of service contracts which represents less than half her pay. How does her commission income affect any overtime compensation?

3. Ralph Scott is a waiter at Good Eats Diner. What are the two ways that his employer might compute his overtime earnings in reference to his tip income?

Portrait Images Asia by
NONWARIT/Shutterstock

LO 3-5   Create a Payroll Register

A *payroll register* is the payroll accountant's internal tool that helps ensure the accuracy of employee compensation. A payroll register can be completed manually, in a spreadsheet program such as Microsoft Excel, in accounting software programs such as QuickBooks, or by payroll outsourcing companies such as ADP or Paychex. Like other worksheets that accountants use, the payroll register is a company confidential document that is subject to the rules about document retention and destruction.

Payroll Register Data

The payroll register is annotated at the top with the beginning and ending dates of the payroll period. Each employee has a separate row in the register. The register contains columns to reflect each employee's specific payroll information, such as

1. Employee name.
2. Filing status.
3. Number and type of dependents.
4. Hourly rate or period salary.
5. The number of regular hours worked.
6. The number of overtime hours worked.
7. Regular pay.
8. Overtime pay.
9. Gross pay.
10. Federal income tax withheld.
11. Social Security tax withheld.
12. Medicare tax withheld.
13. State income tax withheld (where applicable).
14. Other state taxes.
15. Local taxes (if applicable).
16. 401(k) or other retirement plan deductions.
17. Insurance deductions.
18. Garnishments or levies.
19. Union dues.
20. Any other deductions.
21. Net pay.
22. Check or payment ID number.

FIGURE 3-2
Sample Payroll Register

P/R End Date [   ]   Company Name   _____
Check Date [   ]

Name	M/S	# W/H	Hourly Rate or Period Wage	# Regular Hours	# Overtime Hours	# Holiday Hours	Commis-sions	Gross Earnings	401(k)	Sec 125	Taxable Wages for Federal W/H	Taxable Wages for FICA
Totals							-		-	-	-	-

Name	Gross Earnings	Taxable Wages for Federal W/H	Taxable Wages for FICA	Federal W/H	Social Security Tax	State W/H Tax	Medicare W/H	Net Pay	Check No.
Totals	-	-	-	-	-	-	-	-	

It may seem tedious to complete a register each payroll period, but the register offers more information than just the employee compensation. The register also contains information about employer liabilities for taxes and the employees' voluntary deductions that the employer must remit to the appropriate places at a future date. A sample payroll register is shown in Figure 3-2.

Note that other columns may be added to meet the company's needs. Other columns that may appear on a payroll register include commission, piece rate, standby hours, and sleep time. The purpose of the payroll register is to both document the employees' time and hours worked and provide totals of the compensation for each category. Employers use these categorizations as part of labor analysis and planning tasks.

A separate payroll register is maintained for each pay period. To ensure accuracy, the accountant totals, proves, and rules the register.

WHAT DO *TOTAL, PROVE,* AND *RULE* MEAN?

Total: Each column and row are totaled.

Prove: The column totals are added horizontally *and* row totals are totaled vertically. The aggregate column and row totals must be equal.

Rule: Column totals are double underlined to show that the totals have been totaled.

Track Employee Compensation Using a Payroll Register

A payroll register is a tool used by payroll accountants to ensure accurate tracking of employee compensation. The following examples will demonstrate different scenarios using a payroll register.

EXAMPLE 1: WAGE PAYMENTS, NO OVERTIME

Jon Ames is a nonexempt, hourly employee of CM Bakeries. He receives $12.50/hour and receives overtime for any time worked in excess of 40 hours/week. He is single with one dependent. During the week ending April 25, he worked 37 hours. The payroll register would appear as follows:

Name	Filing Status	Hourly Rate or Period Wage	No. of Regular Hours	No. of Overtime Hours	No. of Holiday Hours	Commissions	Gross Earnings
Jon Ames	S-1	$12.50	37				$462.50

In Example 1, the employee's hourly rate is multiplied by the number of hours worked to obtain the gross pay for the period. The use of the Regular Earnings column is introduced here, although no overtime exists. Example 2 will show how overtime is included in a payroll register.

EXAMPLE 2: WAGE PAYMENT WITH OVERTIME

Mike Brown is a nonexempt, hourly employee of Strong Coffee Company and earns $18.50/hour. He is married filing jointly with two dependents. He receives overtime for any hours worked in excess of 40 during a weekly period. During the period ended September 20, he worked 45.75 hours. The payroll register would appear as follows:

Name	Filing Status	Hourly Rate or Period Wage	No. of Regular Hours	No. of Overtime Hours	Reg. Earnings	Overtime Earnings	Gross Earnings
Mike Brown	MJ-2	$18.50	40	5.75	$740.00	$159.56*	$899.56

*Overtime earning = $18.50/hour × 5.75 hours × 1.5 (overtime premium) = $159.56

Notice that the payroll register in Example 2 is expanded to include a breakdown of regular earnings and overtime earnings. The purpose of this practice is to facilitate computations, ensure accuracy, and allow for future analysis of overtime worked during a given period.

Example 3 contains a payroll register for a salaried, exempt employee. Notice the difference in the columns used to record the period salary.

EXAMPLE 3: SALARY PAYMENT

Rae Smith is a manager at Hartshorn Industries. She is a salaried, exempt employee and is married filing jointly with four dependents. She earns a salary of $2,000 per pay period. For the period ending July 31, the payroll register would appear as follows:

Name	Filing Status	Hourly Rate or Period Wage	No. of Regular Hours	No. of Overtime Hours	No. of Holiday Hours	Commissions	Gross Earnings
Rae Smith	MJ-4	$2,000.00					$2,000.00

In a company, it is common to have both salaried and hourly employees, and all employees must be represented on a payroll register. Example 4 contains employees with pay variations that commonly exist in business.

EXAMPLE 4: PAYROLL REGISTER FOR MULTIPLE EMPLOYEES

PBL Freight pays its employees on a biweekly basis. The standard workweek for hourly employees is 40 hours, and employees receive overtime pay for any hours worked in excess of 40 during a week. The following payroll register is for the period ending March 22:

Name	Filing Status	Hourly Rate or Period Wage	No. of Regular Hours	No. of Overtime Hours	Reg. Earnings	Overtime Earnings	Gross Earnings
Mary Jahn	S-1	$ 15.25	40		$ 610.00		$ 610.00
John Charles	MJ-3	$2,750.00			$2.750.00		$ 2.750.00
Ranea Hu	MJ-5	$ 21.50	40	6	$ 860.00	$193.50	$ 1,053.50
					$4,220.00	$193.50	$ 4,413.50

Notice how the columns are totaled in Example 4. Each earnings column is totaled vertically, and the double underline (i.e., ruling) denotes that the computations are concluded. The total in the bottom-right corner proves that the sum of the rows in the Gross Earnings column equals the total of the Regular Earnings and Overtime Earnings columns. Once the payroll register is totaled, proved, and ruled, then it is ready for the next step in the payroll process.

The Payroll Register

Stop & Check

1. What is the purpose of the payroll register?
2. What are five of the columns that usually appear in a payroll register?
3. Why are computations for regular hours and overtime hours entered in different columns?

Billion Photos/Shutterstock

LO 3-6   Apply Combination Pay Methods

Employers often offer their employees *combination pay* methods. Sometimes the employee performs two different jobs for the same employer, and those two tasks have different compensation bases. Other situations involve payroll-based incentives that link to company productivity. Note how the payroll register reflects these combination pay methods.

Base Salary Plus Commission

A common method includes a base salary plus a commission or piece rate, depending on the nature of the work performed. Another method is a combination of salary plus hourly compensation that reflects a standard set of work hours plus additional hours that are paid only when worked. The purpose of the combination pay method is to meet minimum wage requirements and encourage employees to achieve sales or production goals. The base salary offers both the employer and the employee a level of stability in pay amounts because they will know the minimum amount of compensation for each pay period. Whatever the employees earn above the base salary may vary from pay period to pay period, depending on the employee's capabilities, production needs, and customer needs.

EXAMPLE: BASE SALARY PLUS COMMISSION

Henri Jay is a salaried, exempt employee of Night Lights Security. He is single with two dependents. His compensation package includes commission based on sales of security system packages to customers. During the pay period ending January 15, he earned $1,500 in salary and 4 percent commission on $10,000 of sales.

Commission = $10,000 × 0.04 = $400

Name	Filing Status	Hourly Rate or Period Wage	No. of Regular Hours	No. of Overtime Hours	No. of Holiday Hours	Commissions	Gross Earnings
Henri Jay	S-2	$1,500.00				$ 400.00	$1,900.00

Many types of jobs have a combination pay method because it has been found to boost employee productivity and maintain FLSA compliance. Some jobs that use combination pay methods are

District managers	Account executives
Recruiters	Retail sales workers
Farmworkers	Real estate salespersons

Dragon Images/Shutterstock

To compute combination pay methods, knowledge of the employee's base salary plus variable rate is essential.

EXAMPLE: DIFFERENT COMBINATION METHODS, THE SAME COMPANY

Todd Jones is an account executive for Bayfront Watercraft. He earns a base salary of $36,000 plus a commission of 0.5 percent on each sale he makes. He is married with six withholding allowances. Suppose that Todd sold $100,000 of boats during a two-week pay period ending June 15.

Base salary = $36,000/26 = $1,384.62.

Commission = $100,000 × 0.5% = $500.

Total pay for Todd: $1,884.62

The payroll register for Todd's June 15 pay would appear as

Name	Filing Status	Hourly Rate or Period Wage	No. of Regular Hours	No. of Overtime Hours	Piece Rate Pay	Commissions	Gross Earnings
Todd Jones	MJ-6	$1,384.62				$500.00	$1,884.62

Maria Dee installs the seating in the boats for Bayfront Watercraft. She is single with one withholding allowance. In her position, she earns a base salary of $26,000 per year plus a piece rate of $100 for each boat completed during the pay period. During the pay period, Maria installed the seating for eight boats.

Salary = $26,000/26 = $1,000

Piece-rate pay = $100 × 8 = $800

Total Pay for Maria: $1,800

(continued)

(concluded)

The payroll register including both employees for the June 15 pay period would appear as follows:

Name	Filing Status	Hourly Rate or Period Wage	No. of Regular Hours	No. of Overtime Hours	Piece Rate Pay	Commissions	Gross Earnings
Todd Jones	MJ-6	$1,384.62				$500.00	$1,884.62
Maria Dee	S-1	$1,000.00			$800.00		$1.800.00
Totals					$800.00	$500.00	$3,684.62

Like any other type of payment method, the important element in computing combination pay is accurate maintenance of the base salary, the variable rate, and the number of items or sales for which the variable rate must apply. The use of the payroll register facilitates the computations and ensures the accuracy of the employees' gross pay.

Payroll Draw

A special situation in commission-based pay is a situation called a *draw*. A draw generally involves an employee whose regular compensation is little more than the minimum wage, such as a retail sales position. Employees have sales goals they must meet and receive compensation on a commission basis once they meet or exceed those sales goals. If the sales goal is not met, the employee may draw a salary against future commissions. The expectation with a draw is that the employee will eventually generate enough sales to cover any draws during pay periods when sales revenues were lower than expected.

> A draw is generally associated with a commission-only job in which the employer allows new employees to receive money for expected future commissions. With a draw, it is implied that the draw may occur on a regular basis. However, paying employees solely on the basis of commission and draw has been challenged on the basis that it does not recognize employee rest breaks and nonproductive time. In *Bermudez Vaquero v. Stoneledge Furniture LLC*, the court upheld the FLSA rules regarding mandatory rest breaks. (Source: FindLaw)

Salary Plus Commission and Draw

Salaried employees who receive commission may be eligible to draw against that commission at the company's discretion. This pay combination could be for external salespeople who have commissions as a relatively large portion of their regular income.

EXAMPLE: SALARY PLUS COMMISSION AND DRAW

Kari Lee is an employee in the sales department of Fastball Sports. She is single with one dependent, and her annual base salary is $12,000, paid monthly. She is expected to earn between $1,000 and $3,000 in sales commissions each month and may draw up to $3,000 per month against future earnings.

During October, she earned $1,000 in commissions in addition to her salary. She decided to take an additional $1,000 draw against her future earnings. The payroll register would reflect this compensation as follows:

Name	Filing Status	Hourly Rate or Period Wage	No. of Regular Hours	No. of Overtime Hours	Reg. Earnings	Draw	Commissions	Gross Earnings
Kari Lee	S-1	$1,000.00			$1,000.00	$1,000.00	$1,000.00	$3,000.00

> In this case, Kari could have withdrawn up to $3,000 against future earnings. If her employment is terminated before she earns enough sales commission to repay the draw, she will have to repay the company for that money. It is important to keep track of employee draws to ensure that the employee repays the draw.

Another example where the company may allow individuals to draw on their payroll exists when the pay period is monthly. In this situation, many employers allow their employees to draw up to 30–40 percent of their wages at mid-month. Some organizations may not withhold taxes from the draw, and the employee will have the full amount of taxes withdrawn upon the next payroll.

Employers must be careful when allowing employees to draw against future wages. A written and signed authorization must be obtained from the employee that specifies when the draw will be deducted from the employee's future wages to avoid legal issues with deductions, such as wage garnishments, that could be affected by the draw.

EXAMPLE: SALARY PLUS DRAW, EMPLOYEE INELIGIBLE FOR COMMISSION

Scott Fay is a new salesperson with Bayfront Watercraft, hired on September 24. He receives a base salary of $19,500 per year, paid biweekly, plus a 5 percent commission on sales once he achieves his sales quota of $20,000 during a pay period. During the pay period ending September 30, Scott closed $10,000 in sales, making him ineligible for a commission for September. He is eligible to draw up to the minimum commission for the pay period, which is $20,000 × 5%, or $1,000. The payroll register would reflect his pay as follows:

Name	Filing Status	Hourly Rate or Period Wage	No. of Regular Hours	No. of Overtime Hours	Reg. Earnings	Draw	Commissions	Gross Earnings
Scott Fay	S-1	$750.00			$750.00	$1,000.00		$1,750.00

Period salary = $19,500/26 pay periods = $750.00
Commission draw = $20,000 × 0.05 = $1,000.00.

Ken Brown/E+/Getty Images

Incentive Stock Options (ISOs)

Other employee compensation plans, known as *incentive stock options (ISOs)*, allow an employee to report a small base salary for tax purposes and to be issued company stock that must be held for a certain period before being sold. In some instances, the stock option may be exercised after three months of employment, and in other cases, it may be after one year of employment. The purpose of ISO stock option plans is a deferral of taxes and salary liabilities for the employer and employee. This type of compensation is often found in executive pay packages.

In the class-action lawsuit *McElrath v. Uber Technologies,* the plaintiff stated that employees were offered an ISO as a significant part of the compensation package. The issue arose because Uber had accelerated the exercisability of its ISOs to make the compensation attractive. However, when employees exercised their options, the company refused to allow employees to receive the promised compensation on a tax-deferred basis that is consistent with an ISO. Instead, Uber changed the ISOs to nonqualified stock options (NSOs), which changed the taxation on employee compensation. (Source: *Courthouse News*)

EXAMPLE: EXECUTIVE SALARY WITH ISO

Leo Wilde was hired as a regional manager with Amificat International. Amificat International's stock had a market price of $25 per share when Leo was hired. He was offered an annual salary of $78,000 paid biweekly and an ISO of 1,000 shares at $25 per share that could be exercised one year after his hire date.

Biweekly salary = $78,000/26 = <u>$3,000</u>

Note that the ISO, valued at $25,000 at the time of hire, may not be exercised for one year. The value of the stock option would depend on the market price on the date that Leo exercised the stock option by selling his shares. In any case, the ISO does not appear on the payroll register but would be included in the total compensation for the employee.

Combination Pay Methods

Stop & Check

1. Shelly Penzo, a service administrator, receives a base salary of $42,000 per year paid semimonthly, plus $100 commission for each service contract she sells to her customers. During a pay period, she sells five contracts. What is her gross pay for the period?

2. Adam Reininger is a new salesperson with S&D Music. He receives a base salary of $36,000 paid monthly. Company policy allows him to draw 35 percent of his salary on the 15th of each month. How much will Adam receive at mid-month if he elects to take a draw? How much will he receive at the end of the month if he takes the 35 percent draw?

3. Joy Mrowicki, an executive for Adarma Chemicals, receives an annual salary of $75,000 plus an additional 3 percent in an ISO. What is the amount of stock she receives annually? What is her total annual compensation?

LO 3-7   Explain Special Pay Situations

Compensation laws have many exceptions. According to the FLSA, every aspect of labor legislation, including minimum wage and overtime provisions, has its less common applications. The introduction of new types of knowledge-based employment during the 21st century, as well as the continuance of more traditional agricultural tasks, necessitates an examination of these special pay situations.

BassittART/E+/Getty Images

Compensatory Time

The FLSA allows public employees to receive *compensatory (comp) time*, often called "comp time," in lieu of overtime. According to section 3(s)(1)(c) of the FLSA, exempt public employees must receive comp time equal to 1.5 times the overtime hours worked. Therefore, if a public employee worked 5 hours of overtime, the comp time awarded must be 7.5 hours.

Comp time is often misconstrued by the private sector. FLSA provisions for comp time are only for public-sector employees, such as government workers, law enforcement, and seasonally hired laborers. Unless specifically designated by a firm's policies, a private-sector employer is not required to offer comp time. Additionally, many private-sector employers offer comp time on a straight-line basis, meaning that they offer the same number of compensatory hours as the number of overtime hours worked. Firefighters, police, and other emergency workers may receive a maximum of 480 comp hours annually; other public-sector employees are eligible for up to 240 hours of comp time based upon union-negotiated contracts. Certain union comp time contracts will only cover specific peak periods for the work being performed.

When calculating an employee's gross pay, it is prudent to be aware of any effects that a comp time award may have on overtime pay to ensure that the employee's compensation is accurate.

EXAMPLE: PUBLIC EMPLOYEE COMPENSATORY TIME

David Donahue works as an exempt employee of the federal government. In the course of his work, he accrues 8 hours of overtime during a pay period when he completes additional work for an absent co-worker. According to FLSA regulations, David must receive 12 hours of comp time because he is not eligible for paid overtime as an exempt government employee.

On-Call Time

Some professions require employees to be available for work outside of normal working hours. This availability is known as *on-call time*, and two classes of on-call time exist: on-call at the employer's premises, and on-call away from the employer's premises.

- If the employee is required to remain at the employer's premises, the employee's freedom is restricted, and he or she must be compensated for the on-call time.
- If the employee is not restricted to the employer's premises for the on-call time, compensation is not required.

In *Ward v. Tilly's, Inc.,* the employer required its workers to be on-call and be available to report to work within two hours of being requested, even when not being scheduled to work. The employees were not given notice of when they may be called into work, but receive no pay for being on-call. The court found for the employees, in this case, citing California's Work Order 7 that states that employees in on-call situations such as this case must be compensated whether they were required to report for work or not. The judge's reasoning was that the employees could not engage in other occupations or activities because of the requirement to be on-call. (Source: HRDive; California Department of Industrial Relations)

In either case, company policy must be specific regarding the conditions of the on-call time. The number of hours specified for on-call compensation must be added to the employee's gross pay. Company policy should also be specific about the pay rate for the on-call time, especially if the pay rate differs from the employee's regular pay rate.

EXAMPLE: ON-CALL TIME

Kevin Gee works as a service representative for Built Strong, an equipment manufacturer. He earns $19.25/hour for a standard 40-hour workweek and is married filing separately with two dependents. Built Strong requires that each service representative rotate on-call duties in one-week increments, during which they remain available for service calls outside of working hours but may otherwise engage in personal activities. During this on-call time, company policy stipulates that on-call service representatives receive two hours of regular pay for each on-call day. Kevin was on-call during the biweekly pay period ending February 25 and would receive 14 hours of additional straight-time pay for his on-call time. The payroll register would reflect the on-call pay as follows:

Name	Filing Status	Hourly Rate or Period Wage	No. of Regular Hours	No. of On-Call Hours	Reg. Earnings	On-Call Earnings	Gross Earnings
Kevin Gee	MS-2	$19.25	80	14	$1,540.00	$269.50	$1,809.50

Robert Kneschke/Shutterstock

Sleep Time, Travel Time, and Wait Time

Employees have traditionally commuted to and from work, although a growing trend toward telecommuting exists in the 21st century. Travel to and from an office is not compensable time; however, many employees do not work at a single location. Additionally, many employees travel for their employer's benefit for training or other business requirements. Similarly, employees may be required to wait by their employer, as in the case of a chauffeur or a bus driver. Other employees such as firefighters or medical personnel may be required to work 24-hour shifts and must be given at least five hours of paid *sleep time* during that 24-hour period. An agreement between the employer and employee may exist to exclude up to eight hours if the employer provides furnished facilities for uninterrupted sleep.

According to FLSA, the guideline that assists in the determination of compensable activity in these three situations is if the activity is for the employer's benefit. Travel among customer- or business-related sites is compensable as *travel time* because it directly benefits the employer. Requiring a driver to wait as part of the job description also benefits the employer and is compensated as *wait time*. Travel from the employee's home to the office or to the first customer site in the morning and returning home in the evening benefits the employee and is not compensable.

EXAMPLE: SLEEP TIME

Dan Morli is a first-year surgical resident at Mercy Hospital and is classified as a non-exempt employee who earns $124,000 per year, paid semimonthly. The standard workweek is 40 hours. He is single with no dependents. He works two 24-hour shifts per week in the regular course of his employment. His employer provides him a quiet sleeping area, per FLSA requirements. During a single 24-hour shift in the November 15 pay period, he sleeps 7 hours. According to FLSA guidelines, his pay may not be reduced for the first five hours that he sleeps. Dan's gross pay will reflect a two-hour reduction for the additional sleep in excess of the five-hour requirement.

The hourly rate needs to be computed to determine the deduction for the excess sleep time: $124,000/(40 \times 52) = \underline{\$59.62}$

The payroll register would appear as follows:

Name	Filing Status	Hourly Rate or Period Wage	Hourly Rate	Sleep Hours >5	Reg. Earnings	Less Excess Sleep Time	Gross Earnings
Dan Morli	S-0	$5,166.67	$59.62	2	$5,166.67	$(119.24)	$5,047.43

Note the inclusion of the sleep hours in excess of five and the deduction. The purpose of tracking this information is to highlight specific issues with employee performance and related costs, which leads to stronger managerial control.

Jury Duty

Employees may be summoned to serve on a jury for court cases. In the event that an employee is required to serve jury duty, the pay given to employees for the time spent away from work in this capacity is at the discretion of the employer. Some employers pay their employees their full compensation, while others pay a predetermined alternate amount. If an employee receives full compensation while on jury duty, the company may require the employee to return or reject the jury duty pay.

Sub-Minimum Wage Situations

Tipped employees are not the only workers who may legally receive compensation lower than the minimum wage. Other specific classes of employees may receive an hourly wage that is less than the FLSA minimum wage.

A 1996 amendment to the FLSA allows workers younger than the age of 20 to be paid a minimum wage of $4.25 per hour, but only for the first 90 calendar days of employment.

Note that overtime worked by employees who are paid at sub-minimum wage rates may not be less than the federal minimum wage.

EXAMPLE: YOUNG EMPLOYEE

Cady Horn is a new employee of The Big Chicken, a fast-food restaurant in Glendale, Arizona, where new employees are paid minimum wage. Cady is 18 years of age and is single with no dependents. During the weekly pay period ending July 18, she worked 37 hours. The payroll register would appear as follows:

Name	Filing Status	Hourly Rate or Period Wage	No. of Regular Hours	No. of Overtime Hours	Reg. Earnings	Gross Earnings
Cady Horn	S-0	$4.25	37		$157.25	$157.25

An employer may obtain a certificate to pay a worker with disabilities related to the work performed an amount less than the minimum wage. According to section 14(c) of the FLSA, employers must obtain a certificate to pay less than the minimum wage.

EXAMPLE: DISABLED WORKER

Christi Snow is employed as a call-center representative with OEC Dispatch in Bend, Oregon. She is disabled due to a hearing impairment, and OEC Dispatch has obtained a certificate under section 14(c) of the FLSA in order to pay Christi $10.50/hour, which is less than the Oregon minimum wage of $11.25/hour. During the weekly pay period ending March 10, Christi worked 44 hours, 4 hours of which were overtime. She is single with two dependents. The payroll register for the period would appear as follows:

Name	Filing Status	Hourly Rate or Period Wage	No. of Regular Hours	No. of Overtime Hours	Reg. Earning	Overtime Earnings	Gross Earnings
Christi Snow	S-2	$10.50	40	4	$420.00	$63.00	$483.00

Full-time students in the employ of retail establishments, agriculture, colleges, and universities may receive a wage that is 85 percent of the federal minimum wage. Like disabled employees, the employer must obtain a certificate authorizing the sub-minimum wage.

EXAMPLE: FULL-TIME STUDENT WAGE

Kay Stone works in the café at Valparaiso University in Valparaiso, Indiana. She is a full-time student at the university and is 20 years old. According to the FLSA, she may receive 85 percent of the minimum wage.

Indiana minimum wage: $7.25/hour

Full-time student wage = $7.25/hour × 0.85 = $6.16/hour

(continued)

(concluded)

In her employment at the café, Katie may legally be paid $6.16 per hour while she is a full-time student. During the week of May 4, she worked 35 hours. She is single with no dependents. The payroll register would appear as follows:

Name	Filing Status	Hourly Rate or Period Wage	No. of Regular Hours	No. of Overtime Hours	Reg. Earning	Overtime Earnings	Gross Earnings
Kay Stone	S-0	$6.16	35		$215.60		$215.60

According to section 14(a) of the FLSA, student learners in vocational education programs may be paid at a rate of 75 percent of the federal minimum wage. Similar to situations involving disabled employees, the employer must obtain a certificate authorizing the sub-minimum wage.

EXAMPLE: STUDENT WORKER IN VOCATIONAL EDUCATION PROGRAM

Ben Yoo is enrolled at Middlebury High School in Maine and is taking a shop class as part of his program. Ben is 16 and is single with no dependents. He works for Vining's Cabinets as an apprentice woodworker. After obtaining a certificate from the U.S. Department of Labor's Wage and Hour National Certification Team, Vining's Cabinets pays Ben an hourly wage of $9.00 because of his enrollment in the shop class at his high school. During the weekly pay period ending December 18, Ben worked 36 hours. The payroll register would reflect his pay as follows:

Name	Filing Status	Hourly Rate or Period Wage	No. of Regular Hours	No. of Overtime Hours	Reg. Earnings	Overtime Earnings	Gross Earnings
Ben Yoo	S-0	$9.00	36		$324.00		$324.00

Nonqualified Deferred Compensation

Certain employees may be subject to the nonqualified deferred compensation provisions of IRS Code section 409(a). Nonqualified deferred compensation pertains to employees who earn compensation in one period but elect to receive it in a later period. A common example of this practice involves teachers who work during the nine-month academic year but elect to receive compensation for 12 months. Under section 409(a), this type of compensation is taxed like any other employee pay.

Olena Yakobchuk/Shutterstock

Pension Payments

Employers occasionally offer pension plans to their employees. The percent of employees who participate in employer-sponsored pensions has decreased due to the availability of alternate retirement plans (i.e., 401(k), 403(b), etc.), and pension funding has experienced shortfalls among both private and governmental employers. When the pension enters the payout period, the retired employee receives their pension less any federal tax due. FICA taxes do not apply to pension plan payments.

Retroactive Pay

If an employee is due retroactive pay ("back pay") because of compensation increases or labor union negotiations, the wages must be issued at the earliest time and all applicable taxes are due. To receive back pay, the FLSA has three methods available:

1. The Department of Labor's Wage and Hour Division may provide supervision for the payment.

2. A lawsuit for back pay *plus* an equal amount of damages may be brought by the Secretary of Labor.

3. The employee may initiate a lawsuit for the back pay *plus* an equal amount of damages *plus* attorney's fees and court costs.

It is important to note that the statute of limitations for back pay lawsuits is two years. However, if willful nonpayment can be proven, the statute of limitations is three years.

> In early 2019, the Gilroy (California) Federation of Paraeducators came to an agreement to grant pay raises to the educational support staff that was retroactive to July 1, 2017. This pay raise was spread incrementally over two fiscal years to spread the impact on the school district's budget. (Source: *Gilroy Dispatch*)

Wages for Deceased Employees

If an employee dies while a current employee of a firm, it is important to understand the payroll implications associated with gross pay. IRS guidelines stipulate that wages earned prior to the employee's death must be paid as accurately as possible to reflect the amount of work performed. A special note about deceased employee pay is that the employee's pay if issued specifically in a check form may need to be reissued to the deceased employee's estate.

What Is the Correct Pay?

1. Alex Longwith is a nonexempt employee of The Silver Club. He works 10 hours of overtime during a pay period and requests that he receive compensatory time instead of overtime pay. The Silver Club's overtime policy states that that compensatory time may be offered at 1.5 times the number of hours worked in excess of 40. His employer grants his request and offers him 10 hours of compensatory time. How much comp time should Alex receive? Explain.

2. Stacy Albom is a student in a vocational program at a cosmetology school. She accepts employment as a shampooer at Cuts & Styles Hair Salon in Alabama. The agreement between the school and the salon is that students receive the student-learner minimum wage. How much should Stacy be paid per hour?

Summary of Gross Pay Computation

Gross pay is the employee's compensation before taxes and other withholdings are deducted; net pay is the amount of money an employee receives after taxes and other deductions are subtracted. We discussed the different types of methods for pay computation, including salary, hourly, commission, and piece-rate pay. Gross pay is complex and a variety of combinations exist to meet the needs of the traditional and the gig economies.

We looked at the effect of FLSA provisions and applicability of different compensation methods and offered examples of some job classifications that could be compensated using different methods. We discussed the use of a payroll register in computing gross pay and explored the concepts of the total, prove, and rule to ensure accurate computation of gross pay.

EMPLOYEE COMPENSATION

Employee compensation tends to be a hot topic because of the way it affects people on a personal level. Some developments since 2015 in employee compensation include the following:

- Increased diligence in overtime tracking and compensation following a lawsuit involving large companies.
- New types of incentive pay to increase employee engagement, including merchandise rewards, additional company benefits, and other nonmonetary awards.
- Discussions of the legality of differential pay levels for travel time by nonexempt employees.
- Discussions about gaps in wages between people with and without a college education.

Some trends to watch in employee compensation include the following:

- Entry-level employee pay increases due to increases in states' minimum wages.
- Equal pay among genders, races, and other variables will continue to be a driving force in employee compensation
- Bonuses and other short-term incentives will be used more widely among employers to entice other employees.
- Employee pay will become more transparent and less taboo among workers, especially young employees.
- States will drive compensation mandates to meet the living wage needs of their employees.

We explored a variety of situations involving overtime pay and discussed the computations for different pay bases. We concluded with a discussion of special compensation situations, including on-call time, time spent unoccupied for the employer's benefit, and situations in which an employee may receive less than the FLSA minimum wage. The conclusion had an explanation of retroactive pay and other less-common pay situations.

Key Points

- Gross pay is the total amount earned by an employee prior to the deductions for taxes or other withholdings.
- Employees may be subject to the wage and hour provisions of the FLSA (nonexempt) or they may not (exempt), depending on the type of job and employee duties.
- Nonexempt hourly employees are compensated on a basis that recognizes an economic connection between work performed and wages paid.
- Nonexempt salaried employees work a fixed number of working hours per week and receive overtime compensation.
- Exempt employees receive a fixed salary and may work more hours than their nonexempt colleagues.
- Commission-based pay connects employee compensation with sales revenue.
- Piece-rate pay compensates employees based on the manufacturing or completion of goods or services.
- The payroll register is an integral tool to ensure the accuracy of payroll computations, especially in combination pay situations.

- Employees who work on a commission basis may have the option to draw against future earnings.
- ISOs are a means of offering compensation on a tax-deferred basis that is connected to the market price of the company's stock.
- Compensatory time is legally required for public-sector exempt employees and may be offered to private-sector employees at the employer's discretion.
- Overtime pay is computed according to the guidelines published by the IRS, as appropriate to the employee's pay base.
- Employees may be compensated for time that they are unoccupied if they are required to be available for the employer's benefit.
- Retroactive "back pay" and pension pay are situations requiring additional care in processing to avoid lawsuits.
- In certain circumstances, employees may receive less than the FLSA minimum wage.

Vocabulary

Combination pay
Commission
Compensatory (comp) time
Draw
Eight and Eighty (8 and 80)
Exempt
Gross pay
Hourly
Hundredth-hour system

Incentive stock options (ISOs)
Minimum wage
Net pay
Nonexempt
On-call time
Overtime
Payroll register
Piece rate
Prove
Quarter-hour system

Rule
Salary
Sleep time
Time card
Tip credit
Tipped employee
Tipped wages
Total
Travel time
Wait time

Review Questions

1. How is overtime pay computed for nonexempt, salaried workers?
2. When do overtime rates apply?
3. How does minimum wage affect commission employees?
4. How does the tipped minimum wage differ from the FLSA minimum wage?
5. What types of occupations are typically salaried?
6. What is an ISO, and how does it affect employee pay?
7. What is the difference between a salary and a draw?
8. How is overtime computed for piece-rate employees?
9. In what situations could a salaried employee receive overtime pay?
10. What is the primary difference between commission work and piece-rate work?
11. In what situations might an employee draw money against his or her future pay?
12. What is the difference between quarter-hour and hundredth-hour pay?
13. Why are companies moving toward the hundredth-hour system?
14. What is comp time?
15. Under what circumstances may an employee receive compensation for on-call time?
16. When are wait time, travel time, and sleep time compensable?
17. Aside from tipped employees, under what circumstances may an employee receive less than the FLSA minimum wage?
18. What is one of the three methods for employees to receive retroactive pay?
19. What amount did the Final Rule stipulate as the minimum wage for salaried workers?

Exercises Set A

E3-1A.
LO 3-1

Thomas Wilson is a minimum wage worker in Nevada. He is contemplating a move to another state. Which of the following states would be the most favorable in terms of the highest minimum wage?
1. Idaho
2. California
3. Utah
4. Arizona

E3-2A.
LO 3-1

Certain types of businesses are always covered by FLSA provisions. Which of the following businesses are always covered by FLSA? (Select all that apply.)
1. Fruit stands selling only locally obtained goods that conduct no interstate business.
2. A school for children with learning disabilities.
3. A privately run hospital.
4. A Social Security Administration branch office.

E3-3A.
LO 3-1

Marion Barker is a tipped employee in Wisconsin. What is the minimum cash wage for her state?
1. $2.13/hour
2. $2.33/hour
3. $3.32/hour
4. $4.93/hour

E3-4A.
LO 3-1

Rick Richards, a waiter at the Misosis Club in Pennsylvania, receives the tipped minimum wage. During a 40-hour workweek, how much must he earn in tips to meet the minimum wage requirement?
1. $85.20
2. $113.20
3. $176.80
4. $204.80

E3-5A.
LO 3-2

Marty Burgess works for Hyrolated Sports. His compensation is based on sales of store products to customers. Which type of pay basis represents Marty's pay?
1. Piece rate
2. Hourly
3. Commission
4. Salary

E3-6A.
LO 3-3

Lana Reid is an accounting clerk at Tenity Enterprises who is paid $18.15 per hour. During a week's pay period, she worked 39 hours and 41 minutes. Based on a hundredth-hour pay method, what is her gross pay for the period? (Round the final answer to two decimal places.)
1. $726.00
2. $721.46
3. $716.93
4. $720.25

E3-7A.
LO 3-4

According to the FLSA, what is the basis used to determine overtime worked for standard nonexempt workers?
1. The 8 and 80 rule.
2. The excess over 40 hours during a pay period.
3. The excess over 40 hours in seven consecutive days.
4. The excess over 8 hours in a 24-hour period.

E3-8A.
LO 3-4

Eugene Torres works in a shared role for Multiglass Computers. He works in both the programming and the research departments for the company and splits his time equally in both roles. Eugene is paid $20 per hour in the programming department and $28 per hour in the research department. When he works overtime in the research department, what is his pay rate?
1. $30 per hour
2. $36 per hour
3. $42 per hour
4. $48 per hour

E3-9A.
LO 3-5

Of the items in the following list, which one(s) should appear in a payroll register? (Select all that apply.)
1. Name
2. Home address
3. Shifts worked
4. Hours worked

E3-10A.
LO 3-5

Tricia Grey is a salaried, exempt employee with Meganti Inc. She is single with one dependent and earns $45,000 per year. Complete the payroll register for the biweekly pay period ending June 10, 20XX with a pay date of June 15, 20XX.

Run Date:										

P/R Date:						Company:				

Name	Filing Status	Period Wage	Period Salary	Commissions	Draw	No. of Regular Hours	No. of Overtime Hours	Reg. Earnings	Overtime Earnings	Gross Earnings

E3-11A.
LO 3-6

Jeremy Ortiz is an employee of Insulor Flooring, where his job responsibilities include selling service contracts to customers. Jeremy is single with two dependents. He receives an annual salary of $36,000 and receives a 3 percent commission on all sales. During the semimonthly pay period ending September 29, 20XX, Jeremy sold $12,500 of service contracts. Complete the payroll register for the September 29 pay period with a pay date of October 2nd.

Run Date:										

P/R Date:						Company:				

Name	Filing Status	Period Wage	Period Salary	Commissions	Draw	No. of Regular Hours	No. of Overtime Hours	Reg. Earnings	Overtime Earnings	Gross Earnings

E3-12A.
LO 3-7

Jude Sizemore is a full-time student at Sioux City College in Sioux City, Iowa, where he works in the library. What is the minimum hourly wage that he may receive?
1. $7.25 per hour
2. $6.50 per hour
3. $6.16 per hour
4. $5.44 per hour

Problems Set A

P3-1A.
LO 3-3

Edie Manson worked the following schedule: Monday, 8 hours; Tuesday, 9 hours; Wednesday, 7 hours 48 minutes; Thursday, 8 hours; Friday, 8 hours. The employer pays overtime for all time worked in excess of 40 hours per week. Complete the following table. Determine Edie's total time worked according to the (a) quarter-hour method and (b) the hundredth-hour method. Which is the more favorable method for Edie, quarter-hour or hundredth-hour?

	Quarter-Hour Time	Hundredth-Hour Time	More Favorable Method
E. Manson			

P3-2A.
LO 3-2

Bobby Howard is a salaried exempt employee at Coric Industries. He is married filing jointly with two dependents. His contract stipulates a 40-hour workweek at $47,500 per year. During the week ending November 27, there was a company-paid holiday for one day. Calculate Bobby's weekly pay. Round wages to five decimal points.

Name	Filing Status	Annual Salary	Hourly Rate	No. of Regular Hours	No. of Holiday Hours	Reg. Earnings	Holiday Earnings	Gross Earnings

P3-3A.
LO 3-2

Cheryl Bryant completed designing 22 custom cakes on her 18-cake contract as an employee of Frontier Wedding Planners. There is a bonus earned if the individual exceeds 145 percent of her piece contract. How many cakes must Cheryl complete in the remainder of the week to receive the bonus?

P3-4A.
LO 3-5

Ernest Miller works for Skyescent Parachutes. He is a shared employee; he works in the manufacturing department and has been trained to work the sales counter in times of need. During other employees' vacations, he was asked to work in the sales department on two days for six hours each day. When he works in the manufacturing department, he earns $15.50 per hour. Ernest earns a $2.50 pay differential for working the sales counter. He worked a total of 39 hours and 32 minutes during the week. Ernest is single with no dependents. Compute Ernest's pay for the week ending May 22 using the quarter-hour system. (Use a separate line for each job classification.)

Name	Filing Status	Hourly Rate or Period Salary	No. of Regular Hours	Reg. Earnings	Gross Earnings

P3-5A.
LO 3-3

Marcell Teague submitted a pay card reflecting the following hours worked at Kicy Inc. He earns $16.02 per hour. The company pays overtime only on hours worked exceeding 40 per week. The company is considering changing from quarter-hour to hundredth-hour time collection. Under the current quarter-hour system, each time the employee clocks in or out, the time is rounded to the nearest quarter-hour. Calculate Marcell's time for both the quarter-hour and hundredth-hour systems. (Round your intermediate calculations and final answers to two decimal places.)

In	Out	In	Out	Total Hours with Quarter-Hour	Total Hours with Hundredth-Hour
8:00	11:22	12:17	5:22		
7:29	12:30	1:45	4:10		
9:12	11:45	12:28	3:36		
8:00	11:00	12:02	5:00		

What is Marcell's total pay in a quarter-hour system?_____

What is Marcell's total pay in a hundredth-hour system? _____

P3-6A.
LO 3-4

Ranee Tolliver is a nurse at Great Meadows Hospital. She is paid $28 per hour and has a 40-hour standard workweek. During the biweekly pay period from May 15–28, she worked a total of 95 hours. What is her gross pay?

P3-7A.
LO 3-5

Terry McNutt, a single employee with two dependents, is paid $12 per hour and receives a commission on net sales. He does not receive a commission until his net sales exceed $150,000. Once the minimum net sales are reached, he receives a 4 percent commission on all of his sales at Skidoo Sports. During the week of January 24, he sold $87,000 of ski equipment; however, he had $2,250 of returns from the prior week's sales. Company policy requires that commissions on sales returns are deducted from the employee's pay, regardless of current commission earnings. Compute Terry's gross pay for the 40-hour weekly pay period.

Name	Filing Status	Hourly Rate	No. of Regular Hours	Reg. Earnings	Commissions	Gross Earnings

P3-8A.
LO 3-1, 3-2

Renata McCarter, an outside sales representative for Alinda Publications, receives 15 percent commission on all new magazine subscriptions she sells in her sales territory. During the week of March 27, she sold $4,500 of new subscriptions and worked 40 hours.

What is her gross pay?_____

Is she subject to minimum wage laws?_____

Why or why not?_____

P3-9A.
LO 3-1, 3-2

Telemarketers receive $15 commission on all new customers that sign up for cell phone service through Movill Networks. Each telemarketer works 40 hours. The company ran a competition this week to see who could sign up the most new people and the winner would get a bonus of $75. Because these employees are paid solely on commission, the employer must ensure that they earn the federal minimum wage for 40 hours each week. Compute the gross pay for each of the following outbound sales representatives.

Employee	Number of New Customers Signed	Total Commission	Difference Between Commission and Minimum Pay (if the minimum is not met)	Total Gross Pay
S. McCulloch	25			
F. Odell	18			
S. Heller	23			
V. Caro	15			

P3-10A.

LO 3-1, 3-2

For each of the piece-rate workers below, determine gross pay. If the employees have a standard 40-hour workweek, what is their effective hourly wage? Based on the state's minimum wage in South Dakota, calculate each employee's minimum weekly pay. What is the difference the employer must pay between the calculated gross pay and the calculated state's minimum pay? (Reminder: Divide gross pay by 40 hours to determine the hourly wage.)

Worker	Number of Items	Rate per Item	Gross Pay	Gross Pay/ 40 Hours	Minimum Pay	Difference to Be Paid by the Employer
E. McNeal	25 boat hulls	$10				
T. Fair	70 seat covers	$15				
M. Sturgeon	45 steering mechanisms	$ 4				

P3-11A.

LO 3-4

Damien Carranza is a nonexempt employee of Verent Enterprises where he is a salesperson, earning a base annual salary of $30,000 with a standard 40-hour workweek. He earns a 3 percent commission on all sales during the pay period. During the weekly pay period ending August 21, Damien closed $25,000 in sales and worked 4 hours overtime. What is his gross pay for the period?

P3-12A.

LO 3-1, 3-2, 3-4

Nigel McCloskey is a waiter at Albicious Foods in South Carolina. He is single with one dependent. He receives the standard tipped hourly wage. During the week ending October 22, 20XX, he worked 44 hours and received $210 in tips. Calculate his gross pay, assuming his tips are included in the overtime rate determination.

Name	Filing Status	Reg. Hourly Rate	Overtime Rate	No. of Regular Hours	No. of Overtime Hours	Reg. Earnings	Tips	Overtime Earnings	Gross Earnings

Does Albicious Foods need to contribute to Nigel's wages to meet FLSA requirements? _____

If so, how much should be contributed? _____

P3-13A.

LO 3-5

Stephanie Parker is a salaried, nonexempt administrator for Forise Industries and is paid biweekly. Her annual salary is $63,000, and her standard workweek is 45 hours. During the pay period ending February 3, 20XX, she worked 8 hours overtime. She is married filing jointly with two dependents. Complete the following payroll register for Stephanie's pay. (Round intermediate calculations to two decimal points.)

Name	Filing Status	Annual Salary	Hourly Rate	Overtime Rate	No. of Regular Hours	No. of Overtime Hours	Reg. Earnings	Overtime Earnings	Gross Earnings

P3-14A.

LO 3-6

Brigida Masterson is an administrative assistant for Maxilane Fashions. At the end of her shift one day, her employer requires her to deliver a package to a customer before traveling home. Her normal commute is an hour. She spends two hours driving to the customer site, and then another hour driving home for a total of three hours' drive time. How much of Brigida's travel time is compensable?

P3-15A.
LO 3-7

Rico Musgrove is an 18-year-old worker in the receiving department of Trynix Inc. in St. Paul, Minnesota. On his first paycheck, he notices that he received $170.00 gross pay for 40 hours of work. Did his employer pay him correctly? Explain.

Exercises Set B

E3-1B.
LO 3-1

Barbara Hampton is a minimum wage worker in Ohio. She is contemplating moving to a state with a more favorable minimum wage. Which of the following states should she choose?
1. Indiana
2. Michigan
3. Arkansas
4. Kentucky

E3-2B.
LO 3-1

Which one of the following workers is covered by FLSA provisions? (Select all that apply.)
1. Factory manager for an international company.
2. Part-time babysitter earning $1,000 annually.
3. Professional chauffeur earning $25,000 annually.
4. Assistant fire chief for a small town.

E3-3B.
LO 3-1

Julie Stevens is a tipped employee at the Neovee Resort in Hawaii. What is the minimum cash wage for her area, assuming she receives in excess of $20 in tips per pay period?
1. $9.35/hour
2. $2.13/hour
3. $3.62/hour
4. $8.25/hour

E3-4B.
LO 3-1

Rosalie Moran is a waitress at a restaurant in Washington, D.C., named Molly's Diner. She earns the tipped minimum wage. During a 40-hour workweek, how much must she earn in tips to satisfy the minimum wage requirement (without consideration of the tip credit)?
1. $85.20
2. $382.00
3. $190.00
4. $349.20

E3-5B.
LO 3-2

Austin Sherman is an employee of Divacee Designs. He is an interior designer who is paid based on the number and complexity of the customer designs he generates. What pay basis most accurately describes his compensation?
1. Hourly
2. Commission
3. Piece-rate
4. Salary

E3-6B.
LO 3-3

Doreen George, a stocker at Dender Factory Outlet, is paid on an hourly basis and earns $12.45/hour. During a one-week period, she worked 39 hours and 19 minutes. How much would her gross pay be under the quarter-hour system? (Round your final answer to two decimal places.)
1. $485.55
2. $488.66
3. $489.49
4. $491.78

E3-7B.

LO 3-4

Johnny Clark is a tipped employee at Pyrolia Pizza. What are the two methods his employer may use to determine his overtime compensation?

1. Compute gross pay based on the minimum cash wage plus tips.
2. Compute gross pay based on an average of the minimum cash wage and the maximum tip credit.
3. Compute gross pay based on the minimum cash wage, excluding tips.
4. Compute gross pay based on the minimum cash wage multiplied by the overtime rate (i.e., 1.5).

E3-8B.

LO 3-4

Jacques Beasley is a salaried nonexempt accounting clerk for Supplies Enterprises who is contracted to work 45 hours per week. How should his overtime be determined, according to FLSA?

1. Any hours worked in excess of 40 during a consecutive 7-day period.
2. Any hours worked in excess of 45 during a consecutive 7-day period.
3. Any hours worked in excess of 80 during a consecutive 14-day period.
4. Any hours worked in excess of 45 during a consecutive 14-day period.

E3-9B.

LO 3-5

Of the following items listed, which ones should appear in a payroll register? (Select all that apply.)

1. Gross pay
2. Hourly rate
3. Period ending date
4. Office number

E3-10B.

LO 3-4, 3-5

Hubert Jennings is an hourly employee working for Symoid Industries. He is married filing joint with two dependents and earns $22.15 per hour. During a biweekly pay period ending February 21, 20XX, he worked 88.5 hours. Complete the payroll register with the period's information. (Note: round overtime rate computation to 3 decimal places. All earnings should be rounded to two decimal places.)

Name	Filing Status	Hourly Rate	Overtime Rate	No. of Regular Hours	No. of Overtime Hours	Regular Earnings	Overtime Earnings	Gross Earnings

E3-11B.

LO 3-6

Paula Warren is an employee of Archic Outdoor Gear, where she earns a base salary of $27,200 plus an 8 percent commission on all sales. She is married filing jointly with four dependents. During the biweekly pay period ended June 16, 20XX, Paula made $15,000 in sales. Complete the payroll register for the pay period.

Name	Filing Status	Period Salary	Sales	Reg. Earnings	Commission Earnings	Gross Earnings

E3-12B.

LO 3-7

Sherrill Pullman is 18 years of age and is a new employee of Camicero Bank in Hendersonville, Tennessee. What is the minimum hourly wage that she may receive during the first 90 days of employment?

1. $9.47 per hour
2. $2.13 per hour
3. $7.25 per hour
4. $4.25 per hour

Problems Set B

P3-1B.
LO 3-3

Ruben Trout worked the following schedule: Monday, 8 hours, 24 minutes; Tuesday, 7 hours, 44 minutes; Wednesday, 9 hours, 8 minutes; Thursday, 8 hours, 2 minutes; Friday, 8 hours, 36 minutes. The employer pays overtime in accordance with FLSA regulations. Determine Ruben's total time worked according to the (a) quarter-hour method and (b) the hundredth-hour method. Which is the more favorable method for Ruben, quarter-hour or hundredth-hour?

	Quarter-Hour Time	Hundredth-Hour Time	More Favorable Method
R. Trout			

P3-2B.
LO 3-2

Harvey Ramos is a salaried exempt employee at Duodo Scales with a contract that stipulates 35 hours per week at $52,000 per year. He is married filing separately with three dependents. The pay period ending November 26 contained two company-paid holidays. Calculate Harvey's biweekly pay based on a standard five-day workweek. Round wages to five decimal points. (Hint: Determine Harvey's hourly wage to determine holiday pay.)

Name	Filing Status	Period Salary	Hourly Rate	No. of Regular Hours	No. of Holiday Hours	Reg. Earnings	Holiday Earnings	Gross Earnings

P3-3B.
LO 3-2

Doris Black completed 1,750 pieces on her 2,000-piece contract for Make It Work. There is a bonus earned if the individual exceeds 115 percent of the piece contract. How many more pieces must Doris complete in the remainder of the pay period to receive the bonus?

P3-4B.
LO 3-4, 3-5

Katrina Hughes is a shared employee; she works in the accounting department and has been trained to work at the front desk in times of need. During one weekly pay period, she was asked to work at the front desk on four days for five hours each day. When she works in the accounting department, she earns $17.26 per hour and earns $13.75 per hour for working at the front desk. She worked a total of 45 hours during the week. Complete the payroll register using separate lines for each job classification, and place the overtime on her accounting department hours.

Name	Filing Status	Hourly Rate	No. of Regular Hours	No. of Overtime Hours	Reg. Earnings	Overtime Earnings	Gross Earnings

P3-5B.
LO 3-3

Simon Cunningham earns $16.45 per hour at Transist Electronics. Compute his pay under both the hundredth-hour and quarter-hour systems. The company is considering switching from a quarter-hour method to a hundredth-hour method. Simon submitted the following time card:

In	Out	In	Out	Total Hours with Quarter-Hour	Total Hours with Hundredth-Hour
8:08	11:57	12:59	4:57		
9:04	12:17	1:28	5:18		
7:45	11:45	12:43	4:01		
7:57	12:04	1:03	5:06		

Simon's total pay in the hundredth-hour system: _____

Simon's total pay in a quarter-hour system: _____

Which is the most beneficial for Simon?: _____

P3-6B.

LO 3-4

Shelli Quintanilla is the concierge at Hotel Amize where she is a nonexempt employee earning $18 per hour plus a $250 biweekly bonus based on customer reviews. During the pay period of November 27–December 10, she worked 85 hours and earned the entire bonus. What is her gross pay for the pay period, assuming a 40-hour standard workweek?

P3-7B.

LO 3-4, 3-5

Jesse Daniels is a commission-based employee who is single with no dependents. She is paid $13.50/hour and receives a 5 percent commission on net sales. She does not receive commissions until her net sales exceed $55,500 during a weekly period at Perous Pharmaceuticals. For the week ending May 5, 20XX, she worked 48 hours and sold $67,500 of medicinal supplies but had $900 of returns from last week's sales. Company policy requires that commissions on returned sales be deducted from her pay during the next pay period. Compute her gross pay for the week.

Name	Filing Status	Hourly Rate	No. of Regular Hours	No. of Overtime Hours	Reg. Earnings	Overtime Earnings	Net Commissions	Gross Earnings

P3-8B.

LO 3-1, 3-2

Lacie Bingham, an outside sales representative for Redoo Insurance, receives 4 percent commission on all new policies she receives in her sales territory. During the pay period ending April 16, she sold $150,000 of new policies and worked 40 hours.

What is her gross pay? _____

Is she subject to minimum wage laws? _____

Why or why not?_____

P3-9B.

LO 3-1, 3-2

Outbound sales representatives at Alindu Magazines in Arizona receive a $20 commission on all new customers they sign up for new magazine subscriptions. Each outbound sales representative works 40 hours. During a weekly competition, the outbound sales representative who sold the most subscriptions was awarded a $125 bonus. Because these employees are paid solely on commission, the employer must ensure that they earn the federal minimum wage for 40 hours each week. Compute the gross pay for each of the following outbound sales representatives and the difference when the commission pay is less than the gross pay at minimum wage.

Employee	Number of New Customers Signed	Total Commission	Gross Pay at Minimum Wage	Difference Between Commission and Minimum Pay (if the minimum is not met)
H. Meyers	35			
M. Jansen	19			
K. Bartels	42			
T. Macklin	29			

P3-10B.

LO 3-1, 3-2

For each of the piece-rate workers at Perigen Snowsports, determine gross pay. If the employees have a standard 37.5-hour workweek, determine their effective hourly rate. Based on the minimum wage for New Hampshire, what is the minimum wage they must receive each week? If they are not receiving the FLSA minimum wage for the pay period, what is the difference that must be paid by the employer? (Remember: Effective hourly rate equals the gross pay divided by 37.5 hours.)

Worker	Number of Items	Rate per Item	Gross Pay	Gross Pay/ 37.5 Hours	Minimum Pay	Difference to Be Paid by the Employer
S. Jackson	25 snowboards	$9.00				
A. Foster	30 helmets	$7.75				
L. Howard	80 bindings	$4.50				

P3-11B.
LO 3-4

Latoyia Judge is a piece-rate employee at Anible Computers. She receives $30 for each desktop computer that she assembles and has a standard 40-hour workweek. During the weekly pay period ending December 15, she completed the assembly of 48 computers and worked 44 hours, all of which are productive hours. What is her gross pay for the period?

P3-12B.
LO 3-1, 3-2

Clarence Torres is the concierge at the Forise Resort in Oregon. He is single with one dependent. He receives the standard tipped hourly wage for the state. During the week ending December 3, 20XX, he worked 40 hours and received $105 in tips. Compute Clarence's pay for the period.

Name	Filing Status	Hourly Rate	No. of Regular Hours	Reg. Earnings	Tips	Gross Earnings

Does the Forise Resort need to contribute to Clarence's wages to meet FLSA minimum wage requirements?_____
If so, how much must the employer contribute?_____

P3-13B.
LO 3-5

Dennis Murphy is a salaried, nonexempt administrative assistant for Dionti Investments and is paid semimonthly. He is married filing jointly with five dependents. His annual salary is $65,000, and his standard workweek is 37.5 hours. During the pay period, he worked 10 hours overtime. Compute Dennis's gross pay for the period ending August 18, 20XX.

Name	Filing Status	Annual Salary	Hourly Rate	Overtime Rate	No. of Regular Hours	No.of Overtime Hours	Reg. Earnings	Overtime Earnings	Gross Earnings

P3-14B.
LO 3-6

Joshua Peterson is a sales assistant at Cogindu Connectors whose normal commute time is 30 minutes in each direction. At the beginning of his shift one day, his employer requires him to pick up a package from a customer before arriving at work. This activity is considered part of his principal work duties. He spends an additional 60 minutes driving to the customer site and then another 30 minutes driving to the office, for a total of 1.5 hours drive time on his way to his primary work location for the day. How much of Joshua's travel time is compensable?

P3-15B.
LO 3-7

Annie Adams is a 19-year-old accounting clerk with Quijen Accounting Solutions. During the first month of her employment at Quijen, she noticed that she received $369.75 for her first biweekly pay covering 87 regular hours. Did the employer pay her correctly? Explain.

Critical Thinking

3-1. West Virginia State University has a policy of hiring students to work in its bookstores and cafeterias. Assuming that 138 students work for the university at minimum wage rates, what is the amount of pay they will receive for a biweekly pay period, assuming they each work 30 hours per week?

3-2. Thomas Campbell owns Veiled Wonders, a firm that makes window treatments. Some merchandise is custom-made to customer specifications, and some is mass-produced in standardized measurements. He has production workers who work primarily on standardized blinds and some employees who additionally work on custom products on an as-needed basis. How should he structure his pay methods for his production workers?

In the Real World: Scenario for Discussion

Many states offer incentives to hire disabled individuals. When doing so, the employer must receive a specific waiver allowing them to pay sub-minimum wage. This can be a great outreach for the employer in assisting the disabled community to obtain independence and a sense of self-worth.

Review various state agencies, determine the wages that may be paid to the disabled workers and what benefits a couple of states have. What federal incentives are there for hiring disabled workers?

Internet Activities

3-1. Using a search engine such as Google, Yahoo, or Bing, search "commission-based pay." Sites such as the Society for Human Resource Management (www.shrm.com) have a large volume of articles about commission-based pay and workplace cases. Choose a case and find out as much as you can about the company involved. Why do you think that commission-based pay is such a popular topic among human resource professionals?

3-2. Go to www.accountingtools.com/podcasts and look for payroll-related podcasts. Once you have listened to one or more podcasts, what do you feel was the most interesting information you learned?

3-3. Want to learn more about the concepts in this chapter? Check out

www.dol.gov/whd/minwage/america.htm

www.flsa.com/coverage.html

http://webapps.dol.gov/elaws/otcalculator.htm

3-4. Would you like to watch a video to learn more about FLSA treatment of minimum wage, hours worked, and overtime? Check out the following links:

Topic 2: Minimum Wage

Topic 4: Hours Worked

Topic 5: Overtime

Continuing Payroll Project: Prevosti Farms and Sugarhouse

The first day of work for Prevosti Farms and Sugarhouse for all employees is February 3, 2020. February 7 is the end of the first pay period and includes work completed during the week of February 3-7. Compute the employee gross pay using 35 hours as the standard workweek for all employees except Mary Shangraw, who works 20 hours per week and receives overtime for any time worked past that point per company policy. The other hourly employees receive overtime pay when they work more than 35 hours in one week. Joel Schwartz has made $5,000 in case sales at a 3 percent commission rate during this pay period. Remember that the employees are paid biweekly. Note that the first pay period comprises only one week of work, but the pay frequency for federal income tax purposes is biweekly.

Exempt employee pay information is as follows:

Name	Annual Salary	Notes
Millen	$35,000	
Lewis	$32,000	
Schwartz	$24,000	plus 3% commission on sales
Prevosti	$45,000	

The hours for the nonexempt employees are as follows:

Name	Hourly Rate	Hours Worked 2/3–2/7	Regular Time Pay	Overtime Pay	Commission Pay	Gross Pay
Towle	$12.00	35 hours				
Long	$12.50	40 hours				
Shangraw	$11.00	21 hours				
Success (You)	$18.68	35 hours				

Complete the payroll register for the period's gross pay. Pay will be disbursed on February 12, 2020, starting with check number 6628.

February 21, 2020, is the end of the final pay period for the month. Schwartz has sold $7,500 of products during this pay period at a 3 percent commission. Complete the payroll register for the period's gross pay. Pay will be disbursed on February 26, 2020, and check numbers will continue from prior payroll.

The hours for the nonexempt employees are as follows:

Name	Hourly Rate	Hours Worked 2/10–2/21	Regular Time Pay	Overtime Pay	Commission Pay	Gross Pay
Towle	$12.00	80 hours				
Long	$12.50	70 hours				
Shangraw	$11.00	42 hours				
Success (You)	$18.68	70 hours				

P/R End Date ____   Check Date ____   Company Name: ____

Name	Filing Status	Type and Number of Dependents	Hourly Rate or Period Wage	No. of Regular Hours	No. of Overtime Hours	No. of Holiday Hours	Commissions	Gross Earnings	Sec 125	401(k)	Taxable Wages for Federal W/H
Totals											

Name	Gross Earnings	Taxable Wages for Federal W/H	Taxable Wages for FICA	Federal W/H	Social Security Tax	Medicare W/H	State W/H Tax	Garnish-ment	United Way	Net Pay
Totals										

Answers to Stop & Check Exercises

Pay Your Employees Correctly

1. No. Heather should have received time-and-a-half for the additional 8 hours. Her pay should have been $667.00 [(80 × 7.25) + (8 × 1.5 × 7.25)]
2. $398.95 (39.5 × 10.10)
3. $631.40 (32 × 2 × 9.86)
4. $739.50 (75 × 9.86)

Pay Computations for Different Basis

1. $6,744.00 ($224,800 × 3%)
2. $1,100.00. Yes, because $1,100.00/90 hours = $12.22 per hour. South Carolina has no dictated minimum wage so federal minimum wage would apply.
3. With unpaid time, her current pay will be less; if she had vacation time, there would be no difference.

Standard salary per biweekly payroll: $57,000 / 26 = $2,192.310769
($57,000 / (40 × 26 × 2)) = $27.40384 per hour × (8 × 3) for unpaid leave of $657.69216
Current pay $2,192.30769 − 657.69216 = $1,534.62 (rounded)

Quarter-Hour vs. Hundredth-Hour

1. Ann:
   Quarter-hour: 8.25 hours
   Hundredth-hour: 7.93 hours
   Nevada:
   Quarter-hour: 8 hours
   Hundredth-hour: 8.12 hours
   Pat:
   Quarter-hour: 8 hours
   Hundredth-hour: 7.82 hours
2. The difference exists because the time worked during a quarter-hour system is rounded to the nearest quarter hour. In a hundredth-hour system, the worker is paid for the exact number of minutes worked.
3. It would be beneficial to adopt a hundredth-hour system to reduce payroll inaccuracies that may affect both employees and company profits.

How Does Overtime Affect Gross Pay?

1. FLSA Section 7(j) covers the overtime rules for hospital and residential care facilities and would fall under the 8 and 80 rule.
2. Commissions do not have an effect on overtime earnings because overtime only considers worked hours in the calculations.
3. His employer could include Ralph's tips by adding them to his gross pay based on the cash wage. This total with tips becomes the hourly rate used to determine overtime earnings. The other method would be to exclude the tip income, using the cash wage only as the basis for overtime computations.

The Payroll Register

1. To document the employees' time and hours worked as well as to provide totals of the compensation by each category.
2. Name, marital status, number of withholdings, hourly rate, number of regular hours, number of overtime hours, commission, piece rate, regular earnings, overtime earnings, gross earnings.
3. To facilitate calculations of regular and overtime, help ensure accuracy, and allow for analysis of overtime worked.

Combination Pay Methods

1. Base pay = $42,000 ÷ 24 = $1,750
   Commission = $100 × 5 = $500
   Gross pay = $2,250
2. $36,000 ÷ 12 = $3,000 per month
   $3,000 × 0.35 = $1,050 mid-month draw
   $3,000 − $1,050 draw = $1,950 received at the end of the month
3. $75,000 × 0.03 = $2,250 received in stock
   Annual compensation = $75,000 + $2,250 = $77,250

What Is the Correct Pay?

1. 15 hours because compensatory time must be awarded at 1.5 times regular hours.
2. $5.44 per hour ($7.25 × 75%)

Chapter Four

Fringe Benefits and Voluntary Deductions

Fringe benefits are noncash forms of compensation that employers use to reward an employee for company service. Examples of fringe benefits include the use of a company car, health and life insurance, dependent care, gym memberships, and many other perks offered as a privilege of working for a particular employer. Employers are not required to offer fringe benefits, and the presence of certain benefits serves as an incentive for potential employees to join the company. By offering fringe benefits, an employer can avoid the need to rely on high salary and wage amounts to attract employees and build morale. However, the cost of offering fringe benefits can impede the company's cash flow. The challenge is to provide a salary and fringe benefit package that attracts the desired employees at a manageable cost to the company.

The IRS classifies fringe benefits as deductible from an employee's pay on either a pre-tax or a post-tax basis, depending on the type of benefit. Pre-tax deductions reduce the current taxable income of the employee and may be taxed at a later time; for example, contributions to a qualifying retirement program would be a pre-tax deduction. Other fringe benefits are deducted from an employee's compensation after computing taxes, which makes the perk a post-tax benefit. The IRS clearly differentiates between taxable and nontaxable fringe benefits in *Publication 15-b*.

LEARNING OBJECTIVES

After studying Chapter 4, you should be able to:

LO 4-1 Define Fringe Benefits within the Context of Payroll

LO 4-2 Interpret Cafeteria Plan Types

LO 4-3 Describe Fringe Benefit Exclusion Rules

LO 4-4 Explain Fringe Benefit Valuation Rules

LO 4-5 Differentiate between Pre-Tax and Post-Tax Deductions

LO 4-6 Apply Rules for Withholding, Depositing, and Reporting Benefits

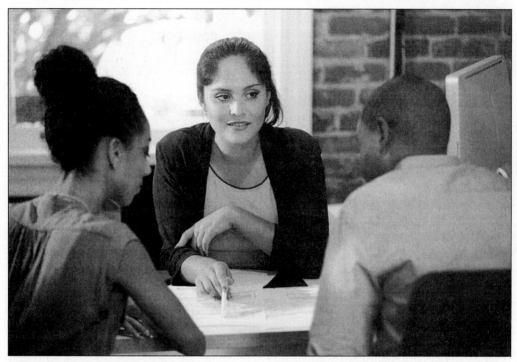

Monkey Business Images/Shutterstock

A New Direction for Fringe Benefits

A popular retirement plan enacted by the Revenue Act of 1978 is commonly known as the 401(k) because of its IRS code. The 401(k) is classified as a defined benefit plan characterized by employee contributions and some level of matched contribution by the employer. The purpose of the 401(k) is to help employees set aside money for retirement on a non-taxed basis and is a deferred compensation plan, meaning that employees who elect to contribute to it plan to withdraw money from it at a later date; in this case, that later date is after the employee retires from the workforce.

In addition to the employer-sponsored retirement plan, Bank of America is one of about one-third of all companies which has added financial education as an employee benefit. This education transcends traditional retirement planning because it helps employees learn to manage their entire financial position, not just their retirement, the purpose of this benefit is to promote financial wellness to complement other types of wellness programs. Previously, financial programs like the one offered by Bank of America have only been available to high-income people as part of a wealth management program. By offering this benefit to all employees, Bank of America has expanded programs to include lower-income employees and their families, thus allowing them to grow wealth at any level. Knowing financial security can ease stress, and lead to more productive employees at work.

Offering this benefit has allowed employers to recruit younger talent and has brought the reassurance of post-retirement security for older employees. It allows employees to manage the nuances of their lives and make necessary adjustments as circumstances change. This type of benefit sets the stage for financial stability by teaching the necessary financial literacy and planning strategies.

(Sources: Employee Benefit News, Workest)

Despite the additional cost involved, fringe benefits are an important part of attracting and retaining high-quality employees. We will explore different types of fringe benefits and their treatment for payroll purposes in Chapter 4.

LO 4.1   Define Fringe Benefits within the Context of Payroll

Payroll has been said to be the intersection of human resources and accounting because of the need to include employee information and to record all financial transactions involving work performed for the business. Fringe benefits are an extension of that notion because these benefits are rewards given to employees in return for their service to the company. The correlation between employee satisfaction and retention is often a result of the fringe benefits offered by the employer.

vetkit/Shutterstock

The term *fringe* was applied to these noncash benefits because they were viewed as an insignificant part of employee *compensation*. Over time, the Bureau of Labor Statistics has proven that fringe benefits actually constitute an additional 25–33 percent of an employee's annual compensation. The importance of fringe benefits, despite the inherent monetary value, is best seen in terms of employee satisfaction and long-term increases in revenue and net income. In this section, we will examine the purpose of fringe benefits and the treatment of this form of noncash compensation as it pertains to pay and taxation.

Purpose of Fringe Benefits

Employees have often been considered one of the costs of conducting business. The employer's obligation to pay employment taxes and supply additional benefits in order to entice employee engagement was viewed as a necessary, albeit expensive, part of the company's financial structure. Research conducted during the past decade has found that the advantages gained from providing fringe benefits far outweigh the related costs in terms of employee productivity, creativity, and revenue production.

Employers continually introduce new or expanded benefit plans to attract, develop, and keep good employees. Some examples of these benefits include

- Amazon, JPMorgan Chase, and Berkshire Hathaway have created a new self-insured health care company called Haven to make health benefits more accessible.

- Bloomberg offers 26 weeks of paid family leave for a caregiver.

- DoorDash and Instacart partnered with the Stride app to give its freelance workers access to benefits.

- Ocean Spray waived mental health copays for all employees to promote mental well-being.

(**Source:** Employee Benefits News)

Hallmarks of fringe benefits include the following indicators:

- All employees have access to the benefit because of their working relationship with the employer.

- Employees enjoy improved living conditions as a result of the benefit.

- The ability to receive the benefit is not related to employee performance.

- Fringe benefits supplement employees' cash compensation.
- These benefits may be either deducted pre- or post-tax.
- Fringe benefits promote the welfare of all employees.
- Legislative treatment of fringe benefits involves certain mandatory tax deductions from employee pay.

FAMILIES FIRST CORONAVIRUS RESPONSE ACT (H.R. 6201)

In response to the COVID-19 outbreak, the U.S. Congress passed the Families First Coronavirus Act, which made certain fringe benefits mandatory for employers with fewer than 500 employees. The act's provisions extended those granted by the Family Medical Leave Act (FMLA). Provisions of the act included the following points that directly affected employers:

- Federal emergency paid leave benefits program to provide payments to employees taking unpaid leave due to the coronavirus outbreak.
- Expanded unemployment benefits and grants to states for processing and paying claims.
- The requirement for employers to provide paid sick leave to employees, full-time or part-time. Part-time employees were granted paid sick leave based on the average number of hours they worked.
- Requirements for providing coronavirus diagnostic testing at no cost to employees.
- Full-time employees were granted up to 80 hours of paid leave if they were unable to work to telecommute because of a COVID-19 diagnosis; if they were advised to self-quarantine because of their symptoms; if they needed time away from work to care for a family member diagnosed with the virus; if they could not obtain the necessary childcare to work due to daycare closures; or if the employee lived in an area was in an area under lockdown due to state or local mandates.

The Families First Coronavirus Act mandated that employers adopt it not later than April 2, 2020, and expired on December 31, 2020. Employers had no continuing legal responsibilities under this Act after December 31. Other stipulations of the Act included

- A cap of $511 per day ($5,110 in total) per employee if the employee was directly affected. After the 10 business days, the employee would receive two-thirds of normal pay unless they had access to other paid sick leave. The total paid leave was capped at $10,000 per employee, and employees could not be paid for unused sick leave granted under the act if they terminated their employment.
- Employees who needed leave to care for family members had their pay capped at $200 per day ($2,000 in total).
- Employees may elect to use the sick leave provided by this Act before using normally granted paid sick leave.
- Employers with 50 or fewer employers were exempt from the Act if doing so would compromise the business's viability (i.e., their going concern).
- Employees must have been employed for 30 days prior to accessing leave granted under the Act.
- Employees who used the leave mandated by this Act could not be discriminated against for using the available paid leave.
- Employee reinstatement rights under FMLA were enforced; however, very small employers with 25 or fewer employees could claim a hardship exemption.

Sources: U.S. Congress; Smith, Gambrell, & Russel, LLP

Fringe benefits may be included in employee pay, although they are not part of the cash compensation package. In the next section, we will explore how fringe benefits appear on an employee's pay advice.

Including Benefits in Pay

In Chapter 3, we discussed the computation of employee gross pay. Some fringe benefits may increase employee pay and would be taxable. Examples of this would include, but are not limited to, employer-provided vehicles, mileage, leasing, and commuting. The items to be included in gross pay are valued at the level as if they were purchased through a third party, often referred to as an *arm's-length transaction.*

State laws regarding fringe benefits, while based on IRS regulations, may vary regarding paid sick time and paid time off. In New Hampshire, all sick and vacation time is considered to be part of employee wages, and employers must notify employees in writing of these benefits. Furthermore, employees must receive an annual notice that contains details about balances accrued in sick time and paid time off categories. Employers are not required to disburse cash compensation for the accrued time at termination and decide if the unused time may be rolled over to the next year. (Source: New Hampshire Business Review)

Fringe Benefits and Payroll Taxes

Certain fringe benefits change the calculations for tax calculations, such as Federal Withholding, Medicare, or Social Security. Others do not affect the calculation for taxes and are considered post-tax benefits. The IRS requires that all fringe benefits that involve deductions from pay or for which the employee contributes part of regular pay must be listed explicitly on the employee's *pay advice.* A sample pay advice is contained in Figure 4-1. The affected taxes include Federal withholding (W/H), SSI, Medicare, and State withholding (W/H), and the fringe benefits include Pretax Insurance and 401(k).

FIGURE 4-1
Sample Pay Advice

Hazlitt Industries						
2210 Secours Way						
Springfield, MA 02312						199203

Stephen Torrisi	Date	11/05/20XX

One-thousand one-hundred twenty-two and 77/100   dollars   1,122.77

Payee: Stephen Torrisi
Address: 3230 Longview Drive
City/State Zip: Agawam, MA 02249   Signed: *Mitchell North*

Payroll End Date	10/31/20XX	Payroll Pay Date	11/05/20XX	Check:	199203
Employee Name	Stephen Torrisi	Employee Number	42850	Rate	21.50

Description	Earnings	YTD Gross	Description	Deductions	YTD Deductions
Regular	1,720.00	32,680.00	Federal W/H	275.47	5,233.93
Holiday			SSI	106.64	2,026.16
Commissions			Medicare	24.94	473.86
			State W/H	88.58	1,683.02
			Pretax Insurance	50.00	950.00
Total Earnings	1,720.00	32,680.00	401(k)	51.60	980.40
			Total Deductions	597.23	11,347.37

An exception to this requirement involves *de minimis* benefits. *De minimis* benefits include items with a value that is so minimal that accounting for it would be unnecessary. These items include an occasional cup of coffee or an isolated postage stamp, both relatively small in value. However, it should be noted that when *de minimis* items become a regular benefit, such as an everyday cup of coffee instead of an occasional one, then the value aggregates to become a sum that could be treated as income.

De minimis benefits, according to IRS Publication 15-b, have such minimal accounting value that the accounting for it is deemed impractical. Examples of de minimis benefits include (but are not limited to)

- Employee use of a company copier, as long as the usage does not exceed 15 percent of the employee's total usage of that equipment for business purposes.
- Noncash, low-value holiday or birthday gifts.
- Similar gifts for family illnesses or birth celebrations.
- Group–term life insurance for the death of a dependent if the life insurance face value does not exceed $2,000.
- Certain meals, occasional picnics, and parties for employees and their guests.
- Occasional tickets to sporting or theater events.
- Personal use of an employer-provided cell phone provided primarily for noncompensatory business purposes.

Notice that *de minimis* benefits are generally classified as occasional use. If the usage becomes more than occasional, such as season tickets to sporting or arts events or club memberships, the benefits are not considered *de minimis*.

(**Source:** IRS)

In *Troester v. Starbucks Corp.,* (2018), the question of the *de minimis* doctrine arose when it was applied to work requested of employees who were off the clock, but were still on the premises. The California Supreme Court ruled that work performed off the clock did not meet the *de minimis* doctrine because of the frequency with which Starbucks requested that its employees perform such tasks. (Sources: APA, Google Scholar)

Voluntary fringe benefits have two basic types of treatments regarding payroll taxes: They may be deducted either before or after *mandatory deductions* (i.e., taxes) have been calculated. The IRS specifies which fringe benefits may be deducted on a pre-tax basis and which must be treated as post-tax deductions in Publication 15-b, which is updated annually. Employers are responsible for remitting amounts withheld for fringe benefits in a timely manner and reporting annual totals to employees on Form W-2. Figure 4-2 details the type of fringe benefit and payroll tax treatment follows.

Freeograph/Shutterstock

EXAMPLE: FRINGE BENEFIT
Phil Cahill is an employee of Cohen Corporation, a company that offers undergraduate educational assistance as a fringe benefit. According to the IRS, the first $5,250 of Phil's tuition is not subject to payroll taxes. During 2020, Phil received reimbursement from his employer of $7,250 in education assistance. The additional $2,000 is taxable income for Phil.

FIGURE 4-2

Fringe Benefits and Payroll Tax Treatment

Fringe Benefits and Payroll Tax Treatment			
Type of Fringe Benefit	Income Tax Exempt	FICA Taxes Exempt	FUTA Tax Exempt
Accident and health benefits*	XX	XX	XX
Achievement awards (up to $1,600 for qualified plan awards, $400 for nonqualified)	XX	XX	XX
Adoption assistance	XX		
Athletic facilities owned or leased by the employer†	XX	XX	XX
De minimis benefits	XX	XX	XX
Dependent care assistance (up to $5,000 annually)	XX	XX	XX
Education (i.e., tuition) assistance (up to $5,250 annually)	XX	XX	XX
Employee discounts (various limits apply)	XX	XX	XX
Employee stock options (depending on the type of option)	XX	XX	XX
Employer-provided cell phone (if not otherwise compensated)	XX	XX	XX
Group term life insurance	XX	XX‡	XX
Health savings accounts (HSAs) for qualified individuals	XX	XX	XX
Lodging on the employer premise (for the employer convenience as a condition of employment)	XX	XX	XX
Meals (if *de minimis* or for employer convenience on employer premises)	XX	XX	XX
No-additional-cost services	XX	XX	XX
Retirement planning services	XX	XX	XX
Transportation benefits (commuting and rail passes up to $270, exempt if *de minimis*)	XX	XX	XX
Tuition reduction for undergraduate education (graduate if the employee engages in teaching or research)	XX	XX	XX
Working condition benefits	XX	XX	XX

*Does not include long-term care benefits if they are included in flexible spending accounts.
† Exempt if substantially all use during the calendar is by employees, their spouses, and their dependent children and the facility is on the employer's premises or a location owned or leased by the employer.
‡ Up to cost of $50,000 of coverage. Excess over $50,000 must appear on the employee's Form W-2.

Fringe Benefits 101

1. What are the two main categories of fringe benefits?

2. Which of the following benefits is not considered a fringe benefit? (Use Figure 4-2 as a reference.)

   a. Educational assistance for undergraduate students.

   b. Group–term life insurance over $250,000.

   c. Overtime hours worked during the year.

   d. Cell phones for business purposes.

   e. Retirement planning services.

3. Which of the following fringe benefits would also be exempt from Social Security and Medicare taxes?

   a. Working condition benefits.

   b. Adoption Assistance.

   c. Qualified Health Savings Accounts.

   d. Qualified Achievement Awards.

LO 4-2 Interpret Cafeteria Plan Types

The Internal Revenue Code has a special program to assist workers with necessary health care expenses. Section 125 of the IRS code was initially enacted in 1978 and has been revised several times. It permits employers to offer employees a choice between two or more cash and qualified benefits. The employer must explicitly describe the plan benefit, rules governing the benefit, and ways that the employee may both pay for and obtain the benefits. Employee-elected deductions for qualified cafeteria plan benefits are withheld on a *pre-tax* basis.

Examples of qualified insurance benefits include

- Accident and health benefits.
- Long-term care benefits.
- Group–term life insurance (including costs not excluded from wages).
- Health Savings Accounts (HSAs).

Comstock/PunchStock

Cafeteria plans, also known as Section 125 plans, are offered by the employer and are usually deducted on a pre-tax basis with the intent of making employer-sponsored benefits more affordable for employees. A cafeteria plan, in essence, allows employees to convert fringe (i.e., non-cash) benefits into tax savings. Although they often pertain to health coverage, cafeteria plans may also include dependent care and other expenses. Participation in cafeteria plans potentially saves employees upwards of 7.65 percent (the FICA taxes) and may save more money, depending on the employee's income tax bracket. Note that if an employee chooses to receive benefits under the cafeteria plan this does not convert a fringe benefit to a taxable one.

Premium Only Plan (POP)

A *premium only plan (POP)* is a type of cafeteria plan that allows employees to deduct premiums for employer-sponsored group insurance on a pre-tax basis. Deducting the premium on a pre-tax basis allows the employee to have a lower tax liability. A list of POPs that employers may provide and are subject to Section 125 pre-tax provisions is provided in Table 4-1. Note that not all employers offer all types of insurance coverage.

Employers benefit by offering POPs because employee premiums deducted on a pre-tax basis reduce the employer's FICA tax liability. Offering pre-tax deductions for group insurance coverage as part of their employee benefits package is also beneficial to employers because participation in health plans has been correlated with reductions in employee sick time and related health care costs. POPs allow employees to offset the cost of rising health care premiums by allowing employees to deduct the premiums on a pre-tax basis.

TABLE 4-1

Types of Insurance that May Be Included in a Premium Only Plan

Health	Dental	Vision
Prescription	Cancer	Medicare Supplement
Accident	Disability	Hospital Indemnity
Employee Group Term Life*		

*Employee Group Term Life insurance premiums are subject to a limit of $50,000 per employee and may be subject to a 10-employee minimum.

EXAMPLE: PRE-TAX DEDUCTION OF HEALTH INSURANCE PREMIUM

Cathie Hollins, an employee of Wolfe & Associates, has the option to deduct her health insurance premium on a pre-tax basis. She consulted her payroll accountant about the difference between pre-tax and post-tax premium deduction and received this analysis:

	Pre-Tax vs. Post-Tax Premium Deduction	
	Pre-Tax	Post-Tax
Period gross pay	$2,500	$2,500
Health insurance premium	250	250
Taxable income	$2,250	$2,500

The pre-tax deduction would lead to lower taxable income, which would result in less federal, state, and local income tax being deducted from Cathie's pay.

Flexible Spending Arrangement (FSA)

Another benefit that can be included in the cafeteria plan is a *flexible spending arrangement (FSA)*. FSAs are available to assist in the payment of medical expenses, including certain co-payments and prescriptions, transportation, and certain child care expenses. According to IRS Publication 502, examples of includible medical expenses are

- Acupuncture.
- Ambulance service.
- Automobile expenses when traveling for medical purposes.
- Braille books and magazines.
- Chiropractor.
- Hearing aids.
- Lead-based paint removal.
- Wheelchair.

It should be noted that any employee contributions to an FSA in excess of $2,750 annually (2020 amount) are treated as taxable income. The purpose of the FSA is not to defer taxable income or to avoid paying taxes, but to reduce the financial burden of health care costs.

Cafeteria plan–based FSAs generally have a "use it or lose it" provision, meaning that any unused funds at the end of the plan year may not be accessed afterward. However, the IRS permits employers to roll over up to $500 annually per employee at the employer's discretion.

EXAMPLE: FSA EFFECT ON ANNUAL GROSS SALARY

For plans that have a year starting after December 31, 2019, the maximum annual amount that an employee may contribute to an FSA offered under Section 125 is $2,750 per person. As an example, Faith Goldman is an employee of Kuzmeckis Doors. She earns $50,000 annually and elects to contribute $2,700 of her annual pay to an employer-sponsored FSA. Her taxable pay would be reduced as follows:

Annual pay – FSA election = $50,000 – $2,750 = $47,250

At the end of the calendar year, Faith has $500 remaining out of her annual FSA election. Her employer allows her to carry over the balance to next year and requires that it be spent by March 15. She would need to spend the remaining balance on qualified medical expenses and provide documentation as required to support the expenditures. Any amount remaining from the prior year may be forfeited by the employee after March 15.

One benefit of cafeteria plans is that employees may choose two or more benefits that consist of cash and noncash elements. For example, they may elect to have health insurance premiums *and* a flexible spending arrangement deducted on a pre-tax basis.

Health Savings Account (HSA)

Another type of cafeteria plan is a *health savings account (HSA)* that can be used to pay for qualified medical expenses. It is important to note that HSAs may only be used in conjunction with a cafeteria plan by employees who have a *high-deductible health plan (HDHP)*. The 2020 definition of a high-deductible health plan includes the following deductible limits:

- $1,400 annual deductible (self-coverage).
- $2,800 annual deductible (family).
- $6,900 out-of-pocket expenses maximum (self-coverage).
- $13,800 out-of-pocket expenses maximum (family).

EXAMPLE: PRE-TAX VS. POST-TAX WITH A FLEXIBLE SPENDING ARRANGEMENT (FSA)

Cathie Hollins also has the option to contribute to an FSA for her annual out-of-pocket medical expenses and decides to use that to meet cafeteria plan requirements. She is paid semimonthly and decides to contribute $2,400 to a qualified FSA. Her taxable income would be as follows:

	Pre-Tax vs. Post-Tax	Premium Deduction
	Pre-Tax	Post-Tax
Period gross pay	$2,500	$2,500
Health insurance premium	250	250
FSA	100	-0-
Taxable income	$2,150	$2,500

Note the difference between her taxable income in both situations. The use of pre-tax deductions can significantly reduce Cathie's tax liability.

FSA vs. HSA

FSA	HSA
Must be offered by an employer.	Only permitted for employees with an HDHP (see deductible rules).
Independent Contractors do not qualify.	Independent contractors do not qualify.
Employees may elect to contribute up to $2,750	Employees may contribute to HSAs as follows: • $3,550 (single) • $7,100 (married) • $1,000 (additional catch-up amount for employees over age 55)
Employees may use any amount of the annual contribution at any time, regardless of how much they have contributed for the year.	Functions like a bank account in that the employee owns the funds contributed, although employers may also contribute funds.
The plan is owned by the employer and unused annual contributions may be retained by the employer	All funds contributed are the property of the employee
The employer decides if they want to give employees a grace period (up to March 15 in most cases) to use annual elections.	Unused funds rollover each year and continue to grow with the account. Unused funds do not affect the yearly contribution limits.
Employees must provide receipts or provider evidence to support used funds.	Employees may not access more funds than they have contributed to the HSA.
FSA contributions are reported on the W-2	Employees must report all used funds with their personal income tax returns.
Annual contributions must be elected each year.	Employees may change their annual contribution at any time.

Dragon Images/Shutterstock

One aspect of HSAs that differentiates them from FSAs is that the amounts that employees contribute to an HSA may remain in the account for use later in life. These funds may be reserved for medical costs and long-term care and are not taxable when used for medical expenses. Money withdrawn for nonmedical expenses is subject to income taxes. Another difference is that anyone with an HDHP may establish an HSA with a trustee, even if their employer does not offer the benefit. However, not all HSAs can be considered tax exempt. Only HSAs included as part of the company's qualifying Section 125 cafeteria plan are deemed exempt from Social Security, Medicare, and federal income taxes.

> HDHPs are a way for employers to offer affordable insurance premiums for their employees. As of 2020, approximately 79 percent of employers offer HDHPs. The problem employers experience is annual deductibles for these plans can exceed $3,500, which is equivalent to three weeks of an employee's pay. The other issue employers face by offering HDHPs is pharmaceutical costs cannot always be included in the plan, so employers either offer pharmacy insurance or employees must seek pharmacy-only plans. (Source: PBMI)

A note about HSAs is the money contributed to the account may roll over from year to year as long as the employee is part of an HDHP. Employees with a single marital status may contribute up to $3,550 tax-free, and married employees may contribute up to $7,100. Additionally, employees age 55 and older may contribute an additional $1,000 per year as a catch-up contribution. Certain HSA plans allow participants to invest money into mutual funds or other investments. It should also be noted HSAs do not have the same restrictions for spending as FSAs.

Employers may make tax-exempt contributions to their employees' HSAs as long as they make comparable contributions to all company employee accounts according to the category or coverage and the employment category (e.g., full-time, part-time). Employer contributions to HSAs are tax exempt as far as federal income tax, FICA, and FUTA because sums contributed are not considered employee wages.

> An issue with cafeteria plans is the exclusion of sole proprietors, partners, shareholders in an S-corporation who have greater than a 2 percent share in the company, and members of limited liability companies (LLCs) who elect to be taxed as partnerships. According to Section 125, these individuals may not participate in a cafeteria plan. The problem is that 73 percent of business owners fall into one of these exclusions, which means that many people cannot access the tax privileges that they offer their employees. (Source: *Financial Regulation News*)

What is served in the cafeteria plan?

Stop & Check

1. Which of the following types of insurance may be included in a POP?
   a. Cancer
   b. Vision
   c. Auto
   d. Dental

2. What are two of the differences between FSAs and HSAs?

3. What constitutes an HDHP?

LO 4-3   Describe Fringe Benefit Exclusion Rules

Remember that fringe benefits are noncash compensation. We have discussed the tax treatment of benefits that may be deducted from employee income on a pre-tax basis using a cafeteria plan. Other fringe benefits may not be included in a cafeteria plan and are also generally not reported as compensation. Employers routinely offer these excluded fringe benefits, and it is important for payroll accountants to understand specific tax rules in order to represent them accurately on employee W-2s when necessary.

Excluded fringe benefits exist that are not part of a cafeteria plan and, despite the cash value, do not generally constitute a taxable portion of employee pay. The value of these fringe benefits is exempt from federal income tax, FICA taxes, and FUTA tax and is not reported on the employee's W-2. The table in Figure 4-2 contains specific details of fringe benefit exclusions and limitations of the exclusions. In this section, we will examine fringe benefits not specifically addressed in *Publication 15-b* that are commonly offered by companies.

ColorBlind Images/Blend Images LLC

Prizes and Awards

Workplace prizes and awards are a way for employers to influence employee morale by offering noncash rewards for winning competitions and achieving milestones such as company tenure. In Publication 15-b, the cash-value limit on achievement awards is $1,600 annually for those given in accordance with a qualified plan; the limit for nonqualified awards is $400. A *qualified plan* is one that considers all employees equally, not favoring highly compensated employees. These types of achievement awards, according to IRS Publication 535, are for improvements to safety programs and for the longevity of service to the employer. The following example contains some context for achievement awards.

Simon Hawkins is a sales employee at Austin Trailers and Motorsports. The company offers achievement awards on a regular basis to reward sales employees for achieving safety goals and longevity of service. All sales staff members are eligible for these awards, including the company officers.

EXCLUDED ACHIEVEMENT AWARD
On June 5, 2020, Simon won an award of $500 for achieving the highest safety record during the month of May. According to Publication 15-b, this achievement award would not be reported on Simon's W-2 as taxable income.

TAXABLE PORTION OF ACHIEVEMENT AWARD: CASH AWARD
As of December 31, 2020, Simon had won the award for compiling a comprehensive safety plan on four separate occasions during the calendar year. The total of his achievement awards is $500 × 4, or $2,000. Because the achievement awards received exceeded $1,600, the additional $400 ($2,000 – $1,600) would be reflected as taxable income on his W-2.

TAXABLE PORTION OF ACHIEVEMENT AWARD: NONCASH AWARD
In addition to winning the cash prizes for safety achievement, Simon received a new smartphone with a value of $1,000 for 10 years of service to the company. As the value of his awards is now $3,000, the excess of value over $1,600 will be reflected as taxable income.

Gym Memberships

Employee discounts for gym memberships are a common fringe benefit that employers use to promote wellness initiatives. If the employer has on-site athletic facilities (either

Sol Stock/Getty Images

on the employer's premises or other premises owned or leased by the employer) that are restricted to use by employees, their spouses, and their dependents, then the benefit would be nontaxable. However, if an employer provides gym memberships to off-site clubs at no additional cost to employees on a qualified plan, the cost of the gym membership is taxable. Likewise, if the athletic facility is open to the public as well as to employees and their dependents, the value of the membership would be taxable.

EXAMPLE: OFF-SITE GYM MEMBERSHIP

Claire Warner is an employee of Althea Productions. Her employer offers memberships at a local gym as an optional benefit for employees. These memberships are at no additional cost to the employee and have a cash value of $75 per month. Because the gym membership has an annual value of $900 and is not an on-site athletic facility, it must be counted as income and reported on Claire's Form W-2.

Personal Use of Company Vehicle

Company cars are a common fringe benefit given to employees who drive regularly as part of their job. Business use of these company cars is considered a nontaxable fringe benefit, deemed Working Condition Benefit, because it is an asset provided to the employee for use

that specifically benefits the company, much like a computer or office equipment. The taxable portion occurs when the employee uses the company-provided vehicle for personal business. Employers often request that employees document personal use of the business vehicle at the end of the calendar year to facilitate proper identification of taxable income associated with the company car.

Mark Dierker/McGraw-Hill Education

In the case of *Scott v. Scott,* an issue that arose was the value of fringe benefits used to determine the defendant's income for use in divorce proceedings. The plaintiff contended that the use of a company truck was not calculated into the value of the defendant's income that was used as the basis of calculating child support. Upon review of the defendant's total compensation, including all fringe benefits, the Supreme Court of Georgia found that the defendant's actual monthly income was substantially more than previously stated and increased the monthly child support obligation. (Source: *Justia*)

Gift Cards

If an employee received gift cards as a fringe benefit, the cash value of those gift cards must be included as compensation on the employee's Form W-2. For example, if an employee entered a company-sponsored raffle at company functions during the year and won a $100 gift card to a local restaurant, the $100 must be added as compensation to the employee's Form W-2. There is no minimum amount of cash or cash equivalent gift cards that would be excluded under *de minimis* fringe benefits.

Employer-Provided Snacks and Meals

Employers often have coffeemakers and kitchen facilities available for employees. If the employer *occasionally* provides food or beverage as an employee perk, the cash value of the benefit is considered *de minimis* and is not taxable. However, if the employer routinely provides food or

Eugenio Marongiu/Image Source

beverages for employee consumption at no additional charge to the employees, then the cash value of those items must be reported as compensation on the employee's Form W-2.

EXAMPLE: PIZZA FRIDAYS

Laurie Ortega works for Excellent Embroidery and Screen Printing. On Fridays, the company provides a pizza lunch for all employees. The intent of the pizza is to promote employee morale on Fridays and to celebrate weekly accomplishments. Although the value per employee of Excellent Embroidery for pizza on Fridays is small on a weekly basis, it aggregates to an additional $100 per employee over a year's time. Laurie would see an additional $100 in compensation added to her Form W-2 for this non-cash fringe benefit.

Keep in mind that fringe benefits may appear in many different forms. It is important for the payroll accountant to be aware of the perks offered to employees as well as Publication 15-b guidelines in order to identify potential additions to employee compensation and to provide accurate reports to employees and governmental authorities.

For a fringe benefit to be excluded, the employer must be prepared to prove that providing the benefit, not simply adding it to employee gross pay, substantially improves conditions at the firm. For example, the addition of an on-site gym must provide significant benefits above what it would cost employers to add the amount associated with a gym membership to employee pay. Proving that the benefit is substantial could include tracking the number of employees that use the on-site facility versus those who would request and use an external gym membership. (Source: Mondaq)

Excluded Fringe Benefits

Stop & Check

1. Clayton Clark is an employee at Glazier Foods Inc., where he is in the shipping and receiving department. His employer provides an athletic facility on the premises for employees to use. Would this benefit be taxable on Clayton's W-2? Why or why not?

2. Marcia Zimmerman is an employee of the Moeller Gallery, and she has a company-issued vehicle to use in order to conduct business. Does this vehicle represent a fringe benefit? Why or why not?

LO 4.4 Explain Fringe Benefit Valuation Rules

Now that we have an idea about what fringe benefits are and how they fit into a payroll context, it is time to address specific rules about the valuation of fringe benefits. As noted in the case of *Scott v. Scott,* the value of fringe benefits potentially increases the total value of an employee's income without directly affecting the cash they receive. Note that the details for fringe-benefit valuation rules appear in Publication 15-b and are updated annually.

Proper valuation of vehicles is very important for benefits evaluation. It is important that employers know the value of the benefits they provide to ensure that they withhold appropriate amounts of tax for the use of company property such as vehicles.

Ssuaphotos/Shutterstock

Alex Varlakov/Hemera/Getty Images Plus

General Valuation Rule

The *general valuation rule (GVR)* is the most common way to determine the value of fringe benefits. The GVR uses *fair market value (FMV)* as the cornerstone of valuation. Fair market value is defined as the price a person would need to pay to obtain a good or service from a third party in an arm's-length transaction. In other words, if an employee needed to obtain a gym membership, the price paid for that individual membership would constitute the fair market value. In this section, we will explore different applications of the GVR with explanations of the method used to determine the value for payroll reporting purposes.

Personal Use of Company Vehicle: Lease Value Rule

Access to a company car can present a challenge in terms of evaluation of the specific amount associated with personal use of the asset. To compute the value of the employee's personal use of the asset, the IRS uses a complex method that involves the age of the car, the fair market value of the asset, and miles driven. Three primary methods exist for determining value: the *lease value rule*, the *commuting rule*, and the *cents-per-mile rule*. Figure 4-3 contains an example of how a company could derive the valuation using the lease value method. Publication 15-b does provide an annual lease amount for vehicles. After the annual amount of the lease has been determined, the amount is then multiplied by the percentage of personal use of the vehicle. This amount is considered taxable income to the employee. When the employer provides the fuel for the vehicle, this must also be included in the previous calculations. Employer-paid fuel is calculated at FMV or 5.5 cents per mile of personal use. If the employer does not provide fuel, then there is no addition for the fuel.

In the form provided in Figure 4-3, the employee, Nina Falco, claims that she uses the company car for personal use 25 percent of the time during the calendar year. By obtaining the data requested in the form and computing the value of the fringe benefit, Nina has received $892.21 in noncash compensation for this fringe benefit. In addition, the company has provided the fuel for the vehicle (at 5.5 cents per mile), and the number of personal miles is used to compute the personal value of fuel consumption. The total value of this benefit for Nina is $1,101.21 and must be added to her Form W-2 as compensation.

Personal Use of a Company Vehicle: Commuting Rule

Like the situation in the lease value rule, the employee has a company vehicle for use. However, the commuting rule applies to employees who are strictly forbidden from using the vehicle outside of work hours and for personal purposes. The vehicle is only available for transport to and from work and during the workday. Under the commuting rule, the employee computes the number of miles driven for commuting to and from work and multiplies that by $1.50 to determine the valuation for this fringe benefit. Figure 4-4 contains an example of how this rule is applied, assuming a 20-mile round-trip commute done each day of the week.

In Figure 4-4, we see that providing a company car and charging an employee based on the number of miles in the commute can lead to a higher fringe benefit valuation than seen in the lease value rule.

Personal Use of a Company Vehicle: Cents-per-Mile Rule

Another way to determine the value of a company car as a fringe benefit is to use the IRS standard mileage rate. This rate is updated each year and for 2020 is sitting at $0.575, and the payroll accountant should refer to Publication 15-b for updated rates. The cents-per-mile rule uses the number of personal miles driven and multiplies it by the standard mileage rate to determine the value of the fringe benefit. The purpose of the cents-per-mile rule is to consider costs of maintenance and insurance for the vehicle, both of which may increase for the

FIGURE 4-3
Value of the Personal Use of a Company Car: Lease-Value Rule

Kascka Incorporated

Worksheet to Calculate Personal Use of Company Vehicle

(LeaseValue Rule)

Employee Name: ____Nina Falco_____

Vehicle Make: _____Ford_____   **Vehicle Year:** _2020_____

Vehicle Model: _____Fusion_____

Odometer Mileage on the First Day of Use During the Year: _____790_____

Odometer Mileage on the Last Day of Use During the Year: _____15,990_____

Annual Lease Method

Fair Market Value of Vehicle: _____$25,000_____

Annual Lease Value: _____$6,850_____*(Use Table 3-1 in Publication 15b)*

Enter Number of Days Available for Use During the Year: _____190_____

Divide by the Number of Days in the Tax Year: ____365_____

Prorated Annual Lease Percentage: ___52.1%_____

Prorated Annual Lease Value: _____$3,568.85 ($6,850 x 52.1%)_____

Percent of Personal Use During the Year (from employee statement): ____25%_____

Personal Annual Lease Value: _____$892.21_____(Prorated Annual Lease Value x % Personal Use)

If fuel is provided by the employer, enter personal miles: 3,800 x $0.055/mile[1] = $209.00

Total Personal Use Taxable Income: _____$892.21 + 209.00 = $1,101.21_____

[1]**Fuel provided by the company is valued at $0.055 per mile per personal use purposes.**

Note: The number of personal miles is computed by determining the total miles driven during the year (15,990–790 = 15,200 miles), then multiplying that total by the percentage of personal use (15,200 × 25% = 3,800 miles).

company when the vehicle is driven for personal purposes. Figure 4-5 contains an example of applying the cents-per-mile rule.

The choice of company car valuation method rule determines the company's policy and the actual use of the vehicle in terms of total miles driven for business, the value of the asset, and the primary user of the vehicle. Publication 15-b contains specific details for the payroll accountant to determine which method is the most appropriate. No matter which method is chosen, it is important to be consistent in the application of personal vehicle use valuations.

Unsafe Conditions

A special rule applies if a company vehicle is provided to an employee only because of unsafe conditions. The foundation of this rule is that the

Scherbinator/Shutterstock

FIGURE 4-4
Value of the Personal Use of a Company Car: Commuting Rule

Kascka Incorporated

Worksheet to Calculate Personal Use of Company Vehicle

(Commuting Rule)

Employee Name: Nina Falco

Vehicle Make: Ford   **Vehicle Year:** 2020

Vehicle Model: Fusion

Odometer Mileage on the First Day of Use During the Year: 790

Odometer Mileage on the Last Day of Use During the Year: 15,990

Commuter Rule

Number of miles driven for daily commute to and from work: 38

Number of Days worked during the year: 350

Total number of commute miles driven during the year (38 x 350): 13,300

Value of company vehicle for commuting: (13,300 x $1.50/mile): $19,950

employee would walk, bicycle, or use public transportation under normal conditions. An example of an unsafe condition in which this rule may apply would be in the event of a sudden snowstorm that makes the employee's normal travel mode unsafe. In this case, the IRS rule is that the employee is charged $1.50 for a one-way commute (i.e., to or from home), and this charge should be either added to the employee's wages or reimbursed to the company by the employee.

Other Transportation Benefits

Another transportation benefit that employers can offer is a transit pass. These provide employees access to commuter vehicles (six or more passengers required) through the use of the pass. Employers in larger cities, where parking is a premium, may provide parking subsidies to their employees. When there are toll roads present, an employer may provide prepaid commuter passes to their employees to assist in meeting the cost of toll roads. Employers may exclude up to $270 (2020 value) from the employee's wages for these benefits. Any amount paid by the employer in excess of $270 for a commuter pass would be taxable income for the employee.

> As of 2020, employers in Seattle are required to provide employees with commuter passes on a pre-tax basis. Employees will have the option to select the benefit and must provide proof with a request for reimbursement to receive this benefit. (Source: APA)

FIGURE 4-5

Value of the Personal Use of a Company Car: Cents-per-Mile Rule

Kascka Incorporated

Worksheet to Calculate Personal Use of Company Vehicle

(Cents-per-Mile Rule)

Employee Name:_____Nina Falco_____

Vehicle Make:_____Ford_____   Vehicle Year: 2020_____

Vehicle Model: _____Fusion_____

Odometer Mileage on the First Day of Use During the Year:_____790_____

Odometer Mileage on the Last Day of Use During the Year:_____15,990_____

Cents-per-Mile Rule

Number of miles driven during the year:_____15,200_____

Number of miles OR percent driven for personal use:__25%_____

Total number of commute miles driven during the year (15,200 x 0.25): **3,800**

Value of company vehicle for commuting: (3,800 x $0.575/mile): **$2,185.00**

Fringe Benefit Valuations

Stop & Check

1. Oliver Robertson is a field service representative whose primary job function is to visit customer sites. His primary base for computing mileage is his home. During 2020, he drove a total of 30,250 miles, 15 percent of which was for personal use. Using the IRS standard mileage rate of 57.5 cents per mile, what is the value of this fringe benefit using the cents-per-mile rule?

2. Katie Turner is a sales representative for a large pharmaceuticals company. She drives a 2020 Lexus ES, which has a fair market value of $47,000 and a lease value of $12,250. Katie has had the use of the vehicle for 180 days during 2020. She drives the vehicle 20 percent for personal use, and fuel is not provided by her employer. Using the lease value rule, what is the value of the fringe benefit? (Round final figure to two decimal places).

LO 4.5 Differentiate between Pre-Tax and Post-Tax Deductions

Two classes of deductions exist: pre-tax and post-tax. Pre-tax deductions are those deductions that are withheld from an employee's *gross pay*, which is the amount of compensation prior to computing tax liability or applying deductions. The effect of pre-tax deductions is that

Rob Byron/Shutterstock

they reduce the taxable income of the employee. Pre-tax deductions are *voluntary deductions* that have been legislated by the federal government as eligible for pre-tax withholding status, including certain types of insurance, retirement plans, and cafeteria plans.

Post-tax deductions are deducted from employee pay after federal, state, and local income taxes and FICA taxes have been deducted. Amounts deducted on a post-tax basis include both voluntary and court-mandated deductions. The voluntary deductions taken on a post-tax basis involve fringe benefits such as gym memberships, charitable contributions, repayment of company loans, optional insurance (e.g., auto, home), and union dues. Court-mandated deductions deducted on a post-tax basis may include child support garnishments, tax liens, credit card garnishments, and other legally directed items.

Insurance

Employers may provide subsidized health insurance coverage for their employees. The employees pay a portion of these health insurance expenses out of their paycheck and the company makes up the difference. How much a company pays is determined by the company and could vary greatly, depending on the costs of health insurance and the policy selected by the employee. For health insurance plans to qualify for pre-tax status, they must meet the guidelines stated in the IRS Code:

According to the IRS, the following guidelines are used to determine if a health insurance plan qualifies for pre-tax status:

- Health plans offered through the state's small or large group market.
- An employer's self-insured health plan.
- The Department of Defense's Non-Appropriated Fund Health Benefits Program.
- A governmental plan.
- COBRA health coverage.
- Retiree health coverage.

(Source: IRS)

The IRS specifies these items as pre-tax because it reflects the belief that health insurance is a necessity, allowing employees to reduce their tax liability, and ultimately reducing the financial burden on families and employers by proactively supporting medical care.

EXAMPLE: PRE-TAX MEDICAL PREMIUM

Kelli Dennis works for Gunderson Associates. Her employer offers medical insurance for which the premiums may be taken on a pre-tax basis. Kelli is a salaried employee who earns $48,000 annually and is paid on a semimonthly basis. Her premium for medical insurance is $125 per pay period. Consider the following difference in taxable income:

	Medical Insurance Deducted on a Pre-Tax Basis	Medical Insurance NOT Deduced on a Pre-Tax Basis
Annual salary	$48,000	$48,000
Period salary	$48,000/24 = $2,000	$48,000/24 = $2,000
Medical insurance deduction	$125	$0
Taxable income	$1,875	$2,000

In 2010, the Affordable Care Act was passed, providing small businesses a tax credit for providing health insurance coverage when their employees are at low- and moderate-income levels. The act extended coverage of children until the age of 26 to be included as an option to employees on a pre-tax basis. This is only for employees covered under a qualifying cafeteria plan.

In response to the Affordable Care Act, IRS Code 6056 changed the reporting requirements for health insurance programs provided to employees. Employers with more than 50 employees are required to file an information return with the IRS and must provide a detailed summary of health coverage to employees. The value of the insurance coverage contributed by the employer must be reported on the employee's W-2 year-end tax statement within box 12 using code DD and should reflect the amounts contributed by both the employee and the employer. It is important to remember that the amounts reported on the W-2 for the employer's contribution to health insurance do not add to the taxable wages of the employee.

According to the Internal Revenue Service, the Affordable Care Act mandates that individuals have "minimum essential coverage." The Tax Cuts and Jobs Act removed the penalty of 2.5 percent after December 31, 2018.

Examples of minimum essential coverage include

- Employer-provided health insurance.
- Health insurance purchased through an approved health insurance exchange.
- Coverage provided under federal auspices such as Medicare and Medicaid.
- Privately purchased health insurance.

Minimum essential coverage does not include the following limited benefit or limited-term coverage plans:

- Vision and dental insurance issued on a stand-alone basis (i.e., not grouped with a medical insurance policy).
- Workers' compensation insurance.
- Accidental death and disability plans maintained by the employer.

(Source: Tax Cuts and Job Act, IRS)

Supplemental Health and Disability Insurance

Another option many employers are offering is a flow-through (i.e., the company does not cover any of the costs) of supplemental health and disability insurance. One of the largest providers of this type of insurance is the American Family Life Assurance Company of Columbus (AFLAC). AFLAC comprises a variety of policies with separate treatment for taxation purposes (whether pre- or post-tax). The IRS Revision Ruling 2004-55 deals specifically with the tax treatment of short- and long-term disability, and IRS Code Sections 104(a)(3) and 105(a) deal with the exclusion of short- and long-term disability benefits from employees' gross wages. Long-term disability insurance is excluded from taxable income under the ruling. If an employer pays for long-term disability insurance, these amounts may be excluded from or included in gross pay, depending upon the election of the company. When determining the tax treatment for the supplemental health insurance, the IRS guidance provides the following: If the income derived will be estimated to be tax-free, then the cost associated will also be tax-exempt. (Note: Supplemental health and disability plan premiums are not tax-exempt for Social Security and Medicare taxes.)

EXAMPLE: SUPPLEMENTAL HEALTH INSURANCE DEDUCTION

Paul Nichols is a salaried exempt employee of Mark One Restoration Services. He earns $78,000 annually and is paid biweekly. The employer offers him medical insurance and supplemental health insurance with premiums of $150 and $75, respectively. Paul elects to have both premiums withheld on a pre-tax basis.

Salary per period ($78,000/26)	$3,000.00
Less: Medical insurance premium	150.00
Less: Supplemental medical insurance premium	75.00
Taxable income*	$2,775.00

*Note: Taxable income computed here pertains to computations of federal income tax. The taxable income for Social Security and Medicare taxes would be $2,850 because supplemental medical insurance premiums are not exempt for FICA taxes.

Retirement Plans

Monkey Business Images/Shutterstock

Retirement plans were covered under the Employee Retirement Income Security Act (ERISA) of 1974 in conjunction with the Internal Revenue Code. There are two basic types of retirement plans: *defined benefit* and *defined contribution*. In a defined benefit plan, the employer guarantees the employee a specific level of income once retirement has been reached. As an example, under a defined benefit plan, the employer may guarantee 10 percent of the average salary earned in the final five years of employment.

In a defined contribution plan, the individual places money from his or her payroll, pre-tax, into a retirement plan and the company may or may not match to a percentage. There are several different types of defined contribution plans, such as *401(k)*, *SIMPLE 401(k)*, *403(b)*, *457*, *IRA*, *SIMPLE*, *SEP*, *ESOP*, and profit-sharing.

Note: Although some qualified 401(k) plans may be considered as cafeteria plans and may be excluded from FICA tax liability, the IRS states in Publication 15-b that most 401(k) plans are subject to Social Security and Medicare taxes. For the purposes of this text, we will assume that the 401(k) plans are not included in federal or state tax calculations but are included in Social Security and Medicare tax calculations. See Table 4-2 for an explanation of the different retirement plan types.

TABLE 4-2
Retirement Plan Types

Type of Plan	Description
401(k)	A group of investments, typically invested in stock market-based or mutual fund-based plans.
403(b)	Similar to a 401(k), but offered by nonprofit employers such as hospitals and schools.
457	Similar to 401(k) and 403(b), but has no penalty for fund withdrawal before age 59-1/2. Generally offered to governmental and certain nongovernmental employees
Savings Incentive Match Plan for Employees (SIMPLE)	The major limitation is employers may not have more than 100 employees. Funds are specifically set aside for the individual employee in a bank, mutual fund account, or stock market SIMPLE 401(k).
Individual Retirement Account (IRA)	Funds are specifically set aside for the individual employee in a bank or mutual fund account.
Employee Stock Ownership Plan (ESOP)	The company offers employees the ability to earn company stock for the duration of their employment.
Simplified Employee Pension (SEP)	A tax-favorable IRA is set up by or for the employee, and the employer contributes the funds into the account. The SEP is tax-favorable because it reduces the employee's income tax liability.

> **EXAMPLE: RETIREMENT PLAN EMPLOYEE CONTRIBUTION**
>
> Whitney Robinson is a salaried, exempt employee of Hovey Heating and Cooling. She is single with one withholding deduction and receives an annual salary of $60,000, paid semimonthly. She elects to contribute 6 percent of her period pay to the company-sponsored 401(k) plan on a pre-tax basis. Her taxable income would be computed as follows:
>
> | | |
> |---|---|
> | Salary per period ($60,000/24) | $2,500.00 |
> | Less: 6% contribution to 401(k)* | 150.00 |
> | Taxable income | $2,350.00 |
>
> *Note: The 401(k) deduction is *not* exempt from Social Security and Medicare taxes.

> Each year, the IRS imposes a cap on pre-tax retirement plan contributions. For 2020, the limit on 401(k) contributions is $19,500. People over 50 years of age may contribute a pre-tax "catch-up" amount up to $6,500.

Post-Tax Deductions

After the employer withholds the pre-tax and mandatory amounts from an employee's pay, other withholdings may apply. These other withholdings, known as post-tax deductions, comprise both voluntary and *mandated deductions*. An example of a voluntary post-tax deduction is a charitable contribution elected by the employee. Mandated post-tax deductions include *garnishments* and *union dues*. Post-tax deductions are amounts that the IRS has declared cannot reduce the employee's tax liability. A general guide to garnishments is in Table 4-3.

TABLE 4-3
Garnishment Rules

Type of Garnishment	Maximum Percentage of DISPOSABLE Income
Child support or alimony	50% if employee is supporting another spouse or child 60% if employee is not supporting another spouse or child NOTE: If child support is >12 weeks in arrears, an additional 5% may be added to the garnishment
U.S. Government debts	15% of earnings in excess of federal minimum wage weekly earnings
Student loans	15% of earnings in excess of federal minimum wage weekly earnings
Consumer credit	25% of earnings in excess of federal minimum wage weekly earnings
Tax levies	See IRS Publication 1494
Personal bankruptcy	Lower of 25% or 30 times the amount of weekly income in excess of federal minimum wage

Charitable Contributions

Many companies offer to deduct funds for approved charitable organizations directly from the employee's pay. This *charitable contribution* is typically withheld *after* taxes have been calculated. The individual will report the charitable contribution on his or her itemized tax return, and there are separate requirements for meeting the deductible percentage that is outside the scope of this text.

EXAMPLE: NET PAY WITH A CHARITABLE CONTRIBUTION

Perry Wallace is an employee at Working Environments in Winchester, New Hampshire. He earns $29,000 annually and is paid weekly. He is single with one withholding allowance. He has pre-tax health insurance of $25 and a charitable contribution to the United Way of $10 per pay period. His taxable income would be as follows:

Period pay	$557.69
Less: Health insurance	25.00
Taxable income	$532.69

Note that Perry's taxable income does *not* reflect his United Way contribution. Because that contribution is computed on a post-tax basis, it does not affect taxable income.

Court-Ordered Garnishments

There are several reasons that a court may order an employer to withhold amounts from an employee's pay and redirect those funds to a regulatory agency. The most common garnishments are for child support, alimony, and student loans. Garnishments apply to *disposable income*, which is the amount of employee pay after legally required deductions such as income taxes have been withheld. If an employee has one garnishment order for 10 percent and receives a second for 15 percent, any further garnishment requests will be deferred until the disposable income is at a level that is available for garnishments.

Consumer credit:

According to Title III of the **Consumer Credit Protection Act (CCPA)**, garnishments may not be more than (a) 25 percent of the employee's disposable earnings OR (b) the amount by which an employee's disposable earnings are greater than 30 times the federal minimum wage, or $217.50.

Child support:

Garnishments for child support or alimony may be up to 50 percent of disposable income, with an additional 5 percent for any child support that is more than 12 weeks in arrears.

Nontax debts owed to federal agencies:

Garnishments for nontax amounts to federal agencies may not total more than 15 percent of disposable income.

Ken Cavanagh/McGraw-Hill Education

Union Dues

When employees are part of a union that requires regular dues, the employer must withhold those dues from the employee as a post-tax payroll deduction. The union uses dues to fund its activities, which include representation in employee-employer negotiations and political activism. Some employers may pay the union dues for their employees as part of their noncash compensation but there is no requirement for them to do so.

As of February 2020, Kickstarter voted to allow employees to form a labor union. Kickstarter, a company that promotes crowdfunding of entrepreneurs, has aided in the successful launch of many companies by allowing people to contribute to the funds for a new product or service, such as games, tech inventions, and many other projects. This unionization at Kickstarter is significant because of the company's tech foundations and the inability of other tech companies such as Google to form labor unions. As a small company, the implications for this union are huge because it signals to other small or tech-oriented companies that their labor is worthy of professional representation in salary, benefits, and working conditions matters. (Source: *The New York Times*)

Pre-tax vs. post-tax deductions

Stop & Check

1. Which act offered a small-business tax credit for employees' health insurance premiums?

2. What are examples of different retirement plans that may qualify as pre-tax withdrawals?

3. Otis Singleton has disposable pay of $1,790.00. He receives a court-ordered garnishment for credit card debt of $15,000. Otis Singleton does not have earnings over 30 times the federal minimum wage. What is the maximum amount that may be withheld from Otis's pay?

4. Otis questioned the amount of the garnishment in question #3, claiming that he has health insurance of $125 and union dues of $45 that must also be withheld from his pay. How much should be withheld for the garnishment? Explain.

LO 4.6 Apply Rules for Withholding, Depositing, and Reporting Benefits

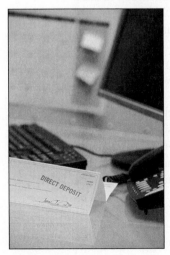

Comstock/PunchStock

Providing benefits as a condition of employment is an important part of employee compensation. In many cases, amounts of money associated with benefits are quantifiable such as insurance premiums, employee contributions, or specific mandatory deductions. In other cases, the fringe benefit valuation rules are needed. The next piece of the puzzle is actually withholding, depositing, and reporting the benefits to the necessary people and organizations.

Rules for Withholding Amounts Related to Benefits

As a general rule, the money associated with employee benefits should be withheld when the benefit is made available. It is up to the employer's discretion if the money should be withheld during a pay period, monthly, annually, and so forth. Therefore, any employee contributions to cafeteria plans, FSAs, HSAs, or other benefits should be deducted from regular pay. A best practice is to document the amounts involved in voluntary deductions in writing for the employee to acknowledge and sign.

Sums of money related to benefits should be deducted from employee pay in a timely manner. The IRS stipulates that the value of all noncash benefits must be determined no later than January 31 of the following year. This deadline facilitates reporting of the fringe benefits on the employees' W-2s. It additionally allows the employer time to deposit any necessary amounts on time.

> The IRS reported that the number of employer audits increased because of the reporting of fringe benefits and taxes due. According to the IRS, when an audit is triggered because of red flags in the computer selection program, one of the first areas checked is employer valuation and reporting of fringe benefits. Other items considered include the employer's internal control system and classification of workers as employees or independent contractors. (Source: *Accounting Today*)

An exception to the general rule is the *special accounting rule* defined by the IRS for noncash benefits provided only in the last two months of the calendar year. Benefits given during this period may be treated as paid during the following calendar year; however, only the value of the benefits may be treated as such. Although employers may opt to use the special accounting period for specific benefits, all employees who receive that benefit must also have it reported in accordance with the special accounting rule.

> **EXAMPLE: SPECIAL ACCOUNTING RULE**
> Marion Morrison is an employee of Connections Inc. and drives a company car. According to the special accounting rule, the company deferred the taxable amount of Marion's personal use of the company car during November and December 2020 until January 2021. This practice would reduce Marion's taxable income for 2020, but she would still be liable for it in her 2021 taxes. Connections Inc. would be required to notify Marion of its use of the special accounting rule for her personal company car use no later than January 31, 2021.

Treatment of Taxable Benefit Withholdings

No matter how the employee receives specific benefits, the employer must treat the benefit as though it was paid annually. The rationale for this treatment is to guarantee that taxable benefits are reflected appropriately on employee W-2s. The employer may change the timing of any amounts withheld for benefits as necessary for the entire company and for individual employees.

One caveat to the rules for withholding involves the transfer of property associated with benefits. For example, if the benefit involved is an investment, any amount withheld from the employee must coincide with the transfer of ownership of the investment.

In regards to the valuation of taxable fringe benefits, employers may choose to add the periodic value of the fringe benefit to period pay and tax it at the employee's regular tax rate. Alternatively, the employer may report the total value and withhold federal income tax at the 25 percent rate. An example of this practice would involve the valuation of personal company car use if reported annually. In that case, the employer may add the full amount of the benefit valuation to a single pay period and deduct the taxes at that time.

> Employees have found that their "free" fringe benefits may be subject to taxes. Wellness programs involving gym memberships, nutritional counseling, and other services provided at no cost to employees may be added to an employee's gross income and subject to income and FICA taxes. (Source: *Forbes*)

Rules for Depositing Amounts Related to Benefits

Employer deposit rules related to benefits are nearly as diverse as the benefits themselves. Like the withholdings, the deposit frequency depends on the timing of deductions from employee pay and recipient requirements (when applicable). A general rule for taxes withheld is that the deposit of these amounts must follow employer deposit rules, which will be covered in Chapter 6. The employer should estimate the amount of the benefit transmitted on a specific date, remit taxes, and transmit any other monies as necessary.

EXAMPLE: DEPOSIT OF EMPLOYEE 401(K) CONTRIBUTIONS

Theresa Bowen, an employee of TMS Physical Therapy, contributes 4 percent of her gross pay to her employer-sponsored employee stock option benefit. Theresa is paid biweekly and earns $52,000 annually. The employer makes quarterly deposits to the stockbroker. In this example, Theresa's contribution is $2,000 x 0.04, or $80, per pay period. The employer would deduct the amounts from Theresa's pay and retain it in a liability account, which they would deposit with the stockbroker at the appropriate time each quarter.

Depositing taxes for noncash fringe benefits will occasionally require an estimate of the taxes due. An example when such an estimate may occur would be employee meals. The employer would estimate the value of the meals and deposit the appropriate amount of tax because it would be a taxable fringe benefit. It is important to note that the estimate needs to be as accurate as possible and that the underpayment of taxes associated with noncash fringe benefits will result in IRS penalties.

Rules for Reporting Benefits

Benefit reports occur in two different places: the employee's Form W-2 and the total compensation report. Each report serves a different purpose.

- Form W-2 serves as a report of all wages and associated taxes for a calendar year. All taxable benefits are reported as wages on the employee's Form W-2. This method of reporting ensures that the employer calculates the correct amount of income taxes and that the employee's annual tax return reflects the proper amounts of income.
- The total compensation report is a report given to the employee from the company that details all benefits in monetary terms. This report allows employees to have an accurate statement of the cash and noncash value of their service to the employer.

Gorodenkoff/Shutterstock

Custom benefits software is becoming more popular among employers. Companies specializing in employee benefits provide integrated custom platforms that address employer withholding, depositing, and reporting needs. These platforms sometimes cost more than $100,000, which makes them too expensive for many small- and some medium-sized employers. Innovations in technology may ultimately make these platforms more affordable. Changes in reporting laws certainly make them necessary. (Source: *Employee Benefit Adviser*)

According to the IRS and the Department of Labor, some of the most common benefits errors are

- Incorrectly defined compensation.
- Delays in the remittance of employees' contributions for benefits.

- Improper definition of employee eligibility and enrollment in benefit plans.
- Incorrect employee vesting in plans.
- Benefit forfeitures.
- Improper use of loans made to participants.
- Incorrect use of hardship distributions.
- Incorrectly recorded plan expenses.

The best way to avoid errors is to involve both the payroll and the human resources departments in benefits determinations to ensure proper implementation and internal classification of related monies. Benefit plans should be reviewed annually to ensure accuracy in legal compliance, remittance procedures, and reconciliation of employee contributions with payroll records.

Employee Benefits reporting

1. When should employers withhold amounts of money associated with benefits from employee pay?

2. Brandon McLaughlin is an employee of Creighton Steel and receives several fringe benefits as a result of his employment. He wants to know the value of his employment, both cash and noncash. What report should he request from his employer?

3. Vivian King is an employee of Nabors Drilling. She receives her Form W-2 in January and notices that her gross pay exceeds her annual salary. As the payroll accountant, you are aware of all fringe benefits available to and used by employees. What would you tell Vivian to help her understand the difference?

Trends to Watch

EMPLOYEE BENEFITS

Employers' attitudes toward employee benefits have undergone changes since 2018. Benefits have become important negotiating tools for employees, which has resulted in the following:

- Large companies such as Google, Facebook, and Costco have developed a reputation for offering generous benefits.
- Employees are using sites such as Glassdoor and Salary.com to rate prospective employers' total compensation packages.
- Values associated with fringe benefits have risen in proportion to employee salaries.
- Employers are starting to offer financial wellness planning—apart from retirement planning.
- Legislation is being introduced to encourage employers and employees in student loan reduction payments.

Trends to watch in fringe benefits and voluntary deductions include the following:

- Increases to paid family sick leave and flexible or remote work options.
- Increased guidance for student loan repayment connections with employee benefits.

- Increases to onsite wellness benefits such as gyms and healthy eating options coupled with fitness incentives.
- Financial wellness and identity theft education resources.
- Auto-enrollment and automatic diversification plans to help employees save more of their earnings and manage their investments.
- The Department of Labor is clarifying the concepts of discretionary and non-discretionary bonuses. This is in response to a number of incorrect calculations seen within industry. Discretionary bonuses are infrequent and at the discretion of management, so employees are not expecting them year over year. These would not be included in the determination of regular wage rate for overtime. Nondiscretionary bonuses are contract driven, commissions, or given frequently enough that employees have come to expect and plan for them. Clarification about inclusion in the calculation of regular wage rate for overtime and retroactive application is under discussion.

Summary of Fringe Benefits and Voluntary Deductions

Fringe benefits are an integral part of employee compensation and often have a significant influence on the cost of an employee. Common forms of fringe benefits are health insurance and retirement, but can encompass an endless variety of employee perks. Certain noncash fringe benefits are subject to employment taxes, which requires an employer to be aware of the taxes associated with offering certain types of benefits.

A primary category of fringe benefits involves employer-sponsored medical insurance plans. Most medical insurance plans may be deducted from an employee's pay on a pre-tax basis, which reduces the employee's tax liability. Employee medical insurance premiums are deducted on a pre-tax basis; this fringe benefit is often part of a cafeteria plan, and other pre-tax benefits such as flexible spending arrangements (FSA) may be included.

Certain types of noncash fringe benefits are excluded from taxation. A common form of excluded fringe benefits is *de minimis* benefits that have a value small enough that accounting for the cost would be unrealistic. Other noncash fringe benefits not subject to taxes involve items provided by the employer for their own convenience, such as on-site meals and company cars. However, the personal use of company cars is subject to tax, based on the valuation method chosen by the employer.

Many voluntary benefits are deducted from employee pay on a post-tax basis. Other post-tax deductions include court-mandated deductions and garnishments. It is important to note the legal limits involved with garnishing employee pay to ensure that an appropriate amount is deducted. Employers are responsible for withholding, depositing, and reporting all deductions from an employee's pay, especially when those deductions are taxes. The total amount of annual compensation including pay, taxes, and benefits may be reported on Form W-2 and the total compensation report.

Key Points

- Fringe benefits are an important part of an employee's compensation package because they help attract and retain high-quality employees.
- Fringe benefits have been correlated with increases in employee productivity and company revenue.
- Fringe benefits may be statutory or voluntary in nature.

- Pre-tax deductions are used for qualified deductions and to reduce the taxable wage base.
- Cafeteria plans allow employees to exclude medical premiums and qualified medical expenses from income tax and FICA taxes.
- Certain pre-tax deductions are subject to FICA taxes.
- Excluded fringe benefits are subject to specific IRS rules that govern amounts and taxation.
- Personal use of company vehicles is evaluated to determine the amount of income the employee is taxed on his or her Form W-2.
- Post-tax deductions include garnishments, union dues, and charitable contributions.
- Garnishments are subject to maximum percentages of disposable income, depending on the type of garnishment.
- Employer withholding of amounts associated with providing employee benefits varies depending on the benefit and if it is subject to taxes.
- Taxes associated with taxable noncash fringe benefits must be deposited when the benefit is transmitted to the employee.
- Employers report the valuation of noncash fringe benefits as part of the employee's Form W-2 and the total compensation report.

Vocabulary

401(k)	ESOP	Lease value rule
403(b)	Fair market value (FMV)	Mandated deductions
457	Flexible spending arrange-	Mandatory deductions
Cafeteria plan	ment (FSA)	Pay advice
Cents-per-mile rule	Fringe benefit	Post-tax deductions
Charitable contribution	Garnishments	Premium only plan (POP)
Commuting rule	General valuation rule	Publication 15-b
Compensation	(GVR)	Qualified plan
Consumer Credit Protection	Gross pay	SEP
Act (CCPA)	Health savings account	SIMPLE
De minimis	(HSA)	SIMPLE 401(k)
Defined benefit	High-deductible health plan	Special accounting rule
Defined contribution	(HDHP)	Union dues
Disposable income	IRA	Voluntary deductions

Review Questions

1. Why do companies offer fringe benefits to their employees?

2. Approximately what percentage of employee compensation includes fringe benefits?

3. What are three examples of voluntary fringe benefits?

4. What are the two reports associated with fringe benefits?

5. What are two examples of voluntary deductions?

6. What are two examples of pre-tax deductions?

7. What are two types of insurance that may be deducted pre-tax under a cafeteria plan?

8. What are the four categories of cafeteria plans?

9. How does an FSA affect an employee's taxable wages?

10. What are three examples of excluded fringe benefits?

11. What are the ways that the value of a company vehicle as a fringe benefit is determined?

12. What are garnishments and how must they be handled?

13. How do post-tax deductions differ from pre-tax deductions?

14. How does the special accounting rule affect withholding of benefits?

15. How often must employers deposit taxes associated with taxable fringe benefits?

Exercises Set A

E4-1A.
LO 4-1, 4-4

Caroline Watts is an employee of Lavender Creek Farm. She has come to you, the payroll accountant, for advice about her health insurance premiums, specifically, whether she should have them deducted pre-tax or post-tax. What reason(s) would you give her for having the medical premiums deducted on a pre-tax basis?
a. The premium amounts are reduced by deducting them on a pre-tax basis.
b. The employee's income that is subject to income tax(es) is reduced.
c. The income subject to Social Security and Medicare taxes is reduced.
d. All health insurance premiums must be deducted on a pre-tax basis.

E4-2A.
LO 4-1

Nora Wade is an employee of WGLO-TV, where she is an on-air news presenter. Which of the following would likely be fringe benefits that her employer would provide because they would be needed as part of her job? (Select all that apply.)
a. Wardrobe consulting services
b. On-site cafeteria
c. Hair and makeup services
d. Personal accounting services

E4-3A.
LO 4-2

Examples of qualified insurance benefits include which of the following? (Select all that apply.)
a. Long-term care benefits
b. Health savings accounts
c. Pet insurance premiums
d. Group–term life insurance (up to $50,000)

E4-4A.
LO 4-2

What is a significant difference between flexible spending arrangements (FSAs) and health savings accounts (HSAs)?
a. Only FSAs may be included as part of a cafeteria plan.
b. HSAs may accompany any type of employer-sponsored health insurance.
c. Amounts contributed to HSAs may remain in the account for use later in life.
d. No annual pre-tax contribution limit exists for FSAs.

E4-5A.
LO 4-3

Dallas Wong is an employee who receives educational assistance in the amount of $10,250 per year. How is this amount treated for tax purposes?
a. None of it is taxable
b. All of it is taxable
c. $5,000 is taxable
d. $5,250 is taxable

E4-6A.
LO 4-4

Ana Cole is an employee of Wilson In-Home Healthcare Services. She is issued a company vehicle so that she may drive to customer sites. Which of the general valuation rules would be appropriate to compute the value of the asset for any personal use? (Select all that apply.)
a. Cents-per-mile rule
b. Commuting rule
c. Unsafe conditions rule
d. Lease value rule

E4-7A.
LO 4-5

Which of the following describes the primary difference between a 401(k) and a 403(b) retirement plan?

a. The 401(k) is a defined benefit only plan.
b. The 403(b) is a defined contribution only plan.
c. The 401(k) is restricted to investments in stocks only.
d. The 403(b) is restricted to use by nonprofit companies.

E4-8A
LO 4-5

Which of the following is true about fringe benefits?

a. They represent additional cash paid directly to employees.
b. They are only available for employees.
c. They represent additional compensation given for services performed.
d. The amount of the fringe benefit is never subject to income tax.

E4-9A.
LO 4-5

How is disposable income computed?

a. Gross pay less pre-tax deductions
b. Gross pay less pre-tax deductions and income taxes
c. Gross pay less mandatory deductions
d. Gross pay less Social Security and Medicare taxes

E4-10A.
LO 4-6

By what date must a company declare the value of noncash benefits used in 2020?

a. January 1, 2021
b. December 31, 2021
c. February 1, 2021
d. January 31, 2021

Problems Set A

P4-1A.
LO 4-1, 4-2

Karen Wilson and Katie Smith are looking at the company's health care options and trying to determine how much their net pay will decrease if they sign up for the qualified cafeteria plan offered by the company. Explain the calculations of taxable income when qualified health care deductions are involved. Karen, a married woman with four exemptions, earns $2,000 per biweekly payroll. Katie, a single woman with one exemption, also earns $2,000 per biweekly payroll. The biweekly employee contribution to health care that would be subject to the cafeteria plan is $100.

Karen	Katie
Karen's taxable income if she declines to participate in the cafeteria plan:	Katie's taxable income if she declines to participate in the cafeteria plan:
Karen's taxable income if she participates in the cafeteria plan:	Katie's taxable income if she participates in the cafeteria plan:

P4-2A.
LO 4-1

Joe Ramsey is a computer programmer at Biosphere Communications. He approaches you, the payroll accountant, about his garnishment for child support, claiming that he wishes to remit it personally because he needs to increase his net pay. What advice should you offer him?

P4-3A.
LO 4-1, 4-2

Yvette Bradbury is an account representative at Commerce Savings Bank, earning $42,000 annually, paid semimonthly. She contributes 3 percent of her gross pay to her qualified 401(k) plan on a pre-tax basis and has a pre-tax medical premium of $120. What is her taxable income per pay period?

P4-4A.
LO 4-3

Keren Wiseman is an employee of Dimensionworks Designs in New Mexico. She received the following achievement awards from her employer during 2020:

- Best safety plan, Santa Fe County: $1,200
- Top emergency plan layout, New Mexico: $1,600
- Ten-year employee award: $750

How much of her achievement award income is taxable?

P4-5A.
LO 4-1, 4-3

Trinidad Schwab is an employee at the Kyletown Fire Department. He received the following benefits from his employer during 2020 for company purposes:
- On-site housing: $250 per month
- Employer-provided cell phone: $50 per month
- Meals: $100 per month

What amount of these benefits is taxable for 2020?

P4-6A.
LO 4-4

Judi Pendergrass is an account representative at Ever Pharmaceuticals. She has a company car for customer visits, which she uses to commute from home to work on Monday mornings and work to home on Friday nights, 50 weeks per year. Her commute is 25 miles in each direction. Using the commuting rule, what is the valuation of the fringe benefit?

P4-7A.
LO 4-4

Brent Bishop is the vice president of operations for Southern Sweets Bakery. He drives a 2020 Toyota Prius as his company car, and it has a fair market value of $41,500. The prorated annual lease value per Publication 15-b for the vehicle is $10,750. He reported driving 34,750 miles during 2020, of which 20 percent were for personal reasons. The company pays his fuel and charges him five cents per mile for fuel charges. Using the lease value rule, what is the valuation of Brent's company car benefit?

P4-8A.
LO 4-5

Geraldine Wolfe is a supervisor at Fantastigifts. She has an annual salary of $45,000, paid biweekly, and a garnishment for consumer credit of $375. Assuming that her disposable income is 80 percent of her gross pay per period, does the garnishment follow the CCPA? If not, what is the maximum garnishment allowed for Geraldine's consumer credit garnishment?

P4-9A.
LO 4-1, 4-2, 4-5

Christine Boone is an employee at Americamp Vehicles. She earns a salary of $34,750 annually, paid biweekly. She contributes to the following fringe benefits and other deductions:
- Medical insurance: $80 per pay period
- Dental insurance: $15 per pay period
- 401(k): 5 percent of gross pay
- Union dues: $100 per month
- Additional withholding: $75 per month

What is the total annual amount of Christine's fringe benefits and other deductions?

P4-10A.
LO 4-6

Gavin Range is the payroll accountant for Comptech Industries. His employer decided to use the special accounting rule for 2020. Which months may be included in the special accounting rule?

P4-11A.
LO 4-1, 4-2, 4-3, 4-5

Elijah Hamilton is the payroll accountant at White Box Builders. He is preparing an information package about voluntary and fringe benefits. Using the following list of fringe benefits, classify each benefit as pre-tax or post-tax *and* as taxable or tax-exempt for federal income taxes.

Employee Benefits				
Benefit	Pre-tax	Post-tax	Taxable	Tax-exempt
401(k)				
Medical insurance				
Off-site gym membership				
United Way contributions				
AFLAC				
Tuition assistance up to $5,250 annually				
Commuter passes up to $270 monthly				

Exercises Set B

E4-1B.
LO 4-1
Which of the following fringe benefits is exempt from federal income tax but subject to FICA tax?
a. Moving expense reimbursements
b. Tuition reduction for undergraduate education
c. Adoption assistance
d. Working condition benefits

E4-2B.
LO 4-1
Robin Mendez is an employee of Pharmiceutics LLC. She is a traveling salesperson who routinely meets with customers at their places of business. Which of the following fringe benefits would be appropriate for her employer to provide for Robin to conduct business? (Select all that apply.)
a. Laptop computer
b. Company car
c. Personal stylist
d. Clothing allowance

E4-3B.
LO 4-2
Which of the following is a co-requisite of a health savings account (HSA)?
a. No employer-provided insurance
b. A high deductible health plan
c. Multiple health insurance plans held by the same employee
d. A flexible spending arrangement

E4-4B.
LO 4-2
What is the annual maximum amount that an employee may contribute to a flexible savings arrangement before it becomes taxable income?
a. $2,250
b. $2,450
c. $2,750
d. $2,850

E4-5B.
LO 4-4
Alejandro McCarthy is an employee of Shiloh Bakery. His regular commute includes paying a toll for a portion of his route. Shiloh Bakery offers commuter passes as a fringe benefit. What is the maximum amount that may be excluded from taxes as a fringe benefit?
a. $150
b. $200
c. $270
d. $300

E4-6B.
LO 4-4
Juan Potter is an employee of Convergent Technologies whose job is strictly based in the company's office. His employer has authorized his use of a company vehicle for commuting purposes, as necessary. Which of the general valuation rules would be appropriate to evaluate the value of this fringe benefit?
a. Lease value rule
b. Unsafe conditions rule
c. Commuting rule
d. Cents-per-mile rule

E4-7B.
LO 4-2
Cameron Levitt is the payroll accountant for Glowing Yoga. He is preparing a presentation about Section 125 cafeteria plans. Which of the following items may qualify for inclusion in a cafeteria plan?
a. Health benefits
b. Adoption assistance
c. Childcare expenses
d. Education assistance

E4-8B.
LO 4-5

Gabrielle Jackson is the payroll accountant of Choice Bakeries. She is researching retirement plan options for her employer. Choice Bakeries has 77 employees and is a for-profit company. Which of the following plans should she consider? (Select all that apply.)
a. 403(b)
b. 401(k)
c. SIMPLE 401(k)
d. IRA

E4-9B.
LO 4-1

Which of the following is/are examples of fringe benefits? (Select all that apply.)
a. Education assistance (up to $5,250 annually)
b. Dependent care assistance (up to $5,000 annually)
c. Vacation packages
d. Retirement planning services

E4-10B.
LO 4-5

Which of the following are always post-tax deductions? (Select all that apply.)
a. Garnishments
b. Qualified health insurance
c. Charitable contributions
d. Retirement plan contributions

E4-11B.
LO 4-6

To which two months does the special accounting rule pertain?
a. January and February
b. November and December
c. The last two months of the company's fiscal year
d. December and January of the following year

Problems Set B

P4-1B.
LO 4-1, 4-2

Will Barrett and Eric Martin are looking at the company's health care options and trying to determine what their taxable income will be if they sign up for the qualified cafeteria plan offered by the company, which will allow them to deduct the health care contributions pre-tax. Will, a single man with one exemption, earns $1,600 per semimonthly payroll. Eric, a married man with six exemptions, earns $1,875 per semimonthly pay period. The semimonthly employee contribution to health care that would be subject to the cafeteria plan is $75 for Will, $250 for Eric. Calculate the taxable income when qualified health care deductions are involved.

Will	Eric
Will's taxable income if he declines to participate in the cafeteria plan:	Will's taxable income if he participates in the cafeteria plan:
Eric's taxable income if he declines to participate in the cafeteria plan:	Eric's taxable income if he participates in the cafeteria plan:

P4-2B.
LO 4-1

Orlando Collier is employed as a concierge at Strawberry Lodge, an upscale resort in the Adirondack Mountains. He wants to know which deductions from his pay are considered voluntary fringe benefits. As the payroll accountant, where would you tell him to look on his pay stub?

P4-3B.
LO 4-1, 4-2

Todd Redden is a supervisor at Pinebank Construction. He contributes $2,400 annually to an FSA and has medical insurance that has a $250 monthly premium. He earns a salary of $64,000 and is paid semimonthly. What is his taxable income per period?

P4-4B.
LO 4-1

Kareem Espinal is employed as a copywriter at Jacksaw Publications. He is receiving education assistance of $10,000 per year from his employer to complete his bachelor's degree from an accredited college. How much of that assistance is taxable?

P4-5B.
LO 4-1, 4-3

Jewel Lyman is a married employee in the office of Salvaggio & Wheelers, Attorneys at Law. She received the following benefits during 2020:
- Medical insurance: $250 per month
- Commuter pass: $500 per month
- Employer-paid membership to Anytime Gym: $75 per year
- Dependent care assistance: $3,600 per year

What is the total annual taxable amount for Jewel's 2020 benefits?

P4-6B.
LO 4-4

Rodney Atwater is a sales representative for American Silk Mills. Because he visits customer sites, he has a company car. He drove 25,500 miles during 2020, of which he reported 15 percent was personal miles. Using the cents-per-mile rule, what is the valuation of this benefit for 2020?

P4-7B.
LO 4-4

Janice Lucas is the president of Miller Custom Coffee Roasters. She drives a 2020 Mercedes E300 with a fair market value of $57,500. The lease value is $14,750. The odometer started at 655 and was reported at 32,855 at the end of the year. The car was available all of 2020. Janice reported that she drove 32,200 miles during 2020, of which 9,800 were for personal reasons. The company pays all her fuel and charges her five cents per personal mile for fuel costs. What is her 2020 valuation using the lease value rule?

P4-8B.
LO 4-5

Doug Barton is an employee at Artlee Collections. He earns a salary of $36,000 per year, paid semimonthly, and has a child support garnishment. Assuming that Doug's disposable income is 80 percent of his gross pay, what is the maximum amount per period that may be deducted for the garnishment?

P4-9B.
LO 4-2, 4-5

Gwen Evans is an employee at Findley Street Financial, where she earns an annual salary of $125,500, paid semimonthly. She has the following fringe and voluntary benefits:
- Medical insurance: $150 per month
- 401(k): 6 percent of gross pay
- Flexible spending arrangement: $2,000 annually
- United Way contribution: $25 per pay period

What is the total amount she contributes to fringe benefits and voluntary deductions annually?

P4-10B.
LO 4-6

Arla Dodson is the payroll accountant for Penn & Associates Investments. The company owner decided on December 15, 2020, that he would invoke the special accounting rule. By what date does Arla need to notify affected employees that the rule is being used?

P4-11B.
LO 4-1, 4-2,
4-3, 4-5

Kerry Palmer is reviewing benefits with you, the payroll accountant for Silly Lemon Films. Classify the following benefits in which she is interested as pre-tax or post-tax deductions *and* as taxable or tax exempt for federal income tax.

K. Palmer Benefits				
Fringe Benefit	Pre-tax	Post-tax	Taxable	Tax-exempt
Medical insurance				
FSA				
AFLAC				
Graduate school tuition at $11,000 annually				
On-site meals				

Critical Thinking

4-1. Malcolm Figueroa is a sales employee of Carefree Pools and Spas Inc. During 2020, he was issued a company car with a fair market value of $35,000. He drove a total of 22,000 miles; used the car for 2,000 miles for personal use; and his employer paid for fuel, charging Malcolm 5.5 cents per mile. Under the lease-value rule, what is the amount that must be added to Malcolm's gross pay for 2020? (Use the following table for lease values.)

4-2. Malcolm's employer offers him the option to use the cents-per-mile rule instead of the lease-value rule for 2020. Which method will yield the lower gross income for Malcolm? (Use 57.5 cents per mile in your calculations.)

(1) Automobile FMV	(2) Annual Lease
$ 0 to 999	$ 600
1,000 to 1,999	850
2,000 to 2,999	1,100
3,000 to 3,999	1,350
4,000 to 4,999	1,600
5,000 to 5,999	1,850
6,000 to 6,999	2,100
7,000 to 7,999	2,350
8,000 to 8,999	2,600
9,000 to 9,999	2,850
10,000 to 10,999	3,100
11,000 to 11,999	3,350
12,000 to 12,999	3,600
13,000 to 13,999	3,850
14,000 to 14,999	4,100
15,000 to 15,999	4,350
16,000 to 16,999	4,600
17,000 to 17,999	4,850
18,000 to 18,999	5,100
19,000 to 19,999	5,350
20,000 to 20,999	5,600
21,000 to 21,999	5,850
22,000 to 22,999	6,100
23,000 to 23,999	6,350
24,000 to 24,999	6,600
25,000 to 25,999	6,850
26,000 to 27,999	7,250

(1) Automobile FMV	(2) Annual Lease
28,000 to 29,999	7,750
30,000 to 31,999	8,250
32,000 to 33,999	8,750
34,000 to 35,999	9,250
36,000 to 37,999	9,750
38,000 to 39,999	10,250
40,000 to 41,999	10,750
42,000 to 43,999	11,250
44,000 to 45,999	11,750
46,000 to 47,999	12,250
48,000 to 49,999	12,750
50,000 to 51,999	13,250
52,000 to 53,999	13,750
54,000 to 55,999	14,250
56,000 to 57,999	14,750
58,000 to 59,999	15,250

In the Real World: Scenario for Discussion

Project labor agreements (PLAs) are used in certain states to promote pay and benefit equity for construction workers. Specifically, PLAs ensure that construction workers who choose not to join a union have access to the same pay and benefits as their union-affiliated colleagues. PLAs ensure that the presence or absence of a labor union is not a factor in the contract bidding process, therefore encouraging more contractors to bid on construction projects. Proponents of PLAs contend that they expand employment opportunities. Opponents claim that the PLA cannot exist in at-will employment states.

Which side is more correct? How can at-will employment laws exist where PLAs are allowed?

Internet Activities

4-1. Health insurance is a rapidly changing and evolving field. Employers have many options and concerns to consider. Check out www.npr.org/sections/health-care/ to listen to podcasts about health insurance and employer issues. What issues do employers currently face?

4-2. Using a site such as Google, Yahoo, or Safari, search for the term "fringe benefits." Sites such as HR360 at www.hr360.com contain insights into fringe benefits and guidance about the tax treatment for benefits. Why do you think that fringe benefits are important enough to influence an employee's choice of employer?

4-3. Go to www.benefitspro.com and search for benefits-related podcasts. Once you have listened to one or more podcast, what insights did you gain from the information presented?

4-4. Want to know more about the topics discussed in this chapter? Go to the following links:

www.healthcare.gov/law/index.html

www.aflac.com

www.investopedia.com

www.irs.gov/pub/irs-pdf/p15b.pdf

www.dol.gov/general/topic/wages/garnishments

4-5. Can employers charge employees for their uniforms? Check out the U.S. Department of Labor video at https://www.youtube.com/watch?v=PoZCux0rTN8&feature=youtu.be

Continuing Payroll Project: Prevosti Farms and Sugarhouse

Although the company has already established medical and retirement plan benefits, Toni Prevosti wants to consider other benefits to attract employees. As the company's accountant, you have been tasked with annotating employee earnings records with benefit elections for each employee. The following sheet contains details of employee choices. These costs are employer-paid and will take effect on the first pay period of March.

To calculate the life insurance benefit, multiply the employee's annual salary by 1 percent. For example, if an employee earned $50,000 per year, the life insurance would be $50,000 × 0.01 = $500.

Employee	Flex-time	Child care assistance (under $5,000 annually)	FSA (annual)	Education assistance ($4,000 annually)	Life insurance (at 1% of annual salary value)	Long-term care insurance $15 per period	Gym membership $15 per month	Cost per employee
Millen	Yes	Yes	19.23077	No	13.46154	No	6.92308	$39.62
Towle	No	No	46.15385	Yes	No	No	6.92308	$53.08
Long	Yes	Yes	26.92308	Yes	8.75000	No	6.92308	$42.60
Shangraw	Yes	No	7.69231	No	4.40000	No	No	$12.09
Lewis	No	No	61.53846	No	12.30769	15.00000	No	$88.85
Schwartz	No	No	17.30769	Yes	9.23077	No	6.92308	$33.46
Prevosti	Yes	No	34.61538	No	17.30769	No	6.92308	$58.85
Student	No	No	11.53846	Yes	No	No	6.92308	$18.46
	*	*		*				

*No assigned cost until employee uses benefit

Annotate the Employee Earning Records with payroll-related benefit elections. The amount per period should be included in the record. As an example, if an employee elected to contribute $1,300 to his or her FSA, the period payroll deduction would be $1,300/26, or $50. The estimated yearly earnings used for insurance purposes for the hourly employees are computed as follows: (hourly wages times number of hours worked per week × 52) then divide by 26 pay periods to get an amount per pay period. For example: If Shangraw worked 20 hours per week, the computation is $11/hour × 52 weeks = $11,440 per year. Insurance is computed as $11,440 × 1% = $114.40/26 = $4.40 per pay period.

EMPLOYEE EARNING RECORD

NAME	Thomas Millen	Hire Date	2/3/2020	Dependent child < 17	3
ADDRESS	1022 Forest School Road	Date of Birth	12/16/1982	Dependent other	1
CITY/STATE/ZIP	Woodstock, VT 05001	Position	Production Manager PT (FT)	Step 4a W-4 Info	none
TELEPHONE	802-478-5055	Filing Status	Married	Step 4b W-4 Info	none
SOCIAL SECURITY NUMBER	031-11-3456	Exempt/Nonexempt	Exempt	Step 4c W-4 Info	none
		Pay Rate	$35,000.00 Hr / Wk / Mo (Yr)		

Flex-Time	Child Care	FSA Amount	Educational Assistance	Life Ins.	Long-Term Care	Gym Membership	Total Benefit

Period Ended	Hrs Worked	Reg Pay	OT Pay	Holiday	Comm	Gross Pay	Ins	401(k)	Taxable Pay for Federal	Taxable Pay for FICA

Taxable Pay for Federal	Taxable Pay for FICA	Fed Inc. Tax	Social Sec. Tax	Medicare	State Inc. Tax	Total Deduc	Net Pay	YTD Net Pay	YTD Gross Pay	YTD FUTA
-	-									

EMPLOYEE EARNING RECORD

NAME	Avery Towle	Hire Date	2/3/2020	Dependent child < 17	0
ADDRESS	4011 Route 100	Date of Birth	7/14/1991	Dependent other	0
CITY/STATE/ZIP	Plymouth, VT 05102	Position	Production Worker PT (FT)	Step 4a W-4 Info	none
TELEPHONE	802-967-5873	Filing Status	Married	Step 4b W-4 Info	none
SOCIAL SECURITY NUMBER	089-74-0974	Exempt/Nonexempt	Non-exempt	Step 4c W-4 Info	none
		Pay Rate	$12.00 (Hr) Wk / Mo / Yr		

Flex-Time	Child Care	FSA Amount	Educational Assistance	Life Ins.	Long-Term Care	Gym Membership	Total Benefit

EMPLOYEE EARNING RECORD

NAME	Charlie Long	Hire Date	2/3/2020	Dependent child < 17	2
ADDRESS	242 Benedict Road S.	Date of Birth	3/16/1987	Dependent other	0
CITY/STATE/ZIP	Woodstock, VT 05002	Position	Production Worker PT (FT)	Step 4a W-4 Info	none
TELEPHONE	802-429-3846	Filing Status	Married	Step 4b W-4 Info	none
SOCIAL SECURITY NUMBER	056-23-4593	Exempt/Nonexempt	Non-exempt	Step 4c W-4 Info	none
		Pay Rate	$12.50 (Hr) Wk / Mo / Yr		

Flex-Time	Child Care	FSA Amount	Educational Assistance	Life Ins.	Long-Term Care	Gym Membership	Total Benefit

EMPLOYEE EARNING RECORD

NAME	Mary Shangraw	Hire Date	2/3/2020	Dependent child < 17	0
ADDRESS	1901 Main Street #2	Date of Birth	8/20/1994	Dependent other	1
CITY/STATE/ZIP	Bridgewater, VT 05520	Position	Administrative Assistant (PT) FT	Step 4a W-4 Info	none
TELEPHONE	802-575-5423	Filing Status	Single	Step 4b W-4 Info	none
SOCIAL SECURITY NUMBER	075-28-8945	Exempt/Nonexempt	Non-exempt	Step 4c W-4 Info	none
		Pay Rate	$11.00 (Hr) Wk / Mo / Yr		

Flex-Time	Child Care	FSA Amount	Educational Assistance	Life Ins.	Long-Term Care	Gym Membership	Total Benefit

EMPLOYEE EARNING RECORD

NAME	Kristen Lewis	Hire Date	2/3/2020	Dependent child < 17	2
ADDRESS	840 Daily Hollow Road	Date of Birth	4/6/1960	Dependent other	1
CITY/STATE/ZIP	Bridgewater, VT 05523	Position	Office Manager PT (FT)	Step 4a W-4 Info	none
TELEPHONE	802-390-5572	Filing Status	Married	Step 4b W-4 Info	none
SOCIAL SECURITY NUMBER	076-39-5673	Exempt/Nonexempt	Exempt	Step 4c W-4 Info	none
		Pay Rate	$32,000.00 Hr / Wk / Mo (Yr)		

Flex-Time	Child Care	FSA Amount	Educational Assistance	Life Ins.	Long-Term Care	Gym Membership	Total Benefit

EMPLOYEE EARNING RECORD

NAME	Joel Schwartz	Hire Date	2/3/2020	Dependent child < 17	2
ADDRESS	55 Maple Farm Way	Date of Birth	5/23/1985	Dependent other	0
CITY/STATE/ZIP	Woodstock, VT 05534	Position	Sales PT (FT)	Step 4a W-4 Info	none
TELEPHONE	802-463-9985	Filing Status	Married	Step 4b W-4 Info	none
SOCIAL SECURITY NUMBER	021-34-9876	Exempt/Nonexempt	Exempt	Step 4c W-4 Info	none
		Pay Rate	$24,000 + Commiss Hr / Wk / Mo (Yr)		

Flex-Time	Child Care	FSA Amount	Educational Assistance	Life Ins.	Long-Term Care	Gym Membership	Total Benefit

EMPLOYEE EARNING RECORD

NAME	Toni Prevosti	Hire Date	2/3/2020	Dependent child < 17	3
ADDRESS	820 Westminster Road	Date of Birth	9/19/1967	Dependent other	2
CITY/STATE/ZIP	Bridgewater, VT 05521	Position	Owner/President	PT (FT) Step 4a W-4 Info	none
TELEPHONE	802-555-3456	Filing Status	Married	Step 4b W-4 Info	none
SOCIAL SECURITY NUMBER	055-22-0443	Exempt/Nonexempt	Exempt	Step 4c W-4 Info	none
		Pay Rate	$45,000.00	Hr / Wk / Mo (Yr)	

Flex-Time	Child Care	FSA Amount	Educational Assistance	Life Ins.	Long-Term Care	Gym Membership	Total Benefit

EMPLOYEE EARNING RECORD

NAME	Student Success	Hire Date	2/3/2020	Dependent child < 17	0
ADDRESS	1644 Smitten Road	Date of Birth	1/1/1991	Dependent other	0
CITY/STATE/ZIP	Woodstock, VT 05001	Position	Accounting Clerk	PT (FT) Step 4a W-4 Info	none
TELEPHONE	555-555-5555	Filing Status	Single	Step 4b W-4 Info	none
SOCIAL SECURITY NUMBER	555-55-5555	Exempt/Nonexempt	Non-exempt	Step 4c W-4 Info	none
		Pay Rate	$34,000.00	Hr / Wk / Mo (Yr)	

Flex-Time	Child Care	FSA Amount	Educational Assistance	Life Ins.	Long-Term Care	Gym Membership	Total Benefit

Answers to Stop & Check Exercises

Fringe Benefits 101

1. Fringe benefits will fall under the pre-tax or post-tax category.
2. b and c
3. a, c, and d

What Is Served in the Cafeteria Plan?

1. a, b, d
2. A flexible spending account (FSA) can be taxable when contributions are over $2,750 annually by the employee. The purpose is to defer, not avoid, paying taxes, and there is typically a "use it or lose it" policy where the funds expire at a point in time when not used. Health savings accounts (HSAs) may only be used in conjunction with a cafeteria plan where there is a high deductible, and the funds may be available longer for related medical care.
3. An HDHP has the following limits: $1,400 annual deductible (single), $2,800 annual deductible (family), $6,900 out-of-pocket expenses maximum (single), and $13,800 out-of-pocket expenses maximum (family).

Excluded Fringe Benefits

1. No, because it is provided on the employer's premises and is operated by the company and restricted to use by its employees, their spouses, and dependents.
2. The portion of the cost of the car that would represent the personal use portion of mileage will be included in Marcia's gross income. However, any amount that is directly related to the job would be excluded under the Working Conditions Benefits.

Fringe Benefit Valuations

1. $2,435.15 (rounded) (30,250 miles × 15% × 0.575).
2. The value of the fringe benefit is $813.70, computed as follows (round final figure to two decimals):

Fair market value of the vehicle:	$ 47,000
Annual lease value:	12,250
Prorated annual lease value:	49.315%
Percent of personal use during the year:	20%
Personal annual lease value:	$1,208.22

Pre-Tax vs. Post-Tax Deductions

1. Affordable Care Act.
2. 401(k); 403(b); Savings Incentive Match Plan for Employees (SIMPLE); Individual Retirement Account (IRA); Employee Stock Ownership Plan (ESOP); Simplified Employee Pension (SEP).
3. $447.50 calculated as: $1,790 disposable income × 25%.
4. Union dues and health insurance are not legally required and thus would not affect the amount of the disposable income available for garnishments.

Employee Benefits Reporting

1. Monies should be withheld from the employee when the benefit is made available; normal practice is to deduct these as the employees receive their pay (daily, weekly, biweekly, semimonthly, monthly, annually).
2. The total compensation report can be given to Brandon to explain the total cost of benefits and compensation received.
3. There are several fringe benefits that must be included in taxable income to the employees. These include personal use of a company-provided vehicle, commuting paid by the employer, or lease of a vehicle.

Chapter Five

Employee Net Pay and Pay Methods

Death and taxes are two certainties in life. Taxes are withheld from employees' earnings and remitted to the governing body. Companies operate as the collector and depositor of income taxes, garnishments, and other deductions on behalf of the employee. The tax code permits certain qualifying deductions to be taken out of an employee's pay prior to the income taxes being calculated. These deductions are called pre-tax deductions. Other deductions are removed from the employee's pay after income taxes have been calculated; these are called post-tax deductions. Circular E, also known as Publication 15 (and all supplemental materials), from the Internal Revenue Service provides a comprehensive list of employee taxes, employer responsibilities, and guidance for special situations. *Publication 15-T* is new in 2020 and contains wage-bracket tables and percentage method computation amounts.

Taxes and both voluntary and mandated deductions all reduce the gross pay that we computed in Chapter 3. In this chapter, we will explore the effects of these deductions and any other fringe benefits on employee take-home pay, also called *net pay*.

LEARNING OBJECTIVES

After studying Chapter 5, you should be able to:

LO 5-1   Compute Employee Net Pay

LO 5-2   Determine Federal Income Tax Withholding Amounts

LO 5-3   Compute Social Security and Medicare Tax Withholding

LO 5-4   Calculate State and Local Income Taxes

LO 5-5   Apply Post-Tax Deductions

LO 5-6   Discuss Employee Pay Methods

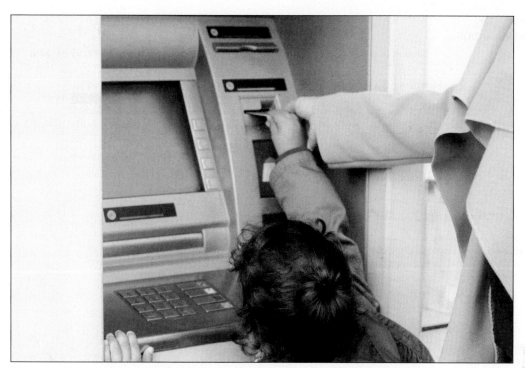

Shutterstock/LumineImages

Paycard Use and Legal Regulations Vary among States

The use of paycards as a means of transmitting employee pay from the employer to the employee has changed the way many employees receive their compensation. In 2017, the Aite Group, a payment consultant group, found that over 5.9 million workers received their compensation—a total exceeding $42 billion—via paycards. Employees who used paycards ranged from being fully banked (meaning that they have a bank account) to being completely unbanked, thus relying on the security of the paycard to receive and use their earned income. These numbers are expected to increase with the entrance of millennial workers into paid employment.

However, not every state allows the use of paycards and only 39 states have regulations to protect employees' access to funds. State legislation exists in some areas to promote full disclosure of any fees associated with paycards and any limits imposed by the card issuer with regards to funds availability and withdrawal via automated teller machines (ATMs). The use of paycards represents a movement away from cash or paper checks as sources of compensation disbursement and involves financial technology that simultaneously promotes transparency in employee compensation and requires additional vigilance against cyberthreats.

(Sources: American Payroll Association, Patriot Software, PYMNTS)

Changes in net pay computations and payment methods affect employee take-home pay and accessibility to earned income. In Chapter 5, we will explore the computations of employee net pay and the methods used to transmit that pay to the employees.

FIGURE 5-1
Prepaid card use in 2020

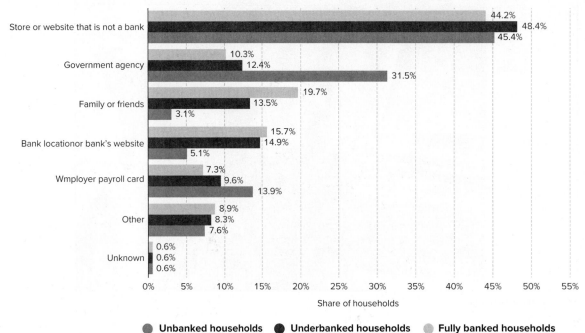

Sources of prepaid cards among households in the United States in 2017, by banking status

Source: **FDIC** via Statista, 2020

Rawpixel.com/Shutterstock

LO 5-1   Compute Employee Net Pay

Now that we have discussed the computation of gross income, it is time to focus on the various taxes and miscellaneous voluntary or court-ordered deductions withheld and to determine the employee's **net pay**, which is the amount of cash an employee receives in a physical check, cash, direct deposit, or a paycard. The process of computing gross pay involves several steps, each of which must be completed accurately. We will explore the details of pre-tax deductions, tax computations, and post-tax deductions in the following sections of this chapter.

In 2020, the Tax Cuts and Jobs Act of 2017 led to a new Form W-4 and different tax tables. An employee's federal income tax, for those who filed the 2020 Form W-4, is computed based on the employee's tax filing status, pay frequency, taxable earnings, and spouse's employment status—a vast difference from prior years. Both methods (i.e., employees with a pre-2020 Form W-4 and those with the new W-4) will be explained during this chapter.

Once the employer has computed the employee's gross pay, the next step is to deduct mandatory (i.e., legislated), voluntary, and mandated (i.e., court-ordered or union-regulated) amounts. These deductions include federal income tax, Medicare, and Social Security taxes, which are the primary mandatory deductions. Other mandatory deductions that the employee may be subject to include *state income taxes*, city or county income taxes, and regional taxes. For example, Denver has a "head tax" for those employees working within the city and county; Mountain View, California, instituted a similar tax because of Google's presence in the city. Federal Unemployment Tax is the sole employer-only tax. Some states require employees to contribute to the State Unemployment Tax, whereas other states consider it an employer-only tax.

Pay Computation Steps

This is the process to compute each employee's pay:

1. Start with the employee's gross pay.
2. Subtract the pre-tax deductions to get the total taxable earnings.

3. Compute the taxes to be withheld from the total taxable earnings.

4. Deduct the taxes.

5. Deduct any other voluntary or mandated deductions.

6. The result is the employee's net pay.

The easiest way to keep track of all deductions and to ensure pay accuracy is to use a payroll register. In the following examples, we will show the computations as well as a sample of the payroll register representation.

EXAMPLE: NET PAY COMPUTATION

Marco Myles receives a salary of $2,000 paid biweekly and has earned $46,000 year-to-date. He is married filing jointly and his spouse is also employed. Marco works for KOR Inc. in Charleston, West Virginia, where his state income tax is 6 percent. His pre-tax deductions include medical insurance of $50, a cafeteria plan of $75, and a 401(k) of 3 percent of his gross salary per pay period. He has charitable contributions of $10, union dues of $62, and a court-ordered garnishment of $120. Taxable income computation is the same for both federal and state income tax purposes. Let us compute Marco's net pay step-by-step:

Gross pay	$2,000.00
Less: pre-tax medical insurance deduction	−50.00
Less: cafeteria plan	−75.00
Less: 401(k) contribution	−60.00
Total taxable earnings	$1,815.00
Less: Federal income tax (using the wage-bracket method)	−154.00
Less: Social Security tax*	−116.25
Less: Medicare tax†	−27.19
Less: West Virginia state income tax‡	−108.90
Less: Charitable contribution	−10.00
Less: Union dues	−62.00
Less: Garnishment	−120.00
Net pay	$1,216.66

*$2,000 − 50 − 75 = 1,875 \times 0.062 = 116.25$
†$2,000 − 50 − 75 = 1,875 \times 0.0145 = 27.19$
‡$1,815 \times 0.06 = 108.90$

The payroll register for Marco Myles's pay would appear as follows:

Name	Filing Status	Hourly Rate or Period Wage	No. of Regular Hours	No. of Overtime Hours	No. of Holiday Hours	Gross Earnings	401(k)	Insurance	Cafeteria Plan	Taxable Wages for Federal W/H	Taxable Wages for FICA
Marco Myles	MJ-2	2,000.00				2,000.00	60.00	50.00	75.00	1,815.00	1,875.00

Name	Gross Earning	Taxable Wages for Federal W/H	Taxable Wages for FICA	Federal W/H	Social Security Tax	Medicare W/H	State W/H Tax	Charitable Contribution	Union Dues	Garnishment	Net Pay
Marco Myles	2,000.00	1,815.00	1,875.00	154.00	116.25	27.19	108.90	10.00	62.00	120.00	1,216.66

Shutterstock/Andy Dean Photography

Grossed-Up Pay

An employer will occasionally want to pay an employee a specific net amount, perhaps as a bonus. However, all federal, state, and local taxes must be applied. The amount of the employee's pay must be "grossed up" to satisfy tax liabilities and achieve the net pay desired.

EXAMPLE: "GROSSING UP" AN EMPLOYEE'S PAY

Caitlyn Lanneker is an employee of Pacifica Enterprises, located in the state of Washington. The firm's president wants to award Caitlyn a $150 bonus at the end of the year to reward her. Use the following steps to compute the gross-up amount:

1. Compute the tax rate for federal income tax and FICA. The tax rate on bonuses is 22 percent, per Publication 15-T. The Social Security (6.2%) and Medicare taxes (1.45%) must be added to this rate. For bonuses, the total tax rate equals 22% + 6.2% + 1.45%, or 29.65%. (For non-bonus gross up, compute the tax rate using amounts from Appendix C.) Add any state or local income tax rates to this computation as necessary.

2. To calculate the net tax rate, subtract the tax rate percentage from 100 percent (i.e., 100% − tax rate) to get the net tax rate. For this bonus, it is 100% − 29.65%, or 70.35%, because no state or local income tax rates apply.

3. Gross-up amount equals the net pay divided by the net tax rate.

For example, for Caitlyn to receive a $150 bonus, the equation to calculate the gross pay is $150/70.35% = $213.22.

Note: Typically, voluntary pre-tax or post-tax deductions are not withheld from bonus checks.

Differentiating Between Gross and Net Pay

Stop & Check

1. What is the difference between gross pay and net pay?
2. What are three items that may be deducted from gross pay?
3. What does it mean to "gross up" an amount paid to an employee?

LO 5-2 Determine Federal Income Tax Withholding Amounts

Now let us shift our focus to *mandatory deductions* that must be withheld from employee pay. The first class of mandatory deductions is the federal income tax. This is an employee-only tax, meaning that the employer does not contribute a matching amount for the federal income tax withheld from an employee's pay.

Federal Income Taxes

Andrii Yalanskyi/Shutterstock

The first tax we will cover is the *federal income tax*. The federal income tax represents amounts to be withheld from employed persons, calculated using the information reported by the employee on Form W-4. The withheld tax is the employee's deposit against income taxes. The employer acts as a collector and depositor for these funds. When an individual files the income tax return, the amount withheld from his or her pay during the year reduces the amount he or she may have to pay with the return. Federal taxable income is reduced by pre-tax deductions discussed previously.

In manual systems, there are two commonly used methods to calculate the employee's federal income tax: Wage bracket and percentage. In 2020, the IRS issued Publication 15-T for the sole purpose of income tax calculations, given that two types of Forms W-4 were in use. We will explain both federal income tax computation methods, using the 2020 Form W-4 and pre-2020 Form W-4. Regardless of the method used for calculating federal income taxes, the reduction for pre-tax items will remain the same. We will also show the results in each example using the IRS Income Tax Withholding Assistant, an Excel spreadsheet that the IRS provided in 2020 to assist with income tax determination.

Federal Income Pre-Tax Computation Examples

EXAMPLE: GROSS PAY LESS 401(K) AND INSURANCE

Amanda Brady's gross wages are $950, she has subscribed to the company's cafeteria plan, and she has agreed to a 10 percent investment of her gross wages in a qualified 401(k) plan. Her portion of the health insurance is $56.90 per pay period. To calculate her taxable pay, we must first determine the 401(k) deduction: $950 × 10% = $95. Therefore, her taxable pay is

$950.00	gross pay
−95.00	401(k) deduction
−56.90	health insurance
$798.10	taxable income

EXAMPLE: EFFECT OF FIXED AMOUNT VS. PERCENTAGE DEDUCTION FOR 401(K) CONTRIBUTION ON TAXABLE WAGES

Daniel Cain has gross wages of $1,125, participates in the company's 401(k) program at $100 per pay period, and has health insurance and AFLAC (all pre-tax) totaling $113.80. The calculation of Daniel's taxable income is

$1,125.00	gross pay
−100.00	401(k) deduction
−113.80	health insurance and AFLAC
$ 911.20	taxable income

Had Daniel participated in the company's 401(k) as a percentage instead of a fixed dollar, the percent would be calculated prior to other deductions. For instance, if he elected to invest 3 percent of his gross pay, his taxable income would be

$1,125.00	
× 0.03	
33.75	401(k) contribution

$1,125.00	gross pay
−33.75	401(k) contribution
−113.80	health insurance and AFLAC
$ 977.45	taxable income

Note: Gross Pay − qualified medical = taxable wages for FICA. $1,125 − 113.80 = $1,011.20 would be the taxable amount for Social Security and Medicare because retirement contributions are not exempt from FICA taxes.

Forms W-4, 2020 Version

Based on changes contained in the Tax Cuts and Jobs Act, Form W-4 in 2020 was very different in appearance and the criteria for amounts withheld from employee payroll. The employee federal income tax criteria used starting in 2020 included the following:

- Filing status (Single, Married Filing Jointly, Married Filing Separately, and Head of Household)
- Multiple jobs or spouse's employment
- Dependents under the age of 17
- Other dependents

The intent of the revised Form W-4 was to reduce the chance that employees would have too little income tax deducted from their pay by claiming too many withholding allowances, which led to employees having under-withheld taxes and owing more money on filing their annual income tax return. The new Form W-4 removes the withholding allowances and focuses on marital status, annual income, and dependents. The filing status was expanded to match the categories used on the annual tax return and the reality of an employee supporting other non-child dependents were included as part of the form. The IRS guidelines to incorporate employee Form W-4 information are included in Publication 15-T and appear as follows:

Worksheet 4. Employer's Withholding Worksheet for Percentage Method Tables for Manual Payroll Systems With Forms W-4 From 2020 or Later

Keep for Your Records

Table 5	Monthly	Semimonthly	Biweekly	Weekly	Daily
	12	24	26	52	260

Step 1.   Adjust the employee's wage amount

1a   Enter the employee's total taxable wages this payroll period . . . .   1a $ _____

1b   Enter the number of pay periods you have per year (see Table 5) . . . .   1b   _____

1c   Enter the amount from Step 4(a) of the employee's Form W-4 . . . .   1c $ _____

1d   Divide line 1c by the number on line 1b . . . .   1d $ _____

1e   Add lines 1a and 1d . . . .   1e $ _____

1f   Enter the amount from Step 4(b) of the employee's Form W-4 . . . .   1f $ _____

1g   Divide line 1f by the number on line 1b . . . .   1g $ _____

1h   Subtract line 1g from line 1e. If zero or less, enter -0-. This is the **Adjusted Wage Amount** . . . . . .   1h $ _____

Step 2.   Figure the Tentative Withholding Amount

based on your pay frequency, the employee's Adjusted Wage Amount, filing status (Step 1(c) of Form W-4), and whether the box in Step 2 of Form W-4 is checked.

2a   Find the row in the *STANDARD Withholding Rate Schedules* (if the box in Step 2 of Form W-4 is NOT checked) or the *Form W-4, Step 2, Checkbox, Withholding Rate Schedules* (if it HAS been checked) of the Percentage Method tables in this section in which the amount on line 1h is at least the amount in column A but less than the amount in column B, then enter here the amount from column A of that row . . . .   2a $ _____

2b   Enter the amount from column C of that row . . . .   2b $ _____

2c   Enter the percentage from column D of that row . . . .   2c   _____ %

2d   Subtract line 2a from line 1h . . . .   2d $ _____

2e   Multiply the amount on line 2d by the percentage on line 2c . . . .   2e $ _____

2f   Add lines 2b and 2e. This is the **Tentative Withholding Amount** . . . .   2f $ _____

Step 3.   Account for tax credits

3a   Enter the amount from Step 3 of the employee's Form W-4 . . . .   3a $ _____

3b   Divide the amount on line 3a by the number of pay periods on line 1b . . . .   3b $ _____

3c   Subtract line 3b from line 2f. If zero or less, enter -0- . . . .   3c $ _____

Step 4.   Figure the final amount to withhold

4a   Enter the additional amount to withhold from Step 4(c) of the employee's Form W-4 . . . .   4a $ _____

4b   Add lines 3c and 4a. **This is the amount to withhold from the employee's wages this pay period** . . . .   4b $ _____

The above worksheet is available from the IRS in Microsoft Excel Format for use by employers who compute payroll manually. The Excel spreadsheet is located at https://www .irs.gov/businesses/small-businesses-self-employed/income-tax-withholding-assistant-for-employers and will be used to compute wage-bracket withholding taxes. If this spreadsheet is used, a separate Excel File should be maintained for each employee. Excel workbooks can be linked to a payroll register and earnings report so that the calculations can flow through.

Publication 15-T contains tax tables to match the new criteria. The following examples reflect how the new tax deductions affect employee pay.

EXAMPLE: WAGE-BRACKET COMPUTATION OF FEDERAL INCOME TAX, MARRIED FILING JOINT, SEMIMONTHLY

Regina Smith is an employee of Centerspot Photo Designs. She earns $36,000 per year and is paid semimonthly. She is married and files taxes jointly with her husband, who is also employed. She has two children under the age of 17 and no other dependents. Using the 2020 wage-bracket tables in Appendix C, we will determine Regina's federal income tax in different situations.

1. NO VOLUNTARY PRE-TAX DEDUCTIONS

Period pay ($36,000/24)	$1,500.00
Taxable income	1,500.00
Federal income tax	-0-

2. PRE-TAX HEALTH INSURANCE DEDUCTION, $150

Period pay ($36,000/24)	$1,500.00
Less: health insurance	150.00
Taxable income	$1,350.00
Federal income tax	-0-

3. PRE-TAX HEALTH INSURANCE DEDUCTION, $150, AND 401(K) CONTRIBUTION, 4%

Period pay ($36,000/24)	$1,500.00
Less: health insurance	150.00
Less: 401(k) contribution	80.00
Taxable income*	$1,270.00
Federal income tax	-0-

*Note: The taxable income for Social Security and Medicare tax is $2,000 − 150 = $1,850.

Notice that Regina would have no federal income tax withheld in any case because she declared two children under the age of 17. The IRS Excel spreadsheet data shows how the calculation arrived at zero federal income tax is to be withheld.

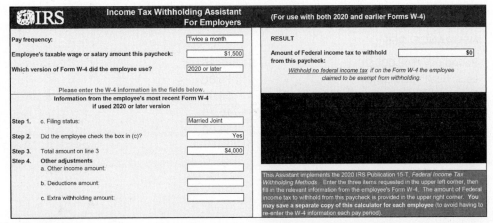

Source: Internal Revenue Service

Wage-Bracket Method: Forms W-4 from 2020

Using the *wage-bracket method*, the payroll clerk identifies the individual's marital status, number of exemptions, and taxable income level and then follows the chart located in Publication 15 for the amount to be withheld. If manually calculating the wage-bracket method, it is important to apply the appropriate number of withholding variables prior to calculating the tax amounts. The wage-bracket method is useful for manual payroll preparation because the process of federal tax withholding is an estimate for the year-end amount of taxes due. To determine taxes to withhold using the wage-bracket method in Appendix C, the payroll clerk may use Publication 15-T. If the payroll clerk is using an automated system, periodic checking and ensuring year-end updates do not run prior to the last payroll are important to ensuring validity in the system.

Note that if the federal income tax withholding assistant spreadsheet is used, the taxable amount should be rounded to the nearest dollar.

EXAMPLE: WAGE-BRACKET COMPUTATION OF FEDERAL INCOME TAX, SINGLE, BIWEEKLY

Steve Bishop is an employee at Vosgienne Farms. He is single with no dependents and earns $48,000 annually, paid biweekly. Using the IRS Income Tax Withholding Assistant we will determine Steve's federal income tax in different situations.

1. NO PRE-TAX DEDUCTIONS

Period pay ($48,000/26)	$1,846.15
Taxable income	1,750.00
Federal income tax	157.00

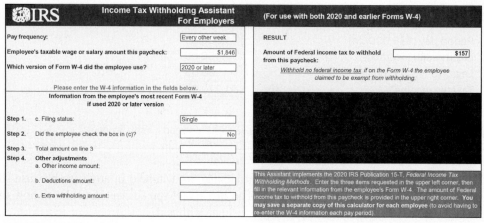

Source: Internal Revenue Service

2. PRE-TAX HEALTH INSURANCE, $75, PRE-TAX SUPPLEMENTAL HEALTH INSURANCE, $55

Period pay ($48,000/26)	$1,846.15
Less: health insurance	75.00
Less: supplemental health insurance	55.00
Taxable income	$1,716.15
Federal income tax	$ 141.00

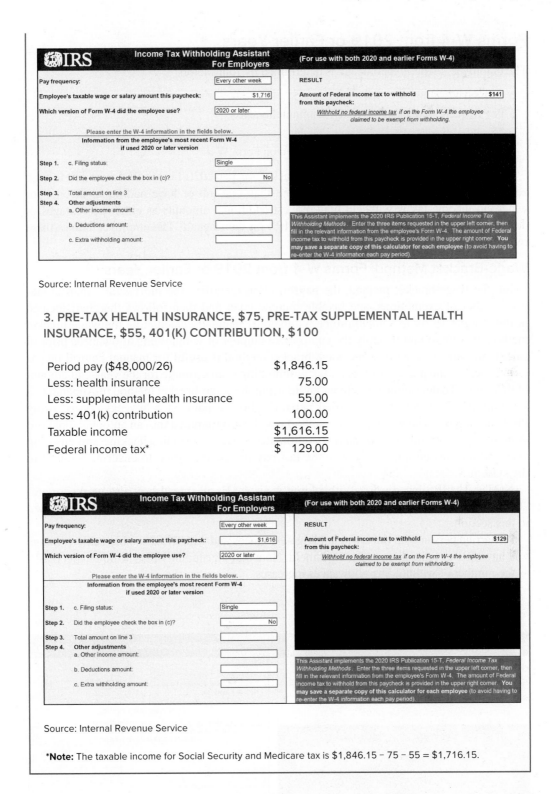

Source: Internal Revenue Service

3. PRE-TAX HEALTH INSURANCE, $75, PRE-TAX SUPPLEMENTAL HEALTH INSURANCE, $55, 401(K) CONTRIBUTION, $100

Period pay ($48,000/26)	$1,846.15
Less: health insurance	75.00
Less: supplemental health insurance	55.00
Less: 401(k) contribution	100.00
Taxable income	$1,616.15
Federal income tax*	$ 129.00

Source: Internal Revenue Service

Note: The taxable income for Social Security and Medicare tax is $1,846.15 – 75 – 55 = $1,716.15.

If the employer uses the percentage method, the Excel spreadsheet may still be used. Automated payroll programs such as Quickbooks are designed to compute the income taxes automatically.

Forms W-4 from 2019 or Earlier Years

The employee's federal income tax is determined by four factors:

1. Gross pay.
2. Pay frequency (weekly, biweekly, semimonthly, etc.).
3. Marital status.
4. Number of withholding allowances claimed on Form W-4.

The highest-taxed federal income tax bracket for per-2020 Forms W-4 was single with zero dependents. Employees who work more than one job or have additional income for which no income tax is withheld may request additional amounts as either percentages or dollars to be withheld and submitted to the IRS on their behalf. The employee makes these requests on Form W-4.

Wage-Bracket Method: Forms W-4 from 2019 or Earlier Years

Using the wage-bracket method, the payroll clerk identifies the individual's marital status, number of exemptions, and taxable income level and then follows the chart located in Publication 15 for the amount to be withheld. If manually calculating the wage-bracket method, it is important to apply the appropriate number of withholding allowances prior to calculating the tax amounts. The wage-bracket method is useful for manual payroll preparation because the process of federal tax withholding is an estimate for the year-end amount of taxes due. To determine taxes to withhold using the wage-bracket method in Appendix C, see Figure 5-2, which is for married persons who are paid on a biweekly basis, using Publication 15-T. The wage-bracket method may be programmed into an automated payroll system. If the payroll clerk is using an automated system, periodic checking and ensuring year-end updates do not run prior to the last payroll are important to ensuring validity in the system.

NOTE: The IRS Income Tax Withholding Assistant Excel spreadsheet also works for pre-2020 Forms W-4. Examples of how it compares with manual computations will be included in this section.

A married person with three withholding allowances and with $1,839 in biweekly earnings will have $91 of federal income tax withheld. Note that the amount of tax withheld decreases as the number of withholding allowances increases.

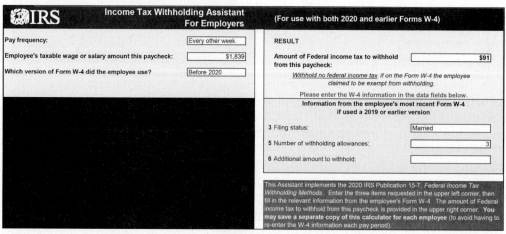

Source: Internal Revenue Service

FIGURE 5-2
Biweekly Payroll Period—Married Persons, Wage-Bracket Method, Pre-2020 W-4

Valerie Ball is married and has three withholding allowances on her 2019 Form W-4. The employee is paid biweekly and earned $1,839. What is the Federal Income Tax for Valerie?

2020 Wage Bracket Method Tables for Manual Payroll Systems With Forms W-4 From 2019 or Earlier
BIWEEKLY Payroll Period

If the **Wage Amount** (line 1a) is		MARRIED Persons And the number of allowances is:										
		0	1	2	3	4	5	6	7	8	9	10
At least	But less than	The Tentative Withholding Amount is:										
$1,430	$1,460	$103	$83	$66	$49	$33	$16	$0	$0	$0	$0	$0
$1,460	$1,490	$107	$87	$69	$52	$36	$19	$3	$0	$0	$0	$0
$1,490	$1,520	$110	$91	$72	$55	$39	$22	$6	$0	$0	$0	$0
$1,520	$1,550	$114	$94	$75	$58	$42	$25	$9	$0	$0	$0	$0
$1,550	$1,580	$118	$98	$78	$61	$45	$28	$12	$0	$0	$0	$0
$1,580	$1,610	$121	$101	$82	$64	$48	$31	$15	$0	$0	$0	$0
$1,610	$1,640	$125	$105	$85	$67	$51	$34	$18	$1	$0	$0	$0
$1,640	$1,670	$128	$109	$89	$70	$54	$37	$21	$4	$0	$0	$0
$1,670	$1,700	$132	$112	$92	$73	$57	$40	$24	$7	$0	$0	$0
$1,700	$1,730	$136	$116	$96	$76	$60	$43	$27	$10	$0	$0	$0
$1,730	$1,760	$139	$119	$100	$80	$63	$46	$30	$13	$0	$0	$0
$1,760	$1,790	$143	$123	$103	$83	$66	$49	$33	$16	$0	$0	$0
$1,790	$1,820	$146	$127	$107	$87	$69	$52	$36	$19	$2	$0	$0
$1,820	$1,850	$150	$130	$110	$91	$72	$55	$39	$22	$5	$0	$0
$1,850	$1,880	$154	$134	$114	$94	$75	$58	$42	$25	$8	$0	$0
$1,880	$1,910	$157	$137	$118	$98	$78	$61	$45	$28	$11	$0	$0
$1,910	$1,940	$161	$141	$121	$101	$82	$64	$48	$31	$14	$0	$0
$1,940	$1,970	$164	$145	$125	$105	$85	$67	$51	$34	$17	$1	$0
$1,970	$2,000	$168	$148	$128	$109	$89	$70	$54	$37	$20	$4	$0

Important facts:

- The employee is married
- Has 3 withholding allowances
- Pay frequency is biweekly
- Earned $1,839

The page of the table is for married employees with biweekly pay

Go to the row that contains the bracket containing the employee's pay. In this example, the pay is $1,839, which is in the $1,820-$1,850 row.

Go to the column that contains the number of withholding allowances. In this case, the employee has 3 withholding allowances.

*The intersection of the table **row and column** is the **withholding tax**, which is **$91**

EXAMPLE: WAGE-BRACKET COMPUTATION OF FEDERAL INCOME TAX, MARRIED, SEMIMONTHLY

Jessa Cunningham is an employee of Rowan Trees. She earns $48,000 per year and is paid semimonthly. She is married with three withholding allowances. Using the Pre-2020 wage-bracket tables in Appendix C, we will determine Jessa's federal income tax in different situations. The IRS income tax withholding assistant results are included.

1. NO VOLUNTARY PRE-TAX DEDUCTIONS

Period pay ($48,000/24)	$2,000.00
Taxable income	2,000.00
Federal income tax	100.00

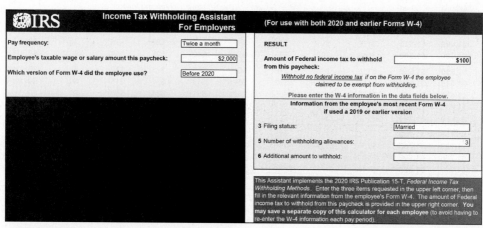

Source: Internal Revenue Service

2. PRE-TAX HEALTH INSURANCE DEDUCTION, $150

Period pay ($48,000/24)	$2,000.00
Less: health insurance	150.00
Taxable income	$1,850.00
Federal income tax	$ 82.00

Source: Internal Revenue Service

3. PRE-TAX HEALTH INSURANCE DEDUCTION, $150, AND 401(K) CONTRIBUTION, 4%

Period pay ($48,000/24)	$2,000.00
Less: health insurance	150.00
Less: 401(k) contribution	80.00
Taxable income*	$1,770.00
Federal income tax	$ 74.00

***Note:** The taxable income for Social Security and Medicare tax is $2,000 − 150 = $1,850

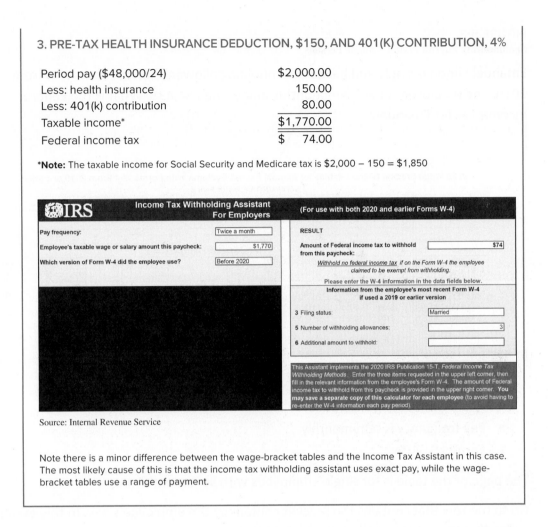

Source: Internal Revenue Service

Note there is a minor difference between the wage-bracket tables and the Income Tax Assistant in this case. The most likely cause of this is that the income tax withholding assistant uses exact pay, while the wage-bracket tables use a range of payment.

The process of using wage-bracket tables for employees claiming single marital status is similar. Figure 5-3 is a sample of the wage-bracket table for a single person with semi-monthly wages.

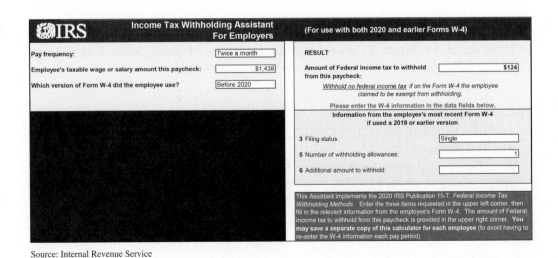

Source: Internal Revenue Service

FIGURE 5-3
Semimonthly Payroll Period—Single Persons

Emanuel Simon is single and has one withholding allowance on his Form W-4 from 2019. The employee is paid semimonthly and earned $1,438. What is the Federal Income Tax for Emanuel?

2020 Wage Bracket Method Tables for Manual Payroll Systems With Forms W-4 From 2019 or Earlier
SEMIMONTHLY Payroll Period

If the Wage Amount (line 1a) is		SINGLE Persons										
		And the number of allowances is:										
		0	1	2	3	4	5	6	7	8	9	10
At least	But less than	The Tentative Withholding Amount is:										
$1,395	$1,425	$142	$120	$99	$77	$56	$36	$18	$0	$0	$0	$0
$1,425	$1,455	$146	$124	$103	$81	$60	$39	$21	$3	$0	$0	$0
$1,455	$1,485	$149	$128	$106	$85	$63	$42	$24	$6	$0	$0	$0
$1,485	$1,515	$153	$131	$110	$88	$67	$45	$27	$9	$0	$0	$0
$1,515	$1,545	$156	$135	$113	$92	$70	$49	$30	$12	$0	$0	$0
$1,545	$1,575	$160	$138	$117	$95	$74	$52	$33	$15	$0	$0	$0

<u>Important facts:</u>

- The employee is single
- Has 1 withholding allowance
- Pay frequency is semimonthly
- Earned $1,438

The page of the table is for single employees with semimonthly pay

Go to the row that contains the bracket containing the employee's pay. In this example, the pay is $1,438, which is in the $1,425-$1,455 row.

Go to the column that contains the number of withholding allowances. In this case, the employee has 1 withholding allowance.

*The intersection of the table **<u>row and column</u>** is the **withholding tax**, which is **<u>$124</u>**

Using the table in Figure 5-3, a single person earning a semimonthly wage of $1,438 with one withholding allowance will have a federal income tax of $124.

EXAMPLE: WAGE-BRACKET COMPUTATION OF FEDERAL INCOME TAX, SINGLE, BIWEEKLY

Alex Castro is an employee at Milliken Metals. He is single with three withholding allowances and earns $45,500 annually, paid biweekly. Using the wage-bracket tables in Appendix C, we will determine Alex's federal income tax in different situations.

1. NO PRE-TAX DEDUCTIONS

Period pay ($45,500/26)	$1,750.00
Taxable income	1,750.00
Federal income tax	125.00

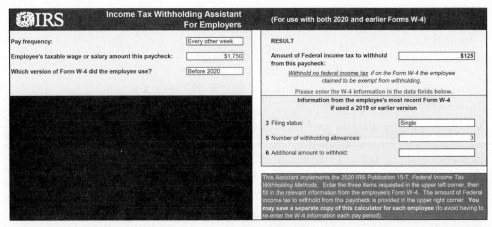

Source: Internal Revenue Service

Note the difference between the wage-bracket tables and the Income Tax Assistant spreadsheet.

2. PRE-TAX HEALTH INSURANCE, $75, PRE-TAX SUPPLEMENTAL HEALTH INSURANCE, $55

Period pay ($45,500/26)	$1,750.00
Less: health insurance	75.00
Less: supplemental health insurance	55.00
Taxable income	$1,620.00
Federal income tax	$ 110.00

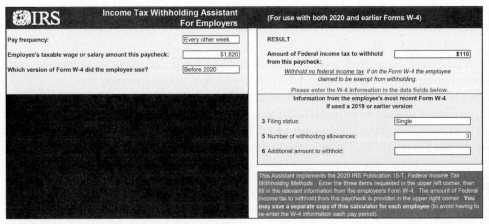

Source: Internal Revenue Service

(continued)

(concluded)

3. PRE-TAX HEALTH INSURANCE, $75, PRE-TAX SUPPLEMENTAL HEALTH INSURANCE, $55, 401(K) CONTRIBUTION, $100

Period pay ($45,500/26)	$1,750.00
Less: health insurance	75.00
Less: supplemental health insurance	55.00
Less: 401(k) contribution	100.00
Taxable income	$1,520.00
Federal income tax*	$ 98.00

*Note:** The taxable income for Social Security and Medicare tax is $1,750 − 75 − 55 = $1,620.

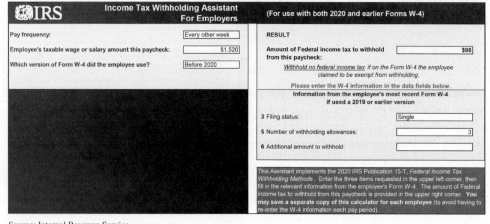

Source: Internal Revenue Service

Again, notice the result was different using the income tax withholding assistant versus the wage-bracket tables. The most likely cause of the difference between the two is the withholding assistant uses exact wages instead of the range found in the wage-bracket tables.

When using the wage-bracket tables, it should be noted that many wage amounts are the same number as the beginning and the end of a range. In these events, if the number is the exact number of the range, the next bracket should be used. For example, refer to the below image. It is important to notice is the language at the top of the column: "And the wages are— At least. . . But less than." If the wages were $3,324.99, then the top row would be used. If the wages were precisely $3,325, then the second row would be used.

Percentage Method: Forms W-4 from 2019 or Earlier Years

There are many tables in Publication 15 from the IRS to assist employers with the correct amount of withholding given the variety of pay period, marital status, and exemption options that can be available. The ***percentage method*** for calculating employee withholding is tiered, with each layer building upon the previous layer. The table that reflects the amount for one withholding allowance using the percentage method is contained in

2020 Wage Bracket Method Tables for Manual Payroll Systems With Forms W-4 From 2019 or Earlier

SEMIMONTHLY Payroll Period

If the **Wage Amount** (line 1a) is		SINGLE Persons										
		And the number of allowances is:										
At least	But less than	0	1	2	3	4	5	6	7	8	9	10
		The Tentative Withholding Amount is:										
$3,285	$3,325	$517	$477	$438	$399	$359	$320	$280	$241	$202	$176	$154
$3,325	$3,365	$526	$486	$447	$407	$368	$329	$289	$250	$210	$181	$159
$3,365	$3,405	$534	$495	$456	$416	$377	$337	$298	$259	$219	$185	$164
$3,405	$3,445	$543	$504	$464	$425	$386	$346	$307	$267	$228	$190	$169
$3,445	$3,485	$552	$513	$473	$434	$394	$355	$316	$276	$237	$197	$174
$3,485	$3,525	$561	$521	$482	$443	$403	$364	$324	$285	$246	$206	$178
$3,525	$3,565	$570	$530	$491	$451	$412	$373	$333	$294	$254	$215	$183
$3,565	$3,605	$578	$539	$500	$460	$421	$381	$342	$303	$263	$224	$188
$3,605	$3,645	$587	$548	$508	$469	$430	$390	$351	$311	$272	$233	$193
$3,645	$3,685	$596	$557	$517	$478	$438	$399	$360	$320	$281	$241	$202
$3,685	$3,725	$605	$565	$526	$487	$447	$408	$368	$329	$290	$250	$211
$3,725	$3,765	$614	$574	$535	$495	$456	$417	$377	$338	$298	$259	$219
$3,765	$3,805	$624	$583	$544	$504	$465	$425	$386	$347	$307	$268	$228
$3,805	$3,845	$633	$592	$552	$513	$474	$434	$395	$355	$316	$277	$237
$3,845	$3,885	$643	$601	$561	$522	$482	$443	$404	$364	$325	$285	$246
$3,885	$3,925	$653	$610	$570	$531	$491	$452	$412	$373	$334	$294	$255
$3,925	$3,965	$662	$619	$579	$539	$500	$461	$421	$382	$342	$303	$263
$3,965	$4,005	$672	$629	$588	$548	$509	$469	$430	$391	$351	$312	$272
$4,005	$4,045	$681	$638	$596	$557	$518	$478	$439	$399	$360	$321	$281
$4,045	$4,085	$691	$648	$605	$566	$526	$487	$448	$408	$369	$329	$290
$4,085	$4,125	$701	$658	$615	$575	$535	$496	$456	$417	$378	$338	$299
$4,125	$4,165	$710	$667	$624	$583	$544	$505	$465	$426	$386	$347	$307
$4,165	$4,205	$720	$677	$634	$592	$553	$513	$474	$435	$395	$356	$316

Figure 5-4. It is important to select the withholding allowance amount that corresponds to the correct pay frequency. If the employee has more than one withholding allowance, the amount in the table should be multiplied by the number of withholding allowances claimed on the employee's Form W-4.

When using the percentage method, the deduction for each withholding allowance is subtracted prior to computing the taxes. The wage-bracket and percentage methods will yield similar results as to income tax withholding; the percentage method shown in Figure 5-5 allows more flexibility for calculations involving high-wage earners or uncommon pay periods.

FIGURE 5-4

Percentage Method for One Withholding Allowance with Forms W-4 from 2019 or Earlier

Payroll Period	One Withholding Allowance
Weekly	$ 83.00
Biweekly	165.00
Semimonthly	179.00
Monthly	358.00
Quarterly	1,075.00
Semiannually	2,150.00
Annually	4,300.00
Daily or miscellaneous (each day of the payroll period)	17.00

FIGURE 5-5

Percentage Method Tables for Income Tax

2020 Percentage Method Tables for Manual Payroll Systems With Forms W-4 From 2019 or Earlier

WEEKLY Payroll Period

MARRIED Persons					SINGLE Persons				
If the Adjusted Wage Amount (line 1d) is		The tentative amount to withhold is...	Plus this percentage ...	of the amount that the wage exceeds...	If the Adjusted Wage Amount (line 1d) is		The tentative amount to withhold is...	Plus this percentage ...	of the amount that the wage exceeds...
at least...	But less than...				at least...	But less than...			
A	B	C	D	E	A	B	C	D	E
$0	$229	$0.00	0%	$0	$0	$73	$0.00	0%	$0
$229	$609	$0.00	10%	$229	$73	$263	$0.00	10%	$73
$609	$1,772	$38.00	12%	$609	$263	$845	$19.00	12%	$263
$1,772	$3,518	$177.56	22%	$1,772	$845	$1,718	$88.84	22%	$845
$3,518	$6,510	$561.68	24%	$3,518	$1,718	$3,213	$280.90	24%	$1,718
$6,510	$8,204	$1,279.76	32%	$6,510	$3,213	$4,061	$639.70	32%	$3,213
$8,204	$12,191	$1,821.84	35%	$8,204	$4,061	$10,042	$911.06	35%	$4,061
$12,191		$3,217.29	37%	$12,191	$10,042		$3,004.41	37%	$10,042

BIWEEKLY Payroll Period

MARRIED Persons					SINGLE Persons				
If the Adjusted Wage Amount (line 1d) is		The tentative amount to withhold is...	Plus this percentage ...	of the amount that the wage exceeds...	If the Adjusted Wage Amount (line 1d) is		The tentative amount to withhold is...	Plus this percentage ...	of the amount that the wage exceeds...
at least...	But less than...				at least...	But less than...			
A	B	C	D	E	A	B	C	D	E
$0	$458	$0.00	0%	$0	$0	$146	$0.00	0%	$0
$458	$1,217	$0.00	10%	$458	$146	$526	$0.00	10%	$146
$1,217	$3,544	$75.90	12%	$1,217	$526	$1,689	$38.00	12%	$526
$3,544	$7,037	$355.14	22%	$3,544	$1,689	$3,436	$177.56	22%	$1,689
$7,037	$13,019	$1,123.60	24%	$7,037	$3,436	$6,427	$561.90	24%	$3,436
$13,019	$16,408	$2,559.28	32%	$13,019	$6,427	$8,121	$1,279.74	32%	$6,427
$16,408	$24,383	$3,643.76	35%	$16,408	$8,121	$20,085	$1,821.82	35%	$8,121
$24,383		$6,435.01	37%	$24,383	$20,085		$6,009.22	37%	$20,085

SEMIMONTHLY Payroll Period

MARRIED Persons					SINGLE Persons				
If the Adjusted Wage Amount (line 1d) is		The tentative amount to withhold is...	Plus this percentage ...	of the amount that the wage exceeds...	If the Adjusted Wage Amount (line 1d) is		The tentative amount to withhold is...	Plus this percentage ...	of the amount that the wage exceeds...
at least...	But less than...				at least...	But less than...			
A	B	C	D	E	A	B	C	D	E
$0	$496	$0.00	0%	$0	$0	$158	$0.00	0%	$0
$496	$1,319	$0.00	10%	$496	$158	$570	$0.00	10%	$158
$1,319	$3,840	$82.30	12%	$1,319	$570	$1,830	$41.20	12%	$570
$3,840	$7,623	$384.82	22%	$3,840	$1,830	$3,722	$192.40	22%	$1,830
$7,623	$14,104	$1,217.08	24%	$7,623	$3,722	$6,963	$608.64	24%	$3,722
$14,104	$17,775	$2,772.52	32%	$14,104	$6,963	$8,798	$1,386.48	32%	$6,963
$17,775	$26,415	$3,947.24	35%	$17,775	$8,798	$21,758	$1,973.68	35%	$8,798
$26,415		$6,971.24	37%	$26,415	$21,758		$6,509.68	37%	$21,758

2020 Percentage Method Tables for Manual Payroll Systems With Forms W-4 From 2019 or Earlier

MONTHLY Payroll Period

MARRIED Persons					SINGLE Persons				
If the Adjusted Wage Amount (line 1d) is		The tentative amount to withhold is...	Plus this percentage ...	of the amount that the wage exceeds...	If the Adjusted Wage Amount (line 1d) is		The tentative amount to withhold is...	Plus this percentage ...	of the amount that the wage exceeds...
at least...	But less than...				at least...	But less than...			
A	B	C	D	E	A	B	C	D	E
$0	$992	$0.00	0%	$0	$0	$317	$0.00	0%	$0
$992	$2,638	$0.00	10%	$992	$317	$1,140	$0.00	10%	$317
$2,638	$7,679	$164.60	12%	$2,638	$1,140	$3,660	$82.30	12%	$1,140
$7,679	$15,246	$769.52	22%	$7,679	$3,660	$7,444	$384.70	22%	$3,660
$15,246	$28,208	$2,434.26	24%	$15,246	$7,444	$13,925	$1,217.18	24%	$7,444
$28,208	$35,550	$5,545.14	32%	$28,208	$13,925	$17,596	$2,772.62	32%	$13,925
$35,550	$52,829	$7,894.58	35%	$35,550	$17,596	$43,517	$3,947.34	35%	$17,596
$52,829		$13,942.23	37%	$52,829	$43,517		$13,019.69	37%	$43,517

QUARTERLY Payroll Period

MARRIED Persons					SINGLE Persons				
If the Adjusted Wage Amount (line 1d) is		The tentative amount to withhold is...	Plus this percentage ...	of the amount that the wage exceeds...	If the Adjusted Wage Amount (line 1d) is		The tentative amount to withhold is...	Plus this percentage ...	of the amount that the wage exceeds...
at least...	But less than...				at least...	But less than...			
A	B	C	D	E	A	B	C	D	E
$0	$2,975	$0.00	0%	$0	$0	$950	$0.00	0%	$0
$2,975	$7,913	$0.00	10%	$2,975	$950	$3,419	$0.00	10%	$950
$7,913	$23,038	$493.80	12%	$7,913	$3,419	$10,981	$246.90	12%	$3,419
$23,038	$45,738	$2,308.80	22%	$23,038	$10,981	$22,331	$1,154.34	22%	$10,981
$45,738	$84,625	$7,302.80	24%	$45,738	$22,331	$41,775	$3,651.34	24%	$22,331
$84,625	$106,650	$16,635.68	32%	$84,625	$41,775	$52,788	$8,317.90	32%	$41,775
$106,650	$158,488	$23,683.68	35%	$106,650	$52,788	$130,550	$11,842.06	35%	$52,788
$158,488		$41,826.98	37%	$158,488	$130,550		$39,058.76	37%	$130,550

SEMIANNUAL Payroll Period

MARRIED Persons					SINGLE Persons				
If the Adjusted Wage Amount (line 1d) is		The tentative amount to withhold is...	Plus this percentage ...	of the amount that the wage exceeds...	If the Adjusted Wage Amount (line 1d) is		The tentative amount to withhold is...	Plus this percentage ...	of the amount that the wage exceeds...
at least...	But less than...				at least...	But less than...			
A	B	C	D	E	A	B	C	D	E
$0	$5,950	$0.00	0%	$0	$0	$1,900	$0.00	0%	$0
$5,950	$15,825	$0.00	10%	$5,950	$1,900	$6,838	$0.00	10%	$1,900
$15,825	$46,075	$987.50	12%	$15,825	$6,838	$21,963	$493.80	12%	$6,838
$46,075	$91,475	$4,617.50	22%	$46,075	$21,963	$44,663	$2,308.80	22%	$21,963
$91,475	$169,250	$14,605.50	24%	$91,475	$44,663	$83,550	$7,302.80	24%	$44,663
$169,250	$213,300	$33,271.50	32%	$169,250	$83,550	$105,575	$16,635.68	32%	$83,550
$213,300	$316,975	$47,367.50	35%	$213,300	$105,575	$261,100	$23,683.68	35%	$105,575
$316,975		$83,653.75	37%	$316,975	$261,100		$78,117.43	37%	$261,100

2020 Percentage Method Tables for Manual Payroll Systems With Forms W-4 From 2019 or Earlier

ANNUAL Payroll Period									
MARRIED Persons					SINGLE Persons				
If the Adjusted Wage Amount (line 1d) is		The tentative amount to withhold is...	Plus this percentage	of the amount that the wage exceeds...	If the Adjusted Wage Amount (line 1d) is		The tentative amount to withhold is...	Plus this percentage	of the amount that the wage exceeds...
at least...	But less than...		...		at least...	But less than...		...	
A	B	C	D	E	A	B	C	D	E
$0	$11,900	$0.00	0%	$0	$0	$3,800	$0.00	0%	$0
$11,900	$31,650	$0.00	10%	$11,900	$3,800	$13,675	$0.00	10%	$3,800
$31,650	$92,150	$1,975.00	12%	$31,650	$13,675	$43,925	$987.50	12%	$13,675
$92,150	$182,950	$9,235.00	22%	$92,150	$43,925	$89,325	$4,617.50	22%	$43,925
$182,950	$338,500	$29,211.00	24%	$182,950	$89,325	$167,100	$14,605.50	24%	$89,325
$338,500	$426,600	$66,543.00	32%	$338,500	$167,100	$211,150	$33,271.50	32%	$167,100
$426,600	$633,950	$94,735.00	35%	$426,600	$211,150	$522,200	$47,367.50	35%	$211,150
$633,950		$167,307.50	37%	$633,950	$522,200		$156,235.00	37%	$522,200

DAILY Payroll Period									
MARRIED Persons					SINGLE Persons				
If the Adjusted Wage Amount (line 1d) is		The tentative amount to withhold is...	Plus this percentage	of the amount that the wage exceeds...	If the Adjusted Wage Amount (line 1d) is		The tentative amount to withhold is...	Plus this percentage	of the amount that the wage exceeds...
at least...	But less than...		...		at least...	But less than...		...	
A	B	C	D	E	A	B	C	D	E
$0.00	$45.80	$0.00	0%	$0.00	$0.00	$14.60	$0.00	0%	$0.00
$45.80	$121.70	$0.00	10%	$45.80	$14.60	$52.60	$0.00	10%	$14.60
$121.70	$354.40	$7.59	12%	$121.70	$52.60	$168.90	$3.80	12%	$52.60
$354.40	$703.70	$35.51	22%	$354.40	$168.90	$343.60	$17.76	22%	$168.90
$703.70	$1,301.90	$112.36	24%	$703.70	$343.60	$642.70	$56.19	24%	$343.60
$1,301.90	$1,640.80	$255.93	32%	$1,301.90	$642.70	$812.10	$127.97	32%	$642.70
$1,640.80	$2,438.30	$364.38	35%	$1,640.80	$812.10	$2,008.50	$182.18	35%	$812.10
$2,438.30		$643.50	37%	$2,438.30	$2,008.50		$600.92	37%	$2,008.50

Source: Internal Revenue Service

Using the percentage method tables can be confusing, so let's look at a step-by-step example.

> How to calculate federal income tax using the percentage method: Caroline Smart is single and claims two withholding allowances on her Form W-4 from 2019. She is paid semimonthly and earns $48,000 per year.
>
> | Step 1: | Total Wage Payment | $48,000 ÷ 24 | = | $ 2,000 |
> |---|---|---|---|---|
> | Step 2: | One withholding allowance for semimonthly pay (Figure 5-3) | | | $ 179.00 |
> | Step 3: | Allowances claimed on W-4 | | | 2 |
> | Step 4: | Multiply Step 2 by Step 3 | | | $ 358.00 |
> | Step 5: | Amount subject to withholding | $2,000 – $358 | = | $1,642.00 |
> | Step 6: | See Figure 5-5 (Semimonthly wages for a single person). Look at the column labeled "of excess over" and choose line 2 "$570.00" from Publication 15-T | | – | $ 570.00 |
> | Step 7: | Subtract Step 6 from Step 5 | | = | $1,072.00 |
> | Step 8: | Multiply Step 7 by 12% (from line 2) | $1,072.00 × 0.12 | = | $ 128.64 |
> | Step 9: | Add Step 8 plus $41.20 (from line 2 in Publication 15-T) to compute the federal income tax to withhold | $128.64 + $41.20 | = | $ 169.84 |

Source: Internal Revenue Service

Note the IRS income tax withholding assistant rounded the result from the percentage method to the nearest dollar. For withholding purposes, the IRS prefers to round earnings and taxes to the nearest dollar.

The amount of federal income tax withholding may differ slightly between the wage-bracket and percentage methods. Let's revisit the tax computation for the married employee, this time using the percentage method.

EXAMPLE: MARRIED EMPLOYEE, PERCENTAGE METHOD VS. WAGE-BRACKET TABLE

Valerie Ball earns $1,839 biweekly and is married with three withholding allowances on her Form W-4 from 2019.

Gross pay	$1,839.00
Less withholding allowances (3 × $165.00)	495.00
Taxable base	1,344.00
Less: "of excess over $1,200" (line 2)	1,217.00
Adjusted taxable base	$ 127.50
Multiplied by tax rate (12% or 0.12)	15.24
Plus marginal tax	75.90
Total tax	$ 91.14

Note the wage-bracket method ended with a result of $91. The reason for the difference in the cents is the rounding used in wage-bracket table computations.

Let's now revisit the single employee and compare the percentage method computations to the wage-bracket table.

EXAMPLE: SINGLE EMPLOYEE, PERCENTAGE METHOD VS. WAGE-BRACKET TABLE

Emanuel Simon earns $1,438 semimonthly and is single with one withholding allowance on his Form W-4 from 2019.

(continued)

(concluded)

Gross pay	$1,438.00
Less: withholding allowance (1 × $179.00)	179.00
Taxable base	$1,259.00
Less: "of excess over $570" (line 2)	570.00
Adjusted taxable base	$ 689.00
Multiplied by tax rate (12% or 0.12)	82.68
Plus marginal tax	41.20
Total tax	$ 123.88

Note that the wage-bracket method resulted in $124.00. Again, the reason for the difference is the rounding used in wage-bracket table computations.

How Much Tax to Withhold?

1. Jennifer Parsons earns $52,000 annually. She is married filing joint with two dependents, not under 17, her spouse does work (box 2 checked), and she is paid semimonthly. Her W-4 is from 2020. Calculate the amount to be withheld using (a) the wage-bracket method and (b) the percentage method.

2. If Jennifer elected to deduct $100 per pay period for her 401(k), how much would that change the tax withheld from her paycheck? (Use the wage-bracket method.)

3. How much would Jennifer's federal income tax be if her $75 health insurance and $55 AFLAC premiums were deducted each pay period pre-tax? (Use the wage-bracket method, independent of question 2.)

LO 5-3   Compute Social Security and Medicare Tax Withholding

zimmytws/iStockphoto/Getty Images

The Social Security Act of 1935 mandated the withholding of certain taxes in addition to federal income tax. Two different taxes were part of the Social Security Act legislation: Social Security tax and Medicare tax. Employers collect only federal income taxes on employees without making a corresponding contribution. Social Security and Medicare, collectively known as *FICA (Federal Insurance Contributions Act) taxes*, contain both the employer's and the employee's portion. When the employer deposits the federal withholding tax, it deposits the Social Security and Medicare amounts at the same time. The deposits are usually done online but may be made by standard mail in certain circumstances. The report provided to the IRS does not provide a breakdown of tax amounts for individual employees. Specific questions about Social Security or Medicare tax situations should be directed to the Social Security Administration at www.ssa. gov or via telephone at 800-772-1213.

Social Security Tax

Kreinick/123RF

Social Security tax, formerly known as OASDI, was designed to cover people for illness, retirement, disability, and old age. As a method of social insurance by which communities will help provide for people who are unable to work, Social Security has evolved into a tax that is levied upon all employees until their annual income reaches a specified level. The maximum income, known as the *wage base*, for the Social Security tax changes annually. In 2020, the wage base is $137,700. This means only the first $137,700 of wages earned are subject to the 6.2% tax. Every dollar earned above $137,700 will not be subject to Social Security tax. The tax rate on employee pay is 6.2 percent of eligible wages. Remember that eligible wages can be different from gross pay because of pre-tax deductions and the wage base maximum.

Examples of Social Security Tax Computations

Employee	Period Wages	YTD Salary at End of Previous Pay Period	Social Security Tax Computation	Social Security Tax Amount to Be Withheld
1	$ 1,700	$ 55,600	$1,700 × 6.2%	$105.40
2	2,850	90,000	2,850 × 6.2%	176.70
3	7,200	130,600	7,100 × 6.2%*	440.20
4	6,200	135,200	2,500 × 6.2%†	155.00
5	10,500	195,000	0‡	0

* The employee's wage base reaches the maximum during this pay period; thus, only the amount under the $137,700 cap is taxed for Social Security: $137,700 − $125,800 = $7,100, so only the $7,100 is taxed.

† The employee's wage base reaches the maximum during this pay period; thus, only the amount under the $137,700 cap is taxed for Social Security: $137,700 − $135,200 = $2,500, so only the $2,500 is taxed.

‡ The employee's wage base maximum was met prior to the current pay period, so no Social Security taxes are withheld.

The employee earnings record is especially important in computing and tracking the Social Security taxes due for each employee. Current records allow payroll accountants to keep track of annual salaries for each employee to avoid exceeding the maximum wage base, preventing excess deductions from employees' pay.

The employer and employee pay the same amount for the Social Security tax. Remember the Social Security tax has a maximum annual wage amount, the wage base, for which taxes may be withheld. After reaching that maximum annual wage, neither the employee nor the employer pays any more Social Security tax for the remainder of the year.

Medicare Tax

Medicare taxes differ from Social Security taxes in a couple of significant ways. *Medicare taxes* were levied on employers and employees to help provide basic health coverage for all individuals qualified to enroll in Medicare benefits. The Medicare tax amount for employee wages is 1.45 percent on all wages earned; there is **no maximum wage base** for Medicare taxes. The Affordable Care Act of 2010 levied an *additional Medicare tax* of 0.9 percent on certain workers Who earn more than $200,000 annually. This made the simple computations and tracking for Medicare taxes a little more challenging for payroll accountants and increased the need for accuracy on the employee earnings report. Note the additional Medicare tax is levied only on the employees, so there is no employer match.

Highly compensated employees are subject to an additional 0.9 percent of Medicare tax as a result of the Affordable Care Act. This additional tax is only paid by the employee, and no employer match is required. The wage base for this additional Medicare tax depends on the marital and tax filing statuses reported on the employee's Form W-4 as follows:

- $200,000 for employees who report that they are single.
- $250,000 for employees who report that they are married and file taxes jointly.
- $125,000 for employees who report that they are married and file taxes separately.

Examples of Medicare Tax Computations

Employee	Period Wages	YTD Salary at End of Previous Pay Period	Medicare Tax Computation	Total Medicare Tax Liability (Employee and Employer)
1	$1,700	$ 55,600	$ 1,700 × 1.45%	$ 24.65 × 2 = $49.30
2	2,850	90,000	2,850 × 1.45%	41.33 × 2 = 82.66
3	7,200	112,600	7,200 × 1.45%	104.40 × 2 = 208.80
4	6,200	118,000	6,200 × 1.45%	89.90 × 2 = 179.80
5	10,500	195,000	Employee: (10,500 × 0.0145[†]) + (5,500[‡] × 0.009) = $201.75	Employee: $201.75 + Employer: $152.25* Total = $354.00

*The employer does not pay the additional Medicare tax.
†10,500*0.0145 = 152.25
‡195,000 + 10,500 = 205,500 − 200,000 = 5,500

Remember the applicable wages may have pre-tax deductions. Social Security and Medicare taxes apply to the employee's gross pay if an employee elects to have a 401(k) deduction. However, qualified Section 125 (cafeteria) plans are exempt from FICA taxes. When computing employee taxes, understanding the tax effect of the pre-tax deductions is important in computing accurate FICA deductions.

EXAMPLE: COMPUTATION OF SOCIAL SECURITY AND MEDICARE TAXES WITH PRE-TAX DEDUCTIONS

Chris McBride is an employee who earns an annual salary of $58,000, paid biweekly. He is single with no dependents. Chris has pre-tax deductions including $155 for health insurance and a contribution of 5 percent of his gross pay to a 401(k) plan. Let's compute Chris's net pay using the IRS Income Tax Assistant spreadsheet to determine federal income tax, using the information for a 2020 Form W-4.

Gross pay per period (58,000/26)	$2,230.77
Less: health insurance	155.00
Less: 401(k) (2,230.77 × 0.05)	111.54
Taxable income*	$1,964.23
Federal income tax	171.00
Social Security tax[†]	128.70
Medicare tax[†]	30.10
Net pay	$1,634.43

*This taxable income is for federal income tax only.
†Social Security and Medicare taxes are computed on taxable income of $2,230.77 − $155.00 = $2,075.77, then $2,075.77 × 0.062 (Social Security) and $2,075.77 × 0.0145 (Medicare)

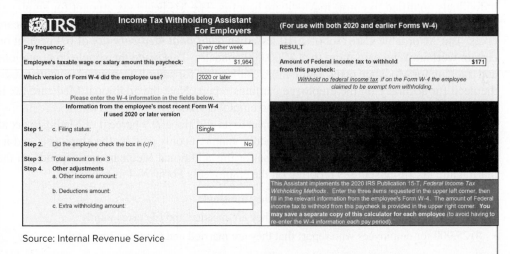

Source: Internal Revenue Service

EXAMPLE: COMPUTATION OF NET PAY, HIGHLY COMPENSATED EMPLOYEE

Morris Malone is the CEO and president of Martens Flooring. His annual salary is $320,000, and he is paid biweekly. He is married with three dependents under the age of 17, files taxes jointly, and has pre-tax deductions for health insurance of $250 and 401(k) of $1,000. His spouse is not employed.

He will exceed the Social Security wage base in May 20XX and will incur the additional Medicare tax in September. Let's look at his net pay computations on January 15, June 15, and October 31.

FEDERAL INCOME TAX COMPUTATION

Federal income tax is computed as follows, using the IRS Income Tax Withholding Assistant spreadsheet

Gross pay per period	$13,333.33
Less: health Insurance	250.00
Less: 401(k)	1,000.00
Taxable income	$12,083.33
Total federal income tax	$ 1,985.00

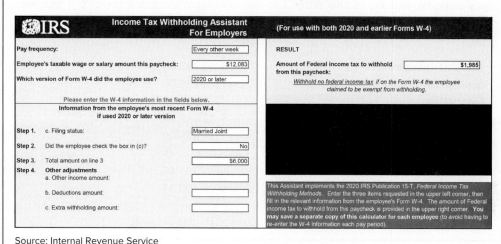

Source: Internal Revenue Service

JANUARY 15 PAY PERIOD

Gross pay per period	$ 13,333.33
Less: health Insurance	250.00
Less: 401(k)	1,000.00
Taxable income*	$ 12,083.33
Federal income tax	1,985.00
Social Security tax[†]	811.17
Medicare tax[†]	189.71
Net pay	$ 9,097.45

* This taxable income is for federal income tax only.
[†] Social Security and Medicare taxes are computed using a base of $13,333 − 250 = $13,083.33.

JUNE 15 PAY PERIOD

As of May 31, Morris has earned year-to-date gross pay of $119,999.97 ($13,333.33 × 9 pay periods). This means that he will exceed the Social Security wage base during the next pay period, which ends May 31. Morris's salary is only taxable for Social Security wages up to the wage base of $137,700 (2020 amount), so the amount that

(continued)

(concluded)

may be taxed is $137,700 − $133,333.30 = $4,366.70. After the June 15 pay period, Morris will have no more Social Security tax deducted from his pay. His net pay for June 15 will be as follows:

Gross pay per period	$ 13,333.33
Less: health Insurance	250.00
Less: 401(k)	1,000.00
Taxable income*	$ 12,083.33
Federal income tax	1,985.00
Social Security tax†	270.73
Medicare tax‡	189.71
Net pay	$ 9,637.89

* This taxable income is for federal income tax only.
† Social Security tax is computed as $4,366.70 × 0.062 = $270.73.
‡ Medicare tax is computed using a base of $13,083.33 as $13,083.33*0.0145 = $189.71.

OCTOBER 31 PAY PERIOD

As of October 15, Morris has earned year-to-date pay of $253,333.27 (13,333.33*19 pay periods). His pay is now subject to the additional Medicare tax of 0.9 percent, levied only on employees (i.e., no employer match). His net pay for October 31 will be computed as follows:

Gross pay per period	$ 13,333.33
Less: health insurance	250.00
Less: 401(k)	1,000.00
Taxable income*	$ 12,083.33
Federal income tax	1,985.00
Social Security tax	-0-
Medicare tax†	307.46
Net pay	$ 9,790.87

* This taxable income is for federal income tax only.
†Medicare taxes are computed as: $13,333.33 − 250.00 = $13,083.33*(0.0145 + 0.009) = $307.46

FICA Taxes

Stop & Check

1. Trent Powell is an employee whose annual salary prior to the current pay period is $63,500. His gross pay for the current pay period is $5,280. What amount must be withheld for Social Security tax? For Medicare tax?

2. For Trent's FICA taxes, what is the total tax liability including employee and employer share?

3. Sarah Erickson is the CEO of a company, and she earns $250,000 per year. Her year-to-date salary for the 19th pay period of the year was $197,916.67. She is single and contributes 5 percent of her pay to her 401(k) and has a qualified Section 125 deduction of $75 per semimonthly pay period.

   a. For the 20th pay period, what is her Social Security tax liability? Medicare tax liability?

   b. For the 21st pay period, what is her Medicare tax liability?

Maintaining accurate records of taxes withheld through payroll registers and employee earnings records is a critical part of calculating proper FICA tax deductions. Whether a company uses a manual system, an automated system, or outsources the payroll duties, it remains responsible for the accuracy of the deductions and maintenance of associated records.

zimmytws/123RF

LO 5-4 Calculate State and Local Income Taxes

Many states and localities apply taxes in addition to the federal income tax, Social Security, and Medicare. According to the IRS, all but nine states withhold income taxes. As budgets become tighter and the unfunded pension liabilities come due, these states may look to income tax as a means for covering budget or pension shortfalls. The nine states are

Alaska	New Hampshire*	Tennessee*
Florida	South Dakota	Washington
Nevada	Texas	Wyoming

* New Hampshire and Tennessee do not charge a payroll tax but obtain revenue from individual taxpayers through taxes on dividends and investments.

State-Specific Taxes

All other states (except the nine above) withhold income tax from their employees, and many apply other taxes as well. For instance, employees in the state of California have State Disability Insurance (SDI) of 1.0 percent of gross pay (up to a maximum wage of $122,909 in 2020), in addition to the personal income tax (PIT) that the state levies. Like federal income tax, California's PIT amounts vary by income level, pay frequency, and marital status. California, like many other states, offers both the wage-bracket and the percentage method of determining the PIT amount due. In contrast, Illinois charges a flat rate of 4.95 percent on all employees for its state withholding tax. (See Appendix D for state income tax information.)

If a firm operates only in one state, deciphering state income tax requirements is reasonably simple, but becomes increasingly complex as the firm does business in more locations. State income tax information is readily available through each state's department of revenue as well as through most computerized payroll software programs. (See Appendix E for a state revenue department list.)

TravnikovStudio/Shutterstock

New York ranks as the highest state in *per capita* state and local income tax. The marginal tax rate in 2020 ranged from 5.0%-8.82%, depending on income, and many localities charge income taxes. Workers who reside or earn income in New York City pay a tax that ranges from approximately 3.078% to 3.876% in addition to any federal and state income taxes. (Source: Smart Asset, Tax Foundation)

Some states require the collection and remittance of income taxes based upon all wages earned within their state. This could result in the company having several state employer identification numbers, even if the company does not have a physical presence in the state.

For example, if a Floridian paper mill worker is stationed at the St. Marys, Georgia, location, the employer could be required to remit the employee's income taxes in Georgia. Other types of payroll taxes can include items like Oregon's public transportation payroll tax for any services performed within the state, regardless of residency status.

EXAMPLE: NET PAY WITH STATE INCOME TAX

Jeremy Underwood receives a salary of $850 per week at his job in Joliet, Illinois. He is married filing jointly (box 2 is not checked) with one dependent under the age of 17 and is paid weekly. We will use the IRS Income Tax Withholding Assistant to determine federal income tax. He has pre-tax deductions of $50 for insurance and $50 for 401(k). Using the Illinois state tax rate of 4.95 percent,

Taxable income ($850 − 50 − 50)	$750.00
State income tax ($750 × 0.0495)	$ 37.13

His net pay would be computed as follows:

Name	Marital Status	Hourly Rate or Period Wage	No. of Regular Hours	No. of Overtime Hours	No. of Holiday Hours	Gross Earnings	401(k)	Insurance	Cafeteria Plan	Taxable Wages for Federal W/H	Taxable Wages for FICA
Jeremy Underwood	MJ-1	850.00				850.00	50.00	50.00		750.00	800.00

Name	Gross Earnings	Taxable Wages for Federal W/H	Taxable Wages for FICA	Federal W/H	Social Security Tax	Medicare W/H Tax	State W/H Tax	Charitable Contribution	Union Dues	Garnishment	Net Pay
Jeremy Underwood	850.00	750.00	800.00	-0-	49.60*	11.60†	37.13				651.67

*Social Security Tax: $800 × 0.062
†Medicare Tax = $800 × 0.0145

IRS	Income Tax Withholding Assistant For Employers	(For use with both 2020 and earlier Forms W-4)

Pay frequency:	Weekly	**RESULT**	
Employee's taxable wage or salary amount this paycheck:	$750	Amount of Federal income tax to withhold from this paycheck:	$0
Which version of Form W-4 did the employee use?	2020 or later		

Withhold no federal income tax if on the Form W-4 the employee claimed to be exempt from withholding.

Please enter the W-4 information in the fields below.
Information from the employee's most recent Form W-4 if used 2020 or later version

Step 1.	c. Filing status:	Married Joint
Step 2.	Did the employee check the box in (c)?	No
Step 3.	Total amount on line 3	$2,000
Step 4.	Other adjustments	
	a. Other income amount:	
	b. Deductions amount:	
	c. Extra withholding amount:	

This Assistant implements the 2020 IRS Publication 15-T, *Federal Income Tax Withholding Methods* . Enter the three items requested in the upper left corner, then fill in the relevant information from the employee's Form W-4. The amount of Federal income tax to withhold from this paycheck is provided in the upper right corner. **You may save a separate copy of this calculator for each employee** (to avoid having to re-enter the W-4 information each pay period).

Source: Internal Revenue Service

Local Income Taxes

Another mandatory tax is ***local income tax*** levied by certain municipalities and counties. Payroll accountants need to be aware of any local taxes that apply to their business. Information about applicable local taxes may be found through city and county governments, often through their Internet sites.

Denver, Colorado, has a local tax called the Occupational Privilege Tax (OPT), also known as the "head tax." The OPT is $5.75 per month for employees and $4.00 for employers of any business that has any activity in Denver, even if the employee or business does not exist or reside in Denver itself, on wages exceeding $500. The local income tax is applied after any pre-tax deductions. (Source: Denver Treasury Division)

EXAMPLE: NET PAY WITH LOCAL INCOME TAX

Shalie Rice is an employee at Keiser and Sons in Denver, Colorado. She earns $39,000 annually and is paid biweekly. She is married filing joint with no dependents (box 2 is not checked). She has pre-tax deductions including $100 for health insurance and a contribution of 6 percent of her gross pay to a 401(k) plan. We will use the IRS Income Tax Withholding Assistant to compute Shalie's federal income tax. Colorado's state income tax is 4.63 percent. Her net pay would be as follows:

Name	Filing Status	Hourly Rate or Period Wage	No. of Regular Hours	No. of Overtime Hours	No. of Holiday Hours	Gross Earnings	401(k)	Insurance	Cafeteria Plan	Taxable Wages for Federal W/H	Taxable Wages for FICA
Shalie Rice	MJ-0	1,500.00				1,500.00	90.00	100.00		1,310.00	1,400.00

Name	Gross Earnings	Taxable Wages for Federal W/H	Taxable Wages for FICA	Federal W/H Tax	Social Security Tax	Medicare W/H Tax	State W/H Tax	Denver OPT	Union Dues	Garnishment	Net Pay
Shalie Rice	1,500.00	1,310.00	1,400.00	36.00	86.80*	20.30†	60.65‡	5.75			1,100.50

*$1,400 \times 0.062 = 86.80$
†$1,400 \times 0.0145 = 20.30$
‡$1,310 \times 0.0463 = 60.65$

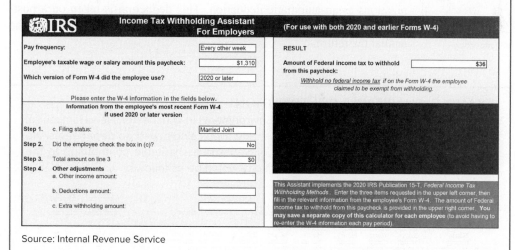

Source: Internal Revenue Service

Legislators in the state of Iowa lowered state income tax rates in 2019 following the passage of Senate File 2417. The underlying premise of their proposal was that lower income tax rates promoted economic growth and injected revenue into the state through sources such as consumer spending and housing expansion, as well as promoted competition with adjacent Midwest states. Future income tax rates will be indexed to prevent inflation-based increases. (Source: Iowa Department of Revenue)

State and Local Income Taxes

Stop & Check

1. April Griffith works as a research scientist in Coeur d'Alene, Idaho. She earns $62,500 annually, is married filing jointly with no dependents (box 2 is not checked), paid biweekly. She has a pre-tax deduction of $150 for her 401(k) and $80 for qualified health insurance. Using the state tax listed in Appendix D, what is her state income tax?

2. Rick Barker works as an accountant in Denver, Colorado. Colorado has a state income tax of a flat 4.63 percent. Colorado's OPT is $5.75 per month per employee. If Rick is paid monthly and earns $2,850 after pre-tax deductions, what are his state and local taxes?

LO 5-5   Apply Post-Tax Deductions

Once the payroll clerk determines each employee's gross pay, pre-tax deductions, and taxes withheld, the post-tax deductions are applied to the remaining amount. All deductions, both voluntary and mandatory, should be listed on an attachment to the paycheck, in both pay-period and year-to-date amounts.

Post-tax deductions may include court-mandated or governmental debts as well as employee repayments of advances or overpayments. In this section, we will explore examples of post-tax deductions and how they are included in net pay computations.

©Markus Mainka/Shutterstock

Charitable Contributions

Employees may choose to contribute part of their pay to charitable organizations as an automatic deduction. This deduction is taken on a post-tax basis because the employee may deduct it from gross income on the annual tax return.

EXAMPLE: CHARITABLE CONTRIBUTION

Perry Wallace is an employee at Working Environments in Winchester, New Hampshire. He earns $29,000 annually and is paid weekly. He is single with no dependents. He has a pre-tax health insurance premium of $25 and a charitable contribution to the United Way of $10 per pay period. His net pay would be as follows:

Name	Filing Status	Hourly Rate or Period Wage	No. of Regular Hours	No. of Overtime Hours	No. of Holiday Hours	Gross Earnings	401(k)	Insurance	Cafeteria Plan	Taxable Wages for Federal W/H	Taxable Wages for FICA
Perry Wallace	S-0	557.69				557.69		25.00		532.69	532.69

Name	Gross Earnings	Taxable Wages for Federal W/H	Taxable Wages for FICA	Federal W/H	Social Security Tax	Medicare W/H	State W/H Tax	Charitable Contribution	Union Dues	Garnishment	Net Pay
Perry Wallace	557.69	532.69	532.69	32.00	33.03	7.72		10.00			449.94

IRS	Income Tax Withholding Assistant For Employers	(For use with both 2020 and earlier Forms W-4)

		RESULT
Pay frequency:	Weekly	
Employee's taxable wage or salary amount this paycheck:	$533	Amount of Federal income tax to withhold from this paycheck: $32
Which version of Form W-4 did the employee use?	2020 or later	*Withhold no federal income tax if on the Form W-4 the employee claimed to be exempt from withholding.*

Please enter the W-4 information in the fields below.

Information from the employee's most recent Form W-4 if used 2020 or later version

Step 1.	c. Filing status:	Single
Step 2.	Did the employee check the box in (c)?	No
Step 3.	Total amount on line 3	$0
Step 4.	**Other adjustments**	
	a. Other income amount:	
	b. Deductions amount:	
	c. Extra withholding amount:	

This Assistant implements the 2020 IRS Publication 15-T, *Federal Income Tax Withholding Methods*. Enter the three items requested in the upper left corner, then fill in the relevant information from the employee's Form W-4. The amount of Federal income tax to withhold from this paycheck is provided in the upper right corner. **You may save a separate copy of this calculator for each employee** (to avoid having to re-enter the W-4 information each pay period).

Source: Internal Revenue Service

Garnishments

Remember garnishments are for court-mandated deductions such as child support obligations, liens, and consumer credit repayment. These deductions are taken on a post-tax basis because they are viewed as an obligation of the employee that must be paid out of post-tax income. Garnishments are subject to a maximum of 25 percent of disposable income for many situations. However, child support garnishment may be up to 60 percent, depending on how many people the person supports financially.

EXAMPLE: CHILD SUPPORT

Andrew Malowitz is an employee of Kennesaw Mills. He earns $49,500 annually, paid semimonthly. He is single with one dependent under 17. He has a pre-tax health insurance deduction of $100 and contributes 3 percent of his gross pay to his 401(k) per pay period. The state income tax rate is 6 percent. He has a court-ordered garnishment of $300 per pay period for child support. His net pay would appear as follows (amounts rounded to the nearest dollar). Specific computations used in the payroll register follow immediately below the register.

Name	Filing Status	Hourly Rate or Period Wage	No. of Regular Hours	No. of Overtime Hours	No. of Holiday Hours	Gross Earnings	401(k)	Insurance	Cafeteria Plan	Taxable Wages for Federal W/H	Taxable Wages for FICA
Andrew Malowitz	S-1	2,062.50				2,062.50	61.88	100.00		1,900.63	1,962.50

Name	Gross Earnings	Taxable Wages for Federal W/H	Taxable Wages for FICA	Federal W/H	Social Security Tax	Medicare W/H	State W/H Tax	Charitable Contribution	Union Dues	Garnish-ment	Net Pay
Andrew Malowitz	2,062.50	1,900.63	1,962.50	75.00	121.68	28.46	114.04			300.00	1,261.44

(continued)

(concluded)

Payroll Register Computations

Payroll Register Column	Computation
Period wage	$49,500/24 = $2,062.50
401(k)	$2,062.50 × 0.03 = $61.88
Taxable wages for federal and state	$2,062.50 − 61.88 −100 = $1,900.63
Taxable wages for FICA	$2,062.50 −100 = $1,962.50
Social Security tax	$1,962.50 × 0.062 = $121.68
Medicare tax	$1,962.50 × 0.0145 = $24.68
State tax	$1,900.63 × 0.06 = $114.04
Net pay	$2,062.50 − 61.88 − 100 − 75 − 121.68 − 28.46 − 114.04 − 300 = $1,261.44

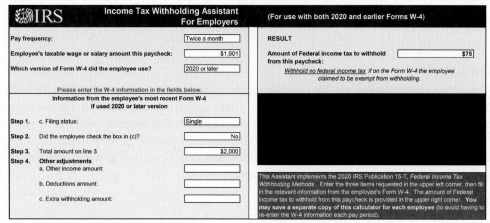

Source: Internal Revenue Service

DISPOSABLE INCOME: CHILD SUPPORT

It is important to consider Andrew's disposable income to ensure the garnishment does not exceed legal maximums. His disposable income is computed as follows:

Gross pay	$ 2,062.50
Less: federal income tax	75.00
Less: state income tax	114.04
Less: Social Security tax	121.68
Less: Medicare tax	28.46
Total disposable income	$ 1,723.32
Percent of garnishment to disposable income	17.4%*

* $300/1,723.32 = 0.174 = 17.4% (rounded)

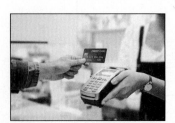

Nattakorn_Maneerat/Shutterstock

Consumer Credit

Like other post-tax deductions such as student loans, consumer credit is considered to be an obligation to be paid out of a person's after-tax earnings. The next example shows the effect of a consumer credit garnishment on an employee's wages. In this case, the 25 percent maximum garnishment rule applies.

EXAMPLE: CONSUMER CREDIT

Mona Todd is an employee of Level Two Gallery in Ogden, Utah. She earns $38,500 annually, paid biweekly. She is single with no dependents. The state income tax rate is 5 percent. She has pre-tax deductions of $50 for health insurance and $30 for her contribution to a 401(k) plan, and she contributes $15 to the United Way. She has a court-ordered consumer credit garnishment of $100 per pay period. Her net pay would appear as follows:

Name	Filing Status	Hourly Rate or Period Wage	No. of Regular Hours	No. of Overtime Hours	Gross Earnings	401(k)	Section 125	Taxable Wages for Federal W/H	Taxable Wages for FICA
Mona Todd	S-0	$1,480.77			$1,480.77	$30.00	$50.00	$1,400.77	$1,430.77

Name	Gross Earnings	Taxable Wages for Federal/ State W/H	Taxable Wages for FICA	Federal W/H	Social Security Tax	Medicare W/H Tax	State W/H Tax	Charitable Contribution	Garnishment	Net Pay
Mona Todd	$1,480.77	$1,400.77	$1,430.77	$107.00	$88.71	$20.75	$70.04	$15.00	100.00	$999.27

DISPOSABLE INCOME: CONSUMER CREDIT

Let's ensure Mona's consumer credit garnishment is within legal guidelines:

Gross pay	$1,480.77
Less: federal income tax	107.00
Less: state income tax	70.04
Less: Social Security tax	88.71
Less: Medicare tax	20.75
Total disposable income	$1,194.27
Percent of garnishment to disposable income	8.4%*

* $100/$1,194.27 = 0.0835 = 8.4% (rounded)

A topic of discussion between the American Payroll Association and the Wage and Hour Division of the Department of Labor has been the treatment of lump-sum distributions when a garnishment is imposed on an employee. The general guideline for considering a distribution as subject to garnishment is the concept of "personal service." If the distribution was for services rendered by the employee, then the amount may be garnished. Specific examples of lump-sum distributions that are subject to garnishment include the following:

- Sign-on bonuses
- Any performance or productivity bonus
- Commissions
- Holiday pay
- Retroactive pay
- Termination pay
- Any other bonuses or incentive payments

(Source: American Payroll Association)

Union Dues

Employees who belong to a collective bargaining unit usually pay dues to the unit for their representation. The CCPA disposable income limits do not pertain to union dues because those dues are not court-mandated. The following example shows how union dues affect employee pay. It should be noted the employee's deduction for union dues is voluntary.

EXAMPLE: UNION DUES

Forester Greer is an employee of Pacific High School in Washington state, where he is a member of a collective bargaining unit (i.e., union) that negotiates his salary, benefits, and working conditions and has dues of $50 per pay period. He earns $67,500 annually and is paid biweekly. He is married filing jointly with 2 dependents under the age of 17 (box 2 is not checked). He has pre-tax deductions of $150 for a 401(k) plan and $100 for a qualified Section 125 cafeteria plan. His net pay would appear as follows:

Name	Filing Status	Hourly Rate or Period Wage	No. of Regular Hours	No. of Overtime Hours	Gross Earnings	401(k)	Section 125	Taxable Wages for Federal W/H	Taxable Wages for FICA
Forester Greer	MJ-2	$2,596.15			$2,596.15	$150.00	$100.00	$2,346.15	$2,496.15

Name	Gross Earnings	Taxable Wages for Federal W/H	Taxable Wages for FICA	Federal W/H	Social Security Tax	Medicare W/H Tax	State W/H Tax	Charitable Contribution	Union Dues	Net Pay
Forester Greer	$2,596.15	$2,346.15	$2,496.15	$0	$154.76	$36.19			$50.00	$2,105.20

According to ADP, the estimated amount of employee wages subject to garnishments totaled over $32.3 billion in 2018. E-Garnishments are becoming more popular, and are often mandated through the use of electronic income withholding orders (e-IWOs), which states transmit to employers for enforcement. (Source: ADP)

Employee Advances and Overpayments

Employees may have an opportunity for an advance of money in anticipation of their pay. The timing of the repayment of advances depends on the agreement between the employee and employer. When the advance becomes due for repayment, it is treated as a post-tax deduction. The same concept applies to situations in which the employee is overpaid due to an error in computation or reporting.

At Maricopa County Community College, a payroll system upgrade caused employees to be under- or overpaid, sometimes by thousands of dollars. The rollout of the new payroll system caused issues with understanding the differences between the new and old systems. Accountants worked with managers and employees to ensure that all discrepancies were addressed in a timely manner. (Source: AZCentral)

Dotshock/Shutterstock

Post-tax deductions

Stop & Check

1. Which of the following is a debt that may be collected via wage garnishment?
   a. Student loans
   b. Child support
   c. Debt to family members
   d. Tax liens
   e. Union dues
   f. Charitable contributions

2. Camden Crosby is an electrician who is a member of the IBEW union. He asks you, the payroll accountant, if he may pay his union dues by using a personal check instead of a post-tax deduction. The IBEW requires that collected dues be remitted by the employer. What advice would you offer him?

LO 5-6   Discuss Employee Pay Methods

Romariolen/Shutterstock

Once the net pay is computed, the next step is to give the employees access to their money. Four common types of payment methods are available: cash, check, direct deposit, and paycard. Each method has its advantages and disadvantages. We will explore each method separately.

Cash

Cash is one of the oldest forms of paying employees but is not widely used as a contemporary payroll practice. The most common use of cash as a payment method involves paying for day laborers, temporary helpers, and odd jobs. Cash is one of the most difficult forms of payroll to manage because it is difficult to track and control. Payments for wages in cash should involve a written receipt signed by the employee. Companies paying by cash must physically have the cash on hand for payroll, which increases the risk of theft from both internal and external sources. Payroll taxes must be withheld, which requires prior preparation so that the appropriate amount of cash is available to pay precisely what is due for each employee. For employees, cash is a very convenient payment method because of its inherent liquidity.

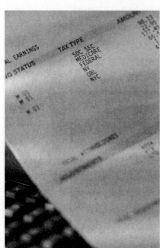

Comstock Images/Getty Images

Cash wage payment challenges the security of the funds for both the employer and the employee. For the employer, ensuring the employee receives and acknowledges the appropriate payment amount is the key. When using cash as a payment method for employees, a receipt that contains information about the gross pay, deductions, and net pay is important. The critical piece is to have the employee sign and date a copy acknowledging the receipt of the correct amount of cash on the specific date. Obtaining the employee's signature and date received can prevent future problems with perceived problems involving timely payments of employee compensation.

Check

Paper checks are a common method of remitting employee compensation. For the employer, a paper check offers traceability and simplicity of accounting records. The use of checks instead of cash means the employer does not have to maintain large amounts of cash, reducing the vulnerability of keeping currency on hand. Programs such as QuickBooks and Sage100

Cloud allow employers to print paychecks directly from the program on specifically designed, preprinted forms. Checks offer a level of security that cash does not because they are issued to a specific employee, the only person who can legally convert the check into cash.

The disadvantage of using paper checks for payroll purposes involves bank account reconciliation. Once issued, the employee may choose not to deposit it into his or her bank account, which can complicate the firm's reconciliation process. Paper checks could be lost or destroyed, requiring voiding of the old check and issuance of a new one. Additionally, employees may not have a bank account, which makes cashing paychecks challenging and potentially costly. Paper checks may soon be phased out of current practice as other methods of employee pay grow in popularity because of the convenience for both the employer and the employee.

According to the Pew Internet and American Life Project in 2014, more than 53 million consumers in the United States use online banking. As of 2017, that number grew to more than two-thirds of Americans. The practice of payroll disbursement using paper checks is declining as people shift from traditional banking methods to a culture of electronic money management. (Sources: Pew research center: http://www.pewinternet.org/2013/08/07/51-of-u-s-adults-bank-online/, American Banking Journal: https://bankingjournal.aba.com/2017/09/aba-survey-two-thirds-of-americans-use-digital-banking-channels-most-often/)

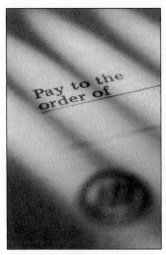

Ingram Publishing

For employers who use paper checks as a compensation method, two significant best practices exist: (1) The use of a payroll-only checking account and (2) a procedure for the handling of the payroll checks themselves. A separate payroll-dedicated checking account prevents problems that could occur if the company has difficulties (such as insufficient funds) in the business's main account. For the checks themselves, the payroll accountant needs to maintain a record that notes the use of each and every check, especially for checks that are voided, lost, or never cashed. If a company issues checks, it needs to maintain an unclaimed property account for payroll checks that are never cashed by the employee. The process of leaving a check uncashed, especially if it is a payroll check, results in the *escheatment* of the payroll check because the payee of the check has never claimed the property (i.e., the payroll money) and is subject to state laws about the handling and distribution of such unclaimed money. Compliance with state escheatment laws is mandatory but not largely enforced—but that does not relieve the employer of the obligation to pay its employees. The use of a record in which the payroll accountant annotates each check's use (i.e., cashed, voided, lost) is imperative.

According to the office of the State Comptroller of New York, the policy for escheatment is that uncashed payroll checks are escheated as of predetermined dated. As of 2020, over $16 billion in escheated funds remained in the custody of the state. (Source: New York Office of the State Comptroller: https://www.osc.state.ny.us/ouf/)

When a company pays employees by check, the numerical amount of the check must also be represented in specific words for the bank to accept the check for payment to the payee. It is important to note banks pay the check based on the amount written in words on the check. The highlighted area in the image in Figure 5-6 shows how the information should appear on the face of the check, specifically the written-out amount of the check. Figure 5-6 contains a sample of a paycheck.

FIGURE 5-6
Sample Paycheck

Wings of the North		
121 Nicholas Street		
North Pole, AK 99705		Check No. 23445

Petra Smith   Date   1/3/20XX

One Thousand One Hundred Twenty-four and 13/100   dollars   1,124.13

Payee: Petra Smith
Address: 426 Candy Cane Lane
City/State Zip: North Pole, AK 99705   Signed: *Rudolph Donner*

A relevant concept in using checks for payroll is the potential for fraud by manipulating the information on checks. The check issuer (i.e., the employer) may be liable for the funds until the fraudulent activity is proven. Some red flags that may indicate check fraud include the following:

- Changes in font type between the company's address and the employee's name.
- Low check numbers (e.g., 1001–1500) because payroll fraud often involves new accounts.
- Evidence of typewriter use on the check (most payroll checks are generated via computerized programs).
- Stains or discolorations on the check.
- Notations in the memo line that contain the word "payroll" or "load."
- Handwritten additions to the check, such as the recipient's phone number.
- Absence of the bank's or the recipient's address.
- Check number is either absent or is the same on all checks.

(Source: National Check Fraud Center: http://www.ckfraud.org/)

Paper checks are more vulnerable to fraud than electronic transfers because of the ease of obtaining preprinted checks. Many employers are transitioning to either direct deposits or paycards to protect company assets.

Direct Deposit

Direct deposit of employee compensation into the individual's bank account offers employers some of the same advantages as checks. Like checks, employee compensation is traceable through both the employer's bank and the optional paper pay advice issued to the employee. Employees often prefer direct deposit because their pay is immediately available in their bank account, eliminating the need to travel to the bank to deposit the paper check. However, for employees to receive their pay through direct deposit, they must have a bank account.

An advantage of direct deposit is that it prevents paper waste, promoting "green" business practices. The savings per employee per pay period is approximately $1.35, according to the National Federation of Independent Business. Although this may seem like a small amount, when multiplied by the number of employees and pay periods annually it creates a potentially large saving for employers. These savings came from lower waste collection,

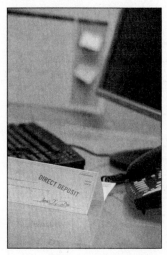

Comstock/PunchStock

paper usage, and recycling costs. Not only does direct deposit save a company money, it reduces the time needed for payroll processing, which frees payroll accountants to complete other tasks.

When using direct deposit as an employee compensation method, a suggested best practice is to grant the employees access to a website or online portal by which they can securely view their *pay advice* and pay history, as this may substitute for paper payroll advice. Because direct deposit involves the use of electronic data transmittal, the posting of the pay advice on a secure site could be linked with the human resources data, allowing the employee an element of self-maintenance in payroll records. The potential pitfall in the use of a website for these highly sensitive records is the vulnerability of the information to computer hacking. If an employer chooses to use a website in this manner, he or she must take steps to prevent hacking through data encryption, identity verification, and site security.

> The Federal Communications Commission (FCC) published guidelines for employer data security procedures, especially as pertains to employee information on websites and the use of paycards. The FCC guidelines include advice about the selection of data to be included on employee-accessible websites, password strength guidelines, update intervals, and data archiving. (Source: FCC: https://transition.fcc.gov/cyber/cyberplanner.pdf)

Tarik Kizilkaya/Getty Images

Paycards

Paycards have been growing in popularity since the beginning of the 21st century. These cards are debit cards onto which an employer electronically transmits the employee's pay. The use of payroll cards started in the 1990s as a convenient way to compensate over-the-road truck drivers who could not be in a predictable place on each payday. Comerica started issuing the paycards that could be used anywhere a conventional MasterCard was accepted, which is nearly everywhere. Unlike the use of paper checks or direct deposit, the paycard does not require an employee to maintain a bank account to access his or her pay. The convenience and ease of use for employees makes the paycard an option that millions of workers in the United States have opted to use.

> Paycards have grown in popularity because of their inherent flexibility for sending and receiving money. The paycard may be used as a debit card by people without bank accounts, which also grants them the ability to participate in online purchases even if they cannot qualify for a credit card. For the 13 million unbanked households in the United States, paycards grant the financial freedom and accessibility that they may otherwise not have and allow unbanked employees to avoid check-cashing fees. (Sources: American Payroll Association)

What is the disadvantage of paycard use? Unlike the limits to access that a bank has for its account holders, a paycard can be lost or stolen. Some employees may encounter challenges such as withdrawal limits or cash back at point-of-sale (POS) purchases. Like paper checks, paycards may be subject to state escheatment laws that govern unclaimed funds.

An issue that haunted the early use of paycards was *Regulation E* of the Federal Deposit Insurance Corporation (FDIC), which protects consumers from loss of the availability of their funds on deposit in the event of bank losses. Until 2006, Regulation E applied to funds on deposit in an FDIC-insured institution. Regulation E was extended to cover payroll funds transferred to paycards, according to 12 CFR Part 205. As a payment method that is growing in popularity among employers and employees, paycards offer more compensation options for employers.

Nito/Shutterstock

Paycards require different types of security than the other types of employee compensation, but most elements remain the same. In addition to tracking hours and accurately compensating employees based on their marital status and withholdings, the employer must keep the employee's paycard number in a secure file. Software such as QuickBooks offers password encryption abilities for the files of employees who have paycards. Like any other debit card, the funds are electronically coded to the account number. The card issuer (not the employer) must remain compliant with Regulation E as far as card loss or theft is concerned, but the employer is responsible to ensure this extra step of payroll security.

> Visa Inc. introduced an improvement to its Visa Advanced Authorization technology, making compensation via paycards more secure and reliable. This new technology improved real-time fraud detection and was projected to prevent nearly $200 million in fraud within a five-year period. Since its inception, technology has evolved to include predictive analytics that detects unusual card usage. (Source: Visa)

Zapp2Photo/Shutterstock

Cryptocurrency

An emerging wage payment method involves *cryptocurrency*, such as Bitcoin or Ethereum, and the use of *blockchain* technology. Cryptocurrency uses Internet technology to transmit money securely from one "wallet," or account, to a recipient. The cryptocurrency itself is not a physical currency, as it exists only in electronic form. Transmission of wages is thought to be secure because the blockchain technology makes it very difficult for wages to be diverted from the intended recipient because the blockchain involves the transmission of packets of data through a very large number of computers, making a single transaction difficult to isolate.

The advantage of using cryptocurrency is it is not subject to international exchange rates and it is transferred nearly instantaneously. The disadvantage of using cryptocurrency is no centralized authority oversees the value of the currency, making it extremely volatile in value, which could lead to the underpayment of employees if the currency loses value. As cryptocurrency becomes more accepted as a payroll payment form, additional governmental guidance will likely emerge.

> The state of Ohio started accepting employer remittance of payroll taxes via blockchain technology in late 2018. The state's revenue department allots a 15-minute time period for the employer to complete entering the data associated with the remittance and a third-party company insures the state against the risk of loss in value during the transmission time. (Source: American Payroll Association)

Pay Methods

Stop & Check

1. What are the different employee pay methods?
2. What regulation governs paycard loss or theft?
3. For which pay method(s) must an employee have a bank account?

TAXES AND PAYMENT METHODS

Employee net pay changes each year because of legal developments regarding deductions and payment methods. Developments in employee withholdings since 2015 include the following:

- Changes to employee net pay because of the Affordable Care Act health insurance requirements for employers.
- Changes to sick-leave compensation at the state and local levels.
- Changes in the amounts that employees may contribute on a tax-deferred basis to pension plans.
- Increased public awareness of the effect of pay raises, especially for the cost of living, on net pay.
- Expanded regulatory guidance regarding data privacy and security, similar to the General Data Protection Regulation (GDPR) mandated in the European Union, to protect electronic employee payroll transmission.

Some trends to watch in employee net pay include the following:

- A continued increase in cashless payroll disbursement methods, including paycards and direct deposit.
- The growing use of mobile payments and electronic wallets with artificial intelligence to facilitate the transmission and accuracy of employee pay.
- Faster payments, including early payroll disbursements through electronic means.
- Increased standardization of payroll methods using non-contact or cloud-based technologies.

Summary of Employee Net Pay and Pay Methods

Employee pay is subject to a variety of deductions that can be mandatory, mandated by a court or other authority, or voluntary. In 2020, the introduction of the new Form W-4 changed the factors by which federal income tax withholding was determined and the IRS provided an Excel-based tool to aid payroll accountants with the preparation of payroll. Deductions such as federal income tax and Medicare tax are virtually inescapable. Other taxes such as Social Security, state taxes, and local taxes are not applicable in every employee's situation and depend on a variety of factors such as year-to-date pay and state of residence. Of the other deductions, some can be withheld from an employee's pay before taxes are deducted, which benefits an employee by reducing their payroll tax liability. Other deductions must be taken after taxes are withheld. Understanding the difference between gross pay and net pay is vital for payroll accountants because the net pay, not the gross, is the pay that the employee actually receives.

The question of employee pay methods is complex. Which payment method is the best? It is not an easy answer. An employer should consider the needs of the employees, as well as the business, to decide if one method will suit everyone. Sometimes a combination of payment methods is the best solution, although it adds complexity for the payroll accountant. The most appropriate method for the organization will depend on many different factors. Attention to these factors, which include payroll frequency, employee types, and the nature of the business itself, helps inform employer decisions about employee pay methods.

Key Points

- Net pay is gross pay less all deductions.
- Federal income tax applies to all workers, and the changes in federal income tax deductions changed because of the implementation of provisions of the Tax Cuts and Jobs Act.
- Employees hired after January 1, 2020, are subject to different factors as part of federal income tax computation. Employees hired in 2019 and prior years may continue to use their existing tax methods.
- Social Security tax has a maximum wage base that can change each year.
- Medicare tax has no maximum wage base, and an additional Medicare tax is levied on highly compensated employees.
- Employees who are subject to mandated deductions such as garnishments for child support and consumer credit liens have certain protections as to the percent of disposable income that may be withheld.
- Employees' pay may be disbursed in cash, by check, by paycard, or via direct deposit.
- Uncashed employee paychecks are turned over to state authorities as escheatments and become unclaimed property.
- Electronic means of transmitting pay such as paycards are growing in popularity because of the ease of access and transmittal.
- Cryptocurrency is becoming a growing way for employers to transmit funds to employees and state agencies, although the standardization of the rules regarding cryptocurrency does not yet exist.

Vocabulary

Additional Medicare tax	Local income tax	Publication 15-T
Blockchain	Mandatory deductions	Regulation E
Cryptocurrency	Medicare tax	Social Security tax
Direct deposit	Net pay	State income taxes
Escheatment	Pay advice	Wage base
Federal income tax	Paycard	Wage-bracket method
FICA tax	Percentage method	

Review Questions

1. What are the factors that affect how much federal income tax is withheld from an employee's pay with a 2020 or later W-4 on file?
2. What factors determine the amount of federal income tax withheld for employees who have a pre-2020 Form W-4 on file with their employer?
3. How is Social Security tax computed? What is the maximum wage base?
4. How is Medicare tax computed? What is the maximum wage base?
5. Name four states that do not have an income tax for employees.
6. How is an employee's net income computed?
7. Why is the difference between gross pay and taxable income important?
8. What are the five different payment methods?
9. What are the advantages and disadvantages of paycards?
10. What are an advantage and disadvantage of direct deposit?
11. How does the percentage method work for W-4s submitted 2020 and later?
12. When should the percentage method be used instead of the wage-bracket method?
13. What are two examples of garnishments?
14. Why are garnishments deducted on a post-tax basis?
15. Why are union dues not considered a garnishment?
16. How does cryptocurrency function as a payroll payment method?
17. Why has cryptocurrency not yet been fully adopted as an employee payment method?

Exercises Set A

E5-1A.
LO 5-1

Lyle Ingram, the payroll accountant, needs to compute net pay for the employees for Hay Industries. Place the following steps in the proper order.
a. Compute income taxes.
b. Subtract pre-tax deductions from gross pay.
c. Compute Social Security and Medicare taxes.
d. Subtract taxes and all other deductions from gross pay.
e. Determine gross pay. Order: _____

E5-2A.
LO 5-1

Daryl Simpson is the owner of Padua Products. During the holiday season, he wants to reward his employees for their work during the year, and he has asked you to gross up their bonuses so that they receive the full amount as net pay. What amount(s) should you consider when computing the grossed-up pay? (Select all that apply.)
a. Desired bonus amount
b. Garnishments
c. Mandated deductions
d. Income tax(es)

E5-3A.
LO 5-2

Teddy Harrington is a new payroll clerk with B&H Farms. As he prepares to use the federal income tax withholding assistant to determine federal income tax withholdings, what information does he need for each employee? (Select all that apply.)
a. Age
b. Taxable income
c. Pay date
d. Pay frequency

E5-4A.
LO 5-3

Under which circumstances could the percentage method be used to determine federal income tax withholding amounts? (Select all that apply.)
a. When the employee's taxable income exceeds the maximum amount on the appropriate wage-bracket table.
b. When using a computerized accounting system to compute payroll deductions.
c. When using a manual accounting system for a small number of low-pay employees.
d. When computational accuracy is critical.

E5-5A.
LO 5-3

Which of the following is true about Social Security and Medicare taxes as they pertain to earnings limits? (Select all that apply.)
a. Social Security tax applies to all earnings, regardless of year-to-date amounts.
b. Highly compensated employees are subject to additional Medicare tax withholding.
c. Once an employee's year-to-date earnings exceed the wage base, no additional Social Security tax is withheld.
d. Employers contribute equally to all Social Security and Medicare taxes.

E5-6A.
LO 5-3

Which of the following are the rates for Social Security and Medicare taxes, respectively?
a. 4.4 percent, 6.2 percent
b. 4.2 percent, 1.5 percent
c. 6.2 percent, 1.45 percent
d. 1.45 percent, 6.2 percent

E5-7A.
LO 5-4

Which of the following statements are true about state and local income taxes? (Select all that apply.)
a. All states tax employee earnings.
b. State tax rates on employee earnings vary among states.
c. Certain states have no personal income tax deduction.
d. Some localities levy income tax on employees.

E5-8A.

LO 5-6

Petra Stevens is the accountant for FAB Products, a newly formed company. She is exploring employee pay methods. Which of the following describes a method in which employee earnings are transferred automatically from the employer's bank account to the employee's bank account?
a. Check
b. Paycard
c. Cash
d. Direct deposit

E5-9A.

LO 5-2

What are the two methods payroll accountants use to determine federal income tax withholding amounts? (Select all that apply.)
a. Percentage method
b. Salary-bracket method
c. Wage-salary method
d. Wage-bracket method

E5-10A.

LO 5-3

At what income level do many employees contribute an additional percentage to their Medicare tax deduction?
a. $128,400
b. $150,000
c. $175,000
d. $200,000

Problems Set A

P5-1A.

LO 5-1, 5-2, 5-3

Compute the net pay for Karen Wilson and Katie Smith. Assume that they are paid a $2,500 salary biweekly, subject to federal income tax (use the wage-bracket method) in Appendix C and FICA taxes, and have no other deductions from their pay. They have a state tax rate of 3 percent. If they choose to participate in the cafeteria plan, the deduction for the pay period is $100; otherwise, there is no deduction for the cafeteria plan. The cafeteria plan qualifies under Section 125. You do not need to complete the number of hours. Additional information for Karen: Box 2 is not checked and the dependents are under 17.

Name	Filing Status	Hourly Rate or Period Wage	No. of Regular Hours	No. of Overtime Hours	No. of Holiday Hours	Commiss-ions	Gross Earnings	Cafeteria Plan	Taxable Wages for Federal / State W/H	Taxable Wages for FICA
Karen Wilson—no cafeteria plan	MJ-2	2,500.00								
Karen Wilson—cafeteria plan	MJ-2	2,500.00								
Katie Smith—no cafeteria plan	S-0	2,500.00								
Katie Smith—cafeteria plan	S-0	2,500.00								

Name	Gross Earnings	Taxable Wages for Federal/ State W/H	Taxable Wages for FICA	Federal W/H	Social Security Tax	Medicare W/H Tax	State W/H Tax	Net Pay
Karen Wilson—no cafeteria plan								
Karen Wilson—cafeteria plan								
Katie Smith—no cafeteria plan								
Katie Smith—cafeteria plan								

P5-2A.

LO 5-1, 5-2, 5-3, 5-5

Tooka's Trees in Auburn, Tennessee, has six employees who are paid biweekly. Calculate the net pay from the information provided below for the November 15 pay date. Assume that all wages are subject to Social Security and Medicare taxes. All 401(k) and Section 125 amounts are pre-tax deductions. The wages are not subject to state taxes. Use the percentage method in Appendix C (or the IRS federal income tax assistant) to compute federal income taxes. You do not need to complete the number of hours.

a. T. Taylor
   Single, two dependents <17
   Gross pay: $1,500 per period
   401(k) deduction: $125 per pay period

b. B. Walburn
   Married/Joint, two dependents <17
   Gross pay: $2,225 per period
   401(k) deduction: $250 per period

c. H. Carpenter
   Single, no dependents
   Gross pay: $2,100 per period
   Section 125 deduction: $75 per period
   401(k) deduction: $50 per period

d. J. Knight
   Married/Joint, one dependent <17
   Gross pay: $1,875 per period
   United Way deduction: $50 per period
   Garnishment: $50 per period

e. C. Lunn
   Single, no dependents
   Gross pay: $1,200 per period
   Section 125 withholding: $50 per period
   401(k) deduction: 6 percent of gross pay

f. E. Smooter
   Married/Joint, 3 dependents <17
   Gross pay: $2,425 per period
   401(k) deduction: $75 per period

Name	Filing Status	Hourly Rate or Period Wage	No. of Regular Hours	No. of Overtime Hours	No. of Holiday Hours	Commiss-ions	Gross Earnings	401(k)	Section 125	Taxable Wages for Federal / State W/H	Taxable Wages for FICA

Name	Gross Earnings	Taxable Wages for Federal W/H	Taxable Wages for FICA	Federal W/H	Social Security Tax	Medicare W/H Tax	State W/H Tax	Garnish-ments	United Way	Net Pay

P5-3A.

LO 5-1, 5-2, 5-3, 5-4, 5-5

The following employees of CIBA Ironworks in Bristol, Illinois, are paid in different frequencies. Some employees have union dues or garnishments deducted from their pay. Calculate their net pay using the percentage method in Appendix C (or the IRS federal income tax assistant) to determine federal income tax. Include Illinois income tax of 4.95 percent of taxable pay. No employee has exceeded the maximum FICA limits. You do not need to complete the number of hours.

Employee	Frequency	Filing Status, Dependents	Pay	Union Dues per Period	Garnishment per Period	Net Pay
C. Whaley	Weekly	MJ-0	$ 850		$ 50	
F. Paguaga	Semimonthly	MJ-2 (<17)	2,800	$120		
K. Harvey	Monthly	S-1 (Other)	8,000	240	75	
L. Bolling	Biweekly	MJ-0	2,500		100	

Name	Frequency	Filing Status	Hourly Rate or Period Wage	No. of Regular Hours	No. of Overtime Hours	No. of Holiday Hours	Commiss- ions	Gross Earnings	401(k)	Section 125	Taxable Wages for Federal / State W/H	Taxable Wages for FICA

Name	Gross Earnings	Taxable Wages for Federal/ State W/H	Taxable Wages for FICA	Federal W/H	Social Security Tax	Medicare W/H Tax	State W/H Tax	Union Dues	Garnish- ment	Net Pay

P5-4A.

LO 5-1, 5-2, 5-3, 5-4, 5-5

Frances Newberry is the payroll accountant for Pack-It Services of Jackson, Arizona. The employees of Pack-It Services are paid semimonthly. An employee, Glen Riley, comes to her on November 6 and requests a pay advance of $750, which he will pay back in equal parts on the November 15 and December 15 paychecks. Glen is married filing jointly (box 2 is checked) with three dependents under 17 and is paid $50,000 per year. He contributes 3 percent of his pay to a 401(k) and has $125 per paycheck deducted for a Section 125 plan. Compute his net pay on his November 15 paycheck. The applicable state income tax rate is 2.88 percent. Use the percentage method in Appendix C to determine the federal income tax.

Name	Filing Status, Dependents	Hourly Rate or Period Wage	No. of Regular Hours	No. of Overtime Hours	No. of Holiday Hours	Commiss-ions	Gross Earnings	401(k)	Section 125	Taxable Wages for Federal/ State W/H	Taxable Wages for FICA
Glen Riley											

Name	Gross Earnings	Taxable Wages for Federal/State W/H	Taxable Wages for FICA	Federal W/H	Social Security Tax	Medicare W/H Tax	State W/H Tax	Advance	Net Pay
Glen Riley									

P5-5A.
LO 5-1, 5-2

Milligan's Millworks pays its employees on a weekly basis. Using the wage-bracket tables from Appendix C to compute the federal income tax withholdings for the following employees of Milligan's Millworks:

Employee	Filing Status	Dependents	Weekly Pay	Federal Tax
D. Balestreri	Single	two <17	$ 845	
Y. Milligan	Single	one Other	1,233	
H. Curran	Married/Joint	two <17, one Other	682	
D. Liberti	Head of Household	One <17	755	

P5-6A.
LO 5-2

Wynne and Associates have employees with pay schedules that vary based on job classification. Compute the federal income tax withholding for each employee using the percentage method in Appendix C (or the IRS federal income tax assistant).

Employee	Filing Status	Dependents	Pay Frequency	Pay Amount	Federal Income Tax
S. Turner	S	None	Weekly	$ 3,000	
D. McGorray	S	One Other	Monthly	15,000	
A. Kennedy	MJ	One <17	Daily	500	
R. Thomas	MJ	Two <17	Semimonthly	5,000	

P5-7A.
LO 5-3

The employees of Agonnacultis Inc. are paid on a semimonthly basis. Compute the FICA taxes for the employees for the November 15 payroll. All employees have been employed for the entire calendar year.

Employee	Semimonthly Pay	YTD Pay for Oct 31 Pay Date	Social Security Tax for Nov. 15 Pay Date	Medicare Tax for Nov. 15 Pay Date
T. Newberry	$ 7,500			
S. Smith	3,500			
D. Plott	4,225			
I. Ost	6,895			
D. Bogard	10,250			
M. Mallamace	4,100			

P5-8A.
LO 5-4

Fannon's Chocolate Factory operates in North Carolina. Using the state income tax rate of 4.75 percent, calculate the state income tax for each employee.

Employee	Amount per Pay Period	North Carolina Income Tax
K. Jamieson	$ 550	
D. Macranie	4,895	
G. Lockhart	3,225	
K. McIntyre	1,795	

P5-9A.

LO 5-2

Using the percentage method from Appendix C calculate the federal withholding amounts for the following employees. No information was included in any Step 4 of the W-4, all W-4s were from 2020, no box was checked in Step 2.

Employee	Filing Status	Dependents	Pay Frequency	Amount per Pay Period	Federal Income Tax
S. Calder	MJ	Three <17	Monthly	$20,000	
P. Singh	HH	One <17	Biweekly	3,300	
B. Nelson	MJ	None	Daily	500	

P5-10A.

LO 5-6

Margaret Wilson is the new accountant for a start-up company, Peaceful Skunk Builders. The company has cross-country drivers, warehouse personnel, and office staff at the main location. The company is looking at options that allow its employees flexibility with receiving their pay. Margaret has been asked to present the advantages and disadvantages of the various payment methods for senior management. Which would be the best option for each class of workers?

Exercises Set B

E5-1B.

LO 5-1

Chastity Santos is in the process of computing net pay for the employees of Happy Crab Marketing. Place the following steps in order after Chastity has determined the amount of gross pay.
a. Compute Social Security and Medicare tax withholding
b. Compute income tax withholding(s)
c. Compute pre-tax deductions
d. Compute post-tax deductions

E5-2B.

LO 5-1

Joey Martel is an employee of Overclock Watches. His employer would like to give him a bonus and has asked you to gross it up to ensure that Joey receives the full amount of the desired award. Which of the following should be considered in the denominator to compute the grossed-up amount? (Select all that apply.)
a. Social Security and Medicare taxes
b. 401(k) contribution
c. Health insurance premium
d. Income tax(es)

E5-3B.

LO 5-2

Liam Figueroa is the payroll accountant for Chop Brothers Coffee. As he prepares to use wage-bracket tables to determine federal income tax withholdings for each employee, which information should he have available? (Select all that apply.)
a. Filing status
b. Job title
c. Year-to-date earnings
d. Number and type of dependents

E5-4B.

LO 5-2

Which of the following are steps in computing federal income tax withholding using the percentage method? (Select all that apply.)
a. Compute and deduct withholding allowance.
b. Apply the tax rate to the taxable portion of the earnings.
c. Determine if the employee is exempt or nonexempt.
d. Add the marginal tax.

E5-5B.

LO 5-3

Which of the following are true about Social Security and Medicare tax deductions? (Select all that apply.)

a. They are applied to the gross pay.

b. Contributions to a 401(k) plan are exempt from these taxes.

c. Medicare taxes apply to all earnings equally.

d. Certain pre-tax deductions are exempt from Social Security and Medicare tax computations.

E5-6B.

LO 5-3

Scout Freeman is the vice president for marketing at Sun Field Industries. She earns $140,000 annually and is paid on a semimonthly basis. As of October 31, Scout has year-to-date earnings of $133,667. The Social Security wage base is $137,700. What is the maximum amount of her taxable earnings that may be subject to Social Security tax for the November 15 pay period?

a. $5,833

b. $1,833

c. $4,033

d. $0

E5-7B.

LO 5-4

Which of the following is true about state and local income tax? (Select all that apply.)

a. Pre-tax deduction rules for federal income tax are generally the same for state and local income taxes.

b. Nine states do not have a personal income tax on earnings.

c. All localities levy income taxes on employees.

d. State income tax computations vary among states.

E5-8B.

LO 5-6

Which of the following is true about employee pay methods? (Select all that apply.)

a. Employees must be able to access the full amount of their net pay upon demand.

b. Employers must keep a record of all pay disbursements.

c. Employees do not need to own a bank account to receive their pay via direct deposit.

d. Paycards may be reloaded with an employee's net pay on the pay date.

E5-9B.

LO 5-4

Which of the following states does not withhold employee income tax? (Select all that apply.)

a. Washington

b. North Dakota

c. Tennessee

d. Alabama

E5-10B.

LO 5-6

Margarita Sutton is preparing a training session for her colleagues about payroll check fraud. Which of the following may be indicators of check fraud? (Select all that apply.)

a. Changes in font type between company address and employee name

b. Company logo on the face of the check

c. The check number is missing from the check

d. Only one signature is required from the company

Problems Set B

P5-1B.

LO 5-1, 5-2, 5-3

Compute the net pay for Will Barrett and Eric Martin. Assume that they are paid biweekly, subject to federal income tax (use wage bracket method) and FICA taxes, and have no other deductions from their pay. Will's deduction if he chooses to participate in the cafeteria plan is $75; Eric's is $250. There is no deduction if they do not participate in the cafeteria plan. The cafeteria plan qualifies for Section 125. There are no state income taxes and you do not need to complete the number of hours. All W-4s were received in 2020 and there is no information for Step 4. Eric did check the box in Step 2.

Name	Filing Status	Dependents	Hourly Rate or Period Wage	No. of Regular Hours	No. of Overtime Hours	No. of Holiday Hours	Commiss-ions	Gross Earnings	Cafeteria Plan	Taxable Wages for Federal / State W/H	Taxable Wages for FICA
Will Barrett—no cafeteria plan	S	None	1,600.00								
Will Barrett—cafeteria plan	S	None	1,600.00								
Eric Martin—no cafeteria plan	MJ	Two <17 One Other	1,875.00								
Eric Martin—cafeteria plan	MJ	Two <17 One Other	1,875.00								

Name	Gross Earnings	Taxable Wages for Federal / State W/H	Taxable Wages for FICA	Federal W/H	Social Security Tax	Medicare W/H	State W/H Tax	Net Pay
Will Barrett—no cafeteria plan								
Will Barrett—cafeteria plan								
Eric Martin—no cafeteria plan								
Eric Martin—cafeteria plan								

P5-2B.

LO 5-1, 5-2, 5-3, 5-5, 5-6

Hark Enterprises in Taft, Wyoming, has six employees who are paid on a semimonthly basis. Calculate the net pay from the information provided for the August 15 pay date. Assume that all wages are subject to Social Security and Medicare taxes. Use the wage-bracket tables in Appendix C (or the IRS federal income tax assistant) to determine the federal income tax withholding. You do not need to complete the number of hours. No one has checked the box in Step 2 and there is no additional information in Step 4.

a. L. Fletcher:
Married/Joint, Two dependents <17
Gross pay: $1,320 per period
401(k) deduction: 2 percent of gross pay per pay period

b. S. Lince
Single, No dependents
Gross pay: $1,745 per period
401(k) deduction: $220 per pay period

c. A. Brown
Single, One dependent <17, One Other
Gross pay: $2,120 per period
Section 125 deduction: $25 per pay period
401(k) deduction: $150 per pay period

d. R. Kimble
Married/Joint, Three dependents <17
Gross pay: $1,570 per period
United Way deduction: $25 per pay period
Garnishment: $75 per period

e. F. Monteiro
Married/Joint, No dependents
Gross pay: $2,200 per period
Section 125 deduction: $100 per period
401(k) deduction: 4 percent of gross pay

f. K. Giannini
Single, One Other dependent
Gross pay: $1,485 per period
401(k) deduction: $120 per period

Name	Filing Status	Dependents	Hourly Rate or Period Wage	No. of Regular Hours	No. of Overtime Hours	No. of Holiday Hours	Commiss-ions	Gross Earnings	401(k)	Section 125	Taxable Wages for Federal / State W/H	Taxable Wages for FICA

Name	Gross Earnings	Taxable Wages for Federal/State W/H	Taxable Wages for FICA	Federal W/H Tax	Social Security Tax	Medicare Tax	State Tax	United Way	Garnishment	Net Pay

P5-3B.

LO 5-1, 5-2, 5-3, 5-4, 5-5

The following employees of Memory Bytes of Titusville, Washington, are paid in different frequencies. Some employees have union dues or garnishments deducted from their pay. Calculate their net pay. Use the percentage method in Appendix C (or the IRS federal income tax assistant) to determine federal income tax unless the amount is over the table. No employee has exceeded the maximum FICA limits. You do not need to complete the number of hours. There is no information for Step 4 and all W-4s were received in 2020. No box was checked in Step 2.

Employee	Frequency	Filing Status/ Dependents	Pay	Union Dues per Period	Garnishment per Period	Net Pay
N. Lawrence	Biweekly	MJ, One dependent <17	$1,680	$102		
D. Gaitan	Weekly	S, No dependents	1,300		$70	
N. Ruggieri	Semimonthly	MJ, No dependents	2,525	110	90	
P. Oceguera	Monthly	HH, One dependent <17	6,600		45	

Name	Filing Status	Dependents	Hourly Rate or Period Wage	No. of Regular Hours	No. of Overtime Hours	No. of Holiday Hours	Commiss-ions	Gross Earnings	401(k)	Section 125	Taxable Wages for Federal/ State W/H	Taxable Wages for FICA

Name	Gross Earnings	Taxable Wages for Federal/ State W/H	Taxable Wages for FICA	Federal W/H Tax	Social Security Tax	Medicare W/H Tax	State W/H	Union Dues	Garnishment	Net Pay

P5-4B.

LO 5-1, 5-2, 5-3, 5-4, 5-5

Jane Heinlein is the payroll accountant for Sia Lights of Carter, Nebraska. The employees of Sia Lights are paid biweekly. An employee, Melinda Gunnarson, comes to her on September 11 and requests a pay advance of $825, which she will pay back in equal parts on the September 25 and October 9 pay-checks. Melinda is single with no dependents and is paid $32,500 per year. She contributes 1 percent of her pay to a 401(k) plan and has $25 per pay-check deducted for a court-ordered garnishment. Compute her net pay for her September 25th paycheck. Her state income tax rate is 6.84 percent. Use the wage bracket tables in Appendix C (or the IRS federal income tax assistant) to determine the federal income tax withholding amount. Her W-4 is from prior to 2020. You do not need to complete the number of hours.

Name	Filing Status	Dependents	Hourly Rate or Period Wage	No. of Regular Hours	No. of Overtime Hours	No. of Holiday Hours	Commiss ions	Gross Earnings	401(k)	Section 125	Taxable Wages for Federal/ State W/H	Taxable Wages for FICA
Melinda Gunnarson												

Name	Gross Earnings	Taxable Wages for Federal / State W/H	Taxable Wages for FICA	Federal W/H	Social Security Tax	Medicare Tax	State Tax	Garnishment	Advance	Net Pay
Melinda Gunnarson										

P5-5B.

LO 5-2

Wolfe Industries pays its employees on a semimonthly basis. Using the wage-bracket tables in Appendix C (or the IRS federal income tax assistant), compute the federal income tax deductions for the following employees of Wolfe Industries. All W-4s were received in 2020, no information was included in Step 4 of any W-4, McCollum checked the box in Step 2c.

Employee	Marital Status	Dependents	Semimonthly Pay	Federal Income Tax
T. Canter	MJ	No dependents	$1,050	
M. McCollum	MJ	Two dependents <17	1,390	
C. Hammond	HH	One dependent <17	1,295	
T. Elliott	S	Two dependents <17	1,165	

P5-6B.
LO 5-2

GL Kennels has employees with pay schedules that vary based on job classification. Compute the federal income tax liability for each employee using the percentage method in Appendix C (or the IRS federal income tax assistant). All W-4s were received prior to 2020 and no one requested additional withholding.

Employee	Filing Status	Exemptions	Pay Frequency	Pay Amount	Percentage Method
C. Wells	MJ	1	Biweekly	$1,825	
L. Decker	MS	0	Weekly	750	
J. Swaby	S	2	Weekly	875	
M. Ohlson	MJ	1	Semimonthly	2,025	

P5-7B.
LO 5-3

The employees of Black Cat Designs are paid on a semimonthly basis. Compute the FICA taxes for the employees for the November 30, 2020, payroll. All employees have been employed for the entire calendar year.

Employee	Semimonthly Pay	YTD Pay for 11-15-2020	Social Security Tax for 11-30-2020 Pay	Medicare Tax for 11-30-2020 Pay
P. Gareis	$4,250			
E. Siliwon	6,275			
G. De La Torre	5,875			
L. Rosenthal	2,850			
C. Bertozzi	5,105			
T. Gennaro	2,940			

P5-8B.
LO 5-4

Christensen Ranch operates in Pennsylvania. Using the state income tax rate of 3.07 percent, calculate the state income tax for each employee.

Employee	Amount per Pay Period	Pennsylvania Income Tax
G. Zonis	$1,325	
V. Sizemore	1,710	
R. Dawson	925	
C. Couture	2,550	

P5-9B.
LO 5-2

Using the percentage method in Appendix C (or the IRS federal income tax assistant), calculate the federal withholding amounts for the following employees. All W-4s were received in 2020, no box was checked in Step 2c and no additional information was included in Step 4.

Employee	Filing Status	Dependents	Pay Frequency	Amount per Pay Period	Federal Income Tax
L. Abbey	HH	Two dependents <17	Semimonthly	$3,500	
G. Narleski	MJ	No dependents	Weekly	1,000	
T. Leider	S	No dependents	Monthly	2,400	

P5-10B
LO 5-6

David Adams has been retained as a consultant for Marionet Industries. The company has had difficulty with its cross-country drivers receiving their pay in a timely fashion because they are often away from their home banks. The company is looking at options that allow its employees flexibility with receiving their pay. Prepare a presentation for senior management depicting the advantages and disadvantages of the various pay methods.

Critical Thinking

For the Critical Thinking problems, use the following steps to compute the gross-up amount:

1. Compute tax rate: The tax rate on bonuses is 22 percent. Social Security (6.2%) and Medicare taxes (1.45%) must be added to this rate. For bonuses, the total tax rate equals 22% + 6.2% + 1.45%, or 29.65%.

2. Subtract 100 percent − tax rate percentage to get the net tax rate. For bonuses, it is 100% − 29.65%, or 70.35%.

3. Gross-up amount = net pay/net tax rate. For example, if you want the employee to receive a $150 bonus, the equation is $150/70.35% = $213.22.

   (Note: Typically voluntary pre-tax and post-tax deductions are not withheld from bonus checks.)

5-1 Vicky Le, an employee of Sweet Shoppe Industries, receives a bonus of $5,000 for her stellar work. Her boss wants Vicky to receive $5,000 on the check. She contributes 3 percent of her pay in a pre-tax deduction to her 401(k). Calculate the gross pay amount that would result in $5,000 paid to Vicky.

5-2 Your boss approaches you in mid-December and requests that you pay certain employees their gross pay amount as if there were no deductions as their year-end bonuses. None of the employees have reached the Social Security wage base for the year. What is the gross-up amount for each of the following employees? (Use the tax rate for bonuses and no state taxes.)

Employee	Regular Gross Pay per Period	Grossed-Up Amount
Yves St. John	$2,500	
Kim Johnson	3,380	
Michael Hale	3,178	

In the Real World: Scenario for Discussion

The state of Kansas passed legislation that allowed employers to select their employee pay method. The legislation was known as the "paperless payroll law," and many employers opted to give their employees paycards instead of cash, check, or direct deposit. This practice spread to many other states, including New York. In 2017, the law was revoked because it made employers into *de facto* financial institutions.

What are the issues with this practice? What are the benefits?

Internet Activities

5-1. Did you know that you can use an online calculator to see how your voluntary deductions will affect your paycheck? Many different payroll calculators exist. Go to one or more of the following sites and use the payroll calculator:

www.paycheckcity.com/

www.surepayroll.com/resources/calculator

www.adp.com/tools-and-resources/calculators-and-tools/payroll-calculators.aspx

5-2. Want to know more about the concepts in this chapter? Check out these sites:

https://www.irs.gov/pub/irs-pdf/p15t.pdf

https://www.irs.gov/businesses/small-businesses-self-employed/income-tax-withholding-assistant-for-employers

www.americanpayroll.org/Visa-Paycard-Portal/

5-3. Would you like to preview employee apps used to enter time and to calculate payroll disbursements? Check out these links:

DOL Timesheet: https://itunes.apple.com/us/app/dol-timesheet/id433638193?mt=8

Intuit payroll: https://payroll.intuit.com/additional-services/mobile-payroll-apps/

Sure payroll: https://www.surepayroll.com/payroll/mobile

Continuing Payroll Project: Prevosti Farms and Sugarhouse

For the February 7, 2020, pay period, use the gross pay totals from the end of Chapter 3 and compute the net pay for each employee. Once you have computed the net pay (using the wage-bracket tables in Appendix C or the IRS federal income tax assistant), state withholding tax for Vermont is computed at 3.35 percent of taxable wages (i.e., gross pay less pre-tax deductions). Note that the first pay period comprises only one week of work during the February 7 pay period and that the federal income tax should be determined using the biweekly tables in Appendix C.

Initial pre-tax deductions for each employee are as follows:

Name	Deduction
Millen	Insurance: $155/paycheck/401(k): 3% of gross pay
Towle	Insurance: $100/paycheck/401(k): 5% of gross pay
Long	Insurance: $155/paycheck/401(k): 2% of gross pay
Shangraw	Insurance: $100/paycheck/401(k): 3% of gross pay
Lewis	Insurance: $155/paycheck/401(k): 4% of gross pay
Schwartz	Insurance: $100/paycheck/401(k): 5% of gross pay
Prevosti	Insurance: $155/paycheck/401(k): 6% of gross pay
You	Insurance: $100/paycheck/401(k): 2% of gross pay

Compute the net pay for the February 7 pay period using the payroll register. All insurance and 401(k) deductions are pre-tax. Update the Employee Earnings Records as of February 7, 2020.

Name	Filing Status	Dependents	Hourly Rate or Period Wage	No. of Regular Hours	No. of Overtime Hours	No. of Holiday Hours	Commissions	Gross Earnings	401(k)	Sec 125	Taxable Wages for Federal / State W/H	Taxable Wages for FICA

Name	Gross Earnings	Taxable Wages for Federal/State W/H	Taxable Wages for FICA	Federal W/H Tax	Social Security Tax	Medicare W/H Tax	State W/H Tax	Total Deduc	Net Pay	Check No.

Compute the net pay for the February 21 pay period using the payroll register. All insurance and 401(k) deductions are pre-tax. Update the Employee Earnings Records as of February 21, 2020.

Name	Filing Status	Dependents	Hourly Rate or Period Wage	No. of Regular Hours	No. of Overtime Hours	No. of Holiday Hours	Commissions	Gross Earnings	401(k)	Sec 125	Taxable Wages for Federal W/H	Taxable Wages for FICA
Thomas Millen				70								
Avery Towle				70	10							
Charlie Long				70								
Mary Shangraw				40	2							
Kristen Lewis				70								
Joe Schwartz				70			225.00					
Toni Prevosti				70								
Student Success				70	1							

Name	Gross Earnings	Taxable Wages for Federal/State W/H	Taxable Wages for FICA	Federal W/H Tax	Social Security Tax	Medicare W/H Tax	State W/H Tax	Total Deduc	Net Pay	Check No.
Thomas Millen										
Avery Towle										
Charlie Long										
Mary Shangraw										
Kristen Lewis										
Joe Schwartz										
Toni Prevosti										
Student Success										

Employee Earnings Register

NAME	Thomas Millen	Hire Date	2/3/2020	Dependent child <17	3
ADDRESS	1022 Forest School Road	Date of Birth	12/16/1982	Dependent other	1
CITY/STATE/ZIP	Woodstock, VT 05001	Position	Production Worker PT /(FT)	Step 4a W-4 Info	none
TELEPHONE	802-478-5055	Filing Status	Married	Step 4b W-4 Info	none
SOCIAL SECURITY		Exempt/Nonexempt	Exempt	Step 4c W-4 Info	none
NUMBER	031-11-3456	Pay Rate	$ 35,000.00 Hr / Wk / Mo /(Yr)		

Flex-Time	Child Care	FSA Amount	Educational Assistance	Life Ins.	Long-Term Care	Gym Membership	Total Benefit
Yes	Yes	$ 500.00	No	Yes	No	Yes	$ 39.62

Period Ended	Hrs Worked	Reg Pay	OT Pay	Holiday	Comm	Gross Pay	Social Sec Tax	Medicare	Fed W/H Tax	State Inc Tax	Sect 125	401 (K)	Total Deduc	Net Pay	YTD

Employee Earnings Register

NAME	Avery Towle	Hire Date	2/3/2020	Dependent child <17	0
ADDRESS	4011 Route 100	Date of Birth	7/14/1991	Dependent other	0
CITY/STATE/ZIP	Plymouth, VT 05102	Position	Production Worker PT /(FT)	Step 4a W-4 Info	none
TELEPHONE	802-967-5873	Filing Status	Married	Step 4b W-4 Info	none
SOCIAL SECURITY		Exempt/Nonexempt	Non-exempt	Step 4c W-4 Info	none
NUMBER	089-74-0974	Pay Rate	$ 12.00 (Hr)/ Wk / Mo / Yr		

Flex-Time	Child Care	FSA Amount	Educational Assistance	Life Ins.	Long-Term Care	Gym Membership	Total Benefit
No	No	$ 1,200.00	Yes	No	No	Yes	$ 53.08

Period Ended	Hrs Worked	Reg Pay	OT Pay	Holiday	Comm	Gross Pay	Social Sec Tax	Medicare	Fed W/H Tax	State Inc Tax	Sect 125	401 (K)	Total Deduc	Net Pay	YTD

Employee Earnings Register

NAME	Charlie Long	Hire Date	2/3/2020	Dependent child <17	2
ADDRESS	242 Benedict Road S.	Date of Birth	3/16/1987	Dependent other	0
CITY/STATE/ZIP	Woodstock, VT 05002	Position	Production Worker PT /(FT)	Step 4a W-4 Info	none
TELEPHONE	802-429-3846	Filing Status	Married	Step 4b W-4 Info	none
SOCIAL SECURITY		Exempt/Nonexempt	Non-exempt	Step 4c W-4 Info	none
NUMBER	056-23-4593	Pay Rate	$ 12.50 (Hr)/ Wk / Mo / Yr		

Flex-Time	Child Care	FSA Amount	Educational Assistance	Life Ins.	Long-Term Care	Gym Membership	Total Benefit
Yes	Yes	$ 700.00	Yes	Yes	No	Yes	$ 42.60

Period Ended	Hrs Worked	Reg Pay	OT Pay	Holiday	Comm	Gross Pay	Social Sec Tax	Medicare	Fed W/H Tax	State Inc Tax	Sect 125	401 (K)	Total Deduc	Net Pay	YTD

Employee Earnings Register

NAME	Mary Shangraw	Hire Date	2/3/2020	Dependent child <17	0
ADDRESS	1901 Main Street #2	Date of Birth	8/20/1994	Dependent other	1
CITY/STATE/ZIP	Bridgewater, VT 05520	Position	Administrative Assistant (PT)/ FT	Step 4a W-4 Info	none
TELEPHONE	802-575-5423	Filing Status	Single	Step 4b W-4 Info	none
SOCIAL SECURITY NUMBER	075-28-8945	Exempt/Nonexempt	Non-exempt	Step 4c W-4 Info	none
		Pay Rate	$ 11.00 (Hr)/ Wk / Mo / Yr		

Flex-Time	Child Care	FSA Amount	Educational Assistance	Life Ins.	Long-Term Care	Gym Membership	Total Benefit
Yes	No	$ 200.00	No	Yes	No	No	$ 12.09

Period Ended	Hrs Worked	Reg Pay	OT Pay	Holiday	Comm	Gross Pay	Social Sec Tax	Medicare	Fed W/H Tax	State W/H Tax	Sect 125	401 (K)	Total Deduc	Net Pay	YTD

Employee Earnings Register

NAME	Kristen Lewis	Hire Date	2/3/2020	Dependent child <17	2
ADDRESS	840 Daily Hollow Road	Date of Birth	4/6/1960	Dependent other	1
CITY/STATE/ZIP	Bridgewater, VT 05523	Position	Office Manager PT /(FT)	Step 4a W-4 Info	none
TELEPHONE	802-390-5572	Filing Status	Married	Step 4b W-4 Info	none
SOCIAL SECURITY NUMBER	076-39-5673	Exempt/Nonexempt	Exempt	Step 4c W-4 Info	none
		Pay Rate	$ 32,000.00 Hr / Wk / Mo /(Yr)		

Flex-Time	Child Care	FSA Amount	Educational Assistance	Life Ins.	Long-Term Care	Gym Membership	Total Benefit
No	No	$ 1,600.00	No	Yes	Yes	No	$ 88.85

Period Ended	Hrs Worked	Reg Pay	OT Pay	Holiday	Comm	Gross Pay	Social Sec Tax	Medicare	Fed Inc Tax	State W/H Tax	Sect 125	401 (K)	Total Deduc	Net Pay	YTD

Employee Earnings Register

NAME	Joel Schwartz	Hire Date	2/3/2020	Dependent child <17	2
ADDRESS	55 Maple Farm Way	Date of Birth	5/23/1985	Dependent other	0
CITY/STATE/ZIP	Woodstock, VT 05534	Position	Sales PT /(FT)	Step 4a W-4 Info	none
TELEPHONE	802-463-9985	Filing Status	Married	Step 4b W-4 Info	none
SOCIAL SECURITY NUMBER	021-34-9876	Exempt/Nonexempt	Exempt	Step 4c W-4 Info	none
		Pay Rate	$ 24,000 + Commiss Hr / Wk / Mo /(Yr)		

Flex-Time	Child Care	FSA Amount	Educational Assistance	Life Ins.	Long-Term Care	Gym Membership	Total Benefit
No	No	$ 450.00	Yes	Yes	No	Yes	$ 33.46

Period Ended	Hrs Worked	Reg Pay	OT Pay	Holiday	Comm	Gross Pay	Social Sec Tax	Medicare	Fed Inc Tax	State W/H Tax	Sect 125	401 (K)	Total Deduc	Net Pay	YTD

Employee Earnings Register

NAME	Toni Prevosti	Hire Date	2/3/2020	Dependent child <17	3
ADDRESS	820 Westminster Road	Date of Birth	9/19/1967	Dependent other	2
CITY/STATE/ZIP	Bridgewater, VT 05521	Position	Owner/President PT /(FT)	Step 4a W-4 Info	none
TELEPHONE	802-555-3456	Filing Status	Married	Step 4b W-4 Info	none
SOCIAL SECURITY NUMBER	055-22-0443	Exempt/Nonexempt	Exempt	Step 4c W-4 Info	none
		Pay Rate	$ 45,000.00 Hr / Wk / Mo /(Yr)		

Flex-Time	Child Care	FSA Amount	Educational Assistance	Life Ins.	Long-Term Care	Gym Membership	Total Benefit
Yes	No	$ 900.00	No	Yes	No	Yes	$ 58.85

Period Ended	Hrs Worked	Reg Pay	OT Pay	Holiday	Comm	Gross Pay	Social Sec Tax	Medicare	Fed Inc Tax	State W/H Tax	Sect 125	401 (K)	Total Deduc	Net Pay	YTD

Employee Earnings Register

NAME	Student Success	Hire Date	2/3/2020	Dependent child <17	0
ADDRESS	1644 Smitten Road	Date of Birth	1/1/1991	Dependent other	0
CITY/STATE/ZIP	Woodstock, VT 05001	Position	Accounting Clerk PT /(FT)	Step 4a W-4 Info	none
TELEPHONE	555-555-5555	Filing Status	Single	Step 4b W-4 Info	none
SOCIAL SECURITY NUMBER	555-555-5555	Exempt/Nonexempt	Non- exempt	Step 4c W-4 Info	none
		Pay Rate	$ 34,000.00 Hr / Wk / Mo /(Yr)		

Flex-Time	Child Care	FSA Amount	Educational Assistance	Life Ins.	Long-Term Care	Gym Membership	Total Benefit
No	No	$ 300.00	Yes	No	No	Yes	$ 18.46

Period Ended	Hrs Worked	Reg Pay	OT Pay	Holiday	Comm	Gross Pay	Social Sec Tax	Medicare	Fed Inc Tax	State W/H Tax	Sect 125	401 (K)	Total Deduc	Net Pay	YTD

Answers to Stop & Check Exercises

Differentiating between Gross and Net Pay

1. Gross pay consists of wages or commissions earned by the employee before deductions. Net pay consists of an employee's salary or wages less all mandatory and voluntary deductions.

2. Student answers may vary but could include qualifying medical or dental plans, Internal Revenue Code Section 125 plans, 401(k) retirement plans, federal income tax, Medicare tax, Social Security tax, state income tax, garnishments, charitable contributions, and union dues.

3. To "gross up" a payroll amount is to calculate the amount of gross pay necessary to receive a net pay result. This is most often done for bonuses.

How Much Tax to Withhold?

1. $52,000 paid semimonthly would give per period of $2,166.67 $52,000/24 = $2,166.67 rounded to $2,167 less dependents of ($1,000 (2 × 500)/24 pay periods for $41.67. Taxable income of $2,125 (2,166.67 − 41.67)
   (a) $185; (b) $189.77

2. $2,166.67 gross pay − $100 for 401(k) deduction per pay period − $41.67 dependents = $2,025 taxable pay. This is the amount used in conjunction with the

wage-bracket table to calculate the federal income tax withheld of $172. The difference in taxes with the 401(k) deduction is $13 = $185 − 172

3. $170 = $2,166.67 gross pay − $75 health insurance − $55 AFLAC − $41.67 dependents = $1,995 taxable pay.

FICA Taxes

1. Social Security = $327.36 = $5,280 × .062; Medicare = $76.56 = $5,280 × 0.0145.
2. Total liability = $807.84 = ($327.36 + $76.56) × 2.
3. a. $0 Social Security liability because the maximum amount of wages taxable for social security is $137,700 and she has exceeded that. Her semimonthly salary is $250,000/24 = $10,416.67. Medicare taxable earnings would be reduced by the qualified insurance deduction $10,416.67 − 75 = $10,341.67. Year-to-date gross wages of $197,916.67 less qualified deduction of $1,425 ($75 × 19) gives $196,491.67 of YTD Medicare taxable earnings. Medicare base for this payroll is $200,000 − 196,491.67 = $3,508.33 to reach the $200,000 cap and $6,833.34 ($10,416.67 − 3,508.33 − 75.00) that will be charged the surcharge. ($3,508.33 × 1.45%) + ($6,833.37 × 2.35%) = $50.87 + 160.58 = $211.45 Medicare tax.
   b. Medicare liability will be: ($10,416.67 − 75.00) × (0.0145 + 0.009) = $243.03

State and Local Income Taxes

1. $65.02 ($62,500 annual salary/26 biweekly = $2,403.85 gross pay − $150 for 401(k) pre-tax deduction − $80 health insurance pre-tax deduction = $2,173.85 taxable pay − $1,827 amount more than on the married person chart = $346.85 × 6.925% = $24.02 + 41 additional amount = $65.02. From Appendix D, Married.
2. $131.96 ($2,850 × 4.63%) state, $5.75 local.

Post-Tax Deductions

1. a, b, d
2. Because the IBEW union requires that employees' union dues be remitted by the employer, the amount due must be deducted on a post-tax basis from his period pay.

Pay Methods

1. Cash, check, direct deposit, paycard, and cryptocurrencies.
2. Regulation E.
3. Direct deposit.

Chapter Six

Employer Payroll Taxes and Labor Planning

All facets of payroll accounting are important because they affect the success of the company and its employees. A particularly important piece of the payroll puzzle is the employer's payroll tax responsibility. The reporting and remittance of payroll taxes is a significant aspect that requires scrupulous attention to detail. Many different tax forms exist that must be filed at regular intervals and with varying governmental bodies. Tax filing requires organizational skills, time management, and continued accuracy. Tax reporting is a huge responsibility for the business and its payroll accountant because of governmental oversight. Additionally, employment tax revenue remittances represent 70 percent of all federal revenue. Therefore, employment tax remittances are a vital part of the U.S. economy.

Employers must also consider payroll responsibilities as part of labor planning. Besides taxes, other aspects of an employer's payroll responsibilities include maintaining workers' compensation insurance, forwarding amounts withheld through employees' voluntary and mandated deductions, and determining both labor expenses and employee benefits. The Internal Revenue Service and state employment departments have websites that contain important information about filing requirements, due dates, guidelines, and penalties (see Appendix E for state employment department contact information). Insurance responsibilities are a vital consideration when determining labor expenses and employee benefits because they are a significant element in the cost of doing business.

LEARNING OBJECTIVES

After studying Chapter 6, you should be able to:

LO 6-1 List Employer-Paid and Employee-Paid Obligations

LO 6-2 Discuss Reporting Periods and Requirements for Employer Tax Deposits

LO 6-3 Prepare Mid-Year and Year-End Employer Tax Reporting and Deposits

LO 6-4 Describe Payroll within the Context of Business Expenses

LO 6-5 Relate Labor Expenses to Company Profitability

LO 6-6 Complete Benefit Analysis as a Function of Payroll

Radius Images

Labor Costs in the Restaurant Industry

A growing economy generally leads to rising costs on a year-over-year basis. The Big Mac Index, jokingly created in the 1980s, is used as an international index to measure changes in the iconic McDonald's sandwich that can be found in most countries. The purpose of the index is to track and compare costs over time and then comparing the price for the same food item to determine currency value. However, this index points to other costs, specifically the labor costs associated with restaurants.

In Austin, Texas, the restaurant industry has noticed a rise in labor costs that has affected the price of food offerings. Employers must consider the cost to have employees and to offer competitive compensation to attract and retain valuable employees. Companies have offered seemingly high compensation to attract managers who will build the culture of the company and maintain the quality of the offerings. In some cases, the amount of money, including employee costs, have caused businesses to close because they cannot remain competitive.

Sources: Community Impact Newspaper, *The Economist*

Labor costs potentially constitute a significant portion of a company's expense. Employee benefits such as company contributions to retirement plans, temporary disability insurance, and educational reimbursements represent additional business expenses. In this chapter, we will examine employer payroll tax responsibilities and how payroll is a tool in labor planning.

LO 6-1   List Employer-Paid and Employee-Paid Obligations

Employers must pay some of the same taxes that the employees do. However, a firm has additional liabilities that employees do not, such as certain unemployment taxes and workers' compensation insurance. A comparison of employee-paid and employer-paid taxes is given in Table 6-1.

The taxes an employer must pay are often known as *statutory deductions*, meaning that governmental statutes have made the tax a mandatory, legally obligated deduction. An important element of employer tax responsibility is that it continues after disbursing the employees' pay, often extending well after an employee leaves the firm. Employers must file mandatory reconciliation reports detailing the amounts they have withheld from employee pay, tracking the employees throughout the company's accounting system, and maintaining the personnel files for both current and terminated employees in accordance with the firm's payroll practices and governmental regulations.

Social Security and Medicare Taxes

The *FICA* taxes, which include both the Social Security and Medicare taxes, are among the statutory withholdings that employees and employers pay. Employees and employers must each contribute 6.2 percent (for a total of 12.4%) of the employee's pay up to the maximum withholding amount for Social Security. Employers must match the employees' payroll

TABLE 6-1

Employee-Paid and Employer-Paid Taxes

Tax	Employee Pays	Employer Pays
Social Security	XX	XX
Medicare	XX	XX
Federal Income Tax	XX	
Federal Unemployment Tax (FUTA)		XX
State Income Tax (where applicable)	XX	
State Unemployment Tax (SUTA)	Sometimes both are responsible at different percentages; see your local taxation authority for specific details.	XX
Local Income Taxes	XX	
Local Occupational Taxes (where applicable)	XX	XX
Workers' Compensation Premiums		XX
401(k)/Pension (if matching policy exists)	XX	XX
Other Voluntary Deductions	XX	

deductions for the Medicare tax in the amount of 1.45 percent (for a total of 2.9%) of the employees' gross pay less applicable deductions. In addition, the Affordable Care Act has mandated an additional 0.9 percent of Medicare tax for employees whose wages exceed $200,000 annually. The employer does not match this additional Medicare tax.

> Due to the COVID-19 outbreak in 2020, remittance of the employer's share of Social Security tax for each employee was changed. Employers were allowed to defer the remittance of their share of Social Security taxes (but not Medicare taxes) due after February 15, 2020. This deferment stipulated that employers had to remit 50 percent of their Social Security tax liability until December 31, 2021. The remainder of the Social Security tax liability needed to be remitted by December 31, 2022. Source: U.S. Congress

Let's look at an example of how the employer's share of the FICA tax works.

EXAMPLE: EMPLOYEE AND EMPLOYER SHARE, SOCIAL SECURITY TAX

Courtney Russo works as an hourly worker who earns an annual salary of $36,000 and is paid biweekly. Her gross pay is $1,384.62 per pay period ($36,000 per year/26 pay periods).

Courtney's share of the Social Security tax:	$1,384.62 × 6.2% = $85.85
Her employer's share of the Social Security tax:	$1,384.62 × 6.2% = $85.85
Total Social Security tax liability for Courtney's pay this period:	$171.70

As shown in the example, the employer and employee contribute the same amounts for the Social Security tax. Remember the Social Security tax has a maximum withholding per year based on the employee's salary, which is $137,700 for 2020. After reaching that maximum, neither the employee nor the employer contributes any more Social Security tax.

EXAMPLE: EMPLOYEE AND EMPLOYER SHARE SOCIAL SECURITY TAXES, HIGHLY COMPENSATED EMPLOYEE

William Perry is the vice president of Sunny Glassworks. His annual salary is $225,000, which is paid semimonthly. His gross pay per period is $9,375.00 ($225,000/24 pay periods). For the 13th pay period of the year, the Social Security tax withholding is as follows:

William's share of the Social Security tax:	$9,375 × 6.2% = $ 581.25
Sunny Glasswork's share of William's Social Security tax:	$9,375 × 6.2% = 581.25
Total Social Security tax liability for William's pay this period:	$1,162.50

After the 14th pay period, William's year-to-date pay is $9,375 × 14 = $131,250. After the 15th pay period, William's year-to-date pay will be $9,375 × 15 = $140,625, which exceeds the Social Security wage base. The amount subject to Social Security tax for the 15th pay period equals the wage base minus the 14th pay period YTD pay:

$137,700 – $131,250 = $6,450 of William's pay during the 15th pay period is included for Social Security tax, which means that he will not be taxed on $2,925.

William's share of the Social Security tax:	$6,450 × 6.2% = $399.90
Sunny Glasswork's share of William's Social Security tax:	$6,450 × 6.2% = 399.90
Total Social Security tax liability for William's pay this period that must be remitted by Sunny Glassworks:	$799.80

Medicare tax, the other piece of the FICA taxes, has no maximum but does have an additional tax for high-wage employees. Let's look at Courtney Russo's pay again to see how the Medicare tax works.

EXAMPLE: EMPLOYEE AND EMPLOYER SHARE, MEDICARE TAXES

Courtney's share of the Medicare tax:	$1,384.62 × 1.45% = $20.08
Her employer's share of the Medicare tax:	$1,384.62 × 1.45% = 20.08
Total Medicare tax liability for Courtney's pay this period that must be remitted by Sunny Glassworks:	$40.16
Total FICA responsibility from Courtney's pay this period ($171.70 + $40.16):	$211.86

Now let's look at the employee and employer share of Medicare taxes for William, who is a highly compensated employee.

EXAMPLE: EMPLOYEE AND EMPLOYER SHARE MEDICARE TAXES, HIGHLY COMPENSATED EMPLOYEE

As of the 22nd pay period of the year, William's YTD pay is $206,250. Amount subject to the additional Medicare tax: $6,250.

Medicare tax amounts:	
William's standard Medicare tax liability:	$9,375 × 1.45% = $135.94
Sunny Glasswork's Medicare tax liability:	$9,375 × 1.45% = 135.94
William's additional Medicare tax liability:	$6,250 × 0.9% = 56.25
Total Medicare tax liability:	$328.13
Total FICA responsibility for William's pay this period:	$328.13

Remember, no Social Security tax applies because William has already exceeded the wage base.

Social Security and Medicare amounts may be listed separately when the company makes its tax deposit. The employer's tax deposit will also include the amount deducted from the employee for federal income tax.

Maintaining accurate records of taxes withheld through payroll registers and employee earnings records is a critical part of calculating proper FICA tax deductions. Whether a company uses a manual system, has an automated system, or outsources the payroll duties, it remains responsible for the accuracy of the deductions and maintenance of associated records.

Federal and State Unemployment Taxes

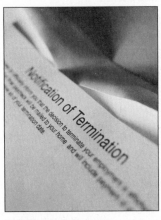

Janis Christie/Getty Images

Another set of employer-paid payroll taxes include those mandated by the Federal Unemployment Tax Act *(FUTA)* and State Unemployment Tax Act *(SUTA).* FUTA and SUTA are unemployment compensation funds established to provide for workers who have lost their jobs. Generally, the rate for FUTA tax is lower than that for SUTA tax because the states govern the disbursement of unemployment funds and because unemployment rates vary by region. FUTA taxes pay for the administrative expenses of the unemployment insurance fund. SUTA tax rates provide a localized and individual focus for employer taxes. The unemployment insurance fund pays for half of the extended unemployment benefits and provides a fund of additional benefits against which states may borrow as necessary to cover unemployment claims. An interesting note is that FUTA and SUTA are employer-only taxes in all *but* three states: Alaska, New Jersey, and Pennsylvania.

FUTA pertains only to U.S. citizens and workers employed by American companies. According to the IRS, to be classified as an American company, an employer must meet the following criteria:

- An individual who is a resident of the United States,
- A partnership, if two-thirds or more of the partners are residents of the United States,
- A trust, if all of the trustees are residents of the United States, or
- A corporation organized under the laws of the United States, of any state, or the District of Columbia.

American citizens who work for companies outside of the United States who are not classified as American employers are not subject to FUTA provisions. Certain resident aliens and professions are exempt from FUTA provisions, as stipulated by Income Tax Regulation §31.3301-1. The professions from which employee compensation is exempt from FUTA provisions are:

- Compensation paid to agricultural workers.
- Compensation paid to household employees unless the compensation exceeds $1,000 during any calendar quarter of the current year or prior year.
- Compensation paid to employees of religious, charitable, educational, or certain other tax-exempt organizations.
- Compensation paid to employees of the U.S. government or any of its agencies.
- Compensation paid to employees of the government of any state of the United States, or any of its political subdivisions.
- Compensation paid to employees of the government of the District of Columbia, or any of its political subdivisions.

The full 2020 rate for FUTA tax is 6.0 percent of the first $7,000 of an employee's wages paid during a calendar year. FUTA is paid by the employer. Employees who move to a different company will have the new employer paying additional FUTA taxes. Therefore, if an employer has a high turnover rate among its employees (i.e., a large number of employees remain employed for only a short period before terminating employment), the firm will pay FUTA tax for all employees for the first $7,000 of earnings, including the ones who remained in their employ for only a short time. FUTA is subject to a 5.4 percent reduction, for which employers may qualify on two conditions:

- Employers make SUTA deposits on time and in full.
- The state is not a credit reduction state.

Due to the COVID-19 outbreak, employers were granted a refundable tax credit of 50 percent of wages paid between April 2, 2020, and December 31, 2020, by certain employers who met the following criteria:

- Operations were suspended, partially or in full, because of the outbreak.
- Gross sales declined 50 percent or more because of the outbreak.*
- Tax-exempt businesses were also eligible for this break.

In addition, a payroll tax credit was extended for businesses that continued to pay wages (up to $10,000 of compensation per employee, including fringe health benefits paid), as follows:

- For businesses with more than 100 employees, compensation for services not provided due to COVID-19 reasons.
- For businesses with fewer than 100 employees, all employee wages qualified for the credit.

* The eligibility for the gross sales tax credit ceased once the business's sales receipts reached 80 percent of the same amount earned during the same quarter of the prior calendar year.

Source: U.S. Congress

With the credit, the employer's FUTA rate will be 0.6 percent on the first $7,000 of every employee's wage. The minimum FUTA tax rate is 0.6 percent, which means that a minimum of $42 ($7,000 × 0.006) may be paid per employee. Note that FUTA tax liability is always reported for the prior year, which means that the FUTA tax liability in 2021 will increase with the first payroll and thus reflect both 2020 and 2021 liability if the 940 has not been filed yet. If the employer makes quarterly deposits, then the full 2020 liability would not be part of the FUTA Tax Payable account in 2021.

EXAMPLE: FUTA TAX COMPUTATION, ALL EMPLOYEES EARNING IN EXCESS OF $7,000

Snowborn Inc. is a company based in Great Falls, Montana. During 2020, the company had 178 employees, all of whom earned in excess of $7,000 in wages and salaries. At the end of the year, only 145 employees remained with the company. The 2020 FUTA tax liability for Snowborn Inc. would be computed as follows:

Number of employees during 2020	Multiplied by the first $7,000 of wages	Multiplied by 0.6% tax rate	FUTA tax liability for 2020
178	$7,000	0.006	$7,476

Note Snowborn Inc. is liable for the FUTA tax on all employees who worked for the company, even if they left employment with the company. The FUTA tax filing is due on January 31, 2021.

What happens when the employees earn less than $7,000 during the calendar year? The employer is still responsible for the FUTA tax on the employees' earnings, but only the amount earned during the calendar year.

EXAMPLE: FUTA TAX, EMPLOYEES WITH EARNINGS LESS THAN $7,000 DURING THE YEAR

Baja Brothers Wines, based in Tucson, Arizona, has 62 employees and the following employee data for FUTA taxes:

Number of employees during 2020	Multiplied by the first $7,000 of wages	Multiplied by 0.6% tax rate	FUTA tax liability for 2020
59	$7,000	0.006	$2,478.00
Employees who earned less than $7,000 during 2020:	**Multiplied by the amount of wages earned in 2019**	**Multiplied by 0.6% tax rate**	
Employee A	$5,894.00	0.006	$ 35.36
Employee B	3,198.00	0.006	19.19
Employee C	975.00	0.006	5.85
		Total FUTA tax	**$2,538.40**

Belterz/iStockphoto

The establishment of the SUTA in each state provided states with the local authority to offer unemployment or jobless benefits. Designed as an unemployment insurance program after the Great Depression of the 1930s, the remittance of SUTA payments follows many of the same procedures as other payroll taxes. As a state-run fund, each state can establish its own qualification requirements for both individual claims and business payments, the wage base for employers in the state, and the tax rate. The SUTA wage base and rate fluctuates among states and can be an incentive for businesses to change operations from one state to another. Note that all states' wage bases exceed the minimum required by the law, but the tax rate is variable.

FUTA Credit Reduction

As we noted, the nominal FUTA tax is 6.0 percent, of which the employer remits 0.6 percent to the federal government. A caveat to this 0.6 percent employer rate involves Title XII advances issued from the federal government to assist with payments of unemployment liabilities. This can occur when a high period of unemployment happens due to layoffs or economic downturns.

In the event a state defaults on its repayment of these federal loans, the credit taken against the 6.0 percent FUTA rate may be reduced. Each year, states have until November 10 to repay the prior year's loan. If the loan remains unpaid for more than one year, the FUTA credit will continue to be reduced in the third and fifth years after the loan is due. An example of the FUTA credit reduction follows.

EXAMPLE: FUTA CREDIT REDUCTION

State Z had a loan taken during 2019 to supplement amounts paid for unemployment insurance liabilities. The balance of that loan would be due on November 10, 2020. If the balance is not paid by that date, the credit against the FUTA rate for the next calendar year would be as follows:

FUTA rate	Standard FUTA rate after credit	FUTA rate after credit reduction
6.0%	0.6%	2.4%

The credit would be reduced further in future years if the loan remains unpaid. The credit reduction is reported by employers on Form 940. For 2020, the FUTA credit reductions only apply to the U.S. Virgin Islands (2.7%). (Source: Paylocity)

State Unemployment Taxes

SUTA is limited to wages collected and the 5.4 percent rate is a guideline. State rates vary based on employee retention and other factors. States examine employee turnover during an established period and determine if employers qualify for a credit against the nominal SUTA rate. Depending upon the state the company is operating in, this limit may be equal to, higher, or lower than the SUTA rate. For example, Alaska's SUTA wage base was $41,500 in 2020. A chart containing the SUTA wage base and rates is shown in Table 6-2.

TABLE 6-2
SUTA Wage Base and Rates 2020

State	Wage Base	Min/Max Rate
Alabama	$ 8,000	0.65%–6.8%
Alaska	$41,500	1.0%–5.4%
Arizona	$ 7,000	0.05%–12.85%
Arkansas	$ 7,000	0.3%–14.2%
California	$ 7,000	1.5%–6.2%
Colorado	$13,600	0.58%–7.40%
Connecticut	$15,000	1.9%–6.8%
Delaware	$16,500	0.3%–8.2%
District of Columbia	$ 9,000	1.6%–7.0%
Florida	$ 7,000	0.1%–5.4%
Georgia	$ 9,500	0.04%–8.1%

(continued)

TABLE 6-2

SUTA Wage Base and Rates 2020 *(concluded)*

State	Wage Base	Min/Max Rate
Hawaii	$48,100	0.0%–5.6%
Idaho	$41,600	0.255%–5.4%
Illinois	$12,740	0.425%–6.875%
Indiana	$ 9,500	0.5%–7.4%
Iowa	$31,600	0.0%–7.5%
Kansas	$14,000	0.0%–7.1%
Kentucky	$10,800	0.225%–8.925%
Louisiana	$ 7,700	0.09%–6.2%
Maine	$12,000	0.6%–5.46%
Maryland	$ 8,500	0.3%–7.5%
Massachusetts	$15,000	0.94%–14.37%
Michigan	$ 9,500	0.06%–10.3%
Minnesota	$35,000	0.2%–9.1%
Mississippi	$ 14,000	0.2%–5.6%
Missouri	$11,500	0.0%–9.45%
Montana	$34,100	0.13%–6.25%
Nebraska	$ 9,000	0.0%–5.4%
Nevada	$32,500	0.3%–5.4%
New Hampshire	$14,000	0.1%–7.0%
New Jersey	$35,300	0.4%–5.4%
New Mexico	$25,800	0.33%–5.4%
New York	$11,600	0.6%–7.9%
North Carolina	$25,200	0.06%–5.76%
North Dakota	$37,900	0.08%–9.69%
Ohio	$ 9,000	0.3%–9.4%
Oklahoma	$18,700	0.1%–5.5%
Oregon	$42,100	0.7%–5.4%
Pennsylvania	$10,000	1.2905%–9.9333%
Rhode Island	$24,000	0.9%–9.4%
South Carolina	$14,000	0.06%–5.46%
South Dakota	$15,000	0.0%–9.35%
Tennessee	$ 7,000	0.01%–10.0%
Texas	$ 9,000	0.31%–6.31%
Utah	$36,600	0.1%–7.1%
Vermont	$16,100	0.8%–6.5%
Virginia	$ 8,000	0.11%–6.21%
Washington	$52,700	0.13%–7.73%
West Virginia	$12,000	1.5%–8.5%
Wisconsin	$14,000	0.0%–12.0%
Wyoming	$26,400	0.18%–8.72%

Sources: American Payroll Association, ADP

An employer's SUTA rate is determined by a mix of state unemployment rates and company experience ratings. The SUTA rate for company A may be different from the rate for company B. For example, a construction company may experience higher unemployment claims because of the seasonal nature and higher risk associated with the industry; therefore, the company's rate may be 4.54 percent, whereas a similar-sized company in a professional services industry may have an unemployment rate of 3.28 percent. States issue letters on an annual basis to companies with the individually determined SUTA rate for the following year.

The first example is a company that has a SUTA rate of 5.4 percent and all employees have earned in excess of $7,000 for the year.

EXAMPLE: FUTA AND SUTA LIABILITY, SUTA = 5.4 PERCENT

JayMac Communications, a California company, has 15 employees, all of whom have met the $7,000 threshold for the FUTA tax. The state portion for which JayMac is liable is 5.4 percent. The unemployment tax obligations are

FUTA:	15 employees × $7,000 × 0.006 = $ 630
SUTA:	15 employees × $7,000 × 0.054 = 5,670
Total unemployment tax liability:	$6,300

The next example is a company in Georgia that has a SUTA rate of 2.3 percent and some employees who have earned less than $7,000 during the year.

EXAMPLE: FUTA AND SUTA LIABILITY, SUTA = 2.3 PERCENT

Charmer Industries of Georgia has 20 employees: 18 employees have met the FUTA and SUTA thresholds, and 2 employees have not, earning $5,400 and $2,500, respectively. The state obligation for Charmer is 2.3 percent owing to a favorable employer rating. Charmer's unemployment taxes would be computed as follows:

FUTA:	18 × $7,000 × 0.006 =	$ 756.00
	($5,400 + $2,500) × 0.006 =	47.40
	Total FUTA liability:	$ 803.40
SUTA:	18 × $9,500 × 0.023 =	$3,933.00
	($5,400 + $2,500) × 0.023 =	181.70
	Total SUTA liability:	$4,114.70
Total unemployment tax liability:		$4,918.10

Tips to Minimize SUTA Taxes

Experience-Rating System
• Know how your company compares to other similar companies in the same industry as far as hiring and retention of employees
Experience Rate Charges
• The employer's account is charged each time a former employee files for unemployment. Be careful to avoid improper use of the account by dumping employees into other states to avoid SUTA taxation
Revew the SUTA Account Regularly
• Ensure that charges to the employer's account are accurate and alert the state unemployment office promptly if inaccuracies occur.

Carefully Select New Employees
• An employee should be assessd prior to hire to ensure that they are an appropriate fit for the company culture and have the needed skills for their job requirements.
Time Temporary or Seasonal Layoffs to Avoid Partial Weeks
• Partial weeks of unemployment can add up to large amounts being charged to the employer's SUTA account.
Employee Separation Review and Documentation
• Maintain documentation about the employee's departure from the company to ensure that they do not improperly claim SUTA benefits.
Former Employees and Retirement
• The offer of retirement with the possibility of rehire can reduce the number of unemployment claims because a retired employee cannot claim unemployment insurance
Use State-Issued Forms if Contesting an Unemployment Claim
• This will make the processing and quicker to ensure accuracy and remediation of any disputes.
Pay SUTA Taxes on Time
• A record of timely SUTA payments adds to the company's experience rating and allows the employer to avoid penalties or other fees.
Use Historical SUTA Reports to Estimate Future Unemployment Charges
• Knowing what to expect ahead of time will help with budgeting, hiring and estimations of future labor costs

Other State and Local Employer-Only Payroll Taxes

Some states have employer-only taxes unique to the area. Delaware, Colorado, Hawaii, and several other states have additional taxes that are remitted under different names. Some examples of these types of taxes include

- Georgia employers pay an administrative assessment of 0.06 percent on employee gross wages with a wage base of $9,500 (2020 figure).
- Maine has an employer-paid Competitive Skills Scholarship Program tax of 0.06 percent.
- In California, employers pay an Employment Training Tax (ETT) of 0.1 percent on all wages up to the first $7,000 of wages.

As a payroll accountant, it is very important to be familiar with the tax withholding and employer responsibilities for each state in which the company has employees residing, even if there is not a business office located there. It is also important to be aware of any forms that are required within the state the company has employees.

Individual counties and cities can also impose occupational taxes on the businesses within their jurisdiction. The reporting periods for the local and city taxes are separate from the filing requirements for federal or state taxes. The payroll accountant must review all tiers of taxes to ensure compliance in collection, submission, and reporting.

Workers' Compensation Insurance

Workers' compensation insurance is another type of employer payroll responsibility. Although it is not considered a tax, states enforce workers' compensation statutes; federal employees are protected by the Federal Employment Compensation Act. Workers' compensation statutes are designed to protect workers who are injured (temporarily or permanently) or killed during the performance of their job-related duties.

Andrey_Popov/Shutterstock

Because workers' compensation is an insurance policy maintained by employers, premiums vary based on employees' job classifications and the risk of injury they typically encounter in the normal course of work. Premium amounts are expressed as amounts per $100 of payroll for each job classification. Premium amounts are estimated based on expected payroll amounts for the coming year and then adjusted at the end of the year once the actual payroll amounts are finalized.

EXAMPLE: WORKERS' COMPENSATION PREMIUM COMPUTATION

Jesse Hildreth is the owner of Eastern Freight Lines. She has three categories of employees: drivers, loaders, and administrative staff. The workers' compensation premium rates are as follows:

- Drivers: $1.45/$100 of payroll
- Loaders: $2.50/$100 of payroll
- Administrative staff: $0.40/$100 of payroll

For 20XX, Eastern Freight Lines payroll is expected to be the following:

Job Classification	Premium per $100 of Payroll	Estimated Payroll	Premium Due Jan. 1
Driver	$1.45	$387,500	$ 5,618.75*
Loader	2.50	435,200	10,880[†]
Administrative Staff	0.40	320,000	1,280[‡]
Total Premium Due, Jan. 1			$ 17,778.75

*($387,500/$100) × $1.45 = $5,618.75
†($435,200/$100) × $2.50 = $10,880
‡($320,000/$100) × $0.40 = $1,280

The 20XX premium is adjusted based on actual payroll. The difference between the paid estimated premium and the premium based on actual payroll results must either be remitted to the insurance company or refunded to the employer. An analysis of the actual payroll as of December 31, 20XX, revealed the following results:

Job Classification	Premium per $100 of Payroll	Actual Payroll	Premium Due Dec. 31
Driver	$1.45	$410,563	$ 5,953.16*
Loader	2.50	478,290	11,957.25[†]
Administrative staff	0.40	338,945	1,355.78[‡]
Total actual premium due December 31			$19,266.19
Less: Premium paid on Jan. 1			17,778.75
Difference to be remitted to the insurance company			$ 1,487.44

*($410,563/$100) × $1.45 = $5,953.16
†($478,290/$100) × $2.50 = $11,957.25
‡($338,945/$100) × $0.40 = $1,355.78

Eastern Freight Lines must remit $1,487.44 to the insurance company due to the difference between the estimated and the actual payroll for 20XX.

Workers' compensation premium rates may also vary based on the employer's safety record. For example, a company with multiple job-related injuries would have a higher premium than another company with few or no injuries. Employer compliance with OSHA guidelines is important to control the cost of workers' compensation insurance.

The majority of workers' compensation insurance claims occur in five main categories of injuries:

1. Sprains and strains.
2. Punctures or cuts.
3. Bruises or other contusions.
4. Inflammation.
5. Fractured bones.

Most work-related injuries can be avoided through employee safety training, attention to the walking and working conditions of the facility, and employer diligence. (Source: Insurance Journal)

FUTA, SUTA, and Workers' Compensation

1. AMS Enterprises in New Mexico has 30 employees. Of these, 25 have exceeded the FUTA and SUTA wage bases. This is the first quarter of the year, and AMS Enterprises has not yet paid FUTA or SUTA taxes for the year. The other five employees' YTD wages are as follows: Employee A, $15,800; Employee B, $7,800; Employee C, $11,115; Employee D, $22,800; Employee E, $2,575. AMS Enterprises receives the full FUTA tax credit and pays a SUTA rate of 4.2 percent (See Table 6-2 for SUTA taxable wage maximum). How much are AMS Enterprises' FUTA and SUTA liabilities?

2. Noodle Noggins of Maine has 12 employees and is eligible for the full FUTA tax credit; the SUTA rate is 3.26 percent. Ten of the 12 employees have exceeded the FUTA wage base. Eight employees have exceeded the SUTA wage base (See Table 6-2 for the SUTA taxable wage maximum). The remaining employees have the following YTD wages: $5,500, $6,800, $11,100, and $9,850. The Competitive Skills Scholarship tax applies to all employees. Noodle's YTD total wages are $279,580. What are the FUTA, SUTA, and Competitive Skills Scholarship tax liabilities for Noodle Noggins?

3. High Flyers Jump School has two classifications of employees: clerical employees and jump instructors. The workers' compensation premium rates are $0.45/$100 for clerical employees and $3.75/$100 for jump instructors. During 20XX, the estimated payroll amounts were $104,550 for clerical employees and $215,690 for jump instructors. How much would the estimated workers' compensation insurance policy cost High Flyers Jump School during 20XX?

Comstock/Getty Images

LO 6-2   Discuss Reporting Periods and Requirements for Employer Tax Deposits

The frequency of depositing federal income tax and FICA taxes depends on the size of the company's payroll. The depositing schedules have nothing to do with a company's pay frequency, although some of the names are similar. The IRS stipulates five different schedules for an employer's deposit of payroll taxes:

*   Annually
*   Quarterly
*   Monthly
*   Semiweekly
*   Next business day

Of these, the most common deposit schedules are monthly and semiweekly. Electronic tax deposits are usually processed through the *Electronic Federal Tax Payment System (EFTPS)* website, although the IRS allows employers to transmit payments through certain financial institutions via *Automated Clearing House (ACH)* or wire transfer. When using the EFTPS, the employer must register with the IRS to access the site. The EFTPS is used for both Form 941 (federal income tax, Social Security tax, and Medicare tax) and the quarterly/annual Form 940 FUTA tax deposit. The website for EFTPS is www.eftps.gov.

Lookback Period

The frequency of each company's deposits is determined through a *lookback period*, which is the amount of payroll taxes an employer has reported in the 12-month period prior to June 30 of the previous year. For example, the lookback period that the IRS would use for 2020 tax deposit frequency would be the period from July 1, 2018, through June 30, 2019. Employers

TABLE 6-3
Lookback Period

Lookback Period for 2020 Taxes			
July 1, 2018, through	October 1, 2018, through	January 1, 2019, through	April 1, 2019, through
September 30, 2018	December 31, 2018	March 31, 2019	June 30, 2019

Source: Internal Revenue Service

receive notification about their deposit requirements in writing from the IRS in October of each year. Table 6-3 shows the lookback period.

During 2020, employer tax remittance dates were extended due to the COVID-19 outbreak as follows:

- Tax payments due by April 15, 2020, were extended to July 15, 2020.
- Returns and payments due by May 15, 2020, were extended to August 15, 2020.

Source: U.S. Congress

Deposit Frequencies

The IRS informs businesses in writing if they need to deposit their payroll taxes annually, monthly, or semiweekly based on the deposits during the lookback period. All new companies are monthly schedule depositors unless they have a total payroll liability in excess of $100,000 during any pay period. It is important to note that the tax deposit due date is based on the payroll disbursement date, not the pay period ending date. For example, if a company's pay period ended on June 28, but the payroll was not disbursed until July 1, the payroll tax deposit date would be based on the July 1 disbursement. Table 6-4 outlines the criteria for differences among deposit frequencies.

EXAMPLE: MONTHLY SCHEDULE DEPOSITOR

Generational Coffee is a company based in Wenatchee, Washington. During the lookback period ending June 30, 2019, the company had **$36,549** in total payroll tax liability. Generational Coffee would be a *monthly* schedule depositor. Payroll tax deposits would be due on the 15th of the following month (e.g., June 15 for May payroll taxes).

TABLE 6-4
Criteria for Deposit Frequencies

Frequency	Criteria	Due Date
Annually	$2,500 or less in employment taxes to be remitted annually with Form 944.	January 31 of the following year.
Quarterly	For any amounts not deposited during the quarter that may be due to rounding errors or other undeposited amounts.	15th of the month following the end of the quarter.
Monthly	$50,000 or less in payroll tax liability during the lookback period. The amount of total tax liability is also found on Form 941, line 10. All new businesses are monthly schedule depositors unless they accrue in excess of $100,000 in payroll taxes for any pay period. (See the Next Business Day rule frequency.)	15th of the month following the month during which the company accrued payroll tax deposits. For example, taxes on March payroll would be due on **April 15,** or the next business day if April 15 falls on a weekend or a holiday.
Semiweekly	More than $50,000 in payroll tax liability during the lookback period. The amount of total tax liability is also found on Form 941, line 10. The exception to the semiweekly deposit schedule is the Next Business Day rule.	For payroll paid on a Wednesday, Thursday, or Friday, the payroll tax deposit is due by the following **Wednesday.** For payroll paid on a Saturday, Sunday, Monday, or Tuesday, the payroll tax is due by the following **Friday.**
Next business day	$100,000 or more in payroll tax liability for any payroll period.	The payroll tax deposit is due on the **next business day.**

Notice the amount of total payroll tax for Generational Coffee. Because the total amount was less than $50,000, it is classified as a monthly schedule payroll tax depositor, and due dates are the 15th of the following month.

EXAMPLE: SEMIWEEKLY SCHEDULE DEPOSITOR

Pollak Woolens is a company based in Sault Ste. Marie, Michigan. During the look-back period ending June 30, 2019, it had **$75,984** in total payroll tax liability. Pollak Woolens would be a semiweekly schedule depositor. Depending on the payroll date, tax deposits are due on either the Wednesday or the Friday following the payroll date.

Notice the total tax liability during the lookback period. For Pollak Woolens, the amount exceeded $50,000 but is less than $100,000; this makes it a semiweekly schedule depositor. Because payroll tax deposits for semiweekly depositors are driven by the day of the week upon which payroll was paid, deposits may be due either on Wednesday or on Friday. For companies with a biweekly payroll frequency, the tax deposit date may remain the same with few exceptions due to holidays. For companies with semimonthly payroll frequencies, the day of the tax deposit will likely vary.

EXAMPLE: NEXT BUSINESS DAY DEPOSITOR

Cornell Companies, based in Ohio, is a semiweekly schedule payroll tax depositor because of the total payroll tax liability of $693,259 during the lookback period ending June 30, 2019. The company had a total payroll tax liability of **$110,290** during the August 21, 2020, payroll period. August 21 is a Friday, so the payroll deposit would be due on Monday, August 24 because it exceeds $100,000.

In this example, Cornell Companies is already a semiweekly schedule depositor because of its payroll tax liability during the lookback period. Because the company's tax liability exceeds $100,000 for the payroll period, Cornell Companies must deposit those payroll taxes by the next business day.

EXAMPLE: ANNUAL SCHEDULE DEPOSITOR

Wallflower Guitars is based in Ocean Springs, Mississippi. During the lookback period ending June 30, 2019, the company had a total payroll tax liability of $2,154. The payroll tax deposit schedule for Wallflower Guitars would be annual because of the small amount of total tax liability. As long as the total payroll tax liability remains less than $2,500 during 2020, the company may deposit its payroll taxes with its annual payroll tax return.

In this example, Wallflower Guitars has a very small payroll tax liability. It should be noted *annual schedule depositors* are assumed to have a very small tax liability. If the company's payroll tax liability grows during the calendar year, the schedule depositors should be mindful of the monthly schedule deposit rules. However, the company will not become a monthly schedule depositor until notified in writing by the IRS.

Reporting Periods

1. Perry Plastics had $46,986 in payroll taxes during the lookback period. How often must the company deposit its payroll taxes?

2. For Perry Plastics, when is the deposit for June payroll taxes due?

3. Charlie's Kitchens has a payroll tax liability of $126,463 on its Friday payroll. When is the payroll tax deposit due?

LO 6-3 Prepare Mid-Year and Year-End Employer Tax Reporting and Deposits

A. and I. Kruk/Shutterstock

Companies and payroll accountants are responsible for the timely filing of the various tax documents required by governmental authorities. Note the dates for depositing and reporting taxes are not always the same. For example, an employer may be required to file payroll tax deposits through the EFTPS on a daily, semiweekly, or monthly basis, depending upon their payroll tax liability during the lookback period. However, that same employer would not be required to file tax forms until after the end of the quarter. Like personal tax reporting, business reporting of statutory tax obligations has specific forms that employers must use. The most common forms used to deposit federal income tax and FICA taxes are Forms 941 (quarterly) and 944 (annual). An additional form used by agricultural businesses is Form 943, which serves the same purpose as Form 941.

Form 941

Monthly payroll tax depositors file *Form 941* (see Figure 6-1), which is the employer's quarterly report of taxes deposited and taxes due. The form is used to reconcile the firm's deposits with the tax liability derived through mathematical computations on the form. It is common to encounter minor adjustments during the process of completing the form owing to rounding differences incurred during monthly tax deposits. Form 941 has specific instructions for its completion, as shown in Table 6-5.

Schedule B

Semiweekly depositors must file Schedule B (Figure 6-2) in addition to Form 941. This form allows firms to enter the details of payroll tax liabilities that occur multiple times during a month. On *Schedule B*, the payroll tax liability is entered on the days of the month on which the payroll occurred. The total tax liability for each month is entered in the right column. The total tax liability for the quarter must equal line 10 of Form 941.

EXAMPLE: PAYROLL TAX LIABILITY

Nicholas Lindeman is the owner of a company that pays its employees on the 15th and the last day of the month. All employees are salaried, exempt workers. Pay dates that fall on the weekend are paid on the preceding Friday. According to the lookback period, the company is required to deposit payroll taxes on a semiweekly basis. Because Lindeman is a semiweekly schedule depositor, he must file Schedule B in addition to Form 941. For the first quarter of 2020, Lindeman's company had the following pay dates and payroll tax liabilities:

Pay Date	Payroll Tax Liability
January 15	$ 41,486.47
January 31	41,486.47
February 14	41,486.47
February 28	41,486.47
March 13	41,486.47
March 31	41,486.47
Total Tax Liability for the Quarter	$248,918.82

Note that the payroll tax liability is (a) listed on the payroll date and (b) includes the FICA taxes (employee and employer share) and the federal income tax withheld.

TABLE 6-5
Instructions for Completing Form 941

Part 1: Data for Chalmette Company

Susan Wagner is the President of Chalmette Company, EIN 67-3983240, located at 572 Rue Bon Temps, New Orleans, Louisiana, 70116. The company's phone number is 504-555-2039. The following Form 941 is for the second quarter of the year.

Name	Gross Earning	Taxable Wages for Federal W/H	Taxable Wages for FICA	Taxable Wages for FUTA	Total Federal W/H	Total Social Security Tax	Total Medicare W/H	FUTA Tax	SUTA Tax	Net Pay
YTD Totals	$128,356.74	$128,356.74	$94,569.00	$84,000.00	$18,432.50	$11,726.56	$2,742.50	$504.00	$5,106.73	
Line # on Form 941		2	5a & 5c		3	5a	5c			

Line 1: The number of employees during the quarter reported, as indicated in the box in the upper right-hand corner.
Line 2: Total wages subject to federal income tax (less pre-tax deductions) for the quarter.
Line 3: Federal income tax withheld from wages paid during the quarter.
Line 4: Check the box only if no wages paid during the quarter were subject to taxes. (This is uncommon.)
Lines 5a–5d: Column 1 is for the wages and tips subject to Social Security and Medicare taxes; column 2 is the amount of wages multiplied by the tax percent specified on the form.
Line 5e: Total of column 2, lines 5a–5d.
Line 5f: Tax on unreported tips.
Line 6: Total taxes due before adjustments.
Lines 7–9: Quarterly tax adjustments.
Line 10: Total tax less adjustments: line 6 minus lines 7, 8, and 9.
Line 11: Qualified business tax credit for research activities
Line 12: Total taxes due, after adjustments and credits
Line 13: Total taxes deposited during the quarter.
Line 14: Balance due.
Line 15: Overpayment.

Part 2:

Check the first box if the tax liability for the quarter is less than $2,500.
OR
Check the second box if the tax liability is greater than $2,500 and enter the taxes deposited each month during the quarter.
The total deposits must equal the total liability in Part 1.
If the business is a semiweekly depositor, then Schedule B must be completed.

FIGURE 6-1
Form 941

Form **941 for 2019:** Employer's QUARTERLY Federal Tax Return

950117

(Rev. January 2020)

Department of the Treasury — Internal Revenue Service

OMB No. 1545-0029

Employer identification number (EIN) 6 7 – 3 9 8 3 2 4 0

Name *(not your trade name)* Susan Wagner

Trade name *(if any)* Chalmette Company

Address 572 Rue Bon Temps
Number / Street / Suite or room number

New Orleans | LA | 70116
City / State / ZIP code

Foreign country name / Foreign province/county / Foreign postal code

Report for this Quarter of 2019
(Check one.)

☐ 1: January, February, March

☒ 2: April, May, June

☐ 3: July, August, September

☐ 4: October, November, December

Go to *www.irs.gov/Form941* for instructions and the latest information.

Read the separate instructions before you complete Form 941. Type or print within the boxes.

Part 1:	**Answer these questions for this quarter.**

1 Number of employees who received wages, tips, or other compensation for the pay period including: *Mar. 12* (Quarter 1), *June 12* (Quarter 2), *Sept. 12* (Quarter 3), or *Dec. 12* (Quarter 4) **1** | 12

2 Wages, tips, and other compensation . . . . **2** | 128356 . 74

3 Federal income tax withheld from wages, tips, and other compensation . . . . **3** | 18432 . 50

4 If no wages, tips, and other compensation are subject to social security or Medicare tax ☐ Check and go to line 6.

	Column 1		Column 2
5a Taxable social security wages . .	94569 . 00	× 0.124 =	11726 . 56
5b Taxable social security tips . . .	.	× 0.124 =	.
5c Taxable Medicare wages & tips. .	94569 . 00	× 0.029 =	2742 . 50
5d Taxable wages & tips subject to Additional Medicare Tax withholding	.	× 0.009 =	.

5e Add Column 2 from lines 5a, 5b, 5c, and 5d . . . . **5e** | 14469 . 06

5f Section 3121(q) Notice and Demand—Tax due on unreported tips (see instructions) . . . **5f** | .

6 Total taxes before adjustments. Add lines 3, 5e, and 5f . . . . **6** | 32901 . 56

7 Current quarter's adjustment for fractions of cents . . . . **7** | . 01

8 Current quarter's adjustment for sick pay . . . . **8** |

9 Current quarter's adjustments for tips and group-term life insurance . . . **9** |

10 Total taxes after adjustments. Combine lines 6 through 9 . . . . **10** | 32901 . 57

11 Qualified small business payroll tax credit for increasing research activities. Attach Form 8974 **11** | .

12 Total taxes after adjustments and credits. Subtract line 11 from line 10 . . . . . . **12** | 32901 . 57

13 Total deposits for this quarter, including overpayment applied from a prior quarter and overpayments applied from Form 941-X, 941-X (PR), 944-X, or 944-X (SP) filed in the current quarter **13** | 32901 . 57

14 Balance due. If line 12 is more than line 13, enter the difference and see instructions . . . **14** | .

15 Overpayment. If line 13 is more than line 12, enter the difference | . | Check one: ☐ Apply to next return. ☐ Send a refund.

▶ **You MUST complete both pages of Form 941 and SIGN it.**

Next ▶

For Privacy Act and Paperwork Reduction Act Notice, see the back of the Payment Voucher.   Cat. No. 17001Z   Form **941** (Rev. 1-2020)

950217

Name *(not your trade name)*	Employer identification number (EIN)
Susan Wagner	67-3983240

Part 2:   Tell us about your deposit schedule and tax liability for this quarter.

If you are unsure about whether you are a monthly schedule depositor or a semiweekly schedule depositor, see section 11 of Pub. 15.

16   Check one: ☐   Line 12 on this return is less than $2,500 or line 12 on the return for the prior quarter was less than $2,500, and you didn't incur a $100,000 next-day deposit obligation during the current quarter. If line 12 for the prior quarter was less than $2,500 but line 12 on this return is $100,000 or more, you must provide a record of your federal tax liability. If you are a monthly schedule depositor, complete the deposit schedule below; if you are a semiweekly schedule depositor, attach Schedule B (Form 941). Go to Part 3.

☒   **You were a monthly schedule depositor for the entire quarter.** Enter your tax liability for each month and total liability for the quarter, then go to Part 3.

Tax liability:	Month 1	10967. 19
	Month 2	10967. 19
	Month 3	10967. 19
	Total liability for quarter	32901. 57 **Total must equal line 12.**

☐   **You were a semiweekly schedule depositor for any part of this quarter.** Complete Schedule B (Form 941), Report of Tax Liability for Semiweekly Schedule Depositors, and attach it to Form 941.

Part 3:   Tell us about your business. If a question does NOT apply to your business, leave it blank.

17   If your business has closed or you stopped paying wages . . . . ☐ Check here, and

enter the final date you paid wages   [/   /   ] .

18   If you are a seasonal employer and you don't have to file a return for every quarter of the year   . . ☐ Check here.

Part 4:   May we speak with your third-party designee?

Do you want to allow an employee, a paid tax preparer, or another person to discuss this return with the IRS? See the instructions for details.

☐ Yes. Designee's name and phone number   [   ]   [   ]

Select a 5-digit Personal Identification Number (PIN) to use when talking to the IRS.   ☐ ☐ ☐ ☐ ☐

☒ No.

Part 5:   Sign here. You MUST complete both pages of Form 941 and SIGN it.

Under penalties of perjury, I declare that I have examined this return, including accompanying schedules and statements, and to the best of my knowledge and belief, it is true, correct, and complete. Declaration of preparer (other than taxpayer) is based on all information of which preparer has any knowledge.

✗ Sign your name here *Susan Wagner*	Print your name here	Susan Wagner
	Print your title here	President
Date 7/13/2020	Best daytime phone	504-555-2039

Paid Preparer Use Only   Check if you are self-employed . . . ☐

Preparer's name		PTIN	
Preparer's signature		Date	/ /
Firm's name (or yours if self-employed)		EIN	
Address		Phone	
City		State	ZIP code	

FIGURE 6-2
Schedule B for Form 941

Schedule B (Form 941):

Report of Tax Liability for Semiweekly Schedule Depositors

(Rev. January 2017)   Department of the Treasury — Internal Revenue Service

960311

OMB No. 1545-0029

Employer identification number (EIN) 1 3 – 2 5 6 9 9 0 4

Name *(not your trade name)* Nicholas Lindeman

Calendar year 2 0 2 0   (Also check quarter)

Report for this Quarter...
(Check one.)

[X] 1: January, February, March

[ ] 2: April, May, June

[ ] 3: July, August, September

[ ] 4: October, November, December

Use this schedule to show your TAX LIABILITY for the quarter; don't use it to show your deposits. When you file this form with Form 941 or Form 941-SS, don't change your tax liability by adjustments reported on any Forms 941-X or 944-X. You must fill out this form and attach it to Form 941 or Form 941-SS if you're a semiweekly schedule depositor or became one because your accumulated tax liability on any day was $100,000 or more. Write your daily tax liability on the numbered space that corresponds to the date wages were paid. See Section 11 in Pub. 15 for details.

Month 1

#		#		#		#		Tax liability for Month 1
1		9		17		25		
2		10		18		26		82972 . 94
3		11		19		27		
4		12		20		28		
5		13		21		29		
6		14		22		30		
7		15	41486 . 47	23		31	41486 . 47	
8		16		24				

Month 2

#		#		#		#		Tax liability for Month 2
1		9		17		25		
2		10		18		26		82972 . 94
3		11		19		27		
4		12		20		28	41486 . 47	
5		13		21		29		
6		14		22		30		
7		15	41486 . 47	23		31		
8		16		24				

Month 3

#		#		#		#		Tax liability for Month 3
1		9		17		25		
2		10		18		26		82972 . 94
3		11		19		27		
4		12		20		28		
5		13		21		29	41486 . 47	
6		14		22		30		
7		15	41486 . 47	23		31		
8		16		24				

Fill in your total liability for the quarter (Month 1 + Month 2 + Month 3) ▶
Total must equal line 12 on Form 941 or Form 941-SS.

Total liability for the quarter

248918 . 82

For Paperwork Reduction Act Notice, see separate instructions.   IRS.gov/form941   Cat. No. 11967Q   Schedule B (Form 941) (Rev. 1-2017)

Source: Internal Revenue Service

State Tax Remittance

Each state that charges income tax has its own form that it uses for employee income *tax remittance* purposes. State tax forms are similar to federal forms as far as the information included is concerned and generally have similar due dates. An important note is that each state has its own unique taxes. For example, California has an employee-only State Disability Insurance (SDI) tax of 1.0 percent on earnings up to $122,909 per employee (2020 figure), as well as an employer-only Employment Training Tax (ETT) of 0.1 percent on the first $7,000 of each employee's earnings. These additional taxes are included on the state's payroll tax return. Figure 6-3 Contains an example of a completed California quarterly tax return.

Additionally, employers are responsible for reporting any other local or regional taxes. Employers must abide by the filing requirements for each of the taxes or face fines or penalties depending upon state/local tax code. The purpose of these taxes can include the provision of social services and the funding of infrastructure costs. The Denver Head Tax was designed to fulfill both of these purposes in response to the increase of infrastructure and the availability of municipal programs for residents. An example of the Denver Occupational Privilege Tax Return quarterly form is located in Figure 6-4.

Form 944

Firms with a total annual tax liability of less than $2,500 use *Form 944* (see Figure 6-5). Like Form 941, the firm enters the details of wages paid and computes the taxes due. The firm reports the monthly deposits and liabilities in Part 2. However, instead of entering a quarterly liability, the firm enters the annual liability, which is the sum of all the monthly liabilities. The IRS must notify a company in writing of the requirement to file Form 944 prior to its use.

EXAMPLE: FORM 944

Sophie Jennings owns Forest Dog Walkers. Forest Dog Walkers is a sole proprietorship with one part-time employee who works only five months of the year. The IRS has notified Ms. Jennings that Forest Dog Walkers is required to report federal payroll tax liabilities using Form 944. The total wages paid to the employee during 2019 were $8,952.20. The federal income tax liability was $800, and the total payroll tax liability for the year was $2,169.98. Because the total annual payroll tax liability is less than $2,500, Forest Dog Walkers must file an annual return. The due date for Form 944 is January 31 of the following year.

Unemployment Tax Reporting

Form 940 is the employer's annual report of federal unemployment taxes due, based on employee wages paid during the year. This report is for a calendar year and is due by January 31 of the following year.

According to 26 IRC Section 3306, certain fringe benefits are not subject to federal unemployment taxes because they represent non-cash compensation that is not intended to be used as disposable income. Specific examples of these fringe benefits are employer contributions to employee retirement plans, such as the 401(k) and 403(b), and payments for benefits excluded under qualified Section 125 cafeteria plans.

EXAMPLE: EMPLOYER CONTRIBUTIONS TO RETIREMENT PLANS

Winterguard Products offers its employees a matching 401(k) contribution of 0.5 percent for each 1 percent of salary that the employee contributes. During 2019, Susanna Stark, an employee of Winterguard Products, contributed 4 percent of her $36,500 annual salary to her 401(k) plan.

Susanna's contribution	$36,500 × 0.04 =	$1,460.00
Winterguard's contribution match	Half of the employee's contribution =	730.00
Amount exempt from FUTA tax		$ 730.00

The $730 would be listed on line 4 of Form 940 as an amount exempt from FUTA taxes.

FIGURE 6-3

Example of Completed California Quarterly Contribution Return and Report of Wages

EDD Employment Development Department
State of California

QUARTERLY CONTRIBUTION RETURN AND REPORT OF WAGES

REMINDER: File your DE 9 and DE 9C together.

00090112

PLEASE TYPE THIS FORM—DO NOT ALTER PREPRINTED INFORMATION

QUARTER ENDED 09/30/2020	DUE 10/15/2020	DELINQUENT IF NOT POSTMARKED OR RECEIVED BY 10/15/2020

YR **20**   QTR **3**

EMPLOYER ACCOUNT NO. 392-1002-3

Four Mountains Inn
19283 Aracita Boulevard
Jackson, California 94453

DO NOT ALTER THIS AREA

DEPT. USE ONLY

P1   P2   C   P   U   S   A

T

EFFECTIVE DATE   Mo.   Day   Yr.

FEIN 58-3020493

A. NO WAGES PAID THIS QUARTER ☐

B. OUT OF BUSINESS/NO EMPLOYEES ☐

B1. OUT OF BUSINESS DATE   M M D D Y Y Y Y

ADDITIONAL FEINS

C. TOTAL SUBJECT WAGES PAID THIS QUARTER 48,394.78

D. UNEMPLOYMENT INSURANCE (UI) (Total Employee Wages up to $ per employee per calendar year)

(D1) UI Rate %	(D2) UI TAXABLE WAGES FOR THE QUARTER	(D3) UI CONTRIBUTIONS
3.8 TIMES	19,840.62 =	753.94

E. EMPLOYMENT TRAINING TAX (ETT)

(E1) ETT Rate %		(E2) ETT CONTRIBUTIONS
0.1 TIMES	UI Taxable Wages for the Quarter (D2) ...... =	19.84

F. STATE DISABILITY INSURANCE (SDI) (Total Employee Wages up to $ per employee per calendar year)

(F1) SDI Rate %	(F2) SDI TAXABLE WAGES FOR THE QUARTER	(F3) SDI EMPLOYEE CONTRIBUTIONS WITHHELD
1 TIMES	19,840.62 =	198.41

G. CALIFORNIA PERSONAL INCOME TAX (PIT) WITHHELD 3,275.29

H. SUBTOTAL (Add Items D3, E2, F3, and G) 4,247.48

I. LESS: CONTRIBUTIONS AND WITHHOLDINGS PAID FOR THE QUARTER 0.00
(**DO NOT** INCLUDE PENALTY AND INTEREST PAYMENTS)

J. TOTAL TAXES DUE OR OVERPAID   (Item H minus Item I) 4,247.48

If amount due, prepare a *Payroll Tax Deposit* (DE 88), include the correct payment quarter, and mail to: Employment Development Department, P.O. Box 826276, Sacramento, CA 94230-6276. **NOTE:** Do not mail payments along with the DE 9 and *Quarterly Contribution Return and Report of Wages (Continuation)* (DE 9C), as this may delay processing and result in erroneous penalty and interest charges. **Mandatory Electronic Funds Transfer (EFT)** filers must remit all SDI/PIT deposits by EFT to avoid a noncompliance penalty.

K. I declare that the above, to the best of my knowledge and belief, is true and correct. If a refund was claimed, a reasonable effort was made to refund any erroneous deductions to the affected employee(s).

Signature *Benjamin Blanco*   Title Owner   Phone (530) 2931004   Date 10/14/2020
(Owner, Accountant, Preparer, etc.)

SIGN AND MAIL TO: State of California / Employment Development Department / P.O. Box 989071 / West Sacramento CA 95798-9071

DE 9 Rev. 1 (1-12) **(INTERNET)**   Page 1 of 2   Fast, Easy, and Convenient!
Visit EDD's Web site at **www.edd.ca.gov**

Sources: American Payroll Association, ADP

FIGURE 6-4
Example of a Denver Occupational Privilege Tax Return

Denver Occupational Privilege Tax Return
Quarterly

City and County of Denver
Department of Finance, Treasury Division
P.O. Box 660859
Dallas, TX 75266-0859
www.DenverGov.org/eBizTax

Business Name	Account Number	Phone Number
Mile High Gifts	203-1495010	303-555-8883

Primary Business Location	Period End Date
6637 16th Avenue, Denver, Colorado	3/31/2020

▶ YOU <u>MUST</u> FILE A RETURN EVEN IF YOU HAVE DETERMINED NO TAX IS DUE
▶ IMPORTANT INFORMATION IS ON THE BACK

If the number of employees for which the business is liable (Line 2) is different from the number of employees from whom the tax was withheld (Line 3) or if no tax is due, you must attach an explanation.

I. BUSINESS OCCUPATIONAL PRIVILEGE TAX

Line 1. Enter the number of self-employed individuals, owners, partners or managers. Multiply this number by $4.00 and enter the total.

NOTE: This line is for self-employed proprietors, partners, or managers of the business. There is no minimum level of monthly earnings required for self-employed proprietors, partners, or managers to be liable.

NOTE: All businesses located in Denver or performing work in Denver, regardless of the length or duration, are required to pay the minimum $4.00 Business Occupational Privilege Tax (OPT) for each month even when there are no taxable employees.

Line 2. Enter the number of employees for which the business is liable. Multiply this number by $4.00 and enter the total.

Liable employees are those who worked all or part of their time in Denver and received gross compensation of at least $500 for the month for services performed in Denver. Include all qualifying employees, even if some have another employer that is withholding this tax. The business is still liable for the business portion if the compensation was $500 or more. In the case of corporations for purposes of this tax, everyone, including all corporate officers, are considered employees.

II. EMPLOYEE OCCUPATIONAL PRIVILEGE TAX

Line 3. Enter the number of employees liable for this tax. Multiply this number by $5.75 and enter the total.

This line is for all employees who received gross compensation of at least $500 for the month for services performed in Denver. Corporations under the Business OPT ordinance are considered to only have employees, not owners. Therefore all corporate officers meeting the earnings requirement in Denver, should be included here. If any employee has another employer who is withholding this tax, Form TD-269 must be furnished to the secondary employer verifying the primary employer is withholding the tax.

Line 4a. If the return is filed or paid after the due date, enter 15% of Line 4, or $25.00, whichever is greater.

Line 4b. If the return is filed or paid after the due date enter 1% of Line 4 for each month or part of a month past due.

Line 5. Add Line 3, Line 4a, Line 4b. Enter the total. This is the total amount owed. Include a check or money order made payable to **Manager of Finance.**

RETURN LOWER PORTION - DETACH HERE

☐ CHECK HERE IF THIS IS AN AMENDED RETURN   **DENVER OCCUPATIONAL PRIVILEGE TAX RETURN**

ACCOUNT NUMBER	TaxType	Period End	Due Date	Media #
203-1495010	Occupational Privilege Tax	3/31	4/15	000000000005

000000000005

NAME
PRIMARY BUSINESS LOCATION 6637 16th Avenue, Denver, Colorado

I hereby certify, under penalty of perjury, that the statements made herein are to the best of my knowledge true and correct.

Signature (Required) *Kira Gardner*	Title	President	Date	4/3/2020

BUSINESS OCCUPATIONAL PRIVILEGE TAX

1 Enter the number of liable self-employed individuals, owners, partners or managers for each month, add across and enter the total.

Month 1	Month 2	Month 3	Total			
1	1	1	1	Multiply Total by $4.00	4	00

2 Enter the number of employees the business is liable for each month, add across and enter total.

Month 1	Month 2	Month 3	Total			
5	5	5	5	Multiply Total by $4.00	20	00

EMPLOYEE OCCUPATIONAL PRIVILEGE TAX

3 Enter the number of liable employees for each month, add across and enter total.

Month 1	Month 2	Month 3	Total			
5	5	5	5	Multiply Total by $5.75	28	75

4 Total Tax: Add Lines 1, 2 and 3

	52	75

5 Late Filing - if return is filed after the due date - Add:

a Penalty: the greater of 15% of Line 4 or $25.00

b Interest: 1% of Line 4 for each month that the return is late

6 TOTAL DUE AND PAYABLE: Add Line 4, 5a, 5b. This is the total due. Include a check or money order payable to **MANAGER OF FINANCE**

	52	75

0000000000005000000000005

FIGURE 6-5
Form 944

Form **944 for 2019:** **Employer's ANNUAL Federal Tax Return**
Department of the Treasury — Internal Revenue Service

OMB No. 1545-2007

Employer identification number (EIN) | 3 | 2 | – | 9 | 8 | 7 | 0 | 9 | 8 | 0

Name *(not your trade name)* | Sophie Jennings

Trade name *(if any)* | Forest Dog Walkers

Address | 403 Lake Road

| Number | Street | Suite or room number |

| Rouse Point | NY | 12809 |
| City | State | ZIP code |

| Foreign country name | Foreign province/county | Foreign postal code |

Who Must File Form 944

You must file annual Form 944 instead of filing quarterly Forms 941 **only if the IRS notified you in writing.**

Go to *www.irs.gov/Form944* for instructions and the latest information.

Read the separate instructions before you complete Form 944. Type or print within the boxes.

Part 1: Answer these questions for this year. Employers in American Samoa, Guam, the Commonwealth of the Northern Mariana Islands, the U.S. Virgin Islands, and Puerto Rico can skip lines 1 and 2, unless you have employees who are subject to U.S. income tax withholding.

1 Wages, tips, and other compensation . . . . | 1 | 2380 ▪ 78

2 Federal income tax withheld from wages, tips, and other compensation . . . . . . | 2 | 274 ▪ 00

3 If no wages, tips, and other compensation are subject to social security or Medicare tax | 3 ☐ Check and go to line 5.

4 Taxable social security and Medicare wages and tips:

	Column 1		Column 2	
4a Taxable social security wages	2380 ▪ 78	× 0.124 =	295 ▪ 22	
4b Taxable social security tips	▪	× 0.124 =	▪	
4c Taxable Medicare wages & tips	2380 ▪ 78	× 0.029 =	69 ▪ 04	
4d Taxable wages & tips subject to Additional Medicare Tax withholding	▪	× 0.009 =	▪	

4e Add Column 2 from lines 4a, 4b, 4c, and 4d . . . . | 4e | 364 ▪ 26

5 Total taxes before adjustments. Add lines 2 and 4e . . . . | 5 | 638 ▪ 26

6 Current year's adjustments (see instructions) . . . . | 6 | ▪

7 Total taxes after adjustments. Combine lines 5 and 6 . . . . | 7 | 638 ▪ 26

8 Qualified small business payroll tax credit for increasing research activities. Attach Form 8974 | 8 | ▪

9 Total taxes after adjustments and credits. Subtract line 8 from line 7 . . . . | 9 | 638 ▪ 26

10 Total deposits for this year, including overpayment applied from a prior year and overpayments applied from Form 944-X, 944-X (SP), 941-X, or 941-X (PR) . . . . . . | 10 | ▪

11 Balance due. If line 9 is more than line 10, enter the difference and see instructions . . . | 11 | ▪

12 Overpayment. If line 10 is more than line 9, enter the difference | ▪ | Check one: ☐ Apply to next return. ☐ Send a refund.

▶ **You MUST complete both pages of Form 944 and SIGN it.**

Next ▶

For Privacy Act and Paperwork Reduction Act Notice, see the back of the Payment Voucher. | Cat. No. 39316N | Form **944** (2019)

Note that a company that files Form 944 has the opportunity to remit payroll taxes using Form 944-V, payment voucher.

Name *(not your trade name)*	Employer identification number (EIN)
Sophie Jennings	32-9870980

Part 2: Tell us about your deposit schedule and tax liability for this year.

13 Check one: [X] **Line 9 is less than $2,500. Go to Part 3.**

[ ] Line 9 is $2,500 or more. Enter your tax liability for each month. If you're a semiweekly depositor or you became one because you accumulated $100,000 or more of liability on any day during a deposit period, you must complete Form 945-A instead of the boxes below.

	Jan.		Apr.		July		Oct.
13a	.	13d	.	13g	.	13j	.

	Feb.		May		Aug.		Nov.
13b	.	13e	.	13h	.	13k	.

	Mar.		June		Sept.		Dec.
13c	.	13f	.	13i	.	13l	.

Total liability for year. Add lines 13a through 13l. Total must equal line 9. 13m ____ .

Part 3: Tell us about your business. If question 14 does NOT apply to your business, leave it blank.

14 If your business has closed or you stopped paying wages...

[ ] Check here and enter the final date you paid wages. ____

Part 4: May we speak with your third-party designee?

Do you want to allow an employee, a paid tax preparer, or another person to discuss this return with the IRS? See the instructions for details.

[ ] Yes. Designee's name and phone number ____

Select a 5-digit Personal Identification Number (PIN) to use when talking to the IRS. [ ][ ][ ][ ][ ]

[X] No.

Part 5: Sign here. You MUST complete both pages of Form 944 and SIGN it.

Under penalties of perjury, I declare that I have examined this return, including accompanying schedules and statements, and to the best of my knowledge and belief, it is true, correct, and complete. Declaration of preparer (other than taxpayer) is based on all information of which preparer has any knowledge.

X Sign your name here *Sophie Jennings*

Date ____

Print your name here Sophie Jennings

Print your title here Owner

Best daytime phone 518-555-4395

Paid Preparer Use Only   Check if you're self-employed [ ]

Preparer's name		PTIN	
Preparer's signature		Date	
Firm's name (or yours if self-employed)		EIN	
Address		Phone	
City		State	ZIP code	

Page **2**   Form **944** (2019)

Detach Here and Mail With Your Payment and Form 944.

- -

Form **944-V**	**Payment Voucher**	OMB No. 1545-2007
Department of the Treasury Internal Revenue Service	▶ **Don't staple this voucher or your payment to Form 944.**	20**19**

1 Enter your employer identification number (EIN).	2 **Enter the amount of your payment.** ▶ Make your check or money order payable to "**United States Treasury**"	Dollars	Cents
32-9870980		638	26

3 Enter your business name (individual name if sole proprietor).

Forest Dog Walkers

Enter your address.

403 Lake Road

Enter your city, state, and ZIP code; or your city, foreign country name, foreign province/county, and foreign postal code.

Rouse Point, NY 12809

Source: Internal Revenue Service

Fringe benefits that may be exempt from FUTA taxes are those excluded from cafeteria plans, such as the ones in the following example:

EXAMPLE: EXCLUDED FRINGE BENEFITS NOT SUBJECT TO FUTA TAXES

Hutcheson Medical Products offers its employees the following fringe benefits:

Benefit	Annual Value	Amount Paid During the Calendar Year
Adoption assistance	$5,000 per employee	$15,000.00
Achievement awards	$250 per employee	10,000.00
Meals	$300 per employee	15,000.00
Total annual value of excluded fringe benefits		$40,000.00

Hutcheson Medical Products would list $40,000 on Form 940 line 4, "Payments exempt from FUTA tax."

Other fringe benefits specifically exempt from FUTA tax and reported on line 4 include

- Dependent care (up to $2,500 per employee or $5,000 per married couple).
- Employer contributions to group–term life insurance.
- Certain other noncash payments, as outlined in the Instructions for Form 940.

For tax reporting purposes, amounts contributed by employees to these exempt items must be treated in one of two ways on Form 940:

- Deducted from Line 3 "Total payments to all employees."
- Reported on Line 4 "Payments exempt from FUTA taxes."

EXAMPLE: ANNUAL FUTA TAX LIABILITY LESS THAN $500

Kimbro Painting has an annual FUTA liability of $392 during 2018. During the first three quarters of 2018, they would leave Part 5 blank because the tax liability is less than $500 and the liability would roll over to the next quarter. They would complete Part 5 to report the year-end FUTA deposit.

According to the IRS Tax Topic 759, they should deposit since it is year-end. "If your total FUTA tax liability for the year is $500 or less, you can either deposit the amount or pay the tax with your Form 940 by January 31." Because they have a total liability of $392 for the year, they should have an amount in Section 5 and make the payment with the year-end filing.

An example of Form 940 for L&L Hay and Grain is found in Figure 6-6.

EXAMPLE: FORM 940

Paige Laparchay owns L&L Hay and Grain, EIN 39-7482936. She filed the Annual FUTA Tax Return (Form 940) to report unemployment tax contributions during 2019. L&L Hay and Grain has 12 employees, all of whom earned over the FUTA wage base. Lines 9 through 11 are adjustments to the FUTA deposited, which are rare and do not apply in this scenario. (See pages 8–10 of Publication 15 for more details.)

(continued)

(concluded)

Name	Gross Earnings (Including fringe benefits and retirement)	Fringe Benefits	Retirement/ Pension	Payments Exempt from FUTA	Payments in Excess of $7,000 per Employee	Taxable Wages for FUTA	FUTA Tax
YTD Totals	$364,039.32	$24,868.00	$38,496.00	$63,364.00	$216,675.32	$84,000.00	$504.00
The line on Form 940	3			4	5	7	8

Line 1a: If the company pays the unemployment tax in only one state, then the state abbreviation is entered here; otherwise, the company must check the box on line 1b and complete schedule A. L&L Hay and Grain has only one location, in Oklahoma.

Line 3: All wages paid during the calendar year are entered here ($364,039.32).

Line 4: Payments exempt from FUTA Tax. L&L has fringe benefits ($24,868.00) and retirement plan contributions ($38,496.00) that are exempt from FUTA.

Line 5: Wages for the year that are in excess of $7,000 per employee are entered here. The FUTA wage base is $7,000 per employee. In this example, all employees worked for the entire calendar year, so L&L is responsible for FUTA tax on $7,000 per employee. To compute Line 5:

Total wages	$364,039.32
Less: payments exempt from FUTA	(63,364.00)
Less: FUTA wage base ($7,000 × 12 employees)	(84,000.00)
Wages in excess of $7,000	$216,675.32

Line 6: This is the sum of lines 4 and 5.

Line 7: FUTA Taxable wages, which are $84,000 for L&L Hay and Grain.

Line 8: FUTA Tax ($84,000 × 0.006) or $504.

Line 12: Total FUTA Tax of $504.

Line 13: Total FUTA Tax deposited during the year. This total must match Line 17 (side 2). Because all of L&L Hay and Grain's employees exceeded their wage base by the end of the second quarter of 2019, all FUTA tax for the year has been deposited prior to completion of the tax return.

Lines 16a and 16b: Tax liability during each quarter. These boxes report the employer's FUTA tax liability based on wages paid or accrued during the quarter. In this case, L&L Hay and Grain had a FUTA liability of $350 for the first quarter of 2019 and $104 for the second quarter of 2019. The sum of these liabilities (and any other quarterly liability, which does not exist in this example) is recorded on Line 17. The total on Line 17 must match the total on Line 13 (side 1).

Matching Final Annual Pay to Form W-2

One of the more common questions payroll accountants receive following the release of W-2s from the employees at the end of the year is, "why doesn't this match my final paycheck?" In short, it should—if you know how to calculate the income that belongs in each block of the W-2. The W-2 reflects all gross wages received by the employee, less any pre-tax deductions: health insurance, qualified retirement contributions, and other deductions adding any taxable fringe benefits. The total federal income taxes that the employer withheld from the employee and remitted as part of the 941 tax deposits also appears on the W-2 and acts as supporting documentation for the total wages reported on Forms 941 and 940.

As a result of the Affordable Care Act, the employer must report their contributions to employee health coverage on Form W-2. Amounts contributed by the employer should appear in Box 12 using code DD to designate that it is the employer's share of the health care premium.

FIGURE 6-6
Form 940

Form **940 for 2019:** **Employer's Annual Federal Unemployment (FUTA) Tax Return**

850113

Department of the Treasury — Internal Revenue Service

OMB No. 1545-0028

Employer identification number (EIN) 3 9 – 7 4 8 2 9 3 6

Name *(not your trade name)* Paige Laparchay

Trade name *(if any)* L&L Hay & Grain

Address 1534 Route 19 West
Number / Street / Suite or room number

Burlington / OK / 73722
City / State / ZIP code

Foreign country name / Foreign province/county / Foreign postal code

Type of Return
(Check all that apply.)

☐ **a.** Amended

☐ **b.** Successor employer

☐ **c.** No payments to employees in 2019

☐ **d.** Final: Business closed or stopped paying wages

Go to *www.irs.gov/Form940* for instructions and the latest information.

Read the separate instructions before you complete this form. Please type or print within the boxes.

Part 1: **Tell us about your return. If any line does NOT apply, leave it blank. See instructions before completing Part 1.**

1a If you had to pay state unemployment tax in one state only, enter the state abbreviation . | **1a** | O K

1b If you had to pay state unemployment tax in more than one state, you are a multi-state employer . . . . | **1b** | ☐ Check here. Complete Schedule A (Form 940).

2 If you paid wages in a state that is subject to CREDIT REDUCTION . . . . | **2** | ☐ Check here. Complete Schedule A (Form 940).

Part 2: **Determine your FUTA tax before adjustments. If any line does NOT apply, leave it blank.**

3 Total payments to all employees . . . . | **3** | 364069 . 32

4 Payments exempt from FUTA tax . . . . . . | **4** | 63364 . 00

Check all that apply: **4a** ☒ Fringe benefits **4c** ☒ Retirement/Pension **4e** ☐ Other
4b ☐ Group-term life insurance **4d** ☐ Dependent care

5 Total of payments made to each employee in excess of $7,000 . | **5** | 216675 . 32

6 Subtotal (line 4 + line 5 = line 6) . . . . | **6** | 280039 . 32

7 Total taxable FUTA wages (line 3 – line 6 = line 7). See instructions . . . . | **7** | 84000 . 00

8 FUTA tax before adjustments (line 7 x 0.006 = line 8) . . . . | **8** | 504 . 00

Part 3: **Determine your adjustments. If any line does NOT apply, leave it blank.**

9 If ALL of the taxable FUTA wages you paid were excluded from state unemployment tax, multiply line 7 by 0.054 (line 7 × 0.054 = line 9). Go to line 12 . . . . | **9** | .

10 If SOME of the taxable FUTA wages you paid were excluded from state unemployment tax, OR you paid ANY state unemployment tax late (after the due date for filing Form 940), complete the worksheet in the instructions. Enter the amount from line 7 of the worksheet . | **10** | .

11 If credit reduction applies, enter the total from Schedule A (Form 940) . . . . | **11** | .

Part 4: **Determine your FUTA tax and balance due or overpayment. If any line does NOT apply, leave it blank.**

12 Total FUTA tax after adjustments (lines 8 + 9 + 10 + 11 = line 12) . . . | **12** | 504 . 00

13 FUTA tax deposited for the year, including any overpayment applied from a prior year . | **13** | 504 . 00

14 Balance due. If line 12 is more than line 13, enter the excess on line 14.
• If line 14 is more than $500, you must deposit your tax.
• If line 14 is $500 or less, you may pay with this return. See instructions . . . . | **14** | .

15 Overpayment. If line 13 is more than line 12, enter the excess on line 15 and check a box below | **15** | .

▶ You **MUST** complete both pages of this form and **SIGN** it.   Check one: ☐ Apply to next return. ☐ Send a refund.

Next ▶

For Privacy Act and Paperwork Reduction Act Notice, see the back of the Payment Voucher.   Cat. No. 11234O   Form **940** (2019)

850212

Name *(not your trade name)*	**Employer identification number (EIN)**
Paige Laparchay	39-7482936

Part 5:   Report your FUTA tax liability by quarter only if line 12 is more than $500. If not, go to Part 6.

16   Report the amount of your FUTA tax liability for each quarter; do NOT enter the amount you deposited. If you had no liability for a quarter, leave the line blank.

16a   **1st quarter** (January 1 – March 31) . . . .   16a | 350 . 00 |

16b   **2nd quarter** (April 1 – June 30) . . . .   16b | 154 . 00 |

16c   **3rd quarter** (July 1 – September 30) . . . . . .   16c | . |

16d   **4th quarter** (October 1 – December 31) . . . . . .   16d | . |

17   **Total tax liability for the year** (lines 16a + 16b + 16c + 16d = line 17)   17 | 504 . 00 | **Total must equal line 12.**

Part 6:   May we speak with your third-party designee?

Do you want to allow an employee, a paid tax preparer, or another person to discuss this return with the IRS? See the instructions for details.

☐ **Yes.**   Designee's name and phone number

Select a 5-digit Personal Identification Number (PIN) to use when talking to IRS

☒ **No.**

Part 7:   Sign here. You MUST complete both pages of this form and SIGN it.

Under penalties of perjury, I declare that I have examined this return, including accompanying schedules and statements, and to the best of my knowledge and belief, it is true, correct, and complete, and that no part of any payment made to a state unemployment fund claimed as a credit was, or is to be, deducted from the payments made to employees. Declaration of preparer (other than taxpayer) is based on all information of which preparer has any knowledge.

✗ **Sign your name here**   *Paige Laparchay*

Print your name here   Paige Laparchay

Print your title here   President

Date   1/29/2020

Best daytime phone   580-555-4932

Paid Preparer Use Only   Check if you are self-employed ☐

Preparer's name		PTIN	
Preparer's signature		Date	/ /
Firm's name (or yours if self-employed)		EIN	
Address		Phone	
City		State		ZIP code	

Source: Internal Revenue Service

REPORTING OF EMPLOYER-SPONSORED HEALTH CARE COVERAGE

Type of Coverage	Form W-2, Box 12, Code DD		
	Must Report	Optional	Do Not Report
Major medical insurance	X		
Dental insurance, either as part of major medical or a separate, voluntary election		X	
Health FSA funded only by salary reduction (reported in Box 14)			X
Health FSA value in excess of employee salary deduction for qualified benefits	X		
Health saving arrangement contribution (employer or employee funded)			X
Hospital indemnity or specified illness funded by employee pre-tax deduction or by employer	X		
Multi-employer plans		X	
Domestic partner coverage included in gross income	X		
Governmental plan provided for members of the military and their families			X
Federally-recognized Indian tribal government plans			X
Accident or disability income			X
Long-term care			X
Workers' compensation			X
Excess reimbursement to highly compensated individual			X
Payment or reimbursement of premium to 2% shareholder-employee, included in gross income			X
Employers required to file fewer than 250 W-2 forms in preceding calendar year		X	
Form W-2 furnished to terminated employee prior to end of calendar year		X	
Form W-2 provided by third-party sick-pay provider to employees of other employers		X	

Source: Internal Revenue Service

Similarly, Form W-2 contains the employee's Social Security and Medicare wages. These wages are not reduced by contributions by the employee to qualified pension accounts (401(k), 403(b), etc.), and therefore may be higher than box 1. The only difference between boxes 3 and 5 will come when employees earn more than the maximum Social Security wage in the given year, i.e., $137,700 for 2020. When this occurs, the Medicare wages reported in box 5 will be greater than the Social Security wages displayed in box 3. Boxes 4 and 6 contain the Social Security and Medicare taxes withheld from the employee and remitted through 941 deposits.

Tipped employees will have amounts represented in boxes 7 and 8 for their reported tips. Box 10 is used to report Dependent Care Benefits. Contributions to nonqualifying retirement plans will be represented in box 11. Employee contributions to qualifying plans are represented in box 12. An alphabetical code is assigned to the specific type of qualified retirement plan the contributions are made to (A through EE). Box 13 denotes specific contributions to deferred compensation plans. Box 14 is used to report other information to employees, such as union dues, health insurance premiums (not pre-tax), educational assistance payments, and other similar items. State and local taxes and wages are represented in boxes 15 through 20.

The following is an explanation of each box and its contents for Form W-2.

Instructions for Completing Form W-2

Box	Explanation
a	Employee's Social Security number based on their Social Security card and/or Form W-4.
b	Employer Identification Number (EIN)
c	Employer address: This should match the address reported on other tax reports such as Form 941 and Form 940.
d	Optional. This could be used for the company's employee number.
e–f	Employee's name and address as shown on the Social Security card and Form W-4.
1	Wages paid during the calendar year, including any additional amounts from • Bonuses • Cash value of prizes • Awards • Noncash value of fringe benefits • Educational assistance programs (over $5,250) • Group-term life insurance • Roth contributions made to certain retirement plans • Payments to statutory employees • HSA contributions • Nonqualified moving expenses and expense reimbursements • Any other compensation
2	Federal income tax withheld during the year.
3	Social Security wages: Wages paid subject to employees Social Security tax but not including Social Security and allocated tips. • Educational assistance programs (over $5,250)
4	Social Security tax withheld (employee share only)
5	Medicare wages and tips: This should be the same as the Social Security wages in box 3, unless employees reach the Social Security wage cap. • Educational assistance programs (over $5,250)
6	Medicare tax withheld (employee share only)
7	Social Security tips: Any tips reported to you by the employee go in this box.
8	Allocated tips: Use this box if the company allocates tips among employees.
9	Verification code: Used if the employer participates in the W-2 Verification Code pilot.
10	Dependent care benefits: Report all dependent care benefits paid during the calendar year under a dependent care benefit program.
11	Nonqualified plans: Used by the Social Security Administration.
12	Codes (see Figure 6-7)
13	Check the boxes for the following circumstances • Statutory employee: Earnings are subject to Social Security and Medicare taxes but not federal income tax. • Retirement plan: If the employee was an active participant in a defined benefit or defined contribution plan. • Third-party sick pay: Used when reporting sick pay benefits.
14	Other: Used to report annual leave value of an employee's company car is the employer paid 100%.
15–20	Used for reporting state and local tax information. Deductions and inclusions would follow state laws.

Source: Internal Revenue Service

When completing *Form W-2*, you will have several copies of the same form. A sample Form W-2 is found in Figure 6-8. According to the order in which they print, the copies of Form W-2 are as follows:

Which Copy?	What Is It For?
Copy A	Social Security Administration
Copy 1	State, City, or Local Tax Department
Copy B	Filing with the Employee's Federal Tax Return
Copy C	Employee's Records
Copy 2	State, City, or Local Tax Department
Copy D	Employer

FIGURE 6-7
Box 12 Codes for Form W-2

Form W-2 Reference Guide for Box 12 Codes

A	Uncollected social security or RRTA tax on tips	L	Substantiated employee business expense reimbursements	Y	Deferrals under a section 409A nonqualified deferred compensation plan
B	Uncollected Medicare tax on tips (but not Additional Medicare Tax)	M	Uncollected social security or RRTA tax on taxable cost of group-term life insurance over $50,000 (former employees only)	Z	Income under a nonqualified deferred compensation plan that fails to satisfy section 409A
C	Taxable cost of group-term life insurance over $50,000	N	Uncollected Medicare tax on taxable cost of group-term life insurance over $50,000 (but not Additional Medicare Tax) (former employees only)	AA	Designated Roth contributions under a section 401(k) plan
D	Elective deferrals under a section 401(k) cash or deferred arrangement plan (including a SIMPLE 401(k) arrangement)	P	Excludable moving expense reimbursements paid directly to members of the Armed Forces	BB	Designated Roth contributions under a section 403(b) plan
E	Elective deferrals under a section 403(b) salary reduction agreement	Q	Nontaxable combat pay	DD	Cost of employer-sponsored health coverage
F	Elective deferrals under a section 408(k)(6) salary reduction SEP	R	Employer contributions to an Archer MSA	EE	Designated Roth contributions under a governmental section 457(b) plan
G	Elective deferrals and employer contributions (including nonelective deferrals) to a section 457(b) deferred compensation plan	S	Employee salary reduction contributions under a section 408(p) SIMPLE plan	FF	Permitted benefits under a qualified small employer health reimbursement arrangement
H	Elective deferrals to a section 501(c)(18)(D) tax-exempt organization plan	T	Adoption benefits	GG	Income from qualified equity grants under section 83(i)
J	Nontaxable sick pay	V	Income from exercise of nonstatutory stock option(s)	HH	Aggregate deferrals under section 83(i) elections as of the close of the calendar year
K	20% excise tax on excess golden parachute payments	W	Employer contributions (including employee contributions through a cafeteria plan) to an employee's health savings account (HSA)		

Source: Internal Revenue Service

Figure 6-8 is an example of a Form W-2 for Joseph A. Balestreri.

FIGURE 6-8
Form W-2

a Employee's social security number **22222**		
OMB No. 1545-0008		

b Employer identification number (EIN) 45-3392039	1 Wages, tips, other compensation 36,523.34	2 Federal income tax withheld 3,671.04
c Employer's name, address, and ZIP code

Crystal GM & Buick
882 First Street
Pawtucket, RI 02862 | 3 Social security wages 38,523.34 | 4 Social security tax withheld 2,388.45 |
	5 Medicare wages and tips 38,523.34	6 Medicare tax withheld 588.89
	7 Social security tips	8 Allocated tips
d Control number	9	10 Dependent care benefits
e Employee's first name and initial   Last name   Suff.

Joseph A. Balestreri
3949 Winchester Street
Pawtucket, RI 02862 | 11 Nonqualified plans | 12a Code D \| 2,000.00 |
	13 Statutory employee ☐ Retirement plan ☒ Third-party sick pay ☐	12b Code
	14 Other	12c Code
		12d Code
f Employee's address and ZIP code		

15 State Employer's state ID number RI | 382948374	16 State wages, tips, etc. 36,523.34	17 State income tax 1,369.63	18 Local wages, tips, etc.	19 Local income tax	20 Locality name

Form **W-2** Wage and Tax Statement   **2020**   Department of the Treasury—Internal Revenue Service

Copy 1—For State, City, or Local Tax Department

Source: Internal Revenue Service

EXAMPLE: FORM W-2

Joseph A. Balestren worked for Crystal GM & Buick during 2019. The following is on his W-2 for 2020:

Box 1 contains the wages, tips, and other compensation. Joseph earned $36,523.34 during 2020.

Box 2 contains the federal income tax withheld: Joseph had $3,671.04 withheld based on his W-4 information.

Boxes 3 and 5 contain the Social Security and Medicare wages. Note that these two boxes contain a higher amount than box 1. Joseph has a retirement plan into which he contributed $2,000 during 2020.

Boxes 4 and 6 contain the Social Security tax withheld ($2,388.45) and the Medicare tax withheld ($558.59).

Box 12 contains amounts for nontaxable items. Codes for box 12 are contained in Figure 6-7.

Boxes 15–17 contain the state tax information. Joseph had $1,369.63 withheld for state taxes based on the state withholding certificate that he filed in January 2020.

Form W-3 is the transmittal form that accompanies the submission of Copy A to the Social Security Administration. It contains the aggregate data for all W-2s issued by an employer. Form W-3 and all accompanying W-2s must be mailed or electronically transmitted by January 31 of the following year (i.e., W-2s and W-3s for 2019 are due on January 31, 2020). The total annual wages reported on the W-3 must match the annual wages reported on Forms 941 and 940. The following is an explanation of the boxes on Form W-3.

	Instructions for Completing Form W-3
Box	**Explanation**
a	Control number (optional)
b	Kind of payer: The employer indicates if one or more of the following applies:
	• Form 941 *and* no other category applies
	• Military
	• Form 943 (agricultural employers)
	• Form 944 *and* no other category applies
	• CT-1 (railroad employers)
	• Hshld. Emp. (Household employers)
	• Medicare govt. emp. (if the Forms W-2 are for employees subject only to Medicare tax)
	Kind of employer: The employer checks the box that applies to them:
	• None, if none of the situations apply
	• 501c non-govt (for tax-exempt non-governmental employers, such as private foundations, charities, social and recreational clubs, and veterans organizations)
	• State/local non-501c (for state/local governments or other entities with governmental authority)
	• State/local 501c (for state/local governments that have a tax-exempt designation)
	• Federal govt. (for federal government entities)
	Third-party sick pay: Employers who have indicated on the Form W-2 that they issue third-party sick pay must check this box
c	Total number of Forms W-2 submitted with the W-3
d	Establishment number: Used to identify separate establishments within the same business.
e	Employer Identification Number (EIN)
f–g	Employer name and address

(continued)

	Instructions for Completing Form W-3
Box	**Explanation**
h	Any other EIN used during the year
	Employer contact information
1–8	Same as boxes 1–8 on Form W-2. The numbers in these boxes should reflect the total of each box for all forms submitted with Form W-3.
9	Leave blank
10	Dependent care benefits: Report all dependent care benefits paid during the calendar year under a dependent care benefit program as a total of all Forms W-2.
11	The total reported in box 11 of Forms W-2
12a	Deferred Compensation: Enter the total of all amounts reported with codes D-H, S, Y, AA, BB, and EE in Box 12 of Forms W-2. No code should be entered in Box 12a.
13	For third-party sick pay use only. Leave the box blank.
15	State/Employer's state ID number: Place the two-letter state abbreviation and the ID number. If the Forms W-2 are from more than one state, enter X in this box and omit the ID number.
16–19	Enter the state/local total wages and income tax withheld in the corresponding boxes.

The following example from Ferrigno Day Spa depicts the completion of Form W-3 for a company. (See Figure 6-9.)

EXAMPLE

Marlene Ferrigno is the owner of Ferrigno Day Spa, 2849 Water Street, Falls Church, Virginia, 22043, EIN 84-9943043, phone number 703-555-0904, fax number 703-555-0906. Her email address is mferrigno@ferrignodayspa.com.

Box b: Ferrigno Day Spa will file Form 941 to report quarterly tax liability, so box 941 is checked.

Box c: Ferrigno Day Spa had 25 employees who received W-2s.

Box 1: Wages and tips for 2019 were $654,087.35.

Box 2: The amount of federal income tax withheld for the 2019 wages was $117,735.

Box 3: Social Security wages were $546,333.35.

Box 4: Social Security tax withheld was $33,872.67.

Box 5: Medicare wages and tips were $570,838.25.

Box 6: Medicare tax withheld was $8,277.16.

Box 7: Social Security tips were $24,505.

Box 12a: Deferred compensation was $83,249.

Box 15: VA; Employer's State ID number: 66-2245538849A-238.

Box 16: State wages, tips, etc. were $654,087.35.

Box 17: State income tax withheld was $41,403.73.

Note: Taxable tips reported in Box 7 should be reported on IRS form 4070.

(Source: Internal Revenue Service)

Employers may occasionally need to correct filed tax forms. In this case, the employer should use the X version of the form (i.e., Form 941-X, Form 940-X, etc.). Note that any additional tax amounts owed that are discovered during the correction process should be remitted as soon as the employer completes the correction form. During the correction process, if an employer has withheld too much federal income tax or FICA from one or more employees, the employee has the option to recover these overages using IRS Form 843.

FIGURE 6-9
Form W-3

DO NOT STAPLE

33333	a Control number	For Official Use Only ▶
		OMB No. 1545-0008

| b **Kind of Payer** (Check one) | 941 [X] CT-1 [ ] | Military [ ] Hshld. emp. [ ] | 943 [ ] Medicare govt. emp. [ ] | 944 [ ] | **Kind of Employer** (Check one) | None apply [ ] State/local non-501c [ ] | 501c non-govt. [ ] State/local 501c [ ] | Federal govt. [ ] | Third-party sick pay (Check if applicable) [ ] |

c Total number of Forms W-2	d Establishment number	1 Wages, tips, other compensation	2 Federal income tax withheld
25		654,087.35	117,735.00

e Employer identification number (EIN)	3 Social security wages	4 Social security tax withheld
84-9943043	546,333.35	33,872.67

f Employer's name	5 Medicare wages and tips	6 Medicare tax withheld
Ferrigno Day Spa	570,838.25	8,277.16

	7 Social security tips	8 Allocated tips
2849 Water Street Falls Church, VA 22043	24,505.00	
	9	10 Dependent care benefits
	11 Nonqualified plans	12a Deferred compensation 83,249.00

g Employer's address and ZIP code		

h Other EIN used this year	13 For third-party sick pay use only	12b

15 State VA	Employer's state ID number 66-2245538849A-238	14 Income tax withheld by payer of third-party sick pay

16 State wages, tips, etc.	17 State income tax	18 Local wages, tips, etc.	19 Local income tax
654,087.35	41,403.73		

Employer's contact person Marlene Ferrigno	Employer's telephone number 703-555-0904	For Official Use Only

Employer's fax number 703-555-0906	Employer's email address mferrigno@ferrignodayspa.com	

Under penalties of perjury, I declare that I have examined this return and accompanying documents, and, to the best of my knowledge and belief, they are true, correct, and complete.

Signature ▶   Title ▶   Date ▶

Form **W-3** **Transmittal of Wage and Tax Statements**   **2020**   Department of the Treasury
Internal Revenue Service

Source: Internal Revenue Service

Tax Forms

1. Jacobucci Enterprises is a monthly schedule depositor. According to the information it reported on Form 941, its quarterly tax liability is $8,462.96. During the quarter, it made deposits of $2,980.24 and $3,068.24. How much must it remit with its tax return?

2. Corrado's Corrals paid annual wages totaling $278,452.76 to 15 employees. Assuming that all employees were employed for the entire year, what is the amount of FUTA wages?

3. For Corrado's Corrals in the previous question, what is the FUTA tax liability?

4. Skyrockets Inc. had the following wage information reported in box 1 of its W-2s:

   Employee A: $25,650

   Employee B: $30,025

   Employee C: $28,550

   Employee D: $31,970

   What amount must it report as total wages on its Form W-3?

LO 6-4 Describe Payroll within the Context of Business Expenses

Understanding employer payroll expenses are important because of the wide range of mandatory activities and lesser-known expenses associated with maintaining employees. Compensation expenses and employer payroll-related liabilities must be accurately maintained in an accounting system. The scope of payroll-related employer responsibilities contributes to the need for knowledgeable payroll accountants.

Jd8/Shutterstock

> According to the Bureau of Labor Statistics, employers' average hourly cost for employees was $36.63, of which wages were $25.03 and benefits totaled $11.60. For private-sector employers, the average hourly cost was $34.53; for governmental employers, the average hourly cost was $50.03. (Source: BLS - September 2019 data)

The amounts withheld from employee pay and the employer liabilities must be deposited in a timely manner with the appropriate authorities. The omission of any of the required filings, activities, or any inaccuracy in the accounting system can lead to problems that could include governmental sanctions and penalties. No statute of limitations exists for unpaid taxes. If a company outsources its payroll processing, it is still liable for any late or unremitted payroll taxes.

The IRS will waive penalties under two conditions:

1. The amount of the shortfall does not exceed the greater of $100 or 2 percent of the required tax deposit.
2. The amount of the shortfall is deposited either (a) by the due date of the period return (monthly and semiweekly depositors) or (b) the first Wednesday or Friday that falls after the 15th of the month (semiweekly depositors only).

Penalties fall into two classifications: (1) failure to deposit and (2) failure to file. The following penalties apply when a ***failure to deposit*** occurs:

2%	Deposits made 1 to 5 days late.
5%	Deposits made 6 to 15 days late.
10%	Deposits made 16 or more days late. It also applies to amounts paid within 10 days of the date of the first notice the IRS sent asking for the tax due.
10%	Amounts (that should have been deposited) paid directly to the IRS or paid with your tax return. See payment with the return, earlier in this section, for an exception.
15%	Amounts still unpaid more than 10 days after the date of the first notice the IRS sent asking for the tax due or the day on which you received notice and demand for immediate payment, whichever is earlier.

Source: Internal Revenue Service

EXAMPLE: FAILURE TO DEPOSIT PENALTY

Mane Street Hairstylists is a monthly schedule payroll tax depositor. The company owed $4,552 in payroll tax liabilities during the month of July. The owner, Billy James, failed to deposit the July payroll taxes until August 27.

The failure to deposit penalty would be calculated as follows:

Tax Due	Number of Days Late	% Penalty	Total Penalty
$4,552.00	12	5%	$227.60

The ***failure to file*** penalty applies to amounts on Form 941 and is 5 percent of the unpaid tax due with the return. This penalty accrues for each month or partial month that the tax remains unpaid.

EXAMPLE: FAILURE TO FILE AND FAILURE TO DEPOSIT PENALTIES

Mary Warren, president of Great Meadows Farms, outsourced the payroll for the company during October 2020. She received a notice on February 15, 2020, that Form 941 for the fourth quarter of 2020 was not filed. After contacting the payroll service, she determined that $32,860 in payroll taxes due with Form 941 was never deposited. The penalties for this oversight would be as follows:

Failure to File Penalty

Tax Due	Number of Months Late	% Penalty per Month	Penalty
$32,860.00	2*	5%	$3,286.00

Failure to Deposit Penalty

Tax Due	Number of Days Late	% Penalty	Penalty
$32,860.00	30	10%	$3,286.00

| | | **Total penalties due** | $6,572.00 |

* The number of months is two because the failure to file penalty is based on both months and partial months. Because the notice was issued in February, the penalty would be for 2 months.

Notice how quickly the penalties can accrue for unfiled and undeposited taxes. The maximum penalty rate for the failure to file is 25% and the maximum for failure to deposit is 15%. Also, keep in mind that the penalties may be subject to interest charges.

A quick summary of general employer payroll expenses and responsibilities follows:

Employee Compensation	Tax Withholding	Tax Matching
Tax remittance	Voluntary deductions from employee pay	Remittance of voluntary deductions
Tax reporting	Tax deposits	Accountability

Singkham/Shutterstock

Employees and Company Framework

Beyond the expenses and responsibilities of the payroll accounting system is the understanding of how the employees fit within the larger framework of the company. Payroll is one part of the cost of employing people. Before the employee ever becomes productive for a company, employers will incur recruiting, hiring, and training costs that vary based on the company's location and minimum job requirements. Other costs include any tools, uniforms, and specific equipment that employees need to perform their jobs. Expenses associated with hiring and retaining well-qualified employees may comprise a significant amount of a company's overhead.

According to a study conducted by Hundred5, the cost to hire and train new employees averages 15 to 25 percent of the employee's salary. For a manager earning $36,000 per year, the cost to hire and train employees could total approximately $9,000. (Source: Hundred5)

It is important to understand the responsibility employers have for remitting the federal income tax and FICA tax amounts withheld from employees. According to IRS §6672, any responsible person within the company who *willfully* does not remit the withheld employee taxes—meaning they did not remit the taxes due to something as innocuous as a lack of funds—is subject to a 100% penalty for those non-remitted funds. It is important to note this penalty only applies to employee federal income tax and FICA taxes, not the employer's share of the FICA taxes or FUTA tax. The following diagram explains who is considered a responsible party for payroll tax deposits.

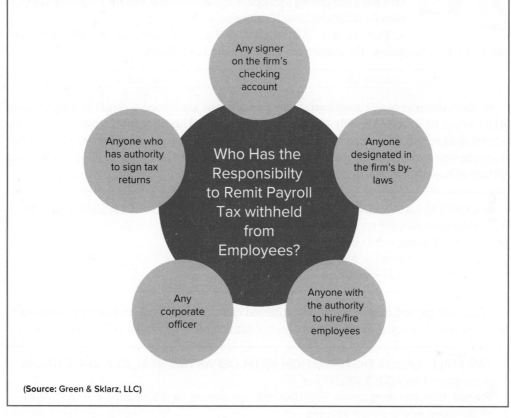

(**Source:** Green & Sklarz, LLC)

Tracking employee payroll expenses is an important duty of payroll accountants. The use of payroll reports fosters cost analysis that informs accounting and human resource professionals of specific details needed for budget purposes. Companies need the information generated by payroll records to ensure profitability and competitiveness.

Payroll-Related Business Expenses

1. What are the two types of penalties associated with payroll taxes?
2. How do payroll expenses relate to other business functions?

LO 6-5 Relate Labor Expenses to Company Profitability

Compensating employees is far more complex than simply paying the hourly wage. The employer's expenses related to taxes, insurance, and benefits are an addition to the employee's annual salary. (See Figure 6-10.) Having employees affects the profitability of a company but is a vital part of doing business. Managers need to associate the proper amount of payroll costs with their department so they can make informed decisions about employee productivity and future budgets.

kitzcorner/Shutterstock

The Labor Distribution Report

The number of employees in a department is known as the *labor distribution*. Payroll accounting is a powerful tool in understanding the labor distribution of a company. Accounting records facilitate departmental identification of the number and type of employees, time worked, overtime used, and benefits paid. Integrating the department information into the employee earnings records facilitates labor distribution analysis.

For example, ABD Industries has three departments: administration, sales, and manufacturing. The employees are distributed as follows:

Administration: 15	Sales: 10	Manufacturing: 60

Without *departmental classification*, the payroll costs associated with the 85 employees at ABD would be allocated evenly among the departments. This allocation would result in the administration and sales departments absorbing an amount of the payroll costs that are disproportionate to the number of employees. The departmental classification yields an accurate picture of how the labor is distributed across a company.

EXAMPLE: LABOR DISTRIBUTION, NO DEPARTMENTAL CLASSIFICATION

Total payroll amount for ABD Industries = $500,000
Number of departments = 3
Payroll cost assigned to each department:
$500,000/3 = $166,666.67

Assigning payroll costs without departmental classification works when each department is composed of an equal number of employees with reasonably similar skills and job titles.

EXAMPLE: LABOR DISTRIBUTION WITH DEPARTMENTAL CLASSIFICATION

Total payroll for ABD: $500,000 or
Payroll cost per employee: $500,000/85 employees = $5,882.35 per employee (if allocated evenly per employee).

Departmental allocation:

Administration payroll costs = $5,882.35 × 15 = $88,235
Sales payroll costs = $5,882.35 × 10 = $58,824
Manufacturing payroll costs = $5,882.35 × 60 = $352,941

FIGURE 6-10

Percent of Employee Compensation Component to Total Payroll Expense

Compensation Component	Civilian Workers	Private Industry	State and Local Government
Wages and salaries	68.7%	70.1%	62.3%
Benefits	31.3%	29.9%	37.7%
Paid leave	7.2%	7.2%	7.5%
Supplemental pay	2.8%	3.2%	1.0%
Insurance	8.7%	8.0%	11.7%
Health benefits	8.2%	7.5%	11.5%
Retirement and savings	5.3%	3.8%	11.9%
Defined benefit	3.3%	1.5%	11.1%
Defined contribution	2.0%	2.3%	0.8%
Legally required	7.3%	7.7%	5.5%

(Source: Bureau of Labor Statistics, 2019)

Allocating costs according to the number of employees in each department yields a more accurate amount than the equal distribution of the labor costs across the three departments at ABD. However, allocating by the number of departmental employees assumes that each employee has equal compensation, which is improbable. A payroll accounting system allows accurate allocation based on the precise amounts paid to each employee per payroll period. Labor distribution reports are among the tools that managers use to determine the productivity and costs specifically associated with their department.

> Labor distribution reports may be used to reveal whatever information is important to a business. Funding sources, payroll accuracy, and budget projections are three common uses of labor distribution reports. Vanderbilt University uses a labor distribution report to ensure that payroll costs are linked to appropriate departments and to specific grant funding. (Source: *Small Business Chronicle:* http://smallbusiness.chron.com/labor-cost-distribution-report-34077.html)

Labor Distribution Report

Stop & Check

1. Pine Banks Tree Farms has 10 employees on staff: three office staff, five agricultural workers, and two drivers. The annual payroll expense is $300,000.

    a. What would be the labor distribution if Pine Banks Tree Farms uses departmental classification?

    b. What would be the labor distribution if Pine Banks Tree Farms does not use departmental classification?

2. Which method—departmental classification or nondepartmental classification—is most appropriate? Why?

LO 6-6 Complete Benefit Analysis as a Function of Payroll

bleakstar/Shutterstock

Companies offer employee benefits both to retain employees after the initial hire and to remain competitive within their industry. The problem with offering benefits is the cost of the benefits directly affects a company's profitability. The challenge is to find ways to promote employee engagement, reduce employee turnover, and maintain company profitability. Payroll data plays an important role in completing an analysis of the benefits offered and their strategic advantage.

Wages and salaries are often a company's largest employee expense. The second-largest expense to employers is employee benefits. According to Paychex, employee benefits potentially add an additional 25–33 percent to an employee's base pay. Benefits can include paid time off, holiday pay, bonuses, and insurance. Many companies pay a percentage of the employee's insurance benefits, ranging from 70 percent to 100 percent in some cases. With the rising costs and mandatory nature of health insurance for certain employers, employee costs have become a major budget concern for many managers.

Payroll-related employee costs need to be compared to the advantages of maintaining the employee, namely, the profitability of the department and the company. To achieve the analysis required, a *benefit analysis* report needs to be compiled. Compiling a benefit analysis report is an important tool in maintaining a balance between employee retention and profitability. The payroll records of the company facilitate the compilation of the benefit analysis report.

The analysis of employee benefits considers all of the variables that comprise their compensation. Many managers are unaware of the full cost of having an employee added to or removed from their department, so the benefit analysis report serves the following purposes:

- Benefit analysis helps employers benchmark their employees' compensation to other companies with similar profiles or in certain geographic locations.
- The report helps employers with labor distribution and budgeting tasks by providing data for decision making.
- The benefit analysis facilitates managerial understanding of departmental impacts prior to hiring or dismissing employees.

Shutterstock/Zodar

Accurate reporting of the benefits costs to employers provides the management with guidance for budget analysis and employee compensation. A sample benefit analysis report is contained in Figure 6-11.

Note the differences between total employee benefit costs and total employer benefit costs. Mandatory and voluntary employee payroll deductions represent a significant monetary investment. When added to the employee's wages and the costs involved with recruitment and hiring, the amount of money dedicated to labor costs becomes a significant portion of a company's expenses.

Taking the information prepared above, the payroll accountant can determine the cost of each employee to the company. This information can also be used to determine the total cost of offering a particular benefit to the employees. The latter is used when the company is looking at annual renewals of health insurance benefits for comparison.

Annual Total Compensation Report

Some companies provide their employees with an *annual total compensation report*. The annual total compensation report is similar to the benefit analysis report because it contains a detailed analysis of employee costs. The difference between the two reports is the intended audience. The benefit analysis report is an internal report for the company's management and the annual total compensation report is meant to be distributed to the employee. The work going into the total compensation report can come from either the human resources department or the accounting department, depending on the structure of the company. Either way, the payroll accountant contributes vital information to the report.

The Credit Union National Association (CUNA) publishes annual total compensation reports that contain the details of CEOs and senior executives at credit unions in the United States. Information from these reports informs each credit union's decisions about base salary, benefits, and retirement packages by providing an industry-wide benchmark. (Source: CUNA)

To prepare the information for the benefit analysis and total compensation reports, the payroll accountant will gather information from many sources: payroll registers, accounts payable invoices, *payroll tax reports*, and contributions to retirement programs (when employer matching is involved). The payroll accountant will start by printing the annual earnings report for the employee in question. A computerized earnings register can be configured to include taxes and other deductions from the employee's pay. When the total compensation report covers periods greater than one year, it may be necessary for the payroll accountant to obtain Social Security and Medicare tax rates for the years in question. Employer portions

GaudiLab/Shutterstock

FIGURE 6-11
Sample Benefit Analysis Report

Statement for: Elizabeth M. Charette

Annual Gross Salary:	$44,137.60	
Total Hours Worked Annually:	2,080 Hours	
Health & Welfare Benefits:	**Annual Employee Cost**	**Annual Employer Cost**
Medical/Dental:	$ 600.00	$ 6,000
Life insurance:	0	1,200
AD&D coverage:	0	980
Dependent life insurance:	300.00	600
Disability insurance:	600.00	3,000
Total health & welfare:	$1,500.00	$ 11,780
Retirement Plan Benefits:	**Employee Cost**	**Employer Cost**
401(k) employee contribution:	$1,324.13	$ 662.07
Profit sharing:	0	3,000
Total retirement plan:	$1,324.13	$ 3,662.07
PTO & Holiday Pay	**Employee Cost**	**Employer Cost**
Paid time off:	$ 0	$ 1,697.60
Holiday pay:	0	1,867.36
Total PTO and holiday pay:	$ 0	$ 3,564.96
Additional Compensation:	**Employee Cost**	**Employer Cost**
Annual bonus:	$ 0	$ 2,500
Bereavement pay:	0	509.28
Production bonus:	0	500
Tuition reimbursement:	0	5,250
Total additional comp:	$ 0	$ 8,759.28
Government Mandated:	**Employee Cost**	**Employer Cost**
Social Security:	$2,736.53	$ 2,736.53
Medicare:	640.00	640.00
Federal unemployment:	0	253.28
State unemployment:	0	2,279.53
Workers' compensation:	0	353.10
Total government mandated:	$3,376.53	6,262.44
Total cost of benefit provided by WLA Industries	$6,200.66	$34,028.75
Total cost of employing E. M. Charette*		$78,166.35

*44,137.60 + 34,028.75 = $78,166.35
Sources: American Payroll Association, ADP

of unemployment insurance, workers' compensation, and taxes are added to the benefits provided to the employees in the determination of the total cost.

The payroll accountant will request copies of invoices for health insurance, life insurance, and any other benefits the employer provides, such as on-site meals and gym facilities/memberships, from the accounts payable accountant. Other items that may be added to the cost per employee for benefit analysis could be: Company-provided awards, meals, clothing, or special facilities (break room, locker room, etc.). Once complete, the annual compensation report is distributed to employees to help them understand the total value of their annual compensation. A sample total compensation report is in Figure 6-12.

FIGURE 6-12
Total Compensation Report

CASH COMPENSATION AND BENEFITS SUMMARY

The amount of your total compensation from ABC Company is much more than what is indicated in your yearly earnings statement. In addition to direct pay, it includes the value of your health care insurance, disability and life insurance, retirement benefits, and government mandated benefits. Below, we break out your total compensation.

CASH COMPENSATION	Amount
Base Salary	$52,000.00
Total:	**$52,000.00**

BENEFITS	Plan	Coverage	Your Contribution	Company Contribution
Medical Insurance	ABC One		$600.00	$5,400.00
Vision Insurance	ABC Vision		$0.00	$600.00
Dental Insurance	NL Dental		$120.00	$1,080.00
Total:			**$720.00**	**$7,080.00**

Your Contribution 9.23%

Company Contribution 90.77%

TOTAL COMPENSATION VALUE

The true value of your ABC Company total compensation includes your direct pay, the company's contribution to your benefits, and the consequent tax savings to you.

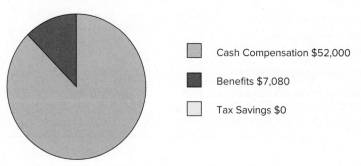

Cash Compensation $52,000

Benefits $7,080

Tax Savings $0

Sources: American Payroll Association, ADP

Benefit Analysis Report

Stop & Check

1. What are the purposes of compiling a benefit analysis report?
2. What is the difference between a benefit analysis report and an annual total compensation report?

EMPLOYER TAXES AND BENEFIT ANALYSIS

Tax rates and remittance methods for employers tend to change annually based on directives issued by federal, state, and local governments. Some developments in employer taxes that have changed since 2016 include the following:

- The use of the EFTPS as a mandatory tax remittance method for new employers and the preferred method for existing employers.
- Additional guidance from the Financial Accounting Standards Board about the reporting of defined benefit and defined contribution plan accounting.
- Increased automation of employer taxes to improve and streamline remittance procedures.
- Continuing focus on employee wellness that includes health incentives as part of employees' total compensation package.

Some trends to watch in employer taxes and benefit analysis include the following:

- The explicit inclusion of mental health as part of comprehensive wellness initiatives.
- Flexibility in benefits choices to allow employees to customize their benefits to suit their needs.
- Changes to stipend requirements that would allow employees to designate amounts to their choice of professional development, wellness, or financial stability needs.
- A strategic focus on benefits offerings as a way to attract qualified employees and boost productivity.

Summary of Employer Payroll Taxes and Labor Planning

Taxes are a part of conducting business. Whether taxes are income or employee related, a business must abide by the regulations for the timely submission and reporting of taxes. Employers have responsibilities for collecting federal income tax, Social Security, and Medicare taxes from their employees. In addition, the company is responsible for setting aside federal unemployment taxes per employee based upon taxable wages. Apart from the federal taxes, employers may be liable for the collecting, reporting, and submission of state and local income and unemployment taxes. Privilege taxes, such as the Denver Head Tax, may also be collected in specific districts. Employers who fail to meet the reporting, deposit, or submission requirements may be subject to fines and penalties.

Understanding the connection between the W-2 Form and the final paycheck of the year can save payroll accountants hours of work in searching to find the answers to each employee's query. When the payroll accountant can explain the elements of the W-2 with confidence, fewer employees will come to ask why the difference, especially if the payroll accountant provides a written explanation with the final annual paycheck or W-2.

Although the human resources department could prepare the benefit analysis report, in smaller companies this duty can fall to the payroll accountant. Even in larger organizations, the human resources department will need specific information from the payroll accountant to feed into the benefit analysis report. Managers can examine the benefit analysis to understand how much their employees cost their department. Once receiving a total annual compensation report, the employee has a more complete understanding of their compensation package, thereby feeding wage discussions and building a data-driven understanding of cost changes.

Key Points

- Employers share some of the same tax obligations as their employees. Some examples are Social Security, Medicare, and (in some states) SUTA taxes.
- FUTA taxes are paid only on the first $7,000 of each employee's annual taxable wage; SUTA tax wage base limits vary by state.
- Workers' compensation is a state-mandated insurance that employers carry to protect employees who are injured or killed while performing normal work duties.
- Workers' compensation insurance premium costs vary according to labor classifications.

- Payroll tax deposit frequency is determined by the amount of payroll taxes paid during a "lookback" period.
- All new employers are monthly schedule depositors until the next lookback period.
- Most employers file quarterly payroll tax returns on Form 941.
- Employers who deposit payroll taxes on a semiweekly basis must also file a Schedule B with their Form 941.
- Employers with less than $2,500 of annual tax liability file a Form 944 at the end of the calendar year.
- Employers report FUTA tax liability on an annual basis by using Form 940.
- Employers file an annual Form W-2 for each employee with the Social Security Administration.
- Form W-3 is the transmittal form used to report a company's aggregate annual wages and withholdings.
- Labor distribution has an effect on company profitability, and benefit costs are a significant factor in managerial decisions.
- A total annual compensation report is used to communicate to employees the complete compensation package that they receive.
- Benefits packages are a strategic part of attracting high-quality candidates.

Vocabulary

Annual schedule depositors	Form 940	Payroll tax reports
Annual total compensation report	Form 941	Quarterly depositors
	Form 944	Schedule B
Automated Clearing House (ACH)	Form W-2	Semiweekly schedule depositors
	Form W-3	
Benefit analysis	FICA	Statutory deductions
Departmental classification	Labor distribution	SUTA
Electronic Federal Tax Payment System (EFTPS)	Lookback period	Tax remittance
	Monthly depositors	
FICA	Next business day depositors	

Review Questions

1. What taxes are paid only by the employer in most states?
2. What taxes are the shared responsibility of the employer and employee?
3. What taxes are paid by the employee only?
4. What determines the deposit requirements for employer taxes?
5. How often must a company report Form 941 earnings/withholdings?
6. How often must a company report Form 940 earnings/withholdings?
7. Which of the mandatory taxes have a maximum wage base?
8. How did the Affordable Care Act change Medicare tax withholding percentages?
9. What is the purpose of Form 941?
10. Which employers must use Schedule B?
11. How do employers know that they must use Form 944?
12. What is the purpose of Form 940?
13. What are three ways an employer could reduce their SUTA tax liability?
14. What is the difference between Form W-2 and Form W-3?
15. What are the employer's payroll responsibilities as far as taxes and other withholdings are concerned?
16. How does payroll relate to a company's costs of doing business?
17. What is meant by the term *labor distribution*?
18. How do payroll records inform managers about labor distribution?
19. What is a benefit analysis report?

20. How can a manager use the benefit analysis report in the decision-making process?

21. How do the payroll reports inform managers about department and company profitability?

Exercises Set A

E6-1A.
LO 6-1

Which of the following are employer-only payroll obligations? (Select all that apply.)
a. Social Security tax
b. SUTA
c. Medicare tax
d. FUTA

E6-2A.
LO 6-1

As of 2020, which of the following accurately represents the full FUTA rate and wage base?
a. 0.6 percent, $137,700
b. Varies by state
c. 6.0 percent, $7,000
d. 0.6 percent, $7,000

E6-3A.
LO 6-1

Davis Reyes is the accounting for Heads Up Hat Corporation. As he pre-pares the payroll for the semimonthly pay period ending December 15, he notices that some of the year-to-date executives' salaries have exceeded $200,000. What payroll tax responsibilities does Heads Up Hat Corporation have, especially regarding FICA taxes? (Select all that apply.)
a. Social Security tax must be deducted from the executives' pay for those under the cap and matched by the corporation
b. An additional 0.9 percent Medicare tax must be deducted from the employees' pay for those over the base and matched by the corporation
c. An additional 0.9 percent Medicare tax must be deducted from the executives' pay for those over the base, but no corporate match is required
d. Medicare taxes should be deducted from all employees' pay and matched by the corporation

E6-4A.
LO 6-2

Rosa Pierce is a payroll clerk at Hot Tree Hand Tools. She receives written notice from the IRS that the company is a semiweekly schedule depositor. How is the deposit schedule determined?
a. The number of employees in the company.
b. The payroll frequency used by the company.
c. The amount of FUTA taxes paid.
d. The payroll tax liability during the lookback period.

E6-5A.
LO 6-2

Match the amount of payroll tax liabilities from the lookback period with the appropriate tax deposit schedule.
a. $42,300 annual payroll taxes.
b. $145,033 annual payroll taxes.
c. $128,450 payroll tax for one pay period.
d. $1,580 annual payroll taxes.

1. Annual
2. Monthly
3. Semiweekly
4. Next business day

E6-6A.
LO 6-3

Which form(s) should be prepared and filed by companies with employees and payroll tax liabilities exceeding $50,000 as of December 31, 20XX? (Select all that apply.)
a. Form 940
b. Form W-4
c. Form 941
d. Form W-2

E6-7A.
LO 6-4

Wade Pools Company made its required tax deposits. However, it filed its second-quarter Form 941 on August 21, after receiving notice from the IRS of the missing form. What is the failure to file penalty?
a. 2 percent
b. 5 percent
c. 10 percent
d. 15 percent

E6-8A.

LO 6-4, 6-5

Which of the following is true about the cost of employees within a business context? (Select all that apply.)

a. Employees constitute a significant cost of conducting business.

b. Hiring employees involves a significant overhead cost.

c. Costs associated with employees include only salary and limited hiring expenses.

d. The cost of providing employee benefits is minimal and of little importance.

E6-9A.

LO 6-6

Which of the following represents the purpose(s) of the benefit analysis report? (Select all that apply.)

a. Benchmarking with other companies.

b. Understanding of employer and employee benefits costs.

c. Billing employees for benefits costs.

d. Identification of opportunities for increasing profitability.

E6-10A.

LO 6-6

Why is it important to prepare the benefit analysis report or the total compensation report? (Select all that apply.)

a. The reports promote employee education about the total value of their salary and benefits.

b. The reports inform labor planning and employer cost strategies.

c. The reports may be used as employee contracts.

d. The reports may be used to accompany benefits billing.

E6-11A.

LO 6-1, 6-4

Which of the following is a characteristic of workers' compensation? (Select all that apply.)

a. Workers' compensation is an insurance policy.

b. Private employers are federally mandated to provide workers' compensation.

c. The cost of workers' compensation represents a labor expense to the business.

d. Workers' compensation is provided to cover employees who are injured or killed while performing work duties.

Problems Set A

P6-1A.

LO 6-1

Bob Higgins works for Red Apple Engines, which pays employees on a semi-monthly basis. Bob's annual salary is $150,000. Calculate the following:

Pay Date	Prior YTD Earnings	Social Security Taxable Wages	Medicare Taxable Wages	Employer Share Social Security Tax	Employer Share Medicare Tax
November 15					
December 31					

P6-2A.

LO 6-1 6-3

White Lemon Cameras has the following employees:

Employee Name	Annual Taxable Wages
Mia Haskell	$26,000
Viktor Papadopoulos	35,000
Puja Anderson	32,000
Cady Billingmeier	29,000
Carl Johnson	46,000

White Lemon Cameras' SUTA tax rate is 5.4 percent and applies to the first $8,000 of employee wages. What is the annual amount due for each employee?

Employee	FUTA Due	SUTA Due
Mia Haskell		
Viktor Papadopoulos		
Puja Anderson		
Cady Billingmeier		
Carl Johnson		

P6-3A.
LO 6-1, 6-2, 6-3

Freedom Inc. has 16 employees within Denver City and County. All of the employees worked a predominant number of hours within the city. The employees earned $10.25 per hour and worked 160 hours each during the month. The employer must remit $4.00 per month per employee who earns more than $500 per month. Additionally, employees who earn more than $500 per month must have $5.75 withheld from their pay. What are the employee and company Occupational Privilege Tax for these employees?

Employee: _____

Employer: _____

P6-4A.
LO 6-1, 6-3

Joseph Farmer earned $128,000 in 2020 for a company in Kentucky. He is single with one dependent under 17 and is paid monthly. Compute the following employee share of the taxes using the percentage method (or the IRS federal income tax withholding assistant) in Appendix C and the state information in Appendix D.

Federal income tax withholding: _____

Social Security tax: _____

Medicare tax: _____

State income tax withholding: _____

P6-5A.
LO 6-3

Using the information from P6-4A, compute the employer's share of the taxes. The FUTA rate in Kentucky for 2020 is 0.6 percent on the first $7,000 of employee wages, and the SUTA rate is 5.4 percent with a wage base of $10,800.

Federal income tax withholding: _____

Social Security tax: _____

Medicare tax: _____

FUTA tax: _____

SUTA tax: _____

State income tax withholding: _____

P6-6A.
LO 6-2

Veryclear Glassware is a new business owned by Samantha Peoples, the company president. Her first year of operation commenced on April 1, 2020. What schedule depositor would she be for the first year of operations?

P6-7A.
LO 6-3

Using the information from P6-6A, complete the following Form 941 for the second quarter of 2020. The report was signed on July 15, 2020

EIN: 78-7654398

Address: 23051 Old Redwood Highway, Sebastopol, California 95482, phone 707-555-5555

Number of employees: 7

Wages, tips, and other compensation paid during the second quarter of 2020: $244,798

Income tax withheld from employees: $48,000

Social Security tax withheld from employees: $15,177.48

Medicare tax withheld from employees: $3,549.57

Monthly tax liability:

April	$28,484.79
May	28,484.79
June	28,484.80

P6-8A.
LO 6-3

Using the information from P6-6A and P6-7A for Veryclear Glassware (California Employer Account Number 999-9999-9), complete the following State of California Form DE-9, Quarterly Contribution and Report of Wages Report. Use 5.4 percent as the UI rate with a cap of $7,000 per employee, 0.1 percent as the ETT rate also with a cap of $7,000 per employee, and 0.9 percent as the SDI rate with a cap of $100,880 per employee. All employees have worked the full quarter with the company, and all wages are subject to UI, ETT, and SDI. The California PIT taxes withheld for the quarter are $4,068. The company has deposited $6,656.18 for the quarter. Samantha Peoples submitted the form on 7/15/2020.

Form **941 for 2020:** **Employer's QUARTERLY Federal Tax Return**

(Rev. January 2020)

Department of the Treasury — Internal Revenue Service

950117

OMB No. 1545-0029

Employer identification number (EIN) [ ][ ] — [ ][ ][ ][ ][ ][ ]

Name *(not your trade name)*

Trade name *(if any)*

Address

Number   Street   Suite or room number

City   State   ZIP code

Foreign country name   Foreign province/county   Foreign postal code

Report for this Quarter of 2020
(Check one.)

☐ **1:** January, February, March

☐ **2:** April, May, June

☐ **3:** July, August, September

☐ **4:** October, November, December

Go to *www.irs.gov/Form941* for instructions and the latest information.

Read the separate instructions before you complete Form 941. Type or print within the boxes.

Part 1:   **Answer these questions for this quarter.**

1   Number of employees who received wages, tips, or other compensation for the pay period including: *Mar. 12* (Quarter 1), *June 12* (Quarter 2), *Sept. 12* (Quarter 3), or *Dec. 12* (Quarter 4)   **1**

2   Wages, tips, and other compensation **2**

3   Federal income tax withheld from wages, tips, and other compensation **3**

4   If no wages, tips, and other compensation are subject to social security or Medicare tax   ☐ **Check and go to line 6.**

		Column 1		Column 2	
5a	Taxable social security wages . .		.	× 0.124 =	.
5b	Taxable social security tips . . .		.	× 0.124 =	.
5c	Taxable Medicare wages & tips. .		.	× 0.029 =	.
5d	Taxable wages & tips subject to Additional Medicare Tax withholding		.	× 0.009 =	.

5e   Add Column 2 from lines 5a, 5b, 5c, and 5d **5e**

5f   Section 3121(q) Notice and Demand—Tax due on unreported tips (see instructions)   . .   **5f**

6   **Total taxes before adjustments.** Add lines 3, 5e, and 5f **6**

7   Current quarter's adjustment for fractions of cents **7**

8   Current quarter's adjustment for sick pay **8**

9   Current quarter's adjustments for tips and group-term life insurance **9**

10   **Total taxes after adjustments.** Combine lines 6 through 9   . . . .   **10**

11   Qualified small business payroll tax credit for increasing research activities. Attach Form 8974   **11**

12   **Total taxes after adjustments and credits.** Subtract line 11 from line 10   . . . . .   **12**

13   Total deposits for this quarter, including overpayment applied from a prior quarter and overpayments applied from Form 941-X, 941-X (PR), 944-X, or 944-X (SP) filed in the current quarter   **13**

14   **Balance due.** If line 12 is more than line 13, enter the difference and see instructions   . . .   **14**

15   **Overpayment.** If line 13 is more than line 12, enter the difference   [.]   Check one: ☐ Apply to next return.   ☐ Send a refund.

▶ **You MUST complete both pages of Form 941 and SIGN it.**   **Next** ➡

For Privacy Act and Paperwork Reduction Act Notice, see the back of the Payment Voucher.   Cat. No. 17001Z   Form **941** (Rev. 1-2020)

950217

Name *(not your trade name)*	Employer identification number (EIN)

Part 2: **Tell us about your deposit schedule and tax liability for this quarter.**

If you are unsure about whether you are a monthly schedule depositor or a semiweekly schedule depositor, see section 11 of Pub. 15.

16 Check one: ☐ **Line 12 on this return is less than $2,500 or line 12 on the return for the prior quarter was less than $2,500, and you didn't incur a $100,000 next-day deposit obligation during the current quarter.** If line 12 for the prior quarter was less than $2,500 but line 12 on this return is $100,000 or more, you must provide a record of your federal tax liability. If you are a monthly schedule depositor, complete the deposit schedule below; if you are a semiweekly schedule depositor, attach Schedule B (Form 941). Go to Part 3.

☐ **You were a monthly schedule depositor for the entire quarter.** Enter your tax liability for each month and total liability for the quarter, then go to Part 3.

Tax liability: Month 1 [.   ]

Month 2 [.   ]

Month 3 [.   ]

Total liability for quarter [.   ] **Total must equal line 12.**

☐ **You were a semiweekly schedule depositor for any part of this quarter.** Complete Schedule B (Form 941), Report of Tax Liability for Semiweekly Schedule Depositors, and attach it to Form 941.

Part 3: **Tell us about your business. If a question does NOT apply to your business, leave it blank.**

17 If your business has closed or you stopped paying wages . . . . ☐ Check here, and

enter the final date you paid wages [/   /   ] .

18 If you are a seasonal employer and you don't have to file a return for every quarter of the year . . ☐ Check here.

Part 4: **May we speak with your third-party designee?**

Do you want to allow an employee, a paid tax preparer, or another person to discuss this return with the IRS? See the instructions for details.

☐ Yes. Designee's name and phone number [   ] [   ]

Select a 5-digit Personal Identification Number (PIN) to use when talking to the IRS. ☐ ☐ ☐ ☐ ☐

☐ No.

Part 5: **Sign here. You MUST complete both pages of Form 941 and SIGN it.**

Under penalties of perjury, I declare that I have examined this return, including accompanying schedules and statements, and to the best of my knowledge and belief, it is true, correct, and complete. Declaration of preparer (other than taxpayer) is based on all information of which preparer has any knowledge.

X **Sign your name here** [   ] Print your name here [   ]

Print your title here [   ]

Date [/   /   ] Best daytime phone [   ]

Paid Preparer Use Only Check if you are self-employed . . . ☐

Preparer's name	[ ]	PTIN	[ ]
Preparer's signature	[ ]	Date	[/ /]
Firm's name (or yours if self-employed)	[ ]	EIN	[ ]
Address	[ ]	Phone	[ ]
City	[ ]	State	[ ]	ZIP code	[ ]

Form **941** (Rev. 1-2020)

P6-9A.
LO 6-3

The Content Rabbit Graphics Company paid its 25 employees a total of $863,428.49 during 2019. Of these wages, $5,400 is exempt fringe benefits (Section 125 cafeteria plans) and $9,850 is exempt retirement benefits (employer contributions to 401(k) plans). All employees have worked there for the full calendar year and reached the FUTA wage base during the first quarter; taxes were deposited then. The Content Rabbit Graphics Company is located at 3874 Palm Avenue, Sebring, Florida, 20394. The owner is Eula Parks, EIN is 99-2039485, and the phone number is 461-555-9485. Complete Form 940, submitting it on January 13, 2020.

P6-10A.
LO 6-3

Leda Inc. is located at 433 Augusta Road, Caribou, Maine, 04736, phone number 207-555-1212. The Federal EIN is 54-3910394, and it has a Maine Revenue Services number of 3884019. Owner Amanda Leda has asked you to prepare Form W-2 for each of the following employees of Leda Inc. as of December 31, 2020.

Sarah C. Niehaus 122 Main Street, #3 Caribou, ME 04736 SSN: 477-30-2234 Dependent Care Benefit: $1,800.00	Total 2020 wages: $34,768.53 401(k) contribution: $1,043.06 Section 125 contribution: $1,500.00 Federal income tax withheld: $2,028.00 Social Security tax withheld: $2,062.65 Medicare tax withheld: $482.39 State income tax withheld $1,869.08
Maxwell S. Law 1503 22nd Street New Sweden, ME 04762 SSN: 493-55-2049	Total 2020 wages: $36,729.37 401(k) contribution: $1,469.18 Section 125 contribution: $1,675.00 Federal income tax withheld: none Social Security tax withheld: $2,173.37 Medicare tax withheld: $508.29 State income tax withheld $1,947.94
Siobhan E. Manning 1394 West Highway 59 Woodland, ME 04694 SSN: 390-39-1002 Tuition in excess of $5,250: $1,575.00 (Include in boxes 1, 3, 5, 16)	Total 2020 wages: $30,034.87 401(k) contribution: $712.75 Section 125 contribution: $1,000.00 Federal income tax withheld: none Social Security tax withheld: $1,897.81 Medicare tax withheld: $443.84 State income tax withheld $1,734.03
Donald A. Hendrix 1387 Rimbaud Avenue Caribou, ME 04736 SSN: 288-30-5940	Total 2020 wages: $22,578.89 401(k) contribution: $1,354.73 Section 125 contribution: $2,250.00 Federal income tax withheld: $648.00 Social Security tax withheld: $1,260.39 Medicare tax withheld: $294.77 State income tax withheld $1,100.50
Alison K. Sutter 3664 Fairfield Street Washburn, ME 04786 SSN: 490-55-0293	Total 2020 wages: $45,908.34 401(k) contribution: $2,754.50 Section 125 contribution: $1,750.00 Federal income tax withheld: $3,288.00 Social Security tax withheld: $2,737.82 Medicare tax withheld: $640.30 State income tax withheld $2,401.42

P6-11A.
LO 6-3

Using the information from P6-10A for Leda Inc., complete Form W-3 that must accompany the company's W-2 Forms. Leda Inc. is a 941-ss payer and is a private, for-profit company. Amanda Leda is the owner; the phone number is 207-555-1212; no e-mail address to disclose; the fax number is 207-555-9898. No third-party sick pay applied for 2020. The form was signed on January 20, 2021.

Employment Development Department State of California

QUARTERLY CONTRIBUTION RETURN AND REPORT OF WAGES

REMINDER: File your DE 9 and DE 9C together.

00090112

PLEASE TYPE THIS FORM—DO NOT ALTER PREPRINTED INFORMATION

				YR	QTR

QUARTER ENDED

DUE

DELINQUENT IF NOT POSTMARKED OR RECEIVED BY

EMPLOYER ACCOUNT NO.

DEPT. USE ONLY

DO NOT ALTER THIS AREA

P1   P2   C   P   U   S   A

T

EFFECTIVE DATE   Mo.   Day   Yr.

FEIN

A. NO WAGES PAID THIS QUARTER ☐   **B.** OUT OF BUSINESS/NO EMPLOYEES ☐

ADDITIONAL FEINS

B1.   OUT OF BUSINESS DATE   M M D D Y Y Y Y

C. TOTAL SUBJECT WAGES PAID THIS QUARTER ....

D. UNEMPLOYMENT INSURANCE (UI) (Total Employee Wages up to $ _____ per employee per calendar year)

(D1) UI Rate %   TIMES   (D2) UI TAXABLE WAGES FOR THE QUARTER   =   (D3) UI CONTRIBUTIONS   0:00

E. EMPLOYMENT TRAINING TAX (ETT)

(E1) ETT Rate %   TIMES   UI Taxable Wages for the Quarter (D2) ...... =   (E2) ETT CONTRIBUTIONS   0:00

F. STATE DISABILITY INSURANCE (SDI) (Total Employee Wages up to $ _____ per employee per calendar year)

(F1) SDI Rate %   TIMES   (F2) SDI TAXABLE WAGES FOR THE QUARTER   =   (F3) SDI EMPLOYEE CONTRIBUTIONS WITHHELD   0:00

G. CALIFORNIA PERSONAL INCOME TAX (PIT) WITHHELD ....

H. SUBTOTAL (Add Items D3, E2, F3, and G) 0:00

I. LESS: CONTRIBUTIONS AND WITHHOLDINGS PAID FOR THE QUARTER ....
(**DO NOT** INCLUDE PENALTY AND INTEREST PAYMENTS)

J. TOTAL TAXES DUE OR OVERPAID   (Item H minus Item I) 0:00

If amount due, prepare a *Payroll Tax Deposit* (DE 88), include the correct payment quarter, and mail to: Employment Development Department, P.O. Box 826276, Sacramento, CA 94230-6276. **NOTE:** Do not mail payments along with the DE 9 and *Quarterly Contribution Return and Report of Wages (Continuation)* (DE 9C), as this may delay processing and result in erroneous penalty and interest charges. **Mandatory Electronic Funds Transfer (EFT)** filers must remit all SDI/PIT deposits by EFT to avoid a noncompliance penalty.

K. I declare that the above, to the best of my knowledge and belief, is true and correct. If a refund was claimed, a reasonable effort was made to refund any erroneous deductions to the affected employee(s).

Signature *Required* _____   Title _____   Phone (____) _____   Date_____
(Owner, Accountant, Preparer, etc.)

◉   SIGN AND MAIL TO: State of California / Employment Development Department / P.O. Box 989071 / West Sacramento CA 95798-9071

DE 9 Rev. 1 (1-12) **(INTERNET)**   Page 1 of 2   Fast, Easy, and Convenient!
Visit EDD's Web site at **www.edd.ca.gov**

Source: Employment Development Department

Form **940 for 2019:** **Employer's Annual Federal Unemployment (FUTA) Tax Return**   850113

Department of the Treasury — Internal Revenue Service

OMB No. 1545-0028

Employer identification number (EIN) ☐☐ – ☐☐☐☐☐☐☐

Name *(not your trade name)*

Trade name *(if any)*

Address

Number   Street   Suite or room number

City   State   ZIP code

Foreign country name   Foreign province/county   Foreign postal code

Type of Return
(Check all that apply.)

☐ **a.** Amended

☐ **b.** Successor employer

☐ **c.** No payments to employees in 2019

☐ **d.** Final: Business closed or stopped paying wages

Go to *www.irs.gov/Form940* for instructions and the latest information.

Read the separate instructions before you complete this form. Please type or print within the boxes.

Part 1:   Tell us about your return. If any line does NOT apply, leave it blank. See instructions before completing Part 1.

1a If you had to pay state unemployment tax in one state only, enter the state abbreviation .   **1a** ☐☐

1b If you had to pay state unemployment tax in more than one state, you are a multi-state employer . . . .   **1b** ☐ Check here. Complete Schedule A (Form 940).

2 If you paid wages in a state that is subject to CREDIT REDUCTION . . . .   **2** ☐ Check here. Complete Schedule A (Form 940).

Part 2:   Determine your FUTA tax before adjustments. If any line does NOT apply, leave it blank.

3 Total payments to all employees . . . .   **3** ☐ .

4 Payments exempt from FUTA tax . . . . . .   **4** ☐ .

Check all that apply: **4a** ☐ Fringe benefits   **4c** ☐ Retirement/Pension   **4e** ☐ Other
                     4b ☐ Group-term life insurance   **4d** ☐ Dependent care

5 Total of payments made to each employee in excess of $7,000 . . . .   **5** ☐ .

6 Subtotal (line 4 + line 5 = line 6) . . . .   **6** ☐ .

7 Total taxable FUTA wages (line 3 – line 6 = line 7). See instructions . . . . . .   **7** ☐ .

8 FUTA tax before adjustments (line 7 x 0.006 = line 8) . . . . . .   **8** ☐ .

Part 3:   Determine your adjustments. If any line does NOT apply, leave it blank.

9 If ALL of the taxable FUTA wages you paid were excluded from state unemployment tax, multiply line 7 by 0.054 (line 7 × 0.054 = line 9). Go to line 12 . . . .   **9** ☐ .

10 If SOME of the taxable FUTA wages you paid were excluded from state unemployment tax, OR you paid ANY state unemployment tax late (after the due date for filing Form 940), complete the worksheet in the instructions. Enter the amount from line 7 of the worksheet . .   **10** ☐ .

11 If credit reduction applies, enter the total from Schedule A (Form 940) . . . .   **11** ☐ .

Part 4:   Determine your FUTA tax and balance due or overpayment. If any line does NOT apply, leave it blank.

12 Total FUTA tax after adjustments (lines 8 + 9 + 10 + 11 = line 12) . . . . . .   **12** ☐ .

13 FUTA tax deposited for the year, including any overpayment applied from a prior year .   **13** ☐ .

14 Balance due. If line 12 is more than line 13, enter the excess on line 14.
• If line 14 is more than $500, you must deposit your tax.
• If line 14 is $500 or less, you may pay with this return. See instructions . . . . .   **14** ☐ .

15 Overpayment. If line 13 is more than line 12, enter the excess on line 15 and check a box below   **15** ☐ .

▶ You **MUST** complete both pages of this form and **SIGN** it.   Check one: ☐ Apply to next return. ☐ Send a refund.

Next ▶

For Privacy Act and Paperwork Reduction Act Notice, see the back of the Payment Voucher.   Cat. No. 11234O   Form **940** (2019)

850212

Name *(not your trade name)*	Employer identification number (EIN)

Part 5: Report your FUTA tax liability by quarter only if line 12 is more than $500. If not, go to Part 6.

16 Report the amount of your FUTA tax liability for each quarter; do NOT enter the amount you deposited. If you had no liability for a quarter, leave the line blank.

16a **1st quarter** (January 1 – March 31) . . . . **16a** [.   ]

16b **2nd quarter** (April 1 – June 30) . . . . **16b** [.   ]

16c **3rd quarter** (July 1 – September 30) . . . . **16c** [.   ]

16d **4th quarter** (October 1 – December 31) . . . . **16d** [.   ]

17 **Total tax liability for the year** (lines 16a + 16b + 16c + 16d = line 17) **17** [.   ] **Total must equal line 12.**

Part 6: May we speak with your third-party designee?

Do you want to allow an employee, a paid tax preparer, or another person to discuss this return with the IRS? See the instructions for details.

☐ **Yes.** Designee's name and phone number [   ] [   ]

Select a 5-digit Personal Identification Number (PIN) to use when talking to IRS [ ] [ ] [ ] [ ] [ ]

☐ **No.**

Part 7: Sign here. You MUST complete both pages of this form and SIGN it.

Under penalties of perjury, I declare that I have examined this return, including accompanying schedules and statements, and to the best of my knowledge and belief, it is true, correct, and complete, and that no part of any payment made to a state unemployment fund claimed as a credit was, or is to be, deducted from the payments made to employees. Declaration of preparer (other than taxpayer) is based on all information of which preparer has any knowledge.

✗ **Sign your name here** [   ]

Print your name here [   ]

Print your title here [   ]

Date [/   /   ]

Best daytime phone [   ]

Paid Preparer Use Only

Check if you are self-employed ☐

Preparer's name	[ ]	PTIN	[ ]
Preparer's signature	[ ]	Date	[/ /]
Firm's name (or yours if self-employed)	[ ]	EIN	[ ]
Address	[ ]	Phone	[ ]
City	[ ] State [ ]	ZIP code	[ ]

22222	**a** Employee's social security number		
	OMB No. 1545-0008		

b Employer identification number (EIN)	**1** Wages, tips, other compensation	**2** Federal income tax withheld
c Employer's name, address, and ZIP code	**3** Social security wages	**4** Social security tax withheld
	5 Medicare wages and tips	**6** Medicare tax withheld
	7 Social security tips	**8** Allocated tips
d Control number	**9**	**10** Dependent care benefits
e Employee's first name and initial Last name Suff.	**11** Nonqualified plans	**12a** Code
	13 Statutory employee / Retirement plan / Third-party sick pay	**12b** Code
	14 Other	**12c** Code
		12d Code
f Employee's address and ZIP code		

15 State Employer's state ID number	**16** State wages, tips, etc.	**17** State income tax	**18** Local wages, tips, etc.	**19** Local income tax	**20** Locality name

Form **W-2** Wage and Tax Statement   **2020**   Department of the Treasury—Internal Revenue Service

Copy 1—For State, City, or Local Tax Department

Source: Internal Revenue Service

DO NOT STAPLE

33333	**a** Control number	**For Official Use Only ▶**
		OMB No. 1545-0008

b Kind of Payer (Check one)	941 ☐ Military ☐ 943 ☐ 944 ☐ CT-1 ☐ Hshld. emp. ☐ Medicare govt. emp. ☐	**Kind of Employer** (Check one)	None apply ☐ 501c non-govt. ☐ State/local non-501c ☐ State/local 501c ☐ Federal govt. ☐	Third-party sick pay (Check if applicable) ☐

c Total number of Forms W-2	**d** Establishment number	**1** Wages, tips, other compensation	**2** Federal income tax withheld
e Employer identification number (EIN)		**3** Social security wages	**4** Social security tax withheld
f Employer's name		**5** Medicare wages and tips	**6** Medicare tax withheld
		7 Social security tips	**8** Allocated tips
		9	**10** Dependent care benefits
		11 Nonqualified plans	**12a** Deferred compensation
g Employer's address and ZIP code			
h Other EIN used this year		**13** For third-party sick pay use only	**12b**
15 State Employer's state ID number		**14** Income tax withheld by payer of third-party sick pay	
16 State wages, tips, etc.	**17** State income tax	**18** Local wages, tips, etc.	**19** Local income tax
Employer's contact person		Employer's telephone number	For Official Use Only
Employer's fax number		Employer's email address	

Under penalties of perjury, I declare that I have examined this return and accompanying documents, and, to the best of my knowledge and belief, they are true, correct, and complete.

Signature ▶   Title ▶   Date ▶

Form **W-3** Transmittal of Wage and Tax Statements   **2020**   Department of the Treasury Internal Revenue Service

Source: Internal Revenue Service

P6-12A.
LO 6-4, 6-6

Clark Patrick owns Camel Customs, a company that restores vintage Ford Mustangs. He has seven employees. Clark wants to perform a benefits analysis report for one of his employees, Gayle Rowe, for the year. Gayle's benefits package is as follows:

Annual salary: $40,000

401(k) contribution: 3 percent of annual salary, company match is 50 percent of employee contribution

Medical insurance deduction: $150 per month

Dental insurance: $25 per month

Complete the following Benefits Analysis Report for Gayle Rowe for the year. Do not include FUTA and SUTA taxes.

Yearly Benefit Costs	Company Cost	Gayle's Cost
Medical insurance	$7,200	$
Dental insurance	1,000	$
Life insurance	200	-0-
AD&D	50	-0-
Short-term disability	500	-0-
Long-term disability	250	-0-
401(k)	$	$
Social Security	$	$
Medicare	$	$
Tuition reimbursement	2,000	-0-
Total yearly benefit costs	$	$
Gayle's annual salary	$	
Total yearly benefit costs	$	
Total value of Gayle's compensation	$	

P6-13A.
LO 6-4, 6-5

Black Sheep Printing has 35 employees distributed among the following departments:

Sales: 10	Factory: 15	Administration: 10

The total annual payroll for Black Sheep Printing is $700,000. Compute the labor distribution based on equal distribution among the departments.

Sales: _____

Factory: _____

Administration: _____

P6-14A.
LO 6-4, 6-5

For Black Sheep Printing in P6-13A, compute the labor distribution based on the number of employees per department:

Sales: _____

Factory: _____

Administration: _____

P6-15A.
LO 6-1, 6-4

Small Orange Fine Foods is a specialty grocery store. The employees are classified according to job titles for workers' compensation insurance premium computation purposes.

a. Based on the payroll estimates as of January 1, what is the total estimated workers' compensation premium for 20XX?

Employee Classification	Rate per $100 of Payroll	Estimated Payroll for 20XX	Workers' Compensation Premium
Grocery Clerk	$0.75	$192,500	
Shelf Stocker	1.90	212,160	
Stock Handler	2.40	237,120	
		Total Premium =	

b. The actual payroll for 20XX is listed below. What is the workers' compensation premium based on the actual payroll?

Employee Classification	Rate per $100 of Payroll	Actual Payroll for 20XX	Workers' Compensation Premium
Grocery Clerk	$0.75	$196,588	
Shelf Stocker	1.90	215,220	
Stock Handler	2.40	242,574	
		Total Premium =	

c. What is the difference between the actual and the estimated premiums?

_____

Exercises Set B

E6-1B.
LO 6-1

Of the following taxes, which one(s) is/are examples of statutory deductions that pertain to employers? (Select all that apply.)
a. Social Security tax
b. Employee federal income tax
c. FUTA
d. 401(k) contributions

E6-2B.
LO 6-1

Which of the following is/are true about FUTA obligations? (Select all that apply.)
a. FUTA is an employer-only tax.
b. FUTA is subject to a 5.4 percent reduction based on employer and state factors.
c. FUTA is subject to a $7,000 wage base per employee.
d. FUTA applies to all companies.

E6-3B.
LO 6-1

Of the IRS-stipulated lookback periods, which one(s) is/are the most commonly used? (Select all that apply.)
a. Monthly
b. Semiweekly
c. Quarterly
d. Annual

E6-4B.
LO 6-2

The Foggy Snail Theater has annual payroll taxes of $49,250 during the most recent lookback period. Which payroll deposit frequency will the company have, based on that lookback period?
a. Quarterly
b. Monthly
c. Semiweekly
d. Annual

E6-5B.
LO 6-3

Joyce Hunter is the new payroll accountant with Rainy Snake Products in Sparks, Nevada. The company had a payroll tax liability of $250,350 during the most recent lookback period. For the quarter ending September 30, 20XX, which federal form(s) should she file? (Select all that apply.)
a. Form 940
b. Form W-2
c. Form ss-8
d. Form 941

E6-6B.
LO 6-3

Which of the following is a form that must accompany all Forms W-2 submitted to the Social Security Administration?
a. Form 941
b. Form 940
c. Form W-3
d. Form W-4

E6-7B.
LO 6-4

What are the penalties associated with the lack of reporting and remitting payroll taxes? (Select all that apply.)
a. Failure to report
b. Failure to file
c. Failure to deposit
d. Failure to remit

E6-8B.
LO 6-4

Winston Briggs is the accounting supervisor for Cheeky Cat Furnishings, which has chosen to maintain its payroll on an in-house basis for this purpose and has hired new accounting clerks. Which of the following are payroll responsibilities of Cheeky Cat Furnishings? (Select all that apply.)
a. Timely remittance of payroll taxes.
b. Remittance of voluntary deductions.
c. Accountability to employees and governmental agencies.
d. Publication of salary data in company-wide publications.

E6-9B.
LO 6-5

Which of the following represents the difference between the benefit analysis report and the annual total compensation report? (Select all that apply.)
a. The benefit analysis report is designed for review by employees.
b. The annual total compensation report's intended audience is company managers.
c. The benefit analysis report reflects actual benefit costs, and the annual total compensation report includes salary data.
d. The reports are maintained as public records.

E6-10B.
LO 6-5

Which of the following represent(s) the purpose(s) of the labor distribution report? (Select all that apply.)
a. Accurate payroll cost allocation among departments.
b. Explanation of individual employee costs.
c. Evaluation of labor planning efforts.
d. Determination of departmental performance.

E6-11B.
LO 6-1, 6-4

Sunny Day Flooring has employees in its manufacturing, sales, and administrative departments. Which department will have the highest rate for its workers' compensation insurance?
a. Manufacturing
b. Sales
c. Administrative
d. All departments will have the same rate.

Problems Set B

P6-1B.
LO 6-1

Doyle Watson works for Clear Pencil Accounting, which pays employees on a semimonthly basis. Doyle's annual salary is $210,000. Calculate the following:

Pay Date	Prior YTD Earnings	Social Security Taxable Wages	Medicare Taxable Wages	Employer Share Social Security Tax	Employer Share Medicare Tax
November 30					
December 31					

P6-2B.
LO 6-1, 6-3

Black Robot Grill of Andrews, Texas, has the following employees as of December 31:

Employee Name	Annual Taxable Wages
Mark English	$45,750
Shelly Morris	21,250
TL Radford	29,850
James Morrow	36,280
Trella Lyons	34,900

The company's SUTA tax rate is 6.25 percent and the wage base is $9,000. What is the annual amount of FUTA and SUTA taxes due for each employee?

Employee Name	FUTA Due	SUTA Due
Mark English		
Shelly Morris		
TL Radford		
James Morrow		
Trella Lyons		

P6-3B.
LO 6-1, 6-2, 6-3

Deep Mouse Designs has 22 employees within Denver City and County. The employees earned $11.50 per hour and worked 160 hours each during the month. The employer must remit $4.00 per month per employee who earns more than $500 per month. Additionally, employees who earn more than $500 per month must have $5.75 withheld from their pay. What is the employee and company Occupational Privilege Tax for these employees?
Employee: _____
Employer: _____

P6-4B.
LO 6-1, 6-2, 6-3

Rosalie Watts earned $155,000 in 2020 for Sad Orange Web Design in King of Prussia, Pennsylvania. Sad Orange's SUTA rate is 4.8 percent and has a wage base for 2020 of $10,000. Compute Sad Orange Web Designs' share of Rosalie's salary.
Social Security tax:_____
Medicare tax:_____
FUTA tax:_____
SUTA tax:_____

P6-5B.
LO 6-2, 6-3

Howard Murphy is the owner of Stormy Banana Films in West Hollywood, California. Stormy Banana Films had 15 employees with total annual wages of $214,750 (no one exceeded the Medicare tax surcharge or Social Security cap). Stormy Banana Films has a SUTA rate of 3.2 percent for 2020 with a wage base of $7,000. Compute the following employer taxes:
Social Security tax:_____
Medicare tax:_____
FUTA tax:_____
SUTA tax:_____

P6-6B.
LO 6-1

Peaceful Cat Pet Foods is a new business owned by Sylvester Hammond. His first year of operations commenced on July 1, 2020. What schedule depositor would his company be for the first year of operations?

P6-7B.
LO 6-3

Using the information from P6-6B, complete the following Form 941 for the third quarter of 2020. The form was signed by the owner on October 10, 2020. EIN: 98-0050036

Address: 1021 Old Plainfield Road, Salina, California 95670

Phone: 707-555-0303

Number of employees: 8

Wages, tips, and other compensation paid during the third quarter of 2020: $302,374

Income tax withheld: $51,000

Monthly tax liability:

July	$32,421.08
August	32,421.08
September	32,421.07

P6-8B.
LO 6-3

Using the information from P6-6B and P6-7B for Peaceful Cat Pet Foods, complete the following State of California Form DE-9, Quarterly Contribution Return and Report of Wages. The California employer account number is 989-8877-1. Use 5.4 percent as the UI rate, 0.1 percent as the ETT rate, and 0.9 percent as the SDI rate. California UI and ETT wage cap is $7,000 while SDI cap is $100,880. No employee has reached the SDI limit. All employees have worked with the company since July 1. The California PIT taxes withheld for the quarter are $40,000. The company has deposited no taxes for the quarter. Form DE-9 was completed and signed on October 10, 2020, with a due date of October 15, 2020.

P6-9B.
LO 6-3

Jealous Frog Toys paid its nine employees a total of $432,586.40 during 2019. All employees have worked there for the full calendar year and reached the FUTA wage base during the first quarter. Taxes were deposited on time. The employer contributed $12,470 to Section 125 plans during the year as a fringe benefit. Jealous Frog Toys is located at 783 Morehead Street, Fargo, ND 68383, phone number 701-555-3432. The owner is Noah Jackson, and the EIN is 73-4029848. Complete Form 940. The form was signed and submitted on January 10, 2020.

Form **941 for 2020:** **Employer's QUARTERLY Federal Tax Return**

(Rev. January 2020) Department of the Treasury — Internal Revenue Service

950117

OMB No. 1545-0029

Employer identification number (EIN) ☐☐ – ☐☐☐☐☐☐☐

Name *(not your trade name)*

Trade name *(if any)*

Address

Number   Street   Suite or room number

City   State   ZIP code

Foreign country name   Foreign province/county   Foreign postal code

Report for this Quarter of 2020
(Check one.)

☐ **1:** January, February, March

☐ **2:** April, May, June

☐ **3:** July, August, September

☐ **4:** October, November, December

Go to *www.irs.gov/Form941* for instructions and the latest information.

Read the separate instructions before you complete Form 941. Type or print within the boxes.

Part 1: **Answer these questions for this quarter.**

1 Number of employees who received wages, tips, or other compensation for the pay period including: *Mar. 12* (Quarter 1), *June 12* (Quarter 2), *Sept. 12* (Quarter 3), or *Dec. 12* (Quarter 4) **1** ☐

2 Wages, tips, and other compensation **2** ☐

3 Federal income tax withheld from wages, tips, and other compensation **3** ☐

4 If no wages, tips, and other compensation are subject to social security or Medicare tax ☐ Check and go to line 6.

	Column 1		Column 2
5a Taxable social security wages . .	☐	× 0.124 =	☐
5b Taxable social security tips . . .	☐	× 0.124 =	☐
5c Taxable Medicare wages & tips. .	☐	× 0.029 =	☐
5d Taxable wages & tips subject to Additional Medicare Tax withholding	☐	× 0.009 =	☐

5e Add Column 2 from lines 5a, 5b, 5c, and 5d **5e** ☐

5f Section 3121(q) Notice and Demand—Tax due on unreported tips (see instructions) **5f** ☐

6 Total taxes before adjustments. Add lines 3, 5e, and 5f **6** ☐

7 Current quarter's adjustment for fractions of cents **7** ☐

8 Current quarter's adjustment for sick pay **8** ☐

9 Current quarter's adjustments for tips and group-term life insurance **9** ☐

10 Total taxes after adjustments. Combine lines 6 through 9 **10** ☐

11 Qualified small business payroll tax credit for increasing research activities. Attach Form 8974 **11** ☐

12 Total taxes after adjustments and credits. Subtract line 11 from line 10 **12** ☐

13 Total deposits for this quarter, including overpayment applied from a prior quarter and overpayments applied from Form 941-X, 941-X (PR), 944-X, or 944-X (SP) filed in the current quarter **13** ☐

14 Balance due. If line 12 is more than line 13, enter the difference and see instructions **14** ☐

15 Overpayment. If line 13 is more than line 12, enter the difference ☐ Check one: ☐ Apply to next return. ☐ Send a refund.

▶ **You MUST complete both pages of Form 941 and SIGN it.** Next ▶

For Privacy Act and Paperwork Reduction Act Notice, see the back of the Payment Voucher. Cat. No. 17001Z Form **941** (Rev. 1-2020)

950217

Name *(not your trade name)*   Employer identification number (EIN)

| **Part 2:** | **Tell us about your deposit schedule and tax liability for this quarter.** |

If you are unsure about whether you are a monthly schedule depositor or a semiweekly schedule depositor, see section 11 of Pub. 15.

16 Check one: ☐ **Line 12 on this return is less than $2,500 or line 12 on the return for the prior quarter was less than $2,500, and you didn't incur a $100,000 next-day deposit obligation during the current quarter.** If line 12 for the prior quarter was less than $2,500 but line 12 on this return is $100,000 or more, you must provide a record of your federal tax liability. If you are a monthly schedule depositor, complete the deposit schedule below; if you are a semiweekly schedule depositor, attach Schedule B (Form 941). Go to Part 3.

☐ **You were a monthly schedule depositor for the entire quarter.** Enter your tax liability for each month and total liability for the quarter, then go to Part 3.

Tax liability: Month 1 ☐ `.`

Month 2 ☐ `.`

Month 3 ☐ `.`

Total liability for quarter ☐ `.`   **Total must equal line 12.**

☐ **You were a semiweekly schedule depositor for any part of this quarter.** Complete Schedule B (Form 941), Report of Tax Liability for Semiweekly Schedule Depositors, and attach it to Form 941.

| **Part 3:** | **Tell us about your business. If a question does NOT apply to your business, leave it blank.** |

17 If your business has closed or you stopped paying wages . . . . ☐ Check here, and

enter the final date you paid wages [/ /] .

18 If you are a seasonal employer and you don't have to file a return for every quarter of the year . . ☐ Check here.

| **Part 4:** | **May we speak with your third-party designee?** |

Do you want to allow an employee, a paid tax preparer, or another person to discuss this return with the IRS? See the instructions for details.

☐ **Yes.** Designee's name and phone number [   ] [   ]

Select a 5-digit Personal Identification Number (PIN) to use when talking to the IRS. ☐ ☐ ☐ ☐ ☐

☐ **No.**

| **Part 5:** | **Sign here. You MUST complete both pages of Form 941 and SIGN it.** |

Under penalties of perjury, I declare that I have examined this return, including accompanying schedules and statements, and to the best of my knowledge and belief, it is true, correct, and complete. Declaration of preparer (other than taxpayer) is based on all information of which preparer has any knowledge.

✗ **Sign your name here** [   ]   Print your name here [   ]

Print your title here [   ]

Date [/ /]   Best daytime phone [   ]

Paid Preparer Use Only   Check if you are self-employed . . . ☐

Preparer's name [   ]   PTIN [   ]

Preparer's signature [   ]   Date [/ /]

Firm's name (or yours if self-employed) [   ]   EIN [   ]

Address [   ]   Phone [   ]

City [   ] State [   ]   ZIP code [   ]

EDD Employment Development Department
State of California

QUARTERLY CONTRIBUTION RETURN AND REPORT OF WAGES
REMINDER: File your DE 9 and DE 9C together.

00090112

PLEASE TYPE THIS FORM—DO NOT ALTER PREPRINTED INFORMATION

QUARTER ENDED

DUE

DELINQUENT IF NOT POSTMARKED OR RECEIVED BY

YR   QTR

EMPLOYER ACCOUNT NO.

DEPT. USE ONLY

DO NOT ALTER THIS AREA
P1   P2   C   P   U   S   A

T

EFFECTIVE DATE   Mo.   Day   Yr.

FEIN

A. NO WAGES PAID THIS QUARTER ☐

B. OUT OF BUSINESS/NO EMPLOYEES ☐

ADDITIONAL FEINS

B1.   OUT OF BUSINESS DATE
M   M   D   D   Y   Y   Y   Y

C. TOTAL SUBJECT WAGES PAID THIS QUARTER ....

D. UNEMPLOYMENT INSURANCE (UI) (Total Employee Wages up to $ per employee per calendar year)

(D1) UI Rate %   TIMES   (D2) UI TAXABLE WAGES FOR THE QUARTER   =   (D3) UI CONTRIBUTIONS   0.00

E. EMPLOYMENT TRAINING TAX (ETT)

(E1) ETT Rate %   TIMES   UI Taxable Wages for the Quarter (D2) ......   =   (E2) ETT CONTRIBUTIONS   0.00

F. STATE DISABILITY INSURANCE (SDI) (Total Employee Wages up to $ per employee per calendar year)

(F1) SDI Rate %   TIMES   (F2) SDI TAXABLE WAGES FOR THE QUARTER   =   (F3) SDI EMPLOYEE CONTRIBUTIONS WITHHELD   0.00

G. CALIFORNIA PERSONAL INCOME TAX (PIT) WITHHELD ....

H. **SUBTOTAL** (Add Items D3, E2, F3, and G) 0.00

I. LESS: CONTRIBUTIONS AND WITHHOLDINGS PAID FOR THE QUARTER ....
(**DO NOT** INCLUDE PENALTY AND INTEREST PAYMENTS)

J. TOTAL TAXES DUE OR OVERPAID   (Item H minus Item I) 0.00

If amount due, prepare a *Payroll Tax Deposit* (DE 88), include the correct payment quarter, and mail to: Employment Development Department, P.O. Box 826276, Sacramento, CA 94230-6276. **NOTE:** Do not mail payments along with the DE 9 and *Quarterly Contribution Return and Report of Wages (Continuation)* (DE 9C), as this may delay processing and result in erroneous penalty and interest charges. **Mandatory Electronic Funds Transfer (EFT)** filers must remit all SDI/PIT deposits by EFT to avoid a noncompliance penalty.

K. I declare that the above, to the best of my knowledge and belief, is true and correct. If a refund was claimed, a reasonable effort was made to refund any erroneous deductions to the affected employee(s).

Signature *Required*   Title _____   Phone (___) _____   Date _____
                                                    (Owner, Accountant, Preparer, etc.)

SIGN AND MAIL TO: State of California / Employment Development Department / P.O. Box 989071 / West Sacramento CA 95798-9071

DE 9 Rev. 1 (1-12) **(INTERNET)**   Page 1 of 2   Services   Fast, Easy, and Convenient!
                                                                    Visit EDD's Web site at **www.edd.ca.gov**

Form **940** for 2019: **Employer's Annual Federal Unemployment (FUTA) Tax Return**

850113

Department of the Treasury — Internal Revenue Service

OMB No. 1545-0028

Employer identification number (EIN) ☐☐ – ☐☐☐☐☐☐☐

Name *(not your trade name)*

Trade name *(if any)*

Address

Number | Street | Suite or room number

City | State | ZIP code

Foreign country name | Foreign province/county | Foreign postal code

Type of Return
(Check all that apply.)

☐ **a.** Amended

☐ **b.** Successor employer

☐ **c.** No payments to employees in 2019

☐ **d.** Final: Business closed or stopped paying wages

Go to *www.irs.gov/Form940* for instructions and the latest information.

Read the separate instructions before you complete this form. Please type or print within the boxes.

Part 1: **Tell us about your return. If any line does NOT apply, leave it blank. See instructions before completing Part 1.**

1a If you had to pay state unemployment tax in one state only, enter the state abbreviation . **1a** ☐☐

1b If you had to pay state unemployment tax in more than one state, you are a multi-state employer . . . . **1b** ☐ Check here. Complete Schedule A (Form 940).

2 If you paid wages in a state that is subject to **CREDIT REDUCTION** . . . . **2** ☐ Check here. Complete Schedule A (Form 940).

Part 2: **Determine your FUTA tax before adjustments. If any line does NOT apply, leave it blank.**

3 Total payments to all employees . . . . **3** [____ . __]

4 Payments exempt from FUTA tax . . . . . . **4** [____ . __]

Check all that apply: **4a** ☐ Fringe benefits   **4c** ☐ Retirement/Pension   **4e** ☐ Other

4b ☐ Group-term life insurance   **4d** ☐ Dependent care

5 Total of payments made to each employee in excess of $7,000 . . . . **5** [____ . __]

6 Subtotal (line 4 + line 5 = line 6) . . . . **6** [____ . __]

7 Total taxable FUTA wages (line 3 – line 6 = line 7). See instructions . . . . . **7** [____ . __]

8 FUTA tax before adjustments (line 7 × 0.006 = line 8) . . . . **8** [____ . __]

Part 3: **Determine your adjustments. If any line does NOT apply, leave it blank.**

9 If ALL of the taxable FUTA wages you paid were excluded from state unemployment tax, multiply line 7 by 0.054 (line 7 × 0.054 = line 9). Go to line 12 . . . . **9** [____ . __]

10 If SOME of the taxable FUTA wages you paid were excluded from state unemployment tax, **OR** you paid **ANY** state unemployment tax late (after the due date for filing Form 940), complete the worksheet in the instructions. Enter the amount from line 7 of the worksheet . . **10** [____ . __]

11 If credit reduction applies, enter the total from Schedule A (Form 940) . . . . . . **11** [____ . __]

Part 4: **Determine your FUTA tax and balance due or overpayment. If any line does NOT apply, leave it blank.**

12 Total FUTA tax after adjustments (lines 8 + 9 + 10 + 11 = line 12) . . . . . . **12** [____ . __]

13 FUTA tax deposited for the year, including any overpayment applied from a prior year . **13** [____ . __]

14 Balance due. If line 12 is more than line 13, enter the excess on line 14.

- If line 14 is more than $500, you must deposit your tax.
- If line 14 is $500 or less, you may pay with this return. See instructions . . . . . . **14** [____ . __]

15 Overpayment. If line 13 is more than line 12, enter the excess on line 15 and check a box below **15** [____ . __]

▶ You **MUST** complete both pages of this form and **SIGN** it.   Check one: ☐ Apply to next return. ☐ Send a refund.

Next ▶

For Privacy Act and Paperwork Reduction Act Notice, see the back of the Payment Voucher.   Cat. No. 11234O   Form **940** (2019)

850212

Name (not your trade name)	Employer identification number (EIN)

Part 5: Report your FUTA tax liability by quarter only if line 12 is more than $500. If not, go to Part 6.

16 Report the amount of your FUTA tax liability for each quarter; do NOT enter the amount you deposited. If you had no liability for a quarter, leave the line blank.

16a **1st quarter** (January 1 – March 31) . . . . 16a ☐ .

16b **2nd quarter** (April 1 – June 30) . . . . 16b ☐ .

16c **3rd quarter** (July 1 – September 30) . . . . 16c ☐ .

16d **4th quarter** (October 1 – December 31) . . . . 16d ☐ .

17 Total tax liability for the year (lines 16a + 16b + 16c + 16d = line 17) 17 ☐ . Total must equal line 12.

Part 6: May we speak with your third-party designee?

Do you want to allow an employee, a paid tax preparer, or another person to discuss this return with the IRS? See the instructions for details.

☐ **Yes.** Designee's name and phone number ☐ ☐

Select a 5-digit Personal Identification Number (PIN) to use when talking to IRS ☐ ☐ ☐ ☐ ☐

☐ **No.**

Part 7: Sign here. You MUST complete both pages of this form and SIGN it.

Under penalties of perjury, I declare that I have examined this return, including accompanying schedules and statements, and to the best of my knowledge and belief, it is true, correct, and complete, and that no part of any payment made to a state unemployment fund claimed as a credit was, or is to be, deducted from the payments made to employees. Declaration of preparer (other than taxpayer) is based on all information of which preparer has any knowledge.

✗ Sign your name here ☐

Print your name here ☐

Print your title here ☐

Date / /

Best daytime phone ☐

Paid Preparer Use Only Check if you are self-employed ☐

Preparer's name		PTIN	
Preparer's signature		Date	/ /
Firm's name (or yours if self-employed)		EIN	
Address		Phone	
City		State		ZIP code	

P6-10B.
LO 6-3

Philip Castor, owner of Castor Corporation, is located at 1310 Garrick Way, Sun Valley, Arizona, 86029, phone number 928-555-8842. The federal EIN is 20-1948348, and the state employer identification number is 9040-2038-1. Prepare Form W-2 (below) for each of the following employees of Castor Corporation as of December 31, 2020. The same deductions are allowed for state income tax as for federal.

Paul M. Parsons 5834 Moon Drive Sun Valley, AZ 86029 SSN: 578-33-3049	Total 2020 wages: $47,203.78 401(k) contribution: $2,832.23 Section 125 contribution: $1,400.00 Federal income tax withheld: $1,794.00 Social Security tax withheld: $2,839.83 Medicare tax withheld: $664.15 State income tax withheld: $1,443.84
Rachel Y. Maddox 32 Second Street Holbrook, AZ 86025 SSN: 734-00-1938 Tuition in excess of $5,250: $750 (Include in boxes 1, 3, 5, 16)	Total 2020 wages: $37,499.02 401(k) contribution: $1,124.97 Section 125 contribution: $500.00 Federal income tax withheld: $1,612.00 Social Security tax withheld: $2,340.44 Medicare tax withheld: $547.36 State income tax withheld: $1,180.92
Ari J. Featherstone 7784 Painted Desert Road Sun Valley, AZ 86029 SSN: 290-03-4992	Total 2020 wages: $41,904.29 401(k) contribution: $1,885.69 Federal income tax withheld: $3,146.00 Social Security tax withheld: $2,598.07 Medicare tax withheld: $607.61 State income tax withheld: $1,344.63
Connor L. Clearwater 7384 Ridge Road Woodruff, AZ 85942 SSN: 994-20-4837	Total 2020 wages: $29,874.37 401(k) contribution: $597.49 Section 125 contribution: $250.00 Federal income tax withheld: $390.00 Social Security tax withheld: $1,836.71 Medicare tax withheld: $429.55 State income tax withheld: $975.30
Tieya L. Millen 229 Second Street #4A Holbrook, AZ 86025 SSN: 477-30-2234	Total 2020 wages: $15,889.04 Federal income tax withheld: $494.00 Social Security tax withheld: $985.12 Medicare tax withheld: $230.39 State income tax withheld: $533.87

Form **W-2** Wage and Tax Statement   **2020**   Department of the Treasury—Internal Revenue Service
Copy 1—For State, City, or Local Tax Department

Source: Internal Revenue Service

DO NOT STAPLE

33333	**a** Control number		**For Official Use Only ▶** OMB No. 1545-0008	

| **b**
Kind
of
Payer
(Check one) | ▶ | 941 ☐
CT-1 ☐ | Military ☐
Hshld.
emp. ☐ | 943 ☐
Medicare
govt. emp. ☐ | 944 ☐ | **Kind**
of
Employer
(Check one) | ▶ | None apply ☐
State/local
non-501c ☐ | 501c non-govt. ☐
State/local 501c ☐ | Federal govt. ☐ | Third-party
sick pay
(Check if
applicable) ☐ |

c Total number of Forms W-2	**d** Establishment number	**1** Wages, tips, other compensation	**2** Federal income tax withheld
e Employer identification number (EIN)		**3** Social security wages	**4** Social security tax withheld
f Employer's name		**5** Medicare wages and tips	**6** Medicare tax withheld
		7 Social security tips	**8** Allocated tips
		9	**10** Dependent care benefits
		11 Nonqualified plans	**12a** Deferred compensation
g Employer's address and ZIP code			
h Other EIN used this year		**13** For third-party sick pay use only	**12b**
15 State Employer's state ID number		**14** Income tax withheld by payer of third-party sick pay	
16 State wages, tips, etc.	**17** State income tax	**18** Local wages, tips, etc.	**19** Local income tax
Employer's contact person		Employer's telephone number	For Official Use Only
Employer's fax number		Employer's email address	

Under penalties of perjury, I declare that I have examined this return and accompanying documents, and, to the best of my knowledge and belief, they are true, correct, and complete.

Signature ▶   Title ▶   Date ▶

Form **W-3** **Transmittal of Wage and Tax Statements**   **2020**   Department of the Treasury
Internal Revenue Service

P6-11B.
LO 6-3

Using the information from P6-10B for Castor Corporation, complete Form W3 (above) that must accompany the company's Form W2s. Castor Corporation is a 941-SS payer and is a private, for-profit company. No third-party sick pay was applied for 2020. The W-3 was signed and submitted on January 12, 2021.

P6-12B.
LO 6-5, 6-6

Cloudy Night Signs is a company that makes custom signs and has 12 employees. The owner wants to perform a benefits analysis report for the year for one of its employees, Howard Nelson. Howard's benefits package is as follows:

Annual Salary: $38,950

401(k) contribution: 5 percent of annual salary, the company match is half of the employee's contribution up to 6 percent

Medical insurance deduction: $140 per month

Dental insurance: $36 per month

Complete the following Benefits Analysis Report for Howard Nelson for the year.

Yearly Benefit Costs	Company Cost	Howard's Cost
Medical insurance	$9,600	$
Dental insurance	800	$
Life insurance	1,200	-0-
AD&D	125	-0-
Short-term disability	500	-0-
Long-term disability	250	-0-
401(k)	$	$
Social Security	$	$
Medicare	$	$
Tuition reimbursement	5,000	-0-
Total yearly benefit costs	$	
Howard's annual salary	$	
Total yearly benefit costs	$	
Total value of Howard's compensation	$	

P6-13B.

LO 6-4, 6-5

Happy Panda Fashions has 52 employees distributed among the following departments:

Sales: 14	Factory: 26	Administration: 12

The total annual payroll for Happy Panda Fashions is $1,280,550. Compute the labor distribution based on the equal distribution among the departments.

Sales: _____

Factory: _____

Administration: _____

P6-14B.

LO 6-4, 6-5

For Happy Panda Fashions in P6-13B, compute the labor distribution based on the number of employees per department:

Sales:

Factory:

Administration:

P6-15B.

LO 6-1, 6-4

At Fox Furniture, employees are classified according to the job title for workers' compensation insurance premium computation purposes.

a. Based on the following payroll estimates as of January 1, what is the estimated workers' compensation insurance premium for the year 20XX?

Employee Classification	Rate per $100 of Payroll	Estimated Payroll for 20XX	Workers' Compensation Premium
Sales Associate	$0.55	$213,680	
Loader	2.15	155,240	
Furniture Builder	2.95	102,590	
		Total Premium =	

b. The actual payroll for 20XX is listed below. What is the workers' compensation premium based on the actual payroll?

Employee Classification	Rate per $100 of Payroll	Actual Payroll for 20XX	Workers' Compensation Premium
Sales Associate	$0.55	$228,944	
Loader	2.15	163,743	
Furniture Builder	2.95	105,389	
		Total Premium =	

c. What is the difference between the actual and the estimated premiums?
_____

Critical Thinking

6-1. Burton Book Memorabilia is a semiweekly depositor. Following the success of a special project, Kelly Burton, the owner, pays each of the 250 employees a $20,000 bonus on August 14, 2020. Assuming a 25 percent income tax rate, when will Kelly need to deposit the payroll taxes?

6-2. Claude Lopez is the president of Zebra Antiques. His employee, Dwight Francis, is due a raise. Dwight's current benefit analysis is as follows:

Yearly Benefit Costs	Company Cost (Current)	Employee Cost (Current)
Medical insurance	$ 8,000	$ 1,200
Dental insurance	120	120
Life insurance	300	-0-
AD&D	150	-0-
Short-term disability	60	-0-
Long-term disability	30	-0-
401(k)	750	1,500
Social Security	3,018.16	3,018.16
Medicare	705.86	705.86
Tuition reimbursement	2,000	-0-
Total yearly benefit costs (employer)	15,134.02	
Employee's annual salary	50,000	
Total value of employee's compensation	65,134.02	

Compute the benefit analysis assuming:
- 7 percent increase in pay.
- 3 percent contribution to 401(k) will remain the same with a company match of 50 percent.
- 10 percent increase in medical and dental insurance premiums.

Yearly Benefit Costs	Company Cost (New)	Employee Cost (New)
Medical insurance	$	$
Dental insurance	$	$
Life insurance	$	-0-
AD&D	$	-0-
Short-term disability	$	-0-
Long-term disability	$	-0-
401(k)	$	$
Social Security	$	$
Medicare	$	$
Tuition reimbursement	$	-0-
Total yearly benefit costs (employer)	$	
Dwight's annual salary	$	
Total value of employee's compensation	$	

In the Real World: Scenario for Discussion

In Shavertown, Pennsylvania, the owner of Wilkes-Barre Bookkeeping LLC was indicted for embezzling over $376,225 of his clients' payroll tax remittances between 2010 and 2016 and for lying to clients about his actions. Additionally, he embezzled nearly $70,000 from a nonprofit for which he was the treasurer. He was sentenced to 38 months in prison and ordered to pay restitution totaling nearly $500,000. Do you think this was a fair sentence? Why or why not?

Internet Activities

6-1. Would you like to know more about the Employment Cost Index? Check out the videos from the Bureau of Labor Statistics: www.bls.gov/eci/videos.htm

6-2. Go to www.bizfilings.com/toolkit/sbg/tax-info/payroll-taxes/unemployment.aspx and check out the unemployment tax laws for your state.

6-3. Want to know more about the concepts in this chapter? Go to one or more of the following sites. What are two or three things you notice about the information on the site? www.smallbusiness.chron.com/example-employee-compensation-plan-10068. html http://yourbusiness.azcentral.com/labor-cost-distribution-report-26061.html www.irs.gov/publications/p80/ar02.html

6-4. Check out the employer payroll tax estimation tool at https://gusto.com/tools/employer-tax-calculator

6-5. Would you like to explore specific topics about being an employer in more depth? Check out https://www.employer.gov/

Continuing Payroll Project: Prevosti Farms and Sugarhouse

The first quarter tax return needs to be filed for Prevosti Farms and Sugarhouse by April 15, 2020. For the purpose of the taxes, assume the second February payroll amounts were duplicated for the March 6 and March 20 payroll periods and the new benefit elections went into effect as planned (see Chapter 4). The form was completed and signed on April 10, 2020.

	Exempt	
Benefit Information	**Federal**	**FICA**
Health Insurance	Yes	Yes
Life Insurance	Yes	Yes
Long-term care	Yes	Yes
FSA	Yes	Yes
401(k)	Yes	No
Gym	No	No

Number of employees	8
Gross quarterly wages	$31,461.36
Federal income tax withheld	367.00
401(k) contributions	1,231.22
Insurance withheld	4,080.00
Gym membership	90.00
Month 1	-0-
Month 2	1,889.36
Month 3	2,667.08

Complete Form 941 for Prevosti Farms and Sugarhouse. Prevosti Farms and Sugarhouse was assigned EIN 22-6654454.

Form **941 for 2020:** **Employer's QUARTERLY Federal Tax Return**

(Rev. January 2020)   Department of the Treasury — Internal Revenue Service

950117

OMB No. 1545-0029

Employer identification number (EIN) ☐☐ – ☐☐☐☐☐☐☐

Name *(not your trade name)*

Trade name *(if any)*

Address

Number   Street   Suite or room number

City   State   ZIP code

Foreign country name   Foreign province/county   Foreign postal code

Report for this Quarter of 2020
(Check one.)

☐ **1:** January, February, March

☐ **2:** April, May, June

☐ **3:** July, August, September

☐ **4:** October, November, December

Go to *www.irs.gov/Form941* for instructions and the latest information.

Read the separate instructions before you complete Form 941. Type or print within the boxes.

Part 1:   Answer these questions for this quarter.

1   Number of employees who received wages, tips, or other compensation for the pay period including: *Mar. 12* (Quarter 1), *June 12* (Quarter 2), *Sept. 12* (Quarter 3), or *Dec. 12* (Quarter 4)   **1** ☐

2   Wages, tips, and other compensation . . . .   **2** ☐

3   Federal income tax withheld from wages, tips, and other compensation . . . . . .   **3** ☐

4   If no wages, tips, and other compensation are subject to social security or Medicare tax   ☐ Check and go to line 6.

		Column 1		Column 2
5a	Taxable social security wages . .	☐	× 0.124 =	☐
5b	Taxable social security tips . . .	☐	× 0.124 =	☐
5c	Taxable Medicare wages & tips. .	☐	× 0.029 =	☐
5d	Taxable wages & tips subject to Additional Medicare Tax withholding	☐	× 0.009 =	☐

5e   Add Column 2 from lines 5a, 5b, 5c, and 5d . . . .   **5e** ☐

5f   Section 3121(q) Notice and Demand—Tax due on unreported tips (see instructions) . .   **5f** ☐

6   Total taxes before adjustments. Add lines 3, 5e, and 5f . . . .   **6** ☐

7   Current quarter's adjustment for fractions of cents . . . .   **7** ☐

8   Current quarter's adjustment for sick pay . . . .   **8** ☐

9   Current quarter's adjustments for tips and group-term life insurance . . . .   **9** ☐

10   Total taxes after adjustments. Combine lines 6 through 9 . . . .   **10** ☐

11   Qualified small business payroll tax credit for increasing research activities. Attach Form 8974   **11** ☐

12   Total taxes after adjustments and credits. Subtract line 11 from line 10 . . . .   **12** ☐

13   Total deposits for this quarter, including overpayment applied from a prior quarter and overpayments applied from Form 941-X, 941-X (PR), 944-X, or 944-X (SP) filed in the current quarter   **13** ☐

14   Balance due. If line 12 is more than line 13, enter the difference and see instructions . . .   **14** ☐

15   Overpayment. If line 13 is more than line 12, enter the difference ☐   Check one: ☐ Apply to next return. ☐ Send a refund.

▶ **You MUST complete both pages of Form 941 and SIGN it.**   Next ▶

For Privacy Act and Paperwork Reduction Act Notice, see the back of the Payment Voucher.   Cat. No. 17001Z   Form **941** (Rev. 1-2020)

950217

Name *(not your trade name)*

Employer identification number (EIN)

| Part 2: | Tell us about your deposit schedule and tax liability for this quarter. |

If you are unsure about whether you are a monthly schedule depositor or a semiweekly schedule depositor, see section 11 of Pub. 15.

16 Check one: ☐ Line 12 on this return is less than $2,500 or line 12 on the return for the prior quarter was less than $2,500, and you didn't incur a $100,000 next-day deposit obligation during the current quarter. If line 12 for the prior quarter was less than $2,500 but line 12 on this return is $100,000 or more, you must provide a record of your federal tax liability. If you are a monthly schedule depositor, complete the deposit schedule below; if you are a semiweekly schedule depositor, attach Schedule B (Form 941). Go to Part 3.

☐ **You were a monthly schedule depositor for the entire quarter.** Enter your tax liability for each month and total liability for the quarter, then go to Part 3.

Tax liability: Month 1 ☐ .

Month 2 ☐ .

Month 3 ☐ .

Total liability for quarter ☐ . Total must equal line 12.

☐ **You were a semiweekly schedule depositor for any part of this quarter.** Complete Schedule B (Form 941), Report of Tax Liability for Semiweekly Schedule Depositors, and attach it to Form 941.

| Part 3: | Tell us about your business. If a question does NOT apply to your business, leave it blank. |

17 If your business has closed or you stopped paying wages . . . . ☐ Check here, and

enter the final date you paid wages ☐ / / .

18 If you are a seasonal employer and you don't have to file a return for every quarter of the year . . ☐ Check here.

| Part 4: | May we speak with your third-party designee? |

Do you want to allow an employee, a paid tax preparer, or another person to discuss this return with the IRS? See the instructions for details.

☐ **Yes.** Designee's name and phone number ☐ ☐

Select a 5-digit Personal Identification Number (PIN) to use when talking to the IRS. ☐ ☐ ☐ ☐ ☐

☐ **No.**

| Part 5: | Sign here. You MUST complete both pages of Form 941 and SIGN it. |

Under penalties of perjury, I declare that I have examined this return, including accompanying schedules and statements, and to the best of my knowledge and belief, it is true, correct, and complete. Declaration of preparer (other than taxpayer) is based on all information of which preparer has any knowledge.

X **Sign your name here** ☐

Print your name here ☐

Print your title here ☐

Date ☐ / /

Best daytime phone ☐

Paid Preparer Use Only

Check if you are self-employed . . . ☐

Preparer's name	☐	PTIN	☐
Preparer's signature	☐	Date	/ /
Firm's name (or yours if self-employed)	☐	EIN	☐
Address	☐	Phone	☐
City	☐	State ☐	ZIP code ☐

Form **941** (Rev. 1-2020)

Answers to Stop & Check Exercises

FUTA, SUTA, and Workers' Compensation

1.

FUTA: $7,000 × 29 × 0.006 =	$ 1,218.00
$2,575 × 0.006 =	15.45
FUTA liability	$ 1,233.45
SUTA: $24,800 × 25 × 0.042 =	$26,040.00
$60,090 × 0.042 =	2,523.78
(under the cap: 15,800 + 7,800 + 11,115 + 22,800 + 2,575)	
SUTA liability	$28,563.78
Total combined FUTA/SUTA liability	$29,787.23

2.

FUTA: $7,000 × 10 × 0.006 =	$ 420.00
($5,500 + 6,800) × 0.006 =	73.80
Total FUTA liability	$ 493.80
SUTA: $12,000 × 8 × 0.0326 =	$ 3,129.60
$33,250 × 0.0326	
(under the cap: 5,500 + 6,800 + 11,100 + 9,850) =	$ 1,083.95
Total SUTA liability	$ 4,213.55
Competitive Skills Scholarship tax liability: $279,580 × 0.0006 =	$ 167.75
Total FUTA, SUTA, and Competitive Skills Scholarship =	$ 4,875.10

3.

Job Classification	Premium per $100 of Payroll	Estimated Payroll	Premium Due
Clerical Workers	$0.45	$104,550	$ 470.48
Jump Instructors	3.75	215,690	8,088.38
			$8,558.86

Reporting Periods
1. Monthly.
2. July 15.
3. Monday, the next business day.

Tax Forms
1. $2,414.48 = $8,462.96 − 2,980.24 − 3,068.24
2. $105,000 (15 employees × $7,000).
3. $630.00 ($105,000 (from problem 2) × 0.006 FUTA rate).
4. $116,195 = $25,650 + 30,025 + 28,550 + 31,970

Payroll-Related Business Expenses
1. Failure to file and failure to deposit penalties.
2. Payroll expenses relate to the company's profitability, worker productivity analyses, employee retention, and business competitiveness.

Labor Distribution Report
1. a. $300,000/10 employees = $30,000 per employee; Office, $90,000; agricultural, $150,000; drivers, $60,000.
   b. Each department would be allocated $100,000 of the payroll.
2. Department classification is the most appropriate because it matches the costs more closely to each department.

Benefit Analysis Report

1. One of the purposes of compiling a benefit analysis report is to represent graphically all of the variables that make up an employee's compensation package. The benefit analysis report provides managers and supervisors a budgetary tool to understand the full cost of hiring or dismissing employees. Additionally, the benefit analysis allows companies to compare benefits and employee costs to geographic or industry standards.

2. The benefit analysis report is an internal report for the company's management, and the annual total compensation report is meant to be distributed to the employee.

Chapter Seven

7

The Payroll Register, Employees' Earnings Records, and Accounting System Entries

In this chapter, we will integrate the payroll register with the employees' earnings records and financial statements. In previous chapters, we have examined the effects of payroll on employees, employers, and governmental agencies. This chapter links *Generally Accepted Accounting Principles (GAAP)* with payroll elements we have explored in Chapters 1–6. We will discuss the debits and credits associated with payroll accrual and payment. For this chapter, we will use the accrual basis of accounting, which means that transactions are recognized at the time that they are incurred.

Accounting entries are the transactions that place the payroll amounts into the correct ledger accounts. In automated systems, the software is designed to code each payroll item automatically to the correct General Ledger account. However, for the payroll accountant to record accurate expenses and period-end accruals in the correct month, manual entries are necessary. This is the final step of the payroll cycle for each pay period and is the most important piece of the process from an accounting perspective. The final piece of this chapter will include the examination of the ways that payroll costs affect a company's financial reports.

LEARNING OBJECTIVES

After studying Chapter 7, you should be able to:

LO 7-1   Connect the Payroll Register to the Employees' Earnings Records

LO 7-2   Describe Financial Accounting Concepts

LO 7-3   Complete Payroll-Related General Journal Entries

LO 7-4   Generate Payroll-Related General Ledger Entries

LO 7-5   Describe Payroll Effects on the Accounting System

LO 7-6   Explain Payroll Entries in Accounting Reports

ra2studio/Shutterstock

Cybercrime Affects Employees' Payroll Like Never Before

The Federal Bureau of Investigation estimated $3.5 billion in cybercrime occurred during 2019, which reflected an increase from $1.1 billion in 2015. Employee payroll has been one of the targets because of the increased use of automation in the payroll industry. The FBI found the way companies become vulnerable to hackers includes email phishing scams in which access to company records through malicious software (aka malware) inserted into an attachment or link in the email. Spoofing attacks, which involve the hacker acting as an employee of the company by using the employee's name on a non-company, private email address, have increased as a means to gain access to business information.

These hacking scams have involved the diversion of payroll through co-opting of employee payroll information. Perpetrators of payroll hacking schemes occasionally use a request to update direct deposit or paycard information and end with a hacker gaining access to an employee's pay. For these reasons, payroll accountants must know how to understand and interpret accounting data to ensure the integrity of payroll records.

(Source: ESET)

Payroll-related accounting entries are often investigated during company audits. Accurate reporting of payroll costs in the financial statement is a key part of GAAP compliance and decision making. In Chapter 7, we will examine the accounting system entries for payroll costs, then the effect on the company's financial reports, and finally how those reports influence managerial decisions.

LO 7-1   Connect the Payroll Register to the Employees' Earnings Records

Shutterstock/Oleksiy Mark

In previous chapters, we have completed the payroll register, which is the primary tool used to compute payroll amounts. The payroll register has a related set of documents called the employee earnings records. The employees' earnings records form the link between the accounting and the human resource departments. The information contained within each row of the payroll register is transferred to the employees' earnings records. Additionally, information from the payroll register is used to complete payroll entries in the General Journal.

Employee earnings records form the link between the accounting and the human resource departments and connect closely with the payroll register. The information contained within each row of the payroll register is transferred to the employee's earnings record, an example of which is shown in Figure 7-1.

FIGURE 7-1
Employee Earnings Record

EMPLOYEE EARNING RECORD

NAME		Hire Date		Dependent child <17	
ADDRESS		Date of Birth		Dependent other	
CITY/STATE/ZIP		Position		Step 4a W-4 Info	
TELEPHONE		Filing Status		Step 4b W-4 Info	
SOCIAL SECURITY				Step 4c W-4 Info	
NUMBER		Pay Rate		Hr/Wk/Mo/Yr	

Period Ended	Hrs Worked	Reg Pay	OT Pay	Holiday	Comm	Gross Pay	Ins	401(k)	Taxable Pay for Federal	Taxable Pay for FICA

Taxable Pay for Federal	Taxable Pay for FICA	Fed Inc. Tax	Social Sec. Tax	Medicare	State Inc. Tax	Total Deduc	Net Pay	YTD Net Pay	YTD Gross Pay	YTD FUTA

The employee earnings record is the master document accountants use to track employees' marital status, deductions (mandatory, voluntary, and mandated), and year-to-date earnings. Remember Social Security, FUTA, and SUTA taxes have annual earnings limits for each employee. Accountants update the employees' earnings records during each pay period to track all pay and tax deductions. Any employee changes, including pay rate, marital status, and the number of dependents should be annotated in the earnings records as soon as possible to ensure the accuracy of the payroll.

EXAMPLE: EMPLOYEE EARNINGS RECORD, INDIVIDUAL EMPLOYEE

Using the example of Lillian Quinn at Granite Hill Products, we will enter her data into her employee earnings record. She is paid semimonthly.

EMPLOYEE EARNING RECORD

NAME	Lillian Quinn	Hire Date	3/1/20XX	Dependent child <17	2
ADDRESS	3450 Pine Street	Date of Birth	12/15/19XX	Dependent other	1
CITY/STATE/ZIP	Laurel, DE 19956	Position	Manager	Step 4a W-4 Info	
TELEPHONE	302-555-3948	Filing Status	Married/Joint	Step 4b W-4 Info	
SOCIAL SECURITY				Step 4c W-4 Info	
NUMBER	392-20-1030	Pay Rate	$5,000	HR/Wk (Mo)	

Period Ended	Hrs Worked	Reg Pay	OT Pay	Holiday	Comm	Gross Pay	Ins	401(k)	Taxable Pay for Federal	Taxable Pay for FICA
8/31/20xx		2,500.00				2,500.00	225.00	150.00	2,125.00	2,500.00

Taxable Pay for Federal	Taxable Pay for FICA	Fed Inc. Tax	Social Sec. Tax	Medicare	State Inc. Tax	Total Deduc	Net Pay	YTD Net Pay	YTD Gross Pay	YTD FUTA
2,125.00	2,500.00	185.00	155.00	36.25	140.25	891.50	1,608.50	16,085.00	30,000.00	7,000.00

Note how the following employee information is reflected in the employee earnings record:

- Address.
- Telephone number.
- Social Security number.
- Amount paid per month.
- Filing status.
- Pay basis.
- Hire date.
- Birth date.
- Position.
- Pay rate.
- Pay period date.

(continued)

(concluded)

- Year-to-date net pay.

- Year-to-date gross pay.

These items are common to most employee earnings records because of the connection between payroll and human resources. The information contained in the employee earnings record is used as the basis for the employee's Form W-2 as well as other company tax and benefits reporting.

The Employees' Earnings Records and Periodic Tax Reports

Period totals are also included in the earnings record. These totals facilitate the preparation of the quarterly and annual reports. Like any payroll record, the earnings records should be retained and destroyed at the same interval as other accounting records. Earnings records are typically included as supporting documents for internal copies of quarterly filings of Form 941 as well as state and local tax returns (where applicable). During a payroll audit, the documentation attached to the tax returns provides verification of the information contained in the reports. A secondary use is that, in the event of computer data failure, documents attached to payroll records can be used to re-create files.

In the village of Bellows Falls, Vermont, employees of the Windham Northeast Supervisory Union, the school district for the area, have experienced payroll problems for several months. These problems involved overpayment or underpayment of earnings, missing or delayed deposits of retirement deductions, and other anomalies. The Supervisory Union attributed the problem to new payroll software upon which employees were undertrained prior to use. The accuracy of employee payroll and remission of deductions is of paramount importance within a business of any type. (Source: *VTDigger:* https://vtdigger.org/2020/01/23/windham-northeast-reckons-with-payroll-woes-there-is-an-avalanche-of-problems/)

Employees' Earnings Register

1. How do the employees' earnings records relate to the payroll register?

2. Which of the following fields exist in both the payroll register and the employees' earnings records?

   a. Name

   b. Pay rate

   c. Job title

   d. Net pay

   e. Address

3. What reports and forms use information from the employees' earnings records?

LO 7-2 Describe Financial Accounting Concepts

Now that we have explored the principles of computing and reporting payroll data, it is time to connect the information to financial accounting concepts. In financial accounting, the fundamental accounting equation is **Assets = Liabilities + Owners' Equity.**

EXAMPLE: FINANCIAL ACCOUNTING CATEGORIES

Assets: Cash or other items that are used in the operation of the business and amounts owed to the business by customers.

Liabilities: Amounts owed by the business to other people or companies.

Owners' equity: The net investment that the owner has in the business, including earnings kept in the business.

Shutterstock/JSep

Financial business transactions, such as the movement of cash used in paying employees and remitting amounts to third parties, are tracked using the accounting system. A fundamental concept in accounting involves the accounting equation, which must remain in balance at all times. As such, transactions will either increase an account (or multiple accounts), decrease an account (or multiple accounts), or a combination thereof. To understand the concept of equation balance, T-accounts are the first step in understanding the classification process that is part of transaction analysis.

EXAMPLE: TRANSACTION ANALYSIS USING T-ACCOUNTS

Phillip Rossman, the owner of Rossman Designs, paid an independent contractor $4,000 for work done during the course of business on August 1, 2020. Accountants classify the transaction into two accounts: assets and owners' equity. The cash account would decrease because the money was paid from the business. Barry's expenses would increase because he paid a contractor, which appears as an expense of the company and decreases the amount of equity Barry has in the business. Using the T-account approach, the transaction would look like this:

Contractor Expense	
Dr.	Cr.
4,000.00	

Cash	
Dr.	Cr.
	4,000.00

Debits and Credits

If accountants were to maintain T-accounts for all of a business's transactions, their work would be tedious and vulnerable to a large number of errors. To simplify the addition and subtraction involved, accountants use the terms *debit* (abbreviated Dr.) and *credit* (abbreviated Cr.) to explain the transaction. In accounting parlance, *debit* simply means "the left side of the T-account," and *credit* simply means "the right side of the T-account." No connotation exists about good or bad with the use of these terms in accounting.

EXAMPLE: DEBIT AND CREDIT RULES

Debits Increase:	Credits Increase:
Expenses	Liabilities
Assets	Equity (Capital)
Dividends	Revenue

The General Journal

To simplify the use of T-accounts, accountants use a journal (called the *General Journal*) to record the daily financial transactions. The General Journal is maintained in chronological order. The General Journal is essentially one big T-account, has columns to record the debits and credits involved in each transaction, and contains a chronologically ordered list of transactions. Complementing the General Journal is the *General Ledger*, in which all journal transactions are recorded chronologically in their specific accounts.

In the transaction above, the transaction would appear in the General Journal as follows:

EXAMPLE: TRANSACTION IN THE GENERAL JOURNAL

Trans.	Date	Account Name & Description	Post Ref	Debit	Credit
1	8/1/2020	Contractor Expense	501	4,000.00	
		Cash	101		4,000.00
		Paid Contractor			

Note certain accounting conventions present in the journal entry:

- The date of the transaction is noted.
- The debit part of the transaction is on the first line and is flush left in the column.
- The credit part of the transaction is on the second line and is indented slightly.
- A brief description of the transaction is on line three.
- Account numbers are annotated in the Post Reference (Post Ref) column.
- The post reference in the General Journal is the General Ledger account number.

The General Ledger

Once the transaction has been recorded in the General Journal, the accountant posts the entry to corresponding General Ledger accounts. In the following table, note that (1) the transaction itself is listed, and (2) the balance of each account is adjusted accordingly.

EXAMPLE: GENERAL LEDGER POSTING

			Account: 101 – Cash		
Date	Description	Post Ref.	Debit	Credit	Balance
8/1/2020	Paid Contractor	J1		4,000.00	4,000.00

			Account: 501 – Contractor Expense		
Date	Description	Post Ref.	Debit	Credit	Balance
8/1/2020	Paid Contractor	J1	4,000.00		4,000.00

The General Ledger account balances are used to generate the payroll reports that we have been discussing so far. The elements of the General Ledger and specific posting practices will appear later in this chapter.

Despite the increase in the use of accounting software, the need for payroll accountants is growing in importance. Accountants are needed to monitor accuracy in recorded transactions and to adapt to industry changes, especially the integration of technology and the growing use of artificial intelligence. Payroll accountants are particularly in demand because of the specific skills involved in and increasing complexity of payroll accounting. (Source: *Bloomberg BNA, In the Black*)

Financial Accounting Concepts

1. What is the fundamental accounting equation?

2. What increases the Wages and Salaries Payable account: a debit or a credit?

3. What increases the Wages and Salaries Expense account: a debit or a credit?

Shutterstock/PointImages

LO 7-3   Complete Payroll-Related General Journal Entries

Recording the specific General Journal entries that correspond to payroll activities is the next step in the process. General Journal entries are the original entry point for events to be recorded within the accounting system. A sample period payroll for L&L Grain follows.

EXAMPLE: L&L GRAIN PAYROLL DATA

L&L Grain pays its employees biweekly and operates on a calendar fiscal year (i.e., the year-end is December 31). The payroll accountant for L&L Grain has completed the payroll register for the January 24, 2020, payroll. Paychecks will be issued on January 30. Payroll totals are as follows:

Gross pay: $18,050.00
Federal income tax withheld: $1,500.00
Social Security tax withheld: $1,084.38
Medicare tax withheld: $253.61
State income tax withheld: $577.60
401(k) contributions withheld: $750.00
Health insurance premiums withheld: $560.00
United Way contributions withheld: $180.00
Net pay: $13,144.41

The totals row of the payroll register would appear as follows:

Name	Gross Earnings	401(k) Contributions	Insurance	Federal W/H	Social Security Tax	Medicare Tax	State W/H	United Way	Net Pay	Check No.
Totals	$18,050.00	$750.00	$560.00	$1,500.00	$1,084.38	$253.61	$577.60	$180.00	$13,144.41	

The payroll register is the tool used by payroll accountants to create the pay-related journal entries. Here's how it works:

EXAMPLE: PAYROLL REGISTER TO GENERAL JOURNAL ENTRIES

Payroll Register Column	General Journal Account	L&L Grain Amount
Gross Earnings	Salaries and Wages Expense	$18,050.00
401(k) Contributions	401(k) Contributions Payable	750.00
Insurance	Health Insurance Premiums Payable	560.00
Federal W/H	FIT Payable	1,500.00
Social Security Tax	Social Security Tax Payable	1,084.38
Medicare Tax	Medicare Tax Payable	253.61
State W/H	State Income Tax Payable	577.60
United Way	United Way Contributions Payable	180.00
Net Pay	Salaries and Wages Payable	13,144.41

As the payroll data is transferred from the payroll register to the General Journal, notice the following accounting categories:

- Account names ending with the word "expense" are classified as Expense accounts (remember Debit increases).
- Account names ending with the word "payable" are classified as Liability accounts (remember Credit increases).

Employee Pay-Related Journal Entries

The General Journal entry to record the employee's portion of the payroll and the issuance of the checks to employees is in two parts:

EXAMPLE: L&L GRAIN GENERAL JOURNAL PAYROLL ENTRIES— EMPLOYEE PAYROLL TRANSACTION

Date	Description	Account	Debit	Credit
Jan. 24	Salaries and Wages Expense	511	$18,050.00	
	FIT Payable	221		$1,500.00
	Social Security Tax Payable	222		1,084.38
	Medicare Tax Payable	223		253.61
	State Income Tax Payable	224		577.60
	401(k) Contributions Payable	225		750.00
	Health Insurance Premiums Payable	226		560.00
	United Way Contributions Payable	227		180.00
	Salaries and Wages Payable	231		13,144.41
Jan. 30	Salaries and Wages Payable	231	13,144.41	
	Cash	101		13,144.41

Employer Payroll-Related Journal Entries

The employer's share of the payroll is similarly recorded. L&L Grain's share of the payroll expenses follows:

EXAMPLE: L&L GRAIN EMPLOYER PAYROLL TAX OBLIGATIONS DATA

Social Security tax: $1,084.38
Medicare tax: $253.61
FUTA tax: $100.44
SUTA tax: $903.96

The General Journal entry for the employer's share of the payroll taxes follows:

**EXAMPLE: L&L GRAIN GENERAL JOURNAL PAYROLL ENTRIES—
EMPLOYER PAYROLL TAX TRANSACTION**

Date	Description	Account	Debit	Credit
Jan. 24	Payroll Taxes Expense	512	$2,342.39	
	Social Security Tax Payable	222		$1,084.38
	Medicare Tax Payable	223		253.61
	FUTA Tax Payable	228		100.44
	SUTA Tax Payable	229		903.96

Other Payroll-Related Journal Entries

What about the other deductions that L&L Grain withheld from its employees' pay? These other deductions, including federal and state income tax, 401(k) contributions, health insurance premiums, and United Way contributions, are liabilities of the company. These amounts will remain in the liability accounts until L&L Grain *remits* them, which means that the company sends the collected money to the appropriate entity. Upon remittance, the General Journal entries will appear as a debit (decrease) to the Liability account and a credit (decrease) to Cash. An example for the January 24 payroll's voluntary deductions, paid to the appropriate companies on January 30, follows:

**EXAMPLE: L&L GRAIN GENERAL JOURNAL PAYROLL ENTRIES—
VOLUNTARY DEDUCTIONS REMITTANCE**

Date	Description	Account	Debit	Credit
Jan. 30	401(k) Contributions Payable	225	$750.00	
	Health Insurance Payable	226	560.00	
	United Way Contribution Payable	227	180.00	
	Cash	101		$1,490.00

Remember the remittance for governmental taxes has a specific schedule. The General Journal entry for the tax remittances would follow the same pattern as the voluntary deductions: debit the Liability account(s) and credit Cash.

Payroll Accruals and Reversals

A common occurrence is a payroll period may be split between two months, as will be the case for L&L Grain. For example, the majority of the pay for the end of March will be paid on the March 27, 2020, pay date, but the payroll for March 30 and 31 will be paid in April. For accounting purposes, the accountant needs to record the *accrual* of the payroll for March to represent the *expenses* and liabilities incurred during the period accurately, according to the matching principle of accounting. Some companies choose to record the period's expenses through *adjusting entries* and then reverse the entries after the start of the next period to prevent confusion in the payroll accounting process.

Employee payroll data for L&L Grain is given below, followed by the related adjusting entry for the end of March:

EXAMPLE: L&L GRAIN ADJUSTING ENTRY—EMPLOYEE PAYROLL DATA

Gross pay: $16,245.00
Federal income tax withheld: $1,350.00
Social Security tax withheld: $1,007.19
Medicare tax withheld: $235.55
State income tax withheld: $519.84
Net pay: $13,132.42

The adjusting entry for March 31, 2020, would be as follows:

EXAMPLE: L&L GRAIN GENERAL JOURNAL—EMPLOYEE DATA ADJUSTING ENTRIES

Date	Description	Account	Debit	Credit
Mar. 31	Salaries and Wages Expense	511	$16,245.00	
	FIT Payable	221		$1,350.00
	Social Security Tax Payable	222		1,007.19
	Medicare Tax Payable	223		235.55
	State Income Tax Payable	224		519.84
	Salaries and Wages Payable	231		13,132.42

The amount for the employer's share would be as follows:

EXAMPLE: L&L GRAIN GENERAL JOURNAL—EMPLOYER PAYROLL TAX DATA ADJUSTING ENTRIES

Date	Description	Account	Debit	Credit
Mar. 31	Payroll Taxes Expense	512	$2,217.17	
	Social Security Tax Payable	222		$1,007.19
	Medicare Tax Payable	223		235.55
	FUTA Tax Payable (16,245 × 0.006)	228		97.47
	SUTA Tax Payable (16,245 × 0.53983)	229		876.96

On April 1, 2020, the accountant could record a reversing entry as follows:

EXAMPLE: L&L GRAIN GENERAL JOURNAL—EMPLOYEE DATA REVERSING ENTRIES

Date	Description	Account	Debit	Credit
Apr. 1	FIT Payable	221	$1,350.00	
	Social Security Tax Payable	222	1,007.19	
	Medicare Tax Payable	223	235.55	
	State Income Tax Payable	224	519.84	
	Salaries and Wages Payable	231	13,132.42	
	Salaries and Wages Expense	511		$16,245.00

The *reversal* of the General Journal entries, used in accrual-based accounting to represent accrued employer payroll expenditures and liabilities at the end of the prior month, would be as follows:

EXAMPLE: L&L GRAIN GENERAL JOURNAL—EMPLOYER PAYROLL TAX DATA REVERSING ENTRIES

Date	Description	Account	Debit	Credit
Apr. 1	Social Security Tax Payable	222	$1,007.19	
	Medicare Tax Payable	223	235.55	
	FUTA Tax Payable	224	97.47	
	SUTA Tax Payable	229	876.96	
	Payroll Taxes Expense	512		$2,217.17

Note that not all companies and accountants use reversing entries. An advantage of using the reversing entry is that it simplifies the payroll process by avoiding calculating partial payroll periods that occur due to the period end. A disadvantage is the reversing entry becomes additional entries that the accountant has to journalize and post. The use of reversing entries is at the company's discretion.

Payroll and the General Journal

Stop & Check

1. In the following General Journal entry, which account represents the employees' gross pay?

Description	Debit	Credit
Wages and Salaries Expense	$124,785.00	
Federal Income Tax Payable		$15,280.00
Social Security Tax Payable		7,736.67
Medicare Tax Payable		1,809.38
State Income Tax Payable		4,741.83
Wages and Salaries Payable		95,217.12

(continued)

(concluded)

2. Based on the preceding General Journal entry, what would be the entry for the employer's share of the payroll taxes? Omit FUTA/SUTA taxes.

3. Cecil's Craft Warehouse has accrued gross pay of $42,795 that will be paid out in the following period. The accrual amounts are as follows:

Wages and Salaries Expense	$42,795.00	
Federal Income Tax Payable		$15,280.00
Social Security Tax Payable		2,653.29
Medicare Tax Payable		620.53
State Income Tax Payable		1,626.21
Wages and Salaries Payable		22,614.97

What would be the reversing entry?

LO 7-4   Generate Payroll-Related General Ledger Entries

As mentioned before, the process of updating the General Ledger accounts with the transactions that the accountant records in the General Journal is called *posting*. Each account used in the General Journal has a corresponding General Ledger account used to track the individual balances of a firm.

For the January 24 payroll and January 30 remittances for L&L Grain that we discussed in the previous section, the postings to the General Ledger would appear as depicted in Figure 7-2. Note that the entries shown reflect only the payroll entries for the end of January and for the end of February.

General Ledger Posting Practices

Note the columns in the General Ledger are similar to those in the General Journal. Some specific practices in the General Ledger are worth noting:

- Each line has a date. (In the General Journal, only the first line of each transaction is dated.)
- The description is usually left blank, except for adjusting, closing, and reversing entries.

Freedomz/Shutterstock

The post reference number is a combination of letters and numbers. The letters denote which journal the entry correlates. In this case, "J" means that the original entry may be found in the General Journal. The number in the Post Ref column reflects the page of the journal on which the entry is recorded.

The first pair of Debit and Credit columns is used to record the General Journal entry. If the account had a debit in the General Journal transaction, then the amount would appear in the Debit column in the first pair of columns in the General Ledger. The same practice is used for credits.

The second pair of Debit and Credit columns is used to maintain a running balance of the total in the account. These account balances are the foundation for the financial reports generated by the accountant and reviewed by managers, officers, customers, vendors, and governmental agencies.

FIGURE 7-2

L&L Grain's General Ledger

			Post Ref	Debit	Credit	Balance Debit	Balance Credit
						Account: 101 – Cash	
Date		Description	Post Ref	Debit	Credit	Debit	Credit
Jan	31	Beginning Balance				122,367.43	
Jan	31		J1		13,144.91	109,222.52*	
Jan	31		J4		750.00	108,472.52	
Jan	31		J4		560.00	107,912.52	
Jan	31		J4		180.00	107,732.52	

* Cash has a normal debit balance. It will decrease when the account is credited. 122,367.43 − 13,144.91 = 109.222.52.

						Account: 221 – FIT Payable	
Date		Description	Post Ref	Debit	Credit	Balance Debit	Balance Credit
Jan	24		J1		1,500.00		1,500.00
Mar	31	Accrue Payroll	J5		1,350.00		2,850.00*
Apr	1	Reverse Payroll	J7	1,350.00			1,500.00

* FIT Payable is a liability account. It will increase with a credit. 1,500 + 1,350 = 2,850.

						Account: 222 – Social Security Tax Payable	
Date		Description	Post Ref	Debit	Credit	Balance Debit	Balance Credit
Jan	24		J1		1,084.38		1,084.38
Jan	24		J1		1,084.38		2,168.76
Mar	31	Accrue Payroll	J5		974.70		3,143.46
Mar	31	Accrue Payroll – Employer	J6		974.70		4,118.16
Apr	1	Reverse Payroll	J7	974.70			3,143.46
Apr	1	Reverse Payroll – Employer	J7	974.70			2,168.76

						Account: 223 – Medicare Tax Payable	
Date		Description	Post Ref	Debit	Credit	Balance Debit	Balance Credit
Jan	24		J1		253.61		253.61
Jan	24		J1		253.61		507.22
Mar	31	Accrue Payroll	J5		235.55		742.77
Mar	31	Accrue Payroll – Employer	J6		235.55		978.32
Apr	1	Reverse Payroll	J7	235.55			742.77
Apr	1	Reverse Payroll – Employer	J8	235.55			507.22

						Account: 224 – State Income Tax Payable	
Date		Description	Post Ref	Debit	Credit	Balance Debit	Balance Credit
Jan	24		J1		577.60		577.60
Mar	31	Accrue Payroll	J5		519.84		1,097.44
Apr	1	Reverse Payroll	J7	519.84			577.60

						Account: 225 – 401(k) Contributions Payable	
Date		Description	Post Ref	Debit	Credit	Balance Debit	Balance Credit
Jan	24		J1		750.00		750.00
Jan	30		J4	750.00			—

(continued)

FIGURE 7-2

L&L Grain's General Ledger (concluded)

					Account: 226 – Health Insurance Payable	
					Balance	
Date		Description	Post Ref	Debit	Credit	Debit	Credit
Jan	24		J1		560.00		560.00
Jan	30		J4	560.00			—

					Account: 227 – United Way Contributions Payable	
					Balance	
Date		Description	Post Ref	Debit	Credit	Debit	Credit
Jan	24		J1		180.00		180.00
Jan	30		J4	180.00			—

					Account: 228 – FUTA Tax Payable	
					Balance	
Date		Description	Post Ref	Debit	Credit	Debit	Credit
Jan	24		J1		144.40		144.40
Mar	31	Accrue Payroll – Employer	J6		129.96		274.36
Apr	1	Reverse Payroll – Employer	J8	129.96			144.40

					Account: 229 – SUTA Tax Payable	
					Balance	
Date		Description	Post Ref	Debit	Credit	Debit	Credit
Jan	24		J1		974.40		974.40
Mar	31	Accrue Payroll – Employer	J6		876.96		1,851.36
Apr	1	Reverse Payroll – Employer	J8	876.96			974.40

					Account: 231 – Salaries and Wages Payable	
					Balance	
Date		Description	Post Ref	Debit	Credit	Debit	Credit
Jan	24		J1		13,144.41		13,144.41
Jan	30		J1	13,144.41			—
Mar	31	Accrue Payroll	J5		13,164.91		13,164.91
Apr	1	Reverse Payroll	J7	13,164.91			—

					Account: 512 – Payroll Taxes Expense	
					Balance	
Date		Description	Post Ref	Debit	Credit	Debit	Credit
Jan	24		J1	2,457.09		2,457.09	
Mar	31	Accrue Payroll	J6	2,217.17		4,674.26	
Apr	1	Reverse Payroll	J7		2,217.17	2,457.09	

					Account: 511 – Salaries and Wages Expense	
					Balance	
Date		Description	Post Ref	Debit	Credit	Debit	Credit
Jan	24		J1	18,050.00		18,050.00	
Mar	31	Accrue Payroll	J6	16,245.00		34,295.00	
Apr	1	Reverse Payroll	J7		16,245.00	18,050.00	

Human input and payroll software have been a growing concern when facing computer security. Phishing attacks, where a computer hacker attempts to breach the security of a company's software, have been increasing in number and type, including situations in which a company's accounting data is compromised. These attacks have led to an increase in training costs for accounting personnel to educate them about the impacts of accounting breaches to ensure payroll accuracy. (Source: ADP)

General Ledger Entries

1. The Medicare Tax Payable account for Gulf Coast Shrimp had a credit balance on June 22 of $2,540. As of the June 30 payroll, credits totaling $220 were posted to the Medicare Tax Payable account. What is the balance in the account as of June 30?

2. The post reference for the June 30 journal entry is J34. What does this post reference mean?

LO 7-5   Describe Payroll Effects on the Accounting System

Shutterstock

Entries in the payroll system are posted into the General Ledger. When a company has an automated payroll system, the journal entries discussed previously are automatically updated to the General Ledger. A payroll accountant needs to understand how the accounts should look after a payroll period is completed to ensure the automated system has performed correctly. Glitches within computer programs may cause the payroll entry to be one-sided, in which only the debit or credit entry will flow through to the General Ledger. When this occurs, the payroll accountant must discover what has not posted to ensure the entire transaction posts correctly.

Payroll-Related Business Expenses

Payroll represents an expense to the business. As such, it reduces the company's profitability proportional to the wages earned and taxes paid. When the payroll accountant accrues the expenses related to the payroll, the company's expenses will also increase. Companies that operate using a cash basis (i.e., recording activities only when cash is received or spent) will witness the payroll expenses reducing the income when wages and salaries are paid to the employees and when taxes are remitted to governmental agencies.

A study conducted in 2019 indicated that many accounting tasks, including payroll, will be automated by 2021. However, the need for educated accountants remains constant because of the rise in cybersecurity issues. Although artificial intelligence and computerized accounting will have replaced the need for manual entry of the majority of accounting transactions, the accounting professional must verify the accuracy of the transactions and the integrity of the information. (Source: Untapped)

Besides administering specific payroll tasks, the responsibility of the payroll accountant is to allocate the employee expenses to specific accounts, departments, or business activities. Regardless of the employee's job description, some amount of time can be allocable to jobs or customers. For example, a fabric manufacturing company will have sewing, accounting, and managerial staff. The bulk of the sewing staff's time will be allocable to specific jobs; however, some time will be considered overhead—cleaning or meetings, for example. The bulk of the accounting department's time will be considered overhead. However, if the accountant is working on the analysis of a specific client's project, that time may be billed to the client. Managerial positions may also have specific times allocated to jobs depending upon the needs of the client and the position.

Shutterstock/Pavel Ignatov

Payroll-Related Liabilities

Unpaid payroll obligations represent a liability to the company. These liabilities include not only amounts due to employees; but also money to be remitted for voluntary, mandatory, and mandated deductions. Until the money is remitted, the company holds it in its accounts. Specific examples of payroll liabilities include, but are certainly not limited to, the following:

- Federal income tax
- FICA taxes
- Health insurance premiums
- Retirement plan contributions
- Child support garnishments
- Union dues

Employers have a *fiduciary* responsibility to remit all amounts withheld from employee pay. Remember that the Current Tax Payment Act requires employers to remit taxes in a timely manner, according to governmental guidelines. For the other deductions, according to 29 CFR 2510, employers are subject to the provisions of ERISA to protect all amounts due to employees and other recipients.

> The Employee Benefits Security Administration, a division of the Department of Labor, oversees employee contributions and estimated that approximately 68 million employees participated in employer-sponsored 401(k) plans and had invested over $425 trillion as of December 2017. The number of participants has historically increased at a rate of about 3 percent per year since 1975. (Source: DOL)

The Business Effects of Payroll

Stop & Check

1. Does the payment of employee wages increase or decrease the profitability of a business?

2. Why is it important to allocate payroll-related expenses properly?

LO 7-6   Explain Payroll Entries in Accounting Reports

Daimond Shutter/Shutterstock

When examining the *income statement*, *balance sheet*, and post-closing *trial balance* (Figures 7-3, 7-4, and 7-5), the payroll accountant must know what effect his or her work has on each statement. The financial statements are the key to integrating payroll accounting data and human resources information.

Let's start with the income statement, which reports all revenue and expenses for a specific time period. These periods are usually monthly,

FIGURE 7-3

Income Statement Presentation (Partial)

L&L Grain Income Statement For the Quarter Ended March 31, 20XX		
Revenue:		
Sales Revenue		$78,303.40
Expenses:		
Salaries and Wages Expense	$34,295.00	
Payroll Taxes Expense	4,674.26	
Utilities Expense	1,725.00	
Telephone Expense	884.00	
Rent Expense	5,175.00	
Total Expenses		46,753.26
Net Income for Quarter		$31,550.14

FIGURE 7-4

Balance Sheet Presentation (Partial)

L&L Grain Balance Sheet March 31, 20XX		
Assets:		
Cash		$ 78,507.89
Accounts Receivable		39,723.67
Equipment		15,289.00
Inventory		225,960.00
Total Assets		$359,480.56
Liabilities:		
Accounts Payable		4,085.27
FIT Payable		2,850.00
Social Security Tax Payable		4,118.16
Medicare Tax Payable		978.32
State Income Tax Payable		1,097.44
Health Insurance Payable		560.00
FUTA Tax Payable		274.36
SUTA Tax Payable		1,851.36
Salaries and Wages Payable		13,164.91
Total Liabilities		28,979.82
Owner's Equity		
L. Wilson, Capital		330,500.74
Total Owner's Equity		330,500.74
Total Liabilities and Owner's Equity		$359,480.56

quarterly, and annually. The function of the income statement is to correlate all money received during the course of business operations with the money spent to earn that income. Within the expense section of the income statement, you will see several accounts that relate to payroll. The Salaries and Wages Expense represents the gross pay from the period. Each

FIGURE 7-5

Post-Closing Trial Balance Presentation

Account	Debit	Credit
L&L Grain Post-Closing Trial Balance March 31, 20XX		
Cash	$ 78,507.89	
Accounts Receivable	39,723.67	
Inventory	225,960.00	
Equipment	15,289.00	
Accounts Payable		$ 4,085.27
FIT Payable		2,850.00
Social Security Tax Payable		4,118.16
Medicare Tax Payable		978.32
State Income Tax Payable		1,097.44
Health Insurance Payable		560.00
FUTA Tax Payable		274.36
SUTA Tax Payable		1,851.36
Salaries and Wages Payable		13,164.91
L. Wilson, Capital		298,950.60
Retained Earnings		31,550.14
	$359,480.56	$359,480.56

of the taxes we have discussed is listed. Note the expenses related to the taxes are paid by the employer and forwarded to the taxing authority; thus, there is no accrued federal income tax expense. Expenses related to the employer portion of retirement fund matching, health benefits, or other benefits are also located within the income statement.

Moving on to the balance sheet, any unpaid liabilities to be paid during the next 12 months will be reported in the current liability section. In accrual accounting, there may also be end-of-period entries to accrue for payroll earned by the employees. Additional liability accounts for accrued salaries, accrued hourly wages, accrued holiday pay, and accrued paid time off could also appear, depending on the timing of the end of the period and the types of employees and benefits with which the company operates. If there are employees who have taken payroll advances, which are amounts to be repaid by the employee, these are reported in the current assets section as receivables.

The trial balance contains all accounts the company uses, spanning all of the financial statements. The accounts listed on the trial balance appear in the order of the chart of accounts. In the United States, these are typically listed assets first: short-term and then long-term. The following are liabilities: short-term and then long-term. Equity accounts are listed next, followed by revenues and expenses. The important thing to remember when examining the trial balance is that it should balance: Debits must equal credits. Should one side not balance with the other, the accountant must determine why and correct the error. A post-closing trial balance will have already closed the revenue and expense accounts into the retained earnings account.

The purpose of all financial statements is to provide information to the stakeholders of a company. Stakeholders of a company include (but are certainly not limited to) company managers, governmental agencies, creditors, and employees who use the information to make decisions about the business. Financial statements are prepared in accordance with GAAP guidelines to facilitate the presentation of the statements among the wide variety of businesses that exist. Managers of a company, in particular, use the financial reports to make decisions about labor and benefits planning.

Companies are increasingly using application programming interfaces (API) to integrate financial data among their departments. The use of API fosters the sharing of information to improve company performance, employee access to their payroll and employment records, and transparency of financial data within the business. This software also allows payroll accountants to engage more fully in decision-making and other functions that involve critical thought and planning. (Source: What's Next Media)

Rawpixel.com/Shutterstock

Labor Reports

The payroll accountant may provide specific *labor reports* to management or department heads. These reports may have a variety of names and content depending on the needs of the business.

- The *labor usage* report designates where the labor is used within the company. When a company has several employees who work in different departments, the labor usage report can be useful in determining overhead *allocations* by the department and the need for increased or decreased staff within a specific department.

- The *billable vs. nonbillable* report tracks the time employees have spent specifically on projects for which customers are paying. This report allows managers to determine if the time allocated to the job in the job costing process is accurate, the company is operating efficiently, or if the employee is taking too long on a specific job.

- *Overtime* reports allow managers to determine how much overtime has been paid to employees during a specified time period. This report allows managers to monitor labor distribution and scheduling to ensure adherence to budget guidelines.

- Employers can also make use of *trend* reports for payroll staffing needs. Trend reports of income over the period of the year or two can reveal seasonal increases or decreases in business. An informed business manager will know if the company needs to have seasonal or temporary workers for short-term increases. If the trend reflects a steady increase in business, the manager may determine that hiring a new employee would be beneficial. Analyzing the staffing needs of the company compared to income projections may also lead managers to know if they need to lay off personnel, reduce hours of existing employees, or restructure company operations.

As of the end of 2019, over 157 million Americans are employed and work at least 15 hours per week. The level of employment in the United States has grown since 2010 and is projected to continue doing so, according to the Bureau of Labor Statistics. As the number of employees grows, the need for payroll professionals will also increase because of the complexity in compensating workers. Understanding payroll accounting is a vital skill needed by all industries, government employers, and private-sector and private-sector companies. It is safe to state that payroll accounting is a profession that will continue to be needed for the foreseeable future. (Source: BLS)

Labor Reports

Stop & Check

1. Which of the following reports are affected by the payroll of an organization?
   a. Trial balance
   b. Statement of owners' equity
   c. Interest statement
   d. Income statement
   e. Balance sheet
2. What is a specific type of report that the payroll accountant provides to managerial staff?
3. What are trend reports?

ECONOMIC EFFECTS OF PAYROLL

Although payroll accounting principles remain relatively stable, the role that payroll plays in the broader context of a business is subject to change. Some developments in payroll accounting in the business context that have changed since 2015 include the following:

- Accountants seeking roles as consultants (as opposed to technicians) because of increases in automation and technology that foster completion of lower-level work.
- Increases in labor costs for employers resulting from changes to the minimum wage.
- Expansion of the gig economy that has led to judicial review of employment practices.
- Employer-sponsored wellness programs have become a part of strategic human resource management because of the correlation with employee sick time and retention.
- Changes to federal reporting requirements to streamline and standardize company submissions.

Some trends to watch in payroll's economic effects include the following:

- Increased diversity in job titles and job duties that reflect consumer trends.
- Expanded integration of financial technology to improve the automation of accounting transactions.
- The introduction of millennial clients into the economy who bring new ideas and business practices to companies.
- A shift in the role of the accountant from being a recorder to becoming a partner in strategic decision-making for businesses.

Summary of the Payroll Register, Employees' Earnings Records, and Accounting System Entries

The payroll register and employees' earnings records are two tools that payroll accountants need to maintain their work accurately. Both records track employee compensation and contain information about company liabilities to governmental agencies and other organizations. These records also provide information for company decision-makers by yielding data about labor distribution and cost allocation. Payroll records provide information about benefits given to employees and how those benefits affect a business's profitability. Information contained in these sources and tools used by payroll accountants provides integral insights for managerial functions.

The final piece of the payroll cycle is the creation of accounting system entries. Similar to other business transactions, recording, paying the payroll, remitting money to governmental agencies and other firms requires General Journal and General Ledger entries. Business owners and departmental managers use this accounting information to measure the effectiveness of business plans and to plan both short- and long-term strategies. As an integral part of business operations, payroll-related expenses and liabilities represent an employer's financial duty, affect the financial reports, and influence the company's viability.

With this chapter's explanation of accounting system entries, we have now completed our journey through the payroll process. We have investigated the history of payroll, its many aspects and functions, and the importance of employee compensation within a business context.

We hope that after finishing this book, you will have gained the understanding that payroll accounting is complex, involves many different decisions along the way, and deserves your close attention. Figure 7-6 is a depiction of the basic elements of the payroll process that we have discussed.

FIGURE 7-6
Payroll Process Flowchart

- **Company with employees?**
  - Is it payday?
  - How much should each employee be paid?
  - Is managerial approval needed?

- **Computed deductions?**
  - Pre-tax deductions?
  - Mandatory deductions?
  - Voluntary deductions?
  - Mandated deductions?

- **Payroll register completion?**
  - Total, prove, and rule?
  - Approval for pay disbursement?
  - Correct pay method selected?
  - Pay disbursed at the right time?

- **Payroll tax remittance?**
  - Payroll tax deposits and remittance forms completed?
  - Forms and remittances checked for accuracy?
  - Payroll taxes deposited on time?

- **Voluntary deductions remittances?**
  - Are all outgoing remittances verified?
  - Are all outgoing remittances submitted on time?

- **Accounting entries?**
  - Journalize and post employee payroll?
  - Journalize and post the employer's share of the payroll?
  - Employee earnings records updated?
  - Are all financial statements completed?

Key Points

- The payroll register connects directly to the employees' earnings records.
- The employees' earnings records are the link between accounting and human resources and contain information from the payroll register.
- Accounting principles assist in the classification of payroll costs and organizational performance.

- Payroll transactions are recorded in the General Journal and posted to General Ledger accounts.
- The balances in the General Ledger accounts form the foundation of financial reports.
- Payroll costs represent an expense of the business.
- Employees are assigned to departments to foster accurate measurements of business segment profitability.
- Accounting reports provide managers with insights into company profitability and stability.
- Payroll-related transactions contain both the expenses and liabilities of a company.
- Employers have a fiduciary duty to ensure that all amounts deducted from employee pay are remitted to the appropriate entity.
- The increase in the automation of accounting information points to a need for educated, competent payroll professionals.
- Trend reports offer business leaders insight about changes in labor costs over a period.
- Financial reports contain the data that connects the payroll and human resources functions within a company.

Vocabulary

Accrual	Fiduciary	Liabilities
Adjusting entries	Generally Accepted	Owners' equity
Allocation	Accounting Principles	Posting
Assets	(GAAP)	Remit
Balance sheet	General Journal	Reversal
Credit	General Ledger	Trial balance
Debit	Income statement	
Expense	Labor reports	

Review Questions

1. What types of accounts does a debit increase?
2. What types of accounts does a credit increase?
3. Where are daily accounting entries recorded?
4. Once recorded, to where are the entries posted?
5. What is the purpose of the payroll register?
6. What information is contained in employees' earnings records?
7. How are the payroll register and the employees' earnings records related?
8. What type of account is debited for the gross pay?
9. What are three of the accounts that may be credited for the employee payroll?
10. What two accounts are affected upon issuance of paychecks?
11. What accounts are debited and credited for the employer share of the payroll expenses?
12. How do payroll expenses affect the income statement and balance sheet?
13. How can companies use payroll information that is reported in the financial statements to determine labor distribution?
14. How can a company's payroll information contained in financial reports assist in corporate planning?
15. How do the payroll register and employees' earnings records help employers meet their responsibilities to different groups, such as the employees and governmental agencies?
16. What is the term for the responsibility that employers have for payroll deductions under ERISA?

Exercises Set A

E7-1A.
LO 7-1
Which column exists in the employees' earnings records but not in the payroll register?
a. Gross pay
b. Net pay
c. YTD net pay
d. 401(k) contributions

E7-2A.
LO 7-1
What is the connection between the employees' earnings records and payroll tax reporting? (Select all that apply.)
a. Employees' earnings records do not connect with payroll tax reporting.
b. Employees' earnings records may be used to ensure the accuracy of payroll tax reporting.
c. Employees' earnings records contain details of payroll tax reporting and may be considered as source documents.
d. Employees' earnings records contain year-to-date gross pay, which reflects when employees reach tax bases.

E7-3A.
LO 7-2
A debit increases which of the following types of accounts? (Select all that apply.)
a. Liabilities
b. Expenses
c. Revenue
d. Assets

E7-4A.
LO 7-3
The total of the Gross Earnings column of the payroll register for a given pay period will appear in which account for the payroll-related General Journal entry?
a. Salaries and Wages Payable
b. Cash
c. Salaries and Wages Expense
d. Expenses

E7-5A.
LO 7-4
What is always true about the General Ledger? (Select all that apply.)
a. The process of transferring amounts from the General Journal to the General Ledger is called posting.
b. The General Ledger is a way to represent monthly groupings of entire General Journal entries.
c. The General Ledger contains information about the individual accounts used in General Journal transactions.
d. A debit to an account in a General Journal transaction is a debit to that account in the General Ledger.

E7-6A.
LO 7-4,
7-5, 7-6
How does a payroll accountant use the information in the General Ledger? (Select all that apply.)
a. The account balances form the basis for accounting reports.
b. The payroll accountant uses General Ledger balances to determine the effectiveness of individual employees.
c. General Ledger account balances aggregate data to determine payroll costs.
d. Payroll expenses contained in the General Ledger are not used to make personnel decisions.

E7-7A.
LO 7-6
Which of the following accounts would appear on the income statement? (Select all that apply.)
a. Payroll taxes expense
b. 401(k) contributions payable
c. 401(k) employer contributions expense
d. Social Security tax payable

E7-8A.
LO 7-6

What is always true about trial balance reports? (Select all that apply.)
a. Only accounts with activity during the period are included on the report.
b. All accounts with balances are included in the report.
c. The total of the debit column must equal the total of the credit column.
d. The report is prepared for a range of dates.

E7-9A.
LO 7-6

The purpose of a labor report is to do what? (Select all that apply.)
a. Report an individual employee's regular time and overtime.
b. Reflect all expenses of a firm.
c. Promote analysis of payroll expenses.
d. Update managers about payroll on a daily basis.

E7-10A.
LO 7-5, 7-6

Which law governs the fiduciary responsibility that employers have with regards to employees' payroll deductions?
a. FICA
b. FLSA
c. ERISA
d. ACA

Problems Set A

P7-1A.
LO 7-1

Charles Merrill owns a housekeeping service, Charles' Cleaners, in Florida. For the weekly payroll ending July 10, 2020, checks dated July 15, 2020, complete the payroll register. Use the wage bracket method in the federal tax table in Appendix C. No employee has exceeded the Social Security tax wage base. Total, prove, and rule the entries.

P/R End Date 7/10/2020   Company Name   Charles' Cleaners
Check Date 7/15/2020

Name	Filing Status	Hourly Rate or Period Wage	No. of Regular Hours	No. of Overtime Hours	No. of Holiday Hours	Commissions	Gross Earnings	401(k)	Cafeteria Plan	Taxable Wages for Federal W/H	Taxable Wages for FICA
Clark, M.	MJ-3	$ 8.50	40	3				$50.00			
Toonen, B.	S-1	$ 9.20	35					$75.00			
Dahl, P.	S-0	$ 10.10	37.5								
Steverman, S.	S-1	$ 8.74	40								
Bromley, L	MJ-4	$ 8.90	38					$60.00	$20.00		
Matte, R.	S-2	$ 10.50	40	5				$75.00			
Maddox, F.	S-1	$ 9.95	40						$15.00		
Totals											

Name	Gross Earnings	Taxable Wages for Federal W/H	Taxable Wages for FICA	Federal W/H	Social Security Tax	Medicare Tax	State W/H	Garnishment	United Way	Net Pay	Check No.
Clark, M.											
Toonen, B.									$10.00		
Dahl, P.								$100.00			
Steverman, S.									$25.00		
Bromley, L											
Matte, R.									$10.00		
Maddox, F.											
Totals											

P7-2A.
LO 7-1

The employee earnings record for Sean Steverman of Charles' Cleaners is listed below. Record his earnings from the July 10 weekly pay in P7-1A.

EMPLOYEE EARNING RECORD

NAME	Sean Steverman	Hire Date	May 22, 2011	Dependent child <17	0
ADDRESS	2326 Vinings Drive	Date of Birth	November 15, 1991	Dependent other	1
CITY/STATE/ZIP	Lodi, FL 32039	Position	Housekeeper	Step 4a W-4 Info	none
TELEPHONE	305-555-5698	Filing Status	Single	Step 4b W-4 Info	none
SOCIAL SECURITY NUMBER	188-56-7316	Pay Rate	8.74/hour	Step 4c W-4 Info	none

Period Ended	Hours Worked	Regular Pay	OT Pay	Holiday	Comm	Gross Pay	401(k)	Section 125	Taxable Wages for Federal W/H	Taxable Wages for FICA
7/3/2020	40	$321.60				$321.60	—	—	$321.60	$321.60

Taxable Wages for Federal	Taxable Wages for FICA W/H	Fed W/H	Social Sec. Tax	Medicare Tax	State W/H	United Way	Net Pay	YTD Net Pay	YTD Sec. Tax
$321.60	$321.60	$17.00	$19.94	$4.66	—	$25.00	$252.00	$3,500.00	$4,502.40

P7-3A.
LO 7-2, 7-3

Using the payroll register from P7-1A for Charles' Cleaners, complete the General Journal entry for the employees' pay for the July 10 pay date. Paychecks will be issued on July 15.

	Date	Description	Post Ref.	Debit	Credit	
1						1
2						2
3						3
4						4
5						5
6						6
7						7
8						8
9						9
10						10
11						11
12						12

P7-4A. Using the payroll register from P7-1A for Charles' Cleaners, complete the General Journal entry for the employer's share of the payroll taxes for the July 10 pay date. Assume 5.4 percent SUTA and 0.6 percent FUTA tax rates and that $1,352.40 is subject to FUTA/SUTA taxes.

LO 7-2, 7-3

	Date	Description	Post Ref.	Debit	Credit	
1						1
2						2
3						3
4						4
5						5
6						6
7						7
8						8
9						9

P7-5A. Using the employee payroll entry from P7-3A, post the July 10 employee pay for Charles' Cleaners to the selected General Ledger accounts shown next.

LO 7-2, 7-3

Account: Salaries and Wages Payable

	Date	Description	Post Ref.	Debit	Credit	Balance Debit	Balance Credit	
1								1
2								2
3								3
4								4
5								5
6								6

Account: Employee Federal Income Tax Payable

	Date	Description	Post Ref.	Debit	Credit	Balance Debit	Balance Credit	
1								1
2								2
3								3
4								4
5								5
6								6

Account: Social Security Tax Payable

	Date	Description	Post Ref.	Debit	Credit	Balance Debit	Balance Credit	
1								1
2								2
3								3
4								4
5								5
6								6

Account: Medicare Tax Payable

	Date	Description	Post Ref.	Debit	Credit	Balance		
						Debit	Credit	
1								1
2								2
3								3
4								4
5								5
6								6

Account: Salaries and Wages Expense

	Date	Description	Post Ref.	Debit	Credit	Balance		
						Debit	Credit	
1								1
2								2
3								3
4								4
5								5
6								6
7								7

P7-6A.

LO 7-2, 7-3

Using the employee payroll entry from P7-3A, complete the General Journal entry for the issuance of the pay for the July 10 pay date. The date of the checks is July 15, 2020.

	Date	Description	Post Ref.	Debit	Credit	
1						1
2						2
3						3
4						4
5						5

P7-7A.

LO 7-2, 7-3, 7-4

Using the employer payroll entry from P7-4A, post the employer's share of payroll taxes for the July 10 pay at Charles' Cleaners to the appropriate General Ledger accounts. Assume that $1,352.40 is subject to FUTA/SUTA taxes.

Account: Social Security Tax Payable

	Date	Description	Post Ref.	Debit	Credit	Balance		
						Debit	Credit	
1								1
2								2
3								3
4								4
5								5
6								6
7								7

Account: Medicare Tax Payable

	Date	Description	Post Ref.	Debit	Credit	Balance Debit	Balance Credit	
1								1
2								2
3								3
4								4
5								5
6								6
7								7

Account: Federal Unemployment Tax Payable

	Date	Description	Post Ref.	Debit	Credit	Balance Debit	Balance Credit	
1								1
2								2
3								3
4								4
5								5
6								6
7								7

Account: State Unemployment Tax Payable

	Date	Description	Post Ref.	Debit	Credit	Balance Debit	Balance Credit	
1								1
2								2
3								3
4								4
5								5
6								6
7								7

Account: Payroll Taxes Expense

	Date	Description	Post Ref.	Debit	Credit	Balance Debit	Balance Credit	
1								1
2								2
3								3
4								4
5								5
6								6
7								7

P7-8A.

LO 7-2, 7-3

KMH Industries is a monthly schedule depositor of payroll taxes. For the month of August 2020, the payroll taxes (employee and employer share combined) were as follows:

Social Security tax: $3,252.28

Medicare tax: $760.61

Employee federal income tax: $2,520

Create the General Journal entry for the remittance of the taxes. The entry should be dated September 15. Use check 2052 in the description.

	Date	Description	Post Ref.	Debit	Credit	
1						1
2						2
3						3
4						4
5						5
6						6
7						7
8						8

P7-9A.

LO 7-2, 7-3

Sophie Sue Breeders has the following voluntary withholdings to remit:

AFLAC payable: $560.00

401(k) payable: $1,280.00

Garnishments payable: $375.00

United Way contributions payable: $200.00

Create the General Journal entry on June 12, 2020, for the remittance of these withheld amounts.

	Date	Description	Post Ref.	Debit	Credit	
1						1
2						2
3						3
4						4
5						5
6						6
7						7

P7-10A.

LO 7-5, 7-6

Sheronda Rowe is the payroll accountant for Great Lake Lamps. The company's management has requested an analysis of the payroll effects on the expenses of the company. Explain which accounting report(s) you would use to construct your analysis. How would you explain the purpose of labor expenses as they affect company productivity?

P7-11A.

LO 7-6

The new vice president of marketing for your company has asked to meet with you regarding the purpose and location of payroll entries in accounting reports. What is your response to the vice president?

Exercises Set B

E7-1B.
LO 7-1
Which of the following information exists in both the employees' earnings records and the payroll register? (Select all that apply.)
a. Filing status
b. Social Security number
c. Hourly rate or period wage
d. Employee home address

E7-2B.
LO 7-1
How do the payroll register and employees' earnings records connect with payroll tax determination and remittance? (Select all that apply.)
a. Payroll register column totals contain information about pay period tax withholdings.
b. Employees' earnings records have pertinent information to determine individual taxable wage base attainment.
c. Payroll registers records reflect which employees have reached the Medicare additional tax.
d. Payroll registers contain specific information about each employee's raise history.

E7-3B.
LO 7-2
Which of the following are categories contained in the fundamental accounting equation? (Select all that apply.)
a. Assets
b. Liabilities
c. Expenses
d. Owners' Equity

E7-4B.
LO 7-2
Which of the following principles are always true about financial accounting? (Select all that apply.)
a. Assets = Owners' Equity
b. Debits = Credits
c. Assets = Liabilities + Owners' Equity
d. Debits + Credits = Owners' Equity

E7-5B.
LO 7-3
What is true about expenses and liabilities? (Select all that apply.)
a. Expenses usually have the word *expense* in the account title.
b. Expenses represent additional sums earned by the company.
c. Liabilities represent sums of money owed by third parties to the company.
d. Liabilities usually have the word *payable* in the account title.

E7-6B.
LO 7-3,
7-4, 7-5
How do payroll-related expenses affect financial statements? (Select all that apply.)
a. Payroll expenses may be allocable to work performed for a firm's vendors.
b. Payroll expense accounts are reported on the Income Statement.
c. The period's gross earnings are reported on the Balance Sheet.
d. Payroll expenses reduce the net income of a company.

E7-7B.
LO 7-6
Which of the following payroll-related accounts appear on the Balance Sheet? (Select all that apply.)
a. Wages and salaries expense
b. Medicare tax payable
c. Employee federal income tax payable
d. Health insurance premiums payable

E7-8B.
LO 7-2, 7-5
What is the purpose of payroll-related accrual and reversal entries on financial statements? (Select all that apply.)
a. Accrual entries represent payroll amounts earned but not yet paid.
b. Reversing entries represent disbursement of accrued payroll prior to the end of the payroll period.
c. Accrual entries are used to improve the accuracy of the net income for a period.
d. Reversing entries are omitted from financial statements.

E7-9B.

LO 7-6

Managers use labor reports to do which of the following? (Select all that apply.)
a. Analyze labor trends
b. Determine staffing needs
c. Ensure FLSA wage and hour compliance
d. Formulate strategic plans for the company

E7-10B.

LO 7-5, 7-6

To which parties does an employer have a fiduciary duty when it incurs payroll liabilities? (Select all that apply.)
a. Customers
b. Employees
c. Government
d. Vendors

Problems Set B

P7-1B.

LO 7-1

Tony Stanford owns Cosmic Comics in Greensboro, North Carolina. For the weekly payroll dated September 11, 2020, complete the payroll register. Checks will be issued on September 16, 2020. Use the wage bracket method in the federal tax table in Appendix C. Assume 5.25 percent state income tax. No employee has exceeded the Social Security wage base. Total, prove, and rule the entries.

P/R End Date | 9/11/2020 Company Name | Cosmic Comics
Check Date | 9/16/2020 Check Date |

Name	Filing Status	Hourly Rate or Period Wage	No. of Regular Hours	No. of Overtime Hours	No. of Holiday Hours	Commissions	Gross Earnings	401(k)	Sec 125	Taxable Wages for Federal W/H	Taxable Wages for FICA
Camacho, N.	MS-2	$ 12.20	40	2				$50.00			
Rea, A.	S-4	$ 9.45	39						$20.00		
Dahl, P.	MJ-5	$ 11.30	40	5				$35.00	$10.00		
Hayes, K.	S-1	$ 8.95	37					$20.00			
Fortanier, Y.	S-0	$ 10.05	38.5								
Cronan, S.	MJ-2	$ 13.45	40	6							
Murner, A.	S-2	$ 10.65	37					$45.00	$10.00		
Zinsli, E.	MS-0	$ 9.50	40	1				$25.00			
Totals											

Name	Gross Earnings	Taxable Wages for Federal W/H	Taxable Wages for FICA	Federal W/H	Social Security Tax	Medicare W/H	State W/H Tax	Garnishment	United Way	Net Pay	Check No.
Camacho, N.									$10.00		
Rea, A.											
Dahl, P.											
Hayes, K.								$ 60.00			
Fortanier, Y.								$ 50.00			
Cronan, S.											
Murner, A.											
Zinsli, E.											
Totals											

P7-2B.   What follows is the employee earnings record for Ally Murner of Cosmic Comics.
LO 7-1   Record her earnings during the September 11, 2020, pay period from P7-1B.

EMPLOYEE EARNING RECORD

NAME	Ally Murner	Hire Date	4/2/2020	Dependents <17	2
ADDRESS	522 Shady Lane	Date of Birth	7/1/1989	Dependents other	0
CITY/STATE/ZIP	Winslow, NC 22203	Position	Night Cashier	Step 4a W-4 Info	none
TELEPHONE	704-553-5967	Filing Status	Single	Step 4b W-4 Info	none
SOCIAL SECURITY NUMBER	680-30-2983	Pay Rate	$10.65/hour	Step 4c W-4 Info	none

Period Ended	Hrs Worked	Reg Pay	OT Pay	Holiday	Comm	Gross Pay	401(k)	Sec 125	Taxable Pay for Federal W/H	Taxable Pay for FICA
9/4/2020	40	$426.00				$426.00	$45.00	$10.00	$371.00	$416.00

Taxable Pay for Federal W/H	Taxable Pay for FICA	Fed Inc.	Social Sec. Tax	Medicare	State Inc. Tax	Garnishment	United Way	Net Pay	YTD Net Pay	YTD Gross Pay
$371.00	$416.00	$14.00	$25.79	$6.03	$19.48			305.70	5,808.30	$8,256.90

P7-3B.   Using the payroll register from P7-1B for Cosmic Comics, complete the
LO 7-1,   General Journal entry for the employees' pay for the September 11, 2020,
7-2, 7-3   pay date. Employees' paychecks will be issued on September 16.

	Date	Description	Post Ref.	Debit	Credit
1					
2					
3					
4					
5					
6					
7					
8					
9					

P7-4B.   Using the payroll register from P7-1B for Cosmic Comics, complete the
LO 7-1,   General Journal entry for the employer's share of the payroll taxes for the
7-2, 7-3   September 11, 2020, pay date. Assume a 5.4 percent SUTA rate and 0.6
percent FUTA rate, and assume that only $954.05 of the gross pay is subject
to SUTA/FUTA taxes.

	Date	Description	Post Ref.	Debit	Credit
1					
2					
3					
4					
5					
6					
7					
8					
9					

P7-5B.   Using the employee payroll entry from P7-3B, post the September 11
LO 7-3, 7-4   employee pay for Cosmic Comics to the selected General Ledger accounts.

Account: Salaries and Wages Payable

	Date	Description	Post Ref.	Debit	Credit	Balance Debit	Balance Credit
1							
2							
3							
4							
5							
6							

Account: Employee Federal Income Tax Payable

	Date	Description	Post Ref.	Debit	Credit	Balance Debit	Balance Credit
1							
2							
3							
4							
5							
6							

Account: Social Security Tax Payable

	Date	Description	Post Ref.	Debit	Credit	Balance Debit	Balance Credit
1							
2							
3							
4							
5							
6							

Account: Medicare Tax Payable

	Date	Description	Post Ref.	Debit	Credit	Balance Debit	Balance Credit
1							
2							
3							
4							
5							
6							

Account: Employee State Income Tax Payable

	Date	Description	Post Ref.	Debit	Credit	Balance Debit	Balance Credit
1							
2							
3							
4							
5							
6							

Account: Salaries and Wages Expense

	Date	Description	Post Ref.	Debit	Credit	Balance Debit	Balance Credit
1							
2							
3							
4							
5							
6							
7							

P7-6B.
LO 7-3, 7-4

Using the employee payroll entry from P7-3B, complete the General Journal entry for the issuance of Cosmic Comics pay on September 16, 2020.

	Date	Description	Post Ref.	Debit	Credit	
1						1
2						2
3						3
4						4
5						5

P7-7B.
LO 7-3, 7-4

Using the employer payroll entry from P7-4B, post the employer's share of payroll taxes for the September 11 pay period at Cosmic Comics to the appropriate General Ledger accounts.

Account: Payroll Taxes Expense

	Date	Description	Post Ref.	Debit	Credit	Balance Debit	Balance Credit	
1								1
2								2
3								3
4								4
5								5
6								6
7								7

Account: Social Security Tax Payable

	Date	Description	Post Ref.	Debit	Credit	Balance Debit	Balance Credit	
1								1
2								2
3								3
4								4
5								5
6								6
7								7

Account: Medicare Tax Payable

	Date	Description	Post Ref.	Debit	Credit	Balance Debit	Balance Credit	
1								1
2								2
3								3
4								4
5								5
6								6
7								7

Account: Federal Unemployment Tax Payable

	Date	Description	Post Ref.	Debit	Credit	Balance Debit	Balance Credit	
1								1
2								2
3								3
4								4
5								5
6								6
7								7

Account: State Unemployment Tax Payable

	Date	Description	Post Ref.	Debit	Credit	Balance Debit	Balance Credit	
1								1
2								2
3								3
4								4
5								5
6								6
7								7

P7-8B.

LO 7-2, 7-3

Legends Leadworks is a monthly schedule depositor of payroll taxes. For the month of April 2020, the payroll taxes (employee and employer share) were as follows:

Social Security tax: $5,386.56

Medicare tax: $1,259.76

Employee federal income tax: $4,978

Create the General Journal entry for the remittance of the taxes on May 15, 2020. Use check 1320 in the description.

	Date	Description	Post Ref.	Debit	Credit	
1						1
2						2
3						3
4						4
5						5
6						6
7						7
8						8

P7-9B.

LO 7-2, 7-3

Candy Farms Inc. has the following voluntary withholdings to remit as of September 30, 2020:

AFLAC payable: $687.00

Workers' compensation insurance payable: $1,042.00

401(k) payable: $2,104.00

Garnishments payable: $450.00

U.S. savings bonds payable: $200.00

Create the General Journal entry for the remittance of these withheld amounts on October 15, 2020.

	Date	Description	Post Ref.	Debit	Credit	
1						1
2						2
3						3
4						4
5						5
6						6
7						7
8						8

P7-10B

LO 7-5, 7-6

Pujah Srinivasan is the controller for HHT Industries. She has been asked to explain the payroll accounts on the financial statements for the preceding month. What information will she find about payroll on the financial statements?

P7-11B

LO 7-5, 7-6

You are interviewing for a position with Limelight Photography. The president of the company, Emma Jankiewicz, asks you to explain how payroll is both an expense and a liability of the company. How will you answer her?

Critical Thinking

7-1. Your boss asks you for a five-year labor cost trend chart. The labor costs per year are as follows:

2016	$175,248
2017	165,225
2018	179,905
2019	182,315
2020	186,417

Construct a line chart to depict the data. What conclusions can you derive from the data about labor costs and trends over the past five years? Why?

7-2. Giblin's Goodies pays employees weekly on Fridays. However, the company notices that April 30th is a Thursday and the pay period will end on May 1. The payroll data for April 27-April 30 is as follows:

Gross pay: $4,500

Federal income tax: $520

Social Security tax: $279

Medicare tax: $65.25

State income tax: $90

Give the adjusting entry in the General Journal to recognize the employee and employer share of the payroll for April 27-30. The date of the entry is April 30. Then record the journal entry to reverse the adjustment on May 1, 2020.

	Date	Description	Post Ref.	Debit	Credit	
1						1
2						2
3						3
4						4
5						5
6						6
7						7
8						8
9						9
10						10
11						11
12						12
13						13
14						14
15						15

In the Real World: Scenario for Discussion

An ongoing discussion among business managers is the return on employee investment (ROEI). Employers want to maximize business profitability, and employees are a significant part of organizational success. Investments in employee training and professional development constitute a significant part of many companies' budgets. Measures including providing tablet computers for employees to pursue flexible learning opportunities and self-paced classes give employers the opportunity to reduce training and development costs. What are the pros and cons of this practice?

Internet Activities

7-1. Would you like to know about personal experiences as a payroll accountant? How about videos that detail the completion of payroll-related forms? Go to www.youtube.com and search the term *payroll accounting* to read personal perspectives about payroll practice, outsourcing, and tax form completion. What were three insights you found that were new to you?

7-2. Would you like to build your own favorites list of payroll accounting tools? Go to one or more of the following sites. What are three important items you noticed?

   www.accountingtools.com

   www.accountantsworld.com

   www.americanpayroll.org

7-3. Join a conversation about payroll accounting with industry professionals. Go to www.linkedin.com and establish a profile (if you do not have one). Search groups for payroll accounting and follow the conversations. Which topics did you choose? Why?

7-4. Want to know more about the concepts in this chapter? Check out

   www.moneyinstructor.com/lesson/accountingconcepts.asp

   https://www.accountingcoach.com/accounting-basics/outline

Continuing Payroll Project: Prevosti Farms and Sugarhouse

Complete the Payroll Register for the February and March biweekly pay periods, assuming benefits went into effect as anticipated. Remember that pre-tax deductions are not subject to FUTA or SUTA.

Use the Wage Bracket Method Tables for Income Tax Withholding in Appendix C (or the IRS federal income tax withholding assistant). Complete the General Journal entries as follows:

February 7	Journalize the employee pay.
February 7	Journalize the employer payroll tax for the February 7 pay period. Use 5.4 percent SUTA and 0.6 percent FUTA. No employees will exceed the FUTA or SUTA wage base.
February 12	Issue employee pay.
February 21	Journalize the employee pay.
February 21	Journalize the employer payroll tax for the February 21 pay period. Use 5.4 percent SUTA and 0.6 percent FUTA. No employee will exceed the FUTA or SUTA wage base.
February 26	Issue employee pay.
February 26	Issue payment for payroll liabilities.
March 6	Journalize employee pay.
March 6	Journalize employer payroll tax for the March 6 pay period. Use 5.4 percent SUTA and 0.6 percent FUTA. No employees will exceed the FUTA or SUTA wage base.
March 11	Issue employee pay.
March 20	Journalize employee pay.
March 20	Journalize employer payroll tax for the March 20 pay period. Use 5.4 percent SUTA and 0.6 percent FUTA. No employees will exceed FUTA or SUTA wage base.
March 25	Issue employee pay.

	Date	Description	Post Ref.	Debit	Credit	
1						1
2						2
3						3
4						4
5						5
6						6
7						7
8						8
9						9
10						10
11						11
12						12
13						13
14						14
15						15
16						16
17						17
18						18
19						19
20						20
21						21
22						22
23						23
24						24
25						25
26						26
27						27
28						28
29						29
30						30
31						31
32						32
33						33
34						34
35						35

Post all journal entries to the appropriate General Ledger accounts.

Account: Cash   **101**

	Date	Description	Post Ref.	Debit	Credit	Balance Debit	Balance Credit	
1		Beg. Bal.				47 0 0 0 00		1
2								2
3								3
4								4
5								5
6								6

Account: Employee Federal Income Tax Payable   **203**

	Date	Description	Post Ref.	Debit	Credit	Balance Debit	Balance Credit	
1								1
2								2
3								3
4								4
5								5
6								6

Account: Social Security Tax Payable   **204**

	Date	Description	Post Ref.	Debit	Credit	Balance Debit	Balance Credit	
1								1
2								2
3								3
4								4
5								5
6								6

Account: Medicare Tax Payable   **205**

	Date	Description	Post Ref.	Debit	Credit	Balance Debit	Balance Credit	
1								1
2								2
3								3
4								4
5								5
6								6

Account: Employee State Income Tax Payable   **206**

	Date	Description	Post Ref.	Debit	Credit	Balance Debit	Balance Credit	
1								1
2								2
3								3
4								4
5								5
6								6

Account: 401(k) Contributions Payable   **208**

	Date	Description	Post Ref.	Debit	Credit	Balance Debit	Balance Credit	
1								1
2								2
3								3
4								4
5								5
6								6

Account: Health Insurance Payable 209

	Date	Description	Post Ref.	Debit	Credit	Balance Debit	Balance Credit	
1								1
2								2
3								3
4								4
5								5
6								6

Account: Salaries and Wages Payable 210

	Date	Description	Post Ref.	Debit	Credit	Balance Debit	Balance Credit	
1								1
2								2
3								3
4								4
5								5
6								6

Account: FUTA Tax Payable 211

	Date	Description	Post Ref.	Debit	Credit	Balance Debit	Balance Credit	
1								1
2								2
3								3
4								4
5								5
6								6

Account: SUTA Tax Payable 212

	Date	Description	Post Ref.	Debit	Credit	Balance Debit	Balance Credit	
1								1
2								2
3								3
4								4
5								5
6								6

Account: Payroll Taxes Expense 514

	Date	Description	Post Ref.	Debit	Credit	Balance Debit	Balance Credit	
1								1
2								2
3								3
4								4
5								5
6								6

Account: Salaries and Wages Expense   **515**

	Date	Description	Post Ref.	Debit	Credit	Balance Debit	Balance Credit	
1								1
2								2
3								3
4								4
5								5
6								6

Answers to Stop & Check Exercises

Employees' Earnings Records

1. The payroll register contains the period payroll information for all employees. The employees' earnings record lists all payroll data for a single employee.
2. a. Name
   b. Pay rate
   c. Net pay
3. Quarterly and annual tax reports use the totals from the employees' earnings records.

Financial Accounting Concepts

1. Assets = Liabilities + Owners' Equity
2. Credit
3. Debit

Payroll and the General Journal

1. Wages and Salaries Expense

2.

Account	Debit	Credit
Payroll Taxes Expense	$9,546.05	
Social Security Tax Payable		$7,736.67
Medicare Tax Payable		$1,809.38

3.

Account	Debit	Credit
Federal Income Tax Payable	$15,280.00	
Social Security Tax Payable	2,653.29	
Medicare Tax Payable	620.53	
State Income Tax Payable	1,626.21	
Wages and Salaries Payable	22,614.97	
Wages and Salaries Expense		$42,795.00

General Ledger Entries

1. $2,760 Cr.
2. The transaction may be found in the General Journal earlier in this section.

The Business Effects of Payroll

1. The payment of employee wages decreases profitability because it increases the expenses of a business.
2. Allocation of payroll expenses to specific jobs, clients, and so on allows the company to understand the costs associated with the activity.

Labor Reports

1. a. Trial balance
   b. Statement of owners' equity
   c. Income statement
   d. Balance sheet
2. Labor reports
3. Trend reports are used by managers to identify business patterns, needs, and opportunities.

Appendix A

Comprehensive Payroll Project: Wayland Custom Woodworking

Wayland Custom Woodworking is a firm that manufactures custom cabinets and woodwork for business and residential customers. Students will have the opportunity to establish payroll records and to complete a month of payroll information for Wayland.

Wayland Custom Woodworking is located at 12850 Old Highway 50, Glenbrook, Nevada, 89413, phone number 775-555-9877. The owner is Mark Wayland. Wayland's EIN is 91-7444533 and the Nevada Employer Account Number is E6462582020-6. Wayland has determined it will pay its employees on a semimonthly basis. Federal income tax should be computed using the percentage method.

Students will complete the payroll for the final quarter of 2020 and will file the fourth quarter and annual tax reports on the appropriate dates. At the instructor's discretion, students may complete a short version, which contains the payroll transactions beginning December 4. Directions for completion of the short version follow the November 30 transactions.

Rounding can create a challenge. For these exercises, the rate for the individuals is not rounded. So take their salary and divide by 2,080 (52 weeks at 40 hours per week) for full-time, nonexempt employees. NOTE: Leave the hourly rate rounded to 5 decimal places as shown in the next example. *After* the gross pay has been calculated, then round the result to two decimal points prior to calculating taxes or other withholdings.

EXAMPLE: ANNUAL SALARY TO HOURLY RATE, NONEXEMPT EMPLOYEE

Employee Cooper's annual salary is $62,000, and he is a nonexempt employee.

Hourly rate = $62,000/ (52 × 40) = $62,000/2,080

Hourly rate = $29.80769 per hour

EXAMPLE: PERIOD GROSS PAY, SALARIED EMPLOYEE

Employee Chinson earns an annual salary of $48,000 and is paid semimonthly.

Period gross pay = $48,000/24 = $2,000 gross pay

For pay periods with holiday hours: determine the amount paid per day, multiply by the number of days applicable to each pay period.

Annual salary: $48,000/(52*5) = $48,000/260 = $184.61538 (rounded to 5 decimal points) per day. Once you have the holiday pay, subtract it from their salary for the period for regular time.

Employees are paid for the following holidays occurring during the final quarter:

- Thanksgiving day and the day after, Thursday and Friday, November 26-27.
- Christmas, which is a Friday. Employees receive holiday pay for Thursday, December 24, and Friday, December 25.

For the completion of this project, the following information can be located in Appendix C. Students will use the percentage method for federal income tax. Employees' 401(k) and insurance are pre-tax for federal income tax. The SUTA (UI) rate for Wayland Custom Woodworking is 3.25% on the first $32,500. There is an additional 0.05% for Career Enhancement Program (CEP). Neither of these has deductions for Section 125 or 401(k) contributions by the employee.

No employee has additional information in Step 4 of their W-4s, all W-4s were received in 2020, no box 2c has been checked.

Federal Unemployment Rate (employer only) (less Section 125)	0.6% on the first $7,000 of wages
Semimonthly Federal Percentage Method Tax Table	Appendix C
State Unemployment Rate (employer only)	3.25% on the first $32,500 of wages
Career Enhancement Program	0.05% on the first $32,500 of wages

October 1

Wayland Custom Woodworking (WCW) pays its employees according to their job classification. Wayland's staff comprises the following employees:

Employee Number	Name and Address	Payroll information
00-Chins	Anthony Chinson	Married/Joint; 2 < 17
	530 Chimney Rock Road	Exempt
	Stateline, NV 89449	$48,000/year + commission
	775-555-1212	Start Date: 10/1/2020
	Job title: Account Executive	SSN: 511-22-3333
00-Wayla	Mark Wayland	Married/Joint; 3 < 17, 1 Other
	1650 Power House Drive	Exempt
	Glenbrook, NV 89413	$85,000/year
	775-555-1110	Start Date: 10/1/2020
	Job title: President/Owner	SSN: 505-33-1775

01-Peppi	Sylvia Peppinico	Married/Joint; 1 < 17, 1 Other
	1575 Flowers Avenue	Exempt
	Glenbrook, NV 89413	$58,500/year
	775-555-2244	Start Date: 10/1/2020
	Job title: Craftsman	SSN: 047-55-9951
01-Coope	Stevon Cooper	Single; None
	2215 Lands End Drive	Nonexempt
	Glenbrook, NV 89413	$62,000/year
	775-555-9981	Start Date: 10/1/2020
	Job title: Craftsman	SSN: 022-66-1131
02-Hisso	Leonard Hissop	Single; 1 Other
	333 Engine House Circle	Nonexempt
	Glenbrook, NV 89413	$51,500/year
	775-555-5858	Start Date: 10/1/2020
	Job title: Purchasing/Shipping	SSN: 311-22-6698

Voluntary deductions for each employee are as follows:

Name	Deduction
Chinson	Insurance: $50/paycheck 401(k): 3% of gross pay
Wayland	Insurance: $75/paycheck 401(k): 6% of gross pay
Peppinico	Insurance: $75/paycheck 401(k): $50 per paycheck
Cooper	Insurance: $50/paycheck 401(k): 4% of gross pay
Hissop	Insurance: $75/paycheck 401(k): 3% of gross pay
Student	Insurance: $50/paycheck 401(k): 3% of gross pay

Complete the headers of the Employees' Earnings Register for all company employees. Enter the YTD earnings for each employee. The departments are as follows:

Department 00: Sales and Administration

Department 01: Factory Workers

Department 02: Delivery and Customer Service

1. You have been hired as of October 1 as the new accounting clerk. Your employee number is 00-SUCCE. Your name is STUDENT SUCCESS. Your address is 16 Kelly Circle #2, Glenbrook, NV 89413. Your phone number is 775-556-1211, you were born July 16, 1985, your Nevada driver's license number is 168575381944 expiring in 7/2024, and your Social Security number is 555-55-5555. You are nonexempt and paid at a rate of $42,000 per year. Complete Form W-4 and, using the given information, complete the I-9 form to start your employee file. Complete it as if you are single with no dependents or other income, you contribute 3 percent to a 401(k), and health insurance is $50 per pay period.

The balance sheet for WCW as of September 30, 2020, is as follows:

Wayland Custom Woodworking
Balance Sheet
September 30, 2020

Assets		Liabilities & Equity	
Cash	$1,125,000.00	Accounts Payable	$ 112,490.00
Supplies	27,240.00	Salaries and Wages Payable	
Office Equipment	87,250.00	Federal Unemployment Tax Payable	
Inventory	123,000.00	Social Security Tax Payable	
Vehicle	25,000.00	Medicare Tax Payable	
Accumulated Depreciation, Vehicle		State Unemployment Tax Payable	
Building	164,000.00	Career Enhancement Program Payable	
Accumulated Depreciation, Building		Employee Federal Income Tax Payable	
Land	35,750.00	Employee State Income Tax Payable	
Total Assets	1,587,240.00	401(k) Contributions Payable	
		Employee Medical Premiums Payable	
		Notes Payable	224,750.00
		Total Liabilities	337,240.00
		Owners' Equity	1,250,000.00
		Retained Earnings	—
		Total Equity	1,250,000.00
		Total Liabilities and Equity	1,587,240.00

October 15

October 15 is the end of the first pay period for the month of October. Employee pay will be disbursed on October 19, 2020. Any time worked in excess of 88 hours during this pay period is considered overtime for nonexempt employees. Remember that the employees are paid on a semimonthly basis. The hours for the employees are as follows:

Name	Hourly Rate or Period Wage (round to 5 decimals)	Pay Period Hours 10/1–10/15	Regular (round to 2 decimals)	Overtime (round to 2 decimals)	Commission
Chinson		88 hours (exempt)			$1,500.00
Wayland		88 hours (exempt)			
Peppinico		88 hours (exempt)			
Cooper		88 hours			
Hissop		93.25 hours			
Student		90 hours			

October

Sunday	Monday	Tuesday	Wednesday	Thursday	Friday	Saturday
				1	2	3
4	5	6	7	8	9	10
11	12	13	14	15	16	17
18	19	20	21	22	23	24
25	26	27	28	29	30	31

Complete the Payroll Register for October 15. Round wages to five decimal points and all other final answers to two decimal points. Update the Employees' Earnings Records for the period's pay and update the YTD amount. Insurance qualifies for Section 125 treatment. Use the wage bracket method in Appendix C for the federal income tax. The starting check number is 4215.

Voluntary deductions for each employee are as follows:

Name	Deduction
Chinson	Insurance: $50/paycheck 401(k): 3% of gross pay
Wayland	Insurance: $75/paycheck 401(k): 6% of gross pay
Peppinico	Insurance: $75/paycheck 401(k): $50 per paycheck
Cooper	Insurance: $50/paycheck 401(k): 4% of gross pay
Hissop	Insurance: $75/paycheck 401(k): 3% of gross pay
Student	Insurance: $50/paycheck 401(k): 3% of gross pay

Complete the Payroll Register for October 15.

P/R End Date _____   Company Name   Wayland Custom Woodworking

Check Date _____

Name	Filing Status	Dependents	Hourly Rate or Period Wage	No. of Regular Hours	No. of Overtime Hours	No. of Holiday Hours	Commissions	Gross Earnings	Insurance	401(k)	Taxable Wages for Federal W/H	Taxable Wages for FICA
Anthony Chinson												
Mark Wayland												
Sylvia Peppinico												
Stevon Cooper												
Leonard Hissop												
Student Success												
Total												

Name	Gross Earnings	Taxable Wages for Federal W/H	Taxable Wages for FICA	Federal W/He	Social Security Tax	Medicare W/H	Union Dues	Net Pay	Check No.
Anthony Chinson									
Mark Wayland									
Sylvia Peppinico									
Stevon Cooper									
Leonard Hissop									
Student									
Total									

Employee Earnings Register

NAME	_____	Hire Date	_____	Dependent child <17	_____
ADDRESS	_____	Date of Birth	_____	Dependent other	_____
CITY/STATE/ZIP	_____	Position	_____ PT / FT	Step 4a W-4 Info	_____
TELEPHONE	_____	Filing Status	_____	Step 4b W-4 Info	_____
SOCIAL SECURITY NUMBER	_____	Exempt/Nonexempt	_____	Step 4c W-4 Info	_____
		Pay Rate	_____ Hr / Wk / Mo / Yr		

Period Ended	Hrs Worked	Reg Pay	OT Pay	Comm	Gross Pay	Social Sec Tax	Medicare	Fed Inc Tax	State W/H Tax	Sect 125	401(k)	Total Deduc	Net Pay	YTD

EMPLOYEE EARNING RECORD

NAME	_____	Hire Date	_____	Dependent child <17	_____
ADDRESS	_____	Date of Birth	_____	Dependent other	_____
CITY/STATE/ZIP	_____	Position	_____	Step 4a W-4 Info	_____
TELEPHONE	_____	Filing Status	_____	Step 4b W-4 Info	_____
SOCIAL SECURITY NUMBER	_____	Pay Rate	_____	Step 4c W-4 Info	_____
				Hr/Wk/Mo/Yr	_____

Period Ended	Hrs Worked	Reg Pay	OT Pay	Holiday	Comm	Gross Pay	Ins	401(k)	Taxable Pay for Federal	Taxable Pay for FICA

Taxable Pay for Federal	Taxable Pay for FICA	Fed Inc. Tax	Social Sec. Tax	Medicare	Total Deduc	Net Pay	YTD Net Pay	YTD Gross Pay	Current Taxable for FUTA	Current Taxable for SUTA

EMPLOYEE EARNING RECORD

NAME	_____	Hire Date	_____	Dependent child <17	_____
ADDRESS	_____	Date of Birth	_____	Dependent other	_____
CITY/STATE/ZIP	_____	Position	_____	Step 4a W-4 Info	_____
TELEPHONE	_____	Filing Status	_____	Step 4b W-4 Info	_____
SOCIAL SECURITY				Step 4c W-4 Info	_____
NUMBER	_____	Pay Rate	_____	Hr/Wk/Mo/Yr	

Period Ended	Hrs Worked	Reg Pay	OT Pay	Holiday	Comm	Gross Pay	Ins	401(k)	Taxable Pay for Federal	Taxable Pay for FICA

Taxable Pay for Federal	Taxable Pay for FICA	Fed Inc. Tax	Social Sec. Tax	Medicare	Total Deduc	Net Pay	YTD Net Pay	YTD Gross Pay	Current Taxable for FUTA	Current Taxable for SUTA

EMPLOYEE EARNING RECORD

NAME	_____	Hire Date	_____	Dependent child <17	_____
ADDRESS	_____	Date of Birth	_____	Dependent other	_____
CITY/STATE/ZIP	_____	Position	_____	Step 4a W-4 Info	_____
TELEPHONE	_____	Filing Status	_____	Step 4b W-4 Info	_____
SOCIAL SECURITY				Step 4c W-4 Info	_____
NUMBER	_____	Pay Rate	_____	Hr/Wk/Mo/Yr	

Period Ended	Hrs Worked	Reg Pay	OT Pay	Holiday	Comm	Gross Pay	Ins	401(k)	Taxable Pay for Federal	Taxable Pay for FICA

Taxable Pay for Federal	Taxable Pay for FICA	Fed Inc. Tax	Social Sec. Tax	Medicare	Total Deduc	Net Pay	YTD Net Pay	YTD Gross Pay	Current Taxable for FUTA	Current Taxable for SUTA

EMPLOYEE EARNING RECORD

NAME _____   Hire Date _____   Dependent child <17 _____

ADDRESS _____   Date of Birth _____   Dependent other _____

CITY/STATE/ZIP _____   Position _____   Step 4a W-4 Info _____

TELEPHONE _____   Filing Status _____   Step 4b W-4 Info _____

SOCIAL SECURITY _____   Step 4c W-4 Info _____

NUMBER _____   Pay Rate _____   Hr/Wk/Mo/Yr

Period Ended	Hrs Worked	Reg Pay	OT Pay	Holiday	Comm	Gross Pay	Ins	401(k)	Taxable Pay for Federal	Taxable Pay for FICA

Taxable Pay for Federal	Taxable Pay for FICA	Fed Inc. Tax	Social Sec. Tax	Medicare	Total Deduc	Net Pay	YTD Net Pay	YTD Gross Pay	Current Taxable for FUTA	Current Taxable for SUTA

EMPLOYEE EARNING RECORD

NAME _____   Hire Date _____   Dependent child <17 _____

ADDRESS _____   Date of Birth _____   Dependent other _____

CITY/STATE/ZIP _____   Position _____   Step 4a W-4 Info _____

TELEPHONE _____   Filing Status _____   Step 4b W-4 Info _____

SOCIAL SECURITY _____   Step 4c W-4 Info _____

NUMBER _____   Pay Rate _____   Hr/Wk/Mo/Yr

Period Ended	Hrs Worked	Reg Pay	OT Pay	Holiday	Comm	Gross Pay	Ins	401(k)	Taxable Pay for Federal	Taxable Pay for FICA

Taxable Pay for Federal	Taxable Pay for FICA	Fed Inc. Tax	Social Sec. Tax	Medicare	Total Deduc	Net Pay	YTD Net Pay	YTD Gross Pay	Current Taxable for FUTA	Current Taxable for SUTA

EMPLOYEE EARNING RECORD

NAME _____   Hire Date _____   Dependent child <17 _____
ADDRESS _____   Date of Birth _____   Dependent other _____
CITY/STATE/ZIP _____   Position _____   Step 4a W-4 Info _____
TELEPHONE _____   Filing Status _____   Step 4b W-4 Info _____
SOCIAL SECURITY _____   Pay Rate _____   Step 4c W-4 Info _____
NUMBER _____   Pay Rate _____   Hr/Wk/Mo/Yr

Period Ended	Hrs Worked	Reg Pay	OT Pay	Holiday	Comm	Gross Pay	Ins	401(k)	Taxable Pay for Federal	Taxable Pay for FICA

Taxable Pay for Federal	Taxable Pay for FICA	Fed Inc. Tax	Social Sec. Tax	Medicare	Total Deduc	Net Pay	YTD Net Pay	YTD Gross Pay	Current Taxable for FUTA	Current Taxable for SUTA

General Journal Entries

Complete the General Journal entries as follows:

15-Oct	Journalize employee pay including the issuance of paychecks (use one entry for all checks).
15-Oct	Journalize employer payroll tax for the October 15 pay date.
19-Oct	Journalize the payment of payroll.

Post all journal entries to the appropriate General Ledger accounts.

Date		Description	Post Ref.	Debit	Credit

October 31

October 31 is the end of the final pay period for the month. Employee pay will be disbursed on November 4, 2020. Any hours exceeding 96 during this pay period are considered overtime for nonexempt employees. Compute the employee pay. Update the Employees' Earnings Records for the period's pay and update the YTD amount.

Complete the Payroll Register for October 31. Round wages to five decimal points and all other final answers to two decimal points.

The hours for the employees are as follows:

Name	Hourly Rate or Period Wage (round to 5 decimals)	Hours Worked 10/16–10/31	Regular (round to 2 decimals)	Overtime (round to 2 decimals)	Commission
Chinson		96 hours (exempt)			$1,750.00
Wayland		96 hours (exempt)			
Peppinico		96 hours (exempt)			
Cooper		100 hours			
Hissop		103 hours			
Student		98 hours			

October						
Sunday	Monday	Tuesday	Wednesday	Thursday	Friday	Saturday
				1	2	3
4	5	6	7	8	9	10
11	12	13	14	15	16	17
18	19	20	21	22	23	24
25	26	27	28	29	30	31

Complete the Payroll Register for October 31.

Run End Date [   ]   Company Name   Wayland Custom Woodworking

P/R Date [   ]

Name	Filing Status	Dependents	Hourly Rate or Period Wage	No. of Regular Hours	No. of Overtime Hours	No. of Holiday Hours	Commissions	Gross Earnings	Insurance	401(k)	Taxable Wages for Federal W/H	Taxable Wages for FICA
Anthony Chinson												
Mark Wayland												
Sylvia Peppinico												
Stevon Cooper												
Leonard Hissop												
Student												
Total												

Name	Gross Earnings	Taxable Wages for Federal W/H	Taxable Wages for FICA	Federal W/H	Social Security Tax	Medicare W/H	State W/H Tax	Union Dues	Net Pay	Check No.
Anthony Chinson										
Mark Wayland										
Sylvia Peppinico										
Stevon Cooper										
Leonard Hissop										
Student										
Total										

General Journal Entries

Complete the General Journal entries as follows:

31-Oct	Journalize employee pay for the period.
31-Oct	Journalize employer payroll tax for the October 31 pay date.
04-Nov	Journalize the payment of payroll to employees. (Use one entry for all disbursements.)
04-Nov	Journalize remittance of 401(k) and Section 125 health insurance premiums deducted.
04-Nov	Journalize remittance of monthly payroll taxes.

Post all journal entries to the appropriate General Ledger accounts.

Date		Description	Post Ref.	Debit	Credit

November 15

Compute the pay for each employee. Update the Employees' Earnings Record for the period's pay and the new YTD amount. Employee pay will be disbursed on November 19, 2020. Any hours exceeding 80 during this pay period are considered overtime for nonexempt employees. Remember that the employees are paid semimonthly.

Complete the Payroll Register for November 15. Round wages to five decimal points and all other final answers to two decimal points.

The hours for the employees are as follows:

Name	Hourly Rate or Period Wage (round to 5 decimals)	Pay Period Hours 11/01–11/15	Regular (round to 2 decimals)	Overtime (round to 2 decimals)	Commission
Chinson		80 hours (exempt)			$1,050.00
Wayland		80 hours (exempt)			
Peppinico		80 hours (exempt)			
Cooper		88 hours			
Hissop		83 hours			
Student		85 hours			

November						
Sunday	Monday	Tuesday	Wednesday	Thursday	Friday	Saturday
1	2	3	4	5	6	7
8	9	10	11	12	13	14
15	16	17	18	19	20	21
22	23	24	25	26	27	28
29	30					

Complete the Payroll Register for November 30.

Run Date		Company Name	Wayland Custom Woodworking
P/R Date			

Name	Filing Status	Dependents	Hourly Rate or Period Wage	No. of Regular Hours	No. of Overtime Hours	No. of Holiday Hours	Commissions	Gross Earnings	Insurance	401(k)	Taxable Wages for Federal W/H	Taxable Wages for FICA
Anthony Chinson												
Mark Wayland												
Sylvia Peppinico												
Stevon Cooper												
Leonard Hissop												
Student												
Total												

Name	Gross Earnings	Taxable Wages for Federal W/H	Taxable Wages for FICA	Federal W/H	Social Security Tax	Medicare W/H	State W/H Tax	Union Dues	Net Pay	Check No.
Anthony Chinson										
Mark Wayland										
Sylvia Peppinico										
Stevon Cooper										
Leonard Hissop										
Student										
Total										

General Journal Entries

Complete the General Journal entries as follows:

15-Nov	Journalize employee pay including the issuance of paychecks (use one entry for all checks).
15-Nov	Journalize employer payroll tax for the November 15 pay date.
19-Nov	Journalize payment of payroll to employees.

Post all journal entries to the appropriate General Ledger accounts.

Date		Description	Post Ref.	Debit	Credit

Post all journal entries to the appropriate General Ledger accounts.

November 30

Compute the Net Pay for each employee. Employee pay will be disbursed on December 4, 2020. Update the Employees' Earnings Records with the November 30 pay and the new YTD amount.

The company is closed and pays for the Friday following Thanksgiving. The employees will receive holiday pay for Thanksgiving and the Friday following. All the hours over 80 are eligible for overtime for nonexempt employees as they were worked during the non-holiday week. When completing the employee earnings report, remember hours worked must be physically worked (holidays do not count).

The hours for the employees are as follows:

Name	Hourly Rate or Period Wage (round to 5 decimals)	Pay Period Hours 11/16—11/30	Regular (round to 2 decimals)	Overtime (round to 2 decimals)	Holiday (round to 2 decimals)	Commission
Chinson		80 hours (exempt — 16 hours Holiday)				$2,325.00
Wayland		80 hours (exempt — 16 hours Holiday)				
Peppinico		80 hours (exempt — 16 hours Holiday)				
Cooper		82 hours (exempt — 16 hours Holiday)				
Hissop		83 hours (exempt — 16 hours Holiday)				
Student		81 hours (exempt — 16 hours Holiday)				

November						
Sunday	Monday	Tuesday	Wednesday	Thursday	Friday	Saturday
1	2	3	4	5	6	7
8	9	10	11	12	13	14
15	16	17	18	19	20	21
22	23	24	25	26	27	28
29	30					

Complete the Payroll Register for November 30. Round wages to five decimal points and all other final answers to two decimal points.

Complete the Payroll Register for November 30.

Run Date [   ]   Company Name   Wayland Custom Woodworking

P/R Date [   ]

Name	Filing Status	Dependents	Hourly Rate or Period Wage	No. of Regular Hours	No. of Overtime Hours	No. of Holiday Hours	Commissions	Gross Earnings	Insurance	401(k)	Taxable Wages for Federal W/H	Taxable Wages for FICA
Anthony Chinson												
Mark Wayland												
Sylvia Peppinico												
Stevon Cooper												
Leonard Hissop												
Student												
Total												

Name	Gross Earnings	Taxable Wages for Federal W/H	Taxable Wages for FICA	Federal W/H	Social Security Tax	Medicare W/H	State W/H Tax	Union Dues	Net Pay	Check No.
Anthony Chinson										
Mark Wayland										
Sylvia Peppinico										
Stevon Cooper										
Leonard Hissop										
Student										
Total										

General Journal Entries

Complete the General Journal entries as follows:

30-Nov	Journalize employee pay including the issuance of paychecks (use one entry for all checks).
30-Nov	Journalize employer payroll tax for the November 30 pay date.
04-Dec	Journalize payment of payroll to employees.
04-Dec	Journalize remittance of 401(k) and health insurance premiums deducted.
04-Dec	Journalize remittance of monthly payroll taxes.

Post all journal entries to the appropriate General Ledger accounts.

Date		Description	Post Ref.	Debit	Credit

Short Version 1 Month option:

Wayland Custom Woodworking
Balance Sheet
November 30, 2020

Assets		Liabilities & Equity	
Cash	$ 1,075,321.77	Accounts Payable	$ 112,747.25
Supplies	42,240.11	Salaries and Wages Payable	12,735.40
Office Equipment	87,250.00	Federal Unemployment Tax Payable	55.09
Inventory	167,099.00	Social Security Tax Payable	3,893.18
Vehicle	25,000.00	Medicare Tax Payable	910.54
Accumulated Depreciation, Vehicle		State Unemployment Tax Payable	1,044.76
Building	164,000.00	Career Enhancement Program Payable	16.08
Accumulated Depreciation, Building		Employee Federal Income Tax Payable	2,949.14
Land	35,750.00	401(k) Contributions Payable	1,182.81
Total Assets	1,596,660.88	Employee Medical Premiums Payable	750.00
		Notes Payable	210,376.63
		Utilities Payable	
		Total Liabilities	346,660.88
		Owners' Equity	1,250,000.00
		Retained Earnings	—
		Total Equity	1,250,000.00
		Total Liabilities and Equity	1,596,660.88

Students will complete the payroll for the final month of 2020 and will file the fourth quarter and annual tax reports on the appropriate dates. Wayland Custom Woodworking is located at 12850 Old Highway 50, Glenbrook, Nevada, 89413, phone number 775-555-9877. The owner is Mark Wayland. Wayland's EIN is 91-7444533. Wayland has determined it will pay its employees on a semimonthly basis. Federal income tax should be computed using the percentage method.

Rounding can create a challenge. For these exercises, the rate for the individuals is not rounded. So take their salary and divide by 2,080 (52 weeks at 40 hours per week) for full-time, nonexempt employees. NOTE: Leave the hourly rate rounded to 5 decimal places as shown in the next example. *After* the gross pay has been calculated, then round the result to two decimal points prior to calculating taxes or other withholdings.

December 15

Compute the net pay and update the Employees' Earnings Records with the December 15 pay and the new YTD information. Employee pay will be disbursed on December 21, 2020. Any hours worked in excess of 88 hours during this pay period are considered overtime for nonexempt employees.

The hours for the employees are as follows:

Name	Hourly Rate or Period Wage (round to 5 decimals)	Pay Period Hours 12/01–12/15	Regular (round to 2 decimals)	Overtime (round to 2 decimals)	Holiday (round to 2 decimals)	Commission
Chinson		88 hours (exempt)				$1,680.00
Wayland		88 hours (exempt)				
Peppinico		88 hours (exempt)				
Cooper		92 hours				
Hissop		88 hours				
Student		91 hours				

December						
Sunday	Monday	Tuesday	Wednesday	Thursday	Friday	Saturday
		1	2	3	4	5
6	7	8	9	10	11	12
13	14	15	16	17	18	19
20	21	22	23	24	25	26
27	28	29	30	31		

Complete the Payroll Register for December 15. Round wages to five decimal points and all other final answers to two decimal points.

Run Date _____   Company Name   Wayland Custom Woodworking

P/R Date _____

Name	Filing Status	Dependents	Hourly Rate or Period Wage	No. of Regular Hours	No. of Overtime Hours	No. of Holiday Hours	Commissions	Gross Earnings	Insurance	401(k)	Taxable Wages for Federal W/H	Taxable Wages for FICA
Anthony Chinson												
Mark Wayland												
Sylvia Peppinico												
Stevon Cooper												
Leonard Hissop												
Student												
Total												

Name	Gross Earnings	Taxable Wages for Federal W/H	Taxable Wages for FICA	Federal W/H	Social Security Tax	Medicare W/H	State W/H Tax	Union Dues	Net Pay	Check No.
Anthony Chinson										
Mark Wayland										
Sylvia Peppinico										
Stevon Cooper										
Leonard Hissop										
Student										
Total										

General Journal Entries

Complete the General Journal entries as follows:

15-Dec	Journalize employee pay including the issuance of paychecks (use one entry for all checks).
15-Dec	Journalize employer payroll tax for the December 15 pay date.
21-Dec	Journalize payment of payroll to employees.

Post all journal entries to the appropriate General Ledger accounts.

Date		Description	Post Ref.	Debit	Credit

December 31

The final pay period of the year will not be paid to employees until January 5, 2021. The company will accrue the wages for the final pay period only. Because the pay period is complete, there will not be an accrual. No reversing entry is needed because that would occur during the first pay period of the next calendar year.

The company pays for Christmas Eve and the day of Christmas for 2020. Employees will be paid for both Thursday and Friday as holiday pay.

Employee pay will be disbursed and reflected on the Employees' Earnings Register when paid. The remainder of the employer liability will be paid with the final filing for the year. Complete all state and federal tax forms for the year-end. Generate Forms W-2 and W-3 for employees, and recall that these forms only reflect wages actually paid during the calendar year. Employer amounts for health coverage should be reported as 1.5 times the employee's premium in Box 12, using Code DD.

The hours for the employees are as follows:

Name	Hourly Rate or Period Wage (round to 5 decimals)	Pay Period Hours 12/16–12/31	Regular (round to 2 decimals)	Overtime (round to 2 decimals)	Holiday (round to 2 decimals)	Commission
Chinson		96 hours (exempt — 16 hours Holiday)				$1,015.00
Wayland		96 hours (exempt — 16 hours Holiday)				
Peppinico		96 hours (exempt — 16 hours Holiday)				
Cooper		98 hours (16 Holiday)*				
Hissop		97 hours (16 Holiday)*				
Student		99 hours (16 Holiday)*				

*Employees worked extra hours on Saturday, 12/28. Reminder, holidays and vacations are not included as hours worked for calculation of overtime.

December						
Sunday	Monday	Tuesday	Wednesday	Thursday	Friday	Saturday
		1	2	3	4	5
6	7	8	9	10	11	12
13	14	15	16	17	18	19
20	21	22	23	24	25	26
27	28	29	30	31		

Complete the Payroll Register for December 31.

Run Date _____

P/R Date _____

Company Name   Wayland Custom Woodworking

Name	Filing Status	Dependents	Hourly Rate or Period Wage	No. of Regular Hours	No. of Overtime Hours	No. of Holiday Hours	Commissions	Gross Earnings	Insurance	401(k)	Taxable Wages for Federal W/H	Taxable Wages for FICA
Anthony Chinson												
Mark Wayland												
Sylvia Peppinico												
Stevon Cooper												
Leonard Hissop												
Student												
Total												

Name	Gross Earnings	Taxable Wages for Federal W/H	Taxable Wages for FICA	Federal W/H	Social Security Tax	Medicare W/H	State W/H Tax	Union Dues	Net Pay	Check No.
Anthony Chinson										
Mark Wayland										
Sylvia Peppinico										
Stevon Cooper										
Leonard Hissop										
Student										
Total										

General Journal Entries

Complete the General Journal entries as follows:

31-Dec	Accrue employee pay including the issuance of paychecks (use one entry for all checks).
31-Dec	Accrue employer payroll tax for the December 31 pay date.

Post all journal entries to the appropriate General Ledger accounts.

Date		Description	Post Ref.	Debit	Credit

Employment Eligibility Verification

Department of Homeland Security

U.S. Citizenship and Immigration Services

USCIS
Form I-9
OMB No. 1615-0047
Expires 10/31/2022

▶START HERE: Read instructions carefully before completing this form. The instructions must be available, either in paper or electronically, during completion of this form. Employers are liable for errors in the completion of this form.

ANTI-DISCRIMINATION NOTICE: It is illegal to discriminate against work-authorized individuals. Employers **CANNOT** specify which document(s) an employee may present to establish employment authorization and identity. The refusal to hire or continue to employ an individual because the documentation presented has a future expiration date may also constitute illegal discrimination.

Section 1. Employee Information and Attestation *(Employees must complete and sign Section 1 of Form I-9 no later than the **first day of employment**, but not before accepting a job offer.)*

Last Name *(Family Name)*	First Name *(Given Name)*	Middle Initial	Other Last Names Used *(if any)*

Address *(Street Number and Name)*	Apt. Number	City or Town	State	ZIP Code

Date of Birth *(mm/dd/yyyy)*	U.S. Social Security Number	Employee's E-mail Address	Employee's Telephone Number
	☐☐☐ - ☐☐ - ☐☐☐☐		

I am aware that federal law provides for imprisonment and/or fines for false statements or use of false documents in connection with the completion of this form.

I attest, under penalty of perjury, that I am (check one of the following boxes):

☐ 1. A citizen of the United States

☐ 2. A noncitizen national of the United States *(See instructions)*

☐ 3. A lawful permanent resident   (Alien Registration Number/USCIS Number): _____

☐ 4. An alien authorized to work   until (expiration date, if applicable, mm/dd/yyyy): _____
     Some aliens may write "N/A" in the expiration date field. *(See instructions)*

Aliens authorized to work must provide only one of the following document numbers to complete Form I-9:
An Alien Registration Number/USCIS Number OR Form I-94 Admission Number OR Foreign Passport Number.

QR Code - Section 1
Do Not Write In This Space

1. Alien Registration Number/USCIS Number: _____

OR

2. Form I-94 Admission Number: _____

OR

3. Foreign Passport Number: _____

   Country of Issuance: _____

Signature of Employee	Today's Date *(mm/dd/yyyy)*

Preparer and/or Translator Certification (check one):

☐ I did not use a preparer or translator.   ☐ A preparer(s) and/or translator(s) assisted the employee in completing Section 1.
(Fields below must be completed and signed when preparers and/or translators assist an employee in completing Section 1.)

I attest, under penalty of perjury, that I have assisted in the completion of Section 1 of this form and that to the best of my knowledge the information is true and correct.

Signature of Preparer or Translator	Today's Date *(mm/dd/yyyy)*

Last Name *(Family Name)*	First Name *(Given Name)*

Address *(Street Number and Name)*	City or Town	State	ZIP Code

 Employer Completes Next Page

Form I-9 10/21/2019

Page 1 of 3

United States Citizenship and Immigration Services

Employment Eligibility Verification
Department of Homeland Security
U.S. Citizenship and Immigration Services

USCIS
Form I-9
OMB No. 1615-0047
Expires 10/31/2022

Section 2. Employer or Authorized Representative Review and Verification

(Employers or their authorized representative must complete and sign Section 2 within 3 business days of the employee's first day of employment. You must physically examine one document from List A OR a combination of one document from List B and one document from List C as listed on the "Lists of Acceptable Documents.")

Employee Info from Section 1	Last Name *(Family Name)*	First Name *(Given Name)*	M.I.	Citizenship/Immigration Status

List A Identity and Employment Authorization	OR	List B Identity	AND	List C Employment Authorization

List A	List B	List C
Document Title	Document Title	Document Title
Issuing Authority	Issuing Authority	Issuing Authority
Document Number	Document Number	Document Number
Expiration Date *(if any) (mm/dd/yyyy)*	Expiration Date *(if any) (mm/dd/yyyy)*	Expiration Date *(if any) (mm/dd/yyyy)*
Document Title		
Issuing Authority	Additional Information	QR Code - Sections 2 & 3 Do Not Write In This Space
Document Number		
Expiration Date *(if any) (mm/dd/yyyy)*		
Document Title		
Issuing Authority		
Document Number		
Expiration Date *(if any) (mm/dd/yyyy)*		

Certification: I attest, under penalty of perjury, that (1) I have examined the document(s) presented by the above-named employee, (2) the above-listed document(s) appear to be genuine and to relate to the employee named, and (3) to the best of my knowledge the employee is authorized to work in the United States.

The employee's first day of employment *(mm/dd/yyyy)*: _____ *(See instructions for exemptions)*

Signature of Employer or Authorized Representative	Today's Date *(mm/dd/yyyy)*	Title of Employer or Authorized Representative
Last Name of Employer or Authorized Representative	First Name of Employer or Authorized Representative	Employer's Business or Organization Name

Employer's Business or Organization Address *(Street Number and Name)*	City or Town	State	ZIP Code

Section 3. Reverification and Rehires *(To be completed and signed by employer or authorized representative.)*

A. New Name *(if applicable)*			B. Date of Rehire *(if applicable)*
Last Name *(Family Name)*	First Name *(Given Name)*	Middle Initial	Date *(mm/dd/yyyy)*

C. If the employee's previous grant of employment authorization has expired, provide the information for the document or receipt that establishes continuing employment authorization in the space provided below.

Document Title	Document Number	Expiration Date *(if any) (mm/dd/yyyy)*

I attest, under penalty of perjury, that to the best of my knowledge, this employee is authorized to work in the United States, and if the employee presented document(s), the document(s) I have examined appear to be genuine and to relate to the individual.

Signature of Employer or Authorized Representative	Today's Date *(mm/dd/yyyy)*	Name of Employer or Authorized Representative

United States Citizenship and Immigration Services

Form **W-4**	**Employee's Withholding Certificate**	OMB No. 1545-0074
Department of the Treasury Internal Revenue Service	▶ Complete Form W-4 so that your employer can withhold the correct federal income tax from your pay. ▶ Give Form W-4 to your employer. ▶ Your withholding is subject to review by the IRS.	2020

Step 1:

Enter Personal Information

(a) First name and middle initial	Last name	(b) Social security number
Address		▶ **Does your name match the name on your social security card?** If not, to ensure you get credit for your earnings, contact SSA at 800-772-1213 or go to *www.ssa.gov*.
City or town, state, and ZIP code		

(c) ☐ **Single or Married filing separately**

   ☐ **Married filing jointly** (or Qualifying widow(er))

   ☐ **Head of household** (Check only if you're unmarried and pay more than half the costs of keeping up a home for yourself and a qualifying individual.)

Complete Steps 2–4 ONLY if they apply to you; otherwise, skip to Step 5. See page 2 for more information on each step, who can claim exemption from withholding, when to use the online estimator, and privacy.

Step 2:

Multiple Jobs or Spouse Works

Complete this step if you (1) hold more than one job at a time, or (2) are married filing jointly and your spouse also works. The correct amount of withholding depends on income earned from all of these jobs.

Do **only one** of the following.

(a) Use the estimator at *www.irs.gov/W4App* for most accurate withholding for this step (and Steps 3–4); **or**

(b) Use the Multiple Jobs Worksheet on page 3 and enter the result in Step 4(c) below for roughly accurate withholding; **or**

(c) If there are only two jobs total, you may check this box. Do the same on Form W-4 for the other job. This option is accurate for jobs with similar pay; otherwise, more tax than necessary may be withheld . . . . . ▶ ☐

TIP: To be accurate, submit a 2020 Form W-4 for all other jobs. If you (or your spouse) have self-employment income, including as an independent contractor, use the estimator.

Complete Steps 3–4(b) on Form W-4 for only ONE of these jobs. Leave those steps blank for the other jobs. (Your withholding will be most accurate if you complete Steps 3–4(b) on the Form W-4 for the highest paying job.)

Step 3:

Claim Dependents

If your income will be $200,000 or less ($400,000 or less if married filing jointly):

Multiply the number of qualifying children under age 17 by $2,000 ▶ $ _____

Multiply the number of other dependents by $500 . . . . ▶ $ _____

Add the amounts above and enter the total here . . . . | **3** | $ |

Step 4 (optional):

Other Adjustments

(a) **Other income (not from jobs).** If you want tax withheld for other income you expect this year that won't have withholding, enter the amount of other income here. This may include interest, dividends, and retirement income . . . . | 4(a) | $ |

(b) **Deductions.** If you expect to claim deductions other than the standard deduction and want to reduce your withholding, use the Deductions Worksheet on page 3 and enter the result here . . . . | 4(b) | $ |

(c) **Extra withholding.** Enter any additional tax you want withheld each **pay period** . | 4(c) | $ |

Step 5:

Sign Here

Under penalties of perjury, I declare that this certificate, to the best of my knowledge and belief, is true, correct, and complete.

▶ _____   ▶ _____

   Employee's signature (This form is not valid unless you sign it.)   **Date**

Employers Only	Employer's name and address	First date of employment	Employer identification number (EIN)

For Privacy Act and Paperwork Reduction Act Notice, see page 3.   Cat. No. 10220Q   Form **W-4** (2020)

Account: Cash   101

	Date	Description	Post Ref.	Debit	Credit	Balance Debit	Balance Credit	
Beg Bal								
1								1
2								2
3								3
4								4
5								5
6								6
7								7
8								8
9								9
10								10
11								11
12								12
13								13
14								14
15								15

Account: Employee Federal Income Tax Payable   203

	Date	Description	Post Ref.	Debit	Credit	Balance Debit	Balance Credit	
1								1
2								2
3								3
4								4
5								5
6								6
7								7
8								8
9								9

Account: Social Security Tax Payable   204

	Date	Description	Post Ref.	Debit	Credit	Balance Debit	Balance Credit	
1								1
2								2
3								3
4								4
5								5
6								6
7								7
8								8
9								9
10								10
11								11
12								12
13								13
14								14
15								15

Account: Medicare Tax Payable   205

	Date		Description	Post Ref.	Debit	Credit	Balance Debit	Balance Credit	
1									1
2									2
3									3
4									4
5									5
6									6
7									7
8									8
9									9
10									10
11									11
12									12
13									13
14									14
15									15

Account: 401(k) Contributions Payable   208

	Date		Description	Post Ref.	Debit	Credit	Balance Debit	Balance Credit	
1									1
2									2
3									3
4									4
5									5
6									6
7									7
8									8
9									9
10									10

Account: Employee Medical Premiums Payable   209

	Date		Description	Post Ref.	Debit	Credit	Balance Debit	Balance Credit	
1									1
2									2
3									3
4									4
5									5
6									6
7									7
8									8
9									9
10									10

Account: Salaries and Wages Payable   210

	Date		Description	Post Ref.	Debit	Credit	Balance Debit	Balance Credit	
1									1
2									2
3									3
4									4
5									5
6									6
7									7
8									8
9									9
10									10
11									11
12									12

Account: Federal Unemployment Tax Payable   211

	Date		Description	Post Ref.	Debit	Credit	Balance Debit	Balance Credit	
1									1
2									2
3									3
4									4
5									5
6									6
7									7
8									8
9									9
10									10

Account: State Unemployment Tax Payable   212

	Date		Description	Post Ref.	Debit	Credit	Balance Debit	Balance Credit	
1									1
2									2
3									3
4									4
5									5
6									6
7									7
8									8
9									9
10									10

Account: Career Enhancement Program Payable   213

	Date		Description	Post Ref.	Debit	Credit	Balance		
							Debit	Credit	
1									1
2									2
3									3
4									4
5									5
6									6
7									7
8									8
9									9
10									10

Account: Payroll Taxes Expense   514

	Date		Description	Post Ref.	Debit	Credit	Balance		
							Debit	Credit	
1									1
2									2
3									3
4									4
5									5
6									6
7									7
8									8
9									9
10									10

Account: Salaries and Wages Expense   515

	Date		Description	Post Ref.	Debit	Credit	Balance		
							Debit	Credit	
1									1
2									2
3									3
4									4
5									5
6									6
7									7
8									8
9									9
10									10

Form **941 for 2020:** **Employer's QUARTERLY Federal Tax Return**

(Rev. January 2020)   Department of the Treasury — Internal Revenue Service

950117

OMB No. 1545-0029

Employer identification number (EIN) ⬚⬚ – ⬚⬚⬚⬚⬚⬚⬚

Name (*not your trade name*) ⬚

Trade name (*if any*) ⬚

Address ⬚

Number   Street   Suite or room number

⬚

City   State   ZIP code

⬚

Foreign country name   Foreign province/county   Foreign postal code

Report for this Quarter of 2020
(Check one.)

☐ **1:** January, February, March

☐ **2:** April, May, June

☐ **3:** July, August, September

☐ **4:** October, November, December

Go to *www.irs.gov/Form941* for instructions and the latest information.

Read the separate instructions before you complete Form 941. Type or print within the boxes.

Part 1:   Answer these questions for this quarter.

1 Number of employees who received wages, tips, or other compensation for the pay period including: *Mar. 12* (Quarter 1), *June 12* (Quarter 2), *Sept. 12* (Quarter 3), or *Dec. 12* (Quarter 4)   **1** ⬚

2 Wages, tips, and other compensation . . . .   **2** ⬚

3 Federal income tax withheld from wages, tips, and other compensation . . . . . .   **3** ⬚

4 If no wages, tips, and other compensation are subject to social security or Medicare tax   ☐ Check and go to line 6.

	Column 1		Column 2
5a Taxable social security wages . .	⬚	× 0.124 =	⬚
5b Taxable social security tips . . .	⬚	× 0.124 =	⬚
5c Taxable Medicare wages & tips. .	⬚	× 0.029 =	⬚
5d Taxable wages & tips subject to Additional Medicare Tax withholding	⬚	× 0.009 =	⬚

5e Add Column 2 from lines 5a, 5b, 5c, and 5d . . . .   **5e** ⬚

5f Section 3121(q) Notice and Demand—Tax due on unreported tips (see instructions) . .   **5f** ⬚

6 Total taxes before adjustments. Add lines 3, 5e, and 5f . . . .   **6** ⬚

7 Current quarter's adjustment for fractions of cents . . . .   **7** ⬚

8 Current quarter's adjustment for sick pay . . . .   **8** ⬚

9 Current quarter's adjustments for tips and group-term life insurance . . . .   **9** ⬚

10 Total taxes after adjustments. Combine lines 6 through 9 . . . .   **10** ⬚

11 Qualified small business payroll tax credit for increasing research activities. Attach Form 8974   **11** ⬚

12 Total taxes after adjustments and credits. Subtract line 11 from line 10 . . . .   **12** ⬚

13 Total deposits for this quarter, including overpayment applied from a prior quarter and overpayments applied from Form 941-X, 941-X (PR), 944-X, or 944-X (SP) filed in the current quarter   **13** ⬚

14 Balance due. If line 12 is more than line 13, enter the difference and see instructions . . .   **14** ⬚

15 Overpayment. If line 13 is more than line 12, enter the difference ⬚   Check one: ☐ Apply to next return. ☐ Send a refund.

▶ **You MUST complete both pages of Form 941 and SIGN it.**

Next ▶

For Privacy Act and Paperwork Reduction Act Notice, see the back of the Payment Voucher.   Cat. No. 17001Z   Form **941** (Rev. 1-2020)

950217

Name *(not your trade name)*

Employer identification number (EIN)

Part 2: **Tell us about your deposit schedule and tax liability for this quarter.**

If you are unsure about whether you are a monthly schedule depositor or a semiweekly schedule depositor, see section 11 of Pub. 15.

16 **Check one:** ☐ **Line 12 on this return is less than $2,500 or line 12 on the return for the prior quarter was less than $2,500, and you didn't incur a $100,000 next-day deposit obligation during the current quarter.** If line 12 for the prior quarter was less than $2,500 but line 12 on this return is $100,000 or more, you must provide a record of your federal tax liability. If you are a monthly schedule depositor, complete the deposit schedule below; if you are a semiweekly schedule depositor, attach Schedule B (Form 941). Go to Part 3.

☐ **You were a monthly schedule depositor for the entire quarter.** Enter your tax liability for each month and total liability for the quarter, then go to Part 3.

Tax liability: Month 1 [.   ]

Month 2 [.   ]

Month 3 [.   ]

Total liability for quarter [.   ] **Total must equal line 12.**

☐ **You were a semiweekly schedule depositor for any part of this quarter.** Complete Schedule B (Form 941), Report of Tax Liability for Semiweekly Schedule Depositors, and attach it to Form 941.

Part 3: **Tell us about your business. If a question does NOT apply to your business, leave it blank.**

17 **If your business has closed or you stopped paying wages** . . . . ☐ Check here, and

enter the final date you paid wages [/   /   ] .

18 **If you are a seasonal employer and you don't have to file a return for every quarter of the year** . . ☐ Check here.

Part 4: **May we speak with your third-party designee?**

Do you want to allow an employee, a paid tax preparer, or another person to discuss this return with the IRS? See the instructions for details.

☐ Yes. Designee's name and phone number [   ] [   ]

Select a 5-digit Personal Identification Number (PIN) to use when talking to the IRS. ☐ ☐ ☐ ☐ ☐

☐ No.

Part 5: **Sign here. You MUST complete both pages of Form 941 and SIGN it.**

Under penalties of perjury, I declare that I have examined this return, including accompanying schedules and statements, and to the best of my knowledge and belief, it is true, correct, and complete. Declaration of preparer (other than taxpayer) is based on all information of which preparer has any knowledge.

X **Sign your name here** [   ]

Print your name here [   ]

Print your title here [   ]

Date [/   /   ]

Best daytime phone [   ]

Paid Preparer Use Only Check if you are self-employed . . . ☐

Preparer's name [ ]	PTIN [ ]
Preparer's signature [ ]	Date [/ /]
Firm's name (or yours if self-employed) [ ]	EIN [ ]
Address [ ]	Phone [ ]
City [ ] State [ ]	ZIP code [ ]

Form **941** (Rev. 1-2020)

Internal Revenue Service

Form **940 for 2019:** **Employer's Annual Federal Unemployment (FUTA) Tax Return**
Department of the Treasury — Internal Revenue Service

850113

OMB No. 1545-0028

Employer identification number (EIN)

Name *(not your trade name)*

Trade name *(if any)*

Address

Number   Street   Suite or room number

City   State   ZIP code

Foreign country name   Foreign province/county   Foreign postal code

Type of Return
(Check all that apply.)

☐ **a.** Amended

☐ **b.** Successor employer

☐ **c.** No payments to employees in 2019

☐ **d.** Final: Business closed or stopped paying wages

Go to *www.irs.gov/Form940* for instructions and the latest information.

Read the separate instructions before you complete this form. Please type or print within the boxes.

Part 1:   **Tell us about your return. If any line does NOT apply, leave it blank. See instructions before completing Part 1.**

1a   If you had to pay state unemployment tax in one state only, enter the state abbreviation .   **1a** ☐ ☐

1b   If you had to pay state unemployment tax in more than one state, you are a multi-state employer .   **1b** ☐ Check here. Complete Schedule A (Form 940).

2   If you paid wages in a state that is subject to **CREDIT REDUCTION** .   **2** ☐ Check here. Complete Schedule A (Form 940).

Part 2:   **Determine your FUTA tax before adjustments. If any line does NOT apply, leave it blank.**

3   Total payments to all employees .   **3**   ⬜ .

4   Payments exempt from FUTA tax .   **4**   ⬜ .

Check all that apply: **4a** ☐ Fringe benefits   **4c** ☐ Retirement/Pension   **4e** ☐ Other
4b ☐ Group-term life insurance   **4d** ☐ Dependent care

5   Total of payments made to each employee in excess of $7,000 .   **5**   ⬜ .

6   Subtotal (line 4 + line 5 = line 6) .   **6**   ⬜ .

7   Total taxable FUTA wages (line 3 – line 6 = line 7). See instructions .   **7**   ⬜ .

8   FUTA tax before adjustments (line 7 x 0.006 = line 8) .   **8**   ⬜ .

Part 3:   **Determine your adjustments. If any line does NOT apply, leave it blank.**

9   If ALL of the taxable FUTA wages you paid were excluded from state unemployment tax, multiply line 7 by 0.054 (line 7 × 0.054 = line 9). Go to line 12 .   **9**   ⬜ .

10   If SOME of the taxable FUTA wages you paid were excluded from state unemployment tax, OR you paid ANY state unemployment tax late (after the due date for filing Form 940), complete the worksheet in the instructions. Enter the amount from line 7 of the worksheet .   **10**   ⬜ .

11   If credit reduction applies, enter the total from Schedule A (Form 940) .   **11**   ⬜ .

Part 4:   **Determine your FUTA tax and balance due or overpayment. If any line does NOT apply, leave it blank.**

12   Total FUTA tax after adjustments (lines 8 + 9 + 10 + 11 = line 12) .   **12**   ⬜ .

13   FUTA tax deposited for the year, including any overpayment applied from a prior year .   **13**   ⬜ .

14   Balance due. If line 12 is more than line 13, enter the excess on line 14.
   • If line 14 is more than $500, you must deposit your tax.
   • If line 14 is $500 or less, you may pay with this return. See instructions .   **14**   ⬜ .

15   Overpayment. If line 13 is more than line 12, enter the excess on line 15 and check a box below   **15**   ⬜ .

▶ You **MUST** complete both pages of this form and **SIGN** it.   Check one: ☐ Apply to next return.   ☐ Send a refund.

Next ▶

For Privacy Act and Paperwork Reduction Act Notice, see the back of the Payment Voucher.   Cat. No. 11234O   Form **940** (2019)

850212

Name *(not your trade name)*	Employer identification number (EIN)

Part 5:   Report your FUTA tax liability by quarter only if line 12 is more than $500. If not, go to Part 6.

16   Report the amount of your FUTA tax liability for each quarter; do NOT enter the amount you deposited. If you had no liability for a quarter, leave the line blank.

16a   **1st quarter** (January 1 – March 31) . . . .   **16a** [_____ . __]

16b   **2nd quarter** (April 1 – June 30) . . . .   **16b** [_____ . __]

16c   **3rd quarter** (July 1 – September 30) . . . .   **16c** [_____ . __]

16d   **4th quarter** (October 1 – December 31) . . . .   **16d** [_____ . __]

17   **Total tax liability for the year** (lines 16a + 16b + 16c + 16d = line 17)   **17** [_____ . __]   **Total must equal line 12.**

Part 6:   May we speak with your third-party designee?

Do you want to allow an employee, a paid tax preparer, or another person to discuss this return with the IRS? See the instructions for details.

[ ] **Yes.**   Designee's name and phone number   [_____]   [_____]

Select a 5-digit Personal Identification Number (PIN) to use when talking to IRS   [ ] [ ] [ ] [ ] [ ]

[ ] **No.**

Part 7:   Sign here. You MUST complete both pages of this form and SIGN it.

Under penalties of perjury, I declare that I have examined this return, including accompanying schedules and statements, and to the best of my knowledge and belief, it is true, correct, and complete, and that no part of any payment made to a state unemployment fund claimed as a credit was, or is to be, deducted from the payments made to employees. Declaration of preparer (other than taxpayer) is based on all information of which preparer has any knowledge.

X **Sign your name here**   [_____]

Print your name here   [_____]

Print your title here   [_____]

Date   __ / __ / __

Best daytime phone   [_____]

Paid Preparer Use Only   Check if you are self-employed [ ]

Preparer's name		PTIN	
Preparer's signature		Date	__ / __ / __
Firm's name (or yours if self-employed)		EIN	
Address		Phone	
City		State	ZIP code

Page **2**   Form **940** (2019)

State of Nevada New Hire Report

All employers are required to report certain information on newly hired or rehired employees (those separated from your employment at least 60 consecutive days). Use of this form is not mandatory. It is provided for your convenience.

Federal Tax I.D. # _____
Company Name: _____
Company Address: _____
City, State, Zip: _____
Contact Person: _____
Phone Number: _____

☐

Social Security Number	First Name Middle Initial Last Name	Address, Street City, State, Zip	Date of Birth	Start Date	State of Hire
Required	**Required**	**Required**		**Required**	

Please return this form by fax to (775) 684-6379 or mail to:
Department of Employment, Training and Rehabilitation
Employment Security Division – New Hire Unit
500 East Third Street, Carson City, Nevada 89713-0033

Revised 02/12

Internal Revenue Service

DO NOT STAPLE THIS FORM

State of Nevada
Department of Employment, Training & Rehabilitation
EMPLOYMENT SECURITY DIVISION
500 E. Third St., Carson City, NV 89713-0030
Telephone (775) 687-4540

EMPLOYER'S QUARTERLY CONTRIBUTION
AND WAGE REPORT

PLEASE CORRECT ANY NAME OR ADDRESS INFORMATION BELOW. 1a. EMPLOYER ACCOUNT NUMBER	1b. FOR QUARTER ENDING	1e. FEDERAL I.D. NO.
	1c. DELINQUENT AFTER	**IMPORTANT** FOR YOUR PROTECTION, VERIFY YOUR FEDERAL I.D. NO. ABOVE. IF IT IS IN ERROR, PLEASE ENTER THE CORRECT NUMBER HERE:
	1d. YOUR RATES	

	Dollars : Cents	A REPORT MUST BE FILED
3. TOTAL GROSS WAGES (INCLUDING TIPS) PAID THIS QUARTER (If you paid no wages, write "NONE," sign report and return.) (See Instructions)	:	INSTRUCTIONS ENCLOSED

4. LESS WAGES IN EXCESS OF   PER INDIVIDUAL
(Cannot exceed amount in Item 3.)   (See Instructions)
	:	2. **REPORT OF CHANGES**
		If any of the following changes have occurred, please check the appropriate box and provide details on page 2.
		☐ Business Discontinued
		☐ Ownership Change
		  ☐ Entire Business Sold
		  ☐ Part of Business Sold
		  ☐ Legal Ownership Change
		☐ Business Added

5. TAXABLE WAGES PAID THIS QUARTER (Item 3 less Item 4.)	:	
6. UI AMOUNT DUE THIS QUARTER (Item 5 x your UI Rate shown in Item 1d.)	:	
7. CEP AMOUNT DUE THIS QUARTER (Item 5 x the CEP Rate in Item 1d.) (Add) (Do not include the CEP amount on federal unemployment tax return Form 940.)	:	
8. PRIOR CREDIT (Attach "Statement of Employer Account") (Subtract)	:	
9. CHARGE FOR LATE FILING OF THIS REPORT (Add) (One or more days late add $5.00 forfeit.)	:	(FOR DIVISION USE ONLY)
10. ADDITIONAL CHARGE FOR LATE FILING, AFTER 10 DAYS (Add) (Item 5 x 1/10% (.001) for each month or part of month delinquent.)	:	
11. INTEREST ON PAST DUE UI CONTRIBUTIONS (Add) (Item 6 x 1% (.01) for each month or part of month delinquent.) (See Instructions)	:	
12. TOTAL PAYMENT DUE (Total Items 6 through 11.) MAKE PAYABLE TO NEVADA EMPLOYMENT SECURITY DIVISION. Please enter Employer Account Number on check.	:	

13. SOCIAL SECURITY NUMBER	14. EMPLOYEE NAME Do not make adjustments to prior quarters.	15. TOTAL TIPS REPORTED	16. TOTAL GROSS WAGES INCLUDING TIPS	
		Dollars : Cents	Dollars : Cents	
:		:	:	
:		:	:	
:		:	:	
:		:	:	17. NUMBER OF WORKERS LISTED ON THIS REPORT ( )
:		:	:	
:		:	:	18. FOR EACH MONTH, REPORT THE NUMBER OF WORKERS WHO WORKED DURING OR RECEIVED PAY FOR THE PAYROLL PERIOD WHICH INCLUDES THE 12TH OF THE MONTH. 1 MO | 2 MO | 3 MO
:		:	:	
19.TOTAL PAGES THIS REPORT [ ]	20. TOTAL TIPS AND TOTAL WAGES THIS PAGE ——→	$:	$:	

21. I certify that the information contained on this report and the attachments is true and correct.

Signed/Title _____   Name of Preparer if Other Than Employer _____

( ) _____   ( ) _____   ( ) _____   _____
Area Code   Fax Number   Area Code   Telephone Number   Area Code   Telephone Number   Date

NUCS-4072 (Rev.9-02)

Internal Revenue Service

22222	**a** Employee's social security number		
	OMB No. 1545-0008		
b Employer identification number (EIN)		**1** Wages, tips, other compensation	**2** Federal income tax withheld
c Employer's name, address, and ZIP code		**3** Social security wages	**4** Social security tax withheld
		5 Medicare wages and tips	**6** Medicare tax withheld
		7 Social security tips	**8** Allocated tips
d Control number		**9**	**10** Dependent care benefits
e Employee's first name and initial Last name Suff.		**11** Nonqualified plans	**12a** Code
		13 Statutory employee Retirement plan Third-party sick pay	**12b** Code
		14 Other	**12c** Code
			12d Code
f Employee's address and ZIP code			

15 State	Employer's state ID number	16 State wages, tips, etc.	17 State income tax	18 Local wages, tips, etc.	19 Local income tax	20 Locality name

Form **W-2** **Wage and Tax Statement**   **2020**   Department of the Treasury—Internal Revenue Service

Copy 1—For State, City, or Local Tax Department

Internal Revenue Service

22222	**a** Employee's social security number		
	OMB No. 1545-0008		
b Employer identification number (EIN)		**1** Wages, tips, other compensation	**2** Federal income tax withheld
c Employer's name, address, and ZIP code		**3** Social security wages	**4** Social security tax withheld
		5 Medicare wages and tips	**6** Medicare tax withheld
		7 Social security tips	**8** Allocated tips
d Control number		**9**	**10** Dependent care benefits
e Employee's first name and initial Last name Suff.		**11** Nonqualified plans	**12a** Code
		13 Statutory employee Retirement plan Third-party sick pay	**12b** Code
		14 Other	**12c** Code
			12d Code
f Employee's address and ZIP code			

15 State	Employer's state ID number	16 State wages, tips, etc.	17 State income tax	18 Local wages, tips, etc.	19 Local income tax	20 Locality name

Form **W-2** **Wage and Tax Statement**   **2020**   Department of the Treasury—Internal Revenue Service

Copy 1—For State, City, or Local Tax Department

Internal Revenue Service

22222	**a** Employee's social security number		
	OMB No. 1545-0008		

b Employer identification number (EIN)	**1** Wages, tips, other compensation	**2** Federal income tax withheld
c Employer's name, address, and ZIP code	**3** Social security wages	**4** Social security tax withheld
	5 Medicare wages and tips	**6** Medicare tax withheld
	7 Social security tips	**8** Allocated tips
d Control number	**9**	**10** Dependent care benefits
e Employee's first name and initial Last name Suff.	**11** Nonqualified plans	**12a** Code
	13 Statutory employee / Retirement plan / Third-party sick pay	**12b** Code
	14 Other	**12c** Code
		12d Code
f Employee's address and ZIP code		

15 State Employer's state ID number	**16** State wages, tips, etc.	**17** State income tax	**18** Local wages, tips, etc.	**19** Local income tax	**20** Locality name

Form **W-2** Wage and Tax Statement   **2020**   Department of the Treasury—Internal Revenue Service

Copy 1—For State, City, or Local Tax Department

Internal Revenue Service

22222	**a** Employee's social security number		
	OMB No. 1545-0008		

b Employer identification number (EIN)	**1** Wages, tips, other compensation	**2** Federal income tax withheld
c Employer's name, address, and ZIP code	**3** Social security wages	**4** Social security tax withheld
	5 Medicare wages and tips	**6** Medicare tax withheld
	7 Social security tips	**8** Allocated tips
d Control number	**9**	**10** Dependent care benefits
e Employee's first name and initial Last name Suff.	**11** Nonqualified plans	**12a** Code
	13 Statutory employee / Retirement plan / Third-party sick pay	**12b** Code
	14 Other	**12c** Code
		12d Code
f Employee's address and ZIP code		

15 State Employer's state ID number	**16** State wages, tips, etc.	**17** State income tax	**18** Local wages, tips, etc.	**19** Local income tax	**20** Locality name

Form **W-2** Wage and Tax Statement   **2020**   Department of the Treasury—Internal Revenue Service

Copy 1—For State, City, or Local Tax Department

Internal Revenue Service

22222	**a** Employee's social security number	OMB No. 1545-0008

b Employer identification number (EIN)	**1** Wages, tips, other compensation	**2** Federal income tax withheld
c Employer's name, address, and ZIP code	**3** Social security wages	**4** Social security tax withheld
	5 Medicare wages and tips	**6** Medicare tax withheld
	7 Social security tips	**8** Allocated tips
d Control number	**9**	**10** Dependent care benefits
e Employee's first name and initial Last name Suff.	**11** Nonqualified plans	**12a** Code
	13 Statutory employee ☐ Retirement plan ☐ Third-party sick pay ☐	**12b** Code
	14 Other	**12c** Code
		12d Code
f Employee's address and ZIP code		

15 State Employer's state ID number	**16** State wages, tips, etc.	**17** State income tax	**18** Local wages, tips, etc.	**19** Local income tax	**20** Locality name

Form **W-2** Wage and Tax Statement   **2020**   Department of the Treasury—Internal Revenue Service
Copy 1—For State, City, or Local Tax Department
Internal Revenue Service

22222	**a** Employee's social security number	OMB No. 1545-0008

b Employer identification number (EIN)	**1** Wages, tips, other compensation	**2** Federal income tax withheld
c Employer's name, address, and ZIP code	**3** Social security wages	**4** Social security tax withheld
	5 Medicare wages and tips	**6** Medicare tax withheld
	7 Social security tips	**8** Allocated tips
d Control number	**9**	**10** Dependent care benefits
e Employee's first name and initial Last name Suff.	**11** Nonqualified plans	**12a** Code
	13 Statutory employee ☐ Retirement plan ☐ Third-party sick pay ☐	**12b** Code
	14 Other	**12c** Code
		12d Code
f Employee's address and ZIP code		

15 State Employer's state ID number	**16** State wages, tips, etc.	**17** State income tax	**18** Local wages, tips, etc.	**19** Local income tax	**20** Locality name

Form **W-2** Wage and Tax Statement   **2020**   Department of the Treasury—Internal Revenue Service
Copy 1—For State, City, or Local Tax Department
Internal Revenue Service

DO NOT STAPLE

33333	a Control number	For Official Use Only ▶ OMB No. 1545-0008		

b **Kind of Payer** (Check one)	941 ☐ Military ☐ 943 ☐ 944 ☐ CT-1 ☐ Hshld. emp. ☐ Medicare govt. emp. ☐	**Kind of Employer** (Check one)	None apply ☐ 501c non-govt. ☐ State/local non-501c ☐ State/local 501c ☐ Federal govt. ☐	Third-party sick pay (Check if applicable) ☐

c Total number of Forms W-2	d Establishment number	1 Wages, tips, other compensation	2 Federal income tax withheld
e Employer identification number (EIN)		3 Social security wages	4 Social security tax withheld
f Employer's name		5 Medicare wages and tips	6 Medicare tax withheld
		7 Social security tips	8 Allocated tips
		9	10 Dependent care benefits
		11 Nonqualified plans	12a Deferred compensation
g Employer's address and ZIP code			
h Other EIN used this year		13 For third-party sick pay use only	12b
15 State Employer's state ID number		14 Income tax withheld by payer of third-party sick pay	
16 State wages, tips, etc.	17 State income tax	18 Local wages, tips, etc.	19 Local income tax
Employer's contact person		Employer's telephone number	For Official Use Only
Employer's fax number		Employer's email address	

Under penalties of perjury, I declare that I have examined this return and accompanying documents, and, to the best of my knowledge and belief, they are true, correct, and complete.

Signature ▶   Title ▶   Date ▶

Form **W-3** **Transmittal of Wage and Tax Statements**   **2020**   Department of the Treasury
Internal Revenue Service

Internal Revenue Service

Appendix B

Special Classes of Federal Tax Withholding

Special Classes of Employment and Special Types of Payments	Treatment Under Employment Taxes		
	Income Tax Withholding	Social Security and Medicare (Including Additional Medicare Tax when Wages are Paid in Excess of $200,000)	FUTA
Aliens, Nonresident:	See Publication 515, "Withholding of Tax on Nonresident Aliens and Foreign Entities," and Publication 519, "U.S. Tax Guide for Aliens."		
Aliens, Resident:			
1. Service performed in the United States.	Same as U.S. citizens.	Same as U.S. citizens. (Exempt if any part of service as a crew member of foreign vessel or aircraft is performed outside the United States.)	Same as U.S. citizens.
2. Service performed outside the United States.	Withhold	Taxable if (1) working for an American employer or (2) an American employer by agreement covers U.S. citizens and residents employed by its foreign affiliates.	Exempt unless on or in connection with an American vessel or aircraft and performed under a contract made in the United States, or alien is employed on such vessel or aircraft when it touches U.S. port.
Cafeteria Plan Benefits Under Section 125:	If an employee chooses cash, subject to all employment taxes. If an employee chooses another benefit, the treatment is the same as if the benefit was provided outside the plan. See Publication 15-B for more information.		
Deceased Worker:			
1. Wages paid to beneficiary or estate in the same calendar year as worker's death. See the "Instructions for Forms W-2 and W-3" for details.	Exempt	Taxable	Taxable
2. Wages paid to beneficiary or estate after calendar year of worker's death.	Exempt	Exempt	Exempt
Dependent Care Assistance Programs:	Exempt to the extent it is reasonable to believe amounts are excludable from gross income under Section 129.		

Special Classes of Employment and Special Types of Payments	Treatment Under Employment Taxes		
	Income Tax Withholding	Social Security and Medicare (Including Additional Medicare Tax when Wages are Paid in Excess of $200,000)	FUTA
Disabled Worker's Wages paid after the year in which worker became entitled to disability insurance benefits under the Social Security Act.	Withhold	Exempt, if the worker did not perform service for the employer during the period for which payment is made.	Taxable
Employee Business Expense Reimbursement:			
1. Accountable plan.			
a. Amounts not exceeding specified government rate for per diem or standard mileage.	Exempt	Exempt	Exempt
b. Amounts in excess of specified government rate for per diem or standard mileage.	Withhold	Taxable	Taxable
2. Nonaccountable plan. See Section 5 of IRS Publication 15 for details.	Withhold	Taxable	Taxable
Family Employees:			
1. A child employed by the parent (or partnership in which each partner is a parent of the child).	Withhold	Exempt until age 18; age 21 for domestic service.	Exempt until age 21.
2. Parent employed by a child.	Withhold	Taxable if in course of the son's or daughter's business. For domestic services, see Section 3 of IRS Publication 15.	Exempt
3. Spouse employed by a spouse. See Section 3 of IRS Publication 15 for more information.	Withhold	Taxable if in course of a spouse's business.	Exempt
Fishing and Related Activities:	See Publication 334, "Tax Guide for Small Business."		
Foreign Governments and International Organizations:	Exempt	Exempt	Exempt
Foreign Service by U.S. Citizens:			
1. As U.S. government employees.	Withhold	Same as within the United States.	Exempt
2. For foreign affiliates of American employers and other private employers.	Exempt if at the time of payment (1) it is reasonable to believe the employee is entitled to an exclusion from income under Section 911 or (2) the employer is required by the law of the foreign country to withhold income tax on such payment.	Exempt unless (1) an American employer by agreement covers U.S. citizens employed by its foreign affiliates or (2) U.S. citizen works for an American employer.	Exempt unless (1) on American vessel or aircraft and work is performed under contract made in United States or worker is employed on vessel when it touches U.S. port or (2) U.S. citizen works for American employer (except in a contiguous country with which the United States has an agreement for unemployment compensation) or in the U.S. Virgin Islands.
Fringe Benefits:	Taxable on the excess of the fair market value of the benefit over the sum of an amount paid for it by the employee and any amount excludable by law. However, special valuation rules may apply. Benefits provided under cafeteria plans may qualify for exclusion from wages for Social Security, Medicare, and FUTA taxes. See Publication 15-B for details.		

Special Classes of Employment and Special Types of Payments	Treatment Under Employment Taxes		
	Income Tax Withholding	Social Security and Medicare (Including Additional Medicare Tax when Wages are Paid in Excess of $200,000)	FUTA
Government Employment: State/local governments and political subdivisions, employees of:			
1. Salaries and wages (includes payments to most elected and appointed officials).	Withhold	Generally taxable for (1) services performed by employees who are either (a) covered under a Section 218 agreement or (b) not covered under a Section 218 agreement and not a member of a public retirement system (mandatory Social Security and Medicare coverage), and (2) (Medicare tax only) services performed by employees hired or rehired after 3/31/86 who are not covered under a Section 218 agreement or the mandatory Social Security provisions, unless specifically excluded by law. See Publication 963.	Exempt
2. Election workers. Election workers are individuals who are employed to perform services for state or local governments at election booths in connection with national, state, or local elections. **Note:** File Form W-2 for payments of $600 or more even if no Social Security or Medicare taxes were withheld.	Exempt	Taxable if paid $1,900 or more in 2020 (lesser amount if specified by a Section 218 Social Security agreement). See Revenue Ruling 2000-6.	Exempt
3. Emergency workers. Emergency workers who were hired on a temporary basis in response to a specific unforeseen emergency and are not intended to become permanent employees.	Withhold	Exempt if serving on a temporary basis in case of fire, storm, snow, earthquake, flood, or similar emergency.	Exempt
U.S. federal government employees.	Withhold	Taxable for Medicare. Taxable for Social Security unless hired before 1984. See Section 3121(b)(5).	Exempt
Homeworkers (Industrial, Cottage Industry):			
1. Common-law employees.	Withhold	Taxable	Taxable
2. Statutory employees. See Section 2 of IRS Publication 15 for details.	Exempt	Taxable if paid $100 or more in cash in a year.	Exempt
Hospital Employees:			
1. Interns.	Withhold	Taxable	Exempt
2. Patients.	Withhold	Taxable (exempt for state or local government hospitals).	Exempt

Special Classes of Employment and Special Types of Payments	Treatment Under Employment Taxes		
	Income Tax Withholding	Social Security and Medicare (Including Additional Medicare Tax when Wages are Paid in Excess of $200,000)	FUTA
Household Employees:			
1. Domestic service in private homes. Farmers, see Publication 51 (Circular A).	Exempt (withhold if both employer and employee agree).	Taxable if paid $2,200 or more in cash in 2020. Exempt if performed by an individual younger than age 18 during any portion of the calendar year and is not the principal occupation of the employee.	Taxable if the employer paid total cash wages of $1,000 or more in any quarter in the current or preceding calendar year.
2. Domestic service in college clubs, fraternities, and sororities.	Exempt (withhold if both employer and employee agree).	Exempt if paid to regular students; also exempt if an employee is paid less than $100 in a year by an income-tax-exempt employer.	Taxable if the employer paid total cash wages of $1,000 or more in any quarter in the current or preceding calendar year.
Insurance for Employees:			
1. Accident and health insurance premiums under a plan or system for employees and their dependents generally or for a class or classes of employees and their dependents.	Exempt (except 2% shareholder-employees of S corporations).	Exempt	Exempt
2. Group-term life insurance costs. See Publication 15-B for details.	Exempt	Exempt, except for the cost of group-term life insurance includible in the employee's gross income. Special rules apply to former employees.	Exempt
Insurance Agents or Solicitors:			
1. Full-time life insurance salesperson.	Withhold only if an employee under common law. See Section 2 of IRS Publication 15.	Taxable	Taxable if (1) employee under common law and (2) not paid solely by commissions.
2. Other salespeople of life, casualty, and so on, insurance.	Withhold only if an employee under common law.	Taxable only if an employee under common law.	Taxable if (1) employee under common law and (2) not paid solely by commissions.
Interest on Loans with Below-Market Interest Rates (forgone interest and deemed original issue discount):	See Publication 15-A.		
Leave-Sharing Plans: Amounts paid to an employee under a leave-sharing plan.	Withhold	Taxable	Taxable
Newspaper Carriers and Vendors: Newspaper carriers younger than age 18; newspaper and magazine vendors buying at fixed prices and retaining receipts from sales to customers. See Publication 15-A for information on statutory non-employee status.	Exempt (withhold if both employer and employee voluntarily agree).	Exempt	Exempt

Special Classes of Employment and Special Types of Payments	Treatment Under Employment Taxes		
	Income Tax Withholding	Social Security and Medicare (Including Additional Medicare Tax when Wages are Paid in Excess of $200,000)	FUTA
Non-cash Payments:			
1. For household work, agricultural labor, and service not in the course of the employer's trade or business.	Exempt (withhold if both employer and employee voluntarily agree).	Exempt	Exempt
2. To certain retail commission salespersons ordinarily paid solely on a cash commission basis.	Optional with the employer, except to the extent employee's supplemental wages during the year exceed $1 million.	Taxable	Taxable
Nonprofit Organizations:	See Publication 15-A.		
Officers or Shareholders of an S-Corporation: Distributions and other payments by an S-corporation to a corporate officer or shareholder must be treated as wages to the extent the amounts are reasonable compensation for services to the corporation by an employee. See the instructions for Form 1120S.	Withhold	Taxable	Taxable
Partners: Payments to general or limited partners of a partnership. See Publication 541, "Partnerships," for partner reporting rules.	Exempt	Exempt	Exempt
Railroads: Payments subject to the Railroad Retirement Act. See Publication 915, Social Security and Equivalent Railroad Retirement Benefits, for more details.	Withhold	Exempt	Exempt
Religious Exemptions:	See Publication 15-A and Publication 517, "Social Security and Other Information for Members of the Clergy and Religious Workers."		
Retirement and Pension Plans:			
1. Employer contributions to a qualified plan.	Exempt	Exempt	Exempt
2. Elective employee contributions and deferrals to a plan containing a qualified cash or deferred compensation arrangement (for example, 401(k)).	Generally exempt, but see Section 402(g) for limitation.	Taxable	Taxable
3. Employer contributions to individual retirement accounts under a simplified employee pension plan (SEP).	Generally exempt, but see Section 402(g) for salary reduction SEP limitation.	Exempt, except for amounts contributed under a salary reduction SEP agreement.	
4. Employer contributions to Section 403(b) annuities.	Generally exempt, but see Section 402(g) for limitation.	Taxable if paid through a salary reduction agreement (written or otherwise).	
5. Employee salary reduction contributions to a SIMPLE retirement account.	Exempt	Taxable	Taxable

Special Classes of Employment and Special Types of Payments	Treatment Under Employment Taxes		
	Income Tax Withholding	Social Security and Medicare (Including Additional Medicare Tax when Wages are Paid in Excess of $200,000)	FUTA
6. Distributions from qualified retirement and pension plans and Section 403(b) annuities. See Publication 15-A for information on pensions, annuities, and employer contributions to nonqualified deferred compensation arrangements.	Withhold, but the recipient may elect exemption on Form W-4P in certain cases; mandatory 20% withholding applies to an eligible rollover distribution that is not a direct rollover; exempt for a direct rollover. See Publication 15-A.	Exempt	Exempt
7. Employer contributions to a Section 457(b) plan.	Generally exempt, but see Section 402(g) limitation.	Taxable	Taxable
8. Employee salary reduction contributions to a Section 457(b) plan.	Generally exempt, but see Section 402(g) salary reduction limitation.	Taxable	Taxable
Salespersons:			
1. Common-law employees.	Withhold	Taxable	Taxable
2. Statutory employees.	Exempt	Taxable	Taxable, except for full-time life insurance sales agents.
3. Statutory nonemployees (qualified real estate agents, direct sellers, and certain companion sitters). See Publication 15-A for details.	Exempt	Exempt	Exempt
Scholarships and Fellowship Grants (Includible in Income Under Section 117(c)):	Withhold	Taxability depends on the nature of employment and the status of the organization. See Students, scholars, trainees, teachers, etc., below	
Severance or Dismissal Pay:	Withhold	Taxable	Taxable
Service Not in the Course of the Employer's Trade or Business (Other Than on a Farm Operated for Profit or for Household Employment in Private Homes):	Withhold only if an employee earns $50 or more in cash in a quarter and works on 24 or more different days in that quarter or in the preceding quarter.	Taxable if an employee receives $100 or more in cash in a calendar year.	Taxable only if an employee earns $50 or more in cash in a quarter and works on 24 or more different days in that quarter or in the preceding quarter.
Sick Pay: See Publication 15-A for more information.	Withhold	Exempt after the end of 6 calendar months after the calendar month employee last worked for the employer.	
Students, Scholars, Trainees, Teachers, etc.: 1. A student enrolled and regularly attending classes, performing services for:			
a. Private school, college, or university	Withhold	Exempt	Exempt
b. The auxiliary nonprofit organization operated for and controlled by the school, college, or university	Withhold	Exempt unless services are covered by a Section 218 (Social Security Act) agreement.	Exempt
c. Public school, college, or university	Withhold	Exempt unless services are covered by a Section 218 (Social Security Act) agreement.	Exempt

Special Classes of Employment and Special Types of Payments	Treatment Under Employment Taxes		
	Income Tax Withholding	Social Security and Medicare (Including Additional Medicare Tax when Wages are Paid in Excess of $200,000)	FUTA
2. Full-time student performing service for academic credit, combining instruction with work experience as an integral part of the program.	Withhold	Taxable	Exempt unless the program was established for or on behalf of an employer or group of employers.
3. Student nurses performing part-time services for nominal earnings at a hospital as an incidental part of the training.	Withhold	Exempt	Exempt
4. A student employed by organized camps.	Withhold	Taxable	Exempt
5. Student, scholar, trainee, teacher, and so on, as nonimmigrant alien under Section 101(a)(15)(F), (J), (M), or (Q) of Immigration and Nationality Act (that is, aliens holding F-1, J-1, M-1, or Q-1 visas).	Withhold unless excepted by regulations.	Exempt if service is performed for the purpose specified in Section 101(a)(15)(F), (J), (M), or (Q) of Immigration and Nationality Act. However, these taxes may apply if the employee becomes a resident alien. See the special residency tests for exempt individuals in Chapter 1 of Pub. 519, Tax Guide for Aliens.	
Supplemental Unemployment Compensation Plan Benefits:	Withhold	Exempt under certain conditions. See Publication 15-A.	
Tips:			
1. If $20 or more in a month.	Withhold	Taxable	Taxable for all tips reported in writing to the employer.
2. If less than $20 in a month. See Section 6 of IRS Publication 15 for more information.	Exempt	Exempt	Exempt
Workers' Compensation:	Exempt	Exempt	Exempt

Internal Revenue Service

Appendix C

Federal Income Tax Tables*

The following is information about federal income tax withholding for 2020 using Publication 15-T. Specific questions about federal income taxes and business situations may be directed to the Internal Revenue Service via the IRS website at https://www.irs.gov/businesses.

Withholding allowance amounts for use with the percentage method for Pre-2020 Form W-4:

Payroll Period	One Withholding Allowance
Weekly	$ 83.00
Biweekly	165.00
Semimonthly	179.00
Monthly	358.00
Quarterly	1,075.00
Semiannually	2,150.00
Annually	4,300.00
Daily or miscellaneous (each day of the payroll period)	17.00

*Note: Appendix C is derived from IRS Publication 15-T. A comment to refer to pages 44 and 47 exists at the section end for wage-bracket tables when the taxable wages exceed the table. These page references are for Publication 15-T itself and not to pages within this text.

Internal Revenue Service

3. Wage Bracket Method Tables for Manual Payroll Systems With Forms W-4 From 2019 or Earlier

If you compute payroll manually and your employee **has not** submitted a Form W-4 for 2020 or later, use the worksheet below and the Wage Bracket Method tables that follow to figure federal income tax withholding.

The Wage Bracket Method tables cover only up to approximately $100,000 in annual wages and up to 10 allowances. If you can't use the Wage Bracket Method tables because taxable wages exceed the amount from the last bracket of the table (based on marital status and pay period) or the employee claimed more than 10 allowances, use the Percentage Method tables in section 5.

Worksheet 3. Employer's Withholding Worksheet for Wage Bracket Method Tables for Manual Payroll Systems With Forms W-4 From 2019 or Earlier

Keep for Your Records

Step 1.	**Figure the tentative withholding amount**	
	1a Enter the employee's total taxable wages this payroll period	1a $ _____
	1b Use the amount on line 1a to look up the tentative amount to withhold in the appropriate Wage Bracket Table in this section for your pay frequency, given the employee's marital status (line 3 of Form W-4) and number of allowances claimed. This is the **Tentative Withholding Amount**	1b $ _____
Step 2.	**Figure the final amount to withhold**	
	2a Enter the additional amount to withhold from line 6 of the employee's Form W-4	2a $ _____
	2b Add lines 1b and 2a. **This is the amount to withhold from the employee's wages this pay period**	2b $ _____

Internal Revenue Service

2020 Wage Bracket Method Tables for Manual Payroll Systems With Forms W-4 From 2019 or Earlier

WEEKLY Payroll Period

If the **Wage Amount** (line 1a) is		MARRIED Persons										
		And the number of allowances is:										
At least	But less than	0	1	2	3	4	5	6	7	8	9	10
		The Tentative Withholding Amount is:										
$0	$230	$0	$0	$0	$0	$0	$0	$0	$0	$0	$0	$0
$230	$240	$1	$0	$0	$0	$0	$0	$0	$0	$0	$0	$0
$240	$250	$2	$0	$0	$0	$0	$0	$0	$0	$0	$0	$0
$250	$260	$3	$0	$0	$0	$0	$0	$0	$0	$0	$0	$0
$260	$270	$4	$0	$0	$0	$0	$0	$0	$0	$0	$0	$0
$270	$280	$5	$0	$0	$0	$0	$0	$0	$0	$0	$0	$0
$280	$290	$6	$0	$0	$0	$0	$0	$0	$0	$0	$0	$0
$290	$300	$7	$0	$0	$0	$0	$0	$0	$0	$0	$0	$0
$300	$310	$8	$0	$0	$0	$0	$0	$0	$0	$0	$0	$0
$310	$320	$9	$0	$0	$0	$0	$0	$0	$0	$0	$0	$0
$320	$330	$10	$1	$0	$0	$0	$0	$0	$0	$0	$0	$0
$330	$340	$11	$2	$0	$0	$0	$0	$0	$0	$0	$0	$0
$340	$350	$12	$3	$0	$0	$0	$0	$0	$0	$0	$0	$0
$350	$360	$13	$4	$0	$0	$0	$0	$0	$0	$0	$0	$0
$360	$370	$14	$5	$0	$0	$0	$0	$0	$0	$0	$0	$0
$370	$380	$15	$6	$0	$0	$0	$0	$0	$0	$0	$0	$0
$380	$390	$16	$7	$0	$0	$0	$0	$0	$0	$0	$0	$0
$390	$400	$17	$8	$0	$0	$0	$0	$0	$0	$0	$0	$0
$400	$410	$18	$9	$1	$0	$0	$0	$0	$0	$0	$0	$0
$410	$420	$19	$10	$2	$0	$0	$0	$0	$0	$0	$0	$0
$420	$430	$20	$11	$3	$0	$0	$0	$0	$0	$0	$0	$0
$430	$440	$21	$12	$4	$0	$0	$0	$0	$0	$0	$0	$0
$440	$450	$22	$13	$5	$0	$0	$0	$0	$0	$0	$0	$0
$450	$460	$23	$14	$6	$0	$0	$0	$0	$0	$0	$0	$0
$460	$470	$24	$15	$7	$0	$0	$0	$0	$0	$0	$0	$0
$470	$480	$25	$16	$8	$0	$0	$0	$0	$0	$0	$0	$0
$480	$490	$26	$17	$9	$1	$0	$0	$0	$0	$0	$0	$0
$490	$500	$27	$18	$10	$2	$0	$0	$0	$0	$0	$0	$0
$500	$510	$28	$19	$11	$3	$0	$0	$0	$0	$0	$0	$0
$510	$520	$29	$20	$12	$4	$0	$0	$0	$0	$0	$0	$0
$520	$530	$30	$21	$13	$5	$0	$0	$0	$0	$0	$0	$0
$530	$540	$31	$22	$14	$6	$0	$0	$0	$0	$0	$0	$0
$540	$550	$32	$23	$15	$7	$0	$0	$0	$0	$0	$0	$0
$550	$560	$33	$24	$16	$8	$0	$0	$0	$0	$0	$0	$0
$560	$570	$34	$25	$17	$9	$1	$0	$0	$0	$0	$0	$0
$570	$580	$35	$26	$18	$10	$2	$0	$0	$0	$0	$0	$0
$580	$590	$36	$27	$19	$11	$3	$0	$0	$0	$0	$0	$0
$590	$600	$37	$28	$20	$12	$4	$0	$0	$0	$0	$0	$0
$600	$610	$38	$29	$21	$13	$5	$0	$0	$0	$0	$0	$0
$610	$625	$39	$31	$22	$14	$6	$0	$0	$0	$0	$0	$0
$625	$640	$41	$32	$24	$16	$7	$0	$0	$0	$0	$0	$0
$640	$655	$43	$34	$25	$17	$9	$1	$0	$0	$0	$0	$0
$655	$670	$44	$35	$27	$19	$10	$2	$0	$0	$0	$0	$0
$670	$685	$46	$37	$28	$20	$12	$4	$0	$0	$0	$0	$0
$685	$700	$48	$38	$30	$22	$13	$5	$0	$0	$0	$0	$0
$700	$715	$50	$40	$31	$23	$15	$7	$0	$0	$0	$0	$0
$715	$730	$52	$42	$33	$25	$16	$8	$0	$0	$0	$0	$0
$730	$745	$53	$44	$34	$26	$18	$10	$1	$0	$0	$0	$0
$745	$760	$55	$45	$36	$28	$19	$11	$3	$0	$0	$0	$0
$760	$775	$57	$47	$37	$29	$21	$13	$4	$0	$0	$0	$0
$775	$790	$59	$49	$39	$31	$22	$14	$6	$0	$0	$0	$0

2020 Wage Bracket Method Tables for Manual Payroll Systems With Forms W-4 From 2019 or Earlier

WEEKLY Payroll Period

If the **Wage Amount** (line 1a) is		MARRIED Persons										
		And the number of allowances is:										
At least	But less than	0	1	2	3	4	5	6	7	8	9	10
		The Tentative Withholding Amount is:										
$790	$805	$61	$51	$41	$32	$24	$16	$7	$0	$0	$0	$0
$805	$820	$62	$53	$43	$34	$25	$17	$9	$0	$0	$0	$0
$820	$835	$64	$54	$44	$35	$27	$19	$10	$2	$0	$0	$0
$835	$850	$66	$56	$46	$37	$28	$20	$12	$3	$0	$0	$0
$850	$865	$68	$58	$48	$38	$30	$22	$13	$5	$0	$0	$0
$865	$880	$70	$60	$50	$40	$31	$23	$15	$6	$0	$0	$0
$880	$895	$71	$62	$52	$42	$33	$25	$16	$8	$0	$0	$0
$895	$910	$73	$63	$53	$43	$34	$26	$18	$9	$1	$0	$0
$910	$925	$75	$65	$55	$45	$36	$28	$19	$11	$3	$0	$0
$925	$940	$77	$67	$57	$47	$37	$29	$21	$12	$4	$0	$0
$940	$955	$79	$69	$59	$49	$39	$31	$22	$14	$6	$0	$0
$955	$970	$80	$71	$61	$51	$41	$32	$24	$15	$7	$0	$0
$970	$985	$82	$72	$62	$52	$43	$34	$25	$17	$9	$0	$0
$985	$1,000	$84	$74	$64	$54	$44	$35	$27	$18	$10	$2	$0
$1,000	$1,015	$86	$76	$66	$56	$46	$37	$28	$20	$12	$3	$0
$1,015	$1,030	$88	$78	$68	$58	$48	$38	$30	$21	$13	$5	$0
$1,030	$1,045	$89	$80	$70	$60	$50	$40	$31	$23	$15	$6	$0
$1,045	$1,060	$91	$81	$71	$61	$52	$42	$33	$24	$16	$8	$0
$1,060	$1,075	$93	$83	$73	$63	$53	$43	$34	$26	$18	$9	$1
$1,075	$1,090	$95	$85	$75	$65	$55	$45	$36	$27	$19	$11	$3
$1,090	$1,105	$97	$87	$77	$67	$57	$47	$37	$29	$21	$12	$4
$1,105	$1,120	$98	$89	$79	$69	$59	$49	$39	$30	$22	$14	$6
$1,120	$1,135	$100	$90	$80	$70	$61	$51	$41	$32	$24	$15	$7
$1,135	$1,150	$102	$92	$82	$72	$62	$52	$43	$33	$25	$17	$9
$1,150	$1,165	$104	$94	$84	$74	$64	$54	$44	$35	$27	$18	$10
$1,165	$1,180	$106	$96	$86	$76	$66	$56	$46	$36	$28	$20	$12
$1,180	$1,195	$107	$98	$88	$78	$68	$58	$48	$38	$30	$21	$13
$1,195	$1,210	$109	$99	$89	$79	$70	$60	$50	$40	$31	$23	$15
$1,210	$1,225	$111	$101	$91	$81	$71	$61	$52	$42	$33	$24	$16
$1,225	$1,240	$113	$103	$93	$83	$73	$63	$53	$43	$34	$26	$18
$1,240	$1,255	$115	$105	$95	$85	$75	$65	$55	$45	$36	$27	$19
$1,255	$1,270	$116	$107	$97	$87	$77	$67	$57	$47	$37	$29	$21
$1,270	$1,285	$118	$108	$98	$88	$79	$69	$59	$49	$39	$30	$22
$1,285	$1,300	$120	$110	$100	$90	$80	$70	$61	$51	$41	$32	$24
$1,300	$1,315	$122	$112	$102	$92	$82	$72	$62	$52	$42	$33	$25
$1,315	$1,330	$124	$114	$104	$94	$84	$74	$64	$54	$44	$35	$27
$1,330	$1,345	$125	$116	$106	$96	$86	$76	$66	$56	$46	$36	$28
$1,345	$1,360	$127	$117	$107	$97	$88	$78	$68	$58	$48	$38	$30
$1,360	$1,375	$129	$119	$109	$99	$89	$79	$70	$60	$50	$40	$31
$1,375	$1,390	$131	$121	$111	$101	$91	$81	$71	$61	$51	$42	$33
$1,390	$1,405	$133	$123	$113	$103	$93	$83	$73	$63	$53	$43	$34
$1,405	$1,420	$134	$125	$115	$105	$95	$85	$75	$65	$55	$45	$36
$1,420	$1,435	$136	$126	$116	$106	$97	$87	$77	$67	$57	$47	$37
$1,435	$1,450	$138	$128	$118	$108	$98	$88	$79	$69	$59	$49	$39
$1,450	$1,465	$140	$130	$120	$110	$100	$90	$80	$70	$60	$51	$41
$1,465	$1,480	$142	$132	$122	$112	$102	$92	$82	$72	$62	$52	$42
$1,480	$1,495	$143	$134	$124	$114	$104	$94	$84	$74	$64	$54	$44
$1,495	$1,510	$145	$135	$125	$115	$106	$96	$86	$76	$66	$56	$46
$1,510	$1,525	$147	$137	$127	$117	$107	$97	$88	$78	$68	$58	$48
$1,525	$1,540	$149	$139	$129	$119	$109	$99	$89	$79	$69	$60	$50
$1,540	$1,555	$151	$141	$131	$121	$111	$101	$91	$81	$71	$61	$51

2020 Wage Bracket Method Tables for Manual Payroll Systems With Forms W-4 From 2019 or Earlier

WEEKLY Payroll Period

If the **Wage Amount** (line 1a) is		MARRIED Persons										
		And the number of allowances is:										
At least	But less than	0	1	2	3	4	5	6	7	8	9	10
		The Tentative Withholding Amount is:										
$1,555	$1,570	$152	$143	$133	$123	$113	$103	$93	$83	$73	$63	$53
$1,570	$1,585	$154	$144	$134	$124	$115	$105	$95	$85	$75	$65	$55
$1,585	$1,600	$156	$146	$136	$126	$116	$106	$97	$87	$77	$67	$57
$1,600	$1,615	$158	$148	$138	$128	$118	$108	$98	$88	$78	$69	$59
$1,615	$1,630	$160	$150	$140	$130	$120	$110	$100	$90	$80	$70	$60
$1,630	$1,645	$161	$152	$142	$132	$122	$112	$102	$92	$82	$72	$62
$1,645	$1,660	$163	$153	$143	$133	$124	$114	$104	$94	$84	$74	$64
$1,660	$1,675	$165	$155	$145	$135	$125	$115	$106	$96	$86	$76	$66
$1,675	$1,690	$167	$157	$147	$137	$127	$117	$107	$97	$87	$78	$68
$1,690	$1,705	$169	$159	$149	$139	$129	$119	$109	$99	$89	$79	$69
$1,705	$1,720	$170	$161	$151	$141	$131	$121	$111	$101	$91	$81	$71
$1,720	$1,735	$172	$162	$152	$142	$133	$123	$113	$103	$93	$83	$73
$1,735	$1,750	$174	$164	$154	$144	$134	$124	$115	$105	$95	$85	$75
$1,750	$1,765	$176	$166	$156	$146	$136	$126	$116	$106	$96	$87	$77
$1,765	$1,780	$178	$168	$158	$148	$138	$128	$118	$108	$98	$88	$78
$1,780	$1,800	$182	$170	$160	$150	$140	$130	$120	$110	$100	$90	$81
$1,800	$1,820	$186	$172	$162	$152	$142	$133	$123	$113	$103	$93	$83
$1,820	$1,840	$190	$175	$165	$155	$145	$135	$125	$115	$105	$95	$85
$1,840	$1,860	$195	$177	$167	$157	$147	$137	$127	$117	$108	$98	$88
$1,860	$1,880	$199	$181	$169	$160	$150	$140	$130	$120	$110	$100	$90
$1,880	$1,900	$204	$185	$172	$162	$152	$142	$132	$122	$112	$102	$93
$1,900	$1,920	$208	$190	$174	$164	$154	$145	$135	$125	$115	$105	$95
$1,920	$1,940	$212	$194	$177	$167	$157	$147	$137	$127	$117	$107	$97

Internal Revenue Service

2020 Wage Bracket Method Tables for Manual Payroll Systems With Forms W-4 From 2019 or Earlier

WEEKLY Payroll Period

If the **Wage Amount** (line 1a) is		SINGLE Persons										
		And the number of allowances is:										
At least	But less than	0	1	2	3	4	5	6	7	8	9	10
		The Tentative Withholding Amount is:										
$0	$75	$0	$0	$0	$0	$0	$0	$0	$0	$0	$0	$0
$75	$85	$1	$0	$0	$0	$0	$0	$0	$0	$0	$0	$0
$85	$95	$2	$0	$0	$0	$0	$0	$0	$0	$0	$0	$0
$95	$105	$3	$0	$0	$0	$0	$0	$0	$0	$0	$0	$0
$105	$115	$4	$0	$0	$0	$0	$0	$0	$0	$0	$0	$0
$115	$125	$5	$0	$0	$0	$0	$0	$0	$0	$0	$0	$0
$125	$135	$6	$0	$0	$0	$0	$0	$0	$0	$0	$0	$0
$135	$145	$7	$0	$0	$0	$0	$0	$0	$0	$0	$0	$0
$145	$155	$8	$0	$0	$0	$0	$0	$0	$0	$0	$0	$0
$155	$165	$9	$0	$0	$0	$0	$0	$0	$0	$0	$0	$0
$165	$175	$10	$1	$0	$0	$0	$0	$0	$0	$0	$0	$0
$175	$185	$11	$2	$0	$0	$0	$0	$0	$0	$0	$0	$0
$185	$195	$12	$3	$0	$0	$0	$0	$0	$0	$0	$0	$0
$195	$205	$13	$4	$0	$0	$0	$0	$0	$0	$0	$0	$0
$205	$215	$14	$5	$0	$0	$0	$0	$0	$0	$0	$0	$0
$215	$225	$15	$6	$0	$0	$0	$0	$0	$0	$0	$0	$0
$225	$235	$16	$7	$0	$0	$0	$0	$0	$0	$0	$0	$0
$235	$245	$17	$8	$0	$0	$0	$0	$0	$0	$0	$0	$0
$245	$255	$18	$9	$1	$0	$0	$0	$0	$0	$0	$0	$0
$255	$265	$19	$10	$2	$0	$0	$0	$0	$0	$0	$0	$0
$265	$280	$20	$12	$3	$0	$0	$0	$0	$0	$0	$0	$0
$280	$295	$22	$13	$5	$0	$0	$0	$0	$0	$0	$0	$0
$295	$310	$24	$15	$6	$0	$0	$0	$0	$0	$0	$0	$0
$310	$325	$26	$16	$8	$0	$0	$0	$0	$0	$0	$0	$0
$325	$340	$27	$18	$9	$1	$0	$0	$0	$0	$0	$0	$0
$340	$355	$29	$19	$11	$3	$0	$0	$0	$0	$0	$0	$0
$355	$370	$31	$21	$12	$4	$0	$0	$0	$0	$0	$0	$0
$370	$385	$33	$23	$14	$6	$0	$0	$0	$0	$0	$0	$0
$385	$400	$35	$25	$15	$7	$0	$0	$0	$0	$0	$0	$0
$400	$415	$36	$26	$17	$9	$0	$0	$0	$0	$0	$0	$0
$415	$430	$38	$28	$18	$10	$2	$0	$0	$0	$0	$0	$0
$430	$445	$40	$30	$20	$12	$3	$0	$0	$0	$0	$0	$0
$445	$460	$42	$32	$22	$13	$5	$0	$0	$0	$0	$0	$0
$460	$475	$44	$34	$24	$15	$6	$0	$0	$0	$0	$0	$0
$475	$490	$45	$35	$25	$16	$8	$0	$0	$0	$0	$0	$0
$490	$505	$47	$37	$27	$18	$9	$1	$0	$0	$0	$0	$0
$505	$520	$49	$39	$29	$19	$11	$3	$0	$0	$0	$0	$0
$520	$535	$51	$41	$31	$21	$12	$4	$0	$0	$0	$0	$0
$535	$550	$53	$43	$33	$23	$14	$6	$0	$0	$0	$0	$0
$550	$565	$54	$44	$34	$25	$15	$7	$0	$0	$0	$0	$0
$565	$580	$56	$46	$36	$26	$17	$9	$0	$0	$0	$0	$0
$580	$595	$58	$48	$38	$28	$18	$10	$2	$0	$0	$0	$0
$595	$610	$60	$50	$40	$30	$20	$12	$3	$0	$0	$0	$0
$610	$625	$62	$52	$42	$32	$22	$13	$5	$0	$0	$0	$0
$625	$640	$63	$53	$43	$34	$24	$15	$6	$0	$0	$0	$0
$640	$655	$65	$55	$45	$35	$25	$16	$8	$0	$0	$0	$0
$655	$670	$67	$57	$47	$37	$27	$18	$9	$1	$0	$0	$0
$670	$685	$69	$59	$49	$39	$29	$19	$11	$3	$0	$0	$0
$685	$700	$71	$61	$51	$41	$31	$21	$12	$4	$0	$0	$0
$700	$715	$72	$62	$52	$43	$33	$23	$14	$6	$0	$0	$0
$715	$730	$74	$64	$54	$44	$34	$25	$15	$7	$0	$0	$0

2020 Wage Bracket Method Tables for Manual Payroll Systems With Forms W-4 From 2019 or Earlier

WEEKLY Payroll Period

At least	But less than	0	1	2	3	4	5	6	7	8	9	10
$730	$745	$76	$66	$56	$46	$36	$26	$17	$9	$0	$0	$0
$745	$760	$78	$68	$58	$48	$38	$28	$18	$10	$2	$0	$0
$760	$775	$80	$70	$60	$50	$40	$30	$20	$12	$3	$0	$0
$775	$790	$81	$71	$61	$52	$42	$32	$22	$13	$5	$0	$0
$790	$805	$83	$73	$63	$53	$43	$34	$24	$15	$6	$0	$0
$805	$820	$85	$75	$65	$55	$45	$35	$25	$16	$8	$0	$0
$820	$835	$87	$77	$67	$57	$47	$37	$27	$18	$9	$1	$0
$835	$850	$89	$79	$69	$59	$49	$39	$29	$19	$11	$3	$0
$850	$870	$92	$81	$71	$61	$51	$41	$31	$21	$13	$4	$0
$870	$890	$97	$83	$73	$63	$53	$43	$33	$24	$15	$6	$0
$890	$910	$101	$86	$76	$66	$56	$46	$36	$26	$17	$8	$0
$910	$930	$105	$88	$78	$68	$58	$48	$38	$28	$19	$10	$2
$930	$950	$110	$92	$80	$70	$61	$51	$41	$31	$21	$12	$4
$950	$970	$114	$96	$83	$73	$63	$53	$43	$33	$23	$14	$6
$970	$990	$119	$100	$85	$75	$65	$55	$45	$36	$26	$16	$8
$990	$1,010	$123	$105	$88	$78	$68	$58	$48	$38	$28	$18	$10
$1,010	$1,030	$127	$109	$91	$80	$70	$60	$50	$40	$30	$21	$12
$1,030	$1,050	$132	$114	$95	$82	$73	$63	$53	$43	$33	$23	$14
$1,050	$1,070	$136	$118	$100	$85	$75	$65	$55	$45	$35	$25	$16
$1,070	$1,090	$141	$122	$104	$87	$77	$67	$57	$48	$38	$28	$18
$1,090	$1,110	$145	$127	$109	$90	$80	$70	$60	$50	$40	$30	$20
$1,110	$1,130	$149	$131	$113	$95	$82	$72	$62	$52	$42	$33	$23
$1,130	$1,150	$154	$136	$117	$99	$85	$75	$65	$55	$45	$35	$25
$1,150	$1,170	$158	$140	$122	$104	$87	$77	$67	$57	$47	$37	$27
$1,170	$1,190	$163	$144	$126	$108	$90	$79	$69	$60	$50	$40	$30
$1,190	$1,210	$167	$149	$131	$112	$94	$82	$72	$62	$52	$42	$32
$1,210	$1,230	$171	$153	$135	$117	$99	$84	$74	$64	$54	$45	$35
$1,230	$1,250	$176	$158	$139	$121	$103	$87	$77	$67	$57	$47	$37
$1,250	$1,270	$180	$162	$144	$126	$107	$89	$79	$69	$59	$49	$39
$1,270	$1,290	$185	$166	$148	$130	$112	$94	$81	$72	$62	$52	$42
$1,290	$1,310	$189	$171	$153	$134	$116	$98	$84	$74	$64	$54	$44
$1,310	$1,330	$193	$175	$157	$139	$121	$102	$86	$76	$66	$57	$47
$1,330	$1,350	$198	$180	$161	$143	$125	$107	$89	$79	$69	$59	$49
$1,350	$1,370	$202	$184	$166	$148	$129	$111	$93	$81	$71	$61	$51
$1,370	$1,390	$207	$188	$170	$152	$134	$116	$97	$84	$74	$64	$54
$1,390	$1,410	$211	$193	$175	$156	$138	$120	$102	$86	$76	$66	$56
$1,410	$1,430	$215	$197	$179	$161	$143	$124	$106	$88	$78	$69	$59
$1,430	$1,450	$220	$202	$183	$165	$147	$129	$111	$92	$81	$71	$61
$1,450	$1,470	$224	$206	$188	$170	$151	$133	$115	$97	$83	$73	$63
$1,470	$1,490	$229	$210	$192	$174	$156	$138	$119	$101	$86	$76	$66
$1,490	$1,510	$233	$215	$197	$178	$160	$142	$124	$106	$88	$78	$68
$1,510	$1,530	$237	$219	$201	$183	$165	$146	$128	$110	$92	$81	$71
$1,530	$1,550	$242	$224	$205	$187	$169	$151	$133	$114	$96	$83	$73
$1,550	$1,570	$246	$228	$210	$192	$173	$155	$137	$119	$101	$85	$75
$1,570	$1,590	$251	$232	$214	$196	$178	$160	$141	$123	$105	$88	$78
$1,590	$1,610	$255	$237	$219	$200	$182	$164	$146	$128	$109	$91	$80
$1,610	$1,630	$259	$241	$223	$205	$187	$168	$150	$132	$114	$96	$83
$1,630	$1,650	$264	$246	$227	$209	$191	$173	$155	$136	$118	$100	$85
$1,650	$1,670	$268	$250	$232	$214	$195	$177	$159	$141	$123	$104	$87
$1,670	$1,690	$273	$254	$236	$218	$200	$182	$163	$145	$127	$109	$91
$1,690	$1,710	$277	$259	$241	$222	$204	$186	$168	$150	$131	$113	$95

Internal Revenue Service

2020 Wage Bracket Method Tables for Manual Payroll Systems With Forms W-4 From 2019 or Earlier

WEEKLY Payroll Period

If the **Wage Amount** (line 1a) is		SINGLE Persons										
		And the number of allowances is:										
At least	But less than	0	1	2	3	4	5	6	7	8	9	10
		The Tentative Withholding Amount is:										
$1,710	$1,730	$281	$263	$245	$227	$209	$190	$172	$154	$136	$118	$99
$1,730	$1,750	$286	$268	$249	$231	$213	$195	$177	$158	$140	$122	$104
$1,750	$1,770	$291	$272	$254	$236	$217	$199	$181	$163	$145	$126	$108
$1,770	$1,790	$296	$276	$258	$240	$222	$204	$185	$167	$149	$131	$113
$1,790	$1,810	$301	$281	$263	$244	$226	$208	$190	$172	$153	$135	$117
$1,810	$1,830	$305	$286	$267	$249	$231	$212	$194	$176	$158	$140	$121
$1,830	$1,850	$310	$290	$271	$253	$235	$217	$199	$180	$162	$144	$126
$1,850	$1,870	$315	$295	$276	$258	$239	$221	$203	$185	$167	$148	$130
$1,870	$1,890	$320	$300	$280	$262	$244	$226	$207	$189	$171	$153	$135
$1,890	$1,910	$325	$305	$285	$266	$248	$230	$212	$194	$175	$157	$139
$1,910	$1,930	$329	$310	$290	$271	$253	$234	$216	$198	$180	$162	$143

Internal Revenue Service

2020 Wage Bracket Method Tables for Manual Payroll Systems With Forms W-4 From 2019 or Earlier

BIWEEKLY Payroll Period

If the **Wage Amount** (line 1a) is		MARRIED Persons										
		And the number of allowances is:										
At least	But less than	0	1	2	3	4	5	6	7	8	9	10
		The Tentative Withholding Amount is:										
$0	$460	$0	$0	$0	$0	$0	$0	$0	$0	$0	$0	$0
$460	$470	$1	$0	$0	$0	$0	$0	$0	$0	$0	$0	$0
$470	$480	$2	$0	$0	$0	$0	$0	$0	$0	$0	$0	$0
$480	$490	$3	$0	$0	$0	$0	$0	$0	$0	$0	$0	$0
$490	$500	$4	$0	$0	$0	$0	$0	$0	$0	$0	$0	$0
$500	$510	$5	$0	$0	$0	$0	$0	$0	$0	$0	$0	$0
$510	$520	$6	$0	$0	$0	$0	$0	$0	$0	$0	$0	$0
$520	$530	$7	$0	$0	$0	$0	$0	$0	$0	$0	$0	$0
$530	$540	$8	$0	$0	$0	$0	$0	$0	$0	$0	$0	$0
$540	$550	$9	$0	$0	$0	$0	$0	$0	$0	$0	$0	$0
$550	$560	$10	$0	$0	$0	$0	$0	$0	$0	$0	$0	$0
$560	$580	$11	$0	$0	$0	$0	$0	$0	$0	$0	$0	$0
$580	$600	$13	$0	$0	$0	$0	$0	$0	$0	$0	$0	$0
$600	$620	$15	$0	$0	$0	$0	$0	$0	$0	$0	$0	$0
$620	$640	$17	$1	$0	$0	$0	$0	$0	$0	$0	$0	$0
$640	$660	$19	$3	$0	$0	$0	$0	$0	$0	$0	$0	$0
$660	$680	$21	$5	$0	$0	$0	$0	$0	$0	$0	$0	$0
$680	$700	$23	$7	$0	$0	$0	$0	$0	$0	$0	$0	$0
$700	$720	$25	$9	$0	$0	$0	$0	$0	$0	$0	$0	$0
$720	$740	$27	$11	$0	$0	$0	$0	$0	$0	$0	$0	$0
$740	$760	$29	$13	$0	$0	$0	$0	$0	$0	$0	$0	$0
$760	$780	$31	$15	$0	$0	$0	$0	$0	$0	$0	$0	$0
$780	$800	$33	$17	$0	$0	$0	$0	$0	$0	$0	$0	$0
$800	$820	$35	$19	$2	$0	$0	$0	$0	$0	$0	$0	$0
$820	$840	$37	$21	$4	$0	$0	$0	$0	$0	$0	$0	$0
$840	$860	$39	$23	$6	$0	$0	$0	$0	$0	$0	$0	$0
$860	$880	$41	$25	$8	$0	$0	$0	$0	$0	$0	$0	$0
$880	$900	$43	$27	$10	$0	$0	$0	$0	$0	$0	$0	$0
$900	$920	$45	$29	$12	$0	$0	$0	$0	$0	$0	$0	$0
$920	$940	$47	$31	$14	$0	$0	$0	$0	$0	$0	$0	$0
$940	$960	$49	$33	$16	$0	$0	$0	$0	$0	$0	$0	$0
$960	$980	$51	$35	$18	$2	$0	$0	$0	$0	$0	$0	$0
$980	$1,000	$53	$37	$20	$4	$0	$0	$0	$0	$0	$0	$0
$1,000	$1,020	$55	$39	$22	$6	$0	$0	$0	$0	$0	$0	$0
$1,020	$1,040	$57	$41	$24	$8	$0	$0	$0	$0	$0	$0	$0
$1,040	$1,060	$59	$43	$26	$10	$0	$0	$0	$0	$0	$0	$0
$1,060	$1,080	$61	$45	$28	$12	$0	$0	$0	$0	$0	$0	$0
$1,080	$1,100	$63	$47	$30	$14	$0	$0	$0	$0	$0	$0	$0
$1,100	$1,120	$65	$49	$32	$16	$0	$0	$0	$0	$0	$0	$0
$1,120	$1,140	$67	$51	$34	$18	$1	$0	$0	$0	$0	$0	$0
$1,140	$1,160	$69	$53	$36	$20	$3	$0	$0	$0	$0	$0	$0
$1,160	$1,180	$71	$55	$38	$22	$5	$0	$0	$0	$0	$0	$0
$1,180	$1,200	$73	$57	$40	$24	$7	$0	$0	$0	$0	$0	$0
$1,200	$1,220	$75	$59	$42	$26	$9	$0	$0	$0	$0	$0	$0
$1,220	$1,250	$78	$61	$45	$28	$12	$0	$0	$0	$0	$0	$0
$1,250	$1,280	$82	$64	$48	$31	$15	$0	$0	$0	$0	$0	$0
$1,280	$1,310	$85	$67	$51	$34	$18	$1	$0	$0	$0	$0	$0
$1,310	$1,340	$89	$70	$54	$37	$21	$4	$0	$0	$0	$0	$0
$1,340	$1,370	$92	$73	$57	$40	$24	$7	$0	$0	$0	$0	$0
$1,370	$1,400	$96	$76	$60	$43	$27	$10	$0	$0	$0	$0	$0
$1,400	$1,430	$100	$80	$63	$46	$30	$13	$0	$0	$0	$0	$0

Internal Revenue Service

2020 Wage Bracket Method Tables for Manual Payroll Systems With Forms W-4 From 2019 or Earlier

BIWEEKLY Payroll Period

If the **Wage Amount** (line 1a) is		MARRIED Persons										
		And the number of allowances is:										
At least	But less than	0	1	2	3	4	5	6	7	8	9	10
		The Tentative Withholding Amount is:										
$1,430	$1,460	$103	$83	$66	$49	$33	$16	$0	$0	$0	$0	$0
$1,460	$1,490	$107	$87	$69	$52	$36	$19	$3	$0	$0	$0	$0
$1,490	$1,520	$110	$91	$72	$55	$39	$22	$6	$0	$0	$0	$0
$1,520	$1,550	$114	$94	$75	$58	$42	$25	$9	$0	$0	$0	$0
$1,550	$1,580	$118	$98	$78	$61	$45	$28	$12	$0	$0	$0	$0
$1,580	$1,610	$121	$101	$82	$64	$48	$31	$15	$0	$0	$0	$0
$1,610	$1,640	$125	$105	$85	$67	$51	$34	$18	$1	$0	$0	$0
$1,640	$1,670	$128	$109	$89	$70	$54	$37	$21	$4	$0	$0	$0
$1,670	$1,700	$132	$112	$92	$73	$57	$40	$24	$7	$0	$0	$0
$1,700	$1,730	$136	$116	$96	$76	$60	$43	$27	$10	$0	$0	$0
$1,730	$1,760	$139	$119	$100	$80	$63	$46	$30	$13	$0	$0	$0
$1,760	$1,790	$143	$123	$103	$83	$66	$49	$33	$16	$0	$0	$0
$1,790	$1,820	$146	$127	$107	$87	$69	$52	$36	$19	$2	$0	$0
$1,820	$1,850	$150	$130	$110	$91	$72	$55	$39	$22	$5	$0	$0
$1,850	$1,880	$154	$134	$114	$94	$75	$58	$42	$25	$8	$0	$0
$1,880	$1,910	$157	$137	$118	$98	$78	$61	$45	$28	$11	$0	$0
$1,910	$1,940	$161	$141	$121	$101	$82	$64	$48	$31	$14	$0	$0
$1,940	$1,970	$164	$145	$125	$105	$85	$67	$51	$34	$17	$1	$0
$1,970	$2,000	$168	$148	$128	$109	$89	$70	$54	$37	$20	$4	$0
$2,000	$2,030	$172	$152	$132	$112	$92	$73	$57	$40	$23	$7	$0
$2,030	$2,060	$175	$155	$136	$116	$96	$76	$60	$43	$26	$10	$0
$2,060	$2,090	$179	$159	$139	$119	$100	$80	$63	$46	$29	$13	$0
$2,090	$2,120	$182	$163	$143	$123	$103	$83	$66	$49	$32	$16	$0
$2,120	$2,150	$186	$166	$146	$127	$107	$87	$69	$52	$35	$19	$2
$2,150	$2,180	$190	$170	$150	$130	$110	$90	$72	$55	$38	$22	$5
$2,180	$2,210	$193	$173	$154	$134	$114	$94	$75	$58	$41	$25	$8
$2,210	$2,240	$197	$177	$157	$137	$118	$98	$78	$61	$44	$28	$11
$2,240	$2,270	$200	$181	$161	$141	$121	$101	$81	$64	$47	$31	$14
$2,270	$2,300	$204	$184	$164	$145	$125	$105	$85	$67	$50	$34	$17
$2,300	$2,330	$208	$188	$168	$148	$128	$108	$89	$70	$53	$37	$20
$2,330	$2,360	$211	$191	$172	$152	$132	$112	$92	$73	$56	$40	$23
$2,360	$2,390	$215	$195	$175	$155	$136	$116	$96	$76	$59	$43	$26
$2,390	$2,420	$218	$199	$179	$159	$139	$119	$99	$80	$62	$46	$29
$2,420	$2,450	$222	$202	$182	$163	$143	$123	$103	$83	$65	$49	$32
$2,450	$2,480	$226	$206	$186	$166	$146	$126	$107	$87	$68	$52	$35
$2,480	$2,510	$229	$209	$190	$170	$150	$130	$110	$90	$71	$55	$38
$2,510	$2,540	$233	$213	$193	$173	$154	$134	$114	$94	$74	$58	$41
$2,540	$2,570	$236	$217	$197	$177	$157	$137	$117	$98	$78	$61	$44
$2,570	$2,600	$240	$220	$200	$181	$161	$141	$121	$101	$81	$64	$47
$2,600	$2,630	$244	$224	$204	$184	$164	$144	$125	$105	$85	$67	$50
$2,630	$2,660	$247	$227	$208	$188	$168	$148	$128	$108	$89	$70	$53
$2,660	$2,690	$251	$231	$211	$191	$172	$152	$132	$112	$92	$73	$56
$2,690	$2,720	$254	$235	$215	$195	$175	$155	$135	$116	$96	$76	$59
$2,720	$2,750	$258	$238	$218	$199	$179	$159	$139	$119	$99	$79	$62
$2,750	$2,780	$262	$242	$222	$202	$182	$162	$143	$123	$103	$83	$65
$2,780	$2,810	$265	$245	$226	$206	$186	$166	$146	$126	$107	$87	$68
$2,810	$2,840	$269	$249	$229	$209	$190	$170	$150	$130	$110	$90	$71
$2,840	$2,870	$272	$253	$233	$213	$193	$173	$153	$134	$114	$94	$74
$2,870	$2,900	$276	$256	$236	$217	$197	$177	$157	$137	$117	$97	$78
$2,900	$2,930	$280	$260	$240	$220	$200	$180	$161	$141	$121	$101	$81
$2,930	$2,960	$283	$263	$244	$224	$204	$184	$164	$144	$125	$105	$85

2020 Wage Bracket Method Tables for Manual Payroll Systems With Forms W-4 From 2019 or Earlier

BIWEEKLY Payroll Period

If the **Wage Amount** (line 1a) is		MARRIED Persons										
		And the number of allowances is:										
At least	But less than	0	1	2	3	4	5	6	7	8	9	10
		The Tentative Withholding Amount is:										
$2,960	$2,990	$287	$267	$247	$227	$208	$188	$168	$148	$128	$108	$88
$2,990	$3,020	$290	$271	$251	$231	$211	$191	$171	$152	$132	$112	$92
$3,020	$3,050	$294	$274	$254	$235	$215	$195	$175	$155	$135	$115	$96
$3,050	$3,080	$298	$278	$258	$238	$218	$198	$179	$159	$139	$119	$99
$3,080	$3,110	$301	$281	$262	$242	$222	$202	$182	$162	$143	$123	$103
$3,110	$3,140	$305	$285	$265	$245	$226	$206	$186	$166	$146	$126	$106
$3,140	$3,170	$308	$289	$269	$249	$229	$209	$189	$170	$150	$130	$110
$3,170	$3,200	$312	$292	$272	$253	$233	$213	$193	$173	$153	$133	$114
$3,200	$3,230	$316	$296	$276	$256	$236	$216	$197	$177	$157	$137	$117
$3,230	$3,260	$319	$299	$280	$260	$240	$220	$200	$180	$161	$141	$121
$3,260	$3,290	$323	$303	$283	$263	$244	$224	$204	$184	$164	$144	$124
$3,290	$3,320	$326	$307	$287	$267	$247	$227	$207	$188	$168	$148	$128
$3,320	$3,350	$330	$310	$290	$271	$251	$231	$211	$191	$171	$151	$132
$3,350	$3,380	$334	$314	$294	$274	$254	$234	$215	$195	$175	$155	$135
$3,380	$3,410	$337	$317	$298	$278	$258	$238	$218	$198	$179	$159	$139
$3,410	$3,440	$341	$321	$301	$281	$262	$242	$222	$202	$182	$162	$142
$3,440	$3,470	$344	$325	$305	$285	$265	$245	$225	$206	$186	$166	$146
$3,470	$3,500	$348	$328	$308	$289	$269	$249	$229	$209	$189	$169	$150
$3,500	$3,530	$352	$332	$312	$292	$272	$252	$233	$213	$193	$173	$153
$3,530	$3,560	$355	$335	$316	$296	$276	$256	$236	$216	$197	$177	$157
$3,560	$3,600	$363	$340	$320	$300	$280	$260	$240	$221	$201	$181	$161
$3,600	$3,640	$372	$344	$325	$305	$285	$265	$245	$225	$206	$186	$166
$3,640	$3,680	$381	$349	$329	$310	$290	$270	$250	$230	$210	$190	$171
$3,680	$3,720	$389	$354	$334	$314	$295	$275	$255	$235	$215	$195	$175
$3,720	$3,760	$398	$362	$339	$319	$299	$279	$260	$240	$220	$200	$180
$3,760	$3,800	$407	$371	$344	$324	$304	$284	$264	$245	$225	$205	$185
$3,800	$3,840	$416	$379	$349	$329	$309	$289	$269	$249	$230	$210	$190
$3,840	$3,880	$425	$388	$353	$334	$314	$294	$274	$254	$234	$214	$195

Internal Revenue Service

2020 Wage Bracket Method Tables for Manual Payroll Systems With Forms W-4 From 2019 or Earlier

BIWEEKLY Payroll Period

If the **Wage Amount** (line 1a) is		SINGLE Persons										
		And the number of allowances is:										
		0	1	2	3	4	5	6	7	8	9	10
At least	But less than	The Tentative Withholding Amount is:										
$0	$150	$0	$0	$0	$0	$0	$0	$0	$0	$0	$0	$0
$150	$160	$1	$0	$0	$0	$0	$0	$0	$0	$0	$0	$0
$160	$170	$2	$0	$0	$0	$0	$0	$0	$0	$0	$0	$0
$170	$180	$3	$0	$0	$0	$0	$0	$0	$0	$0	$0	$0
$180	$190	$4	$0	$0	$0	$0	$0	$0	$0	$0	$0	$0
$190	$200	$5	$0	$0	$0	$0	$0	$0	$0	$0	$0	$0
$200	$210	$6	$0	$0	$0	$0	$0	$0	$0	$0	$0	$0
$210	$220	$7	$0	$0	$0	$0	$0	$0	$0	$0	$0	$0
$220	$230	$8	$0	$0	$0	$0	$0	$0	$0	$0	$0	$0
$230	$240	$9	$0	$0	$0	$0	$0	$0	$0	$0	$0	$0
$240	$250	$10	$0	$0	$0	$0	$0	$0	$0	$0	$0	$0
$250	$270	$11	$0	$0	$0	$0	$0	$0	$0	$0	$0	$0
$270	$290	$13	$0	$0	$0	$0	$0	$0	$0	$0	$0	$0
$290	$310	$15	$0	$0	$0	$0	$0	$0	$0	$0	$0	$0
$310	$330	$17	$1	$0	$0	$0	$0	$0	$0	$0	$0	$0
$330	$350	$19	$3	$0	$0	$0	$0	$0	$0	$0	$0	$0
$350	$370	$21	$5	$0	$0	$0	$0	$0	$0	$0	$0	$0
$370	$390	$23	$7	$0	$0	$0	$0	$0	$0	$0	$0	$0
$390	$410	$25	$9	$0	$0	$0	$0	$0	$0	$0	$0	$0
$410	$430	$27	$11	$0	$0	$0	$0	$0	$0	$0	$0	$0
$430	$450	$29	$13	$0	$0	$0	$0	$0	$0	$0	$0	$0
$450	$470	$31	$15	$0	$0	$0	$0	$0	$0	$0	$0	$0
$470	$490	$33	$17	$0	$0	$0	$0	$0	$0	$0	$0	$0
$490	$510	$35	$19	$2	$0	$0	$0	$0	$0	$0	$0	$0
$510	$530	$37	$21	$4	$0	$0	$0	$0	$0	$0	$0	$0
$530	$560	$40	$23	$7	$0	$0	$0	$0	$0	$0	$0	$0
$560	$590	$44	$26	$10	$0	$0	$0	$0	$0	$0	$0	$0
$590	$620	$47	$29	$13	$0	$0	$0	$0	$0	$0	$0	$0
$620	$650	$51	$32	$16	$0	$0	$0	$0	$0	$0	$0	$0
$650	$680	$55	$35	$19	$2	$0	$0	$0	$0	$0	$0	$0
$680	$710	$58	$38	$22	$5	$0	$0	$0	$0	$0	$0	$0
$710	$740	$62	$42	$25	$8	$0	$0	$0	$0	$0	$0	$0
$740	$770	$65	$46	$28	$11	$0	$0	$0	$0	$0	$0	$0
$770	$800	$69	$49	$31	$14	$0	$0	$0	$0	$0	$0	$0
$800	$830	$73	$53	$34	$17	$1	$0	$0	$0	$0	$0	$0
$830	$860	$76	$56	$37	$20	$4	$0	$0	$0	$0	$0	$0
$860	$890	$80	$60	$40	$23	$7	$0	$0	$0	$0	$0	$0
$890	$920	$83	$64	$44	$26	$10	$0	$0	$0	$0	$0	$0
$920	$950	$87	$67	$47	$29	$13	$0	$0	$0	$0	$0	$0
$950	$980	$91	$71	$51	$32	$16	$0	$0	$0	$0	$0	$0
$980	$1,010	$94	$74	$55	$35	$19	$2	$0	$0	$0	$0	$0
$1,010	$1,040	$98	$78	$58	$38	$22	$5	$0	$0	$0	$0	$0
$1,040	$1,070	$101	$82	$62	$42	$25	$8	$0	$0	$0	$0	$0
$1,070	$1,100	$105	$85	$65	$46	$28	$11	$0	$0	$0	$0	$0
$1,100	$1,130	$109	$89	$69	$49	$31	$14	$0	$0	$0	$0	$0
$1,130	$1,160	$112	$92	$73	$53	$34	$17	$1	$0	$0	$0	$0
$1,160	$1,190	$116	$96	$76	$56	$37	$20	$4	$0	$0	$0	$0
$1,190	$1,220	$119	$100	$80	$60	$40	$23	$7	$0	$0	$0	$0
$1,220	$1,250	$123	$103	$83	$64	$44	$26	$10	$0	$0	$0	$0
$1,250	$1,280	$127	$107	$87	$67	$47	$29	$13	$0	$0	$0	$0
$1,280	$1,310	$130	$110	$91	$71	$51	$32	$16	$0	$0	$0	$0

2020 Wage Bracket Method Tables for Manual Payroll Systems With Forms W-4 From 2019 or Earlier
BIWEEKLY Payroll Period

If the **Wage Amount** (line 1a) is		SINGLE Persons										
		And the number of allowances is:										
At least	But less than	0	1	2	3	4	5	6	7	8	9	10
		The Tentative Withholding Amount is:										
$1,310	$1,340	$134	$114	$94	$74	$54	$35	$19	$2	$0	$0	$0
$1,340	$1,370	$137	$118	$98	$78	$58	$38	$22	$5	$0	$0	$0
$1,370	$1,400	$141	$121	$101	$82	$62	$42	$25	$8	$0	$0	$0
$1,400	$1,430	$145	$125	$105	$85	$65	$45	$28	$11	$0	$0	$0
$1,430	$1,460	$148	$128	$109	$89	$69	$49	$31	$14	$0	$0	$0
$1,460	$1,490	$152	$132	$112	$92	$72	$53	$34	$17	$1	$0	$0
$1,490	$1,520	$155	$136	$116	$96	$76	$56	$37	$20	$4	$0	$0
$1,520	$1,550	$159	$139	$119	$100	$80	$60	$40	$23	$7	$0	$0
$1,550	$1,580	$163	$143	$123	$103	$83	$63	$44	$26	$10	$0	$0
$1,580	$1,610	$166	$146	$127	$107	$87	$67	$47	$29	$13	$0	$0
$1,610	$1,640	$170	$150	$130	$110	$90	$71	$51	$32	$16	$0	$0
$1,640	$1,670	$173	$154	$134	$114	$94	$74	$54	$35	$19	$2	$0
$1,670	$1,700	$177	$157	$137	$118	$98	$78	$58	$38	$22	$5	$0
$1,700	$1,740	$184	$161	$142	$122	$102	$82	$62	$42	$25	$9	$0
$1,740	$1,780	$193	$166	$146	$127	$107	$87	$67	$47	$29	$13	$0
$1,780	$1,820	$202	$171	$151	$131	$111	$92	$72	$52	$33	$17	$0
$1,820	$1,860	$211	$176	$156	$136	$116	$96	$77	$57	$37	$21	$4
$1,860	$1,900	$220	$183	$161	$141	$121	$101	$81	$62	$42	$25	$8
$1,900	$1,940	$228	$192	$166	$146	$126	$106	$86	$66	$46	$29	$12
$1,940	$1,980	$237	$201	$170	$151	$131	$111	$91	$71	$51	$33	$16
$1,980	$2,020	$246	$210	$175	$155	$135	$116	$96	$76	$56	$37	$20
$2,020	$2,060	$255	$218	$182	$160	$140	$120	$101	$81	$61	$41	$24
$2,060	$2,100	$264	$227	$191	$165	$145	$125	$105	$86	$66	$46	$28
$2,100	$2,140	$272	$236	$200	$170	$150	$130	$110	$90	$70	$51	$32
$2,140	$2,180	$281	$245	$208	$175	$155	$135	$115	$95	$75	$55	$36
$2,180	$2,220	$290	$254	$217	$181	$159	$140	$120	$100	$80	$60	$40
$2,220	$2,260	$299	$262	$226	$190	$164	$144	$125	$105	$85	$65	$45
$2,260	$2,300	$308	$271	$235	$198	$169	$149	$129	$110	$90	$70	$50
$2,300	$2,340	$316	$280	$244	$207	$174	$154	$134	$114	$94	$75	$55
$2,340	$2,380	$325	$289	$252	$216	$180	$159	$139	$119	$99	$79	$60
$2,380	$2,420	$334	$298	$261	$225	$188	$164	$144	$124	$104	$84	$64
$2,420	$2,460	$343	$306	$270	$234	$197	$168	$149	$129	$109	$89	$69
$2,460	$2,500	$352	$315	$279	$242	$206	$173	$153	$134	$114	$94	$74
$2,500	$2,540	$360	$324	$288	$251	$215	$178	$158	$138	$118	$99	$79
$2,540	$2,580	$369	$333	$296	$260	$224	$187	$163	$143	$123	$103	$84
$2,580	$2,620	$378	$342	$305	$269	$232	$196	$168	$148	$128	$108	$88
$2,620	$2,660	$387	$350	$314	$278	$241	$205	$173	$153	$133	$113	$93
$2,660	$2,700	$396	$359	$323	$286	$250	$214	$177	$158	$138	$118	$98
$2,700	$2,740	$404	$368	$332	$295	$259	$222	$186	$162	$142	$123	$103
$2,740	$2,780	$413	$377	$340	$304	$268	$231	$195	$167	$147	$127	$108
$2,780	$2,820	$422	$386	$349	$313	$276	$240	$204	$172	$152	$132	$112
$2,820	$2,860	$431	$394	$358	$322	$285	$249	$212	$177	$157	$137	$117
$2,860	$2,900	$440	$403	$367	$330	$294	$258	$221	$185	$162	$142	$122
$2,900	$2,940	$448	$412	$376	$339	$303	$266	$230	$194	$166	$147	$127
$2,940	$2,980	$457	$421	$384	$348	$312	$275	$239	$202	$171	$151	$132
$2,980	$3,020	$466	$430	$393	$357	$320	$284	$248	$211	$176	$156	$136
$3,020	$3,060	$475	$438	$402	$366	$329	$293	$256	$220	$184	$161	$141
$3,060	$3,100	$484	$447	$411	$374	$338	$302	$265	$229	$192	$166	$146
$3,100	$3,140	$492	$456	$420	$383	$347	$310	$274	$238	$201	$171	$151
$3,140	$3,180	$501	$465	$428	$392	$356	$319	$283	$246	$210	$175	$156
$3,180	$3,220	$510	$474	$437	$401	$364	$328	$292	$255	$219	$182	$160

2020 Wage Bracket Method Tables for Manual Payroll Systems With Forms W-4 From 2019 or Earlier

BIWEEKLY Payroll Period

If the **Wage Amount** (line 1a) is		SINGLE Persons										
		And the number of allowances is:										
At least	But less than	0	1	2	3	4	5	6	7	8	9	10
		The Tentative Withholding Amount is:										
$3,220	$3,260	$519	$482	$446	$410	$373	$337	$300	$264	$228	$191	$165
$3,260	$3,300	$528	$491	$455	$418	$382	$346	$309	$273	$236	$200	$170
$3,300	$3,340	$536	$500	$464	$427	$391	$354	$318	$282	$245	$209	$175
$3,340	$3,380	$545	$509	$472	$436	$400	$363	$327	$290	$254	$218	$181
$3,380	$3,420	$554	$518	$481	$445	$408	$372	$336	$299	$263	$226	$190
$3,420	$3,460	$563	$526	$490	$454	$417	$381	$344	$308	$272	$235	$199
$3,460	$3,500	$572	$535	$499	$462	$426	$390	$353	$317	$280	$244	$208
$3,500	$3,540	$582	$544	$508	$471	$435	$398	$362	$326	$289	$253	$216
$3,540	$3,580	$592	$553	$516	$480	$444	$407	$371	$334	$298	$262	$225
$3,580	$3,620	$601	$562	$525	$489	$452	$416	$380	$343	$307	$270	$234
$3,620	$3,660	$611	$571	$534	$498	$461	$425	$388	$352	$316	$279	$243
$3,660	$3,700	$620	$581	$543	$506	$470	$434	$397	$361	$324	$288	$252
$3,700	$3,740	$630	$590	$552	$515	$479	$442	$406	$370	$333	$297	$260
$3,740	$3,780	$640	$600	$560	$524	$488	$451	$415	$378	$342	$306	$269
$3,780	$3,820	$649	$610	$570	$533	$496	$460	$424	$387	$351	$314	$278
$3,820	$3,860	$659	$619	$579	$542	$505	$469	$432	$396	$360	$323	$287

Internal Revenue Service

2020 Wage Bracket Method Tables for Manual Payroll Systems With Forms W-4 From 2019 or Earlier

SEMIMONTHLY Payroll Period

If the Wage Amount (line 1a) is		MARRIED Persons										
		And the number of allowances is:										
At least	But less than	0	1	2	3	4	5	6	7	8	9	10
		The Tentative Withholding Amount is:										
$0	$500	$0	$0	$0	$0	$0	$0	$0	$0	$0	$0	$0
$500	$510	$1	$0	$0	$0	$0	$0	$0	$0	$0	$0	$0
$510	$520	$2	$0	$0	$0	$0	$0	$0	$0	$0	$0	$0
$520	$530	$3	$0	$0	$0	$0	$0	$0	$0	$0	$0	$0
$530	$540	$4	$0	$0	$0	$0	$0	$0	$0	$0	$0	$0
$540	$550	$5	$0	$0	$0	$0	$0	$0	$0	$0	$0	$0
$550	$560	$6	$0	$0	$0	$0	$0	$0	$0	$0	$0	$0
$560	$570	$7	$0	$0	$0	$0	$0	$0	$0	$0	$0	$0
$570	$580	$8	$0	$0	$0	$0	$0	$0	$0	$0	$0	$0
$580	$590	$9	$0	$0	$0	$0	$0	$0	$0	$0	$0	$0
$590	$600	$10	$0	$0	$0	$0	$0	$0	$0	$0	$0	$0
$600	$625	$12	$0	$0	$0	$0	$0	$0	$0	$0	$0	$0
$625	$650	$14	$0	$0	$0	$0	$0	$0	$0	$0	$0	$0
$650	$675	$17	$0	$0	$0	$0	$0	$0	$0	$0	$0	$0
$675	$700	$19	$1	$0	$0	$0	$0	$0	$0	$0	$0	$0
$700	$725	$22	$4	$0	$0	$0	$0	$0	$0	$0	$0	$0
$725	$750	$24	$6	$0	$0	$0	$0	$0	$0	$0	$0	$0
$750	$775	$27	$9	$0	$0	$0	$0	$0	$0	$0	$0	$0
$775	$800	$29	$11	$0	$0	$0	$0	$0	$0	$0	$0	$0
$800	$825	$32	$14	$0	$0	$0	$0	$0	$0	$0	$0	$0
$825	$850	$34	$16	$0	$0	$0	$0	$0	$0	$0	$0	$0
$850	$875	$37	$19	$1	$0	$0	$0	$0	$0	$0	$0	$0
$875	$900	$39	$21	$3	$0	$0	$0	$0	$0	$0	$0	$0
$900	$925	$42	$24	$6	$0	$0	$0	$0	$0	$0	$0	$0
$925	$950	$44	$26	$8	$0	$0	$0	$0	$0	$0	$0	$0
$950	$975	$47	$29	$11	$0	$0	$0	$0	$0	$0	$0	$0
$975	$1,000	$49	$31	$13	$0	$0	$0	$0	$0	$0	$0	$0
$1,000	$1,025	$52	$34	$16	$0	$0	$0	$0	$0	$0	$0	$0
$1,025	$1,050	$54	$36	$18	$0	$0	$0	$0	$0	$0	$0	$0
$1,050	$1,075	$57	$39	$21	$3	$0	$0	$0	$0	$0	$0	$0
$1,075	$1,100	$59	$41	$23	$5	$0	$0	$0	$0	$0	$0	$0
$1,100	$1,125	$62	$44	$26	$8	$0	$0	$0	$0	$0	$0	$0
$1,125	$1,150	$64	$46	$28	$10	$0	$0	$0	$0	$0	$0	$0
$1,150	$1,175	$67	$49	$31	$13	$0	$0	$0	$0	$0	$0	$0
$1,175	$1,200	$69	$51	$33	$15	$0	$0	$0	$0	$0	$0	$0
$1,200	$1,225	$72	$54	$36	$18	$0	$0	$0	$0	$0	$0	$0
$1,225	$1,250	$74	$56	$38	$20	$3	$0	$0	$0	$0	$0	$0
$1,250	$1,275	$77	$59	$41	$23	$5	$0	$0	$0	$0	$0	$0
$1,275	$1,300	$79	$61	$43	$25	$8	$0	$0	$0	$0	$0	$0
$1,300	$1,325	$82	$64	$46	$28	$10	$0	$0	$0	$0	$0	$0
$1,325	$1,355	$85	$67	$49	$31	$13	$0	$0	$0	$0	$0	$0
$1,355	$1,385	$88	$70	$52	$34	$16	$0	$0	$0	$0	$0	$0
$1,385	$1,415	$92	$73	$55	$37	$19	$1	$0	$0	$0	$0	$0
$1,415	$1,445	$96	$76	$58	$40	$22	$4	$0	$0	$0	$0	$0
$1,445	$1,475	$99	$79	$61	$43	$25	$7	$0	$0	$0	$0	$0
$1,475	$1,505	$103	$82	$64	$46	$28	$10	$0	$0	$0	$0	$0
$1,505	$1,535	$106	$85	$67	$49	$31	$13	$0	$0	$0	$0	$0
$1,535	$1,565	$110	$89	$70	$52	$34	$16	$0	$0	$0	$0	$0
$1,565	$1,595	$114	$92	$73	$55	$37	$19	$1	$0	$0	$0	$0
$1,595	$1,625	$117	$96	$76	$58	$40	$22	$4	$0	$0	$0	$0
$1,625	$1,655	$121	$99	$79	$61	$43	$25	$7	$0	$0	$0	$0

Internal Revenue Service

2020 Wage Bracket Method Tables for Manual Payroll Systems With Forms W-4 From 2019 or Earlier

SEMIMONTHLY Payroll Period

If the **Wage Amount** (line 1a) is		MARRIED Persons										
		And the number of allowances is:										
		0	1	2	3	4	5	6	7	8	9	10
At least	But less than	The Tentative Withholding Amount is:										
$1,655	$1,685	$124	$103	$82	$64	$46	$28	$10	$0	$0	$0	$0
$1,685	$1,715	$128	$107	$85	$67	$49	$31	$13	$0	$0	$0	$0
$1,715	$1,745	$132	$110	$89	$70	$52	$34	$16	$0	$0	$0	$0
$1,745	$1,775	$135	$114	$92	$73	$55	$37	$19	$1	$0	$0	$0
$1,775	$1,805	$139	$117	$96	$76	$58	$40	$22	$4	$0	$0	$0
$1,805	$1,835	$142	$121	$99	$79	$61	$43	$25	$7	$0	$0	$0
$1,835	$1,865	$146	$125	$103	$82	$64	$46	$28	$10	$0	$0	$0
$1,865	$1,895	$150	$128	$107	$85	$67	$49	$31	$13	$0	$0	$0
$1,895	$1,925	$153	$132	$110	$89	$70	$52	$34	$16	$0	$0	$0
$1,925	$1,955	$157	$135	$114	$92	$73	$55	$37	$19	$1	$0	$0
$1,955	$1,985	$160	$139	$117	$96	$76	$58	$40	$22	$4	$0	$0
$1,985	$2,015	$164	$143	$121	$100	$79	$61	$43	$25	$7	$0	$0
$2,015	$2,045	$168	$146	$125	$103	$82	$64	$46	$28	$10	$0	$0
$2,045	$2,075	$171	$150	$128	$107	$85	$67	$49	$31	$13	$0	$0
$2,075	$2,105	$175	$153	$132	$110	$89	$70	$52	$34	$16	$0	$0
$2,105	$2,135	$178	$157	$135	$114	$92	$73	$55	$37	$19	$1	$0
$2,135	$2,165	$182	$161	$139	$118	$96	$76	$58	$40	$22	$4	$0
$2,165	$2,195	$186	$164	$143	$121	$100	$79	$61	$43	$25	$7	$0
$2,195	$2,225	$189	$168	$146	$125	$103	$82	$64	$46	$28	$10	$0
$2,225	$2,255	$193	$171	$150	$128	$107	$85	$67	$49	$31	$13	$0
$2,255	$2,285	$196	$175	$153	$132	$110	$89	$70	$52	$34	$16	$0
$2,285	$2,315	$200	$179	$157	$136	$114	$93	$73	$55	$37	$19	$1
$2,315	$2,345	$204	$182	$161	$139	$118	$96	$76	$58	$40	$22	$4
$2,345	$2,375	$207	$186	$164	$143	$121	$100	$79	$61	$43	$25	$7
$2,375	$2,405	$211	$189	$168	$146	$125	$103	$82	$64	$46	$28	$10
$2,405	$2,435	$214	$193	$171	$150	$128	$107	$85	$67	$49	$31	$13
$2,435	$2,465	$218	$197	$175	$154	$132	$111	$89	$70	$52	$34	$16
$2,465	$2,495	$222	$200	$179	$157	$136	$114	$93	$73	$55	$37	$19
$2,495	$2,525	$225	$204	$182	$161	$139	$118	$96	$76	$58	$40	$22
$2,525	$2,555	$229	$207	$186	$164	$143	$121	$100	$79	$61	$43	$25
$2,555	$2,585	$232	$211	$189	$168	$146	$125	$103	$82	$64	$46	$28
$2,585	$2,615	$236	$215	$193	$172	$150	$129	$107	$86	$67	$49	$31
$2,615	$2,645	$240	$218	$197	$175	$154	$132	$111	$89	$70	$52	$34
$2,645	$2,675	$243	$222	$200	$179	$157	$136	$114	$93	$73	$55	$37
$2,675	$2,705	$247	$225	$204	$182	$161	$139	$118	$96	$76	$58	$40
$2,705	$2,735	$250	$229	$207	$186	$164	$143	$121	$100	$79	$61	$43
$2,735	$2,765	$254	$233	$211	$190	$168	$147	$125	$104	$82	$64	$46
$2,765	$2,795	$258	$236	$215	$193	$172	$150	$129	$107	$86	$67	$49
$2,795	$2,825	$261	$240	$218	$197	$175	$154	$132	$111	$89	$70	$52
$2,825	$2,855	$265	$243	$222	$200	$179	$157	$136	$114	$93	$73	$55
$2,855	$2,885	$268	$247	$225	$204	$182	$161	$139	$118	$96	$76	$58
$2,885	$2,915	$272	$251	$229	$208	$186	$165	$143	$122	$100	$79	$61
$2,915	$2,945	$276	$254	$233	$211	$190	$168	$147	$125	$104	$82	$64
$2,945	$2,975	$279	$258	$236	$215	$193	$172	$150	$129	$107	$86	$67
$2,975	$3,005	$283	$261	$240	$218	$197	$175	$154	$132	$111	$89	$70
$3,005	$3,035	$286	$265	$243	$222	$200	$179	$157	$136	$114	$93	$73
$3,035	$3,065	$290	$269	$247	$226	$204	$183	$161	$140	$118	$97	$76
$3,065	$3,095	$294	$272	$251	$229	$208	$186	$165	$143	$122	$100	$79
$3,095	$3,125	$297	$276	$254	$233	$211	$190	$168	$147	$125	$104	$82
$3,125	$3,155	$301	$279	$258	$236	$215	$193	$172	$150	$129	$107	$86
$3,155	$3,185	$304	$283	$261	$240	$218	$197	$175	$154	$132	$111	$89

2020 Wage Bracket Method Tables for Manual Payroll Systems With Forms W-4 From 2019 or Earlier

SEMIMONTHLY Payroll Period

If the **Wage Amount** (line 1a) is		MARRIED Persons										
		And the number of allowances is:										
At least	But less than	0	1	2	3	4	5	6	7	8	9	10
		The Tentative Withholding Amount is:										
$3,185	$3,215	$308	$287	$265	$244	$222	$201	$179	$158	$136	$115	$93
$3,215	$3,245	$312	$290	$269	$247	$226	$204	$183	$161	$140	$118	$97
$3,245	$3,275	$315	$294	$272	$251	$229	$208	$186	$165	$143	$122	$100
$3,275	$3,305	$319	$297	$276	$254	$233	$211	$190	$168	$147	$125	$104
$3,305	$3,335	$322	$301	$279	$258	$236	$215	$193	$172	$150	$129	$107
$3,335	$3,365	$326	$305	$283	$262	$240	$219	$197	$176	$154	$133	$111
$3,365	$3,395	$330	$308	$287	$265	$244	$222	$201	$179	$158	$136	$115
$3,395	$3,425	$333	$312	$290	$269	$247	$226	$204	$183	$161	$140	$118
$3,425	$3,455	$337	$315	$294	$272	$251	$229	$208	$186	$165	$143	$122
$3,455	$3,485	$340	$319	$297	$276	$254	$233	$211	$190	$168	$147	$125
$3,485	$3,515	$344	$323	$301	$280	$258	$237	$215	$194	$172	$151	$129
$3,515	$3,545	$348	$326	$305	$283	$262	$240	$219	$197	$176	$154	$133
$3,545	$3,575	$351	$330	$308	$287	$265	$244	$222	$201	$179	$158	$136
$3,575	$3,605	$355	$333	$312	$290	$269	$247	$226	$204	$183	$161	$140
$3,605	$3,635	$358	$337	$315	$294	$272	$251	$229	$208	$186	$165	$143
$3,635	$3,665	$362	$341	$319	$298	$276	$255	$233	$212	$190	$169	$147
$3,665	$3,695	$366	$344	$323	$301	$280	$258	$237	$215	$194	$172	$151
$3,695	$3,725	$369	$348	$326	$305	$283	$262	$240	$219	$197	$176	$154
$3,725	$3,755	$373	$351	$330	$308	$287	$265	$244	$222	$201	$179	$158
$3,755	$3,785	$376	$355	$333	$312	$290	$269	$247	$226	$204	$183	$161
$3,785	$3,815	$380	$359	$337	$316	$294	$273	$251	$230	$208	$187	$165
$3,815	$3,845	$384	$362	$341	$319	$298	$276	$255	$233	$212	$190	$169
$3,845	$3,885	$390	$366	$345	$323	$302	$280	$259	$237	$216	$194	$173
$3,885	$3,925	$399	$371	$350	$328	$307	$285	$264	$242	$221	$199	$178
$3,925	$3,965	$408	$376	$354	$333	$311	$290	$268	$247	$225	$204	$182
$3,965	$4,005	$417	$381	$359	$338	$316	$295	$273	$252	$230	$209	$187
$4,005	$4,045	$426	$386	$364	$343	$321	$300	$278	$257	$235	$214	$192
$4,045	$4,085	$434	$395	$369	$347	$326	$304	$283	$261	$240	$218	$197
$4,085	$4,125	$443	$404	$374	$352	$331	$309	$288	$266	$245	$223	$202
$4,125	$4,165	$452	$413	$378	$357	$335	$314	$292	$271	$249	$228	$206
$4,165	$4,205	$461	$421	$383	$362	$340	$319	$297	$276	$254	$233	$211

Internal Revenue Service

2020 Wage Bracket Method Tables for Manual Payroll Systems With Forms W-4 From 2019 or Earlier

SEMIMONTHLY Payroll Period

If the **Wage Amount** (line 1a) is		SINGLE Persons										
		And the number of allowances is:										
At least	But less than	0	1	2	3	4	5	6	7	8	9	10
		The Tentative Withholding Amount is:										
$0	$160	$0	$0	$0	$0	$0	$0	$0	$0	$0	$0	$0
$160	$170	$1	$0	$0	$0	$0	$0	$0	$0	$0	$0	$0
$170	$180	$2	$0	$0	$0	$0	$0	$0	$0	$0	$0	$0
$180	$190	$3	$0	$0	$0	$0	$0	$0	$0	$0	$0	$0
$190	$200	$4	$0	$0	$0	$0	$0	$0	$0	$0	$0	$0
$200	$210	$5	$0	$0	$0	$0	$0	$0	$0	$0	$0	$0
$210	$220	$6	$0	$0	$0	$0	$0	$0	$0	$0	$0	$0
$220	$230	$7	$0	$0	$0	$0	$0	$0	$0	$0	$0	$0
$230	$240	$8	$0	$0	$0	$0	$0	$0	$0	$0	$0	$0
$240	$250	$9	$0	$0	$0	$0	$0	$0	$0	$0	$0	$0
$250	$260	$10	$0	$0	$0	$0	$0	$0	$0	$0	$0	$0
$260	$285	$11	$0	$0	$0	$0	$0	$0	$0	$0	$0	$0
$285	$310	$14	$0	$0	$0	$0	$0	$0	$0	$0	$0	$0
$310	$335	$16	$0	$0	$0	$0	$0	$0	$0	$0	$0	$0
$335	$360	$19	$1	$0	$0	$0	$0	$0	$0	$0	$0	$0
$360	$385	$21	$4	$0	$0	$0	$0	$0	$0	$0	$0	$0
$385	$410	$24	$6	$0	$0	$0	$0	$0	$0	$0	$0	$0
$410	$435	$26	$9	$0	$0	$0	$0	$0	$0	$0	$0	$0
$435	$460	$29	$11	$0	$0	$0	$0	$0	$0	$0	$0	$0
$460	$485	$31	$14	$0	$0	$0	$0	$0	$0	$0	$0	$0
$485	$510	$34	$16	$0	$0	$0	$0	$0	$0	$0	$0	$0
$510	$535	$36	$19	$1	$0	$0	$0	$0	$0	$0	$0	$0
$535	$560	$39	$21	$3	$0	$0	$0	$0	$0	$0	$0	$0
$560	$585	$41	$24	$6	$0	$0	$0	$0	$0	$0	$0	$0
$585	$615	$45	$26	$8	$0	$0	$0	$0	$0	$0	$0	$0
$615	$645	$48	$29	$11	$0	$0	$0	$0	$0	$0	$0	$0
$645	$675	$52	$32	$14	$0	$0	$0	$0	$0	$0	$0	$0
$675	$705	$56	$35	$17	$0	$0	$0	$0	$0	$0	$0	$0
$705	$735	$59	$38	$20	$2	$0	$0	$0	$0	$0	$0	$0
$735	$765	$63	$41	$23	$5	$0	$0	$0	$0	$0	$0	$0
$765	$795	$66	$45	$26	$8	$0	$0	$0	$0	$0	$0	$0
$795	$825	$70	$48	$29	$11	$0	$0	$0	$0	$0	$0	$0
$825	$855	$74	$52	$32	$14	$0	$0	$0	$0	$0	$0	$0
$855	$885	$77	$56	$35	$17	$0	$0	$0	$0	$0	$0	$0
$885	$915	$81	$59	$38	$20	$3	$0	$0	$0	$0	$0	$0
$915	$945	$84	$63	$41	$23	$6	$0	$0	$0	$0	$0	$0
$945	$975	$88	$66	$45	$26	$9	$0	$0	$0	$0	$0	$0
$975	$1,005	$92	$70	$49	$29	$12	$0	$0	$0	$0	$0	$0
$1,005	$1,035	$95	$74	$52	$32	$15	$0	$0	$0	$0	$0	$0
$1,035	$1,065	$99	$77	$56	$35	$18	$0	$0	$0	$0	$0	$0
$1,065	$1,095	$102	$81	$59	$38	$21	$3	$0	$0	$0	$0	$0
$1,095	$1,125	$106	$84	$63	$41	$24	$6	$0	$0	$0	$0	$0
$1,125	$1,155	$110	$88	$67	$45	$27	$9	$0	$0	$0	$0	$0
$1,155	$1,185	$113	$92	$70	$49	$30	$12	$0	$0	$0	$0	$0
$1,185	$1,215	$117	$95	$74	$52	$33	$15	$0	$0	$0	$0	$0
$1,215	$1,245	$120	$99	$77	$56	$36	$18	$0	$0	$0	$0	$0
$1,245	$1,275	$124	$102	$81	$59	$39	$21	$3	$0	$0	$0	$0
$1,275	$1,305	$128	$106	$85	$63	$42	$24	$6	$0	$0	$0	$0
$1,305	$1,335	$131	$110	$88	$67	$45	$27	$9	$0	$0	$0	$0
$1,335	$1,365	$135	$113	$92	$70	$49	$30	$12	$0	$0	$0	$0
$1,365	$1,395	$138	$117	$95	$74	$52	$33	$15	$0	$0	$0	$0

2020 Wage Bracket Method Tables for Manual Payroll Systems With Forms W-4 From 2019 or Earlier

SEMIMONTHLY Payroll Period

If the **Wage Amount** (line 1a) is		SINGLE Persons										
		And the number of allowances is:										
At least	But less than	0	1	2	3	4	5	6	7	8	9	10
		The Tentative Withholding Amount is:										
$1,395	$1,425	$142	$120	$99	$77	$56	$36	$18	$0	$0	$0	$0
$1,425	$1,455	$146	$124	$103	$81	$60	$39	$21	$3	$0	$0	$0
$1,455	$1,485	$149	$128	$106	$85	$63	$42	$24	$6	$0	$0	$0
$1,485	$1,515	$153	$131	$110	$88	$67	$45	$27	$9	$0	$0	$0
$1,515	$1,545	$156	$135	$113	$92	$70	$49	$30	$12	$0	$0	$0
$1,545	$1,575	$160	$138	$117	$95	$74	$52	$33	$15	$0	$0	$0
$1,575	$1,605	$164	$142	$121	$99	$78	$56	$36	$18	$0	$0	$0
$1,605	$1,635	$167	$146	$124	$103	$81	$60	$39	$21	$3	$0	$0
$1,635	$1,665	$171	$149	$128	$106	$85	$63	$42	$24	$6	$0	$0
$1,665	$1,695	$174	$153	$131	$110	$88	$67	$45	$27	$9	$0	$0
$1,695	$1,725	$178	$156	$135	$113	$92	$70	$49	$30	$12	$0	$0
$1,725	$1,755	$182	$160	$139	$117	$96	$74	$53	$33	$15	$0	$0
$1,755	$1,785	$185	$164	$142	$121	$99	$78	$56	$36	$18	$0	$0
$1,785	$1,815	$189	$167	$146	$124	$103	$81	$60	$39	$21	$3	$0
$1,815	$1,845	$192	$171	$149	$128	$106	$85	$63	$42	$24	$6	$0
$1,845	$1,885	$200	$175	$154	$132	$111	$89	$68	$46	$27	$9	$0
$1,885	$1,925	$209	$180	$158	$137	$115	$94	$72	$51	$31	$13	$0
$1,925	$1,965	$218	$185	$163	$142	$120	$99	$77	$56	$35	$17	$0
$1,965	$2,005	$226	$189	$168	$146	$125	$103	$82	$60	$39	$21	$4
$2,005	$2,045	$235	$196	$173	$151	$130	$108	$87	$65	$44	$25	$8
$2,045	$2,085	$244	$205	$178	$156	$135	$113	$92	$70	$49	$29	$12
$2,085	$2,125	$253	$213	$182	$161	$139	$118	$96	$75	$53	$33	$16
$2,125	$2,165	$262	$222	$187	$166	$144	$123	$101	$80	$58	$37	$20
$2,165	$2,205	$270	$231	$192	$170	$149	$127	$106	$84	$63	$41	$24
$2,205	$2,245	$279	$240	$200	$175	$154	$132	$111	$89	$68	$46	$28
$2,245	$2,285	$288	$249	$209	$180	$159	$137	$116	$94	$73	$51	$32
$2,285	$2,325	$297	$257	$218	$185	$163	$142	$120	$99	$77	$56	$36
$2,325	$2,365	$306	$266	$227	$190	$168	$147	$125	$104	$82	$61	$40
$2,365	$2,405	$314	$275	$236	$196	$173	$151	$130	$108	$87	$65	$44
$2,405	$2,445	$323	$284	$244	$205	$178	$156	$135	$113	$92	$70	$49
$2,445	$2,485	$332	$293	$253	$214	$183	$161	$140	$118	$97	$75	$54
$2,485	$2,525	$341	$301	$262	$223	$187	$166	$144	$123	$101	$80	$58
$2,525	$2,565	$350	$310	$271	$231	$192	$171	$149	$128	$106	$85	$63
$2,565	$2,605	$358	$319	$280	$240	$201	$175	$154	$132	$111	$89	$68
$2,605	$2,645	$367	$328	$288	$249	$210	$180	$159	$137	$116	$94	$73
$2,645	$2,685	$376	$337	$297	$258	$218	$185	$164	$142	$121	$99	$78
$2,685	$2,725	$385	$345	$306	$267	$227	$190	$168	$147	$125	$104	$82
$2,725	$2,765	$394	$354	$315	$275	$236	$197	$173	$152	$130	$109	$87
$2,765	$2,805	$402	$363	$324	$284	$245	$205	$178	$156	$135	$113	$92
$2,805	$2,845	$411	$372	$332	$293	$254	$214	$183	$161	$140	$118	$97
$2,845	$2,885	$420	$381	$341	$302	$262	$223	$188	$166	$145	$123	$102
$2,885	$2,925	$429	$389	$350	$311	$271	$232	$192	$171	$149	$128	$106
$2,925	$2,965	$438	$398	$359	$319	$280	$241	$201	$176	$154	$133	$111
$2,965	$3,005	$446	$407	$368	$328	$289	$249	$210	$180	$159	$137	$116
$3,005	$3,045	$455	$416	$376	$337	$298	$258	$219	$185	$164	$142	$121
$3,045	$3,085	$464	$425	$385	$346	$306	$267	$228	$190	$169	$147	$126
$3,085	$3,125	$473	$433	$394	$355	$315	$276	$236	$197	$173	$152	$130
$3,125	$3,165	$482	$442	$403	$363	$324	$285	$245	$206	$178	$157	$135
$3,165	$3,205	$490	$451	$412	$372	$333	$293	$254	$215	$183	$161	$140
$3,205	$3,245	$499	$460	$420	$381	$342	$302	$263	$223	$188	$166	$145
$3,245	$3,285	$508	$469	$429	$390	$350	$311	$272	$232	$193	$171	$150

2020 Wage Bracket Method Tables for Manual Payroll Systems With Forms W-4 From 2019 or Earlier

SEMIMONTHLY Payroll Period

If the **Wage Amount** (line 1a) is		SINGLE Persons										
		And the number of allowances is:										
At least	But less than	0	1	2	3	4	5	6	7	8	9	10
		The Tentative Withholding Amount is:										
$3,285	$3,325	$517	$477	$438	$399	$359	$320	$280	$241	$202	$176	$154
$3,325	$3,365	$526	$486	$447	$407	$368	$329	$289	$250	$210	$181	$159
$3,365	$3,405	$534	$495	$456	$416	$377	$337	$298	$259	$219	$185	$164
$3,405	$3,445	$543	$504	$464	$425	$386	$346	$307	$267	$228	$190	$169
$3,445	$3,485	$552	$513	$473	$434	$394	$355	$316	$276	$237	$197	$174
$3,485	$3,525	$561	$521	$482	$443	$403	$364	$324	$285	$246	$206	$178
$3,525	$3,565	$570	$530	$491	$451	$412	$373	$333	$294	$254	$215	$183
$3,565	$3,605	$578	$539	$500	$460	$421	$381	$342	$303	$263	$224	$188
$3,605	$3,645	$587	$548	$508	$469	$430	$390	$351	$311	$272	$233	$193
$3,645	$3,685	$596	$557	$517	$478	$438	$399	$360	$320	$281	$241	$202
$3,685	$3,725	$605	$565	$526	$487	$447	$408	$368	$329	$290	$250	$211
$3,725	$3,765	$614	$574	$535	$495	$456	$417	$377	$338	$298	$259	$219
$3,765	$3,805	$624	$583	$544	$504	$465	$425	$386	$347	$307	$268	$228
$3,805	$3,845	$633	$592	$552	$513	$474	$434	$395	$355	$316	$277	$237
$3,845	$3,885	$643	$601	$561	$522	$482	$443	$404	$364	$325	$285	$246
$3,885	$3,925	$653	$610	$570	$531	$491	$452	$412	$373	$334	$294	$255
$3,925	$3,965	$662	$619	$579	$539	$500	$461	$421	$382	$342	$303	$263
$3,965	$4,005	$672	$629	$588	$548	$509	$469	$430	$391	$351	$312	$272
$4,005	$4,045	$681	$638	$596	$557	$518	$478	$439	$399	$360	$321	$281
$4,045	$4,085	$691	$648	$605	$566	$526	$487	$448	$408	$369	$329	$290
$4,085	$4,125	$701	$658	$615	$575	$535	$496	$456	$417	$378	$338	$299
$4,125	$4,165	$710	$667	$624	$583	$544	$505	$465	$426	$386	$347	$307
$4,165	$4,205	$720	$677	$634	$592	$553	$513	$474	$435	$395	$356	$316

Internal Revenue Service

2020 Wage Bracket Method Tables for Manual Payroll Systems With Forms W-4 From 2019 or Earlier

MONTHLY Payroll Period

If the **Wage Amount** (line 1a) is		MARRIED Persons										
		And the number of allowances is:										
At least	But less than	0	1	2	3	4	5	6	7	8	9	10
		The Tentative Withholding Amount is:										
$0	$995	$0	$0	$0	$0	$0	$0	$0	$0	$0	$0	$0
$995	$1,015	$1	$0	$0	$0	$0	$0	$0	$0	$0	$0	$0
$1,015	$1,035	$3	$0	$0	$0	$0	$0	$0	$0	$0	$0	$0
$1,035	$1,055	$5	$0	$0	$0	$0	$0	$0	$0	$0	$0	$0
$1,055	$1,075	$7	$0	$0	$0	$0	$0	$0	$0	$0	$0	$0
$1,075	$1,095	$9	$0	$0	$0	$0	$0	$0	$0	$0	$0	$0
$1,095	$1,145	$13	$0	$0	$0	$0	$0	$0	$0	$0	$0	$0
$1,145	$1,195	$18	$0	$0	$0	$0	$0	$0	$0	$0	$0	$0
$1,195	$1,245	$23	$0	$0	$0	$0	$0	$0	$0	$0	$0	$0
$1,245	$1,295	$28	$0	$0	$0	$0	$0	$0	$0	$0	$0	$0
$1,295	$1,345	$33	$0	$0	$0	$0	$0	$0	$0	$0	$0	$0
$1,345	$1,395	$38	$2	$0	$0	$0	$0	$0	$0	$0	$0	$0
$1,395	$1,445	$43	$7	$0	$0	$0	$0	$0	$0	$0	$0	$0
$1,445	$1,495	$48	$12	$0	$0	$0	$0	$0	$0	$0	$0	$0
$1,495	$1,545	$53	$17	$0	$0	$0	$0	$0	$0	$0	$0	$0
$1,545	$1,595	$58	$22	$0	$0	$0	$0	$0	$0	$0	$0	$0
$1,595	$1,645	$63	$27	$0	$0	$0	$0	$0	$0	$0	$0	$0
$1,645	$1,695	$68	$32	$0	$0	$0	$0	$0	$0	$0	$0	$0
$1,695	$1,745	$73	$37	$1	$0	$0	$0	$0	$0	$0	$0	$0
$1,745	$1,795	$78	$42	$6	$0	$0	$0	$0	$0	$0	$0	$0
$1,795	$1,845	$83	$47	$11	$0	$0	$0	$0	$0	$0	$0	$0
$1,845	$1,895	$88	$52	$16	$0	$0	$0	$0	$0	$0	$0	$0
$1,895	$1,945	$93	$57	$21	$0	$0	$0	$0	$0	$0	$0	$0
$1,945	$1,995	$98	$62	$26	$0	$0	$0	$0	$0	$0	$0	$0
$1,995	$2,045	$103	$67	$31	$0	$0	$0	$0	$0	$0	$0	$0
$2,045	$2,095	$108	$72	$36	$0	$0	$0	$0	$0	$0	$0	$0
$2,095	$2,145	$113	$77	$41	$5	$0	$0	$0	$0	$0	$0	$0
$2,145	$2,195	$118	$82	$46	$10	$0	$0	$0	$0	$0	$0	$0
$2,195	$2,245	$123	$87	$51	$15	$0	$0	$0	$0	$0	$0	$0
$2,245	$2,295	$128	$92	$56	$20	$0	$0	$0	$0	$0	$0	$0
$2,295	$2,345	$133	$97	$61	$25	$0	$0	$0	$0	$0	$0	$0
$2,345	$2,395	$138	$102	$66	$30	$0	$0	$0	$0	$0	$0	$0
$2,395	$2,445	$143	$107	$71	$35	$0	$0	$0	$0	$0	$0	$0
$2,445	$2,495	$148	$112	$76	$40	$5	$0	$0	$0	$0	$0	$0
$2,495	$2,545	$153	$117	$81	$45	$10	$0	$0	$0	$0	$0	$0
$2,545	$2,595	$158	$122	$86	$50	$15	$0	$0	$0	$0	$0	$0
$2,595	$2,645	$163	$127	$91	$55	$20	$0	$0	$0	$0	$0	$0
$2,645	$2,705	$169	$133	$97	$61	$25	$0	$0	$0	$0	$0	$0
$2,705	$2,765	$176	$139	$103	$67	$31	$0	$0	$0	$0	$0	$0
$2,765	$2,825	$183	$145	$109	$73	$37	$1	$0	$0	$0	$0	$0
$2,825	$2,885	$191	$151	$115	$79	$43	$7	$0	$0	$0	$0	$0
$2,885	$2,945	$198	$157	$121	$85	$49	$13	$0	$0	$0	$0	$0
$2,945	$3,005	$205	$163	$127	$91	$55	$19	$0	$0	$0	$0	$0
$3,005	$3,065	$212	$169	$133	$97	$61	$25	$0	$0	$0	$0	$0
$3,065	$3,125	$219	$176	$139	$103	$67	$31	$0	$0	$0	$0	$0
$3,125	$3,185	$227	$184	$145	$109	$73	$37	$1	$0	$0	$0	$0
$3,185	$3,245	$234	$191	$151	$115	$79	$43	$7	$0	$0	$0	$0
$3,245	$3,305	$241	$198	$157	$121	$85	$49	$13	$0	$0	$0	$0
$3,305	$3,365	$248	$205	$163	$127	$91	$55	$19	$0	$0	$0	$0
$3,365	$3,425	$255	$212	$169	$133	$97	$61	$25	$0	$0	$0	$0
$3,425	$3,485	$263	$220	$177	$139	$103	$67	$31	$0	$0	$0	$0

Internal Revenue Service

2020 Wage Bracket Method Tables for Manual Payroll Systems With Forms W-4 From 2019 or Earlier

MONTHLY Payroll Period

If the Wage Amount (line 1a) is		MARRIED Persons										
		And the number of allowances is:										
		0	1	2	3	4	5	6	7	8	9	10
At least	But less than	The Tentative Withholding Amount is:										
$3,485	$3,545	$270	$227	$184	$145	$109	$73	$37	$2	$0	$0	$0
$3,545	$3,605	$277	$234	$191	$151	$115	$79	$43	$8	$0	$0	$0
$3,605	$3,665	$284	$241	$198	$157	$121	$85	$49	$14	$0	$0	$0
$3,665	$3,725	$291	$248	$205	$163	$127	$91	$55	$20	$0	$0	$0
$3,725	$3,785	$299	$256	$213	$170	$133	$97	$61	$26	$0	$0	$0
$3,785	$3,845	$306	$263	$220	$177	$139	$103	$67	$32	$0	$0	$0
$3,845	$3,905	$313	$270	$227	$184	$145	$109	$73	$38	$2	$0	$0
$3,905	$3,965	$320	$277	$234	$191	$151	$115	$79	$44	$8	$0	$0
$3,965	$4,025	$327	$284	$241	$198	$157	$121	$85	$50	$14	$0	$0
$4,025	$4,085	$335	$292	$249	$206	$163	$127	$91	$56	$20	$0	$0
$4,085	$4,145	$342	$299	$256	$213	$170	$133	$97	$62	$26	$0	$0
$4,145	$4,205	$349	$306	$263	$220	$177	$139	$103	$68	$32	$0	$0
$4,205	$4,265	$356	$313	$270	$227	$184	$145	$109	$74	$38	$2	$0
$4,265	$4,325	$363	$320	$277	$234	$191	$151	$115	$80	$44	$8	$0
$4,325	$4,385	$371	$328	$285	$242	$199	$157	$121	$86	$50	$14	$0
$4,385	$4,445	$378	$335	$292	$249	$206	$163	$127	$92	$56	$20	$0
$4,445	$4,505	$385	$342	$299	$256	$213	$170	$133	$98	$62	$26	$0
$4,505	$4,565	$392	$349	$306	$263	$220	$177	$139	$104	$68	$32	$0
$4,565	$4,625	$399	$356	$313	$270	$227	$184	$145	$110	$74	$38	$2
$4,625	$4,685	$407	$364	$321	$278	$235	$192	$151	$116	$80	$44	$8
$4,685	$4,745	$414	$371	$328	$285	$242	$199	$157	$122	$86	$50	$14
$4,745	$4,805	$421	$378	$335	$292	$249	$206	$163	$128	$92	$56	$20
$4,805	$4,865	$428	$385	$342	$299	$256	$213	$170	$134	$98	$62	$26
$4,865	$4,925	$435	$392	$349	$306	$263	$220	$177	$140	$104	$68	$32
$4,925	$4,985	$443	$400	$357	$314	$271	$228	$185	$146	$110	$74	$38
$4,985	$5,045	$450	$407	$364	$321	$278	$235	$192	$152	$116	$80	$44
$5,045	$5,105	$457	$414	$371	$328	$285	$242	$199	$158	$122	$86	$50
$5,105	$5,165	$464	$421	$378	$335	$292	$249	$206	$164	$128	$92	$56
$5,165	$5,225	$471	$428	$385	$342	$299	$256	$213	$170	$134	$98	$62
$5,225	$5,285	$479	$436	$393	$350	$307	$264	$221	$178	$140	$104	$68
$5,285	$5,345	$486	$443	$400	$357	$314	$271	$228	$185	$146	$110	$74
$5,345	$5,405	$493	$450	$407	$364	$321	$278	$235	$192	$152	$116	$80
$5,405	$5,465	$500	$457	$414	$371	$328	$285	$242	$199	$158	$122	$86
$5,465	$5,525	$507	$464	$421	$378	$335	$292	$249	$206	$164	$128	$92
$5,525	$5,585	$515	$472	$429	$386	$343	$300	$257	$214	$171	$134	$98
$5,585	$5,645	$522	$479	$436	$393	$350	$307	$264	$221	$178	$140	$104
$5,645	$5,705	$529	$486	$443	$400	$357	$314	$271	$228	$185	$146	$110
$5,705	$5,765	$536	$493	$450	$407	$364	$321	$278	$235	$192	$152	$116
$5,765	$5,825	$543	$500	$457	$414	$371	$328	$285	$242	$199	$158	$122
$5,825	$5,885	$551	$508	$465	$422	$379	$336	$293	$250	$207	$164	$128
$5,885	$5,945	$558	$515	$472	$429	$386	$343	$300	$257	$214	$171	$134
$5,945	$6,005	$565	$522	$479	$436	$393	$350	$307	$264	$221	$178	$140
$6,005	$6,065	$572	$529	$486	$443	$400	$357	$314	$271	$228	$185	$146
$6,065	$6,125	$579	$536	$493	$450	$407	$364	$321	$278	$235	$192	$152
$6,125	$6,185	$587	$544	$501	$458	$415	$372	$329	$286	$243	$200	$158
$6,185	$6,245	$594	$551	$508	$465	$422	$379	$336	$293	$250	$207	$164
$6,245	$6,305	$601	$558	$515	$472	$429	$386	$343	$300	$257	$214	$171
$6,305	$6,365	$608	$565	$522	$479	$436	$393	$350	$307	$264	$221	$178
$6,365	$6,425	$615	$572	$529	$486	$443	$400	$357	$314	$271	$228	$185
$6,425	$6,485	$623	$580	$537	$494	$451	$408	$365	$322	$279	$236	$193
$6,485	$6,545	$630	$587	$544	$501	$458	$415	$372	$329	$286	$243	$200

2020 Wage Bracket Method Tables for Manual Payroll Systems With Forms W-4 From 2019 or Earlier

MONTHLY Payroll Period

If the **Wage Amount** (line 1a) is		MARRIED Persons										
		And the number of allowances is:										
		0	1	2	3	4	5	6	7	8	9	10
At least	But less than	The Tentative Withholding Amount is:										
$6,545	$6,605	$637	$594	$551	$508	$465	$422	$379	$336	$293	$250	$207
$6,605	$6,665	$644	$601	$558	$515	$472	$429	$386	$343	$300	$257	$214
$6,665	$6,725	$651	$608	$565	$522	$479	$436	$393	$350	$307	$264	$221
$6,725	$6,785	$659	$616	$573	$530	$487	$444	$401	$358	$315	$272	$229
$6,785	$6,845	$666	$623	$580	$537	$494	$451	$408	$365	$322	$279	$236
$6,845	$6,905	$673	$630	$587	$544	$501	$458	$415	$372	$329	$286	$243
$6,905	$6,965	$680	$637	$594	$551	$508	$465	$422	$379	$336	$293	$250
$6,965	$7,025	$687	$644	$601	$558	$515	$472	$429	$386	$343	$300	$257
$7,025	$7,085	$695	$652	$609	$566	$523	$480	$437	$394	$351	$308	$265
$7,085	$7,145	$702	$659	$616	$573	$530	$487	$444	$401	$358	$315	$272
$7,145	$7,205	$709	$666	$623	$580	$537	$494	$451	$408	$365	$322	$279
$7,205	$7,265	$716	$673	$630	$587	$544	$501	$458	$415	$372	$329	$286
$7,265	$7,325	$723	$680	$637	$594	$551	$508	$465	$422	$379	$336	$293
$7,325	$7,385	$731	$688	$645	$602	$559	$516	$473	$430	$387	$344	$301
$7,385	$7,445	$738	$695	$652	$609	$566	$523	$480	$437	$394	$351	$308
$7,445	$7,505	$745	$702	$659	$616	$573	$530	$487	$444	$401	$358	$315
$7,505	$7,565	$752	$709	$666	$623	$580	$537	$494	$451	$408	$365	$322
$7,565	$7,625	$759	$716	$673	$630	$587	$544	$501	$458	$415	$372	$329
$7,625	$7,685	$767	$724	$681	$638	$595	$552	$509	$466	$423	$380	$337
$7,685	$7,765	$780	$732	$689	$646	$603	$560	$517	$474	$431	$388	$345
$7,765	$7,845	$797	$742	$699	$656	$613	$570	$527	$484	$441	$398	$355
$7,845	$7,925	$815	$751	$708	$665	$622	$579	$536	$493	$450	$407	$364
$7,925	$8,005	$832	$761	$718	$675	$632	$589	$546	$503	$460	$417	$374
$8,005	$8,085	$850	$771	$727	$684	$641	$598	$555	$512	$469	$426	$383
$8,085	$8,165	$868	$789	$737	$694	$651	$608	$565	$522	$479	$436	$393
$8,165	$8,245	$885	$806	$747	$704	$661	$618	$575	$532	$489	$446	$403
$8,245	$8,325	$903	$824	$756	$713	$670	$627	$584	$541	$498	$455	$412
$8,325	$8,405	$920	$842	$766	$723	$680	$637	$594	$551	$508	$465	$422

Internal Revenue Service

2020 Wage Bracket Method Tables for Manual Payroll Systems With Forms W-4 From 2019 or Earlier

MONTHLY Payroll Period

If the **Wage Amount** (line 1a) is		SINGLE Persons										
		And the number of allowances is:										
At least	But less than	0	1	2	3	4	5	6	7	8	9	10
		The Tentative Withholding Amount is:										
$0	$320	$0	$0	$0	$0	$0	$0	$0	$0	$0	$0	$0
$320	$340	$1	$0	$0	$0	$0	$0	$0	$0	$0	$0	$0
$340	$360	$3	$0	$0	$0	$0	$0	$0	$0	$0	$0	$0
$360	$380	$5	$0	$0	$0	$0	$0	$0	$0	$0	$0	$0
$380	$400	$7	$0	$0	$0	$0	$0	$0	$0	$0	$0	$0
$400	$420	$9	$0	$0	$0	$0	$0	$0	$0	$0	$0	$0
$420	$470	$13	$0	$0	$0	$0	$0	$0	$0	$0	$0	$0
$470	$520	$18	$0	$0	$0	$0	$0	$0	$0	$0	$0	$0
$520	$570	$23	$0	$0	$0	$0	$0	$0	$0	$0	$0	$0
$570	$620	$28	$0	$0	$0	$0	$0	$0	$0	$0	$0	$0
$620	$670	$33	$0	$0	$0	$0	$0	$0	$0	$0	$0	$0
$670	$720	$38	$2	$0	$0	$0	$0	$0	$0	$0	$0	$0
$720	$770	$43	$7	$0	$0	$0	$0	$0	$0	$0	$0	$0
$770	$820	$48	$12	$0	$0	$0	$0	$0	$0	$0	$0	$0
$820	$870	$53	$17	$0	$0	$0	$0	$0	$0	$0	$0	$0
$870	$920	$58	$22	$0	$0	$0	$0	$0	$0	$0	$0	$0
$920	$970	$63	$27	$0	$0	$0	$0	$0	$0	$0	$0	$0
$970	$1,020	$68	$32	$0	$0	$0	$0	$0	$0	$0	$0	$0
$1,020	$1,070	$73	$37	$1	$0	$0	$0	$0	$0	$0	$0	$0
$1,070	$1,120	$78	$42	$6	$0	$0	$0	$0	$0	$0	$0	$0
$1,120	$1,170	$83	$47	$11	$0	$0	$0	$0	$0	$0	$0	$0
$1,170	$1,230	$90	$53	$17	$0	$0	$0	$0	$0	$0	$0	$0
$1,230	$1,290	$97	$59	$23	$0	$0	$0	$0	$0	$0	$0	$0
$1,290	$1,350	$104	$65	$29	$0	$0	$0	$0	$0	$0	$0	$0
$1,350	$1,410	$111	$71	$35	$0	$0	$0	$0	$0	$0	$0	$0
$1,410	$1,470	$118	$77	$41	$5	$0	$0	$0	$0	$0	$0	$0
$1,470	$1,530	$126	$83	$47	$11	$0	$0	$0	$0	$0	$0	$0
$1,530	$1,590	$133	$90	$53	$17	$0	$0	$0	$0	$0	$0	$0
$1,590	$1,650	$140	$97	$59	$23	$0	$0	$0	$0	$0	$0	$0
$1,650	$1,710	$147	$104	$65	$29	$0	$0	$0	$0	$0	$0	$0
$1,710	$1,770	$154	$111	$71	$35	$0	$0	$0	$0	$0	$0	$0
$1,770	$1,830	$162	$119	$77	$41	$5	$0	$0	$0	$0	$0	$0
$1,830	$1,890	$169	$126	$83	$47	$11	$0	$0	$0	$0	$0	$0
$1,890	$1,950	$176	$133	$90	$53	$17	$0	$0	$0	$0	$0	$0
$1,950	$2,010	$183	$140	$97	$59	$23	$0	$0	$0	$0	$0	$0
$2,010	$2,070	$190	$147	$104	$65	$29	$0	$0	$0	$0	$0	$0
$2,070	$2,130	$198	$155	$112	$71	$35	$0	$0	$0	$0	$0	$0
$2,130	$2,190	$205	$162	$119	$77	$41	$5	$0	$0	$0	$0	$0
$2,190	$2,250	$212	$169	$126	$83	$47	$11	$0	$0	$0	$0	$0
$2,250	$2,310	$219	$176	$133	$90	$53	$17	$0	$0	$0	$0	$0
$2,310	$2,370	$226	$183	$140	$97	$59	$23	$0	$0	$0	$0	$0
$2,370	$2,430	$234	$191	$148	$105	$65	$29	$0	$0	$0	$0	$0
$2,430	$2,490	$241	$198	$155	$112	$71	$35	$0	$0	$0	$0	$0
$2,490	$2,550	$248	$205	$162	$119	$77	$41	$5	$0	$0	$0	$0
$2,550	$2,610	$255	$212	$169	$126	$83	$47	$11	$0	$0	$0	$0
$2,610	$2,670	$262	$219	$176	$133	$90	$53	$17	$0	$0	$0	$0
$2,670	$2,730	$270	$227	$184	$141	$98	$59	$23	$0	$0	$0	$0
$2,730	$2,790	$277	$234	$191	$148	$105	$65	$29	$0	$0	$0	$0
$2,790	$2,850	$284	$241	$198	$155	$112	$71	$35	$0	$0	$0	$0
$2,850	$2,910	$291	$248	$205	$162	$119	$77	$41	$6	$0	$0	$0
$2,910	$2,970	$298	$255	$212	$169	$126	$83	$47	$12	$0	$0	$0

2020 Wage Bracket Method Tables for Manual Payroll Systems With Forms W-4 From 2019 or Earlier

MONTHLY Payroll Period

If the **Wage Amount** (line 1a) is		SINGLE Persons										
		And the number of allowances is:										
At least	But less than	0	1	2	3	4	5	6	7	8	9	10
		The Tentative Withholding Amount is:										
$2,970	$3,030	$306	$263	$220	$177	$134	$91	$53	$18	$0	$0	$0
$3,030	$3,090	$313	$270	$227	$184	$141	$98	$59	$24	$0	$0	$0
$3,090	$3,150	$320	$277	$234	$191	$148	$105	$65	$30	$0	$0	$0
$3,150	$3,210	$327	$284	$241	$198	$155	$112	$71	$36	$0	$0	$0
$3,210	$3,270	$334	$291	$248	$205	$162	$119	$77	$42	$6	$0	$0
$3,270	$3,330	$342	$299	$256	$213	$170	$127	$84	$48	$12	$0	$0
$3,330	$3,390	$349	$306	$263	$220	$177	$134	$91	$54	$18	$0	$0
$3,390	$3,450	$356	$313	$270	$227	$184	$141	$98	$60	$24	$0	$0
$3,450	$3,510	$363	$320	$277	$234	$191	$148	$105	$66	$30	$0	$0
$3,510	$3,570	$370	$327	$284	$241	$198	$155	$112	$72	$36	$0	$0
$3,570	$3,630	$378	$335	$292	$249	$206	$163	$120	$78	$42	$6	$0
$3,630	$3,690	$385	$342	$299	$256	$213	$170	$127	$84	$48	$12	$0
$3,690	$3,770	$400	$350	$307	$264	$221	$178	$135	$92	$55	$19	$0
$3,770	$3,850	$418	$360	$317	$274	$231	$188	$145	$102	$63	$27	$0
$3,850	$3,930	$435	$369	$326	$283	$240	$197	$154	$111	$71	$35	$0
$3,930	$4,010	$453	$379	$336	$293	$250	$207	$164	$121	$79	$43	$7
$4,010	$4,090	$471	$392	$346	$303	$260	$217	$174	$131	$88	$51	$15
$4,090	$4,170	$488	$409	$355	$312	$269	$226	$183	$140	$97	$59	$23
$4,170	$4,250	$506	$427	$365	$322	$279	$236	$193	$150	$107	$67	$31
$4,250	$4,330	$523	$444	$374	$331	$288	$245	$202	$159	$116	$75	$39
$4,330	$4,410	$541	$462	$384	$341	$298	$255	$212	$169	$126	$83	$47
$4,410	$4,490	$559	$480	$401	$351	$308	$265	$222	$179	$136	$93	$55
$4,490	$4,570	$576	$497	$418	$360	$317	$274	$231	$188	$145	$102	$63
$4,570	$4,650	$594	$515	$436	$370	$327	$284	$241	$198	$155	$112	$71
$4,650	$4,730	$611	$532	$454	$379	$336	$293	$250	$207	$164	$121	$79
$4,730	$4,810	$629	$550	$471	$392	$346	$303	$260	$217	$174	$131	$88
$4,810	$4,890	$647	$568	$489	$410	$356	$313	$270	$227	$184	$141	$98
$4,890	$4,970	$664	$585	$506	$428	$365	$322	$279	$236	$193	$150	$107
$4,970	$5,050	$682	$603	$524	$445	$375	$332	$289	$246	$203	$160	$117
$5,050	$5,130	$699	$620	$542	$463	$384	$341	$298	$255	$212	$169	$126
$5,130	$5,210	$717	$638	$559	$480	$402	$351	$308	$265	$222	$179	$136
$5,210	$5,290	$735	$656	$577	$498	$419	$361	$318	$275	$232	$189	$146
$5,290	$5,370	$752	$673	$594	$516	$437	$370	$327	$284	$241	$198	$155
$5,370	$5,450	$770	$691	$612	$533	$454	$380	$337	$294	$251	$208	$165
$5,450	$5,530	$787	$708	$630	$551	$472	$393	$346	$303	$260	$217	$174
$5,530	$5,610	$805	$726	$647	$568	$490	$411	$356	$313	$270	$227	$184
$5,610	$5,690	$823	$744	$665	$586	$507	$428	$366	$323	$280	$237	$194
$5,690	$5,770	$840	$761	$682	$604	$525	$446	$375	$332	$289	$246	$203
$5,770	$5,850	$858	$779	$700	$621	$542	$464	$385	$342	$299	$256	$213
$5,850	$5,930	$875	$796	$718	$639	$560	$481	$402	$351	$308	$265	$222
$5,930	$6,010	$893	$814	$735	$656	$578	$499	$420	$361	$318	$275	$232
$6,010	$6,090	$911	$832	$753	$674	$595	$516	$438	$371	$328	$285	$242
$6,090	$6,170	$928	$849	$770	$692	$613	$534	$455	$380	$337	$294	$251
$6,170	$6,250	$946	$867	$788	$709	$630	$552	$473	$394	$347	$304	$261
$6,250	$6,330	$963	$884	$806	$727	$648	$569	$490	$411	$356	$313	$270
$6,330	$6,410	$981	$902	$823	$744	$666	$587	$508	$429	$366	$323	$280
$6,410	$6,490	$999	$920	$841	$762	$683	$604	$526	$447	$376	$333	$290
$6,490	$6,570	$1,016	$937	$858	$780	$701	$622	$543	$464	$385	$342	$299
$6,570	$6,650	$1,034	$955	$876	$797	$718	$640	$561	$482	$403	$352	$309
$6,650	$6,730	$1,051	$972	$894	$815	$736	$657	$578	$499	$421	$361	$318
$6,730	$6,810	$1,069	$990	$911	$832	$754	$675	$596	$517	$438	$371	$328

Internal Revenue Service

2020 Wage Bracket Method Tables for Manual Payroll Systems With Forms W-4 From 2019 or Earlier
MONTHLY Payroll Period

If the **Wage Amount** (line 1a) is		SINGLE Persons										
		And the number of allowances is:										
		0	1	2	3	4	5	6	7	8	9	10
At least	But less than	The Tentative Withholding Amount is:										
$6,810	$6,890	$1,087	$1,008	$929	$850	$771	$692	$614	$535	$456	$381	$338
$6,890	$6,970	$1,104	$1,025	$946	$868	$789	$710	$631	$552	$473	$395	$347
$6,970	$7,050	$1,122	$1,043	$964	$885	$806	$728	$649	$570	$491	$412	$357
$7,050	$7,130	$1,139	$1,060	$982	$903	$824	$745	$666	$587	$509	$430	$366
$7,130	$7,210	$1,157	$1,078	$999	$920	$842	$763	$684	$605	$526	$447	$376
$7,210	$7,290	$1,175	$1,096	$1,017	$938	$859	$780	$702	$623	$544	$465	$386
$7,290	$7,370	$1,192	$1,113	$1,034	$956	$877	$798	$719	$640	$561	$483	$404
$7,370	$7,450	$1,210	$1,131	$1,052	$973	$894	$816	$737	$658	$579	$500	$421
$7,450	$7,530	$1,228	$1,148	$1,070	$991	$912	$833	$754	$675	$597	$518	$439
$7,530	$7,610	$1,247	$1,166	$1,087	$1,008	$930	$851	$772	$693	$614	$535	$457
$7,610	$7,690	$1,267	$1,184	$1,105	$1,026	$947	$868	$790	$711	$632	$553	$474
$7,690	$7,770	$1,286	$1,201	$1,122	$1,044	$965	$886	$807	$728	$649	$571	$492
$7,770	$7,850	$1,305	$1,219	$1,140	$1,061	$982	$904	$825	$746	$667	$588	$509
$7,850	$7,930	$1,324	$1,238	$1,158	$1,079	$1,000	$921	$842	$763	$685	$606	$527
$7,930	$8,010	$1,343	$1,257	$1,175	$1,096	$1,018	$939	$860	$781	$702	$623	$545
$8,010	$8,090	$1,363	$1,277	$1,193	$1,114	$1,035	$956	$878	$799	$720	$641	$562
$8,090	$8,170	$1,382	$1,296	$1,210	$1,132	$1,053	$974	$895	$816	$737	$659	$580
$8,170	$8,250	$1,401	$1,315	$1,229	$1,149	$1,070	$992	$913	$834	$755	$676	$597
$8,250	$8,330	$1,420	$1,334	$1,248	$1,167	$1,088	$1,009	$930	$851	$773	$694	$615
$8,330	$8,410	$1,439	$1,353	$1,267	$1,184	$1,106	$1,027	$948	$869	$790	$711	$633

Internal Revenue Service

2020 Wage Bracket Method Tables for Manual Payroll Systems With Forms W-4 From 2019 or Earlier

DAILY Payroll Period

If the **Wage Amount** (line 1a) is		MARRIED Persons										
		And the number of allowances is:										
At least	But less than	0	1	2	3	4	5	6	7	8	9	10
		The Tentative Withholding Amount is:										
$0	$50	$0	$0	$0	$0	$0	$0	$0	$0	$0	$0	$0
$50	$60	$1	$0	$0	$0	$0	$0	$0	$0	$0	$0	$0
$60	$70	$2	$0	$0	$0	$0	$0	$0	$0	$0	$0	$0
$70	$80	$3	$1	$0	$0	$0	$0	$0	$0	$0	$0	$0
$80	$90	$4	$2	$1	$0	$0	$0	$0	$0	$0	$0	$0
$90	$100	$5	$3	$2	$0	$0	$0	$0	$0	$0	$0	$0
$100	$110	$6	$4	$3	$1	$0	$0	$0	$0	$0	$0	$0
$110	$120	$7	$5	$4	$2	$0	$0	$0	$0	$0	$0	$0
$120	$130	$8	$6	$5	$3	$1	$0	$0	$0	$0	$0	$0
$130	$140	$9	$7	$6	$4	$2	$1	$0	$0	$0	$0	$0
$140	$150	$10	$8	$7	$5	$3	$2	$0	$0	$0	$0	$0
$150	$160	$12	$10	$8	$6	$4	$3	$1	$0	$0	$0	$0
$160	$170	$13	$11	$9	$7	$5	$4	$2	$0	$0	$0	$0
$170	$180	$14	$12	$10	$8	$6	$5	$3	$1	$0	$0	$0
$180	$190	$15	$13	$11	$9	$7	$6	$4	$2	$1	$0	$0
$190	$200	$16	$14	$12	$10	$9	$7	$5	$3	$2	$0	$0
$200	$210	$18	$16	$14	$12	$10	$8	$6	$4	$3	$1	$0
$210	$220	$19	$17	$15	$13	$11	$9	$7	$5	$4	$2	$0
$220	$230	$20	$18	$16	$14	$12	$10	$8	$6	$5	$3	$1
$230	$240	$21	$19	$17	$15	$13	$11	$9	$7	$6	$4	$2
$240	$250	$22	$20	$18	$16	$15	$13	$11	$9	$7	$5	$3
$250	$260	$24	$22	$20	$18	$16	$14	$12	$10	$8	$6	$4
$260	$270	$25	$23	$21	$19	$17	$15	$13	$11	$9	$7	$5
$270	$280	$26	$24	$22	$20	$18	$16	$14	$12	$10	$8	$6
$280	$290	$27	$25	$23	$21	$19	$17	$15	$13	$11	$9	$7
$290	$300	$28	$26	$24	$22	$21	$19	$17	$15	$13	$11	$9
$300	$310	$30	$28	$26	$24	$22	$20	$18	$16	$14	$12	$10
$310	$320	$31	$29	$27	$25	$23	$21	$19	$17	$15	$13	$11
$320	$330	$32	$30	$28	$26	$24	$22	$20	$18	$16	$14	$12
$330	$340	$33	$31	$29	$27	$25	$23	$21	$19	$17	$15	$13
$340	$350	$34	$32	$30	$28	$27	$25	$23	$21	$19	$17	$15
$350	$360	$36	$34	$32	$30	$28	$26	$24	$22	$20	$18	$16
$360	$370	$38	$35	$33	$31	$29	$27	$25	$23	$21	$19	$17
$370	$380	$40	$36	$34	$32	$30	$28	$26	$24	$22	$20	$18
$380	$390	$42	$39	$35	$33	$31	$29	$27	$25	$23	$21	$19
$390	$400	$44	$41	$37	$34	$33	$31	$29	$27	$25	$23	$21
$400	$410	$47	$43	$39	$36	$34	$32	$30	$28	$26	$24	$22
$410	$420	$49	$45	$42	$38	$35	$33	$31	$29	$27	$25	$23
$420	$430	$51	$47	$44	$40	$37	$34	$32	$30	$28	$26	$24
$430	$440	$53	$50	$46	$42	$39	$35	$33	$31	$29	$27	$25
$440	$450	$55	$52	$48	$45	$41	$37	$35	$33	$31	$29	$27
$450	$460	$58	$54	$50	$47	$43	$40	$36	$34	$32	$30	$28
$460	$470	$60	$56	$53	$49	$45	$42	$38	$35	$33	$31	$29
$470	$480	$62	$58	$55	$51	$48	$44	$40	$37	$34	$32	$30
$480	$490	$64	$61	$57	$53	$50	$46	$42	$39	$35	$33	$31
$490	$500	$66	$63	$59	$56	$52	$48	$45	$41	$37	$35	$33
$500	$510	$69	$65	$61	$58	$54	$51	$47	$43	$40	$36	$34
$510	$520	$71	$67	$64	$60	$56	$53	$49	$45	$42	$38	$35
$520	$530	$73	$69	$66	$62	$59	$55	$51	$48	$44	$40	$37
$530	$540	$75	$72	$68	$64	$61	$57	$53	$50	$46	$43	$39
$540	$550	$77	$74	$70	$67	$63	$59	$56	$52	$48	$45	$41

2020 Wage Bracket Method Tables for Manual Payroll Systems With Forms W-4 From 2019 or Earlier

DAILY Payroll Period

If the **Wage Amount** (line 1a) is		MARRIED Persons										
		And the number of allowances is:										
		0	1	2	3	4	5	6	7	8	9	10
At least	But less than	The Tentative Withholding Amount is:										
$550	$560	$80	$76	$72	$69	$65	$62	$58	$54	$51	$47	$43
$560	$570	$82	$78	$75	$71	$67	$64	$60	$56	$53	$49	$46
$570	$580	$84	$80	$77	$73	$70	$66	$62	$59	$55	$51	$48
$580	$590	$86	$83	$79	$75	$72	$68	$64	$61	$57	$54	$50
$590	$600	$88	$85	$81	$78	$74	$70	$67	$63	$59	$56	$52
$600	$610	$91	$87	$83	$80	$76	$73	$69	$65	$62	$58	$54
$610	$620	$93	$89	$86	$82	$78	$75	$71	$67	$64	$60	$57
$620	$630	$95	$91	$88	$84	$81	$77	$73	$70	$66	$62	$59
$630	$640	$97	$94	$90	$86	$83	$79	$75	$72	$68	$65	$61
$640	$650	$99	$96	$92	$89	$85	$81	$78	$74	$70	$67	$63
$650	$660	$102	$98	$94	$91	$87	$84	$80	$76	$73	$69	$65
$660	$670	$104	$100	$97	$93	$89	$86	$82	$78	$75	$71	$68
$670	$680	$106	$102	$99	$95	$92	$88	$84	$81	$77	$73	$70
$680	$690	$108	$105	$101	$97	$94	$90	$86	$83	$79	$76	$72
$690	$700	$110	$107	$103	$100	$96	$92	$89	$85	$81	$78	$74
$700	$710	$113	$109	$105	$102	$98	$95	$91	$87	$84	$80	$76
$710	$720	$115	$111	$108	$104	$100	$97	$93	$89	$86	$82	$79
$720	$730	$118	$114	$110	$106	$103	$99	$95	$92	$88	$84	$81
$730	$740	$120	$116	$112	$108	$105	$101	$97	$94	$90	$87	$83
$740	$750	$122	$118	$114	$111	$107	$103	$100	$96	$92	$89	$85
$750	$760	$125	$121	$117	$113	$109	$106	$102	$98	$95	$91	$87
$760	$770	$127	$123	$119	$115	$111	$108	$104	$100	$97	$93	$90

Internal Revenue Service

2020 Wage Bracket Method Tables for Manual Payroll Systems With Forms W-4 From 2019 or Earlier

DAILY Payroll Period

If the **Wage Amount** (line 1a) is		SINGLE Persons										
		And the number of allowances is:										
At least	But less than	0	1	2	3	4	5	6	7	8	9	10
		The Tentative Withholding Amount is:										
$0	$15	$0	$0	$0	$0	$0	$0	$0	$0	$0	$0	$0
$15	$25	$1	$0	$0	$0	$0	$0	$0	$0	$0	$0	$0
$25	$35	$2	$0	$0	$0	$0	$0	$0	$0	$0	$0	$0
$35	$45	$3	$1	$0	$0	$0	$0	$0	$0	$0	$0	$0
$45	$55	$4	$2	$0	$0	$0	$0	$0	$0	$0	$0	$0
$55	$65	$5	$3	$1	$0	$0	$0	$0	$0	$0	$0	$0
$65	$75	$6	$4	$2	$1	$0	$0	$0	$0	$0	$0	$0
$75	$85	$7	$5	$3	$2	$0	$0	$0	$0	$0	$0	$0
$85	$95	$8	$6	$4	$3	$1	$0	$0	$0	$0	$0	$0
$95	$105	$10	$8	$6	$4	$2	$0	$0	$0	$0	$0	$0
$105	$115	$11	$9	$7	$5	$3	$1	$0	$0	$0	$0	$0
$115	$125	$12	$10	$8	$6	$4	$2	$1	$0	$0	$0	$0
$125	$135	$13	$11	$9	$7	$5	$3	$2	$0	$0	$0	$0
$135	$145	$14	$12	$10	$8	$6	$4	$3	$1	$0	$0	$0
$145	$155	$16	$14	$12	$10	$8	$6	$4	$2	$0	$0	$0
$155	$165	$17	$15	$13	$11	$9	$7	$5	$3	$1	$0	$0
$165	$175	$18	$16	$14	$12	$10	$8	$6	$4	$2	$1	$0
$175	$185	$20	$17	$15	$13	$11	$9	$7	$5	$3	$2	$0
$185	$195	$22	$19	$16	$14	$12	$10	$8	$6	$4	$3	$1
$195	$205	$25	$21	$18	$16	$14	$12	$10	$8	$6	$4	$2
$205	$215	$27	$23	$20	$17	$15	$13	$11	$9	$7	$5	$3
$215	$225	$29	$25	$22	$18	$16	$14	$12	$10	$8	$6	$4
$225	$235	$31	$28	$24	$20	$17	$15	$13	$11	$9	$7	$5
$235	$245	$33	$30	$26	$23	$19	$16	$14	$12	$10	$8	$6
$245	$255	$36	$32	$28	$25	$21	$18	$16	$14	$12	$10	$8
$255	$265	$38	$34	$31	$27	$23	$20	$17	$15	$13	$11	$9
$265	$275	$40	$36	$33	$29	$25	$22	$18	$16	$14	$12	$10
$275	$285	$42	$39	$35	$31	$28	$24	$20	$17	$15	$13	$11
$285	$295	$44	$41	$37	$34	$30	$26	$23	$19	$16	$14	$12
$295	$305	$47	$43	$39	$36	$32	$28	$25	$21	$18	$16	$14
$305	$315	$49	$45	$42	$38	$34	$31	$27	$23	$20	$17	$15
$315	$325	$51	$47	$44	$40	$36	$33	$29	$26	$22	$18	$16
$325	$335	$53	$50	$46	$42	$39	$35	$31	$28	$24	$20	$17
$335	$345	$55	$52	$48	$45	$41	$37	$34	$30	$26	$23	$19
$345	$355	$58	$54	$50	$47	$43	$39	$36	$32	$29	$25	$21
$355	$365	$60	$56	$53	$49	$45	$42	$38	$34	$31	$27	$23
$365	$375	$63	$59	$55	$51	$47	$44	$40	$37	$33	$29	$26
$375	$385	$65	$61	$57	$53	$50	$46	$42	$39	$35	$31	$28
$385	$395	$67	$63	$59	$56	$52	$48	$45	$41	$37	$34	$30
$395	$405	$70	$66	$62	$58	$54	$50	$47	$43	$40	$36	$32
$405	$415	$72	$68	$64	$60	$56	$53	$49	$45	$42	$38	$34
$415	$425	$75	$71	$67	$63	$59	$55	$51	$48	$44	$40	$37
$425	$435	$77	$73	$69	$65	$61	$57	$53	$50	$46	$42	$39
$435	$445	$79	$75	$71	$67	$63	$60	$56	$52	$48	$45	$41
$445	$455	$82	$78	$74	$70	$66	$62	$58	$54	$51	$47	$43
$455	$465	$84	$80	$76	$72	$68	$64	$60	$56	$53	$49	$45
$465	$475	$87	$83	$79	$75	$71	$67	$63	$59	$55	$51	$48
$475	$485	$89	$85	$81	$77	$73	$69	$65	$61	$57	$53	$50
$485	$495	$91	$87	$83	$79	$75	$72	$68	$64	$60	$56	$52
$495	$505	$94	$90	$86	$82	$78	$74	$70	$66	$62	$58	$54
$505	$515	$96	$92	$88	$84	$80	$76	$72	$68	$64	$60	$56

Internal Revenue Service

2020 Wage Bracket Method Tables for Manual Payroll Systems With Forms W-4 From 2019 or Earlier

DAILY Payroll Period

If the **Wage Amount** (line 1a) is		SINGLE Persons										
		And the number of allowances is:										
		0	1	2	3	4	5	6	7	8	9	10
At least	But less than	The Tentative Withholding Amount is:										
$515	$525	$99	$95	$91	$87	$83	$79	$75	$71	$67	$63	$59
$525	$535	$101	$97	$93	$89	$85	$81	$77	$73	$69	$65	$61
$535	$545	$103	$99	$95	$91	$87	$84	$80	$76	$72	$68	$64
$545	$555	$106	$102	$98	$94	$90	$86	$82	$78	$74	$70	$66
$555	$565	$108	$104	$100	$96	$92	$88	$84	$80	$76	$72	$68
$565	$575	$111	$107	$103	$99	$95	$91	$87	$83	$79	$75	$71
$575	$585	$113	$109	$105	$101	$97	$93	$89	$85	$81	$77	$73
$585	$595	$115	$111	$107	$103	$99	$96	$92	$88	$84	$80	$76
$595	$605	$118	$114	$110	$106	$102	$98	$94	$90	$86	$82	$78
$605	$615	$120	$116	$112	$108	$104	$100	$96	$92	$88	$84	$80
$615	$625	$123	$119	$115	$111	$107	$103	$99	$95	$91	$87	$83
$625	$635	$125	$121	$117	$113	$109	$105	$101	$97	$93	$89	$85
$635	$645	$127	$123	$119	$115	$111	$108	$104	$100	$96	$92	$88
$645	$655	$130	$126	$122	$118	$114	$110	$106	$102	$98	$94	$90
$655	$665	$134	$128	$124	$120	$116	$112	$108	$104	$100	$96	$92
$665	$675	$137	$131	$127	$123	$119	$115	$111	$107	$103	$99	$95
$675	$685	$140	$135	$129	$125	$121	$117	$113	$109	$105	$101	$97
$685	$695	$143	$138	$133	$127	$123	$120	$116	$112	$108	$104	$100
$695	$705	$146	$141	$136	$130	$126	$122	$118	$114	$110	$106	$102
$705	$715	$150	$144	$139	$134	$128	$124	$120	$116	$112	$108	$104
$715	$725	$153	$147	$142	$137	$132	$127	$123	$119	$115	$111	$107
$725	$735	$156	$151	$145	$140	$135	$129	$125	$121	$117	$113	$109
$735	$745	$159	$154	$149	$143	$138	$133	$128	$124	$120	$116	$112
$745	$755	$162	$157	$152	$146	$141	$136	$131	$126	$122	$118	$114
$755	$765	$166	$160	$155	$150	$144	$139	$134	$129	$124	$120	$116
$765	$775	$169	$163	$158	$153	$148	$142	$137	$132	$127	$123	$119

Internal Revenue Service

Appendix D

State Income Tax Information

The employee income tax rates for each state for 2020 are presented below. *Tax Bracket* refers to the year-to-date earnings of the individual. *Marginal Tax Rate* refers to the amount of tax actually collected on each dollar the employee earns and is subject to change as the employee's earnings increase during the year. Note that the tax bracket, although generally pertaining to payroll-related income, also applies to other sources of personal revenue such as interest and dividends.

State	Tax Bracket (Single)	Tax Bracket (Married)	Marginal Tax Rate
Alabama	$0+	$0+	2.0%
	$500+	$1,000+	4.0%
	$3,000+	$6,000+	5.0%
Alaska	$0+	$0+	0%
Arizona	$0+	$0+	2.59%
	$26,500+	$53,000+	3.34%
	$53,000+	$106,000+	4.17%
	$159,000+	$318,000+	4.50%
Arkansas	$0+	$0+	2.0%
	$4,000+	$4,000+	4.0%
	$8,000+	$8,000+	5.9%
	$79,300+	$79,300+	6.6%
California	$0+	$0+	1.0%
	$8,809+	$17,618+	2.0%
	$20,883+	$41,766+	4.0%
	$32,960+	$65,920+	6.0%
	$45,753+	$91,506+	8.0%
	$57,824+	$115,648+	9.3%
	$295,373+	$590,746+	10.3%
	$354,445+	$708,890+	11.3%
	$590,742+	$1,000,000+	12.3%
	$1,000,000+	$1,181,484+	13.3%

State	Tax Bracket (Single)	Tax Bracket (Married)	Marginal Tax Rate
Colorado	$0+	$0+	4.63%
Connecticut	$0+	$0+	3.0%
	$10,000+	$20,000+	5.0%
	$50,000+	$100,000+	5.50%
	$100,000+	$200,000+	6.0%
	$200,000+	$400,000+	6.50%
	$250,000+	$500,000+	6.90%
	$500,000+	$1,000,000+	6.99%
Delaware	$2,000+	$2,000+	2.20%
	$5,000+	$5,000+	3.90%
	$10,000+	$10,000+	4.80%
	$20,000+	$20,000+	5.20%
	$25,000+	$25,000+	5.55%
	$60,000+	$60,000+	6.60%
District of Columbia	$0+	$0+	4.0%
	$10,000+	$10,000+	6.0%
	$40,000+	$40,000+	6.50%
	$60,000+	$60,000+	8.50%
	$350,000+	$350,000+	8.75%
	$1,000,000+	$1,000,000+	8.95%
Florida	$0+	$0+	0%
Georgia	$0	$0+	1.0%
	$750+	$1,000+	2.0%
	$2,250+	$3,000+	3.0%
	$3,750+	$5,000+	4.0%
	$5,250+	$7,000+	5.0%
	$7,000+	$10,000+	6.0%
Hawaii	$0+	$0+	1.40%
	$2,400+	$4,800+	3.20%
	$4,800+	$9,600+	5.50%
	$9,600+	$19,200+	6.40%
	$14,400+	$28,800+	6.80%
	$19,200+	$38,400+	7.20%
	$24,000+	$48,000+	7.60%
	$36,000+	$72,000+	7.90%
	$48,000+	$96,000+	8.25%
	$150,000+	$300,000+	9.00%
	$175,000+	$350,000+	10.00%
	$200,000+	$400,000+	11.00%
Idaho	$0+	$0+	1.125%
	$1,541+	$3,082+	3.125%
	$3,081+	$6,162+	3.625%
	$4,622+	$9,244+	4.625%
	$6,162+	$12,324+	5.625%

State	Tax Bracket (Single)	Tax Bracket (Married)	Marginal Tax Rate
	$7,703+	$15,406+	6.625%
	$11,554+	$23,108+	6.925%
Illinois	$0+	$0+	4.95%
Indiana	$0+	$0+	3.23%
Iowa	$0+	$0+	0.33%
	$1,638+	$1,638+	0.67%
	$3,276+	$3,276+	2.25%
	$6,552+	$6,552+	4.14%
	$14,742+	$14,742+	5.63%
	$24,570+	$24,570+	5.96%
	$32,760+	$32,760+	6.25%
	$49,140+	$49,140+	7.44%
	$73,710+	$73,710+	8.53%
Kansas	$0+	$0+	3.10%
	$15,000+	$30,000+	5.25%
	$30,000+	$60,000+	5.70%
Kentucky	$0+	$0+	5.0%
Louisiana	$0+	$0+	2.0%
	$12,500+	$25,000+	4.0%
	$50,000+	$100,000+	6.0%
Maine	$0+	$0+	5.80%
	$22,200+	$44,450+	6.75%
	$52,600+	$105,200+	7.15%
Maryland	$0+	$0+	2.00%
	$1,000+	$1,000+	3.00%
	$2,000+	$2,000+	4.00%
	$3,000+	$3,000+	4.75%
	$100,000+	$150,000+	5.00%
	$125,000+	$175,000+	5.25%
	$150,000+	$225,000+	5.50%
	$250,000+	$300,000+	5.75%
Massachusetts	$0+	$0+	5.0%
Michigan	$0+	$0+	4.25%
Minnesota	$0+	$0+	5.35%
	$26,960+	$39,410+	7.05%
	$88,550+	$156,570+	7.85%
	$164,400+	$273,470+	9.85%
Mississippi	$1,000+	$1,000+	3.0%
	$5,000+	$5,000+	4.0%
	$10,000+	$10,000+	5.0%
Missouri	$105+	$105+	1.5%
	$1,053+	$1,053+	2.0%
	$2,106+	$2,106+	2.5%
	$3,159+	$3,159+	3.0%

State	Tax Bracket (Single)	Tax Bracket (Married)	Marginal Tax Rate
	$4,212+	$4,212+	3.5%
	$5,265+	$5,265+	4.0%
	$6,318+	$6,318+	4.5%
	$7,371+	$7,371+	5.0%
	$8,424+	$8,424+	5.5%
Montana	$0+	$0+	1.0%
	$3,100+	$3,100+	2.0%
	$5,400+	$5,400+	3.0%
	$8,200+	$8,200+	4.0%
	$11,100+	$11,100+	5.0%
	$14,300+	$14,300+	6.0%
	$18,400+	$18,400+	6.9%
Nebraska	$0+	$0+	2.46%
	$3,290+	$6,570+	3.51%
	$19,700+	$39,410+	5.01%
	$31,750+	$63,500+	6.84%
Nevada	$0+	$0+	0%
New Hampshire	$0+	$0+	0%
New Jersey	$0+	$0+	1.40%
	$20,000+	$20,000+	1.75%
	$35,000+	$50,000+	3.50%s/2.45%m
	$40,000+	$70,000+	5.525%s/3.50%m
	$75,000+	$80,000+	6.37%s/5.525%m
	$500,000+	$150,000+	8.97%s/6.37%m
	$5,000,000+	$500,000+	10.75%s/8.97%m
		$5,000,000+	10.75%
New Mexico	$0+	$0+	1.70%
	$5,500+	$8,000+	3.20%
	$11,000+	$16,000+	4.70%
	$16,000+	$24,000+	4.90%
New York	$0+	$0+	4.00%
	$8,500+	$17,150+	4.50%
	$11,700+	$23,600+	5.25%
	$13,900+	$27,900+	5.90%
	$21,400+	$43,000+	6.09%
	$80,650+	$161,550+	6.41%
	$215,400+	$323,200+	6.85%
	$1,077,550+	$2,155,350+	8.82%
North Carolina	$0+	$0+	5.25%

State	Tax Bracket (Single)	Tax Bracket (Married)	Marginal Tax Rate
North Dakota	$0+	$0+	1.10%
	$39,450+	$69,500+	2.04%
	$95,500+	$159,200+	2.27%
	$199,250+	$242,550+	2.64%
	$433,200+	$433,200+	2.90%
Ohio	$21,750+	$21,750+	2.850%
	$43,450+	$43,450+	3.326%
	$86,900+	$86,900+	3.802%
	$108,700+	$108,700+	4.413%
	$217,400+	$217,400+	4.797%
Oklahoma	$0+	$0+	0.5%
	$1,000+	$2,000+	1.0%
	$2,500+	$5,000+	2.0%
	$3,750+	$7,500+	3.0%
	$4,900+	$9,800+	4.0%
	$7,200+	$12,200+	5.0%
Oregon	$0+	$0+	5.0%
	$3,550+	$7,100+	7.0%
	$8,900+	$17,800+	9.0%
	$125,000+	$250,000+	9.9%
Pennsylvania	$0+	$0+	3.07%
Rhode Island	$0+	$0+	3.75%
	$65,250+	$65,250+	4.75%
	$148,350+	$148,350+	5.99%
South Carolina	$0+	$0+	0%
	$3,070+	$3,070+	3.0%
	$6,150+	$6,150+	4.0%
	$9,230+	$9,230+	5.0%
	$12,310+	$12,310+	6.0%
	$15,400+	$15,400+	7.0%
South Dakota	$0+	$0+	0%
Tennessee	$0+	$0+	0%
Texas	$0+	$0+	0%
Utah	$0+	$0+	4.95%
Vermont	$0+	$0+	3.35%
	$39,600+	$66,150+	6.60%
	$96,000+	$159,950+	7.60%
	$200,200+	$243,750+	8.75%

State	Tax Bracket (Single)	Tax Bracket (Married)	Marginal Tax Rate
Virginia	$0+	$0+	2.0%
	$3,000+	$3,000+	3.0%
	$5,000+	$5,000+	5.0%
	$17,000+	$17,000+	5.75%
Washington	$0+	$0+	0%
West Virginia	$0+	$0+	3.0%
	$10,000+	$10,000+	4.0%
	$25,000+	$25,000+	4.5%
	$40,000+	$40,000+	6.0%
	$60,000+	$60,000+	6.5%
Wisconsin	$0+	$0+	4.0%
	$11,970+	$15,960+	5.84%
	$23,930+	$31,910+	6.27%
	$263,480+	$351,310+	7.65%
Wyoming	$0+	$0+	0%

Source: Tax Foundation

Appendix E

State Revenue Department Information

The following are state revenue offices. Where possible, the email address is included. Many states have an Internet email submission form or live chat availability to answer questions.

Alabama

Alabama Department of Revenue
50 North Ripley Street
Montgomery, AL 36104
334-242-1170 Option #7
www.revenue.alabama.gov

Alaska

Juneau Commissioner's Office
P.O. Box 110400
Juneau, AK 99811-0400
907-465-2300
www.revenue.state.ak.us

Arizona

Arizona Department of Revenue
1600 West Monroe Street
Phoenix, AZ 85007-2650
602-255-3381
www.azdor.gov

Arkansas

Little Rock Revenue Central Office
1900 West 7th St., Room 1040
Little Rock, AR 72201
501-682-4663
www.dfa.arkansas.gov

California

Employment Development Department
3321 Power Inn Road, Suite 220
Sacramento, CA 95826
888-745-3886
www.edd.ca.gov

Colorado

Colorado Department of Revenue
1375 Sherman Street
P.O. Box 17087
Denver, CO 80217-0087
303-238-7378
www.colorado.gov/revenue

Connecticut

Department of Revenue Services
450 Columbus Blvd., Suite 1
Hartford, CT 06103
860-297-5962
www.ct.gov/drs

Delaware

Delaware Department of Revenue
Carvel State Office Building
820 North French Street
Wilmington, DE 19801
302-577-8200
www.revenue.delaware.gov

District of Columbia

Office of Tax and Revenue
1101 4th Street SW, Suite 270
Washington, DC 20024
202-727-4829
otr.cfo.dc.gov

Florida

Florida Department of Revenue
5050 West Tennessee Street
Tallahassee, FL 32399
850-488-6800
floridarevenue.com

Georgia

Georgia Department of Revenue
1800 Century Blvd. NE
Atlanta, GA 30345
404-417-2100
dor.ga.gov/withholding-0

Hawaii

Department of Taxation (Oahu District)
Princess Ruth Keelikolani Building
830 Punchbowl Street
Honolulu, HI 96813-5094
808-587-4242
www.tax.hawaii.gov

Idaho

Idaho State Tax Commission
P.O. Box 36
Boise, ID 83722-0036
208-334-7660
www.tax.idaho.gov

Illinois

Illinois Department of Revenue
James R. Thompson Center—7th Floor
100 West Randolph Street
Chicago, IL 60601-3274
800-732-8866
www2.illinois.gov/rev/Pages/default.aspx

Indiana

Indiana Department of Revenue
Indianapolis Taxpayer Services
100 North Senate IGCN Room N105
Indianapolis, IN 46204
317-232-2240
www.in.gov/dor

Iowa

Iowa Department of Revenue
Hoover State Office Building, 4th Floor
1305 East Walnut
Des Moines, IA 50319
800-367-3388
tax.iowa.gov

Kansas

Kansas Department of Revenue
Scott State Office Building
120 SE 10th Avenue
Topeka, KS 66612-1103
785-368-8222
www.ksrevenue.org

Kentucky

Kentucky Department of Revenue

501 High Street

Frankfort, KY 40601

502-564-4581

www.revenue.ky.gov

Louisiana

Louisiana Department of Revenue

617 North Third Street

Baton Rouge, LA 70802

855-307-3893

revenue.louisiana.gov

Maine

Maine Revenue Services

51 Commerce Drive

P.O. Box 9107

Augusta, ME 04332-9107

207-626-8475

withholding.tax@maine.gov

www.maine.gov/revenue

Maryland

Comptroller of Maryland

State Office Building

301 West Preston Street, Room 206

Baltimore, MD 21201-2384

800-638-2937

www.comp.state.md.us

Massachusetts

Massachusetts Department of
Revenue

100 Cambridge Street, 2nd Floor

Boston, MA 02114

800-392-6089

www.mass.gov/orgs/
massachusetts-department-of-revenue

Michigan

Michigan Department of Treasury

Lansing, MI 48922

517-636-6925

www.michigan.gov/treasury

Minnesota

Minnesota Department of Revenue

600 North Robert Street

St. Paul, MN 55146

651-282-5225

www.revenue.state.mn.us

Mississippi

Mississippi Department of Revenue

500 Clinton Center Drive

Clinton, MS 39056

601-923-7700

www.dor.ms.gov

Missouri

Missouri Department of Revenue

Harry S. Truman State Office
Building

301 West High Street

Jefferson City, MO 65101

573-751-3505

www.dor.mo.gov

Montana

Montana Department of Revenue

P.O. Box 1712

Helena, MT 59624-1712

406-444-6900

mtrevenue.gov

Nebraska

Nebraska Department of Revenue

Nebraska State Office Building

301 Centennial Mall South

PO Box 94818

Lincoln, NE 68509-4818

402-471-5729

www.revenue.nebraska.gov

Nevada

Nevada Department of Taxation

1550 College Parkway, Suite 115

Carson City, NV 89706

775-684-2000

tax.nv.gov

New Hampshire

New Hampshire Department of Revenue Administration

Governor Hugh Gallen State Office Park

109 Pleasant Street (Medical & Surgical Building)

Concord, NH 03301

603-230-5000

www.revenue.nh.gov

New Jersey

New Jersey Division of Taxation

Trenton Taxation Building

50 Barrack Street, 1st Floor Lobby

Trenton, NJ 08695

609-826-4400

www.state.nj.us/treasury/taxation

New Mexico

Taxation & Revenue New Mexico

1100 South St. Francis Drive

Santa Fe, NM 87504

505-827-0700

www.tax.newmexico.gov

New York

New York State Department of Taxation and Finance

Building 9

W. A. Harriman Campus

Albany, NY 12227

518-485-6654

www.tax.ny.gov

North Carolina

North Carolina Department of Revenue

501 North Wilmington Street

P.O. Box 25000

Raleigh, NC 27604

877-252-3052

www.dornc.com

North Dakota

Office of State Tax Commissioner

600 East Boulevard Avenue, Department 127

Bismarck, ND 58505-0599

701-328-1241

www.nd.gov/tax

Ohio

Ohio Department of Taxation

Attn: Business Compliance Division

P.O. Box 1090

Columbus, OH 43216-1090

888-405-4039

www.tax.ohio.gov

Oklahoma

Oklahoma Tax Commission

Connors Building, Capitol Complex

2501 North Lincoln Blvd.

Oklahoma City, OK 73194

405-521-3160

www.ok.gov/tax

Oregon

Oregon Department of Revenue

955 Center Street NE

Salem, OR 97301-2555

503-945-8091

payroll.help.dor@oregon.gov

www.oregon.gov/dor

Pennsylvania

Pennsylvania Department of Revenue

Strawberry Square Lobby, First Floor

Fourth and Walnut Streets

Harrisburg, PA 17128

717-787-1064

www.revenue.pa.gov

Rhode Island

Rhode Island Division of Taxation

One Capitol Hill

Providence, RI 02908

401-574-8484

www.tax.ri.gov

South Carolina

South Carolina Department of Revenue

300A Outlet Pointe Blvd.

Columbia, SC 29210

844-898-8542, option 2 then option 4

WithholdingTax@dor.sc.gov

www.dor.sc.gov

South Dakota

South Dakota Department of Labor and Regulation

123 West Missouri Avenue

Pierre, SD 57501

605-773-3101

dlr.sd.gov

Tennessee

Tennessee Department of Labor and Workforce Development

220 French Landing Drive, 3-B

Nashville, TN 37243

844-224-5818

www.tn.gov/workforce

Texas

Texas Comptroller of Public Accounts

Lyndon B. Johnson State Office Building

111 East 17th Street

Austin, TX 78774

512-223-5400

comptroller.texas.gov/taxes/

Utah

Utah State Tax Commission

210 North 1950 West

Salt Lake City, UT 84134

801-297-2200

www.tax.utah.gov

Vermont

Vermont Department of Taxes

133 State Street

Montpelier, VT 05633

802-828-2505

tax.vermont.gov

Virginia

Virginia Tax

1957 Westmoreland Street

Richmond, VA 23230

804-367-8037

www.tax.virginia.gov

Washington

Washington State Employment Security Department

212 Maple Park Avenue SE

Olympia, WA 98501-2347

360-902-9500

www.esd.wa.gov

West Virginia

West Virginia Department of Revenue

Taxpayer Services

1124 Smith Street

Charleston, WV 25301

304-558-3333

TaxHelp@WV.Gov

revenue.wv.gov

Wisconsin

Wisconsin Department of Revenue

2135 Rimrock Road

Madison, WI 53713

608-266-2772

www.revenue.wi.gov

Wyoming

Workforce Center

5221 Yellowstone Blvd.

Cheyenne, WY 82002

307-777-3700

www.wyomingworkforce.org/

Appendix F

Payroll Certification Information

Payroll certification examinations are available to document mastery of payroll accounting topics. The National Association of Certified Professional Bookkeepers (NACPB), the American Institute of Professional Bookkeepers (AIPB), and the American Payroll Association (APA) each offer certification exams. Contact details for each examination are at the end of this appendix.

Correlation of Certification Exam Topics and Specific Learning Objectives

The following table contains information about the topics covered by each payroll certification and the location of that information in this text.

Payroll Certification Exam Topics	Learning Objective
401(k) plans	4-2, 4-5
Account classification	7-2, 7-3
Accounting terminology	7-2
Additional Medicare tax—highly compensated employees	1-2, 5-3
Advances and overpayments	5-5
Affordable Care Act Form 1095	1-2
Benefits costs and benchmarking	6-6, 7-6
Bonuses and commissions	3-2, 3-6
Cafeteria (Section 125) plans	4-2
Calculation of FICA taxes (Social Security and Medicare): Employee	5-3
Calculation of FICA taxes (Social Security and Medicare): Employer	6-1, 6-3
Calculation of involuntary (mandated) deductions	4-5, 5-5
Communication with IRS and SSA	2-2, 4-6
Data privacy	1-4
Data retention	2-5
Deceased employee pay	3-7
De minimis fringe benefits	4-1, 4-3
Deferred compensation	3-6
Docking exempt employee pay	3-2

Payroll Certification Exam Topics	Learning Objective
Employee benefits	4-1, 4-2
Employee classification	1-6
Employee vs. independent contractor	1-2, 1-6, 2-2
Employer-provided benefits: Cafeteria plan, awards, personal use of company vehicle, group-term life insurance	4-2, 4-3, 4-4
Employment forms	2-2
Enterprise test	3-1
Exempt vs. nonexempt	1-6
Expatriate taxation	2-2
Fair Labor Standards Act	1-2
Federal forms	1-4, 6-3
Federal income tax calculation: Taxable wages, tax computation	5-2
Fiduciary responsibility	7-5
FLSA provisions	1-2
Form W-4: Additional withholding, employee changes	2-2
Form 843 treatment	6-3
Fringe benefits	4-1, 4-3, 4-4
FUTA, including credit reduction states	5-3
General Journal entries	7-3
General Ledger entries	7-4
Gross pay calculation	3-2, 3-3, 3-4, 3-5, 3-6
Gross-up of compensation	5-1
Identifying payroll job requirements	3-2, 3-4, 6-1, 6-2, 7-2
Internal controls	2-4
IRS regulations	5-2, 6-1, 6-2
Jury duty	3-7
Leased employees	2-3
Legislation affecting payroll, contract acts	1-1, 1-2
Multiple worksite reporting	1-4, 1-5, 2-2
Net pay calculations	5-1, 5-2, 5-3, 5-4, 5-5
New hire documentation	2-2
Nonproductive time	3-7
Nonqualified deferred compensation	3-7
Nonqualified plans	4-2, 4-3
Nontaxable benefits	4-3
On-premises benefits: Athletic facilities, child care, etc.	4-3
Overtime premium calculation: FLSA, weighted average, commission, salary, piece-rate	3-4
Pay calculation: Regular, tipped, time worked, other pay situations	3-2, 3-3, 3-5, 3-6
Payment methods: Cash, check, direct deposit, paycard	5-6
Payroll in the United States: Employee documentation	2-2
Payroll practices, confidentiality	1-4, 1-5, 2-3
Payroll systems	1-4, 1-5, 7-5
Payroll: Process and challenges	1-4, 1-5, 7-5, 7-6
Payroll trending	7-6
Penalties	6-4
Pension payments and withholding	4-1, 4-6
Planning and organizing payroll operations	1-4, 1-5, 2-1

Payroll Certification Exam Topics	Learning Objective
Qualified employee discounts	4-3, 4-4
Qualified moving expenses	4-3, 4-4
Reconciling wages and taxes	6-3
Recording accruals and reversals	7-4, 7-5
Recordkeeping requirements, including retention	2-3, 2-4, 2-5
Repaying employer loans	5-5
Resident nonalien	2-2
Retirement plans: Qualified	4-2
Retroactive pay	3-7
State wage and hour laws	3-1
State withholding certificates	2-2
Stock compensation	3-2, 3-6
Tax deposits: Requirements, lookback period, deposits	6-2, 6-3
Taxable tips	6-3
Temporary employees	2-3
Time management	1-4, 1-5
Trends: Technology	1-4, 1-5
Unemployment and disability taxes	6-1, 6-3
Voluntary deductions/other deductions calculations computation	4-5, 4-6
Withholding taxes, FICA taxes	5-2, 5-3, 5-4

Contact Information for Payroll Certifications

National Association of Certified Professional Bookkeepers

844-249-3551

info@certifiedpublicbookkeeper.org
http://certifiedpublicbookkeeper.org/certification.cfm

Requirement

- Successful completion of the NACPB Payroll Certification Exam.

American Institute of Professional Bookkeepers

800-622-0121

info@aipb.org
https://aipb.org/certification-program/

Requirements

- A minimum of two years' professional full-time (or part-time equivalent) experience, which may be obtained either before or after the exam.
- Successful completion of a two-part exam.
- Signed acknowledgment of the AIPB's Code of Ethics.

American Payroll Association

(210) 224-6406
http://www.americanpayroll.org/certification

Two levels of payroll certification are available from the American Payroll Association: Certified Payroll Professional (CPP) and Fundamental Payroll Certification (FPC). The following are the criteria for eligibility for each certification available from the APA.

Certified Payroll Professional

The Certification Board of the American Payroll Association (APA) requires that payroll professionals fulfill **ONE** of the following criteria before they take the Certified Payroll Professional Examination.

Criteria 1

The payroll professional has been practicing a total of three (3) years out of the five (5) years preceding the date of the examination. The practice of payroll is defined as direct or related involvement in at least one of the following:

- Payroll production, payroll reporting, payroll accounting.
- Payroll systems and payroll taxation.
- Payroll administration.
- Payroll education/consulting.

Criteria 2

Before a candidate takes the examination, the payroll professional has been employed in the practice of payroll as defined in Criteria 1 for at least the past 24 months *and* has completed within the last 24 months ALL of the following courses within **ONE** of the following three options offered by the APA:

Option 1
- Payroll Practice Essentials (three-day course: live or virtual) and
- Intermediate Payroll Concepts (two-day course: live or virtual) and
- Advanced Payroll Concepts (two-day course: live or virtual) and
- Strategic Payroll Practices (two-day course: live or virtual)

Option 2
- Payroll 101: Foundations of Payroll Certificate Program and
- Payroll 201: The Payroll Administration Certificate Program

Option 3
- Certified Payroll Professional Boot Camp

Criteria 3

Before a candidate takes the examination, the payroll professional has been employed in the practice of payroll as defined in Criteria 1 for at least the past 18 months, has **obtained** the **Fundamental Payroll Certification (FPC),** *and* has completed within the past 18 months ALL of the following courses within **ONE** of the following two options offered by the APA:

Option 1
- Intermediate Payroll Concepts (two-day course: live or virtual) and
- Advanced Payroll Concepts (two-day course: live or virtual) and
- Strategic Payroll Practices (two-day course: live or virtual)

Option 2
- Payroll 201: The Payroll Administration Certificate Program

Fundamental Payroll Certification (FPC)

The Fundamental Payroll Certification (FPC) is open to all those who wish to demonstrate a baseline of payroll competency. The FPC is designed for all of the following:

- Entry-level payroll professionals.
- Sales professionals/consultants serving the payroll industry.
- Systems analysts/engineers writing payroll programs.
- Payroll Service Bureau client representatives.

APA membership and payroll experience are not required to take the FPC examination.

Glossary

401(k)   A defined contribution plan in which employees may contribute either a specific amount or a percentage of their gross pay on a pre-tax or post-tax basis through payroll deductions.

403(b)   A retirement plan designed for employees of certain nonprofit organizations.

457   A retirement plan offered by governmental and certain nongovernmental employers in which contributions are deducted on a pre-tax basis.

A

ACA   Affordable Care Act of 2010. Mandated health care coverage for all Americans regardless of employment status.

Accrual   An accounting method in which revenues and expenses are recorded when they occur, not necessarily when any cash is exchanged.

ADA   The Americans with Disabilities Act of 1990.

ADAAA   The Americans with Disabilities Act Amendments Act of 2008, which extended the definition of disabilities.

Additional Medicare tax   An additional 0.9% Medicare tax levied upon employees who earn in excess of a certain amount per year, as mandated by the Affordable Care Act.

ADEA   The Age Discrimination in Employment Act of 1967 that protects workers over age 40 from age-based discrimination.

Adjusting entries   Journal entries created at the end of an accounting period to allocate income and expenses to the proper accounts.

Allocation   The storing of costs in one account and then dividing the costs based on a quantifiable activity.

Annual schedule depositors   Employers who have an annual payroll tax liability of less than $1,000 during the lookback period and are notified in writing by the IRS that they submit Form 944 and remit taxes on an annual basis.

Annual total compensation report   A list of all compensation that an employee earns per year, including (but not limited to) salary, commissions, bonuses, and all fringe benefits; examples include health insurance, employer contributions to the employee's retirement plan, life insurance, and tuition reimbursement.

ARRA   The American Recovery and Reinvestment Act of 2009.

Asset   An item of value that a business uses in the course of its operations and from which it expects future economic benefit.

ATRA   The American Taxpayer Relief Act of 2012.

Automated Clearing House (ACH)   The electronic network of financial institutions in the United States through which monetary transactions are transmitted in batches.

B

Balance sheet   A financial statement that lists the totals in the assets, liabilities, and owners' equity accounts of a firm for a specific date.

Benefit analysis   A calculation of the costs and benefits of a company, department, project, or employee.

Biweekly payroll   A pay frequency in which employees are paid 26 times per year.

Blockchain   A digital means of transferring electronic currency using small amounts of data transmitted via multiple computers.

C

Cafeteria plan   A benefit plan pursuant to Section 125 of the Internal Revenue Code that allows employees to designate specific amounts to be deducted from their payroll to pay for health and child care expenses on a pre-tax basis.

Cents-per-mile rule   A method used to determine the value of a company car fringe benefit based on a fixed amount times the number of miles driven for personal purposes.

Certified payroll   A report mandated for certain federal government contracts that verifies the accuracy of labor expenses incurred during completion of contract-related activities.

Charitable contribution   A payroll deduction in which an employee designates a specific amount of gross pay to be paid to community, religious, educational, or another IRS-designated charitable organization.

Circular E   See Publication 15.

Civil Rights Act of 1964   Federal legislation that protects employees from discrimination based on race, color, religion, sex, or national origin.

Civil Rights Act of 1991   Federal law that instituted monetary penalties for companies found guilty of discrimination as described under the Civil Rights Act of 1964.

COBRA   The Consolidated Omnibus Budget Reconciliation Act of 1985.

Combination pay   Employee compensation that reflects two or more discrete pay bases during the same pay period.

Commission   Employee compensation paid upon completion of a task, often pertaining to sales-based activities.

Commuting rule   A valuation method used to determine the personal use of a company vehicle based on the number of miles driven for commuting to and from work.

Compensation   The total amount of cash and noncash salary/ wages and benefits that an employee receives in return for working for a company.

Compensatory (comp) time   Paid time off granted to employees instead of paid overtime.

Consolidated Appropriations Act of 2018   Signed into law in March 2018, this act increased the funding for the E-Verify program, which is an Internet-based system that offers employers instant verification of an employee's eligibility to work in the United States. It is important to note that the E-Verify program does not replace the need for the completion of Form I-9 upon employee hire because it is a voluntary service.

Consumer Credit Protection Act (CCPA)   Federal law that pertains to the percentage of wage garnishment that may be withheld from employee pay to satisfy legal obligations.

Copeland Anti-Kickback Act Federal legislation enacted in 1934 that prohibits a federal contractor or subcontractor from inducing an employee to forgo a portion of the wages guaranteed by the contract.

Credit The right side of the T-account.

Cryptocurrency A form of currency that is digitally encrypted and transmitted.

Current Tax Payment Act of 1943 Federal law enacted in 1943 that required employers to submit a timely remittance to the government of any taxes withheld from the employee pay.

D

Daily payroll A pay frequency in which employees are paid each business day.

Davis–Bacon Act of 1931 Federal legislation enacted in 1931 that requires federal contractors to pay employees an amount commensurate with the prevailing local wage.

De minimis A benefit with a very small monetary value that is deemed impractical in terms of tracking using an accounting system.

Debit The left side of the T-account.

Defined benefit A company-sponsored pension plan that uses the employee's salary and length of service to compute the amount of the benefit.

Defined contribution A retirement plan to which the employee, and sometimes the employer, makes a regular contribution.

Departmental classification The division of payroll-related costs by employee function or organizational department.

Direct deposit The electronic transmission of employee wages from the employer to the employee's account at a financial institution.

Disposable income The amount of employee wages remaining after withholding federal, state, and local taxes.

Document destruction The act of destroying documents that contain sensitive payroll and employee information.

DOMA The Defense of Marriage Act of 1996, which was repealed in 2013.

Draw A loan against future earnings that employees will repay from commissions.

Due care The caution that a reasonable person would exercise to avoid being charged with negligence.

E

EEOC The Equal Employment Opportunity Commission.

Eight and Eighty (8 and 80) A two-week, 80-hour pay period used to determine overtime for employees who work for hospitals and emergency providers.

Electronic Federal Tax Payment System (EFTPS) The Electronic Federal Tax Payment System, a free tax payment service provided for use for employers in the United States.

Equal Pay Act of 1963 Federal legislation mandating that males and females receive equal compensation for comparable work.

ERISA The Employee Retirement Income Security Act of 1974.

Escheatment The transfer of personal property to the employee's state of residence when no legal owner claims the property.

ESOP Employee Stock Ownership Plan.

Ethics An individual's definition of right and wrong.

Exempt An employee who is not subject to the overtime provisions of the Fair Labor Standards Act.

Expense The cost of doing business, which may contain both cash and noncash amounts.

F

Fair market value (FMV) The amount of money that a person would spend to obtain a good or service in an arm's-length transaction.

Federal income tax A tax levied by the federal government on individuals.

FICA The Federal Insurance Contributions Act of 1935.

FICA tax The collective term for the combination of Social Security and Medicare taxes.

Fiduciary A relationship, specifically financial, built on trust between a trustee and a beneficiary.

File maintenance The application of all transactions, including any necessary modifications, to an employee's file.

File security The protection of sensitive payroll information by restricting access and securely storing files.

Flexible spending arrangement (FSA) A tax-advantaged employee spending account as designated by the Internal Revenue Code.

FLSA The Fair Labor Standards Act of 1935.

FMLA The Family and Medical Leave Act.

Foreign Account Tax Compliance Act (FATCA) Federal law that regulates the income tax withholdings of foreign employees.

Form 940 The Employer's Annual Federal Unemployment Tax Return.

Form 941 The Employer's Quarterly Federal Tax Return.

Form 944 The Employer's Annual Federal Tax Return.

Form W-2 Wage and Tax Statement.

Form W-3 Transmittal of Wage and Tax Statements.

Fringe benefit A company-sponsored benefit that supplements an employee's salary, usually on a noncash basis.

FUTA Federal Unemployment Tax Act of 1939.

G

Garnishments A legal procedure for the collection of money owed to a plaintiff through payroll deductions.

General Journal A chronological record of a firm's financial transactions.

General Ledger A record of a firm's financial transactions, grouped by account.

General valuation rule (GVR) The method used to determine the value of most fringe benefits using fair market value.

Generally Accepted Accounting Principles (GAAP)   A framework relating to accounting practice including rules, procedures, and standards defined by industry professionals and used by U.S. companies.

Gross pay   The amount of wages paid to an employee based on work performed, prior to any deductions for mandatory or voluntary deductions.

H

Health savings account (HSA)   A savings account that provides tax advantages for individuals with health plans that have high deductions via pre-tax payroll deductions.

High-deductible health plan (HDHP)   A health care plan with an annual deductible that is at least $1,400 for self-coverage and $2,800 for family coverage; annual out-of-pocket limits are $6,900 for self-coverage and $13,800 for family coverage.

HIPAA   The Health Insurance Portability and Accountability Act of 1996.

Hiring packet   A package of forms that a firm issues to new employees; examples are Form W-4, Form I-9, and health insurance enrollment.

Hourly   Wage determination based on the number of complete and partial hours during which an employee performs work-related tasks.

Hundredth-hour system   The division of an hour into 100 increments used to compute employee wages as accurately as possible.

I

I-9   The Employment Eligibility Verification.

Incentive stock options (ISOs)   A type of employee compensation in which the employee receives a firm's stock on a tax-advantaged basis.

Income statement   A financial report used to determine a firm's net income by computing the difference between revenues and expenses for a period; also known as the profit and loss statement.

Independence   The ability of an accountant to act professionally without external pressures that would cause a third party to question the integrity of actions and decisions.

Independent contractor   An individual who contracts to do work for a firm using his or her own tools and processes without being subject to direction by a firm's management.

Integrity   Possessing honesty and high moral principles.

Internal control   A firm's process of maintaining efficiency and effectiveness, work quality, accurate and reliable financial reports, and legal compliance.

IRA   Individual Retirement Account.

IRCA   Immigration Reform and Control Act of 1986.

L

Labor distribution   The classification of a firm's labor by internally designated classifications.

Labor reports   Reports that contain details about the number of hours worked and the wages paid to employees.

Leased employee   A person who provides services for a company subject to the provisions of IRS code section 414(n).

Lease value rule   A method of determining the value of a company car as a fringe benefit using the fair market value and the annual lease as the basis.

Liability   A financial obligation of the firm arising from revenues received in advance of services or sales or expenses incurred but not paid.

Lilly Ledbetter Fair Pay Act of 2009   Federal law that removed the 180-day statute of limitations in allegations of unfair pay practices.

Local income taxes   Payroll taxes levied by a city or county government.

Lookback period   The time frame used by the IRS to determine the payroll tax deposit schedule for a firm.

M

Mandated deductions   Post-tax payroll deductions ordered by a court of law or otherwise nonvoluntary in nature.

Mandatory deductions   Payroll deductions over which the employee has no control; examples include taxes, garnishments, and certain retirement contributions.

Medicare tax   A payroll tax mandated to be paid by all employees of a firm to fund the Medicare program.

Minimum wage   The minimum hourly amount that employers may legally pay to employees.

Monthly depositor   A firm that must deposit its Federal Income Tax and FICA payroll withholdings and contributions on a monthly basis, based on the lookback period.

Monthly payroll   A pay frequency in which employees are paid 12 times per year.

N

Net pay   An employee's wages or salary less all mandatory and voluntary deductions.

New hire reporting   A process by which a firm notifies governmental authorities of any new hires shortly after the hire date.

Next business day depositor   A semiweekly schedule depositor whose payroll tax liabilities exceed $100,000 for any pay period.

Nonexempt   An employee who is subject to all overtime provisions of the Fair Labor Standards Act; generally, an hourly employee.

O

OASDI   Old-Age, Survivors, and Disability Insurance; synonymous with Social Security.

Objectivity   Making decisions that are free from bias or subjectivity.

On-call time   The nonwork time that an employee is expected to be available for workplace-related emergencies.

OSHA   The Occupational Safety and Health Act of 1970.

Outsourced vendor   A party external to a firm that provides goods or services.

Overtime   Time that an employee works beyond his or her normal working hours.

Owners' equity   The financial investment and any accumulated profits or losses of the owner of a firm.

P

Pay advice   A document detailing employee pay and deductions that either accompanies the paycheck or notifies the employee of the direct deposit of net pay.

Pay period   The recurring period during which a firm collects employee labor data and pays employees in accordance with wage or salary agreements.

Paycard   A debit card, issued to employees, that contains electronically transmitted wages.

Payroll audit   An examination of a firm's payroll records to determine legal compliance.

Payroll register   A payroll register is the payroll accountant's internal tool that helps ensure accuracy of employee compensation.

Payroll review   Verification of payroll accuracy for a period.

Payroll tax reports   Report offering details of the period's tax liability that an employer must file with governmental authorities.

Percentage method   A method used to compute an employee's income tax liability that involves computations based on the employee's wages, marital status, pay frequency, and number of withholdings claimed on Form W-4.

Personal Responsibility, Work and Family Promotion Act of 2002   Act that reauthorized PRWOR when it expired

Piece rate   Employee compensation based on production of unit or completion of an action during a specified time period.

Post-tax deductions   Amounts deducted from employee pay after all income and FICA taxes have been deducted; amounts may be voluntary or court mandated.

Posting   Transferring the details of General Journal entries to the General Ledger accounts.

Premium only plan (POP)   A form of cafeteria plan in which employee portions of employer-provided insurance plans may be deducted on a pre-tax basis.

Privacy Act of 1974   Protecting employees by removing personal identifiers from payroll records and restricting access to personnel records.

Professional competence   The continuing capability to perform professional duties with an agreed-upon standard of quality.

Professionalism   A process reflecting the transparency and public accountability of accounting records.

Protecting Americans from Tax Hikes (PATH) Act   An act to prevent tax fraud that extended the Work Opportunity Tax Credit.

Prove   Ensuring that the sum of the rows of the payroll register equals the sum of the columns.

PRWOR   Personal Responsibility and Work Opportunity Reconciliation Act of 1996.

Publication 15   The Employer's Tax Guide published by the Internal Revenue Service.

Publication 15-b   The IRS Employer's Guide to Fringe Benefits.

Publication 15-T   The Federal Income Tax Withholding Methods.

Q

Qualified plan   A written plan for the issuance of employee achievement awards that does not favor highly compensated employees.

Quarter-hour system   The division of an hour into 15-minute increments as a means of computing hourly work.

Quarterly depositors   Monthly schedule depositors who have a payroll tax liability of less than $2,500 during the preceding or current quarter may remit the payroll tax liability when filing Form 941.

R

Regulation E   Federal legislation protecting consumers who use electronic funds transfer to access their net pay.

Remit   To send money in payment of an obligation.

Resignation   Voluntary termination of employment.

Reversal   A general journal entry recorded at the start of the following month to undo the accruals recorded in the prior month.

Review process   Examination and analysis of accounting records to ensure accuracy and completeness.

Rule   The accounting practice in which the final totals of financial reports are double-underlined.

S

Salary   A fixed amount paid to an employee on a regular basis, often expressed in annual terms.

Schedule B   The report of tax liability for semiweekly depositors.

SECURE   An Act that incentivizes small employers to offer retirement plans, either alone or collectively with other small employers, to improve retirement security for U.S. workers.

Semimonthly payroll   The payroll frequency in which employees are paid 24 times per year.

Semiweekly depositor   A firm that must deposit its federal income tax and FICA payroll withholdings and contributions within three days of the pay date, based on the lookback period.

SEP   A Simplified Employee Pension individual retirement account.

Separation of duties   An internal control method in which payroll duties are spread among two or more employees.

SIMPLE   The Savings Incentive Match Plan for Employees.

SIMPLE 401(k)   A retirement plan for employees of companies that employ 100 or fewer workers. An annual investment limit of $11,500 exists for this type of retirement plan.

Sixteenth Amendment to the U.S. Constitution   Allowed the United States government to levy and collect income taxes on individuals.

Sleep time   Employees who are required to be on duty for 24 hours or more may be allowed up to 5 hours of sleep without a reduction in pay.

Social Security Act (SSA)   An act that was passed to promote social welfare for old-age workers and surviving families of workers who had been disabled or deceased in the course of their employment.

Social Security tax   A tax paid by both employers and employees that is used to fund the Social Security program.

SOX   The Sarbanes–Oxley Act of 2002. Public law 107-204, concerning publicly owned companies and auditing firms to ensure appropriate internal controls and the integrity of financial statements.

Special accounting rule   Employers may elect to treat employee amounts for noncash fringe benefits used during November and December as not being paid until January of the following year; employees must be notified in writing by January 31 of the following year if the special accounting rule was used.

State income taxes   Income taxes levied by a state government on employee payroll.

Statutory deductions   Payroll deductions mandated by law.

Statutory employee   A special class of employees who run their own business but must be treated as employees for tax reasons.

SUTA   The State Unemployment Tax Act of 1939.

T

Tax Cuts and Jobs Act   An act to provide a budget resolution that represented changes to individual and business tax rates.

Tax remittance   The payment of a firm's payroll tax liability.

Tax table   A set of precalculated tables issued by federal and state governments to facilitate income tax computations for employee payroll.

Temporary employee   A worker who is employed by a temporary staffing agency and works under the direction of the agency on a temporary basis for different companies.

Termination   Ceasing employment with a firm.

Time card   A record of the time worked during a period for an individual employee.

Tipped employee   An employee who engages in an occupation in which he or she customarily and regularly receives more than $30 per month in tips.

Tipped wage   The base wage paid to employees who earn the majority of their income through customer tips.

Total   Computing the sum of each row and each column of the payroll register.

Travel time   Time that an employee spends traveling for the employer's benefit.

Trial balance   An internal accounting statement in which the accountant determines that the debits equal the credits for the amounts in the General Ledger.

U

Union dues   Amounts paid on a regular basis by employees who are required to be part of a union as a condition of their employment.

USERRA   The Uniformed Services Employment and Reemployment Rights Act of 1994.

V

Voluntary deductions   Amounts that an employee elects to have deducted from his or her paycheck and remitted to a third party; examples include charitable contributions, savings bond purchases, and health club fees.

VPN   Virtual private network.

W

W-4   The Employee Withholding Allowance Certificate.

Wage base   The maximum annual salary that is subject to tax liability, commonly used for Social Security, FUTA, and SUTA taxes.

Wage-bracket method   The use of tax tables located in federal and state publications that facilitate the determination of employee income tax deductions for payroll.

Wait time   The time that an employee is paid to wait on the employer's premises for the benefit of the employer.

Walsh–Healey Public Contracts Act   Legislation enacted in 1936 that required employers working on federal contracts in excess of $10,000 to pay employees the federal minimum wage and follow the overtime provisions of the Fair Labor Standards Act.

Weekly payroll   The payroll frequency in which employees are paid 52 times per year.

Workers' compensation   A mandatory insurance policy paid by employers that provides wage replacement and medical benefits to employees who are injured in the course of their employment.

Index